The Successor of Prophet Muhammad

Understanding Shia Islam: Beliefs, History, and Practices Explained

FADHIL RAHMI

Contents

1. THE MISSION OF THE PROPHET 19

    1.1. The Three Possibilities 20

    1.2. The First Possibility 21

        1.2.1. Challenges Faced by Islam and the Muslims 22

        1.2.2. Sincerity of the Prophet 22

        1.2.3. The Importance of Leadership Among the Companions ... 23

        1.2.4. The Prophet's Position 24

        1.2.5. A Project Manager 25

    1.3. The Second Possibility 26

        1.3.1. Did Prophet Envisage a Shura (Consultation) to be Established by the Companions? 27

        1.3.2. The Shura (Consultation) of Saqifah 28

        1.3.3. Brief Analysis of the Meeting (Shura) of Saqifah 30

        1.3.4. Threatening to Use Force 32

        1.3.5. A Political Adjustment 32

        1.3.6. The Spontaneous Nature of Saqifah 34

        1.3.7. The Principle of Shura (Consultation) and the Companions ... 35

    1.4. The Third Possibility 36

        1.4.1. A Teacher and a Mentor 37

        1.4.2. A Reformatory Movement 38

        1.4.3. The Ground Realities at the Time 39

        1.4.4. Islam is the Word of Allah 40

2. THE PROPHET AND HIS SUCCESSOR 43

    2.1. Ali's Companionship with the Prophet 44

        2.1.1. The Birth of Ali 44

        2.1.2. The Prophet Adopts Ali 45

    2.1.3. The Prophet's Closeness with Ali..47

  2.2. Ali and the Quran...48

  2.3. Ali Acquires Knowledge from the Prophet..50

  2.4. Ali's Conversion to Islam...52

  2.5. The First to Pray Behind the Prophet...53

  2.6. Ali Defends the Prophet as a Child...53

  2.7. The Prophet Marries Fatima to Ali...54

  2.8. Ali and the Death of the Prophet...56

3. ALI AND THE ESTABLISHMENT OF THE ISLAMIC STATE.............58

  3.1. The Role of Abu Talib..58

  3.2. The Role of Ali..59

  3.3. The Birth of the Islamic State...60

  3.4. The Night of the Hijrah (Migration to Madinah)..................................61

    3.4.1. Ali is to Sleep in Prophet's Bed...62

    3.4.2. Ali is to Give Back the Trusts in the Prophet's Possession............63

    3.4.3. The Prophet Meets Caliph Abu Bakr who Accompanies him........64

  3.5. Laying the Foundations of the Islamic State of Madinah....................64

  3.6. The Battle of Badr...66

    3.6.1. The Importance of the Battle of Badr..67

    3.6.2. Ali's Distinct Performance...67

  3.7. The Battle of Uhud..68

    3.7.1. Ali Kills the Majority of the Flag Bearers..68

    3.7.2. The Tables Turn Against the Muslims..69

    3.7.3. Ali Saves the Life of the Prophet...69

  3.8. The Battle of Moat...71

    3.8.1. Amr's Adventure..72

    3.8.2. Ali's Response..72

    3.8.3. The Difference between Victory and Defeat..................................73

  3.9. The Battle of Khaibar...74

    3.9.1. The Victory was Eluding the Muslims...75

    3.9.2. The Prophet calls Upon Ali..75

    3.9.3. The Victory of Khaibar...77

  3.10. The Biggest and the Most Important Project...77

    3.10.1. The Differentiating Factor..78

    3.10.2. The Prophet's Plan and Strategy..80

4. ISLAMIC GOVERNMENT, THE COMPANIONS AND THE PROPHET'S SUNNAH..81

  4.1. Islam Allows Two Kinds of Governments..81

  4.2. Why should the Prophet Choose?...82

    4.2.1. The Future is Secured and Guaranteed...82

    4.2.2. Islam is a Reformatory Movement..83

  4.3. The Custodian of the Sunnah...85

    4.3.1. The Documentation of the Holy Quran...85

    4.3.2. The Documentation of the Sunnah (Traditions).................................86

  4.4. Were Companions the Custodian of the Sunnah?...................................87

    4.4.1. Caliph Abu Bakr and the Sunnah of the Prophet...............................88

    4.4.2. Caliph Umar and the Sunnah of the Prophet.....................................90

    4.4.3. Erasing the Sunnah of the Prophet..92

    4.4.4. The Rest of the Companions and the Sunnah of the Prophet.........93

        4.4.4.1. A Mixed Bag...95

        4.4.4.2. Still Being Guided..96

        4.4.4.3. The Sheer Number of Companions...96

        4.4.4.4. Not to be Confused...97

5. THE LEADERSHIP OF THE AHLULBAYT...98

  5.1. The Hadith of Two Weighty Things (Thaqalayn).......................................98

    5.1.1. Creating Doubt about the Hadith of Two Weighty Things...............103

  5.2. The Prophet Prays for the Purification of Ahlulbayt...............................104

    5.2.1. Creating Doubt about the Quranic Verse 33:33................................107

  5.3. The Ahlulbayt and the Ark of Noah...108

5.4. Do not be Ahead of the Ahlulbayt..109
5.5. The Reward of the Prophet..110
5.6. The Blessings and Salutations on the Ahlulbayt in Daily Prayer.....................114
5.7. The Challenge from the People of Book (Mubahila)..116

6. THE LEADERSHIP OF ALI...121

6.1. The Home Conference (Dawat-Dhul-Ashira)..121
    6.1.1. The Precedents in History..124
    6.1.2. The Negative Attitude Towards the Leadership of Ali................................126
6.2. The Tradition of Analogy..127
    6.2.1. The Reason for the Analogy..130
    6.2.2. The Negative Attitude Towards the Tradition of Analogy..........................132
        6.2.2.1. Ali's Appointment was for a Specific Occasion..................................132
        6.2.2.2. Ali was a Temporary Successor of the Prophet................................133
6.3. Ali the Heir of the Prophet's Knowledge...134
    6.3.1. The Most Knowledgeable After the Prophet..135
    6.3.2. Muslims Should Come to the Door of Ali...136
6.4. Ali is the Mawla (Guardian) of the Muslims..138
    6.4.1. The Tradition of Ghadeer..138
    6.4.2. Analysing the Tradition of Ghadeer..141
    6.4.3. The Meaning of the Word Mawla (Guardian)...143
    6.4.4. The Word "Mawla" and "Wali" in Quran...144
    6.4.5. The Meaning of "Mawla" and "Wali" as Explained by the Prophet.............147
    6.4.6. The Meaning of "Mawla" and "Wali" as Understood by the Companions....149
    6.4.7. The Meaning of "Mawla" and "Wali" as Understood by Caliph Abu Bakr and Umar..150
    6.4.8. When the Authority of Ali was Challenged...153
    6.4.9. The Prophet Keeps Ali in Madinah...155
    6.4.10. An Observation...156

7. WHY WAS ALI NOT CHOSEN?..158

7.1. The Two Trends..158
7.2. The Trend of Al-Ijtihad (Independent Judgment)..............................159
    7.2.1. Example 1: The Treaty of Hudaybiyya......................................159
    7.2.2. Example 2: The Incident of the Pen and Paper.........................161
    7.2.3. Example 3: The Military Detachment Under Usama..................162
    7.2.4. Example 4: The Burning of the Sunnah of the Prophet.............164
7.3. After the Prophet's Death..165
7.4. The Meeting of Saqifah...166
7.5. The Approach of the Ansar...168
    7.5.1. An Unannounced Meeting...169
    7.5.2. A Dubious location..169
    7.5.3. The Ansar were Willing to Wage War...170
    7.5.4. Ali Does Get Mentioned..171
    7.5.5. The Interest of the Ansar Came First..171
    7.5.6. Ignoring the Funeral of the Prophet..173
    7.5.7. Our Approach..173
7.6. The Approach of the Muhajireen..174
    7.6.1. Both Caliph Abu Bakr and Caliph Umar Did Not Inform Others...174
    7.6.2. The Core of Caliph Abu Bakr's Argument.................................175
    7.6.3. The Merits of a Group..176
    7.6.4. The First to Embrace Islam..177
    7.6.5. We Suffered and Supported the Prophet More.........................178
        7.6.5.1. The Night of the Hijrah...179
        7.6.5.2. The Battle of Badr..179
        7.6.5.3. The Battle of Uhud...179
        7.6.5.4. The Battle of Khandaq (Moat)...180
        7.6.5.5. The Battle of Khaibar...180
        7.6.5.6. The Support and Sacrifice of Ali was Unique................181
    7.6.6. We are the Relatives of the Prophet..181
    7.6.7. The Caliph should be from the Quraysh...................................182
    7.6.8. The Offer of Ministry and a Political Adjustment.....................184

- 7.6.9. The Proposal of the Candidates..185
- 7.6.10. Leading the Prayer and Companion of the Cave......................185
  - 7.6.10.1. It wasn't the Deciding Factor...186
  - 7.6.10.2. Caliph Abu Bakr had Led the Prayers..............................187
  - 7.6.10.3. Caliph Abu Bakr is the Companion of the Cave...............188
- 7.6.11. The Real Reason...189
  - 7.6.11.1. Many Years Later..190
  - 7.6.11.2. Ali and the Quraysh...191
  - 7.6.11.3. Caliph Abu Bakr, Caliph Umar and the Quraysh...............192
  - 7.6.11.4. The Irony...192
- 7.6.12. Our Approach..192

8. DEFIANCE OF THE PROPHET AND THE LEGALITY OF SAQIFAH 194

- 8.1. How could the Companions Defy the Prophet?...................................194
  - 8.1.1. The Trend of Al-Ijtihad (Independent Judgment).........................194
  - 8.1.2. Not the First Time...195
  - 8.1.3. They Believed they were Right..195
- 8.2. Why did the Majority Accept the Mandate of Saqifah?........................196
  - 8.2.1. The Quraysh of Makkah...196
  - 8.2.2. The Key Companions in Madinah..197
  - 8.2.3. The Tribal Vote...197
  - 8.2.4. Caliph Umar's Speech at Prophet's Mosque...............................198
- 8.3. The Legality of Saqifah...199
  - 8.3.1. The influence of Quraysh...199
  - 8.3.2. The Quran and the Sunnah..200
  - 8.3.3. The Prophet's Nominee..201
  - 8.3.4. The Process of Fairness..201
  - 8.3.5. A Key Point...202

9. THE APPROACH OF ALI..204

9.1. The Funeral of the Prophet..205
9.2. Saqifah took Precedence over the Prophet's Funeral.......................................205
9.3. The News from Saqifah Reaches Ali..207
9.4. The Demand of Allegiance..207
9.5. Threatening the Ahlulbayt..209
9.6. Enforcing the Verdict of Saqifah...210
9.7. The Issue of Fadak...211
9.8. The Rift Between the Ahlulbayt and Caliph Abu Bakr and Umar......................212
9.9. Why did Ali not Raise his Sword?...213
   9.9.1. The Ground Reality..214
   9.9.2. The Frightening Prospect of Multiple Civil Wars......................................215
   9.9.3. The Offer of Abu Sufyan...216
   9.9.4. The Testimony of History..217
   9.9.5. The Prophet is a Mercy for Mankind...217
   9.9.6. The Ruling of the Quran..218
   9.9.7. The Progeny of the Prophet..219
   9.9.8. Last but not least, the Mandate of the Prophet.......................................219
9.10. The Acceptance of Political Authority..220
   9.10.1. The Spiritual Leadership and Political Authority....................................220
   9.10.2. Ali had Refused to Pay Allegiance to Abu Bakr.....................................221
   9.10.3. The Movement of Apostasy and the False Prophets..............................221
   9.10.4. Ali had no Personal or Political Ambition...223
   9.10.5. Abu Bakr Happened to be the Caliph..223
   9.10.6. Not an Acceptance of Abu Bakr's Sunnah...224
   9.10.7. A Man of Character...225
   9.10.8. Ali Establishes his Spiritual Authority..225
9.11. Our Approach...227

10. ALI IS DENIED THE CALIPHATE FOR THE SECOND TIME.........228
10.1. No Seeming Emergency Now...229
10.2. Time Constraint..230

10.3. Caliph Abu Bakr Dictates his Will...231
10.4. Companions Complain about Caliph Abu Bakr's Nominee.........................232
10.5. Another Peculiar Shura (Consultation)..233
10.6. The Choice of the Successor is not Left to the Ummah................................233

11. ALI IS DENIED THE CALIPHATE FOR THE THIRD TIME............235

11.1. The Proceedings of the Shura..237
11.2. The Rules of the Shura...240
    11.2.1. The Killing of the Companions and the Ahlulbayt.................................240
11.3. The Ansar are Barred from the Shura..241
11.4. The Choice of the Shura members...244
11.5. Head-to-Head...245
11.6. Ammar Ibn Yasir and Abdullah Ibn Abu Sarh..247
    11.6.1. Ammar Ibn Yasir..247
    11.6.2. Abdullah Ibn Abu Sarh...249
    11.6.3. The Difference in the Two Camps...250
11.7. An Unwarranted Stipulation..251
    11.7.1. Elevating the Traditions of the First Two Caliphs..................................252
    11.7.2. Their Traditions were Not in Line in the First Place...............................252
    11.7.3. The Authority of Ali's Knowledge...253
    11.7.4. A Self Contradiction...253
    11.7.5. Abdul Rahman was not Naive...253
11.8. Ali's Exemplary Character...255
11.9. Ali in his Own Words...256
    11.9.1. Ali's Participation was Essential..257
    11.9.2. The Dignified Path Adopted by Ali and the Ahlulbayt............................258

12. THE LEGACY OF SAQIFAH..260

12.1. The Caliphate of Uthman..260
12.2. The Authority of the Key Provinces...262
    12.2.1. Syria...262

12.2.2. Egypt..262

12.2.3. Iraq (Kufa)..263

12.2.4. Iraq (Basra)..264

12.3. Loose Monetary Policy..265

12.3.1. Al-Hakam Ibn Al-Auss..265

12.3.2. Marwan bin al-Hakam..266

12.3.3. Al-Harith Ibn Al-Hakam..267

12.3.4. Abdullah bin Khalid..268

12.3.5. Waleed Ibn Uqba...268

12.3.6. Muawiyah...269

12.3.7. Abu Sufyan...269

12.3.8. When Challenged on Corruption and Nepotism..270

12.4. The Consequences..270

12.4.1. The Wealthy Class...271

12.4.2. Over Taxation..271

12.4.3. Misinformation by the Umayyads..272

12.4.4. Inflamed Ambitions..273

12.5. The Start of the Opposition..273

12.5.1. Abu Dhar..273

12.5.2. Abdullah Ibn Masud...274

12.5.3. Ammar Ibn Yasir..275

12.5.4. Malik al-Ashtar...276

12.6. The Opposition Grows..277

12.6.1. Abdul Rahman Ibn Auf...277

12.6.2. Talhah and Al-Zubair...278

12.6.3. Lady Aisha...279

12.6.4. Amr Ibn al-Auss...280

12.7. Ali's Role in the Crisis..280

12.7.1. The Genuine Opposition..281

12.7.2. The Politically Motivated Opposition...282

12.7.3. The Opportunistic Opposition..282

12.7.4. Ali's Strategy to Defuse the Crisis..282

12.7.5. Ali Advises the Caliph and the Opposition.....................................283

12.8. The End Game...285

12.8.1. A Glimmer of Hope..286

12.8.2. A Colossal Disappointment..287

12.8.3. An Inevitable End..288

12.9. A few Observations...290

12.9.1. Preventing the Killing of Caliph Uthman.......................................290

12.9.2. The Inhabitants of Madinah..291

12.9.3. The Incredible Choices...291

12.9.4. The Character of Ali...292

12.9.5. The Vindication of the Prophet's Strategy....................................293

12.9.5.1. Shura was not Part of the Prophet's Strategy......................293

12.9.5.2. The Prophet's Plan..294

12.9.5.3. Our Responsibility..295

13. THE MAKINGS OF THE TRAGEDY..296

13.1. The Caliphate of Ali..297

13.1.1. The Elite Class and the Privileged Companions..........................299

13.1.2. The Politically Ambitious Companions...299

13.1.3. Lady Aisha Starts a Ferocious Campaign Against Ali................301

13.1.4. Lady Aisha, Talha and Al-Zubair Launch a War Against Ali.....302

13.1.5. Talha and Al-Zubair's Revolt Against Ali......................................303

13.1.6. The Responsibility of Lady Aisha..305

13.1.7. Muawiyah and the Umayyad Clan..307

13.1.8. The Umayyad's Used Lady Aisha and her Group.........................307

13.1.9. Muawiyah Refused to Accept Ali and Launches a War..............308

13.1.10. An Observation..310

13.1.11. The Khawarij...310

13.1.12. The Assassination of Ali...311

13.2. The Caliphate of Hasan..312

13.2.1. Muawiyah Refuses to Accept the Caliphate of Hasan..................312
13.2.2. The Reasons for the Peace Treaty..................313
13.2.3. The Peace Treaty is Signed on Six Points..................314
13.2.4. Muawiyah must Rule by the Quran and the Sunnah..................314
13.2.5. Muawiyah would not Appoint a Successor..................315
13.2.6. Protection for All..................315
13.2.7. The Life and Honour of Shias to be Protected..................315
13.2.8. Muawiyah would not Kill Members of the Ahlulbayt..................316
13.2.9. Muawiyah would Stop the Practice of Cursing Ali..................317
13.3. The Caliphate of Muawiyah..................318
   13.3.1. The Character of Muawiyah..................319
      13.3.1.1. The Killing of the Ahlulbayt (Family of the Prophet)..................322
      13.3.1.2. The Killing of the Companions and the Ordinary Muslims..................323
   13.3.2. Muawiyah Changed the Sunnah of the Prophet..................326
      13.3.2.1. Muawiyah Changed the Talbya Practice in Haj..................326
      13.3.2.2. Muawiyah Changed the Eid Prayer..................327
      13.3.2.3. Muawiyah Made Changes to the Daily Prayers..................327
      13.3.2.4. Muawiyah Blurred the Islamic Concept of Legitimacy..................327
   13.3.3. The Cursing of Ali and Instigating People Against the Ahlulbayt..............328
      13.3.3.1. Muawiyah Instructs his Governors to Curse Ali..................330
      13.3.3.2. Muawiyah Refused to Stop the Cursing of Ali..................332
   13.3.4. Muawiyah Turns the Islamic Caliphate into an Umayyad Dynasty..........333
      13.3.4.1. Muawiyah Uses Deception to Gather Support for Yazid..................334
      13.3.4.2. Muawiyah Pays People to Support Yazid's Nomination..................335
      13.3.4.3. Muawiyah Killed People to Secure Yazid's Succession..................335
      13.3.4.4. Muawiyah Leaves a Will for Yazid..................336
   13.3.5. An Unfortunate Defence..................337
      13.3.5.1. The Merits of Muawiyah..................338
      13.3.5.2. Muawiyah was the Writer of the Revelations..................341
      13.3.5.3. Muawiyah was a Companion of the Prophet..................343
         13.3.5.3.1. The Elite Class of Muslims..................343

13.3.5.3.2. The Testimony of the Holy Quran..344

13.3.5.3.3. The Tradition of the Prophet, Do not Abuse my Companions......345

13.3.5.3.4. The Later Generations can be Superior to the Generation of the Companions...347

13.3.5.3.5. The Highest Honour of a Human Being..349

13.3.5.3.6. Some Companions will be driven to Hellfire................................351

13.3.6. The Prophecy of the Prophet...352

13.3.7. A True Talent would Always Shine..353

13.3.8. The Legitimacy of Muawiyah's Caliphate..354

13.3.9. Imam Hussain Sums up the Caliphate of Muawiyah.............................357

14. THE TRAGEDY OF KARBALA AND THE STAND OF HUSSAIN..360

14.1. The Inauguration of Yazid..360

14.2. Yazid Demands Allegiance..362

14.3. Hussain Refuses...363

14.3.1. The Peace Treaty with the Umayyads..364

14.3.2. In Defence of the Prophet's Revolution..365

14.3.3. A Protest Against Oppression..365

14.3.4. Hussain, the Last Man Standing...366

14.4. Hussain Leaves Madinah and Heads to Makkah..367

14.5. The Invitation from Kufa..368

14.5.1. Hussain Sends his Ambassador to Kufa..368

14.5.2. The Situation Deteriorates in Kufa...369

14.5.3. Yazid Appoints a New Governor in Kufa...370

14.5.4. Ubaydullah Asserts his Authority...371

14.5.5. Ubaydullah Hires a Spy..372

14.5.6. Muslim bin Aqeel's Network is Compromised..372

14.5.7. Muslim bin Aqeel calls upon his Supporters..373

14.5.8. Ubaydullah Pacifies Supporters of Muslim bin Aqeel............................374

14.5.9. The Killing off Muslim bin Aqeel...374

14.5.10. Muslim bin Aqeel's Young Sons are Slaughtered too..........................376

14.6. Hussain Starts his Journey..376
    14.6.1. Hussain Learns about the Killing of Muslim bin Aqeel...................377
    14.6.2. Ubaydullah's Men Intercept the Caravan of Hussain......................378
14.7. Hussain Arrives in Karbala..379
    14.7.1. Hussain Purchases the Land in Karbala...379
    14.7.2. Hussain is Surrounded, Food and Water is Cut Off........................380
    14.7.3. The Night Before the Battle..382
14.8. The Day of Ashura...384
    14.8.1. Hussain Identifies Himself..384
    14.8.2. The Discipline of Hussain's Contingent...386
    14.8.3. The Sacrifice of the Ahlulbayt and the Banu Hashim Begins..........387
    14.8.4. Ali Akbar (Son of Imam Hussain)...387
    14.8.5. Qasim (Son of Hasan)...389
    14.8.6. Ali Asghar (Six Month Old Son of Hussain).....................................391
    14.8.7. Hussain, the Grandson of the Prophet..394
    14.8.8. Hussain Bids Farewell to his Son..394
    14.8.9. Hussain Bids Farewell to the Women and Children........................395
    14.8.10. Hussain Heads to the Battlefield..397
    14.8.11. Hussain's Body is Trampled with Hooves......................................399
14.9. The Tyranny Against Hussain's Women and Children.........................401
    14.9.1. Sakina, the Beloved Daughter of Hussain.......................................401
    14.9.2. Headscarves are Snatched from the Women of the Prophet's Family......402
    14.9.3. The Parading of Women and Children from the Prophet's Family............403
    14.9.4. The Women and Children are Paraded Again in Damascus...................404
    14.9.5. The Imprisonment of the Prophet's Family....................................405
    14.9.6. A Place to Remember and Mourn the Tragedy...............................405
14.10. How could this Happen?...406
14.11. Defaming the Stand of Hussain..409
    14.11.1. Was the Stand of Hussain Initiated by the People of Kufa?.........410
    14.11.2. Hussain could have been Killed in Madinah..................................411
    14.11.3. Hussain could have been Killed in Makkah...................................412

14.11.4. Hussain could have Returned Home from the Outskirts of Kufa............413
14.11.5. Hussain's Life could have been Spared in Karbala................413
14.11.6. The Shias of Kufa Invited, Betrayed and Killed Hussain..............414
14.11.7. The Shias of Kufa and its History 415
14.11.8. The Invitation of Hussain to Kufa..................418
14.11.9. The Betrayal of Hussain.....................420
    14.11.9.1. What Actually Happened?....................420
    14.11.9.2. Brief Analysis....................422
14.11.10. The Killing of Hussain......................423
    14.11.10.1. Who Killed Hussain?..................423
    14.11.10.2. The Opportunist Killers of Hussain.................426
    14.11.10.3. The Individuals Switching Sides...................428
    14.11.10.4. Ubaydullah Prevents the Supporters of Hussain............430
14.11.11. In Present Day Terms.....................432
14.11.12. The Shias of Ali in Kufa and the Companions of the Prophet..............433
14.11.13. The First Attempt to Avenge the Killing of Hussain Fails.................434
14.11.14. The Second attempt to Avenge the Killing of Hussain Succeeds.........436
14.11.15. Hussain did not Listen to the Advice of the Key Companions..............439
14.11.16. When Hasan Signed a Deal then Why did Hussain Take a Stand........442
14.11.17. Hussain was Going for Power and was After the Caliphate.................445
14.11.18. The Fabricated Story of Imam Baqir....................447
14.11.19. Yazid was Forgiven by the Prophet..................449
    14.11.19.1. The Attack on Madinah....................451
    14.11.19.2. The Attack on Makkah....................452
14.12. Hussain the Magnificent....................453
14.13. Visiting the Shrine of Hussain....................456

15. A LOGICAL APPROACH....................459

15.1. The Best Man....................459
15.2. The Majority and the Minority....................462
15.3. Our Approach....................464

16. A COUPLE OF ADDITIONAL TOPICS FOR COMPLETENESS.....467

16.1. The Justification of Saqifah..467
16.2. The Consensus of the Ummah (Ijma)..469
16.3. Bottom of the Pile..470
16.3.1. The Order of Saqifah..471
16.3.2. The Merits...472
16.3.2.1. Companionship with the Prophet...472
16.3.2.2. Piousness and Piety..472
16.3.2.3. Knowledge and Wisdom..473
16.3.2.4. Bravery and Contribution in the Service of Islam......................473
16.4. Burden, Binding, an Indication, and an Indirect Appointment.........................475
16.4.1. Burden and Binding...476
16.4.2. An Indication or an Indirect Appointment......................................479
16.5. Our Approach...482
16.6. The Jewish Conspiracy...483
16.7. The Theories Attributed to Ibn Saba...484
16.7.1. The Return of the Prophet..485
16.7.2. Ali is the Successor of the Prophet..485
16.7.3. Ibn Saba and the Caliphate of Uthman..487
16.7.3.1. The Reasons for the Jewish Card..489
16.7.3.2. The Genuine opposition..489
16.7.4. The Politically Motivated Opposition..489
16.7.4.1. The Opportunistic Opposition...489
16.7.4.2. Lady Aisha, Talhah and Zubair..489
16.7.4.3. The Events Dispel the Existence of Ibn Saba..............................490
16.8. Ibn Saba in the Eyes of History..491
16.8.1. Ibn Saba according to Sunni History...491
16.8.1.1. Sayf Ibn Umar..491
16.8.1.2. Ibn Asakir..493
16.8.2. Ibn Saba according to Shia History..493
16.8.3. An Interesting Theory..495

16.9. The Mythical Saba'iya Group..495

    16.9.1. The Perishing Arabs..496

    16.9.2. The Adnaniya Arabs..496

    16.9.3. The Qathanian Arabs..496

    16.9.4. Saba'iya is an Ethnic Group...496

16.10. Why would a Jew Exalt Ali?..497

16.11. Caliph Umar and Jewish Influence..498

    16.11.1. Caliph Umar and Kaab Al-Ahbar...499

    16.11.2. The Advice of the Prophet to Caliph Umar...............................499

Copyright © 2026 by Fadhil Rahmi

All rights reserved. No part of this publication may be reproduced, distributed, or transmitted in any form or by any means, including photocopying, recording, or other electronic or mechanical methods, without the prior written permission of the publisher, except in the case of brief quotations embodied in critical reviews or certain other noncommercial uses permitted by copyright law.

ISBN eBook   : 979-8-90046-849-5

ISBN Paperback   : 979-8-90243-552-5

Disclaimer: The views and opinions expressed in this book are those of the author and do not necessarily reflect the official policy or position of any organization, institution, or religious group. This book is intended for educational and informational purposes only.

1. THE MISSION OF THE PROPHET

Islam was a revolution that had swept through Arabia challenging each and every custom of the Arabs. Prophet Mohammad, as the head of this revolutionary movement of Islam had introduced a radical transformation to the customs, traditions, and structures of this primitive and medieval society.

The Arabs were mostly nomadic people living in small towns and settlements dotted around the vast desert. Taif and Madinah had slightly better means of livelihood compared to the harsh reality facing most people living in the open desert. Makkah was the city of the iconic temple, its residents were mostly tradesmen who valued a dinar more than the life of a human being.

The Arabs were so ignorant that they used to bury their daughters alive, for no reason except that it was a custom that they had been following for generations. They used to kill each other on trivial matters and the bloodshed would last for generations to come. They used to kill their own brothers and would glorify and rejoice their death. Tribal wars, tribal rivalry and tribal jealously were entrenched in their way of life.

The Arabs were the most proud and egoistic people who used to regard non-Arabs as inferior and even sub-human. The women had no respect or value in this undeveloped and uncivilized society. They were openly bought and sold and were given away to settle disputes and wars.

An existence devoid of morality and decency was the way of life in the inhospitable desert, where present was full of despair and future without any hope. This was the land called Arabia where existence of righteousness and piety were a novelty.

In this deeply uncivilized and uncultured society the Prophet of Allah had arrived as a reformer, as a teacher and as a revolutionary guide. He took on the traditions and customs of this medieval society and brought about justice, brotherhood, equality, fair play, and structure to this backward and unsophisticated nation.

Through his intellectual and spiritual leadership, the Prophet had introduced a comprehensive system of governance, something that Arabs had never seen or experienced before. The system that Prophet had formulated constituted all the elements needed to successfully run and defend the newly established way of life for the Muslims of Arabia. The defence and the survival of the Islamic nation was pitched under the umbrella of the Islamic State of Madinah that Prophet had establish as a base for the Muslims.

The notions of being part of the Muslim Ummah and living under the authority of an Islamic State were concepts that Arabs had never imagined or envisaged before the arrival of Islam.

Once the Islamic State of Madinah was established the Prophet came up with the idea of a public treasury, that would we used for the welfare of poor and needy. This was a new and a unique concept which was unheard off in the medieval Arabia, that the State would look after and help the underprivileged and the disadvantaged in the society. The Prophet introduced a foreign policy element to the newly established State of Madinah, where the ambassadors would go out to other nations inviting them to the path of Allah. The army was given a structure and an order to work as a cohesive force for the defence and the survival of the Islamic State.

These revolutionary steps were unheard of in the primitive land of Arabia, where prior to the coming of Islam people had no structured or organized way of life. The Arabs used to aimlessly wonder in the desert and their lives mostly revolved around internal conflicts, tribal rivalry, tribal jealously and wars. They had no sense of living together as one nation or as one people, where everybody was equal in the eyes of the creator.

Apart from establishing the key elements of the Islamic State, the system of governance that Prophet had introduced comprised of rules and laws that governed each and every aspect of an individual's life. The Islamic ideology introduced a new way of dealing with the family, conducting of business and settling of disputes amicably. And above all it created a notion of a sense of responsibility for others, something that was missing in the Arab societies of that era.

The tribal leaders and the ordinary tribesmen were all subjected to the same set of rules without any discrimination or favouritism, a philosophy that was completely new for the Arabs.

The road from Jahiliya (backwardness) to Islam was long and protracted. It was spread over a period of twenty-three years, and was littered with opposition, sacrifices, patience and wars. The Messenger of Allah had brought an astonishing and amazing transformation to this inhumane and uncivilized society in a very short span of time. The reformatory movement of the Prophet began with a Jahili (backward) man and raised him to the status of a Muslim.

The successful revolution that Prophet had started had to continue and had to be kept on the right track even after his death, since the revolutionary movement of Islam was not going to end after the death of the Prophet.

The Prophet of Islam knew very well that he was the final messenger, and Allah will not send any more Prophets to guide humanity after his death. The Prophet knew that he could not rely on future Messengers to carry the revolution of Islam forward.

The Prophet also knew that his death was approaching. He openly discloses it at the Farewell Pilgrimage (Hujjat-al-Wada). His death was not sudden, unexpected or accidental.

As the head of the revolutionary movement of Islam that was sweeping through Arabia, the Prophet had ample time to contemplate and think about the future of the Islamic State that he had established.

There were primarily three possibilities or options available to the Prophet before his death.

1.1. The Three Possibilities

The three possibilities available to the Prophet before his demise were:

The First Possibility

The Prophet adopts a passive attitude towards the future of the Islamic movement. The Prophet is contend and satisfied with the part that he has already played in bringing the people to the path of Allah. The

Prophet has no plans or thoughts for the future leadership of the Islamic movement that he had started. The Prophet was only concerned with the message of Islam during his lifetime, and he leaves the choice of the future leadership of the Islamic Sate into the hands of the Muslim Ummah. The Prophet does not give any clear guidelines for choosing the future leader of the Muslims, and he does not explicitly choose one either. The Prophet was happy to leave the future of the Islamic State to the turn of events.

The Second Possibility

The Prophet is concerned about the future of the Islamic movement that he had worked so hard to establish. He is actively contemplating as to how the future leadership of the Islamic State would be chosen. He advocates the institution of Shura (consultation) as a means of selecting the future leader of the Muslims. The Shura would be composed of the faithful from the first generation of Muslims. It will comprise of the prominent companions from the Ansar (natives of Madinah), Muhajireen (immigrants from Makkah), and the Ahlulbayt (family of the Prophet). The Shura would be responsible for choosing the future leader of the Muslims who would take the mantle of the Islamic State of Madinah after the demise of the Prophet.

The Third Possibility

The Prophet is actively thinking about the future of the revolution that he had started, a revolution that is a source of inspiration and guidance for the entire mankind. The Prophet chooses a capable person who has been deeply involved in this revolution from the very beginning, to lead the ideological movement of Islam in his absence. The Prophet trains this individual from an early age and breathes into him the spirit and the ideals of Islam. The Prophet prepares him spiritually, intellectually, religiously and politically to guide and lead the Muslims after his death.

We will now discuss all three possibilities in depth.

1.2. The First Possibility

The Prophet adopts a passive attitude towards the future of the Islamic movement. The Prophet is contended and satisfied with the part that he has already played in bringing the people to the path of Allah. The Prophet has no plans or thoughts for the future leadership of the Islamic movement that he had started. The Prophet was only concerned with the message of Islam during his lifetime, and he leaves the choice of the future leadership of the Islamic Sate into the hands of the Muslim Ummah. The Prophet does not give any clear guidelines for choosing the future leader of the Muslims, and he does not explicitly choose one either. The Prophet was happy to leave the future of the Islamic State to the turn of events.

It is of course unthinkable to associate any kind of passivity with the Prophet especially when it came to the message of Islam. The Prophet of Allah was the embodiment of Islam in every sense. He knew that the message of Islam had not just come for his era and was not limited to his lifetime. On the contrary, the message of Islam was for all of humanity including all the future generations of mankind, until the end of time.

The Prophet had sacrificed everything for the sake of Allah and for spreading the message of Islam. He had left his home in Makkah for the survival of his mission. He had spent all his personal wealth and fortune in the service of Allah. He had sacrificed his family and his companions in this path. He had lost his uncle al-Hamzah in the battle of Uhud. Many of his most loyal companions had been brutally tortured and killed by the enemies of the Islamic movement.

The Prophet had no option but to guarantee and ensure the success of the Islamic revolution even after his death.

Let us see if it was even wise or viable for the Prophet to stay passive and leave the future of the Islamic movement that he had setup to the turn of events.

1.2.1. Challenges Faced by Islam and the Muslims

The Islamic revolution was facing a series of challenges and threats both from within the Muslim ranks and also from the outside powers.

The Khosrows (Kings of Persia) and Caesars were lying in wait to ambush the Muslims at any opportunity. Any vacuum created by the death of the Prophet would give them the perfect opportunity to strike the Islamic movement.

In addition to this there was danger to the Islamic cause from the hypocrites (Munafiqun), who were also planning and plotting against the Muslims from time to time. The Holy Quran has dedicated a whole chapter on the faction of Munafiqun. They were an anonymous group of companions whose names are not known but they act treacherously against the Prophet and his mission. The Quran addresses them in the following way:

> *When the hypocrites come to you, [O Muhammad], they say, "We testify that you are the Messenger of Allah ." And Allah knows that you are His Messenger, and Allah testifies that the hypocrites are liars. They have taken their oaths as a cover, so they averted [people] from the way of Allah. Indeed, it was evil that they were doing. That is because they believed, and then they disbelieved; so their hearts were sealed over….. They are the enemy, so beware of them. May Allah destroy them"*
>
> - *Quran (63:1-4)*

Then there were large number of new converts who had entered the faith after various conquests, many of whom had become Muslims out of material gains rather than out of spiritual awakening. Abu Sufyan heads this list. He had fought the Muslims from the very beginning of Islam. He only accepted Islam after the conquest of Makkah, realizing that he could no longer take on the might of the Muslims. It was now better for these people to become Muslims rather than pay jizya (a tax paid by the non-Muslims).

In the absence of a guiding leadership these elements and groups would find a chance to grow if there was a sudden vacuum at the helm. It would be totally impossible to think that an ideological leader like the Prophet would not have assessed or envisaged this danger and remain passive about the future of the Islamic movement.

It is obvious that the Prophet could not possibly have taken a passive approach and leave the future of the Islamic movement that he had worked so hard to the turn of events.

1.2.2. Sincerity of the Prophet

One possibility as to why the Prophet could have taken a passive approach would be to assume that although the Prophet was aware of the dangers facing Islam, and he knew how important the question of leadership was for the movement of Islam, but he did not seek to protect Islam after his death since he did not care about its future and its progress, and he was unconcerned about the Islamic movement after his demise.

Such a notion undoubtably would question the sincerity of the Prophet. This explanation is of course unthinkable in the case of our beloved Prophet. Even if someone does not believe in Islam and does not consider him to be a Prophet, they cannot question the sincerity of the Prophet towards his mission. His passion, his commitment, his sacrifice and his devotion to the cause of Islam cannot be questioned. His entire life until his death proves how attached and concerned he remained to the cause of the Islamic movement that he had begun.

We can see that Prophet was profoundly ill in his final days, he was coming in and out of consciousness, but even on his death bed the Prophet is deeply concerned about the army that he had dispatched under the leadership of Usama.

According to Tarikh al-Kamil of Ibn Athir, the Prophet orders his companions:

> *"Stand ready with Usama's forces! Help the forces of Usama! Send out Usama's contingents!"*
> - *Tarikh al-Kamil of ibn Athir*

This event and others clearly show that the Prophet was deeply concerned and mindful about the future of the Islamic movement. The Prophet was about to die, he does not stand to gain militarily or materialistically from the success of Usama's campaign. He will not be there to reap the rewards of Usama's success. But his deep concern about Usama's campaign shows his immense sincerity towards his mission.

To somehow consider that the Prophet had adopted a passive attitude towards the future of the Islamic movement is to question the sincerity and the integrity of the Prophet himself.

1.2.3. The Importance of Leadership Among the Companions

As soon as the Prophet passed away some of the prominent companions rushed to a place called Saqifah to choose the future leader of the Muslims. Caliph Abu Bakr had come to pay his respects to the Prophet after his death. But as soon as he and other notable companions like Caliph Umar heard that the Ansar had gathered in Saqifah to decide the future leadership of the Muslims, they also left Prophet's house and rushed to Saqifah.

This is how important and critical the issue of the leadership of the Muslims was that the most prominent companions did not even wait for the burial of the Prophet. The future leader of the Islamic movement was decided even before the Prophet was buried. Many of the prominent companions did not even participate in his burial because they considered the issue of leadership to be so critical.

Clearly, if the companions had considered this issue to be so critical and important that they could not even wait for Prophet's burial, then surely the Prophet who was the founder of the Islamic faith must have given some consideration and thought to the future leadership of the Muslims!

We read in history that Caliph Abu Bakr who became the first Caliph did not take a passive approach towards the future leadership of Islam. Before his death he meets a number of companions and then gets Caliph Uthman to write his will. In his will he nominates the second Caliph Umar to be his successor.

It is worth noting that in the last couple of days of his life Caliph Abu Bakr was extremely ill. He was coming in and out of consciousness. Even in that state he was not going to neglect the issue of his successorship. He was so weak that he could not even write his own will, but he got Caliph Uthman to write it for him. It shows how important and paramount it was for Caliph Abu Bakr to have considered and done something about the future leadership of the Muslims. He clearly does not leave anything to a chance or turn of events, even though he is on his death bed.

Similarly, Caliph Umar was deeply concerned and worried about the future of the Caliphate. The famous scholar Allama Shibli Nomani from South Asia wrote in his book Al-Farooq, (page176):

> *"Umar pondered a lot about his successor in his last days and people often found him sitting alone absorbed in thought. When asked, he said he was worried about the Caliphate (after him)."*

The second Caliph Umar appoints a committee of six people before his death to choose his successor. The second Caliph was stabbed with a dagger by a Persian slave called Firoz also known as Abu Lulu. The second Caliph was in immense pain and fell unconscious several times. But even in this condition he did not ignore the question of his successorship. This is how important and critical the issue of Islamic leadership was among the Companions.

Caliph Umar indeed gave some very clear guidelines as to how the future leader of the Muslims should be chosen after his death. He stated the following.

> *"O group of Muhajireen! Verily, the Apostle of God died, and he was pleased with all six of you. I have, therefore, decided to make it (the selection of Khalifa) a matter of consultation among you, so that you may select one of yourselves as Khalifa. If five of you agree upon one man, and there is one who is opposed to the five, kill him. If four are one side and two on the other, kill the two. And if three are on one side and three on the other, then Abdur Rahman Ibn Auf will have the casting vote, and the Khalifa will be selected from his party. In that case, kill the three men on the opposing side. You may, if you wish, invite some of the chief men of the Ansar as observers but the Khalifa must be one of you Muhajireen, and not any of them. They have no share in the khilafat. And your selection of the new Khalifa must be made within three days."*

- Al-Tabari, Vol 3, pp. 294-295

We observe that even on his death bed, Caliph Umar does not take a passive attitude towards the future leadership of the Muslims. On the contrary, he sets up a committee of notables during his lifetime with clear instructions as to how the next ruler of the Muslims should be chosen. He gives them a strict deadline of three days to choose his successor and even orders the killing of the committee members who would oppose the majority consensus of the Shura.

These actions show how prudent and conscious both Caliph Abu Bakr and Caliph Umar were about choosing their successors. Caliph Abu Bakr had written a will in which he nominated his successor whereas Caliph Umar had setup a committee of six people before his death to select his successor.

To say that Prophet had not considered or given any clear guidelines or instructions about his successor and the future leadership of the Islamic movement, and that he had left it to the Ummah is an insult to the intellect and the wisdom of the Prophet.

1.2.4. The Prophet's Position

The Prophet of Allah was not just a political leader, he was a spiritual authority as well as a religious guide. He oversaw of all aspects of the Muslim Ummah. The Muslims would turn to him for guidance in all spheres of life including political, social, religious, and even personal. All roads led to the Prophet. He was the refuge of the Muslims for any problems and challenges that they would face, especially after adopting the new faith.

The Prophet, more than anybody else knew his pivotal role as the head of the Muslim Ummah. If a leader of Prophet's stature and standing would leave or die without thoroughly and proactively thinking about the future, it would plunge the entire Muslim Ummah into a crisis and uncertainty. Also, a vacuum would be left right at the top which could easily be exploited by the enemies of the Muslims.

The Prophet being the final messenger of Allah could not possibly allow such a crisis to engulf the Ummah on his death. He was far too wise and smart not to have considered such a scenario in his lifetime and thought about all such eventualities before his death.

Also, if the Prophet stays passive about the future leadership of Muslims, it means that he was putting the entire burden on the newly established Muslim Ummah, to decide the future course of Islamic governance on their own. This would have meant that the Muslim would be totally responsible for securing the future of the Islamic state and Islamic faith without any guidance, advice or thought from the Prophet on this matter.

The Prophet could not possibly put such a burden on the Ummah and potentially jeopardize the future of the Islamic State, while he stays passive during his lifetime.

We read in the Holy Quran in chapter 33 verse 6 that:

> *"Prophet has more authority over the believers than they have over themselves".*

The clearly implies that Prophet has more right to manage the affairs of the Muslims then the Muslims themselves. When Allah has given Prophet such an authority, then it would be inconceivable to think that Prophet would not use his authority and define a clear path for the future leadership of Islam.

Let us look at an example from everyday life to further clarify this issue.

1.2.5. A Project Manager

Let's say that you are the project manager of a team and you are leading and managing a project. When you go on vacation you have two options.

- You can either delegate your responsibilities to each of the team members, clearly defining the tasks that would need to be carried out by the team while you are away.

Or

- You can choose somebody from your team and make them in charge in your absence. When you make somebody in charge you will choose the most capable person from the team, somebody who understands the project thoroughly, somebody who is most knowledgeable about the project, somebody who has ideally been involved in the project from the beginning and of course somebody who is capable of leading.

If you neglect either of the above options and go away on vacation, you will be considered as an unprofessional project manager. Your superiors will question your managerial skills and your commitment to the project. In addition to this your project will suffer from lack of leadership and would lose direction while you are away.

The revolution of Islam was the most important project that Prophet Mohammad had embarked upon in the history of humanity. The Prophet of Allah was not going away on vacation, he was in fact leaving this world for good and he knew that his death was approaching fast.

To think that Prophet would just leave the project of Islam without either clearly delegating the responsibilities to his most prominent companions or appointing a successor is a travesty. It goes against wisdom, common sense, reason, and logic.

Islam is a complete way of life. It governs every aspect of a person's life i.e., from the moment a child is born to the moment he or she dies, Islam has defined rules and regulations for each and every step. How is it possible that a religion which is so thorough and so comprehensive would be passive about the question of governance and leadership, and would leave it to the Ummah to figure it out?

The Prophet of Islam knows that he is the seal of the Prophets, he is the final messenger of Allah. There will be no more divine messengers after him. The buck stops with him. He cannot possibly stay passive about the future leadership of the Muslims.

He needs to clearly define and lay down the foundations for choosing his successor.

1.3. The Second Possibility

The Prophet is concerned about the future of the Islamic movement that he had worked so hard to establish. He is actively contemplating as to how the future leadership of the Islamic State would be chosen. He advocates the institution of Shura (consultation) as a means of selecting the future leader of the Muslims. The Shura would be composed of the faithful from the first generation of Muslims. It will comprise of the prominent companions from the Ansar (natives of Madinah), Muhajireen (immigrants from Makkah), and the Ahlulbayt (family of the Prophet). The Shura would be responsible for choosing the future leader of the Muslims who would take the mantle of the Islamic State of Madinah after the demise of the Prophet.

This approach makes sense that the Prophet had thought about the future of the Islamic movement, and the Prophet of Allah wanted the future leader of the Muslims to be chosen by Shura (Consultation) after his death. This is certainly plausible.

If Prophet wanted Shura to be the way forward for selecting his successor, then at least he would have taken one of the following steps.

- Either setup a council of Muslims elders from all sections of the Islamic society during his lifetime and give them the responsibility for choosing his successor after his death.

Or

- The Prophet would have educated his companions on the modalities and the legal requirements of a Shura, so that the companions could setup a Shura themselves after the death of the Prophet and choose his successor.

It is clear and transparent from the sources of history that Prophet of Islam never established a council of Muslim elders during his lifetime, who would have been responsible for choosing his successor. There is no mention of such a council in the books of hadith or history of any of the Islamic schools. For instance, we have seen clear evidence in the previous section that Caliph Umar appointed a committee of six people to choose his successor during his lifetime. The names of the committee members with clear instructions from the Caliph on how to choose his successor are found in the books of hadith and Islamic history. But there is no such evidence that Prophet had ever initiated a Shura or a consultative body to appoint his successor during his lifetime.

Any student of Islamic history or hadith can confirm that Prophet of Allah did not take this path for the future leadership of the Muslims.

Now we come to the second point.

1.3.1. Did Prophet Envisage a Shura (Consultation) to be Established by the Companions?

If the Prophet wanted his companions to establish a Shura after his death, then the Prophet of Allah would have thoroughly and clearly defined the modalities and the legal requirements of a Shura during his lifetime. It would have been necessary for the Prophet to educate the first generation of Muslims on the concepts, the rules and the regulations concerning the principle of Shura. The Prophet of Allah would have specifically prepared the newly established Islamic society both mentally and spiritually to accept the system of Shura as a means of selecting his successor.

The education of the first generation of Muslims on the practical aspects of Shura and the implementation of its principles would have been vital on the part of the Prophet. This is because the Islamic society grew from a confederation of clans and tribes where the leaders were chosen based on their ethnic and tribal lineages, and not according to the Islamic principle of Shura. In fact, the leadership among the Arabs prior to the coming of Islam was primarily based around the tribal customs of power, wealth, and inheritance.

It would have been essential for the Prophet to at least teach his foremost companions about the political and the legal aspects of Shura. The likes of Caliph Abu Bakr, Caliph Umar, Caliph Uthman, Ali, Talha, Zubair, Ibn Abbas and other leading Islamic personalities should have been trained and educated in the structure and the legalities of Shura.

However, there is no evidence to suggest that the Prophet had ever trained or educated any of his companions on the practical, legal, or political aspects of Shura, which would then become the basis for selecting his successor or a ruler over the Muslims.

We are not debating the principle of Shura itself, the principle of Shura certainly exists in Islam. But the point I am making is whether the Prophet had envisaged or wanted the methodology of Shura to be used as a means of selecting his immediate successor? If he wanted the first generation of Muslims to use the principle of Shura to choose his successor, then he would have given them clear guidelines on how to establish the Shura after his death.

The Prophet would have consciously taught and trained his prominent companions from both the Ansar and the Muhajireen on the system and the methodology of Shura. The Prophet would have at least informed his companions on the very basic principle of Shura (Consultation) that a Shura can only be conducted when all the concerned parties are present.

We would shortly see that Prophet did not educate or train anybody from the first generation of Muslims on various rules and regulations regarding the system of Shura. If Prophet had done such a thing, then it would have been embodied in the hadith and the history that has been reported from that era, and above all it would have been reflected in the actions and the practices of the companions.

There are no traditions of the Prophet or reports of history that one could find which would show that Prophet wanted Muslims to choose his successor through the system of Shura. This theory is also endorsed and vindicated by the behaviour and the actions of the companions as we will shortly see.

1.3.2. The Shura (Consultation) of Saqifah

In fact, the history of events that took place after the death of the Prophet testify that the first generation of Muslims as far as the Ansar and the Muhajireen were concerned had no idea about the modalities of Shura!

To see what actually took place immediately after the death of the Prophet I will briefly mention the Shura (Consultation) of Saqifah where Caliph Abu Bakr was chosen as the leader of the Muslims. This would clarify the position of the companions as far as their understanding of Shura (Consultation) was concerned.

A Comprehensive discussion and analysis on the event of Saqifah will be done in Chapter 7.

The Muslim community at the time of the death of the Prophet was made up of three distinct groups namely the Ansar (companions from Madinah), Muhajireen (companions from Makkah) and the Ahlulbayt (the family of the Prophet).

Saqifah was a place which was about two or three miles from Madinah. This is where the Shura (Consultation) for selecting the first Caliph of the Muslims was done, and hence it is known as the Shura of Saqifah.

The Shura of Saqifah began with the news of the death of the Prophet. As soon as the Ansar (companions from Madinah) heard that Prophet had passed away they started gathering in Saqifah with the intention of selecting the next Caliph. The Ansar without wasting anytime selected Saad ibn Ubaadah as the future leader of the Muslims, and almost finalized him as the new Caliph to rule over the entire Muslim Ummah. The Ansar even declared that in case the Muhajireen refused to accept their choice, they would drive the Muhajireen out of Madinah on the point of their swords.

However, some companions who were present in Saqifah and were observing its proceedings left the meeting, and informed Caliph Umar about the pre-emptive move of the Ansar for the Caliphate of the Muslims. On hearing the news of the meeting of Ansar in Saqifah Caliph Umar immediately informs Caliph Abu Bakr as to what was happening in Saqifah.

Caliph Abu Bakr at the time was present in the house of the Prophet where the Ahlulbayt (family of the Prophet) were busy in preparing the Prophet's body for burial. As Caliph Abu Bakr receives the news from Caliph Umar that Ansar had gathered in Saqifah he leaves the house of the Prophet and goes to Saqifah with Caliph Umar.

Once they reach Saqifah both Caliph Umar and Caliph Abu Bakr witness that the Ansar had almost finalized Saad ibn Ubaadah as the new Caliph. The Ansar were remunerating their merits and were claiming that since they had given refuge and protection to the Prophet, and since Madinah was their city the future Caliph should be from the Ansar.

Caliph Abu Bakr intervenes in the meeting of Saqifah and acknowledges the merits of Ansar but says that the leadership of the Muslims is only the right of the Muhajireen, since they were the first to accept Islam, and since they had sacrificed more in the path of Allah, and because the Quraysh would not accept the leadership of the Ansar, so it was essential that the new Caliph should be from the Muhajireen.

Both Caliph Abu Bakr and Umar were from the Muhajireen.

The Ansar disagreed and insisted that the Caliph had to be from one of them, as they deserved the Caliphate more than the Muhajireen. A serious discord and dispute began to emerge between the Ansar and the Muhajireen, to the extent that it seemed that the Shura of Saqifah might lead to an open war between the two groups.

Despite the extremely serious and tense situation with the Ansar Caliph Abu Bakr and Caliph Umar refused to budge and did not give into their demands. They kept insisting that the Caliph must be from the Muhajireen, since the Quraysh would not accept the leadership of anyone other than the Muhajireen.

As the meeting of Saqifah reached a stalemate the Ansar proposed a compromise. They offered Caliph Abu Bakr and Caliph Umar to have one ruler from the Ansar and one from the Muhajireen. Caliph Abu Bakr and Caliph Umar declined the offer of the Ansar and said that there could only be one leader of the Muslims, and that leader had to be from Muhajireen since they are from Quraysh, and Quraysh would not accept an Ansar as the new Caliph.

There was a lot of commotion, disagreement and turmoil in the meeting of Saqifah and threats are openly flying. On seeing the situation Caliph Abu Bakr proposed a compromise. He said to the Ansar that we the Muhajireen should become the rulers and you the Ansar should become our advisors, essentially offering Ansar the position of the advisory to the Caliph. Caliph Abu Bakr further stated that the Muhajireen would not make any decisions without consulting the Ansar, giving the Ansar a further incentive to accept his offer.

The Ansar at this stage had suffered a setback, they had lost unity within their own ranks. The old rivalry between the two tribes of Ansar i.e., Al-Aws and Al-Khazraj began to resurface, and the political advantage was shifting to the Muhajireen who were now leading the proceedings of Saqifah.

The Ansar began to contemplate the offer of Caliph Abu Bakr.

Despite the offer of Caliph Abu Bakr, the arguments and the wrangling between the Ansar and the Muhajireen continued unabated, where each side was still vying for power. However, the Ansar could feel that the balance of power was shifting to the Muhajireen who were in the ascendency and were now dictating the proceedings and the terms of the Shura.

On seeing that the Caliphate was slipping away from them and into the hands of the Muhajireen, the Ansar shifted their position and reluctantly accepted the offer of Caliph Abu Bakr to become the advisors to the Caliph.

The Ansar at that stage realized that the top-most position that they could possibly acquire in the presence of the Muhajireen was the position offered by Caliph Abu Bakr. The position of the advisors (vazirs) would give them a say in the decision-making process of the State, something that the Ansar had always desired and wished for, and hence they eventually accepted the offer of being the advisors (vazirs) to the Caliph.

As soon as Caliph Umar sensed that the Ansar had conceded and some sort of an agreement was in the making, he seized the moment and asked Caliph Abu Bakr to stretch out his hand. As Caliph Abu Bakr stretched out his hand Caliph Umar immediately paid allegiance to him to pacify any further discourse or wrangling between the Ansar and the Muhajireen.

The impromptu allegiance of Caliph Umar on the hand of Caliph Abu Bakr sealed the Caliphate for the Muhajireen. This was followed by the allegiance from Abu Ubaydah Ibn al-Jarrah who was the other Muhajir (immigrant from Makkah) present in the meeting of Saqifah.

On seeing that the key Muhajireen present in the meeting had paid allegiance to Abu Bakr, Bashir ibn Saad from the al-Khazraj tribe of Ansar paid allegiance to Abu Bakr, in order not to lose out on the position of being the advisor (vazir).

On witnessing that the members of al-Khazraj have paid allegiance to Abu Bakr, the leaders of al-Aws also paid allegiance to Abu Bakr, in order not to lose favour in the eyes of the new Caliph, and also to acquire the promised position of being the advisors (vazirs).

This is how the meeting of Saqifah ended with Abu Bakr becoming the first Caliph and the leader of the entire Muslim Ummah.

1.3.3. Brief Analysis of the Meeting (Shura) of Saqifah

The Ansar who were the companions of the Prophet from Madinah had gathered in Saqifah without informing anybody about their plans or motives that they were about to select a new caliph over the Muslims. If a Shura is to be conducted which is going to decide the successor of the Prophet, then surely the time when it is going to take place and the location where it is going to be held should be made public to all the concerned parties.

By not informing anybody about the timing and the location of the Shura of Saqifah, the Ansar had shown that they had no understanding of even the very basic principle of Shura, and at the same time they had completely contradicted the spirit of justice and fair play.

The Ansar had not only kept the timing and the location of the Shura a secret, but they had ignored and side lined all the other stake holders who had a say and an interest in this matter. The Ansars had ignored the Ahlulbayt (family of the Prophet) and the Muhajireen (immigrants from Makkah). They included companions like Ibn Abbas, Caliph Abu Bakr, Caliph Umar, Caliph Uthman, Talha, Zubair and Ali.

The system of Shura ensures that you consult with all the relevant groups and parties. This is a very basic and a fundamental principle of Shura. One group cannot just decide to hold a Shura among themselves and impose its decision on the rest of the Muslims. This kind of a meeting or gathering could not be classed as a Shura (Consultation).

By taking this course of action the Ansar had clearly shown that the concept of Shura that they had in mind was certainly not taught or advocated by the Prophet. The Prophet would have never advocated such a Shura for his successor where nobody is informed about its timing or location, and where the relevant parties are not even represented in the Shura.

The role of the Muhajireen, the companions of the Prophet from Makkah was not much different from the Ansar either. We observe that when Caliph Umar finds out about the meeting of Saqifah he only informed Caliph Abu Bakr, but he did not inform Ali or the Ahlulbayt or rest of the prominent Islamic personalities who were present at the time.

Caliph Abu Bakr was in fact present in the house of the Prophet when he finds out about the Shura of Saqifah, but he also did not inform Ali, Ibn Abbas or others who were also present in the house of the Prophet at the same time.

Only Caliph Abu Bakr, Caliph Umar and Abu Ubaydah Ibn al-Jarrah who they met on the way leave for the meeting at Saqifah, but rest of the stakeholders are kept in the dark.

The meeting of Saqifah was immensely important and critical for the future of the Muslims. Both Caliph Abu Bakr and Caliph Umar were early Muslims who had accepted Islam in Makkah. They had the privilege of spending a great deal of time in the company of the Prophet. But both of them fail to inform all the relevant parties about this key meeting, which was going to choose the future leader of the Muslims.

After all, this was no ordinary meeting, this meeting was going to decide the successor of the Prophet.

It was expected that at least the companions of Caliph Abu Bakr and Caliph Umar's stature would adhere to the basic principles of Shura and give all the Muslim factions a fair chance. But it is clear from the events of Saqifah that even the most prominent companions of the Prophet had no understanding of the principles of Shura.

The location of Saqifah and its timing clearly show that it could not possibly have been the wish of the Prophet.

Saqifah is a place which is around three miles from Madinah. During the lifetime of the Holy Prophet the Mosque of the Prophet was the centre of all Islamic activities. It was here that the decisions of war and peace were made. Foreign dignitaries were received here, sermons were delivered, and even court cases were heard here, hence when the news spread about the death of the Prophet the Muslims naturally assembled in that very mosque.

It would have made perfect sense to hold the Shura in the mosque of the Prophet. This would have allowed all the eminent Islamic personalities and the tribal elders to take part in the Shura. The proceedings of the Shura would have been open and transparent for all to see.

If Prophet of Allah had wanted his successor to be chosen by Shura then surely, he would have instructed the Muslims to carry out the proceedings of Shura in his mosque. Prophet's mosque would have been the most suitable and appropriate location for such a gathering.

Also, we observe that the proceedings of the Shura start as soon as the news of the death of the Prophet is announced, and it ends before the Prophet is buried. Islam clearly instructs that you bury your dead as soon as possible.

The Prophet had famously said:

> *Hurry up with the dead body for if it was righteous, you are forwarding it to good; and if it was otherwise, then you are putting off an evil thing from your necks.*
> - Sahih al Bukhari, 1315

If the instructions of the Shura had come from the Prophet, then surely, he would have asked his companions to at least bury him first before proceeding with the Shura. It is inconceivable to think that Prophet would have advised his companions to conduct the Shura to choose his successor even before his burial!

This is contrary to simple logic and common sense.

1.3.4. Threatening to Use Force

The Ansar were threatening to use force against the Muhajireen in case the Muhajireen did not accept an Ansar as the new Caliph. The Ansar had vowed in Saqifah to drive the Muhajireen out of their city on the point of their swords and the war between the two groups seemed likely.

> *(The) Ansar said: "In case they reject our Caliph, we shall drive them out from Al-Madinah at the point of our swords." However, the few Muhajirs in the assembly protested against this attitude and this led to a dispute and disorder of a serious nature and a war between the Muhajirs and Ansars seemed possible.*
>
> - Tareekh Al-Islam, Vol.1, p.273-274

A Shura (Consultation) where one group threatens another group of Muslims with their swords could not possibly have been based on the guidelines given by the Prophet. The Islamic principle of Shura has no room for threats and violence.

A Shura where a group of Muslims is threatened with swords has no validity in the eyes of Allah.

It was the Prophet who had brought the Muhajireen to the city of Madinah. It was under the leadership of the Prophet that Muhajireen had made their homes in Madinah. Threatening to kick the Muhajireen out of Madinah was to threaten and challenge the Sunnah of the Prophet.

It is clear that the Shura which took place in Saqifah could not have been based on the vision or the imagination of the Prophet. The Prophet of Allah could not possibly have left the choice of his successor into the hands of the companions who were threatening other Muslims with violence and war.

1.3.5. A Political Adjustment

Once Caliph Abu Bakr and Caliph Umar reached Saqifah the Ansar had almost finalized their candidate Saad ibn Ubaadah who conveys the following message to Ansar:

> *"So keep control of this matter (i.e. the Caliphate) to yourselves, to the exclusion of others, for it is yours and yours alone."*
>
> - The History of al-Tabari, Vol.10, p.2

Saad ibn Ubaadah who is the companion of the Prophet from Madinah and head of one of the Ansar tribes, wanted the leadership of Muslims to be confined to his tribe only. This could not possibly have been the way of the Prophet. Prophet of Islam had come to move people away from tribal, ethnic and racial persuasions. If Prophet wanted a Shura as a way forward, then surely all the notable personalities from all the tribes would have been considered for the role of the Caliphate based on their merit.

Both Caliph Abu Bakr and Caliph Umar object to the nominee of the Ansar and Challenge Saad ibn Ubaadah. They point out that Muhajireen who were from the tribe of Quraysh have more right to be the rulers than the Ansar.

Caliph Abu Bakr says to the Ansar

> *"(O Ansar) you are our brethren in Islam and our partners in religion...but the Arabs will not submit themselves except to this clan of Quraysh...we (the Quraysh) are in the center among the Muslims with respect to our position..."*
>
> - The History of al-Tabari, Volume 9, p.193

The Ansar then propose a compromise by stating that there should be two leaders, one from the Ansar and one from the Muhajireen.

> *"O Quraysh. There should be one ruler from us and one from you."*
>
> - Sahih Bukhari, Volume 8, Book 82, Number 817

Obviously, there was a tribal custom to have a leader from each tribe, but this approach could not work for the Islamic movement. The Islamic revolution had come to end the tribal, ethnic and racial system which was dominant during the time of Jahilliyah. However, by this action the Ansar had clearly demonstrated that the methodology they had in mind for choosing the successor of the Prophet could not possibly have come from the Prophet himself.

Caliph Umar opposes this move of the Ansar by saying that we cannot have two swords in one sheath. A lot of commotion, disorder and anger broke out in the room between the Ansar and the Muhajireen.

Caliph Abu Bakr then proposes a compromise on part of the Muhajireen. He offers the Ansar the position of being the advisors to the Caliph.

> *"....We (the Muhajirs) are the leaders, and you (Ansars) are the helpers; matters shall not be settled without consultation, nor shall we decide on them without you."*
>
> - The History of al-Tabari, Vol.10, pp.4-5

The Ansar at this stage had lost the political advantage in Saqifah. Their own unity had disappeared and the old rivalry between the two clans of Ansar i.e., Al-Aws and Al-Khazraj had resurfaced. The Ansar could see that with the resurgence of Muhajireen in Saqifah and with their own unity in disarray, the best outcome that they could hope for was the offer of Abu Bakr.

The offer gave them a say in the decision-making process of the State by becoming advisors to the Caliph. It was something that they had always desired and aspired to, and hence they reluctantly conceded to the Muhajireen and accepted the offer of Caliph Abu Bakr.

> *"What you say is correct: we are your advisors, and you are our rulers."*
>
> - Musnad Ahmad, Vol.1, p.5

This is how the meeting of Saqifah ended with Caliph Abu Bakr who was from the Muhajireen becoming the first Caliph and the leader of the Muslims.

However, the offer of becoming the advisors to the Caliph never materialized for the Ansar, as Caliph Abu Bakr never created such a position for the Ansar once he acquired the Caliphate.

At best the Shura of Saqifah could be classed as a political adjustment between the Ansar and the Muhajireen, where the former agreed to become the advisors and the later agreed to become the rulers.

The kind of Shura that took place in Saqifah could not possibly have been introduced or advocated by the Prophet, a Shura where nobody even knew where and when it was going to be held except one group, and where the Shura ends in a power sharing deal, a deal which is never even implemented.

The Prophet of Allah who had tirelessly worked for the revolution of Islam could not possibly have left the future leadership of Muslims on a political adjustment that took place in the Shura of Saqifah, an adjustment which is only done to pacify the Ansar at the time, but it is not even put in practice once Caliph Abu Bakr becomes the head of the State.

1.3.6. The Spontaneous Nature of Saqifah

Another very important principle that transpires from the words of Caliph Umar in the below narration is that the event of Saqifah was an un-premeditated and a spontaneous affair.

Caliph Umar says:

> *"The pledge of allegiance given to Abu Bakr was an un-premeditated spontaneous affair which was (then only later) ratified."*
> - *Sahih Bukhari, Volume 8, Book 82, Number 817*

As per the above words of Caliph Umar the Shura of Saqifah was a spontaneous event, and indeed the proceedings of Saqifah itself testify that Saqifah wasn't a planned, organized or a thought through process. It was something that happened in the heat of the moment, it was a spontaneous event.

Surely, the Prophet of Allah could not have left the future of his mission to the turns of a spontaneous event like Saqifah.

As one reads through the history of Saqifah it becomes abundantly clear that the Shura which took place by the first generation of Muslims after the death of the Prophet could not have been advocated by the Prophet of Allah.

The Prophet would have never allowed an unplanned and a spontaneous event like Saqifah to choose his successor. The Shura of Saqifah came about because of the personal and the political ambitions of the Ansar and the Muhajireen, based on their tribal and ethnic allegiances.

The spontaneous nature of Saqifah is yet another proof that Prophet had not trained or taught his companions on the modalities and the legal structure of an Islamic Shura.

In spite of the fact that the first generation of Muslims was composed of some great Islamic personalities, there is no evidence to suggest that Prophet of Allah had ever given any specific guidelines or instructions to prepare the early generation of Muslims for choosing his successor.

If he really wanted the principle of Shura as a way of selecting his successor, he would have established a clear process for the Shura, so that the Shura could progress according to a definite set of steps where personal desires, political ambitions, tribal and ethnic allegiances would have no part to play.

After analysing the events of Saqifah it becomes clear that Prophet had never given any instructions or guidelines about choosing his successor through the process of Shura or consultation.

1.3.7. The Principle of Shura (Consultation) and the Companions

The principle of Shura is found in the Quran and in some traditions (Sunnah) of the Prophet. However, the rules, regulations and the modalities of Shura were developed much later by the scholars of jurisprudence (Fiqh), which were unavailable to the early generation of Muslims. Even the scholars who developed the rules and regulations of Shura profoundly disagreed on its various aspects, like whether the Shura is a discretionary non-binding decision-making process or whether it is a binding decision-making process.

The concept of Shura was a new concept for the first generation of Muslims who had not experienced any sort of highly developed government before the time of the Prophet. The Companions were unfamiliar and unaware of the details, rules and guidelines surrounding the principle of Shura.

In the meeting of Saqifah there was no assemblance or a structure of a Shura. If the system of Shura was to be put into practice immediately after the death of the Prophet, then Prophet would have disseminated this concept to the early generation of Muslims. He would have prepared his followers both physiologically and intellectually for this system, and filled in any gaps in their understanding, while also explaining the details which would make it a workable solution.

Even if we assume for a moment that Prophet had guided and instructed the Muslims to choose his successor through Shura, the events that took place in Saqifah clearly show that this gathering was certainly not based on the theological principle of Shura found in Islam.

Even Caliph Abu Bakr whose Caliphate was based on the Shura of Saqifah did not adhere to the kind of Shura that gave him the authority. When the first Caliph was nearing his death, he separately spoke to some of the companions and then nominated Caliph Umar as his successor. Abu Bakr dictated his last testament to Caliph Uthman as follows:

> "In the name of Most Merciful God. This is the last will and testament of Abu Bakr bin Abu Quhafa, when he is in the last hour of the world, and the first of the next; an hour in which the infidel must believe, the wicked be convinced of their evil ways, I nominate Umar bin al Khattab as my successor. Therefore, hear to him and obey him….."

- *At-Tabsirah, by ibn Al-Jawzee (1/477-479); and Ashaab Ar-Rasool (1/108)*
- *Abu Bakr, Umar, Usman, Ali (ra) 4 Vol. Set, Professor Masud al-Hasan, 1982*

Caliph Abu Bakr himself did not follow the principle of Shura established in the gathering of Saqifah for his own successor. He distanced himself from the Shura of Saqifah by meeting some of the companions individually, and then nominating his own successor during his lifetime, rather than leaving the decision to the Ummah.

Similarly, we read the sentiments of Caliph Umar on the events of Saqifah.

Ibn Abbas narrated that Umar while serving as a Caliph once said in a speech:

> ".... the pledge of allegiance given to Abu Bakr was given at spur of the moment and it was successful. No doubt, it was like that, but Allah saved (the people) from its evil, and there is none among you who has the qualities of Abu Bakr. Remember that whoever gives the pledge of allegiance to anybody among you without consulting the other Muslims, neither that person, nor the person to whom the pledge of allegiance was given, are to be supported, lest they both should be killed ………"

- *Sahih al-Bukhari: Volume 8, Book 82, Number 817*
- *al-Musnad: vol.1, Narration 391*

The second Caliph Umar himself pours scorn on the events of Saqifah by saying that it was Allah who had saved the Ummah from its evil. Caliph Umar was in fact the very person who had nominated Abu Bakr for the position of the Caliphate, and he was the first person to give him the allegiance.

Caliph Umar does not stop there, he further states:

> *"whoever gives the pledge of allegiance to anybody among you without consulting the other Muslims, neither that person, nor the person to whom the pledge of allegiance was given, are to be supported ..."*

By these statements, in his later life, Caliph Umar in a way had invalidated his own allegiance and nomination of Abu Bakr, since the nomination and the allegiance of Abu Bakr were done without proper consultation and without the presence of all the relevant parties. The only people present in Saqifah were the Ansar and the three Muhajireen i.e., Caliph Abu Bakr, Caliph Umar and Ubaydah Ibn al-Jarrah. Even all the Muhajireen were not represented and certainly there was no representation from the family of the Prophet (Ahlulbayt).

It appears that in later life, when Caliph Umar had time to ponder over the events of Saqifah, and realized its frailties, he completely discredits the gathering of Saqifah and clearly distances himself from its ramifications.

Caliph Umar not only distances himself from the Shura of Saqifah but goes a step further, and states that if anybody in future follows a similar path (i.e., if a ruler is appointed without proper consultation) then both the nominee and the one who gives allegiance to the nominee should be killed!

It becomes absolutely clear that both Caliph Abu Bakr and Caliph Umar who were the most influential participants of Saqifah neither believed in and nor followed its principle in later lives.

We read in the History of al-Tabari, Vol.1, p.195.

> *"Amir asked: "When was the oath of allegiance given to Abu Bakr?"*
> *"The very day the Messenger of Allah died," he (Saeed) replied. "People disliked to be left even part of the day without being organized into a community (jama'ah)."*

This shows the mentality of the Arabs of that era. They disliked to be left leaderless even for half a day. This is how important and critical the issue of leadership was among the Arabs.

This begs the question, was the Prophet not aware of this mentality? Was he not an Arab? Did he not live among the Arabs?

The answer to all these questions is of course a resounding yes!

In the next section I will outline as to how the Prophet had in fact envisaged the continuity of the Islamic leadership after his demise.

1.4. The Third Possibility

The Prophet is actively thinking about the future of the revolution that he had started, a revolution that is a source of inspiration and guidance for the entire mankind. The Prophet chooses a capable person who has been deeply involved in this revolution from the very beginning to lead the ideological movement of Islam in his absence. The Prophet trains this individual from an early age and breathes into him the spirit and the ideals of Islam. The Prophet prepares him spiritually, intellectually, religiously, and politically to guide and lead the Muslims after his death.

Islam was not a superficial reformatory movement that had come to bring about some cosmetic reforms to the Arabian Peninsula. On the contrary, Islam was a revolution that the Prophet of Allah had started to completely change and eradicate the status quo. The religion of Islam had brought a completely new ideology, a completely new definition of life and a complete new set of rules and ideas to transform and change the existing backward (Jahiliyyah) customs and traditions, which were prevalent among the Arabs at the time.

The Prophet of Allah as the head of the revolutionary movement of Islam held a unique and a distinct position, a position that was unlike any other head of the State.

1.4.1. A Teacher and a Mentor

The Prophet of Allah was not just a political leader, he did not just hold a political position. The Prophet of Allah was an ideological leader, he was a spiritual leader, he was an intellectual guide, he was a religious guide, he was a moral authority, he was a military commander, he was judge (Qazi) and a teacher and a mentor in all disciplines of life.

All the attributes that I have mentioned above were found in one person i.e., Prophet Muhammad. Obviously, nobody can acquire the status and the genius of the Prophet. But surely someone who immediately succeeds the Prophet after his death should have some of those traits and attributes, to be able to justify their position as the successor of the Prophet.

If Prophet had just been a political figure, then it was possible that others could have selected someone as his successor. For example, the mayor of a city takes his power from the people living in the city. He is elected by their popular vote. When the mayor dies, or his term ends people of the city can choose someone else to replace the mayor.

However, let's say a thinker or a teacher who has introduced a new ideology or a new phenomenon, or has brought a new school of thought into this world, or has initiated a new way of thinking, where the teacher gives special lessons and classes, and where no one else can teach the class in the way the teacher can, and when that teacher passes away, then one cannot simply choose his replacement by popular vote.

Also, as the ideology introduced by the teacher gains momentum and as people start believing in the doctrine initiated by the teacher, and when his disciples and students find faith in him, and in the ideals that he is proposing, then it is the teacher who will recognize his best pupil, his best student, and the one who is most worthy of continuing his ideology in his absence.

The Prophet of Allah was exactly such a teacher and Islam was exactly such an ideology which the Prophet had initiated.

A teacher or a professor is not selected from the votes of the people or from allegiances given to him as a result of tribal connections or ethnic groupings. It is a teacher who will appoint another teacher based on his ability and knowledge in the field of teaching.

A teacher cannot be simply chosen based on his tribal and ethnic background, a trend that we saw in Saqifah. In Saqifah, the Ansar wanted to choose a leader from their clan, whereas the Muhajireen had insisted on having the leadership of Islam confined to their tribe.

If an expert cardiologist is going away on a trip or passes away, the people cannot hold a referendum or a consultation and choose someone as a cardiologist. This is because the people cannot decide who will be an expert in the field of cardiology, as they may select someone who knows nothing about the heart. It would only be another cardiologist who will appoint a cardiologist based on the expertise of an individual in the field of cardiology. The aim is to choose the right man for the job and choose a person who is most capable and qualified for the post.

The Prophet of Islam held a similar position, he was a teacher and a mentor and a master in all disciplines of life. The Prophet was the head of the new ideological and the revolutionary movement called Islam. The Prophet had introduced a completely new religion, a completely new faith and a completely new way of life which had transformed the Arabian society beyond recognition.

It was the Prophet who would recognize his best pupil and his best student who could lead the ideological movement of Islam in his absence.

The Prophet himself was not appointed by the people around him. Allah, the creator of the universe had appointed the Prophet to lead the message of Islam. And as the head of this newly established divine mission, the Prophet had a right to tell his followers and appoint for them a person who was most worthy to continue his revolutionary path.

It is only logical that Prophet would have chosen someone who was closest to him, someone who was carefully trained by him, someone who was most familiar with his thoughts and teachings, and someone who he had trusted from the very beginning to lead the ideological movement of Islam.

1.4.2. A Reformatory Movement

Islam was not simply a set of beliefs which were kept in one's heart. Islam was a reformatory movement which had come to completely reform the lives and the mindset of the Arabs and the society at large.

Even in secular and non-religious reformatory movements the selection of the new leader is done by its founding fathers. This is because in any reformatory movement the choice of a new leader cannot be left to a popular vote or elections among the masses, or to a Shura conducted by the elders of various tribes or ethnic groups, since either of these methods could possibly select an individual who may not adhere to the principles and the ideals of the reformatory movement.

The selection by Shura or a leader elected from elections cannot guarantee that the best and the most able candidate is chosen to lead the reformatory movement in the future. Both elections and a Shura tend to bring a centrist candidate to the top, i.e., a person who is acceptable to the majority, regardless of whether that individual is totally in line with the reformatory principles or not.

However, a reformatory movement by its very nature is not in line with the view of the majority. On the contrary, by its very nature a reformatory movement is led by a minority whose aim is to reform the majority. It is not a movement which is initiated or run under the guidance of the majority. It is in fact a movement which is designed to reform and bring about a change in the majority.

A wrong choice at the very top could jeopardize the entire reformatory movement itself, and potentially destroy or dilute its message. In a reformatory movement the choice of a new leader cannot be left to the chances of a popular election or a Shura, where potentially any individual acceptable to the majority could be chosen.

Inevitably in elections or in a Shura, personal preferences, tribal and ethnic allegiances play a part in the choice of the future leader, something that the reformatory movement of Islam could not possibly allow. The Prophet of Allah as the founder of the reformatory movement of Islam could not allow such a process to choose his successor.

The ideal and the most suitable person to choose the future leader of a reformatory movement has to be its founding father. In the case of the reformatory movement of Islam the best-placed person was none other than the Prophet of Allah. The Prophet knew all his close and foremost companions extremely well. He knew their strengths and their weaknesses more than anyone else. The Prophet of Allah was the right person to decide who would be the most suitable among his companions to lead the movement of Islam in his absence.

Any other method of choosing the future leader of the Muslims could not guarantee that the best and the most deserving individual would be selected and would come on top.

This theory is further vindicated by considering the ground realities which were faced by the first generation of Muslims at the time of the death of the Prophet.

1.4.3. The Ground Realities at the Time

The total time span of Prophet's mission had barely exceeded two decades. This goes for his earliest companions who had accompanied him from the start of his mission. The time that he had spent with the vast majority of the Ansar did not exceed a single decade. And the time that he had spent with the large number of converts to Islam after the Truce of Hudaybiyya until the conquest of Makkah was no more than three to four years.

On top of this there was a huge chunk of Muslims who were known as Muslimat al-Fath. These were Muslims who had converted to Islam after the conquest of Makkah. They had only become Muslims after Islam had become the most powerful political and military force in the Arabian Peninsula.

The Prophet had very limited contact with these Muslims due to the short span of time between the conquest of Makkah and his death. And most of this contact was in the capacity as a ruler and a leader rather than as a teacher or a mentor. Also, the Prophet used to live in Madinah and these new converts were all in Makkah, so Prophet really had very little contact with these new Muslim converts.

At the same time the Islamic state was going through a critical phase. The issue of Muallifa Qulubuhum had appeared, where to win the hearts of the new Muslims converts, they were given the rights of zakat and offered other bounties and incentives to keep them on the path of Islam.

During this period the Islamic revolution was also facing a danger from the Munafiqun (hypocrites) and Mundisun (infiltrators) who had joined the ranks of the companions and the ordinary Muslims to harm the message of Islam from within. Various Quranic verses testify to the presence of Munafiqun within the ranks of the Muslim community. Here are some of those verses.

> *When the hypocrites come to you (O Prophet), they say, "We bear witness that you are certainly the Messenger of Allah"—and surely Allah knows that you are His Messenger—but Allah bears witness that the hypocrites are truly liars.*

- Quran 63:1

> *They have made their (false) oaths as a shield, hindering (others) from the Way of Allah. Evil indeed is what they do!*

- Quran 63:2

This is because they believed and then abandoned faith. Therefore, their hearts have been sealed, so they do not comprehend.

- Quran 63:3

Then there were threats of a counter-revolution against Islam due to the social and the religious challenge posed by the people of the book. Naturally there was opposition to the Islamic faith by people who were adherents of the previous scriptures, especially the Jews of Arabia. They proved to be a constant source of challenge, unrest, and provocation for the Muslims. The challenge to the Islamic ideology from the Jewish faith is evident from various verses of the Holy Quran.

And the Jews will not be pleased with you, nor the Christians until you follow their religion.

- Quran 2:120

Considering all the internal and external threats and dangers that were faced by the Islamic movement, in addition to the various trends, thoughts and influences that the first generation of Muslims were subjected to, in such circumstances it was incumbent on the Prophet to train and educate someone in the art of leadership, so that this individual could take on the mantle from the Prophet and carry his ideological message forward, and at the same time guard it from the forces that were trying to change, challenge or destroy it.

1.4.4. Islam is the Word of Allah

Islam was not an ideology made by man whose principles or ideals could be defined as a result of a Shura, or some kind of a political adjustment that took place between the Ansar and the Muhajireen in Saqifah, where the Ansar had agreed to become the advisors giving Muhajireen the sole responsibility for the leadership of the Muslims.

The concept of the Islamic governance and the fundamentals of the Islamic system, or the Islamic way of life could not be established on the basis of experimentation or thrashing out of ideas by the first generation of Muslims, something that we witnessed in Saqifah.

For instance, in Saqifah the Ansar suggested that there should be two Caliphs, one from the Ansar and one from the Muhajireen. In response the Muhajireen suggested that there could only be one Caliph over the Muslims.

Ansar said in Saqifah:

"O Quraysh. There should be one ruler from us and one from you."

- Sahih Bukhari, Volume 8, Book 82, Number 817

The Muhajireen responded:

"How preposterous! Two swords cannot be accommodated in one sheath. By Allah, the Arabs will never accept your rule…"

- History of al-Tabari, p.194

Islam was not some kind of an experiment where the Ansar or the Muhajireen could introduce their own suggestions or thoughts, which would then form the basis of the Islamic government. On the contrary,

Islam was the message of Allah whose rules, regulations and beliefs had been divinely ordained by Allah to his Messenger.

It is inconceivable to think that the Islamic leadership which would be responsible for guarding the foundations of this eternal religion could be allowed to experiment and make decisions based on random suggestions by the first generation of Muslims, where one group wants to have two Caliphs and the other considers that idea preposterous.

The hasty and the spontaneous experiment that took place in Saqifah was a testament to the political immaturity of the companions, and the lack of understanding that they had about the Islamic leadership and the system of governance that Islam had laid out.

In spite of the loyalty and the devotion of many among the first generation of Muslims, the majority of the companions did not possess the necessary qualifications which would have enabled them to lead the intellectual and the ideological revolution of Islam that Prophet had shaped.

This does not mean that the companions were not capable of adhering or performing the basic tenants or rituals of the Islamic faith. On the contrary, many of them were pious and devout Muslims who had sacrificed everything in the path of Islam.

As long as the mature and the guiding leadership of the Prophet was present, the companions gelled together as a group and a force, but as soon as the Prophet passed away, cracks appeared among the ranks of the companions, the old rivalry between the Ansar and the Muhajireen resurfaced, where each group was vying for power.

The Ansar who had once welcomed the Muhajireen into their city as brothers were now threatening to drive them out of their city on the point of their swords, and a war between the two groups seemed likely.

> *(The) Ansar said: "In case they reject our Caliph, we shall drive them out from Al-Madinah at the point of our swords." .... this led to a dispute and disorder of a serious nature and a war between the Muhajirs and Ansars seemed possible.*
>
> - *Tareekh Al-Islam, Vol.1, p.273-274*

This is because the companions at this stage were not ready to take on the mantle of the Islamic leadership. Although, there were some inspiring individuals among the companions, but the first generation of Muslims as a whole had not attained the intellectual and the political maturity where they could assume the guardianship of the Islamic faith, and this is obvious from the proceedings of Saqifah itself.

The event of Saqifah was a premature step which was taken before its natural course. It is however illogical to think or accept that Prophet would have ever guided or wished the Muslims to take such a step.

An event like Saqifah could potentially bring the best, or the second best, an average person, or possibly a person who does not deserve to be the leader of the Muslims. In following such a process there is no guarantee that the most deserving and the most able person would end up leading the Islamic nation. The Prophet could not possibly leave the future of Islam to the chances of an election or the kind of Shura which took place in Saqifah, where there was no guarantee that the right and the best person would be selected as the leader of the Muslim Ummah.

The only remaining possibility which is consistent with logic and the facts on the ground is that the Prophet of Allah had adopted a positive attitude towards the future leadership of Islam, and Prophet had chosen someone who had a deep involvement in the revolution of Islam from its very start, and Prophet had trained this individual from an early age, and specifically prepared him so that he could exemplify the religious, intellectual and political leadership of Islam.

This notion is also in line with the actions of the Prophet throughout his life. The Prophet of Allah was so conscious about the issue of leadership that even when he would temporarily leave Madinah for a few days, he would appoint someone to administer the affairs of the Muslims in his absence.

For instance, when Prophet left for the Battle of Badr he appointed Abu Lubabah as his successor, when he left for the battle of Khyber he appointed Numeila as his deputy, when he left for Makkah he chose Abu Raham to replace him, and when Prophet went for the Valedictory Pilgrimage he left Abu Dujanah in charge in Madinah (Ibn Husahm Biography of the Prophet – Journeys of the Prophet).

It was the Sunnah of the Prophet that even when he would leave Madinah temporarily, he would appoint a successor. To say and to accept that Prophet did not choose a successor before leaving this world, would not only tantamount to challenging the wisdom of the Prophet, but it would also be tantamount to challenging his Sunnah.

2. THE PROPHET AND HIS SUCCESSOR

The successor of the Prophet would be someone who was most familiar with the revolutionary message of Islam, someone whose personality had melted around the Islamic thought, someone who resembled the Prophet in terms of his manners, in terms of his knowledge, in terms of his piety, in terms of his bravery, in terms of his spirituality and above all in terms of his wisdom and intellect.

A person of such calibre would not just come out of the wood works one day. A person who would succeed the Prophet would not simply appear on the horizon after the death of the Prophet.

A person who would have the above qualities and traits would have to be trained and ingrained by the Prophet from an early age. The Prophet would have to nurture and groom his successor in the ideals of the Islamic spirit, so that he could ideologically and intellectually lead the movement of Islam in Prophet's absence.

Ali is at the tender age of thirteen when the verse 26:214 is revealed to the Prophet. The Holy Quran says:

> *"And warn your tribe who are of near kindred."*
> - Quran, 26:214

Allah tells the Prophet to invite his near ones to the path of Islam. Prophet organizes a feast where he invites the elders and notables of Banu Hashim, his own clan to the path of Allah. This is the first ever invitation of its kind where the Prophet is openly inviting people to follow the Message of Islam.

Prophet chooses Ali to help him in organizing and preparing for the occasion. The gathering is going to be held in Abu Talib's house who is Ali's father and Prophet's uncle. Ali goes with the Prophet and invites the guests, Ali helps the Prophet in preparing the food, Ali lays out the table where the guests will sit and eat, and when the guests arrive Prophet welcomes them to the house alongside Ali.

The feast lasts for three days and on the final day the Prophet of Allah speaks to the audience. He invites people to the path of Tawheed (oneness of Allah) and informs them that he is the Prophet of Allah. The Prophet then asks the audience to support him and help him in his mission. The audiences stay silent, nobody offers to support the Prophet's mission except Ali, who stood up and offers his allegiance and support to the Prophet.

The Prophet again asks the audience to support him and support the path of truth, again nobody offers to help except Ali. On the third Occasion when Prophet repeats his invitation, again nobody responds to the Prophet's call, again only Ali endorses Prophet's mission and promises to offer his full support.

The Prophet puts his hand on the back of 'Ali's neck and said:

> *"This is my brother, my inheritor (legatee), and my successor (Khalifha) over you, so listen to him and obey him."*
>
> *"Arabic version - Inna hadha akhhi wa wasiyyi wa khalifati fikum, fasma'u lahu wa ati'u"*

- *at-Tabari, at-Ta'rikh, vol. 1 (Leiden, 1980 offset of the 1789 edition) p. 171-173*
- *Ibn al-Athir, al-Kamil, vol. 5 (Beirut, 1965) p. 62-63*
- *Abu 'l-Fida', al-Mukhtasar fi Ta'rikhi 'l-Bashar, vol. 1 (Beirut, n.d.) p. 116-117*
- *as-Suyuti, ad-Durru 'l-Manthur, vol. 5 (Beirut, n.d.) p. 97*
- *al-Bayhaqi, Dala'ilu 'n-Nubuwwa, vol. 1 (Cairo, 1969) p. 428-430*
- *Muttaqi al-Hindi, Kanzu 'l-'Ummal, vol. 15 (Hyderabad, 1968) pp. 100, 113, 115*

Prophet chooses his successor on the very day that he invites people to the path of Tawheed (Oneness of Allah) and Prophethood. This is how critical and important the issue of leadership is in Islam. The Prophet declares and announces Ali to be his brother, his helper/inheritor and his successor and asks the audience to follow and obey him.

Islam is an ideology that Prophet of Allah had initiated. The Islamic ideology had challenged all the previous ideologies, philosophies and theories that existed among the Arabs. There was no way that Prophet would have left the ideological message of Islam without a proper guardian, especially when the ideology of Islam was still in its infancy.

This event is known as the event of Dawat-dhul-Ashira and formally marks the beginning of Ali's training at the hands of the Prophet. This would be the first of many occasions throughout his life where Prophet would announce Ali to be his successor.

The training of Ali had in fact begun even earlier. In the feast of Dawat-dhul-Ashira Ali was inviting the guests, he was laying out the table, he was preparing the food, he was organizing the whole event alongside the Prophet. Ali was not one of the invitees, Ali was in fact the host alongside the Prophet, Ali was already on the path of truth and Ali was already helping the Prophet in this mission even as a child.

Let us see when the training and the grooming of Ali actually began, and the merits and the traits that Ali acquired as a result of Prophet's upbringing.

2.1. Ali's Companionship with the Prophet

Ali was born some thirty years after the birth of the Holy Prophet. Just like the Prophet Ali also belonged to the most respected clan of Quraysh called the Banu Hashim. Ali's mother Fatima bint Assad also belonged to Banu Hashim, making Ali a direct descendant of Prophet Ismael and Prophet Ibrahim. Ali's father Abu Talib was Prophet's real uncle. He was the custodian of the Kaaba and one of the most respected leaders of Banu Hashim. When Prophet lost his grandfather, it was Abu Talib (the father of Ali) who took charge and custody of his nephew (the Prophet) and brought him up like his own son.

2.1.1. The Birth of Ali

It has been documented in many books of history that Ali was born in the Holy Kaaba, the house of Allah. The great historian Masoodi, writes on page 76, Volume II of his book, Murooj-udh-Dhahab (The Golden Meadows) that one of the greatest distinctions that Ali enjoyed was that he was born in the House of Allah.

Some of the other authorities who have affirmed Ali's birth in the Kaaba are:

- *Muhammad Ibn Talha el-Shafei in Matalib-us-saool, page 11.*
- *Hakim in Mustadrak, page 483, Vol. III.*
- *El-Umari in Sharh Ainia, page 15.*
- *Halabi in Sira, page 165, Vol. I.*
- *Sibt Ibn al-Jauzi in Tadhkera Khawasil Ummah, page 7.*
- *Ibn Sabbagh Maleki in Fusoolul Mohimma, page 14.*
- *Muhammad bin Yousuf Shafei in Kifayet al-Talib, page 261.*
- *Shablanji in Nurul Absar, page 76.*
- *Ibn Zahra in Ghiyathul Ikhtisar, page 97.*
- *Edvi in Nafhatul Qudsia, page 41.*

Among the modern historians, Abbas Mahmood al-Akkad of Egypt writes in his book Al-'Abqarriyet al-Imam Ali (Cairo, 1970), that Ali Ibn Abi Talib was born inside the Kaaba.

Another contemporary historian Mahmood Saeed al-Tantawi who was once a member of the Supreme Council of Islamic Affairs in the Arab Republic of Egypt, writes on page 186 of his book Min Fada-il al-'Ashrat al-Mubashireen bil Janna, published in 1976 by Matab'a al-Ahram at-Tijariyya, Cairo Egypt:

> *"May God have mercy upon Ali Ibn Abi Talib. He was born in the Kaaba. He witnessed the rise of Islam; he witnessed the Da'wa of Muhammad, and he was a witness of the Wahi (Revelation of Al-Qur'an al-Majid). He immediately accepted Islam even though he was still a child, and he fought all his life so that the Word of Allah would be supreme."*

The Prophet was really thrilled and excited when he heard about Ali's birth. Ali was only three days old when Prophet came to see his little cousin. It is reported that Ali did not open his eyes for three days until the Prophet arrived. When Prophet held the little boy in his lap, Ali opened his eyes. The first thing that Ali saw was the blessed face of the Prophet.

It is also reported that when Prophet held Ali in his arms, he puts his tongue in Ali's mouth, and the little Ali exuberantly starts sucking it, as if the successor of the Prophet had already started learning from his mentor.

The birth of Ali had filled the heart of the Prophet with joy and happiness. The Prophet of Allah had many other cousins and children around him, but Ali was special. Ali himself had three elder brothers who had exactly the same blood relation with the Prophet, but the Prophet did not show any interest in any of them. Ali and Ali alone remained the focus of his interest and attention.

2.1.2. The Prophet Adopts Ali

After Prophet's marriage with lady Khadija Prophet formally adopts Ali who was only four or five at the time. The Prophet's Uncle Abu Talib had a large family so Prophet and his other uncle Ibn Abbas decided to lessen Abu Talib's burden by adopting his sons. Ibn Abbas chose Jafar, Ali's elder brother and Prophet choses Ali, his favourite cousin.

Ali was no longer going to stay with his parents, instead Ali was now going to be brought up by the Prophet of Allah himself. After all, the little boy would one day succeed the Prophet, so Prophet had to bring up Ali in the house of knowledge and guidance. There were no schools or colleges in those days where the children could go and learn. Prophet's lap is the school of Ali, Prophet's house is the fountain of knowledge which nurtures Ali.

The Prophet of Allah became Ali's guide, Ali's teacher, and Ali's mentor. This was a key distinction that separated Ali from the rest of the companions that Ali was in fact trained, taught, and raised by the Prophet in his own house.

Prophet begins his training on a clean slate. Ali had opened his eyes in the lap of the Prophet. Ali had never been exposed to any other religion, ideology, thoughts, or influences. Ali had never practiced any other faith or religion. The only faith that Ali had ever known was the faith of the Prophet. The Prophet had sheltered Ali in his home and kept him away from the backward (Jahilliyah) traditions, which were prevalent in the society at the time.

The only influence that Ali had was the influence of the immaculate character of the Prophet, which is described in the Holy Quran as "Khuluqin Azeem" i.e., the lofty character of the Prophet. The verse 68:4 of the Holy Quran states:

> "And Indeed you (O' Muhammad), are on character lofty"
> - Quran 68:4

It was indeed under the guidance of this lofty character that Ali was brought up, so that one day he could become a representative of the Prophet.

It was a custom of the Arabs that when a child was born, he was placed at the feet of the tribal idol, thus symbolically dedicating him to the pagan deity. Most of the Arab children were dedicated to the idols but that wasn't the case with Ali, who was in fact greeted by the Prophet of Allah at birth. This is another distinction that Ali had over almost all the other companions since they had all worshipped idols for years before coming to the fold of Islam.

It is for this very reason that many Muslim scholars have chosen to use the words "Karam Allahu Wajhahu" rather than "Radhiallah Anhu" when they mention the name of Ali. "Karam Allahu Wajhahu" means: "he whose face was honoured by Allah". The reason why Ali's face was honoured was because Ali's face had never bowed before an idol, unlike other companions.

Al-Hakim has reported on the authority of Ibn Masud that Prophet had said:

> "To look at the face of Ali is ibadah (worship)"
> - Al-Mustadrak, III, 152-153
> - Mustadrak al Hakim (3/151)

The Prophet says that looking at the face of Ali was worship. The hadith implies that Ali face was so blessed with the virtues of Islam that simply looking at Ali's face was regarded by the Prophet as an act of worship. This hadith of course does not mean that one worships Ali, worship is only for Allah and Allah alone.

However, the face of Ali just like the character of Ali was unique and distinct among all the companions. The first thing that Ali's face had seen was the light of the Prophet. Prophet had kissed the face of Ali on many occasions, and Ali's face had never bowed before an idol. Ali's face embodied the essence of Islam. Ali's face reflected the characters and manners of Prophet's upbringing. Ali was so pious and virtuous that his face reflected the spirit and the ideals of Islam.

By simply looking at Ali's face reminded the companions about Allah, such was the closeness of Ali to Allah and to his Prophet. After all Ali was going to be the successor of the Prophet, his face needed to reflect his position and stature. It was for this reason that Prophet had said that looking at Ali's face was ibadah (worship).

The Prophet had made every effort to ensure that Ali was kept away from idol worship and pagan rituals. This is why Prophet goes and greets Ali at birth and adopts him at a very young age, to make sure that Ali has no influence from the un-Islamic practices prevalent at the time. Prophet goes to great lengths in protecting Ali from the backward customs and traditions of the Arab culture ingrained in the society during that era.

This is another distinction that Ali had over every other companion that he was not exposed to the pagan way of life, and this was part of the plan of the Prophet that Ali was brought up on the monolithic faith, and never worshipped any God other than Allah.

2.1.3. The Prophet's Closeness with Ali

The closeness of Ali with the Prophet was unique and unusual. It wasn't like the relationship that Prophet had with any of his other companions.

Ali describes his closeness with the Prophet in his own words:

> *"...you know what my relations with the Holy Prophet Muhammad were. From the very beginning of my life, he loved me, and I loved him. He took me in his lap when I was a baby and thence, I was always with him. He often kept me embraced to his heart. He used to lay me next to him. We used to be so close to each other that I felt the warmth of his body and smelled the fragrance of his odour.*
>
> *When I was a baby, he fed me with his hands, often chewing hard bits for me. He never found me lying nor weak and wavering. From the time of his [Holy Prophet Muhammad] infancy, Allah had appointed the greatest of His angels to always be with him, and His Arch Angel was leading him towards exemplary qualities and high moral values, and I followed him step by step as a baby camel follows its mother. Daily he used to place before me a fresh standard of efficiency and used to order me to follow it.*
>
> *Every year he used to stay in a grotto of the Hira Mountain for some time, and nobody used to be with him but me. None could then see or hear him but me. During those days Islam was the religion of only the Prophet and his wife, Khadija. I was the third of the trio. Nobody else in this world had accepted Islam. Even then I used to see the divine light of revelation and Prophethood and smell the heavenly fragrance of Prophethood."*
>
> - *Nahjul Balagha sermon of al-Qasi'ah*

The words of Ali are both enlightening and historic. They give us a remarkable picture of Ali's companionship with the Prophet of Allah.

The Prophet grooms and nurtures Ali in the ideals of the Islamic faith from the very start of his life. As a child Prophet always kept Ali by his side, and Ali would follow the Prophet just like a baby camel would follow its mother. Ali grew up under the immaculate supervision of the Prophet, following the best of the creation at every step of the way. The Prophet became the guardian and the mentor of Ali.

The Prophet was indeed building Ali's character from an early age. He wanted to leave a lasting impression on the mind of this young boy. The house of the Prophet became the nursery and the kindergarten for Ali. The house of the Prophet was the academy and the institution that nurtured Ali.

The difference between Ali and the rest of the companions would be clearly evident through their actions after the death of the Prophet.

In Saqifah we witnessed that the Ansar (companions from Madinah) had planned to keep the leadership of Muslims confined to their own tribe. And when Caliph Abu Bakr and Caliph Umar found out about the plans of the Ansar, they also failed to inform any of the other stakeholders. This was because the residue of the tribal and ethnic allegiances was still prevalent in their minds and in their character and was also evident from their actions. Since none of these companions were trained and groomed by the Prophet in the way that he had trained and groomed Ali.

Caliph Abu Bakr had accepted Islam at the age of forty. He was indulged in the customs and traditions of the Arabian society that Prophet had come to reform for four decades. Caliph Umar had accepted Islam around the age of twenty-five, so he had spent two and a half decades in the Jahiliyyah (backward) traditions before coming to the fold of Islam.

The companions of the Prophet had accepted Islam at different stages of their lives. They had entered Islam with previous ideologies and influences which used to govern their lives. It was inevitable that when these individuals make a decision or take an action then some of those decisions or actions would be based on their previous influences, influences which were contrary to Islam.

This is why Prophet had done his level best to protect his successor from the pre-Islamic (Jahilliyah) principles by adopting him as a child.

And it was for this reason that Prophet had famously said:

> *"The one who wants to live my life and die my death will attach himself to Ali."*

- *Musnad of Ahmad, 5/94;*
- *Mustadrak Al-Sahihain of Al-Hakim Al-Nisaburi, 3/128;*
- *Kanz Al Umal, 6/217;*
- *Al-Tabarani*

This tradition of the Prophet is clearly meant for a time when Prophet is not going to be around, since in the presence of the Prophet it is the life of the Prophet which is the source of inspiration and guidance for all to follow. The Prophet was telling his companions that after his death if one wants to see how he had lived then they should look at the life of Ali, since it was the Prophet himself who had shaped Ali's life and nurtured him in the ideals of Islam.

The successor of the Prophet could only be a person whose life had a reflection of the life of the Prophet.

2.2. Ali and the Quran

The Prophet makes sure that Ali grows up in the character and the manners of "Khuluqin Azeem" i.e., Ali is brought up under the guidance of the lofty character of the Prophet. Ali is always with the Prophet and he accompanies the Prophet everywhere.

Ibn Hisham, the famous historian writes that even when Prophet goes for meditation in the cave which was on top of a mountain called Jabl-al-Noor, he often takes Ali with him (Sira Ibn Hisham – Biography of the Prophet). Ali was with the Prophet even when Prophet used to meditate in the cave. This was an honour and a privilege that no other companion shared with Ali. It was another unique distinction of Ali that he was the companion of the Prophet in the cave where the message of Islam had begun.

On many occasions Ali was present in the cave when Quran was being revealed to the Prophet. Ali became a witness to the revelations that had come to the Prophet of Allah. Ali writes down the verses of Quran and discusses them with the Prophet after they have been revealed to the Messenger of Allah. Ali becomes the first Hafiz-e-Quran (a person who memorizes Quran by heart) after the Prophet. Prophet not only teaches the verses of Quran to Ali as they are revealed, but he also explains their meaning (Tafseer) and the context in which these verses were revealed.

Ali is growing up in the very house where Quran is being sent. Ali's character is being built around the verses of Quran. Ali is learning the wisdom of Quran directly from the Prophet himself. Ali and Quran have grown up together in the house of Mohammad and that is why the Prophet had famously said:

> *"Ali is with Quran, and Quran is with Ali. They shall not separate from each other till they both return to me by the Pool (of Paradise)."*
> - *Al-Mustadrak, by al-Hakim, v3, p124 on the authority of Umm Salama*
> - *Al-Sawa'iq al-Muhriqah, by Ibn Hajar, Ch. 9, section 2, pp 191,194*
> - *Al-Awsat, by al-Tabarani; also, in al-Saghir*
> - *Tarikh al-Khulafa, by Jalaluddin al-Suyuti, p173*

The Prophet of Allah clearly states that Ali is with Quran and Quran is with Ali, and Ali and Quran will not separate from each other until they meet the Prophet in Paradise, such was the closeness of Ali with the book of Allah.

The first part of the Hadith states that Ali is with Quran, which implies that Ali works within the guidelines laid out by the Book of Allah. However, if one analyses the hadith a little further the Prophet also says that "Quran is with Ali". This is a very big statement indeed and its significance is immense.

The Prophet is implying that Ali's decisions, Ali's actions, Ali's judgment and Ali's path in fact reflects the verses of Quran. The only reason why Prophet could make such a statement about Ali was because Ali's character, Ali's manners, Ali's personality and Ali's life had moulded around the teachings of Quran, so much so that Ali became a mirror and a reflection of Quran. Ali and Quran became inseparable and hence Prophet had said that both Ali and Quran will meet him in paradise.

Essentially what Prophet is implying in this tradition is that if one wants to understand Quran in Prophet's absence, then they have to come to the door of Ali.

People who desire paradise and crave for success in hereafter have to follow the path of Ali, since the path of Ali is in fact the path laid out by the Holy Quran. And just as Ali and Quran will meet in paradise people who follow Ali and Quran sincerely will also Inshallah end up in Paradise.

The successor of the Prophet could only be someone who would lead the people to the path of Paradise in his absence.

Also, Ali was not someone who simply lived the life of Quran, but Ali was someone who also defended the meaning and the teachings of Quran too. In another tradition Prophet further clarified the position of Ali with regards to the Holy Quran.

The Prophet had said:

> *"There is amongst you a person who will fight for the interpretation of the Quran just as I fought for its revelation. The people around him raised their heads and cast inquisitive glances at the Prophet and at one another. Abu Bakr and Umar were there. Abu Bakr inquired if he was that person and the Prophet replied in the negative. Then Umar inquired if he was that person and*

the Prophet said no. The Prophet said, he is the one who is repairing my shoes, and it was Ali who was repairing Prophet's shoes."

- al-Mustadrak, by al-Hakim, v3, p122, who said this tradition is genuine based on the criteria of al-Bukhari and Muslim.
- al-Dhahabi, also records it in his Talkhis al-Mustadrak and admitted that it is genuine according to the standard of the two Shaikhs.
- Khasa'is, by al-Nisa'i, p40
- Musnad Ahmad Ibn Hanbal, v3, pp 32-33
- Kanz al-Ummal, by al-Muttaqi al-Hindi, v6, p155
- Majma' al-Zawa'id, by al-Haythami, v9, p133

This is another amazing tradition of the Prophet regarding the closeness of Ali with Quran. The Prophet of Allah says that just as I have fought for the revelation of Quran Ali would fight for its interpretation. There are two clear points which come out from the above tradition of the Prophet.

Firstly, this tradition is meant for a time when Prophet wasn't going to be around i.e., it is meant for a time after the death of the Prophet, since in the presence of the Prophet there was no need for anybody else to interpret the Holy Quran.

Secondly, the Prophet had chosen Ali to fight and defend the interpretation of Quran, just as Allah had chosen Prophet for the revelations of Quran, clearly implying that in the absence of the Prophet it was Ali who would be the right source for the correct interpretation of Quran.

The successor of the Prophet had to be someone who was able to defend the teachings and the knowledge of the Book of Allah. This was not a physical defence of Quran. On the contrary, the Prophet was implying that Ali would defend the ideological message of Quran, since it was the Prophet himself who had given Ali the knowledge of Quran.

That is why the companions like ibn Masud, who had witnessed Ali's knowledge of Quran had stated:

> *"The Holy Qur'an has outward and inward meanings, and 'Ali Ibn Abi Talib has the knowledge of both."*

- Hilyatul Awliyaa, by Abu Nu'aym, v1, p65

The early companions had recognized the supremacy of Ali's knowledge in Quran. They were well aware of the fact that Ali knew both the hidden and the literal meaning of Quran.

2.3. Ali Acquires Knowledge from the Prophet

Islam essentially comprises of two kinds of knowledge, the first one being the Holy Quran and the second one being the Sunnah of the Prophet. Ali had acquired both these pearls of knowledge and wisdom from the company of the Prophet.

We read in Nahjul Balagha, a book which is a compilation of Ali's sermons and lectures. Ali says:

> *"The Holy Prophet brought me up in his own arms and fed me with his own morsel. I followed him wherever he went like a baby-camel following its mother. Each day a new aspect of his character would beam out of his noble person and I would accept it and follow it as a command"*

- Nahj-ul-Balagha

Everyday Ali learns a new skill, a new trait and a new pearl of wisdom from the immaculate company of the Prophet. Ali would ask numerous questions and Prophet would respond with intellectual answers, in order to cultivate the character and the personality of Ali in the spirit and the ideals of Islam.

The successor of the Prophet could only be someone who would have shadowed the Prophet throughout his life.

Al-Nisai reported that Ali used to say:

> *"Whenever I asked the Messenger of Allah a question, he replied, and when I was silent, he would speak to me"*
> - *Al-Nisai and Al-Hakim in his Mustadrak*

This is how Ali had gained knowledge from the Prophet and this is how Ali had acquired the wisdom and the intellect from the Prophet.

The Prophet of Allah had dedicated hours and hours to train Ali. The Prophet of Allah used to train Ali both during the day and during the night as documented by Al-Nisa'i.

Al-Nisa'i reported on the authority of Ibn Abbas that Ali used to say:

> *"I had a privileged relationship with the Messenger of Allah which was not granted to any other mortal, as I used to visit the Prophet of Allah every night. If he was praying I would wait until he said the tasbih and then enter, and if he wasn't praying he would permit me and I would enter."*
> - *Al-Nisai*

The Prophet had opened Ali's eyes not just to the concept of religion, but also to the disciplines of social justice, human interaction and fair play, freedom of thought and expression. These were values and notions which were evidently missing from the Arabian society at that time. Ali has to have the command of all the various faculties of knowledge if he was going to succeed the Prophet in its true sense.

Such was the proximity and the closeness of Ali to the Prophet that we read in Hulyat al-Awliya on the authority of Ibn Abbas where he narrates the following:

> *"We used to say that Prophet had entrusted Ali with seventy pledges, which he did not entrust to anyone else"*
> - *Hulyat al-Awliya*

Ali was the trustee of Prophet's secrets and knowledge, and this was a fact known to many prominent companions like Ibn Abbas.

Ibn Abbas said also confessed that:

> *"My knowledge and the knowledge of the Companions of Muhammad is but a drop in seven seas if compared with 'Ali's knowledge."*

Even the likes of Caliph Abu Bakr and Caliph Umar would come to the door of Ali seeking answers to questions and problems that they could not resolve. Hence Caliph Abu Bakr once said:

> *"May Allah never put me in a predicament that Abu Al-Hasan (Ali) cannot solve."*

- *Al Isti'ab, vol 3 p 39*
- *Manaqib al Khawarizmi, p 48*
- *Al Riyadh al Nadirah, vol 2 p 194*

Similarly, Caliph Umar had famously said:

> "If it was not for Ali, 'Umar would have perished."

- *Al Isti'ab, vol 3 p 39*
- *Manaqib al Khawarizmi, p 48*
- *Al Riyadh al Nadirah, vol 2 p 194*

When Caliph Umar had to solve complex disputes among the Muslims during his caliphate he would often resort to Ali's help, and hence he famously said that without Ali he would have perished, implying that without Ali's wisdom he could not have resolved those difficult and challenging cases.

The Prophet had illuminated Ali's mind with knowledge, wisdom, and purity, to such an extent that as Ali grew up in the house of the Prophet, he became a reflection and a mirror of Prophet's ideals and principles and a guiding star for everyone around him.

2.4. Ali's Conversion to Islam

Ali's acceptance of Islam is often not called a conversion because Ali had grown up in the house of the Prophet, and Ali had only ever practiced the faith of the Prophet. Ali was never an idol worshipper like the people of Makkah. It is acknowledged without controversy that Prophet's grandfather Abdul Mutalib alongside with some members of Banu Hashim clan were followers of a monotheistic belief system (Hanifs), prior to the coming of Islam.

Prophet himself was not an idol worshipper before announcing the message of Islam. The Prophet and his close family had always believed in one God and followed the religion of Prophet Ibrahim. Hence, Ali who was born in the same family had only ever practiced the monotheistic belief system that Prophet used to follow.

When Prophet informed Ali about the revelations, Ali immediately accepted Prophet's status as the Prophet of Allah, since Ali himself had witnessed the revelations coming to the Prophet on many occasions. He had no doubt that Prophet Muhammad was the seal of the Prophets.

Anas bin Malik reports:

> "The Prophet began his mission on Monday, and 'Ali embraced Islam on Tuesday."
> - *al-Hakim, al-Mustadrak, Vol. III, p. 312*

Ibn Hisham, the well-known historian writes that Ali was the first person to believe in the Prophet.

> "Ali b. Abi Talib was the first man to believe in the Prophet......."
> - *Ibn Hisham, al-Sirah, Vol. I, p.245.*

2.5. The First to Pray Behind the Prophet

Ali was the first person who prayed behind the Prophet alongside Lady Khadija, the wife of the Prophet. Prophet Mohammad used to enter Kaaba and pray there with Khadija and Ali. Ibn Hisham writes in his Sirah:

> *"One day Ibn Abbas, the uncle of the Prophet was sitting on a hill near the Kaaba. A trader from Yemen was sitting with him. He asked Ibn Abbas who these three persons were, praying in such a strange manner. Ibn Abbas said that the man was his nephew Mohammad , the woman was Mohammad's wife Khadija, and the boy was Abu Talib's son Ali. Ibn Abbas further adds that they follow some strange religion which we are not familiar with yet"*

Ibn Hisham reports along similar lines in another part of his book that Ali was the first person to pray behind the Prophet.

> "Ali b. Abi Talib was the first man to believe in the Prophet, …… to pray together with him, and to affirm the veracity of that which God gave him……."

- *Ibn Hisham, al-Sirah, Vol. I, p.245.*

Ali was praying with the Prophet at a time when nobody even knew what Islam was. The message of Islam had not even begun for the general public, but Ali was already praying alongside the Prophet. Islam at that time was confined to Prophet's closest circle i.e., Ali and his wife Lady Khadija.

The successor of the Prophet had to be someone who was indeed part of his inner circle.

Ibn Majah in his *al-Sunan* and al-Hakim in his *al-Mustadrak* have recorded that Ali had prayed seven years before any of the other companions.

> "I am the servant of God and the brother of His Messenger. …….. I made the prayer seven years before anyone else did."

- *Ibn Majah, al-Sunan, Vol. I, p. 44.*
- *al-Hakim, al-Mustadrak, Vol. III, p. 112.*

Ali had been praying alongside the Prophet while others were still worshipping the idols. The training and the grooming of Ali had begun way before the Prophet even announced his mission to the public.

2.6. Ali Defends the Prophet as a Child

Ali was not only raised on the monotheistic belief system, but Ali also defends the path of truth even as a child. The elders of Quraysh had used many tactics to try and disrupt and stop the mission of the Prophet. One of their clever strategies was to employ their own children to attack and abuse the Prophet of Allah, knowing very well that Prophet would never harm the children. Whenever Prophet leaves his house, the youth of Quraysh would follow him, hurl abuse at him, call him names and throw stones and rubbish at him. The Prophet was really disturbed and upset by this behaviour, but he was powerless to do anything about it, as he could not possibly take on the children of Quraysh.

When Ali finds out that Prophet is being verbally and physically abused, Ali decides to accompany the Prophet, the youth of Quraysh again try to abuse the Prophet, but this time Ali confronts them, he warns them against attacking the Prophet, he throws the stones back at them, and chases them away into the alleyways of Makkah. Ali is alone, the youth of Quraysh are many, but they scatter in all directions.

Ali sets out his metal from an early age on the streets of Makkah. And as per Ali's promise in Dawat-dhul-Ashira Ali successfully defends and protects the Prophet as a young boy. This is another unique honour and distinction that separates Ali from the rest of the companions that Ali defended and protected the Prophet even when he was a child.

However, because of defending the Prophet from an early age Ali had gained many enemies among the Quraysh. The youth of the Quraysh had gone back to their homes and complained to their elders about Ali and how he had attacked and hurt them. The people who were the enemies of the Prophet were now the enemies of Ali too.

The Quraysh make a note of the person who had attacked their kids, and now Ali is on their hit list too. As Ali defends the Prophet for the sake of Islam, he is continuously building enemies around him. The youth of Quraysh will one day grow up and face Ali again in the battles of Badr, Uhud and Hunayn. This time they will face the sword of Ali.

Many of them will be killed and the hatred and the enmity of Ali will be set in blood forever.

Ali was brought up to defend the Prophet and his mission and to lay down his life in the path of Islam from an early age. During the period of economic boycott and social ban against the Muslims in Makkah, Abu Talib had sheltered the clan of Banu Hashim in a valley between the two mountains. The Quraysh were not only boycotting the Muslims, but they were looking to harm the Prophet of Allah too. Abu Talib would order Ali to sleep on Prophet's bed and would move the Prophet from bed to bed in the night, in order to keep his location a secret.

Ali knows that his life could be sacrificed to save the life of the Prophet. The Prophet of Allah must stay alive, the life of the Prophet's is precious, the mission of the Prophet is sacred. Such was the training of Ali from his own father. Ali had grown up to be the defender and the protector of the Prophet and his mission from the very beginning of Islam.

The successor of the Prophet could only be a person who had been acting as shield of the Prophet from an early age.

2.7. The Prophet Marries Fatima to Ali

The Prophet of Allah had trained and nurtured Ali to be his closest and most trusted disciple. One of the key distinctions of Ali was his marriage to Lady Fatima, the daughter of the Prophet. Prophet had given the hand of his beloved daughter into the hand of Ali.

The status of Fatima in the eyes of the Prophet was unique and distinct.

The Prophet had said:

> *"Fatima is part of me. Whoever upsets her upsets me, and whoever harms her harms me."*
>
> - *Sahih Muslim, v. 5, p. 54;*
> - *Al-Tirmidhi, v. 3, Chapter on the Virtues of Fatima, p. 241;*
> - *Khasa'is Al-Imam Ali of Nisa'i, p. 121-122;*
> - *Masabih Al-Sunnah, v. 4, p. 185;*
> - *Al-Isabah, v. 4, p. 378;*
> - *Seir Alam Al-Nubala', v. 2, p. 119;*
> - *Kanz Al-Umal, v. 13, p. 97;*
> - *Haliyat Al-Awliya', v.2, p. 40;*
> - *Muntakhab Kanz Al-Omal, in the margins of Al-Musnad, v. 5, p. 96;*

Because of the status and the closeness of Fatima to the Prophet, many companions had asked for her hand in marriage, including both Caliph Abu Bakr and Caliph Umar. But Prophet refused to give his daughter's hand to any of his prominent companions. However, when the proposal of Ali came, the Prophet of Allah could not possibly refuse, because it was the Prophet who had brought up Ali in his own house. Prophet already knew Ali's merits and qualifications, and his dedication and resolve to defend and expand the message of Islam.

> *When Ali approached the Prophet for Fatima's hand, the Prophet of Allah turned to Ali and asked:*
> "Do you have something to stipulate as your wife's dowry?"
> Ali replied: "As you well know, my belongings consist of nothing more than my sword, armour, and a camel."
> The Prophet said: "That is right. Your sword is needed during battles with the enemies of Islam. And you must water your palm orchards with your camel and also use it on journeys. Therefore, you may only stipulate your armour as your wife's dowry – and I give my daughter Fatima to you against this very armour."
>
> - *(Ihqaq al-Haq)*

Piety and humility were the trademark of Ali's upbringing at the hands of the Prophet, which could be clearly seen in Ali's proposal to Fatima. Ali only owned three things, a sword, an armour, and a camel. The Prophet of Allah gives his daughter's hand to Ali in marriage for the dowry of Ali's armour. Prophet knew very well that Ali had no material possessions, and Prophet of Allah was not going to marry his daughter for material gains either.

Prophet said to Fatima:

> *"I gave you in marriage to the best in my Ummah, the most knowledgeable in them, the best in patience in them, and the first Muslim among them."*
>
> - *Kanz al-Ummal, by al-Muttaqi al-Hindi, v6, p398*
> - *Musnad Ahmad Ibn Hanbal, v3, p136; v5, p26*

The Prophet of Allah justifies his decision to Fatima by stating that he had chosen the best man from his nation for her, since he was the first Muslim and since he was the most patient and the most knowledgeable among all his companions. The reason why Prophet gave Fatima to Ali was because the Prophet himself had nurtured Ali in the ideals of the Islamic spirit, to an extent that Ali became a reflection of Prophets piety and humility.

The Prophet asked Ali to sell his armour so that Prophet could buy some basic items for the marriage of his daughter. The Prophet divided the money into three parts, he gave one part to Bilal to buy scented perfume and the other two parts were put aside for buying clothes and household goods. The historical records show that around 18 items were bought from the proceeds of the armour.

I have listed the most important items below:

- One large scarf for four dirhams
- One piece of dress material for one dirham
- One bed made of wood and palm leaves
- Four pillows of sheep skin filled with a sweet-smelling grass called Azkhar
- One woollen curtain
- One mat
- One hand mill

- One leather water-skin
- One copper washtub
- One large container for milking
- One large earthen pitcher

With the most basic of the items Ali begins his life with the daughter of the Prophet. The marriage ceremony itself was incredibly simple, but the words of the Prophet tell a different story.

The Prophet of Allah said about Ali:

> "There would not be one sufficient for Fatima if God had not created Ali."
>
> - Hiliyat Al-Awliya', 1/34;
> - Al-Riyadh Al-Nudhra, 2/177;
> - Ibn Al-Maghazeli, 242;
> - Al-Khawarizmi, 42;
> - Yanabi' Al-Mawda, 112;

The words of the Prophet were blunt and enlightening. The Prophet stated that if Ali hadn't proposed Fatima, then there was no one good enough to be her match. It was clear from the proceedings of the marriage itself that the match that Prophet was talking about was not a match of wealth or power. The match that Prophet had in mind was the match of Fatima in terms of her character, in terms of her ideals, in terms of her upbringing, and above all a match in terms of her closeness and attachment to the Prophet of Allah and to the message of Islam.

The reason why Ali was a match for Fatima was because the Prophet had brought up Ali on the same ideals of piety, knowledge and humility, and Ali's closeness with the Prophet was at par with the closeness of the prophet to her beloved daughter Fatima.

That is why Prophet had also said:

> "Fatima is more beloved to me than you, oh Ali, and you are dearer to me than her."
>
> - Majmu'a Al-Zawa'id, v. 9, p. 202;
> - Al-Jami' Al-Sagheer, v. 2, p. 654, n. 5761;
> - Muntakhab Kanz Al-Omal, v. 5, 97;
> - Asad Al-Ghaba, v. 5, p. 522;
> - Yanabi' Al-Mawadda, v. 2, ch. 56, p. 79;
> - Al-Sawaiq Al-Muhariqa, ch. 3, p. 191

Since both Ali and Fatima were so close to the Prophet in terms of their understanding and grasp of the message of Islam that the Prophet of Allah had said: "Fatima is more beloved to me than you, oh Ali, and you are dearer to me than her."

2.8. Ali and the Death of the Prophet.

This theme of Ali's closeness to the Prophet continued even after the death of the Prophet.

When the news of Prophet's death spreads, the first thing that the leaders of the Ansar (companions from Madinah) did was to make sure that they select a leader from their own clan to lead the Muslims. These companions (Ansar) had no interest in the burial or the funeral of the Prophet. Caliph Abu Bakr and Caliph Umar had come to the house of the Prophet after his death, but when they are informed that the Ansar had gathered in Saqifah to choose the future leader of the Muslims, they also leave the body of the Prophet and head towards Saqifah.

But Ali was by the side of the Prophet, from the moment he closed his eyes to the moment his body was lowered into the grave. Ali was not going to leave the Prophet alone at that moment. How could Ali even contemplate leaving the body of the Prophet? The Prophet of Allah was his mentor, his trainer, his teacher, and his ultimate guide. Ali had indeed become Ali (Ali means the exalted one) as a result of Prophet's training. The sole focus of Ali after Prophet's death was the burial and the funeral of the Prophet, unlike many of the prominent companions who had other priorities.

Ali washes and baths the pure body of the Prophet alongside Ibn Abbas. Ali then shrouds the body of the Prophet. Ali offers Prophet's funeral prayers alongside the rest of the Ahlulbayt and some of the companions who had gathered in Prophet's house. The Prophet is not immediately buried to allow other companions to catch the last glimpse of the Prophet. Finally, after two days the Prophet's body is lowered into the grave by Ali, and the Prophet of Allah is buried in his own house. Ali had been the companion of the Prophet even after his death. This is again a distinction and an honour that separates Ali from almost all the prominent companions.

The companionship of Ali and the Prophet was unique and distinct, it began with the birth of Ali when Prophet came to see his nephew and ended with the lowering of the Prophet's body into the grave. Ali's entire life until the death of the Prophet was spent in the company of the Prophet, which was unlike the companionship of any of the other companions with the Prophet since they had accepted Islam at different stages of their lives. This is why Ali was inseparable from the Prophet even after his death.

The successor of the Prophet could only be someone who had been his companion both in life and after his death.

3. ALI AND THE ESTABLISHMENT OF THE ISLAMIC STATE

When one looks at the history or the evolution of ideological movements which have survived the test of time, one would often find that there are certain individuals and personalities whose role and service in the growth and the expansion of that movement was indispensable.

The big and key events which take place in the evolutionary phase of such movements are strongly connected to a few individuals who would play a decisive role in its early stages. Their actions and contribution would not only define and secure the movement in its infancy but would also be responsible for shaping its future.

The presence of a solider, a trader, a merchant or a farmer who also supports the movement certainly matters, but these small role performers as individuals do not shape or impact the key and the important events in the life of any movement. Their presence and their role as individuals can be termed as dispensable or incidental, since their individual work could be replaced by another person of similar ability and calibre, without impacting the key events which would shape the future of the movement.

The Islamic movement started by the Prophet of Allah was no different. When one looks at the onset of Islam and its gradual spread, we find that the key events which secured and shaped the future of the Islamic movement were strongly linked and connected to a few individuals, whose role and service in its early stages was unique and indispensable.

Apart from the Prophet who was the founder of the revolutionary movement of Islam, the history presents us with two men whose presence and contribution were indispensable and distinguished in defending and securing the movement of Islam. These two towering personalities were at the core of almost all the key events which shaped and secured the Islamic movement in its early days.

3.1. The Role of Abu Talib

The first of these individuals was Abu Talib, the uncle of the Prophet and the father of Ali, who was also the head of Banu Hashim clan.

Abu Talib was not only the guardian of the Prophet from his childhood, but he became the main defender and the protector of the Prophet after Prophet had publicly announced his Prophethood to the clans of Quraysh. The protection offered by Abu Talib to his nephew against the constant threats and intimidation from the Qurayshite clans was the main factor in the continuity of Prophet's life and his mission in the hostile environment of Makkah.

The non-Hashemite Makkan clans were burning with hatred and animosity towards the Prophet after he had challenged their Gods and their way of life. They were ready to shed his blood and end his movement at the earliest opportunity. It was Abu Talib, who prevented the Qurayshites from harming the Prophet and supported his nephew at every step of the way, despite the great danger and risk to both himself and his family.

The Quraysh of Makkah formed a strong alliance against Abu Talib and his family. The Quraysh had imposed economic and social embargo against Abu Talib and his clan and used the weapon of starvation to subdue the Muslims and their supporters. Abu Talib and Banu Hashim endured unimaginable sufferings including hunger, starvation, and torture, but still he and his clan stood in the way of the Quraysh like a fortress and kept supporting the Prophet and his mission.

Abu Talib tied his fate with the fate of his nephew, and he was unconcerned about the repercussions to himself and his family.

Abu Talib made Ali and his other sons sleep in Prophet's bed in order to save the life of the Prophet from possible assassination attempts by the Quraysh. He was willing to sacrifice every single member of his family to defend the Prophet and his message. The protection offered by Abu Talib to the Prophet was the main physical deterrence that kept the Quraysh of Makkah at bay.

The testimony of history is clear that without the protection of Abu Talib and his family the mission of the Prophet would have never got off the ground. The support and the protection of Abu Talib was instrumental and indispensable in nurturing the plant of Islam in its infancy, especially in the harsh and violent environment of Makkah.

3.2. The Role of Ali

The other great personality with whom the continuity of the faith of Islam was strongly connected and whose contribution in its path was indispensable was Ali, the son of Abu Talib and Prophet's first cousin. The role and the service of Ali in defending and securing the Islamic movement in its early stages was unique and distinguished among all the companions.

The readers of Islamic history would confirm that the message of Islam remained unannounced during the first three years of Prophethood. The Prophet of Allah did not publicly invite people to the path of Islam during this period. He knew very well that any confrontation with the clans of Makkah at this stage would have been fatal for the newly professed faith.

However, the Islamic ideology was not revealed to be kept a secret and the confrontation with the pagans and the opponents of the Islamic thought was inevitable. The environment of Makkah was extremely dangerous and violent for any new ideology to succeed and eventually take over that society. The Arabs of Makkah would attack and kill each other on minor disputes and arguments, and the animosity that would be created as a result would last for generations to come.

It wasn't a society that was based on the principles of justice, fair play, reason, or logic.

The Prophet had to propagate the message of Islam in that extremely harsh and non-conducive environment. If the new ideological message of Islam was to prosper and grow, it needed relative peace and security for both the messenger of Allah and the new converts to Islam.

Even if an individual was inspired by the call to Islam, it was difficult for them to accept the new faith, since it would mean challenging and going against the established traditions of the society. A new convert would have to confront and take on the society that they were part of since birth. This would inevitably mean loss of position, loss of wealth, loss of status and even loss of life if they went against the uncivilized Makkan society that existed at the time of the inception of Islam.

Only a handful of souls would be willing to accept the new faith in such an unwelcoming and hostile circumstances. Most people would not dare to accept the new ideology which required such a big sacrifice, and where the chances of survival after accepting the new faith were bleak. A person of average courage and resolve would be unlikely to embrace the new faith unless his life, wealth and status were protected and safe.

Due to the constant threats and intimidation from the Quraysh of Makkah, the Muslims were not able to prosper and expand their influence in Makkah, and it meant that the new ideology and the new faith would have little success if any in attracting the masses.

As for the man of the message i.e., the Prophet of Allah, his capacity, and his ability to propagate the message of Islam in the harsh reality of Makkah was pretty limited too, especially when his own life and freedom were under constant threat. Even though Prophet of Allah was a fearless soul, in a violent society like Makkah, the death of the Prophet by assassination before the establishment of the Islamic faith would bring the whole Islamic movement to an immediate end.

To counter all these threats and challenges and to ensure that the movement of Islam reaches out to the masses, the Prophet of Allah with all his wisdom and divine guidance devised a strategy to expand Islam to the entire Arabian Peninsula and beyond.

The Prophet of Allah needed a protective shield around him that would give him the space and the freedom which was essential to deliver the message of Islam to the masses, and for the masses to feel safe and secure once they had accepted the new faith. This would be the only way Islam would grow and expand, and the word of Allah would prevail and become supreme in the Arabian desert.

The Prophet of Allah devised a plan and a strategy to expand the message Islam to the masses.

3.3. The Birth of the Islamic State

The Prophet's strategy was to establish a base for the Muslims where they would be free to practice their faith without danger or intimidation from its enemies. The plan of the Prophet was to establish an Islamic State, a state where new converts would not be threatened or attacked, a state that would protect the honour and the dignity of the Muslims, and a state that would become a launching pad for carrying forward the message of Islam to the corners of the world.

The Prophet could not possibly establish the Islamic state without taking on its advisories and without destroying its enemies. The strategy of the pagans and the enemies of Islam was to deny the Prophet any space or freedom to carry forward his message. Their mission was not just to stop the message of Islam but was also to kill the Prophet and his supporters, and to completely eradicate the Islamic movement from the Arabian Peninsula. If the forces which were bent upon wiping out Islam prevailed on the battlefield, then the Islamic State could not be established, and even if it was established it would not survive.

Thus, the Islamic State was destined to be born on the battlefield, not to forcefully spread Islam, but to secure the future of the Islamic ideology which was under threat from its enemies. This was where the sacrifice, the bravery and the support of Ali was unique and distinguished. Ali became Prophet's right-hand man in establishing the Islamic State to secure the future of the Muslims. Ali defended the Prophet of

Allah at every step of the way and carried forward the same role that his father Abu Talib had performed in Makkah, but Ali did it on a much larger scale.

The Prophet was the architect and the founder of the Islamic State of Madinah, and Ali was the eliminator of the obstructive forces which stood in the way of its establishment.

Ali was the flag bearer of the Prophet in every decisive battle. He never placed Ali under anybody else's command, and whenever Ali carried the flag of Islam, he came back victorious. Ali was not a commander who was defended by his soldiers. On the contrary, he always led from the front, and on more than one occasion his soldiers would take refuge in him, and he would become their protector.

Ali attended 18 battles with the Prophet and led countless expeditions. In the following sections I will briefly mention Ali's unique and distinct contribution to the key events that shaped the early Islamic history. These included the event of the night of the Hijrah and the four decisive battles i.e., the battle of Badr, the battle of Uhud, the battle of Moat and the battle of Khaibar. These four battles were truly the battles for the destiny of Islam, and all these battles took place during the early years of the Islamic movement.

If Prophet would have been harmed in any of these events, or Muslims would have been decisively defeated in any of these battles, then that would have been the end of the Islamic revolution in Arabia as we know it.

The first decisive event was the night of the Hijra (Migration to Madinah).

3.4. The Night of the Hijrah (Migration to Madinah)

Ali had pledged to support the Prophet and his mission in every possible way during the feast of Dawat-dhul-Ashira, and in return Prophet had given Ali the titles of being his successor, his brother, and his inheritor. The pledge of Ali in Dawat-dhul-Ashira had literally put Ali at the disposal of the Prophet. The Prophet can now call upon this brother and his successor whenever he wants to, and Ali is obliged to respond to his call. The Islamic State is yet to be born and the titles of being the successor and the brother of the Prophet at this stage are as much an honour for Ali as they are an obligation, where Ali needs to support the mission of the Prophet and fulfil the pledge that he has made.

The first test of Ali's pledge came when the Quraysh of Makkah had planned to assassinate the Prophet on a specific night. The tribal chiefs of Quraysh had decided to bring the life of the Prophet to an end to stifle the movement of Islam in its tracks. They conferred secretly and concluded that the only way they could stop the message of Islam was to kill the Prophet himself. A strong and a courageous man was selected from each clan of Makkah to participate in the assassination plot of the Prophet. This would ensure that if the plot was successful no one clan would get the blame. Allah revealed the conspiracy to the Prophet and ordered him to leave for Madinah.

Prophet mentioned the conspiracy to Ali and asked him to support his mission by executing two key tasks.

- Prophet wants Ali to sleep in his bed on the night of the planned attack.
- Prophet also wants Ali to give back the trusts to the people of Makkah that Prophet had in his possession.

3.4.1. Ali is to Sleep in Prophet's Bed

The time had come for Ali to fulfil his pledge of support practically by sacrificing his life for the life of the Prophet.

When Prophet mentioned the conspiracy to Ali and asked him to sleep in his bed on the night of the planned attack, Ali asks the Prophet:

> *"Messenger of God Will you be safe if I sleep in your bed?" The Prophet said "Yes"*
> - Majlisi, Biḥar al-Anwar, vol. 19, p. 60.
> - Musnad Imam Ahmad (3241/3251)

When Prophet confirmed that he would be safe, Ali immediately bows down in prostration thanking Allah that he would be able to save the life of the Prophet. Ali had absolutely no qualms about his own life. The only thing that mattered to Ali was the safety and the well-being of the Prophet. This was the nature of the commitment that Ali had pledged to the Prophet in the feast of Dawat-dhul-Ashira.

The titles of being the successor and the brother of the Prophet were not simply gifts, that were given to Ali without any obligation. These titles demanded the ultimate sacrifice on the part of Ali, especially when the Islamic State of Madinah was still just a dream.

The ten most renowned warriors from the clans of Makkah were chosen to ambush the Prophet. Once the assassins would enter the house, they would surely kill whoever was on Prophet's bed. Only the bravest of the companions would dare to sleep in Prophet's bed that night. Also, when the assassins would find out that the Prophet had already left and their plot had been foiled, they would inevitably torture that person to gain the information about Prophet's whereabouts. So, the person who would sleep on Prophet bed would have to be prepared for both death and torture at the hands of Quraysh.

As Ali slept on the bed of the Prophet the men of Quraysh entered the house in the dead of the night. Their swords drawn, with the intention to kill the Prophet, but to their surprise they came face to face with Ali. The heavily armed men surrounded Ali and harassed him for information on Prophet's whereabouts. As Ali denied any knowledge about Prophet's whereabouts violence erupted and Ali was attacked and tortured.

We read in Ibn-al-Atheer history al-Kamil part 2 p72

> *"Where is Mohammad?" they asked. "I do not know "Ali replied. They beat Ali up, tortured him and detained him"*
> - al-Kamil by Ibn-al-Atheer part2 p72

Unphased by the strength and the number of enemy combatants Ali pressed the hand of their leader making the sword drop from his hand. Ali seized the sword and managed to drive them out.

On the night of Hijrah Ali distinguished himself by not only offering to sacrifice his life for the Prophet of Allah, but by also refusing to inform the heavily armed Qurayshite tribesmen about the whereabouts of the Holy Prophet, despite being tortured.

Generally, in a battlefield one fights in a group and there is support and help from fellow combatants. On the night of Hijrah Ali is on his own, he is all alone, he has no support or help from anyone, he is surrounded by ten armed men, but he still successfully takes on all the warriors of Makkah who had come to kill the Prophet without any fear or trepidation.

Only a person whose love and obedience of the Prophet exceeded the love they had for their own life could have stepped in Prophet's shoes on the night of the Hijra, and Ali happened to be that unique individual.

Islam was still in its infancy and there were no more than one hundred and fifty to two hundred Muslims at the time of Hijra. There wasn't a big pool of people that Prophet could choose from for such a daring mission. However, there were some gems from the early companions in this small pool of Muslims, and Ali stood out among those companions too.

The Prophet therefore chooses Ali who had pledged him allegiance in the feast of Dawat-dhul-Ashira for the most dangerous of the missions. This was the biggest threat that Prophet had faced at the hands of the Quraysh until now. Allah recognizes the courage and the commitment of Ali to the path of Islam by revealing the following verse in the honour of Ali.

> *"And among men is he who sells his Nafs (self) in exchange for the pleasure of Allah."*
> - *Quran 2:207*

Ali had physically put his life at risk to save the life of his mentor, the Prophet of Islam. Ali sold himself on the night of the Hijra for the pleasure of Allah, and the Holy Quran confirmed the huge significance of Ali's achievement in the above verse.

3.4.2. Ali is to Give Back the Trusts in the Prophet's Possession

The other key task that Prophet had given to Ali was to give back the trusts that Prophet had kept for the Quraysh of Makkah. The Prophet of Allah was the most trustworthy person for both friends and foes. Even though the Quraysh of Makkah were against the Prophet and the message of Islam, they still trusted him with their money and valuable possessions. Hence Prophet was known among the Arabs as the trustworthy one.

Although on the face of it, it seemed like a non-significant task that Ali would return the trusts of the Quraysh in Prophet's possession, but if one digs a little deeper the significance of this task in fact clarifies the unique position of Ali in relation to the Prophet.

Prophet had asked Ali to sleep in his bed in order to foil the plot of the would-be assassins, so there was no guarantee that Ali would have survived the night. On seeing Ali in Prophet's bed, the assassins could have easily killed Ali just as they had planned to kill the Prophet. Despite the fact that there was no guarantee of Ali's survival, Prophet still chooses Ali to deliver his trusts.

It seemed as if Prophet wanted to give a message to the companions that the only person who could keep the trusts of the Prophet was Ali. Prophet could have chosen any other companion to deliver the trusts such as Caliph Abu Bakr, Caliph Umar or Caliph Uthman, since their survival was not in question. However, Prophet only chooses Ali to be his trustee and his representative on the night of the Hijra, as a prelude to show the world that one day Ali would indeed become the trustee and inheritor of Prophet's mandate.

As mentioned in the previous section there were around one hundred and fifty to two hundred Muslims who had accepted Islam by this time. These were Prophet's earliest companions, and in many ways were the elite group of companions since they had accepted Islam in the harsh anti-Islamic society of Makkah.

Out of these top companions Prophet only chose Ali to take on the would-be assassins, and to give back his trusts. This clearly reveals that at least in the mind of the Prophet, the only person who he would rely upon to save his life would be Ali, and the only person who he would trust to give back the possessions of the people would also be Ali.

And Ali indeed repaid Prophet's trust in him by rising to the occasion on the night of the Hijra. Ali became the redeemer of the Prophet that night and justified his claim to be the true successor and the inheritor of the Prophet.

3.4.3. The Prophet Meets Caliph Abu Bakr who Accompanies him

The Prophet leaves his house in the dead of the night while Ali sleeps in his bed. The house of the Prophet is surrounded by the men of Quraysh who are waiting to kill him. As Prophet comes out of his house, he throws some sand towards the men while reciting the following verse of Quran.

> *"And we have put before them a barrier and behind them a barrier and covered them, so they do not see."*
>
> - *Quran 36:9*

With the miracle of Allah, the assailants of Quraysh are unable to see the Prophet and he passes through them without being noticed. As Prophet walks through the city of Makkah, he meets Caliph Abu Bakr who accompanies the Prophet, and they both head to Madinah. When Quraysh realized that their plot to assassinate the Prophet had been foiled, they immediately sent out search parties to track down the Prophet.

The Prophet and Caliph Abu Bakr took refuge in a cave on the outskirts of Makkah to hide from the search parties sent out by Quraysh of Makkah. However, one of the expert trackers managed to track down the footsteps of the Prophet to the mouth of the cave. On hearing the rumbles of the approaching search party Caliph Abu Bakr became nervous and whispered into the ear of the Prophet:

> *Abu Bakr said: If one of them looks under his feet he will see us.*
> *Prophet Replies: Be not afraid God is with us.*
>
> - *Fath Al Bari 8:176*

This incident is also mentioned in the Holy Quran.

> *Allah did indeed help him [Muhammad] when the disbelievers drove him out, the second of two, when they both [Muhammad and Abu Bakr] were in the cave, and he said to his companion [Abu Bakr]: "Be not sad (or afraid), surely Allah is with us"*
>
> - *Quran At-Tawbah 9:40*

The Prophet of Allah reassures Caliph Abu Bakr that there was no need to be afraid and Allah will protect them. Despite being at the entrance of the cave the search party was unable to discover the Prophet and Allah saved his Messenger from the evil designs of the Quraysh.

3.5. Laying the Foundations of the Islamic State of Madinah

The migration to Madinah was probably the most significant event in the lifetime of the Prophet. This event rejuvenated a new life and vigour into the message of Islam, which was being threatened at every step of the way by the Quraysh of Makkah. The migration to Madinah brought a breath of fresh air for both the Prophet and the ordinary Muslims. Unlike the Quraysh of Makkah who had plotted to kill the

Prophet, the inhabitants of Madinah had lined up on the streets to welcome and catch a glimpse of the Prophet as he arrived.

There was an air of excitement on the streets of Madinah at the arrival of the Prophet. Everyone was keen and eager to host the Prophet in their house. As per the wish of the Prophet his camel would decide where he was going to stay. The camel stopped outside the house of Abu Ayyub Ansari, who became the host of the Prophet and Prophet stayed in his house.

The migration to Madinah was the very first step in the plan and the strategy of the Prophet to establish a base for the Muslims. The State of Madinah would indeed become a hub and a nucleus for the Muslims of Arabia. It gave Muslims the much-needed security required for the propagation and survival of Islam at the time. The Prophet starts to lay the foundations of the Islamic State by giving the State of Madinah a constitution. This in fact became the very first written document in the history of Islam, other than the Holy Quran. The document was preserved by Ibn Ishaq in his historical work.

Following are some of the key points from the document.

- All disputes between any two parties in Yathrib would be referred to Muhammad for his decision on them.
- Muslims and Jews would enjoy the same rights.
- Each group in Yathrib would follow its own faith, and no one group would meddle in the affairs of any other group.
- In the event of an external attack upon Yathrib, both groups, i.e., the Muslims and the Jews, would defend the city.
- Both groups would refrain from shedding blood in the city.
- Muslims would not go to war against other Muslims for the sake of non-Muslims.

Ibn Husham has also recorder similar points in his biography of the Prophet (Ibn Husham Biography of Prophet Part 1 p. 503). At that time apart from the Muslims the Jews were the other main inhabitants of Madinah. The constitution of Islam is all inclusive and values the rights of all the inhabitants of Madinah regardless of their faith.

The Prophet establishes a mosque in Madinah which was going to be known as Al-Masjid-an-Nabawi, the mosque of the Prophet. This mosque would become the heart of the Islamic State. This is where the Prophet of Allah would give his sermons and meet his companions and resolve any issues and disputes that would arise. The mosque of the Prophet would become the hub and the focal point of Islamic activity.

The decisions of war and peace would be made in this very mosque. Both peace delegations and Muslim armies would be sent from this mosque, while the mosque would also host delegations from non-Muslim regions. The mosque would serve as the headquarters of the Islamic State, and the city of Madinah would become the military and the constitutional base of Islam.

To further cement the notion of one Muslim Ummah (nation), the Prophet initiates the concept of Islamic brotherhood and fraternity, something that was new and unique for that era. The Islamic concept of brotherhood introduced the idea that a Muslim would desire for his brother what he desires for himself. A Muslim would help his brother when his brother needed help, and a Muslim would feel the pain of his brother as if it was his own pain.

The Prophet of Allah laid out the concept of Islamic brotherhood at three levels:

- The Global Islamic brotherhood that exists among all Muslims.

- The brotherhood among certain muslin groups like the Ansar and the Muhajireen.
- And the notion of brotherhood among specific individuals.

The Prophet created brotherhood between the Ansar (inhabitants Of Madinah) and the Muhajireen (immigrants from Makkah). The Muhajireen had left their family, their friends, and their possessions behind in Makkah, and most of them had migrated to Madinah with absolutely nothing. They needed all the help that they could get from the Ansars, who were the indigenous population of Madinah. The Prophet had established a brotherhood between the Ansar and the Muhajireen to allow the Muhajireen to settle down in Madinah, without feeling alienated or out of place in a new city.

The Prophet had also established brotherhood between the two tribes of Ansar i.e., al-Aws and al-Khazraj. These tribes had been bitter enemies for decades and had fought numerous wars against each other where hundreds of people had been killed. The Prophet wanted to ensure that there was peace and tranquillity in the headquarters of the Islamic State.

The Prophet also laid the foundation of specific brotherhood among certain individuals. This brotherhood was based on the merits and similarities in one's character and traits. It is recorded in Al-Seerat Al-Halabeyah (Ali Ibn Burhanudeen Al-Halabi Biography of the Prophet Part 2 p.97) that Prophet established brotherhood between Caliph Abu Bakr and Caliph Umar, and between Caliph Abu Bakr and Kharijah Ibn Zeid, and between Caliph Omar and Atban Ibn Malik, since the status and the stature of these companions was similar and close to each other.

The Prophet also established brotherhood among various other companions, however when it came to his own brotherhood, Prophet inevitably chooses Ali, to show the rest of the companions that the person who was closest to him and the person who was most similar to him in his character and in his manners was the person who had been personally trained and brought up by him in his own house.

The Prophet said to Ali:

> *"You are my brother in this life and the Hereafter."*
> - *Mustadrak al-Hakim, vol 3, #32/4288*
> - *Al-Khasa'is of Al-Nisa'i, 5;*
> - *Tirmizi, vol. 5, p. 401, Hadith 3741*
> - *Yanabi Al-Mawda, 61;*
> - *Ibn Al-Maghazeli, 37;*
> - *Ibn Husham Part 1 p.505*
> - *Ibn Shahrashub, Manaqib, V, 100.*

The title of being successor of the Prophet could only be given to a person whom Prophet had called his brother in his world and in hereafter.

3.6. The Battle of Badr

The battle of Badr was one of the most important battles for the destiny of Islam. The Islamic State of Madinah had just been established and the Muslims had just begun to enjoy the freedoms of a sovereign Islamic nation when the Quraysh of Makkah decided to attack Madinah. The Muslims were still settling into the newly established Islamic State when the Quraysh of Makkah decided to send an army to attack the bastion of Islam. It was the very first time that the followers of the new faith were put to a serious test. If the Qurayshite army coming from Makkah had won this battle, then the newly established Islamic state of Madinah would have been destroyed in its infancy.

The pagan army consisted of around a thousand fighters. On the side of the Muslims there were 313 men. The Muslim defence was a combination of three elements:

- The personality of the Prophet and his firm leadership.
- The clan of Banu Hashim (Prophet's clan) led by Ali.
- Hundreds of companions who were ready to sacrifice their lives in the path of Islam.

3.6.1. The Importance of the Battle of Badr

There was no one who was more aware of the importance and the decisiveness of this battle than the Prophet of Allah himself. He prays to Allah before the battle begins in the following words.

> *"God this is Quraysh. It has come with all its arrogance and boastfulness trying to discredit Thy Apostle. God I ask Thee to humiliate them tomorrow. God if this Muslim band will perish today Thou shall not be worshiped!"*
> - *Ibn Husham Biography of the Prophet Part 2 p. 621.*

The prayer of the Prophet itself testifies the importance of this battle in his eyes. The Prophet knew that if Muslims were to be defeated in this battle it would be the end of Islam in Arabia.

The battle began with Utbah Ibn Rabi-ah, his son Al-Waleed and his brother Sheibah, all from the Umayyad clan of Quraysh challenging the Muslim army. Prophet sent Ali, Al-Hamzah and Obeidah Ibn Al-Harith, all from the clan of Banu Hashim to face the three Umayyad warriors. Ali killed Al-Waleed and Al-Hamzah killed Utbah, then they both helped Obeidah against his opponent Sheibah who was also killed. However, Obeidah lost his leg and became the first martyr of this battle.

When the general offensive began hundreds of companions participated in the battle and fought bravely against a much larger enemy. They killed many enemy combatants, and they offered sacrifices in the path of Allah and pleased their creator.

However, Ali and Banu Hashim distinguished themselves in the battle with their bravery and skill, and especially Ali's whose endeavour was unique in the battle. When Hanthala Ibn Abu Sufyan faced Ali, Ali finished him off with one blow. Ali also annihilated Al-Auss Ibn Sa-eed and transfixed Tuaima Ibn Oday to his spear, saying:

> *"You shall not dispute with us in God after today".*
> - *Ibn Hisham Biography of the Prophet Part 2 p. 621/708-713*

3.6.2. Ali's Distinct Performance

Around Seventy pagans met their death at the hands of the Muslims army and a similar number were taken prisoners by the Muslims. History has preserved the names of 50 pagans out of 70 who were killed. Twenty-two or twenty-three of these fifty pagans whose names are known were killed by Ali. This means that Ali alone had killed more than 40% of the known enemy combatants, while the rest of the three hundred and twelve companions had killed the remaining 60% percent of the enemy.

By simple maths the performance of Ali was unique and distinguished. Ali had clearly changed the destiny of this battle in favour of Islam and Muslims. If we take out the performance of any one companion, then the outcome of the battle of Badr would not be affected. However, if we take out the performance of Ali, the outcome of the battle of Badr would be different. The individual efforts of the rest of the companions were similar and comparable, but the effort of Ali was unique and distinct, and the facts speak for themselves.

It would not be an exaggeration to say that Ali's endeavour was indispensable in bringing the victory to the Muslims in the battle of Badr. The other companions also fought bravely for the defence of Islam, but their individual effort and endeavour was replaceable by the effort and endeavour of another companion, whereas the effort and the endeavour of Ali was unique, and no other companion could match what Ali had achieved.

The skill and the bravery of Ali on the battlefield was in fact the key differentiating factor which had brought victory to the Muslims in the battle of Badr.

This victory laid the foundation of the Islamic State of Madinah. It made Muslims a force to be reckoned with by the people of the Arabian Peninsula. The bravery and the skill of Ali on the battlefield became the talk of the town. Ali came relatively obscure into the battle of Badr but became an instant hero among the Muslims once the battle was over. Ali's bravery became the subject of conversations among the Arab caravans and Ali suddenly acquired the status of a legendary warrior.

3.7. The Battle of Uhud

The Qurayshite clans were never going to sit idle after their defeat in the battle of Badr. They were burning with hatred against Islam and the Muslims. They could not stand the newly established Islamic State in the heart of the Arabian Peninsula. The Qurayshite clans mobilized three thousand fighters to avenge their defeat in the battle of Badr, and to remove the humiliation that they had suffered at the hands of the Muslims.

The pagan army of Makkah arrived in the area of Uhud which is about five miles from Madinah to take on the Muslims. The Prophet had deployed his forces at strategic positions. He placed fifty marksmen at the slope of the Mount of Uhud, directing them to protect the back of the Muslims against the pagan cavalry. The pagan cavalry was led by Khalid Ibn Al-Waleed. Prophet had commanded these marksmen not to leave their positions even if Muslims had won the battle.

The Islamic defence consisted of the same three elements which defeated the pagans in Badr:

- The impeccable leadership of the Prophet.
- Ali and the members of the Prophet's clan, the Banu Hashim.
- An Islamic army consisting of seven hundred companions who were ready to fight in the defence of Islam.

The start of the Battle of Uhud was similar to the Battle of Badr. Talhah Ibn Abu Talhah, the flag bearer of the pagans challenged the Muslims army. Prophet asked Ali to take him on and Ali swiftly dealt a blow with his sword splitting his head into two. Then Abu Saad Ibn Abu Talhah (brother of Talhah) carried the banner for the pagans and challenged the Muslims, again Ali stepped forward and finished him off. The pagan army kept replacing their flag bearers and Ali kept killing them.

3.7.1. Ali Kills the Majority of the Flag Bearers

According to Ibn Al-Atheer (Ibn Al-Atheer, Al-Kamil Part 3 Page 107), Ali alone killed all the flag bearers of the enemy in the Battle of Uhud. However, some historians say that al-Hamzah, the uncle of the Prophet and a few other companions also killed some of the flag bearers. So, based on the historical accounts of all the historians it would be correct to say that Ali had killed the majority of the enemy flag bearers if not all of them.

The death of the flag bearers of the enemy heightened the morale of the Muslims, and as a result they undertook a general offensive led by Ali, Al-Hamzah, Abu Dujanah and others. The Islamic offensive terrified the pagan army but unfortunately Muslims lost Al-Hamzah, the uncle of the Prophet in this offensive. The Quraysh of Makkah were forced to flee, and Muslims entered their camps and started collecting the spoils of war without meeting any resistance.

This scene watered the mouths of the fifty companions whom the Prophet had placed at the slope of the Mount of Uhud to protect the back of the Muslims against the pagan cavalry. The majority of these companions left their place and joined the collectors of the spoils against the command of the Prophet. Noticing the small number of the companions near the mount of Uhud, Khalid Ibn Al-Waleed and his horsemen overpowered them and began a general offensive against the Muslims.

3.7.2. The Tables Turn Against the Muslims

On seeing the turnaround on the battlefield, the fleeing pagans came back while the companions were still preoccupied collecting the spoils. The companions were shocked and confused on seeing the pagan army back on the battlefield. The pagan army charged the companions, but the companions were not able to sustain the onslaught. Many companions were killed by the pagans and then the companions began to flee, turning their backs and refusing to look behind while the Messenger was calling them back to the battlefield. The Holy Quran records this incident in the following words:

> *Behold! ye were climbing up the high ground, without even casting a side glance at anyone, and the Messenger in your rear was calling you back.*
> - *Quran (3:153)*

As the Holy Quran states the Prophet of Allah was calling the companions back, but the companions paid no heed and fled the battlefield. Even prominent companions like Caliph Umar had run away from the battlefield. Some of the companions ran so far that it took them two or three days to come back to Madinah. The companions fled and took refuge in the hills around Uhad. Caliph Umar gives an account of the battle of Uhad in his own words:

> *Caliph Umar said that on the day of Uhud, the Muslims fled for their lives from the field of battle, and that he himself fled and climbed a hill, jumping from place to place like a mountain goat.*
> - *As-Sayyuti: Ad-Dur Al-Manthur. Vol. 2, p. 88*

As most of the companions had fled, this created a serious danger to the life of the Prophet. The Prophet himself fought extremely bravely but as the pagans started to surround him, he got exposed. The key aim of the Qurayshite army was to kill the Prophet of Allah, in order to bring the movement of Islam to an end once and for all. The death of the Prophet at such an early stage would have been a catastrophe for the Islamic State of Madinah and the movement of Islam as a whole.

3.7.3. Ali Saves the Life of the Prophet

Again, it was Ali who stepped up to the mark and saved the Prophet from certain death. He was among a handful of companions who had stayed back despite the turnaround in the fortunes on the battlefield. The Messenger of Allah witnessed a group of pagans coming towards him. According to Al-Tabari, Prophet asked Ali to charge them, which he did. This forced the pagans to retreat and Amr Ibn Abdullah Al-

Jumahi was killed by Ali in this operation. The Prophet saw another group of pagans approaching him, Prophet again orders Ali to charge them. Again, Ali manages to scatter them and in the encounter that followed he killed Sheibah Ibn Malik, who was one of the pagans trying to harm the Prophet.

Ibn Husham reported:

> *that the Messenger fell into one of the pits which were excavated and covered up by Abu Amir who expected the Muslims to fall in them. The knee of the Messenger was cut. Ali held the hand of the Messenger and pulled him up and Talhah Ibn Ubaydullah helped him until the Prophet stood up.*
>
> • *Ibn Husham Biography of the Prophet Part 2 p.80.*

Muslim in his Sahih reported that Sahl Ibn Saad said the following:

> *"The face of the Messenger was cut and one of his teeth was broken and the protective dress of his head was broken. Fatima daughter of the Messenger was washing the blood and Ali was pouring water he brought by his shield from Al-Mihras. Beholding that the water increased the flow of blood, she burned a mat put some of its ashes on the wound and the blood stopped."*
>
> • *Muslim in his Sahih Part 12 p. 148*

Ali stayed by the side of the Prophet throughout the duration of the battle of Uhud. Ali had helped the Prophet when he fell in the pit and pulled him out of danger. Ali had washed the wounds of the Prophet which he had suffered at the hands of the pagans. There were other Companions like Talha and Umm Umara (a lady) who also defended the Prophet. Talha stopped an arrow coming towards the Prophet, and Umm Umara fought against the pagans to defend the Prophet.

The Battle of Uhud was one of the key battles for the future of Islam. Ali had almost single headedly killed all the flag bearers of the pagan army, and Ali had almost won the battle for the Muslims. Unfortunately, some companions disobeyed the Prophet and left their positions to go after the spoils of war. This turned the battlefield success on its head, and a certain victory became a bitter defeat for the Muslims.

As the tables turned, the biggest threat came to the life of the Prophet itself. Unlike the majority of the companions who choose to flee, Ali again stayed back to save the life and honour of his mentor and guide. Ali became the saviour of the Prophet in Uhud. If Ali had not saved the life the Prophet in Uhud the movement of Islam would have been stopped right in its tracks.

On witnessing the amazing courage of Ali, Angel Gabriel said:

> *"Messenger of God what a redeemer Ali is!" The Prophet replied: "He is from me and I am from him." Gabriel said: "And I am from both of you."*
>
> • *Al-Fairoozbadi in his book: Fada-il Al-Khamsah Part 2 p.317 (conveying from Al-Tabari)*

And Ibn Al-Atheer also recorded something similar about Ali in the battle of Uhud:

> *"There is no youth (full of manhood) but Ali and no sword comparable to Zulfiqar (Ali's sword)"*
>
> • *Ibn Al-Atheer in his History Al-Kamil Part 2 p. 107*

The unique endeavour of Ali in the battle of Uhud was unrivalled by any account and there was praise even from angle Gabriel. Ali had been by the side of the Prophet throughout his life, even on occasions when others had fled. In the battle of Uhud most of the prominent companions including Caliph Umar had fled the battlefield. But Ali kept fighting the unbelievers and defended the Prophet until he was safe.

This is why Ibn Abbas had said:

> *"Ali has four distinctions no one shares with him: He was the first male who prayed with the Messenger of God. He was the bearer of his banner in every battle and he was the one who stayed with the Prophet at the Battle of Uhud and he is the one who washed his blessed body and laid him in his tomb."*
>
> - Al-Hakim recorded in his Al-Mustadrak, Part 3, p.111

As ibn Abbas mentioned, one of the key distinctions of Ali was that he stayed back with the Prophet in the battle of Uhud and saved his life. Ali had kept his promise which he made in Dawat-dhul-Ashira that he would support and help the Prophet of Allah at every step of the way. This was in fact the difference between Ali and the rest of the companions who did not have the kind of upbringing that Ali had at the hands of the Prophet.

Ali was indeed the differentiating factor in the strategy and the plan of the Prophet to establish Islam, and it was this difference which in fact justifies Ali's claim of being the successor of the Prophet.

3.8. The Battle of Moat

The Muslims had lost the battle of Uhud however a key objective of the Quraysh was to kill the Prophet which had not been achieved. The movement of Islam under the leadership of the Prophet was still going strong, and Islam was still expanding and was a force to be reckoned with. The Quraysh of Makkah and the pagans around it were determined to put an end to the movement of Islam and the Islamic State at any cost.

The situation outside Madinah wasn't great for the Muslims either. There were clashes between the Muslims and the neighbouring tribes of Madinah who belonged to the Jewish faith. A delegation from the Jewish tribes went to Makkah during the fifth year after the Hijrah proposing a war against the Muslims. The Makkans needed little persuasion to launch a new offensive against their Muslim enemies and the newly established Islamic State. The Quraysh and the pagans of Makkah mobilized around ten thousand fighters who would invade Madinah and subdue the Muslims.

The Holy Prophet received the news of an imminent invasion of Madinah a few days before the arrival of the Makkan army. The Prophet consulted his companions, and Salman Al-Farisi (one of the companions) suggested to the Prophet to dig a moat around Madinah to prevent the invaders from entering it. The Messenger of Allah liked this idea and commanded the Muslims (who were about three thousand) to implement the plan. A moat was dug around the city of Madinah within six days.

As the invading army arrived they were surprised to see the moat and realized that it had become extremely difficult to enter Madinah. Thus, they decided to besiege the city instead. As the news spread about the besiegement of Madinah it created a huge sense of fear and trepidation among the Muslims. Their city had been surrounded by an army which was more than three times the size of their army, and which possessed far superior weaponry and armour.

The fear among the Muslims went up another notch as the news began to filter through that Banu Quraidhah, a Jewish tribe outside Madinah had also joined the Makkan army, breaking its covenant of peace with the Prophet. Their treacherous actions were another frightening surprise for the Muslims who were besieged and were already under immense physiological pressure. There were also many hypocrites among the Muslims who were spreading frightening rumours which added to the fear and the nervousness among the Muslim population.

The Holy Qur'an informs us about the psychological crisis which the Muslims were experiencing.

> "Behold! They came upon you from above you and from below you and when the eyes grew wild and the hearts gaped up to the throats and ye imagined various (vain) thoughts about God! In that situation the believers were tried: ... The hypocrites ... (even) say: God and His Apostle promised us nothing but delusion! Behold! A party among them said: O people of Yathrib (Madinah) you cannot stand (the attack) therefore turn back! And a band of them ask to leave the Prophet saying: Truly our houses are bare and exposed though they were not exposed; they intended nothing but to flee."

- (Quran 33:10-22)

The Muslims were fearful, panicky, and scared. They were not only besieged but they also had hypocrites within their own ranks who were spreading rumours, adding to the sense of fear and vulnerability.

On the contrary the moral of the pagan army was very high. They were laying a complete siege of the Islamic State of Madinah with around ten thousand men. For them the victory was almost certain. The Quraysh knew that the Muslims did not possess the courage or the means to come out and fight them. Their confidence and moral were further boasted when the Jewish tribe of Banu Quraidhah joined their ranks, breaking their covenant with the Muslims. As a result, the Makkan army changed its strategy from the siege of Madinah to a direct invasion.

3.8.1. Amr's Adventure

Amr Ibn Abd Wudd, who was one of the most feared Arab warriors led a group of fighters and crossed the moat from a narrow opening. Their horses leaped over the moat and entered the city of Madinah. This was a frightening new development for the Muslims who were already jittery and nervous. This move by the enemy further eroded the Muslim confidence and affected their moral even more. Amr Ibn Abd Wudd was a fierce warrior. His very passage from one side of the moat to the other with only a handful of fighters indicated that the man was exceptionally courageous and bold. He was the only combatant from an army of ten thousand fighters who had tried to invade the Muslims directly and challenged them on their own turf.

The passage of Amr and his fighters into Madinah presented a serious danger and a frightening new development which the Muslims were not expecting. The door was about to be opened for hundreds and thousands of enemy soldiers who would follow Amr's example if he wasn't stopped.

After crossing over into Madinah Amr challenged the Muslims for a duel. Amr arrogantly asked, "Is there any dueller?" He repeated this call several times but there was no response on the part of the companions. There were hundreds of companions who had heard the challenge of Amr but none of them had the courage to take him on. The companions and the ordinary Muslims a like stood silently in the face of Amr's daring advance and had no answer to the challenge that Amr had thrown at them.

3.8.2. Ali's Response

The response of Ali was again characteristically unique and distinguished. The new danger did not scare or frighten Ali who was unfazed by the move of Amr into the Muslim territory. History informs us that it was Ali's present-mindedness and fast response that not only confined the danger presented by Amr, but

Ali in fact completely neutralized Amr's move in a very short time. Leading a small number of believers Ali immediately went to the location where the Islamic defence line had been breached. Ali and his fighters stood there and prevented others from attempting to cross the moat. (Ibn Husham Biography of the Prophet Part 2 p. 224)

As Amr was challenging the Muslims for a duel, Ali approached Amr and without any hesitation accepted his challenge. Amr arrogantly replied: "I would not like to kill you." Ali replied: "But by God I would love to kill you." A short and an extremely violent duel took place between the two and Amr quickly lost his life to Ali's sword. As Amr was killed his fighters lost their nerve and ran away trying to cross the moat back to the pagan side. Ali shouted: "Allahu Akbar " (God is Great) and so did the rest of the Muslims.

The death of Amr at the hands of Ali brought an abrupt end to the daring advance of the pagan army. Ali again makes a remarkable contribution to the defence of the Islamic State which none of the other companions could match, even though they all had a chance to take on the challenge laid down by Amr.

The overall role of the Muslim army during the Battle of Uhud was less important than their role during the Battle of Badr, and the contribution of the Muslim army in the Battle of the Moat was almost negligible. In the battle of Moat, the companions and the Muslim army did not fight the enemy. They only dug the moat around the city before the arrival of the pagan army and then stood behind the moat until the battle was over.

3.8.3. The Difference between Victory and Defeat

The contribution of Ali was indeed the difference between victory and defeat in the battle of Moat.

Ali's initiative to block the passage point from where Amr had crossed the moat prevented others from following Amr's lead, and it stopped the danger right in its tracks. If the narrow passage in the moat had remained opened, then a large number of the Qurayshite soldiers would have followed Amr. Their passage would have resulted in establishing a bridge which would have enabled the enemy to cross into Madinah. If Ali had not responded right at that moment to stop Amr, then it would have been a decisive defeat for the Muslims by an enemy which was more than three times their size. It was the courage, the present mindedness, and the experience of Ali on the battlefield which prevented a large-scale invasion of Madinah.

Also, the killing of Amr had frightened the Qurayshite army and their moral suddenly dipped. They were not expecting Amr to lose the duel to Ali. Amr was one of their most courageous and skilled fighters. If Amr was unable to initiate an invasion of Madinah, then it was impossible for anyone else from the Qurayshite army to do so either. The physiological war had dramatically turned in favour of Muslims with the killing of Amr.

The pagan army was left with two choices: To either withdraw or continue the siege until the Muslims surrender. The continuity of the siege of Madinah was beyond the capability of the Qurayshite army. It did not have the food supplies for ten thousand fighters and their horses to continue besieging Madinah. Also, after the killing of Amr an argument had broken out between the pagans and their Jewish allies, as it usually happens when one starts losing. This impacted their cooperation on the battlefield in a negative way.

In addition, a desert storm had hit the city of Madinah making the life of the besieging army a misery. Thus, there was only one alternative left for the pagan army and that was to follow in the footsteps of Amr's defeat and remove the siege. As the siege of Madinah was lifted the Muslims rejoiced and their hope in the continuity of their lives as Muslims was revived. The Muslims regained their confidence in the future of the Islamic State which was in doubt when they were besieged and surrounded by ten thousand armed fighters.

The Messenger said after the withdrawal of the pagan army:

> "After today we shall invade them, and they will not invade us."
> - Ibn Husham in his Biography of the Prophet, Part 2, p. 254.

Ali had again played a unique role in this key victory which had changed the destiny of the Islamic State. This was acknowledged by the Prophet of Allah in the following words:

> "The duel of Ali Ibn Abu Talib against Amr Ibn Abd Wudd at the Battle of the Moat outweighs the good deeds of my whole nation until the Day of Judgment."
> - Al-Mustadrak, Part 3, p. 32.

The Prophet recognizes the importance of Ali's victory over Amr by stating that the victory of Ali outweighs the good deeds of the whole nation until the Day of Judgment. The Prophet had made such a strong statement in favour of Ali because Prophet knew that if Amr had been successful in invading the city of Madinah, the Islamic State would have been destroyed, and the movement of Islam would have come to an end in the Arabian Peninsula.

The position of Ali was unique and distinguished in the eyes of the Prophet. It was based on the achievements and the service of Ali in establishing and defending the Islamic State of Madinah. The sacrifice, the courage, the support, and the intense loyalty that Ali had shown in strengthening the Islamic movement and in supporting the mission of the Prophet was unparalleled and unmatched by any other companion.

It is for this very reason that Ali is the only individual who could lay the claim to be the true inheritor and the successor of the Prophet.

3.9. The Battle of Khaibar

As mentioned previously from the onset of the Islamic State of Madinah the Prophet of Allah had secured the rights of the Jewish nation. These rights were also enshrined in the constitution of the Islamic State. However, for a variety of reasons the Jewish leadership choose not to accept this constitution in its letter and spirit. As mentioned earlier the tribe of Banu Quraidhah from the Jewish community broke their covenant with the Holy Prophet and joined the pagan army when it had surrounded Madinah. This was an act of treason against the constitution of Madinah.

The bulk of the Jewish community was now settling in Khaibar and its numerous fortresses which were about eighty miles from Madinah. The Jews of Khaibar had become a real threat and a menace for the Muslims. They were the same people who had initiated the battle of Moat by persuading the Quraysh of Makkah and the pagan tribes to attack the Muslims in Madinah. They represented a great danger to the safety and the security of the Islamic State, and the time had come to secure the State of Madinah form all the external threats.

When Prophet came back from Al-Hudaibiya where a temporary truce was signed with the pagans of Makkah, the Prophet of Allah turned his attention to the Jewish threat coming from Khaibar. The Prophet organized an army and marched towards Khaibar with about sixteen hundred companions. After reaching

Khaibar the Muslim army began besieging it various fortresses. The Jews of Khaibar were shocked and surprised to see the Muslims at their doorstep.

The siege of Khaibar continued for many days where skirmishes between the two sides took place daily but the frontlines never moved. The Muslims were not able to breach the Jewish defence and none of the companion's present were able to give Muslims an upper hand on the battlefield. The supplies of the Muslims were dwindling rapidly and some of the companions started cooking the meat of donkeys to feed themselves. This was against the teachings of Islam, so the Prophet had to intervene and put an end to this practice.

3.9.1. The Victory was Eluding the Muslims

The Victory was eluding the Muslims and a decisive outcome of the battle became a necessity, since Muslims were not able to continue the siege indefinitely. To conquer the fortresses of Khaibar and to bring the siege to an end the Prophet of Allah gave the flag of the Islamic army to Caliph Abu Bakr. He led the army towards the fortress of Naim. The Jews came out and fought the Muslims, but Caliph Abu Bakr and the other companions could not prevail against the Jewish fighters and were forced to retreat.

Next day the Prophet gave the flag of the Islamic army to Caliph Umar. Caliph Umar led his contingent of soldiers towards the fortresses, but the outcome was exactly the same. He and his pluton also could not conquer any of the fortresses and were forced to retreat like the previous day. On seeing failure after failure and with supplies running low the moral of the Muslims Army began to sink too. The Prophet was bitterly disappointed to see that for two consecutive days both Caliph Abu Bakr and Caliph Umar had failed to secure a victory for the Muslims.

The Prophet found himself in a serious dilemma. The siege had already continued way beyond his expectations. The companions had so far been unable to subdue even a single Jewish fortress. The food supplies had dwindled and had become scarce. The moral of the Muslim army was also on a downward spiral. Should the Prophet continue the siege of Khaibar, or should he lift the siege and go back to Madinah?

If the Prophet goes back to Madinah without conquering Khaibar it would be seen as a monumental failure. The Muslims would not only lose face but their reputation as a military force would be severely dented too. At the same time the Jewish threat around Madinah would magnify and would threaten the very existence of the Islamic State in the future.

3.9.2. The Prophet calls Upon Ali

As the stakes were raised in the battle of Khaibar and the Muslims were facing an embarrassing retreat, the Prophet of Allah called upon his most trusted lieutenant to give him the victory that he so desired. Ali had been the backbone of the Muslim army in every decisive battle, but Ali was missing from the battle of Khaibar. Ali was suffering from the inflammation of the eyes and was excused from the battlefield. However, as Muslim army was on the verge of defeat the Prophet was left with no choice but to call upon Ali to remove the threat emanating from Khaibar.

The Prophet announced to the companions that tomorrow he would give the banner of the Islamic army to a person who would bring victory to the Muslims. The companions spent the whole night contemplating as to who would be that lucky individual. As the dawn broke Prophet asked: "Where is Ali?". Ali was brought to the Prophet, and he saw that Ali was suffering from the inflammation of the eyes. Prophet puts his saliva on Ali's eyes and by a miracle they were cured instantly.

The words of the Prophet are preserved by Sahih al-Bukhari and Sahih al-Muslim as below:

> "The Messenger of God said at Khaibar: I shall give this banner to a man through whom God will bring the victory. He loves God and His Messenger and God and His Messenger love him. "The companions spent the night asking each other: 'Who is the man whom the Holy Prophet meant?' They came in the morning to the Messenger and every one of them was hoping that he would be the man of the banner. "Where is Ali Ibn Abu Talib?" the Prophet asked. "He is suffering from inflammation of his eyes " they said. The Prophet sent for him. When Ali was brought to the Prophet he treated Ali's eyes with his blessed saliva and prayed for him. Ali's eyes were cured instantly as if they did not have any inflammation. The Prophet gave Ali the banner and Ali asked: "Messenger of God shall I fight them until they become Muslims like us?" The Messenger said: "Go on until you reach their dwelling. Invite them to Islam and inform them of their duty towards God and Islam…………"

- Sahih Al-Bukhari Part 5 p. 171
- Muslim in his Sahih Part 15 pp. 178-179

Prophet gave the banner of the Muslim army to Ali and tasked him with conquering the fortresses of Khaibar. As always Ali led from the front carrying the banner of Islam towards the Jewish strongholds and attacked the enemy in its heart.

We read in Ibn Husham Biography of the Prophet that Salamah Ibn Al-Akwa said:

> "By God Ali went out with the banner running, We went following him until he planted the banner into a pile of stones near the fortress." A man from the fortress went up and asked Ali: Who are You? And he replied: I am Ali Ibn Abu Talib. The man said: By what was revealed to Musa you have the upper hand. As the Holy Prophet forecast the Almighty granted Ali the victory. He conquered the enemy before he returned to the Prophet."

- Ibn Husham Biography of the Prophet Part 2 p. 335

Salamah also said:

> "Marhab (the outstanding warrior of the Khaibarites) came out boasting and challenging Ali. Ali struck a single blow with his sword splitting Marhab's head into two, and victory was immediately accomplished."

- Al-Hakim Al-Mustadrak Part 3 pp.28-29.

Marhab was one of the most feared Jewish warriors and no one would dare take him on in a duel. Ali not only accepted his challenge for a duel but finished him off with a single blow, completely demoralizing the rest of the enemy fighters.

Another companion of the Prophet Abu Rafi said:

> "We went with Ali Ibn Abu Talib when the Messenger of God sent him with his banner. When he came near the fortress the dwellers of the fortress came out and he fought them. A man from them hit Ali and made him lose his shield. Ali took a door at the fortress and shielded himself with it. He kept it in his hand until the battle ended. I found myself with seven men trying to move that door, but we could not."

- Ibn Husham Biography of the Prophet Part 2 p.335.

As Ali continued his attacks the retreating enemy fighters took refuge inside the fortress. They tried to defend themselves by entering the fortress and locking its door. But there was no avail, Ali broke down the door of the fortress and used it as a shield, a door which even seven people were unable to move. As Ali entered the fortress, he brought the defensive capability of the Khaibarites to an end. They did not have the courage to challenge Ali either individually or collectively, especially after seeing the death of Marhab. The fortress of Naim fell to the Muslim army due to the offensive that Ali had led. The remaining fortresses fell one after the other until the area of Khaibar was completely subdued by the Muslims.

3.9.3. The Victory of Khaibar

The Battle of Khaibar was another key battle for the destiny of Islam and a victory in this battle was an absolute must for the Muslims. The Jews around Madinah had become extremely powerful and were posing a serious threat to the newly formed Islamic state. They had to be pacified to ensure the safety of the Muslims and to secure the future of the Islamic State of Madinah.

The battle of Khaibar was preceded by two battles in which the Muslims were not in the best of shapes. The Muslims were defeated in the Battle of Uhud where most of the companions ran away from the battlefield except a few. This was followed by the Battle of the Moat in which the Muslims were on the defensive. They were frightened and terrified except a handful of them. Their hearts went up to their throats as testified by the Holy Quran. The battle of Moat ended without the Muslims ever facing their enemy or even attempting to cross the Moat. They simply stood behind the moat until the siege was lifted.

The Muslims in the Battle of Khaibar had outnumbered their enemy. If the Muslims had failed to win here their failure would be seen as a sign of weakness. This would entice many hostile tribes around Madinah to attack the Muslims. Also, the Jewish threat from Khaibar itself would increase and would become the nucleus of future invading forces. In addition, if the Muslims had failed in Khaibar, they would also lose confidence in winning future battles against their numerous enemies.

Ali had once again delivered a key success to the Prophet in his mission to expand the religion of Allah. If there had been another companion who could fulfil Ali's role then Prophet would not have called upon Ali, since Ali was unwell at the time and was suffering from the inflammation of eyes and was excused from the duty of Jihad because of his condition. But Prophet was unable to fill the void left by Ali's absence and there was no other companion who was able to step in Ali's shoes.

The whole of the Muslim army for days was unable to conquer any of the fortress in Ali's absence. Prophet had tried both Caliph Abu Bakr and Caliph Umar, but they were unable to fill this void and deliver the success that Prophet was hoping for. The Prophet had to specifically call upon Ali, cure his eyes and then send him to the battlefield to secure a key victory for the newly established Islamic State.

The presence of Ali alone was the difference between victory and defeat in the battle of Khaibar.

3.10. The Biggest and the Most Important Project

The establishment of the Islamic State of Madinah was the biggest and the most important project that Prophet of Allah had undertaken during his lifetime. If for whatever reason the Prophet had been unsuccessful in establishing the State of Madinah, Islam would have never flourished in the Arabian Desert.

Muslims were a small minority before the Islamic State of Madinah came into existence. It was the State of Madinah which allowed the Muslims to flourish and expand the message of Allah and increase their numbers many folds. The establishment of the Islamic State of Madinah gave Muslims the strength and the recognition that they needed for the movement of Islam to succeed and flourish in the harsh reality of Arabia.

Without the establishment of the Islamic State of Madinah the Muslims would have never been able to grow, and the Islamic movement would have been stopped in its tracks. During the first ten years of Prophet's life in Makkah no more than 200 people had accepted Islam. It was the success of the Islamic State which turned a couple of hundred Muslims into many thousands over the next 10 years.

The conquest of Makkah was the final nail in the coffin of the Qurayshite clans who had opposed Islam and Muslims for almost two decades. The conquest of Makkah was only possible because Muslims had been able to establish a base in Madinah. It was this base which enabled the Muslims to finally subdue the Quraysh of Makkah, and Islam became the most powerful force in the Arabian Peninsula. The Islamic State of Madinah was the launch pad that Muslims had needed to take on their advisories, and Ali was the star performer in its establishment and defence.

The establishment of the Islamic State in Madinah was a unique project in the history of Arabs. Prior to the coming of Islam, the Arabs had not known of any ideological State which comprised of both a set of beliefs and a system of governance. For instance, the other belief systems which were prevalent in Arabia were simply a set of beliefs, such as Christianity, Judaism or the pagan faith. These belief systems did not constitute a way of life or a system of governance which Islam was offering.

The Prophet of Allah with all his wisdom and determination managed to achieve a remarkable success by setting up an Ideological power base for the Muslims in the heart of Arabia. The Muslims were now secure and free to practice their faith in accordance with the book of Allah, and at the same time they could use the newly established State as a launch pad to expand the message of Islam.

It would not be out of place to say that the establishment of the Islamic State of Madinah was probably the single biggest achievement of the Prophet during his lifetime, as it secured the future of Muslims for good.

In Prophet's biggest achievement and in his most important and critical project Ali's performance was unique and distinguished. Ali was the unique hero who tipped the balance in favour of Islam and the Muslims at every critical juncture. Ali was that amazing individual who ensured that Prophet's vision would in fact become a reality.

It is not possible that Prophet of Allah would leave his biggest and the most critical project without a leader or a guide. The Prophet had to ensure that the leadership to guide the Islamic State was in place before his death.

3.10.1. The Differentiating Factor

As we have seen the history itself testifies that Ali was that unique person whom Prophet physically relied upon at every step of the way. Ali's contribution was key and critical in securing the future of the Muslims in the very early days of Islam.

Ali became the differentiating factor in every single battle for the defence of the Islamic State. Whether it was the battle of Badr, the battle of Uhud, the battle of Moat or the battle of Khaibar, it was the amazing courage, bravery and skill of Ali which had given the Muslims an edge over their enemies. Ali was the main contributor after the Prophet in founding the Islamic State of Madinah, as he was the implementer of Prophet's strategy and the eliminator of Prophet's adversaries.

The reason why Ali's performance was unique and distinguished among all the companions was because the Prophet had specifically trained Ali for this mission, and Islamic history is a testament to this difference. The Prophet had adopted Ali as a child to ensure that Ali was brought up to be the defender of his mission. The Prophet more than anybody else knew the calibre, the stature, and the capabilities of Ali, after all it was his own training that had made Ali the man he was.

There is no doubt that numerous companions made great efforts for the sake of Islam and for the establishment of the Islamic State of Madinah. Caliph Abu Bakr, Caliph Umar, Caliph Uthman, Al-Zubeir, Talhah, Salman al-Farsi, Ammar Ibn Yasir, Ibn Masood, Abdul Rahman Ibn Auf, Abu Obeidah Ibn Al-Jarrah along with Madinahites companions such as Abu Dujana, Qais Ibn Saad, Saad Ibn Ubaadah, Saad Ibn Maath and others played their part in the path of Islam.

But their individual contribution, their individual achievements, their individual efforts were comparable and similar to each other. A companion of similar calibre could have replaced the work of another companion without having any effect on the destiny of Islam as a whole. For example, if Caliph Umar had been the companion of the Prophet in the cave at the night of Hijrah instead of Caliph Abu Bakr, the destiny of Islam would not have been affected by this exchange. However, if Ali had not guarded the life of the Prophet in the battle of Uhud, when other companions had fled, the destiny of Islam would have been impacted.

As a group these companions may be classed as indispensable, but not as individuals.

Similarly, in the battle of Badr, Ali alone had killed over 40% of the enemy combatants, whereas the rest of the companions all together had killed the remaining 60% of the enemy forces, again the contribution of Ali was the differentiating factor. In the battle of Moat when Amr had challenged the Muslims for a duel, no other companion had the courage to step forward. It was the sword of Ali which had eliminated Amr and stopped a large-scale invasion of the city of Madinah.

Ali had indeed tipped the scales in favour of Muslims in all the historical battles which were decisive in establishing the destiny of Islam. The endeavour and the bravery of Ali was the key differentiating factor in both the birth and the defence of the Islamic State of Madinah.

The successor of the Prophet could only be someone whose role in the service and support of Islam was indispensable and unique. Only a person whose efforts and endeavours created the difference between victory and defeat for the newly established state of Madinah would be justified to hold the title of the successor of the Prophet.

A companion of average performance whose efforts were not a differentiating factor in the service of Islam, and whose contribution could be replaced by another companion of similar stature, could not possibly lay claim to the successorship of the Prophet. Islam rewards service and sacrifice in its path, and it would have been completely unfair and illogical for the Prophet of Allah to nominate anyone else other than Ali to be his successor.

However, this does not mean that the honour of the other companions is diminished. Being a companion of the Prophet is certainly a great honour, but to be the successor of the Prophet a companion would have to clearly outshine and distinguish himself from the rest of the companions.

And history is a testament that Ali had outshined and distinguished himself among all the companions in the establishment and the defence of the Islamic State of Madinah.

It would only be logical and fair that Prophet would nominate Ali to lead the Muslim Ummah after his demise to carry forward the revolution of Islam which he had so vigorously defended. It was this unique and the distinct service of Ali in the path of Islam that had earned Ali the title of being the successor and the inheritor of the Prophet.

Only the very best and the most virtuous companion deserves to be the successor of the Prophet. The decision of the Prophet undoubtedly would be based on merit and the service of a companion in the path of Islam.

3.10.2. The Prophet's Plan and Strategy

A key point, which must be understood from the above discussion is that the unique link between the efforts of Ali and the birth of the Islamic State did not just happen by chance, where Ali suddenly found himself defending the Islamic State and working for its establishment. The Prophet of Allah does not leave things to chances or turn of events. The unique link between Ali and the birth of the Islamic State was a product of the spiritual evolution that Prophet had started in Ali when he adopted him as a child. Ali had been specifically prepared for this unique honour since he was a little boy.

Prophet Muhammad was the final messenger of Allah. He knew very well that there would be no Prophets after him. He not only has to ensure that the Islamic movement is successful during his lifetime, but he also has to ensure that the future of the Islamic faith is safe and secure even after he had departed this world. That is why Prophet had established a base for the Muslims, to first secure their present where Muslims could live in peace and security, and secondly to secure their future, so that the movement of Islam could flourish even when he is gone.

The establishment of the Islamic State of Madinah itself is a clear proof that Prophet had thought about the future of Islam. It would be completely illogical to think or assume that Prophet of Allah on one hand would establish a State to secure the future of the Muslims, but on the other hand he would remain passive or silent about the future leadership of the very State that he had established.

Just as the Prophet had established a State for the Muslims during his lifetime, the Prophet also had to secure the future leadership of that State during his lifetime too.

4. ISLAMIC GOVERNMENT, THE COMPANIONS AND THE PROPHET'S SUNNAH

Prophet Muhammad was the last of the Prophets, his message was the conclusion of all the heavenly messages. Allah would not send any more Prophets after him, therefore the message of the Prophet and the Islamic movement started by him must succeed, and its future must be secured and guaranteed. The successor of the Prophet would be responsible for the continuity of the Islamic government and the Islamic State which was established by the Prophet with so much determination and with so much sacrifice.

The successor of the Prophet would be responsible for not only defending the borders of the Islamic State, but more importantly his task would be the ideological defence of the message of Islam, ensuring that the newly formed Muslim Ummah stays on the path established by the Prophet of Allah, and the new converts to the faith are guided by the true spirit and principles of Islam as laid down by the Prophet.

The successor of the Prophet would have to lead the Muslim Ummah by example in terms of his knowledge, in terms of his character, in terms of his piety, in terms of his bravery and above all in terms of his wisdom and intellect.

Before we discuss the actual sayings of the Prophet which further clarify the issue of Prophet's successorship, it would make sense to briefly discuss whether the future leader of the Muslims should be chosen by the Prophet or whether he should be selected by the Muslims themselves.

4.1. Islam Allows Two Kinds of Governments

In broad terms there are two types of governments allowed in Islam.

- A government established by Allah.
- A government established through Shura or elected by the people (as long as the government rules by the Islamic framework and does not transgress the laws of Allah).

The readers may think that the appointment of a government or a ruler by Allah is a mere hypothesis and is only an academic theory which has no practical relevance in this day and age. They assume that the only form of Islamic government available to them is where the Muslims elect their own Islamic government through popular vote or through Shura which works within the laws laid out by Allah.

This is certainly true at the moment.

But this wasn't the case during the time of the Prophet. The establishment of a government by divine choice was certainly possible and feasible during the lifetime of the Prophet. The Prophet himself was a ruler by divine selection and choice. Allah had chosen the Prophet to lead mankind out of darkness. The Islamic State of Madinah itself was established with divine guidance and support.

The Prophet was not chosen by the people around him to lead the revolution of Islam. The companions did not have a right to choose who would lead the Islamic State of Madinah. Allah had appointed the Prophet to be the head the Islamic State and to spread the Islamic thought and ideology to the world. Since Prophet Mohammad was the choice of Allah, the government established to run the Islamic State of Madinah was a government appointed by Allah.

So, during the lifetime of the Prophet Muslims had a government that was appointed by Allah.

As Prophet was chosen by Allah to lead the Islamic nation the Prophet also had the right to choose a person to lead the Islamic state that he had established. Just as Allah had chosen the Prophet to lead the Islamic State of Madinah, the Prophet also had the right to choose the most qualified and the most deserving individual to lead that State in his absence.

We read in Holy Quran that Allah commands the believers to obey the Prophet and he also gives Prophet authority over the believers.

> *"O you who have believed, obey Allah and obey the Messenger and those in authority among you. And if you disagree over anything, refer it to Allah and the Messenger…………"*
> - *Quran 4:59*
>
> *"The Prophet has more authority over the believers than they have over themselves..."*
> - *Quran 33:6*

Since the Prophet has more authority over the believers and since Muslims are required to obey the Prophet, the Prophet has a right to choose for the Muslims a government that would secure their future, and Muslims would be required to follow the choice of the Prophet.

Nobody was more attached or concerned for the future of the Islamic State than the Prophet himself, as he was the founder and the architect of this State. As Allah had given Prophet the authority, he would use that authority to select the most deserving and the most qualified individual to lead that ideological State in his absence.-

4.2. Why should the Prophet Choose?

This is a key question which would be clarified and explored in this section.

4.2.1. The Future is Secured and Guaranteed

When Prophet chooses someone to lead the government then the future of that government is secured and guaranteed. This is because the Prophet of Allah knows through divine guidance as to who would be the most righteous and the most able person to lead the Islamic nation.

The Prophet of Allah had thousands of companions and some of the earliest companions had been with him for over two decades. The Prophet of Allah knew the calibre and the stature of each and every prominent companion. He knew their contribution and their sacrifices in the path of Islam. He was well aware of their strengths and their weakness in all aspects of their character and personality. The Prophet also knew through the light of God as to what the future of these companions would be like. He knew more than anybody else as to who would be the best candidate to lead the newly established Islamic State in his absence.

The success of the Prophet's nominee and Prophet's choice is guaranteed since that choice is made with divine guidance.

On the other hand, when people select or elect a ruler through Shura (consultation) or voting, they cannot guarantee that the individual they are choosing would definitely perform and deliver as per their expectations. Even if they are absolutely sincere in choosing the most qualified individual, they cannot be sure if that individual would succeed in the continuity of the Islamic mission, because they cannot see the future that Prophet could see through divine revelation and guidance.

Only the Prophet had that divine link with Allah that allowed him to judge and know as to who would have been the best candidate for the future leadership of Islam. That is why the Prophet's nominee has a huge advantage over the choice of a Shura or elections. When the successor of the Prophet and the succeeding government comes through appointment by the Prophet, it is indirectly a government appointed by Allah as Prophet's appointment and his decisions are supported by Allah's will and knowledge.

The companions could not possibly know with certainty as to who would be the best man to rule over them as they could not foresee their future or the future of the ruler they might choose. On the other hand, Allah could foresee their future, and his messenger could choose the right individual to lead them in his absence.

The righteousness and the suitability of a government established by the Prophet cannot be compared to a government established by Shura (consultation) of the companions.

4.2.2. Islam is a Reformatory Movement

I have briefly discussed this topic in chapter one but for the completeness of the current chapter I will discuss it here in bit more detail.

Islam as a movement had come to reform the primitive and the uncivilized Arabian society that existed at the time of the Prophet. A reformatory movement like Islam was not only destined to change the beliefs of the people but it had also come to completely eradicate their previous way of life and thinking.

By its very nature a reformatory movement is led by a minority which has come to reform the majority. A reformatory movement challenges the traditions and practices prevalent among the majority population in the society. The nucleus of such a movement revolves around the founder of the ideology who would decide as to how the movement should move forward and what its future should look like.

Islam was exactly such a movement established by the Prophet of Allah.

The question of the future leader of a reformatory movement like Islam could not be left to an election or a Shura (consultation) where the majority opinion would prevail, which may or may not adhere to the reformatory principles established by its founder. Leaving the future of a reformatory movement to the chances of an election could seriously jeopardise the entire movement itself, and potentially undo all the reforms started by its founder, especially if the majority votes for a wrong individual to head the new government.

Generally, in Shura (consultation) or elections a candidate with centrist tendencies gets the majority backing i.e., a person who would be able to please and be acceptable to the majority population would come on top. Rarely an election or a Shura (consultation) would bring the most deserving or the most able individual to power. The process of Shura or elections could bring the best, an average person and even an individual who does not deserve to the forefront. The reformatory movement of Islam could not possibly afford such a gamble!

We saw at first hand in our brief discussion of the gathering of Saqifah (chapter 1) that the main issue that divided its participants was tribal lineage. Both groups i.e., the Muhajireen and the Ansar were keen to have the successor of the Prophet from their own clan. The actual merits and the qualification of the new head of the Islamic State were not the primary concern of the Shura. Caliph Abu Bakr won the day as a result of a political adjustment that took place between the Muhajireen and the Ansar, where the Ansar agreed to become the advisors to the Caliph, giving the leadership of the Islamic State to the Muhajireen.

However, it is clear that the Prophet could not allow such a system to choose his successor.

The principles of a reformatory movement are not in line with the reality of elections or a Shura, as it is evident from the event of Saqifah itself, where the majority vote decided the outcome in favour of one of the candidates, regardless of their merits or service in the path of Islam. The government that is established on reformatory principles is in fact a government of the minority, a minority which has started the reformatory process and which in fact intends to reform the majority. It is not a government run by the people. On the contrary, it is a government which is established to reform the people.

In such circumstances it is the founder of the reformatory movement who chooses the most sincere and able person to lead the movement after his demise, to ensure that the reformatory process is carried forward in its spirit and essence, and at the same time it is guarded against both the physical and the ideological threats that it may encounter in the future.

The aim of the Islamic movement established by the Prophet was the supremacy of the rules of the Holy Quran, and the eradication of all other ideologies and religions that stood in its path. Allah declares in his book chapter 9 verse 33:

> *"He (The Almighty) is the One who sent His Messenger with the guidance and the religion of truth to make it prevail over all religions though the Pagans may be averse."*

The Prophet has to ensure that the commands of Allah are fulfilled and the continuity of the Islamic movement is guaranteed, and that Islam prevails over all other religions and ideologies even after his own demise.

For the Prophet to rely on others, or on a group of people, or on any other system or mechanism to choose his successor would inevitably be a risky prospect. As none of these methods could guarantee that the best and the most able candidate would be chosen. It was a risk which the wisdom and the intellect of the Prophet could not possibly afford to take.

Islam is the final message of Allah and Prophet was the last messenger of Allah. The Prophet with all his wisdom and prudence could not let such a critical decision, a decision on which the future of the Islamic movement hinged to be taken by others, whereas he himself does nothing in this regard and simply stays passive.

The only way that Prophet could ensure that the future of Islam was secured and guaranteed in his absence was to handpick someone from his own team, someone who he trusted, and someone who he had trained since they were a child. This was the only logical approach that Prophet could have taken to ensure that the future of Islam was in the right hands.

4.3. The Custodian of the Sunnah

Islam comprises of two inseparable entities, one being the Holy Quran and the other being the Sunnah (traditions) of the Prophet. These two sets of instructions and knowledge constitute guidance for mankind until the Day of Judgment. Islam remains incomplete if one ignores either the book of Allah or the traditions of the Prophet, as both these sources explain and complement each other.

These two invaluable sources together form the basis of the Islamic law and the Islamic faith. And this was exactly what Prophet had told his companions before his death, during his final pilgrimage to Makkah. It is recorded in Al-Muwatta of Imam Malik and in Al-Mustadrak by Al-Hakim that Prophet of Allah on his last pilgrimage said to the companions:

> *"I have left among you two matters by holding fast to which, you shall never be misguided: the Book of God and my Sunnah"*
> - *Dar Al-Hijra Malik ibn Anas in Al-Muwatta. Vol. 2, Pg. # 480, H # 2618.*
> - *Al-Hakim Al-Nishaburi in Al-Mustadrak Alaa Al-Sahihain. Vol. 1, Pg. # 160 - 161, H. # 318.*

The Prophet was clearly telling his companions that after his death if they wanted to stay on the path of salvation, then they needed to follow the book of Allah and the Sunnah (traditions) of the Prophet. These were the two critical and complementary sets of knowledge that the companions were required to adhere to, in order to remain on the correct path.

However, when Prophet instructs his companions to follow certain pieces of knowledge after his death which would keep them on the right path, then it is imperative on the Prophet that he either leaves documentary evidence of that knowledge, so that the companions can refer back to it, or he leaves behind someone or a group who knows and has that knowledge.

Without leaving behind any documentary evidence or without leaving behind someone or a group who has that knowledge, the Prophet could not expect his companions to simply rely on their memory to remember the verses of the Quran or his Sunnah (traditions).

It would be both illogical and unrealistic for the Prophet of Allah to command his companions to follow the Holy Quran and his Sunnah, and at the same time he leaves behind no practical means for them to do so, especially when Quran and Sunnah were so critical that they were the only mechanism by which the companions would stay on the path of righteousness.

The Prophet of Allah was the wisest of the creation, such illogical and unrealistic expectations could not possibly come from a man of Prophet's intellect.

For this very reason the Prophet had documented the Holy Quran while he was still alive, so that the companions could refer to the Book of Allah after his death.

4.3.1. The Documentation of the Holy Quran

The documentation of the Holy Quran was a key objective of the Prophet during his lifetime. The Prophet of Allah had nominated over forty scribes whose sole job was to write the verses of the Quran as and when

Prophet would instruct them to do so. The Prophet had to ensure that he documents the Holy Quran during his lifetime so that his companions could refer to it after his death.

The Prophet of Allah was so conscious of his duty of writing the Holy Quran down that he would even go back and check for scribal mistakes or possible errors that a scribe might make.

Zaid bin Thabit, one of the chief scribes, narrates:

> "I used to write down the revelation for the blessed Prophet ……….I used to fetch a shoulder bone or a piece of something else. He used to go on dictating and I used to write it down. When I finished writing the sheer weight of transcription gave me the feeling that my leg would break, and I would not be able to walk anymore. Anyhow when I finished writing, he would say, 'Read!' and I would read it back to him. If there was an omission or error, he used to correct it and then let it be brought before the people."
>
> - at-Tabarani, Mu'jam al-Awst, (Dar al-Haramain, Cairo, 1415 AH) Hadith 1913; authenticated by al-Haithami in Majma' az-Zawa'id, Hadith 13938

This clearly shows the diligence of the Prophet in documenting and preserving the Holy Quran. The Prophet would personally dictate the words of the Holy Book to the scribes, and he would even ask them to read out what they had written down. This was to ensure that the scribes do not make a mistake in the documenting the words of Allah. The Prophet had personally ensured that the Holy Quran would be documented and preserved without any errors during his lifetime.

After all the Holy Quran was one of the primary sources of guidance for the companions and mankind. There was no way that Prophet would simply rely on the memory of the companions to remember the verses of the Holy Quran or leave such an important and a critical source of knowledge undocumented or without a guide.

4.3.2. The Documentation of the Sunnah (Traditions)

Although, Quran was written down during the lifetime of the Prophet but there was never any concerted effort made by the Prophet or the companions to document the Sunnah (traditions) of the Prophet, which was the other primary source of knowledge and guidance. Some companions on their own did write down some of the traditions of the Prophet, but the bulk of the traditions of the Prophet were not documented during his lifetime.

In fact, most of the Prophet's traditions were not written down in any of the known books of hadith during the first century, i.e., most of the Prophet's traditions were not documented during the first hundred years after the death of the Prophet. Only a small number of Prophet's hadith were written down and documented during this period. The companions of the Prophet only wrote a handful of his traditions during his lifetime or even in their own lifetimes.

Most of the books of hadith present today were written after the first century i.e., these books were written long after the death of the Prophet and the death of all his companions. The companions did not have access to any books of Hadith where they could see the documented Sunnah of the Prophet.

The question now arises that if the Prophet had not instructed the companions to document his Sunnah, and the companions on their own also did not document his traditions except some, then how could the Prophet expect the companions to know and follow his exact and actual Sunnah?

The Prophet was doing his final pilgrimage, he knew his death was near, he was instructing the companions to follow his Sunnah alongside the Quran, but the bulk of his Sunnah was not even documented. So how could he then expect the companions to follow his Sunnah after he had departed from this world?

To answer this key question, we need to look at the makeup of the Islamic nation (Ummah) at the time of the death of the Prophet.

The Islamic movement comprised of two distinct groups, the companions of the Prophet and his Ahlulbayt i.e., the family of the Prophet.

There are two possible answers to the above question:

- It was possible that companions themselves were the custodians of Prophet's Sunnah, and that they had memorized all of his traditions, i.e., they knew with certainty the entire Sunnah of the Prophet, and hence the Prophet was simply asking them to follow his Sunnah which they already knew.

Or

- Another possibility could have been that the Ahlulbayt (family of the Prophet) were the custodians of Prophet's Sunnah, who knew with certainty what Prophet had said and done, and they were the ones who would guide the movement of Islam after Prophet's demise.

I will discuss each one of these possibilities in the following section.

4.4. Were Companions the Custodian of the Sunnah?

The books of history inform us that the Prophet of Allah had thousands of companions. It is estimated that by the time the Prophet of Allah passed away he had over one hundred thousand companions. These companions had obviously accepted Islam at different times in the life of the Islamic movement. Some companions had accepted Islam during the very early days of the Islamic movement, while others had accepted Islam after the conquest of Makkah, and as a result had only spent a very short amount of time in the company of the Prophet.

The knowledge of the Sunnah of the Prophet also varied immensely from companion to companion. It was dependent on the length of time that a companion had spent with the Prophet, and also on their own ability to grasp and understand the message of Islam. The understanding and the grasp of the Sunnah of the Prophet was further complicated by the fact that most of the companions were illiterate and uneducated, as there were no schools, colleges, or universities at that time.

After the announcement of the Prophethood the Prophet had lived in Makkah for ten years before he decided to do the Hijrah (migration to Madinah). History informs us that when Prophet was leaving Makkah, he had no more than two hundred companions. This means that the vast majority of the companions had in fact accepted Islam after the Hijrah, i.e., after the Prophet had moved to Madinah.

If any companions were to be the custodians of the Sunnah of the Prophet, then surely those companions would be the early companions i.e., the companions who were with the Prophet from the very beginning of Islam, meaning the companions from Makkah.

The companions from Makkah could possibly become the custodians of Prophet's Sunnah, since they had spent time with the Prophet in both Makkah and Madinah. They would have witnessed the Sunnah of the Prophet from the very start of his mission, whereas the companions from Madinah could not hold this position as they had missed out on the ten years of Makkan life with the Prophet.

Let's see who could possibly have been the custodian of the Prophet's Sunnah.

4.4.1. Caliph Abu Bakr and the Sunnah of the Prophet

Caliph Abu Bakr had been one of the earliest companions of the Prophet. He had been with the Prophet since the early days of Islam. He had been a companion of the Prophet both in Makkah and in Madinah, and his companionship with the Prophet was longer than any other companion.

However, when we look at examples from his life after the death of the Prophet, it becomes clear that he could not have been the custodian of Prophet's Sunnah.

We read the words of lady Aisha about her father Caliph Abu Bakr in Tadhkirat al-Huffaz, and also in Hujiyat al-Sunnah. Lady Aisha narrates the following:

> *My father collected the hadith of the Messenger of Allah and they numbered five hundred. He spent the night turning back and forth. He saddened me and I said to him, "Are you turning around because of pain, or because of bad news which you have received?" In the morning, he said to me, "Bring me the hadith of the Prophet which I have left with you." I brought him all the hadith. At this point, he asked for fire and burned all the hadith in the fire. I said to him, "Why do you burn these hadith?" He said, "I fear that I will die while I have these hadith. I took them from the man I trusted, but maybe some hadith are not his or maybe the sayings are not authentic."*

- *Tadhkirat al-Huffaz, 1:5*
- *Hujiyat al-Sunnah, p. 394*
- *Muhammed Zakaria, Faza'il-E-Amaal Chapter "stories of Sahabah", page 140*

A man gave Caliph Abu Bakr five hundred traditions (hadith) of the Prophet. Caliph Abu Bakr spent the whole night turning and twisting as he could not figure out if the traditions given to him were genuine or not. In the morning he asked lady Aisha to bring all the five hundred traditions and then he burned every single one of them.

It is clear that the reason why Caliph Abu Bakr burned every single one of those traditions was because he could not differentiate between the authentic and the non-authentic traditions. If Caliph Abu Bakr was able to differentiate between the authentic and the fabricated traditions, then he would have only burned the fabricated traditions, and he would have kept the authentic traditions safe.

This incident took place after the death of the Prophet. It clearly shows that Caliph Abu Bakr was not certain that the narrations that were with him were the actual words and sayings of the Prophet, or if they were fabricated. He could not distinguish which traditions in his possession were authentic and which weren't, and hence he decided to burn all those traditions.

Even though Caliph Abu Bakr was one of the earliest companions and had been with the Prophet the longest, but he still lacked knowledge about the hadith and the traditions of the Prophet, and as a result he ended up burning all five hundred of Prophet's hadith that were given to him.

It also shows that the Oral transmission of the hadith, or simply relying on the memory of the companions was not sufficient to preserve the authentic Sunnah of the Prophet. Even a companion of Caliph Abu Bakr's standing, and stature was unable to recognize and recall the traditions of the Prophet and was unable to verify that the documented traditions he was given were genuine or not.

If a companion of Caliph Abu Bakr stature was unable to distinguish between the right and the wrong Sunnah, then there was little chance that any of the other companions would be able to do the same, since Caliph Abu Bakr had spent the most amount of time in the company of the Prophet.

The most unfortunate thing about this incident was the fact that many of the authentic traditions of the Prophet which were written down in that era were also burned alongside the fabricated ones, which meant that the rest of the companions and the later generation of Muslims had forever been denied of this Sunnah of the Prophet.

The Sunnah of the Prophet was the second most critical source of knowledge and guidance for the companions in Prophet's absence. A person, who heads the Islamic State after the Prophet of Allah must be able to differentiate between the right and the wrong Sunnah. At the same time, he should also know with certainty and without conjecture as to what the authentic Sunnah of the Prophet should be.

After all, this person would need to guide and lead the rest of the companions and the new converts to Islam, and he would also be responsible for carrying forward the process of Dawah (invitation to Islam) in Prophet's absence. If he himself is not certain and sure about the actual Sunnah of the Prophet, and if he himself is not able to distinguish between the real and the fake Sunnah, then what chance does he have of guiding others in this key source of knowledge that Prophet wanted his companions to follow.

Caliph Abu Bakr not only burned the traditions of the Prophet in his possession, but he in fact barred other companions from narrating and even discussing the traditions of the Prophet. Caliph Abu Bakr gave a speech and said to the companions:

> *"You squabble among yourselves over hadith, this habit will increase as time goes by. Do not, therefore, narrate any saying of Messenger. If anyone wants to know, you can tell him the Quran is there between you and him. Whatever is allowed ought to be done, and refrain from what has been prohibited in the Quran."*
>
> - *Tazkara tul Hifaaz e Zuhby*

This statement or decree of Caliph Abu Bakr was indeed most puzzling and absurd. Caliph Abu Bakr prohibited the companions from narrating and even discussing the hadith of the Prophet during his Caliphate. It is difficult to ascertain as to why Caliph Abu Bakr would take such an approach towards the Sunnah of the Prophet.

It would have been only logical to expect that the first Caliph after the Prophet would do everything in his capacity to encourage the companions to narrate as many hadith of the Prophet as possible, so that the Sunnah and the traditions of the Prophet could be documented and preserved, while they were still fresh in the minds of the companions. However, the approach taken by Caliph Abu Bakr clearly goes against this logic, and in fact it also goes against the Sunnah of the Prophet.

The Prophet of Allah had said:

> *Whoever memorizes and conveys forty hadith from my tradition, I will admit him into my intercession on the Day of Judgment,"*
>
> - *Kanz al-Ummal, 10:158, hadith 28817*

The Prophet also said:

> *"Whoever from my ummah memorizes forty hadith, Allah will raise him on the Day of Judgment as a scholar."*
>
> • Kanz al-Ummal, 10:158, hadith 28818

The words of the Prophet clearly contradict the judgement of Caliph Abu Bakr. The Prophet of Allah had encouraged the companions to not only convey and narrate his traditions but also to memorize them, whereas Caliph Abu Bakr was prohibiting the companions from even narrating the traditions of the Prophet.

This was indeed tragic to say the least.

A person who burns the Sunnah of the Prophet because he could not differentiate between the right and the wrong Sunnah, and a person who bars others from narrating the traditions of the Prophet, may become a Caliph over the Muslims, but he cannot claim to be the successor of the Prophet or the custodian of his Sunnah.

4.4.2. Caliph Umar and the Sunnah of the Prophet

Another prominent and one of the earliest companions of the Prophet was Caliph Umar. He had been a companion of the Prophet both in Makkah and in Madinah, and as a result he had the honour of witnessing the Sunnah of the Prophet in both cities.

During his Caliphate he consulted other companions about recording and documenting the traditions of the Prophet. The companions encouraged him and insisted that he should record and preserve the traditions of the Prophet. After considering the matter for a month, Caliph Umar declared the following:

> *"My intention was to record hadith but then I realized that some people (nations) before you kept writing down the sayings of their Prophets, and kept reading them, as a result, they forgot the book of Allah (their scriptures). I fear that same will happen If I order you to document the sayings of the Prophet, or if I do it myself. I do not want to make the book of Allah a victim here because of the hadith, nothing has precedence over the book of Allah"*
>
> • *(Kanzl Ummal, 10, hadith 29474)*

He then wrote to the Ansar and asked them to erase any traditions of the Prophet that they had written down.

> *"Whoever has anything should erase it"*
>
> • *(Taqiad ali-Ilm, 49, hujjiyat al-Sunnah, 3:95)*

And later on Caliph Umar further decreed:

> *"These (the hadith of the Prophet) are just like the Jewish scripts (mushnat), and they must be burnt"*
>
> • *(Ibn Sa'd, Tabaqat al-Kubra, 1:140)*
>
> *He then gathered all of the hadith written on leather, tablets, and pieces of wood and ordered them to be burnt.*

- *(Kanzl Ummal, 5:239)*

The testimony of history is clear, in the eyes of Caliph Umar Quran alone was the primary source of knowledge, to the extent that he had ordered the entire Sunnah of the Prophet to be erased and burned during his reign as a Caliph. In case of Caliph Abu Bakr, he had burned the hadith of the Prophet because he could not differentiate between the authentic and the non-authentic hadith, so he decided to burn them all.

But Caliph Umar had burned the hadith because in his opinion if the hadith (traditions of the Prophet) would have been preserved, i.e., if the Sunnah of the Prophet was preserved, the companions would potentially ignore and neglect the Holy Quran. Since he considered Quran to be the main source of legislation in Islam, he decided to burn the Sunnah of the Prophet.

Even when the rest of the companions advised him and insisted that he should preserve the Sunnah of the Prophet, he chooses to do exactly the opposite, and ordered the companions to erase and burn the traditions of the Prophet, which had been written down on leather, tablets, and pieces of wood.

He even compared the hadith of the Prophet to Jewish scriptures which indeed was most unfortunate.

Nobody knows to this day as to how many traditions of the Prophet were erased and burned down as a result of Caliph Umar's decision. The little Sunnah of the Prophet that was actually written down and documented in the early phase of Islam was lost due to Caliph Umar's decree. This indeed could not be called anything other than a catastrophe for the companions at the time, and for the Muslims who came in the later generations, since the very few hadith which were documented in the era of the Prophet were lost forever!

The fact that Caliph Umar considered the Holy Quran as the primary source of guidance would become even more glaringly obvious when Caliph Umar had indeed said in the presence of the Prophet that the book of Allah was enough for the Muslims. This incident took place just before the death of the Prophet when he was unwell. The Prophet of Allah asked the companions who were present around him to bring him some writing material so that he could write something which would keep them on the path of truth.

In response to Prophet's request for writing his Sunnah, Caliph Umar said to the companions that we have the Book of Allah and that is sufficient for us.

> *Prophet said: "Come, I may write for you a document; you would not go astray after that."*
> *Thereupon Umar said: "Verily Allah's Messenger is deeply afflicted with pain. You have the Quran with you. The Book of Allah is sufficient for us."*

- Sahih Muslim, Book 013, Number 4016

This was the attitude of Caliph Umar towards the Sunnah of the Prophet while the Prophet was still live. Unfortunately, his approach towards the Sunnah of the Prophet became even more negative after the demise of the Prophet.

It is reported that once Caliph Umar accompanied a group of companions on the way to Iraq. They reached a place called Siraar where Caliph Umar said to the companions that you have come to a place where the voice of Quran echoes like honeybees, but do not involve the people living here in hadith (Sunnah), or narrate any traditions of the Prophet to them.

> "………you are going, where the voice of Quran echoes like honeybees. Do not involve those people in Ahadith, and stop them from the Quran or narrate any traditions to them." ….. after that day, they did not remember narrating any hadith again."

- *(Qarza bin Ka'ab reports in Jama ul Biyaan)*

The above incident further confirms Caliph Umar's view regarding the Sunnah of the Prophet, where he was actively advocating the companions not to even narrate any traditions of the Prophet.

Caliph Umar in fact went a step further and more or less tried to put a complete ban on narrating the Sunnah of the Prophet. Some of the prominent companions like Abdullah Ibn Hudaafah, Ibn Masud, Abu Dardah, Abu Dharr al-Ghifari, Uqbaah Ibn Aamir and others who tried to spread the Sunnah of the Prophet to places outside Madinah were summoned by Caliph Umar to his office. Fearing that these companions were spreading the Sunnah of the Prophet to other towns and cities, he confined and restricted their movements to the city of Madinah. These companions were not able to leave Madinah until Caliph Umar was assassinated.

Caliph Umar said to these prominent companions:

> "What is it that you have done! You spread the hadith of the Prophet in other places. You have to stay here (in Madinah) and you will not depart or separate from me as long as I live." Thus, they were confined to Madinah until Umar was assassinated."

- *Mustadrak al-Hakim, 1:110*
- *Tarikh Abu Zarah, 270*
- *Kanz al-Ummal, 10, hadith 29479*

Contrary to the views of Caliph Umar, the Prophet during his last pilgrimage was strictly instructing the companions to follow both the Holy Quran and the Sunnah of the Prophet. The Prophet had made it compulsory for the companions to follow both these sources of knowledge and guidance if they were to stay on the right path.

> "I have left among you two matters by holding fast to which, you shall never be misguided: the Book of God and my Sunnah"

- *Dar Al-Hijra Malik ibn Anas in Al-Muwatta. Vol. 2, Pg. # 480, H # 2618.*
- *Al-Hakim Al-Nishaburi in Al-Mustadrak Alaa Al-Sahihain. Vol. 1, Pg. # 160 - 161, H. # 318.*

It is clear from the actions of Caliph Umar that he possibly could not have been the custodian of Prophet's Sunnah, since he primarily considered the Holy Quran as the main source of knowledge and guidance in Islam.

A person who burns the Sunnah of the Prophet, a person who orders others to erase the Sunnah of the Prophet, and a person who confines the companions of the Prophet to Madinah, just because they had spread the Sunnah of the Prophet to other places, may become a Caliph over Muslims, but he cannot claim to be the successor of the Prophet or custodian of his Sunnah.

4.4.3. Erasing the Sunnah of the Prophet

It is astonishing that both Caliph Abu Bakr and Caliph Umar who had spent over two decades in the company of the Prophet would end up erasing his Sunnah, when indeed they had the honour of leading the Muslims after the death of the Prophet.

They became the first and the second Caliphs and ruled for over twelve years after the demise of the Prophet. It was in fact their responsibility to preserve and document the Sunnah of the Prophet, while the companions were still alive, and while the traditions of the Prophet were still fresh in the minds of the companions. They had the full State machinery behind them to carry out such a task, especially in the case of Caliph Umar whose Caliphate lasted for around ten years.

Instead, they choose to erase and destroy the Sunnah of the Prophet by burning the hadith of the Prophet that they had in their possession, and by instructing others to burn the traditions of the Prophet that they had in their possession, and by stopping the companions from even narrating and relaying the traditions of the Prophet, essentially stopping the transmission of the Sunnah of the Prophet to the masses.

The Sunnah of the Prophet was erased and destroyed on various grounds and pretexts. Sometimes the Sunnah of the Prophet was torched because Caliph Abu Bakr could not distinguish between the authentic and the non-authentic Sunnah. Sometimes the Sunnah of the Prophet was erased because Caliph Umar gave preference to the Book of Allah over the traditions of the Prophet.

Contrary to the actions of the first two Caliphs the words of the Prophet tell a different story. The Prophet had said:

> *"By Allah, I have commanded and admonished and prohibited things, and just like the Qur'an, you have to follow what I say,"*
> - *Ibn Hazm, Al-Ahkam, 1:159*

The Sunnah of the Prophet had to be followed just like the Book of Allah. Prophet had given his Sunnah the same importance and significance as the Book of Allah.

As a student of history, it is difficult to ascertain as to what the real reason was or what the actual motives were, which led Caliph Abu Bakr and Caliph Umar to take such a negative and a harsh approach towards the Sunnah of the Prophet.

Even if one assumes that Caliph Abu Bakr and Caliph Umar were busy in the governance of the Islamic State and in the affairs of the Muslims, and they did not have the time to document or preserve the Sunnah of the Prophet, then at least one should not burn the Prophet's Sunnah that had already been preserved, and of course one should not prohibit others from narrating and transmitting the traditions of the Prophet either.

It would not be unfair to say that if scholars like Bukhari and Muslim had lived in the times of Caliph Abu Bakr or Caliph Umar, then there would not be a Sahih Bukhari or a Sahih Muslim in our midst today. The entire collection of hadith that we have today would have been impossible to gather or document in the reign of the first two Caliphs.

4.4.4. The Rest of the Companions and the Sunnah of the Prophet

As mentioned previously the Prophet of Allah had thousands of companions who had accepted Islam at different times in the life of the Islamic movement. There were companions who had accepted Islam at the beginning of Prophet's mission and there were companions who had accepted Islam right towards the end of Prophet's life.

Some of the companions knew very little about the Sunnah of the Prophet while others knew a lot more. Some companions could only remember one or two traditions of the Prophet whereas others had memorized hundreds of his traditions.

Some of the companions were truly sincere towards the mission of Islam and had sacrificed everything in its path. The Holy Quran has praised these companions with the following words.

> "Muhammad is the Apostle of God; and those who are with him are firm against unbelievers, compassionate towards one another. You see them bowing and prostrating, seeking grace from God and His satisfaction ... The mark of prostration shows on their faces... Allah has promised those among them who believe and do righteous deeds forgiveness, and a great reward."
>
> - Quran (48:29)

On the other hand, some of the companions were hypocrites and had disbelieved after accepting Islam. The Holy Quran addresses these companions in the following way:

> When the hypocrites come to you, [O Muhammad], they say, "We testify that you are the Messenger of Allah ." And Allah knows that you are His Messenger, and Allah testifies that the hypocrites are liars. They have taken their oaths as a cover, so they averted [people] from the way of Allah. Indeed, it was evil that they were doing. That is because they believed, and then they disbelieved; so their hearts were sealed over..... They are the enemy, so beware of them. May Allah destroy them"
>
> - Quran (63:1-4)

The Quran further mentions that there were hypocrites among the companions who were living in Madinah, and even the Prophet was not aware of their hypocrisy.

> And among the Bedouins around you, some are hypocrites, and so are some among the people of Al-Madinah who persist in hypocrisy; you know them not, We know them. We shall punish them twice, and thereafter they shall be brought back to a great (horrible) torment.
>
> - Holy Quran (9:101)

In another verse of the Holy Quran Allah informed the messenger of how some of the companions had pretended to be Muslims but in fact had turned away from Islam.

> They swear by Allah that they did not say [anything against the Prophet] while they had said the word of disbelief and disbelieved after their [pretence of] Islam and planned that which they were not to attain. And they were not resentful except [for the fact] that Allah and His Messenger had enriched them of His bounty........... Allah will punish them with a painful punishment in this world and the Hereafter. And there will not be for them on earth any protector or helper.
>
> - Quran (9:74)

The Prophet of Allah had also predicted the deviation of his companions.

> "Some men from my companions will come to my Lake-Fount and they will be driven away from it, and I will say, 'O Lord, my companions!' It will be said, 'You have no knowledge of what they innovated after you left: they turned apostate as renegades (reverted from Islam).'"
>
> - Saheeh Al-Bukhari 8:586
> - Saheeh Al-Bukhari. Pg. # 20, H. # 3349
> - Saheeh Al-Bukhari. Pg. # 1747, H. # 7049
> - Saheeh Al-Bukhari. Pg. # 1634, H. # 6593

Many companions will in fact end up in hellfire as predicted by Prophet.

"While I am standing, a group of persons came (to me). and once I will recognize them, a man will come between me and them, saying (to them), "Let's go." I will say, "To where?" He will say, "To Hellfire, I swear by Allah (swt)!" I will say, "What is their offence?" He will say, "They apostated after your death!" Then, another group will come, and when I recognize them, a man will come between me and them, saying (to them), "Let's go." I will say, "To where?" He will say, "To Hellfire, I swear by Allah (swt)!" I will say, "What is their offence?" He will say, "They apostated after your death." I do not see any of them escaping except very few."

- Saheeh Al-Bukhari 8:587
- Saheeh Al-Bukhari. Pg. # 1633, H. # 6587
- Saheeh Muslim. Pg. # 1082, H. # 2290 / 26

Along similar lines another tradition of the Prophet which confirms that companions would be taken away from the Prophet because they had introduced innovations in the religion.

"Some persons from amongst those who accompanied me will meet me at the Lake-Fount. I will see them, and they will be presented to me. Then, they will be blocked away from me. I will say: 'O my Lord, They are my companions! They are my companions.' It will be said to me: 'You do not know what innovations they introduced after your death.'"

- Saheeh Muslim. Pg. # 1090, H. # 2304 / 40
- Musnad Ahmad ibn Hanbal. Vol. 38, Pg. # 363, H. # 23337
- Musnad Ahmad ibn Hanbal. Vol. 23, Pg. # 322 - 323, H. # 15121

4.4.4.1. A Mixed Bag

The key point that comes out from the above verses of the Holy Quran and from the narrations of the Prophet is the fact that the companions were not a coherent group, either in terms of their sincerity or in terms of their Islamic character.

Among the companions of the Prophet were some towering personalities who had given everything in the way of Allah. They were praised in the Holy Quran where Allah had testified that they were firm against the unbelievers, compassionate among each other and that they would bow and prostrate to seek Allah's pleasure and reward. These were the righteous companions of the Prophet.

At the same time there were companions who have been called hypocrites in the Holy Quran. They would come to Holy Prophet and swear allegiance, but their allegiance was a cover to harm Islam and Muslims. They had disbelieved after believing in Islam and they had in fact become apostates. Allah promises such companions a painful end in this world and hereafter.

The narrations of the Prophet also paint a similar picture of the companions. The Prophet had informed the Muslims during his lifetime that he would recognize some of his companions on the lake-fountain i.e., on the Day of Judgment, and those companions would be taken away to hell fire in front of his eyes. He would ask Allah as to why his companions were being sent to hell. The Prophet would be told that he does not know what they had innovated after his death, and that some of his companions had become apostates.

Considering the fact that Prophet had such a large number of companions (over one hundred thousand), it was both natural and logical to expect that when so many people had joined the movement of Islam, some of them would be righteous and sincere to the highest degree as they were truly inspired by the message of Islam, whereas others had joined the movement of Islam for their own self-interest or personal gain. And as soon as they would realize that their goals would not be fulfilled or perhaps their goals had already been fulfilled, they would ditch the revolutionary message of Islam and turn against it.

If one reads and analyses the history of other great movements that have left their mark on the history of mankind, a similar pattern could be observed, where some people who have joined the movement are truly sincere while others have ulterior motives, and the movement of Islam was no different.

The companions were a large and a varied group with some very sincere Muslims and some hypocrites in their ranks as testified by both the Holy Quran and the traditions of the Prophet. A group as big as the companions with mixed tendencies could not possibly become the custodian of Prophet's Sunnah. When the faith and the sincerity of a number of the companions was in doubt, and when the Prophet himself had predicted that some of his companions would go astray, then there was no way that Prophet would make them or allow them to become the custodian of his Sunnah.

4.4.4.2. Still Being Guided

The companions were in fact the very people that Prophet had come to reform and guide towards the Islamic faith. They were the Bedouin Arabs of yesterday who were indulged in all kinds of Jahiliya (pre-Islamic) customs before the advent of Islam. They were the very people who were burying their daughters alive not too long ago. They were the same people who used to fight and kill each other on trivial matters and those blood feuds would then last for generations to come.

The vast majority of the companions had only been Muslims for a few years i.e., they had only accepted Islam after the conquest of Makkah, and the Prophet of Allah was still guiding and supporting them on the path of Islam. Many of the companions were simply being kept on the path of Islam by being showered with gifts of war booty and Zakat, in order to soften their hearts towards the faith of Islam.

It made no logical sense that the very people who were new to the faith, and who were still being guided and steered towards the path of Allah, would somehow become the custodian of Prophet's Sunnah, and would somehow be allowed by the Prophet to take on the mantle of the Islamic leadership after his death.

4.4.4.3. The Sheer Number of Companions

There is no definitive figure on the exact number of Prophet's companions. Nobody knows to this day with any certainty as to what was the actual number of the Prophet's companions. It is reported that in Madinah alone there were around ten thousand companions. It is also said that in the battle of Tabuk which took place after the conquest of Makkah, Prophet took over thirty thousand companions with him to the battlefield. Imam Shafi had estimated the number of companions to be roughly around sixty thousand. Most scholars today estimate the number of companions to be over one hundred thousand.

The early scholars did various studies into the lives and the history of the companions, but even these early scholars could only come up with the names of less than five thousand companions. Assuming the widely agreed figure of say one hundred thousand companions, which has been estimated by many scholars, we only know the names of less than five percent of the companions. And when I say names, I mean in many cases we simply know the name of a companion and nothing else about him.

Considering the fact that Prophet of Allah had thousands of companions, and even if we were to assume that every single companion of the Prophet was righteous, i.e., even if we were to ignore all the previous verses of the Holy Quran and the hadith that I have quoted earlier, the sheer number of companions made it impossible for them to be the custodian of Prophet's Sunnah.

A group of sixty to one hundred thousand people scattered between the cities and towns of Makkah and Madinah, with a distance of hundreds of miles between them, and with no modern means of travel or communication, could not possibly coordinate or defend the Sunnah of the Prophet.

Also, as each companion individually had only spent a small amount of time in the company of the Prophet, they only knew certain bits of Prophet's Sunnah, i.e., they only knew the Sunnah that they had observed or heard from the Prophet's mouth. For instance, a companion would only see or meet the Prophet when he was in the mosque or in a public place, so individually each companion had only spent a limited amount of time in the presence of the Prophet, and hence their knowledge of the Sunnah of the Prophet was also limited.

A companion living in Madinah had only been with the Prophet in that city. They had no knowledge of what Prophet did or said in Makkah, unless the Prophet himself informs them about his Sunnah, or a Makkan companion informs them about the Sunnah of the Prophet.

These individual companions in their thousands with bits of knowledge about the Prophet's Sunnah, were spread all over the Arabian Peninsula at the time of the death of the Prophet, with no real means of communication between them, other than the word of mouth or travelling to another city or town on a horse.

It was practically impossible that such a big and a dispersed group of people would be able to even communicate or coordinate with each other, let alone become the custodian or the defender of Prophet's Sunnah.

The Prophet of Allah knew these facts more than anybody else, after all the Prophet of Allah was divinely guided and was the last apostle of Allah. He knew and understood these ground realities better than anyone else at that time. The Prophet had planned for this eventuality at a very early stage in the life of the Islamic movement, and had subsequently announced it on many occasions, especially on his final pilgrimage as we will see in the next chapters.

4.4.4.4. Not to be Confused

The readers must not be confused about the actual point that I am trying to make here. I am not stating that the companions did not know or were not aware of the Sunnah of the Prophet. As I said previously, some companions knew hundreds of traditions of the Prophet while others only knew a handful. The point that I am trying to make here is that the Sunnah of the Prophet did not exist in a compiled or a consolidated state at the time of the death of the Prophet. The Sunnah of the Prophet was scattered among the companions across the Arabian Peninsula, with each companion only knowing a bit of the Prophet's Sunnah.

When Prophet says that he is leaving behind both the Book of Allah and his Sunnah as the two sources of knowledge and guidance after him, then he must ensure that his entire Sunnah is accessible and available to the companions and the rest of the Muslims before he departs this world.

It is a historical fact that the Prophet did not document his Sunnah during his lifetime except some of his traditions. The compilation and the documentation of the Sunnah began almost a century after the death of the Prophet. Hence it was imperative that when Prophet was about to depart from this world, he must leave behind someone or a group of people who have the knowledge and the understanding of his entire Sunnah.

5. THE LEADERSHIP OF THE AHLULBAYT

As I have discussed previously that Islam is a complete way of life, which entails both the book of Allah and the Sunnah of the Prophet, and without either one of these sources Islam remains incomplete.

I will reproduce the tradition (hadith) of the Prophet where Prophet said to his companions on his last pilgrimage that:

> *"I have left among you two matters by holding fast to which, you shall never be misguided: the Book of God and my Sunnah"*
>
> - Dar Al-Hijra Malik ibn Anas in Al-Muwatta. Vol. 2, Pg. # 480, H # 2618.
> - Al-Hakim Al-Nishaburi in Al-Mustadrak Alaa Al-Sahihain. Vol. 1, Pg. # 160 - 161, H. # 318.

When Prophet tells his companions on his final pilgrimage that he was leaving behind his Sunnah as a source of guidance, then he must make sure that he leaves behind a clear means for the companions by which they could refer back to his Sunnah.

A means which was able to differentiate between the right and the wrong Sunnah of the Prophet, and a means which actually regarded the Sunnah of the Prophet as the second most critical source of knowledge after the Holy Quran, and above all a means which had the complete knowledge and understanding of the Sunnah of the Prophet.

5.1. The Hadith of Two Weighty Things (Thaqalayn)

To ensure that the companions had a definitive means of guidance about the Sunnah of the Prophet, which was not documented during the lifetime of the Prophet, the Prophet also announced the following on his final pilgrimage, which is reported by over 20 companions such as Abu Dhar, Saeed Al Khudri, Zayd bin Arqam and Hudiafah and by around 185 narrators.

We read in Al-Tirmidhi in his authentic Sunan reported by Jabir Ibn Abdullah (Al-Ansari):

> *"I witnessed the Messenger of God in his pilgrimage (in the tenth year after the Hijrahh) speaking while he was riding his camel called: Al-Qaswa. I heard him saying: 'O people I have left in you that which if you adhere to you will never go astray: The Book of God and the members of my House."*
>
> - Sunan Al-Tirmidhi. Vol. 3, Pg. # 543 - 544, H. # 3786 – 3788
> - Sunan Al -Tirmidhi. Vol. 6, Pg. # 335

These two traditions of the Prophet complement and support each other. The Prophet clarifies exactly as to who was the custodian of his Sunnah. The Prophet tells his companions that if they follow the Quran and the Ahlulbayt after his death, they will attain salvation, just as he had told them that if they followed the Quran and his Sunnah they would stay on the right path.

The Prophet replaces the word Sunnah with the Ahlulbayt, implying that it was the Ahlulbayt who in fact had the knowledge of the actual Sunnah of the Prophet. The Prophet had mentioned both the Quran and the Ahlulbayt in the same tradition, as they were the two inseparable sources of knowledge and guidance for the companions. The Prophet had considered the Ahlulbayt to be the custodian of his Sunnah, and he wanted his companions to follow the Ahlulbayt after his death, as he expected the Ahlulbayt to guide the companions according to his Sunnah.

It was not possible that Prophet would have left his Sunnah without a guide or without documenting it. The reason why Prophet did not document his Sunnah during his lifetime was because while he was still alive and present among the companions, he was the embodiment and the source of the Sunnah, and the companions could ask him questions or refer to him to access his Sunnah.

And after his death he wanted the companions to refer to the Ahlulbayt to access his Sunnah. Since Prophet was leaving behind a clear and a living source i.e., his Ahlulbayt, who had the complete knowledge and understanding of his Sunnah, he did not need to document his traditions and only documented the Book of Allah.

The Ahlulbayt of the Prophet were indeed the custodian of Prophet's Sunnah in his absence, otherwise the Prophet would not have left his Sunnah undocumented or scattered across the Arabian Peninsula in bits with thousands of companions.

This hadith of the two weighty things is also a proof that Prophet had a plan and a strategy for the movement of Islam both during his lifetime and after his death. The Prophet of Allah had planned for all eventualities. He could not possibly leave the future of the Islamic movement to the turns of history, or to the chances of an election, or in the hands of the very people who he had come to reform.

To say and accept that the Prophet of Allah had not thought about the future of Islam after his death, and that he had left it to the Ummah to decide, is a clear negation of the wisdom and the thought that Prophet had given for securing the future of the Islamic movement during his lifetime.

As long as Prophet was alive the Islamic movement obviously revolved around him, but after his death he wanted that nucleus to be shifted to the Ahlulbayt, as evident from the above hadith and from other hadiths that I will shortly quote.

The Ahlulbayt were a small close nit family of the Prophet, unlike the companions who were in their thousands. They had always been with the Prophet, and they had the maximum company of the Prophet since they were his family. They had been with him in both Makkah and Madinah, and they had witnessed the entire life span of the Islamic movement from its very beginning until the death of the Prophet.

Also, unlike the companions who had both righteous and non-righteous Muslims in their ranks, the Ahlulbayt had no such discrepancy about them. They only had righteous individuals who had been praised by both the Holy Quran and the Prophet on numerous occasions. It is for this reason that Prophet had designated them to lead the Ummah after his death as he had considered his Ahlulbayt to be the custodian of his Sunnah and a security against deviation.

I will give a few variations of hadith-e-Thaqalayn (two weighty things), to give the readers a gist of what Prophet had envisaged for the future of the Muslims after his demise. The Prophet had mentioned this hadith on a number of occasions, including on his final pilgrimage to Makkah, on the day of Ghadeer which took place in the last three months of Prophet's life, and in the mosque of the Prophet.

The Prophet of Allah had not only called the Holy Quran and his Ahlulbayt as the two weighty things, but he had also called them as his two successors (Khalifatayn).

> *"I will leave among you the two Khalifahs (Successors) after me: The Book of Allah and my Itrah (Ahlulbayt). Both shall never separate until they meet me at the 'lake-fount."*

- *Ibn Abi Hasim in Zilal Al-Jannah. Vol. 2, Pg. # 643. H. # 1049.*
- *Musnad Ahmad Ibn Hanbal (Published in 1995) Vol. 35, Pg. 512. H. # 21654.*
- *Musnad Ahmad ibn Hanbal. Pg, # 5065.*
- *Musnad Ahmad ibn Hanbal research by Hamza Ahmed Zain, Darul Hadith Pg 28/51*
- *Abu Bakr 'Abd Allah b. Abi Shaybah, Musnad Ibn Abi Shaybah (Riyadh: Dar al-Watan; 1st edition, 1418 H) [annotators: 'Adil b. Yusuf al-'Azazi and Ahmad b. Farid al-Mazidi], vol. 1, p. 108*
- *Faiz ul Qadeer Sharh Jame Sagheer by Abdul Raouf Al-Manawi Vol 3, Hadith 2631*

On similar lines the Prophet also said:

> *"I left you two things to follow, what is most important to me is the Khalifatayn (Successors). The book of Allah (swt) and my progeny Ahlulbayt (a.s) and they will not separate until they return to me at the pond (of Kawthar in paradise)."*

- *Al-Haythami in Majma Al-Zawa'id. Vol. 9, Pg. # 256, H # 14957.*
- *Al-Suyuti in Jamia Al-Sageer. Vol. 1, Pg. # 482, H # 2457 - 2456.*
- *Jamia Al-Sageer research by Albani Vol 1 Pg 482*
- *Musnad Ahmad ibn Hanbal research by Shoaib Arnaout Hadith Vol 35, Pg 456/512*
- *Majum Al-Kabir research by Ahmed Abdul Majid al-Salafi Vol 5 Pg 4921*
- *Ahmad b. 'Ali b. Hajar al-'Asqalani, Taqrib al-Tahdhib (Beirut: Dar al-Maktabah al-'Ilmiyyah; 2nd edition, 1415 H) [annotator: Mustafa 'Abd al-Qadir 'Ata], vol. 1, p. 718, # 4920*

The Prophet had declared the Holy Quran and the Ahlulbayt to be his two Khalifas, i.e., his two successors, who must be followed after him. Both the Book of Allah and the Ahlulbayt were a source of knowledge and guidance for the rest of the Ummah. The Ahlulbayt were the custodian of Prophet's Sunnah and the Holy Quran was the word of Allah.

The Prophet puts the Ahlulbayt at par with Quran by stating that the Ahlulbayt and the Quran would not separate from each other until they meet him in paradise, giving both the companions and ordinary Muslims a clear direction for the future leadership of the Muslims. The Prophet had chosen the Ahlulbayt to be his successor (Khalifa) over the Muslims during his lifetime, so that the Ahlulbayt could guide the Muslims according to his Sunnah after his death.

In another variation of the hadith the Prophet of Allah had said:

> *"I (my soul) am about to be called for then I would answer, and I am leaving among you the two weighty things, the book of Allah (swt) and my family, the book of Allah which is an extended rope from the skies to the land (Earth) and my family whom they are my household and the Most Kind and the Most Knowing informed me that they shall never separate until they return to me at the Basin (Kawthar). ...."*

- *Musnad Ahmad ibn Hanbal. Pg, # 2317.*
- *Musnad Ahmad ibn Hanbal. Vol. 16, Pg. # 28, H # 21470.*
- *Ahmad ibn Hanbal in Fada'il Al-Sahaba. Vol. 2, Pg. # 603, H # 1032 - 1403.*
- *Musnad Ahmad ibn Hanbal. Pg, # 2307, 5048.*
- *Al Sharah Al Tayyabi al Miskatil Masabi research by Abdullah bin Muhammad al Tayyabi Pg 3909 Hadith 6153*

- Al-Sawa'iq Al-Muhriqah by Hajar Al Haythami Pg 439
- Sharh Al-Maqasid by Al-Taftazani Vol 5, Pg 303
- Sharh Al-Shifa by Qazi Iyaz Vol 2, Pg 83

The Prophet describes the Book of Allah as a rope which is extended from the sky to the earth. The Prophet tells his companions that they would need to hold on to the rope of Allah and his Ahlulbayt after him, as they would not separate from each other until they meet him in paradise.

In another variation the Prophet tells the companions to adhere to the Book of Allah and to follow his Ahlulbayt.

> *"Oh people, I am a human being and the Messenger of my Lord [the angel responsible of taking the soul back to His Lord] is about to come to me and I would answer him [His soul will answer the call of Her lord to go back to Him] and I am leaving among you the two weighty things, the first of Them is the Book of Allah (swt) which has guidance and enlightenment therefore adhere firmly to the Book of Allah (swt) and take it as your leader" …….. " And my household (Ahlulbayt), I remind you to obey Allah by obeying my household (Ahlulbayt) [he said it three times]"*

- Abd Rahman Darimi in Sunan Al Darimi. Vol.4, Pg. 2090 - 2091. H. # 3359.

In a shorter version of the above hadith the Prophet says that the Muslims would never go astray as long as they adhere to the book of Allah and his Ahlulbayt.

> *"Allah's Messenger when performing the hajj seated on his she camel Al-Qaswa on the day of Arafah, saying, "O people, I have left among you something of such a nature that if you adhere to it you will not go astray: Allah's Book and my close relatives, my Ahlulbayt (a.s)."*

- l-Rafi'i Al-Qazweeni in Al-Tadween Fi Akhbar Al-Qazween. Vol.2, Pg. # 266.
- Muttaqi Al-Hindi in Kanz-ul-Ummal. Vol. 1, Pg. # 379 - 380.
- Musnad Ahmad ibn Hanbal research by Shoaib Arnaout Hadith 11561 page 114
- Sunan Al-Tirmidhi research by Jamal Sideeq Jameel Attar Pg 1078, Hadith 3811
- Sunan Al-Tirmidhi research by Nasir Uddin Al Bani Vol 3 g 43 (Published in Riyadh)
- Anees Al Sari by Hajar Asqalani research by Yaqoob Al Basara Pg 1413 (Published in Beirut)
- Al-Sawa'iq Al-Muhriqah by Hajar Al Haythami Pg 653 Vol 1, Pg 439
- Istiglab Irtaqa Al Guraf by Al-Hafiz Saqavi research by Khalid bin Ahmed Sami Babtain Vol 1 Pg 342/343 Hadith No 65/66/67
- Subul al-Huda wa al-Rashad by Muhammad bin Yusuf al-Salehi al-Shami Vol.12 Pg 494

A similar hadith was also mentioned on the day of Ghadeer some three months before the death of the Prophet, clearly highlighting the plan that Prophet had laid out for the future of the Muslims.

> *"I have left among you something that if you abide by, you shall never astray. The Book of Allah, with one side of it in the hand of Allah and the other side in your hands, and my Ahlulbayt."*

- Muttaqi Al-Hindi in Kanz-ul-Ummal. Vol. 13, Pg. # 140, H # 32441.
- ibn Hajar in Al-Matalib Al-Aliya bi Zawa'id Al-Masanid Al-Thamaniya. Vol. 14, Pg. # 132. H. # 3943.
- Al-Busiri in Et'haf Khiratul Mohra. Vol. 9, Pg. # 279, H # 7984.
- ibn Hajar in Al-Matalib Al-Aliya bi Zawa'id Al-Masanid Al-Thamaniya. Vol. 14, Pg. # 132. H. # 3943.
- Ibn Kathir in Tafsir ibn Kathir. Vol. 7, Pg. # 201.
- Al-Tabarani in Al-Mu'jam Al-Kabir. Vol. 5, Pg. # 169 - 170, H # 4980 - 4981.
- Wirasatul Labib fe Seerat ul Habib by Moin Sindhi Pg 207
- Al Nuskatul Musnada Min Nawdiral Usual by Al-Hakeem Tirmizi Vol. 1 Pg 207

In another variation the Prophet had asked the companions to follow the book of Allah and reminded them about the rights of the Ahlulbayt and the way they should be treated.

> "I am about to receive a messenger (the angel of death) from my Lord and I, in response to Allah's call, (would bid good-bye to you), but I am leaving among you two weighty things: the one being the Book of Allah in which there is right guidance and light, so hold fast to the Book of Allah and adhere to it. He exhorted (us) (to hold fast) to the Book of Allah and then said: The second are the members of my household I remind you of God with regard to the People of my Household (Ahlul Bayt), People of my Household (Ahlul Bayt), People of my Household (Ahlul Bayt)..."

- Sahih Muslim Hadith 6225

A similar tradition is also found in Musnad ibn Humayd

> "'O Mankind, I am a mortal, it could be that a messenger of death may visit me soon and I will have to submit, and I have left behind two weighty things. The first one is the Book of Allah (swt), in it there is guidance and light and so hold fast to the Book of Allah (swt) and follow it............ and then he said, "And (hold fast) with my family members, I remind you Allah in my family members, I remind you Allah in my family members." He said this three times!"

- Abd ibn Humayd in Musnad Abd ibn Humayd. Vol. 1, Pg. # 225, H. # 265.

The Prophet reminded the companions about the rights of the Ahlulbayt too, by stressing it at least three times in the same tradition. This further clarifies the position and the status of the Ahlulbayt in the eyes of the Prophet.

The key points that come out from the Hadith-e-Thaqlayn are:

- This tradition was mentioned by the Prophet on several occasions towards the end of his life.
- The Prophet considered both the Quran and the Ahlulbayt as the two valuable and weighty assets which must be followed and adhered to after his demise.
- Prophet informs his companions that both the Quran and the Ahlulbayt will never separate from each other until they meet him in paradise.
- Both the book of Allah and the Ahlulbayt were a source of guidance and knowledge for the companions and the wider Ummah.
- If the companions followed these two key sources of knowledge and guidance they would never go astray.
- The Prophet described both the Book of Allah and the Ahlulbayt as his two successors i.e., his two Khalifas after him.
- The Prophet also tells the companions to be careful in how they would treat his Ahlulbayt, implying that they must also love and respect the Ahlulbayt and treat them well.

As we go through the various versions of this hadith it becomes obvious and clear that Prophet of Allah had carefully thought about the future of the Muslims and the Islamic movement before his death.

He informed his companions towards the end of his life on various occasions that if they wanted to stay on the right path then they must follow both the Quran and the Ahlulbayt, clearly placing the Ahlulbayt in the position of leadership. The Prophet called both the Quran and the Ahlulbayt as the two weighty things (valuable assets) and his two successors, which must be followed in his absence for the companions to stay on the path of salvation.

Just as he had earlier said that they must follow the Quran and his Sunnah, the Prophet of Allah also told his companions that they must follow the Quran and his Ahlulbayt, since the Quran and the Ahlulbayt would never separate from each other. Clearly implying that the teachings of the Ahlulbayt would always be in line with the book of Allah, because the teachings of the Ahlulbayt in fact represented the actual Sunnah of the Prophet.

As Prophet considered the Ahlulbayt to be the custodian of his Sunnah, he wanted the future leadership of Muslims to be in the hands of his Ahlulbayt, since he wanted his Ahlulbayt to guide and lead the companions and the wider Muslim community after his death.

Islam is an all-encompassing way of life and it does not separate religion from the state. In the Islamic State of Madinah which Prophet of Allah had established, he was both a religious authority and the head of the State. Similarly, when he wanted his Ahlulbayt to lead the Ummah after his death, he wanted them to have the same religious and political authority which he enjoyed as the head of the Islamic State.

5.1.1. Creating Doubt about the Hadith of Two Weighty Things

Unfortunately, when this hadith is presented to ordinary Muslim some scholars would come forward and start creating doubts about the authenticity of this Hadith, even though this Hadith is found in some of the most authentic books of Islamic traditions and history. In this context I would like to refer to the work of Khalid bin Ahmed who had researched the book of Al-Hafiz Saqavi who had narrated this Hadith in his book called Istiglab Irtaqa Al Guraf. Al-Hafiz Saqavi writes the names of some of the companions of the Prophet who had narrated this tradition, since it is a mutawatir tradition of the Prophet which means a tradition that is narrated by many companions.

The names of some of the companions who have narrated this tradition are as follows:

- Jabir
- Huzaifah
- Khuzaifa bin Sabit
- Zayd bin Sabit
- Sahal bin Saad
- Zumaira
- Amir bin Laili
- Abdur Rehman bin Auf
- Abdullah ibn Abbas
- Abdullah bin Umar
- Adi bin Hatim
- Uqba bin Amir
- Ali bin Abi Talib
- Abu Dharr
- Abu Rafay
- Abu Shuray Al Khuzai
- Abu Khudamay Ansari
- Abu Hurairah
- Abul Haytam
- Umm Salam
- Umm Hani bint Abi Talib
    - *Istiglab Irtaqa Al Guraf by Al-Hafiz Saqavi research by Khalid bin Ahmed Sami Babtain Vol 1 Pg 342/343 Hadith No 65/66/67*

5.2. The Prophet Prays for the Purification of Ahlulbayt

One may wonder as to why the Ahlulbayt were so righteous that Prophet had asked the companions and the wider Muslim Ummah to follow them and to adhere to their path in his absence. Why was it that the Prophet had asked the companions to follow the Ahlulbayt alongside the Quran? What made the Ahlulbayt to be at par with the Book of Allah? Were the Ahlulbayt righteous simply because they were the family and the relatives of the Prophet?

The answer to the above question is a clear no.

The Holy Quran clearly states:

> "Surely the noblest among you in the sight of God is the most righteous of you"
> - (Chapter 49, verse 13)

To dispel this notion, the word "Aal Muhammad" or "Ahlulbayt" only refers to the chosen relatives of the Prophet, and not to all of the Prophet's relatives and family members, because if all the Prophet's family was included in the Ahlulbayt then it would advocate clannish and tribal supremacy, which goes against the very ethos of Islamic thought and principles.

For instance, we find a chapter in the Holy Quran which defames Abu Lahab, who was the uncle of the Prophet.

> "Perish the two hands of the Father of Flame and perished he. His wealth and whatever he gained did not avail him.... "
> - Chapter 31 verse 33.

The above verse was revealed condemning the uncle of the Prophet, and it clearly shows that even Prophet's uncle who was his blood relation was not immune from the wrath of Allah. Simply being the family or a close relative of the Prophet does not guarantee righteousness, and neither does it make that family member part of the Ahlulbayt.

The word "Ahlulbayt" refers to the chosen relatives of Prophet Muhammad. These relatives were chosen by the Prophet through divine guidance. The Prophet prayed to Allah to make those relatives (Ahlulbayt) righteous and pure, so that they could lead the Muslim Ummah after his demise and become role models for the Muslims.

The wife of the Prophet Umm Salama reports as to how the Prophet had prayed to Allah All Mighty, asking him to make his Ahlulbayt pure and righteous, and how Allah had revealed the verse of purification to remove sins and misguidance from the Ahlulbayt.

Umm Salam reports that when the following Quranic verse of purification was revealed:

> "Verily Allah intends only to remove from you the impurity [of sin], O people of the [Prophet's] household, and to purify you with [extensive] purification."
> - Quran 33:33

The Prophet of Allah was in her house, and he started gathering his Ahlulbayt.

> *Upon that, the Prophet gathered Fatimah, al-Hasan, and al-Hussain, and covered them with a cloak, and he also covered Ali who was behind him. Then the Prophet said: "O' Allah! These are the Members of my House (Ahlulbayt). Keep them away from every impurity and purify them with a perfect purification."*
>
> *Umm Salama (the wife of Prophet) asked: "Am I also included among them O Apostle of Allah?" the Prophet replied: "You remain in your position and you are toward a good ending."*
>
> - *Sunan Al-Tirmidhi. Vol. 3, Pg. # 543, H. # 3787*
> - *Sunan Al-Tirmidhi. Vol. 3, Pg. # 570*
> - *Musnad Ahmad ibn Hanbal. Vol. 44, Pg. # 118-119*
> - *Fath Al Bari. Vol. 7, Pg. # 169*

The above hadith informs us that when the verse of purification (Quran 33:33) was revealed, the Prophet of Allah gathered Ali, Fatima, Hasan, and Hussain and covered them with a cloak, he then prayed to Allah to purify them from all kinds of impurity, sins and misguidance and make them pious and righteous.

This is why the Ahlulbayt were so righteous and pure because Prophet had asked Allah to make them righteous and pure. It was the prayers of the Prophet with divine guidance which had made his Ahlulbayt pious and righteous and worthy of the Islamic leadership. And that is why the Prophet had put them at par with the Book of Allah in hadith-e-Thaqalayn (two weighty things).

The above hadith also gives the names of the Ahlulbayt i.e., Ali, Fatima, Hasan, Hussain and of course the Prophet is also included in the Ahlulbayt, and he was indeed the head of the Ahlulbayt. The end of the hadith further clarifies that when Umm Salama, the wife of the Prophet asked if she was part of the Ahlulbayt, the Prophet replied that although she was on the right path, but she was not part of the Ahlulbayt.

Here is another version of "The Tradition of Cloak" which is narrated by Jaffar Ibn Abi Talib:

> *When the Messenger of Allah noticed that a blessing from Allah was to descent, he told Safiya (one of his wives): "Call for me! Call for me!"*
>
> *Safiya said: "Call who, O the Messenger of Allah?" He said: "Call for me my Ahlulbayt who are Ali, Fatimah, al-Hasan, and al-Husain." Thus, we sent for them and they came to him.*
> *Then the Prophet spread his cloak over them and raised his hand (toward sky) saying: "O Allah! These are my family (Aalee), so bless Muhammad and the family (Aal) of Muhammad."*
>
> *And Allah, to whom belong Might and Majesty, revealed:*
> *"Verily Allah intends to keep off from you every kind of uncleanness O' People of the House (Ahlulbayt), and purify you a thorough purification (Quran 33:33)".*
>
> - *al-Mustadrak by al-Hakim, Chapter of "Understanding (the virtues) of Companions, v3, p148. The author then wrote: "This tradition is authentic (Sahih) based on the criteria of the two Shaikhs (al-Bukhari and Muslim)."*
> - *Talkhis of al-Mustadrak, by al-Dhahabi, v3, p148*
> - *Usdul Ghabah, by Ibn al-Athir, v3, p33*

Again, in this tradition the Prophet of Allah asked his wife Safiya to call his Ahlulbayt i.e., Ali, Fatima, Hasan, and Hussain. Once they all gathered the Prophet covered them under a cloak and raised his hands towards the sky and said to Allah that this is my family, and then he prayed for the blessings and purification of his family. And in the honour of Prophet's prayer Allah revealed the verse of purification in Quran (Quran 33:33), which stated that Allah had removed all kind of uncleanness (meaning sins and misguidance) from the Ahlulbayt.

Lady Aisha narrates a similar tradition of the Prophet where the Prophet again prayed for the purification and righteousness of the Ahlulbayt.

> One day the Prophet (pbuh) came out in the afternoon wearing a black cloak (upper garment or gown; long coat), then al-Hasan Ibn Ali came, and the Prophet accommodated him under the cloak, then al-Husain came and entered the cloak, then Fatimah came and the Prophet entered her under the cloak, then Ali came and the Prophet entered him to the cloak as well. Then the Prophet recited: "Verily Allah intends to keep off from you every kind of uncleanness O' People of the House (Ahlulbayt), and purify you a perfect purification (last part of Quran verse 33:33)."

- Sahih Muslim, Hadith 5955.
- Sahih Muslim. Vol. 2, Pg. # 1136.
- ibn Kathir Tafsir ibn Kathir. Vol. 6, Pg. # 414.
- Musnad Ishaq ibn Rahwayh. Vol. 3, Pg. # 678.
- Al-Hakim Al-Nishaburi in Al-Mustadrak of Al-Hakim. Vol. 3, Pg. # 158-159.

Just like the previous version, the Prophet gathered the Ahlulbayt under a cloak and recited the last part of the verse of Quran (33:33), which states that Allah intends to remove all forms of uncleanness from the Ahlulbayt. The removal of uncleanness is not to physically cleanse the Ahlulbayt as that is absurd and serves no purpose. The removal of uncleanness of course implies to remove all kinds of misguidance, wrongdoing, and sins, and make the Ahlulbayt righteous, pure, and noble, so that they could lead the Muslims on the right path in Prophet's absence. Again, the names of the Ahlulbayt are also clearly mentioned in this tradition.

It is also widely reported that after the Quranic verse 33:33 was revealed the Prophet started coming to the House of Fatimah and Ali before every prayer, and he used to recite the Quranic verse 33:33 on their door. The Prophet continued this practice for many months as he wanted to remind the companions everyday about the status and the righteousness of the Ahlulbayt.

Anas Ibn Malik has narrated:

> The Messenger of Allah from the time of the revelation of the verse "Verily Allah intends to keep off from you every kind of uncleanness O' People of the House (Ahlulbayt) …. Quran 33:33)", and for six (6) months thereafter, (Prophet) stood by the door of the House of Fatimah and said: "Time for Prayer Ahlul-Bayt; No doubt! Allah wished to remove all abomination from you and make you pure and spotless."

- Sahih al-Tirmidhi, v12, p85
- Musnad Ahmad Ibn Hanbal, v3, p258
- Mustadrak, by al-Hakim, v3, p158 who wrote this tradition is authentic as per the criteria of Tafsir al-Durr al-Manthoor, by al-Suyuti, v5, pp 197,199
- Tafsir Ibn Jarir al-Tabari, v22, pp 5,6 (saying seven month)
- Tafsir Ibn Kathir, v3, p483
- Musnad, by al-Tiyalasi, v8, p274
- Usdul Ghabah, by Ibn al-Athir, v5, p146

Abu al-Hamra has narrated:

> "The Messenger of God continued eight (8) months in Madinah, coming to the door of Ali at every morning prayer, putting his two hands on the two sides of the door and exclaiming: "Assalat! Assalat! (prayer! prayer!) Certainly, God ward off all uncleanness from you, O Members of the House of Muhammad, and to make you pure and spotless."

- Tafsir al-Durr al-Manthoor, by al-Suyuti, v5, pp 198-199
- Tafsir Ibn Jarir al-Tabari, v22, p6
- Tafsir Ibn Kathir, v3, p483

- *Dhakha'ir al-Uqba, by Muhibbuddin al-Tabari, p24 on the authority of Anas Ibn Malik*
- *Isti'ab, by Ibn Abd al-Barr, v5, p637*
- *Usdul Ghabah, by Ibn al-Athir, v5, p146*
- *Majma' al-Zawa'id, by al-Haythami, v9, pp 121,168*
- *Mushkil al-Athar, by al-Tahawi, p338*

Also, Ibn Abbas has narrated:

> *"We have witnessed the Messenger of God for nine (9) months coming to the door of Ali, son of Abu Talib, at the time of each prayer and saying: 'Assalamu Alaykum Wa Rahmatullah Ahlulbayt (Peace and Mercy of God be upon you, O Members of the House). Certainly, God wants only to keep away all the evil from you, Members of the House, and purify you with a thorough purification.' He did this seven times a day."*

- *al-Durr al-Manthoor, by al-Hafidh al-Suyuti, v5, p198*

The above-mentioned traditions testify that the Prophet went to the door of Ali and Fatima every day, for at least six months and prayed for the righteousness and the purification of his Ahlulbayt. The actions and the words of the Prophet were not without wisdom or thought or a sense of purpose. The Prophet of Allah had a plan and a strategy for the Islamic movement both during his lifetime and after his demise.

The Prophet of Allah could not possibly make a group or an individual in charge of the Islamic movement without first ensuring that the people he was putting at the helm, and in the position of leadership were themselves righteous and guided and were on the path of truth. There was no point in making someone in charge when their own credentials were not fully in line with the Islamic thought and principles.

Since Prophet had chosen the Ahlulbayt to lead the Ummah, the only way that the Prophet could guarantee that the Ahlulbayt were pure and righteous was to ask Allah to make them pure, pious, and righteous, so that they would be able to lead the rest of the Islamic nation on the path of righteousness too.

For this very reason the Prophet of Allah could confidently say that he was leaving behind two weighty things, one was the book of Allah and the other were his Ahlulbayt, since it was Allah who had ensured the righteousness and the purification of the Ahlulbayt through the prayers of the Prophet.

5.2.1. Creating Doubt about the Quranic Verse 33:33

It is a most unfortunate fact among the Islamic scholars that whenever anyone brings up the issue of the leadership of the Ahlulbayt, doubts and confusion is created in the minds of the ordinary Muslims, to keep them away from recognising the true position of the Ahlulbayt as the guardians of the faith

Regarding the Quranic verse 33:33 these scholars would argue that since the verses before and the verses after the Quranic verse 33:33 are about the wives of the Prophet, hence the verse 33:33 must also be about the wives of the Prophet. They argue that the verse (33:33) needs to be looked at in the context of the verses before it and the verses after it.

The problem is that these scholars are deliberately trying to mislead the ordinary Muslims while knowing full well that the order in which the verses of the Holy Quran currently appear is not necessarily the order in the which the verses of the Holy Quran were revealed. This is a known fact to any student of the Islamic history. The current order in which the verses of the Holy Quran are compiled was devised during the rule of the third Caliph Uthman, but it is not necessarily the order in which these verses were revealed to the Prophet as well.

The order of the revelation of the verses is different from the order of the compilation of verses in the Holy Quran. These are known facts about the Book of Allah.

It would have been very silly of the Prophet to go to the door of Ali, Fatima, Hasan, and Hussain every day for at least six months and recite the Quranic verse 33:33, and pray for their purification, if this verse was indeed revealed for the wives of the Prophet, since none of these personalities were his wives.

The actions of the Prophet itself proves that this verse (33:33) was only revealed for the members his Ahlulbayt and not for his wives, despite the fact that the verses before and after it are for the wives of the Prophet.

5.3. The Ahlulbayt and the Ark of Noah

Along similar lines as hadith of Thaqalayn (two weighty things), the Prophet of Allah had also compared his Ahlulbayt to the ark of Noah.

The Prophet stated:

> "Behold! My Ahlul-Bayt are like the Ark of Noah. Whoever embarked in it was SAVED, and whoever turned away from it was PERISHED."

- al-Mustadrak, by al-Hakim, v2, p343, v3, pp 150-151 on the authority of Abu Dhar. al-Hakim said this tradition is authentic (Sahih).
- Fadha'il al-Companions, by Ahmad Ibn Hanbal, v2, p786
- Tafsir al-Kabir, by Fakhr al-Razi, under the commentary of verse 42:23, Part 27, p167
- al-Bazzar, on the authority of Ibn Abbas and Ibn Zubair with the wording "drowned" instead of "perished".
- al-Sawa'iq al-Muhriqah, by Ibn Hajar Haythami, Ch. 11, section 1, p234 under Verse 8:33. Also in section 2, p282. He said this Hadith has been transmitted via numerous authorities.
- Tarikh al-Khulafaa and Jami' al-Saghir, by al-Suyuti al-Kabir, by al-Tabarani, v3, pp 37,38 al-Saghir, by al-Tabarani, v2, p22
- Hilyatul Awliyaa, by Abu Nu'aym, v4, p306
- al-Kuna wal Asmaa, by al-Dulabi, v1, p76
- Yanabi al-Mawaddah, by al-Qundoozi al-Hanafi, pp 30,370

Around eight companions of the Prophet as well as eight disciples of the companions have narrated this famous hadith. Also, around sixty scholars and authors have recorded it in their books. I have given some of the references above to clarify the authenticity and the importance of this tradition of the Prophet. Some of the well-known companions who have narrated this hadith are Ibn Abbas, Abdullah Ibn Zubair, Abu Saeed, Anas bin Malik, and Abu Dharr.

Just like the hadith of Thaqalayn, the Prophet told his companions that the Ahlulbayt were like the Ark of Noah i.e., if the companions followed the Ahlulbayt they would be guided and they would be saved, whereas if they turned away from the Ahlulbayt they would perish and drown. Again, Prophet is clearly implying that it would be the leadership of Ahlulbayt which would guide the Islamic nation after his demise.

The content and the context of both these traditions clearly prove that they were meant for a time when Prophet had departed from this world. Because while the Prophet was alive and was at the helm of the Islamic State there was no need to follow anybody else, as the Prophet was the ultimate guide who was designated by Allah to lead mankind. The hadith of the Ark of Noah, or the Hadith of Thaqalayn mentioned previously would only come into play after the death of the Prophet, when he is no longer present to guide the companions and the wider Muslim Ummah.

The comparison by the Prophet of his Ahlulbayt to the Ark of Noah was also not without wisdom. Prophet Noah had constructed his ark towards the end of his mission, and whoever embarked on his ark found salvation i.e., whoever followed and accepted the leadership of Prophet Noah was saved and guided, and whoever refused to accept his leadership and authority was doomed.

Similarly, Prophet is telling his companions towards the end of his mission that my Ahlulbayt are like the ark of Noah, if you follow their leadership and accept their authority then you will be guided and you will stay on the path of salvation, and if you don't, then you will perish.

The reason why Prophet was so clear and explicit in his words was because the Prophet wanted his companions to clearly understand the fact that the leadership of the Muslim nation belonged to the Ahlulbayt. Since they were the only people whom Prophet had designated and trained to lead his Ummah (Muslim nation), and he had considered his Ahlulbayt to be the custodian of his Sunnah.

Again, these traditions of the Prophet testify and confirm the fact that Prophet was not passive about the future of the Islamic movement that he had started. On the contrary, he had decided in his lifetime as to who would lead that movement in his absence.

5.4. Do not be Ahead of the Ahlulbayt

Another famous tradition of the Prophet which follows a similar pattern where the Prophet instructs his companions that they should neither lead the Ahlulbayt nor should they turn away from them.

The Prophet had famously said about the Ahlulbayt:

> *"Do not be ahead of them for you will perish, do not turn away from them for you will perish, and do not try to teach them since they know more than you do!"*
>
> - *al-Durr al-Manthoor, by al-Suyuti, v2, p60*
> - *Al-Sawa'iq Al-Muhriqah by Hajar Al Haythami Vol 1, Pg 439*
> - *al-Sawa'iq al-Muhriqah, by Ibn Hajar al-Haythami, Ch. 11, section 1, p230, quoted from al-Tabarani, also in section 2, p342*
> - *Usdul Ghabah, by Ibn al-Athir, v3, p137*
> - *Yanabi' al-Mawaddah, by al-Qundoozi al-Hanafi, p41, and P335*
> - *Kanz al-Ummal, by al-Muttaqi al-Hindi, v1, p168*
> - *Majma' al-Zawa'id, by al-Haythami, v9, p163*
> - *Aqabat al-Anwar, v1, p184*
> - *A'alam al-Wara, pp 132-133*
> - *Tadhkirat al-Khawas al-Ummah, Sibt Ibn al-Jawzi al-Hanafi, pp 28-33*
> - *al-Sirah al-Halabiyyah, by Noor al-Din al-Halabi, v3, p273*

Once again both the content and the context of the hadith clearly refers to an era after the demise of the Prophet, as during the lifetime of the Prophet the leadership of the Muslim Ummah was solely in the hands of the Prophet. And neither the Ahlulbayt nor any other group had a right to lead the Ummah while the Prophet was still alive.

The above hadith of the Prophet could not be any more explicit or clear. This hadith is split into three parts which I will briefly discuss.

In the first part of the hadith the Prophet of Allah is commanding the companions that they should not be ahead of the Ahlulbayt, explicitly telling the companions that the right of the leadership only belonged to the Ahlulbayt, and they are the ones who would lead the Islamic nation. The Prophet does not stop there but he further warns the companions that if they did try to lead the Ahlulbayt, or if they went ahead of the Ahlulbayt then they would perish and they would be doomed.

The second part of the hadith commands the companions to follow the Ahlulbayt and not to turn away from them, clearing telling the companions that their job was to accept and follow the leadership of the Ahlulbayt. Again, the Prophet warns the companions that if they did not follow the Ahlulbayt and turned away from them then they would perish.

The third part of the hadith informs the companions that the Ahlulbayt were more knowledgeable than them, clearly stating that the knowledge of the Ahlulbayt was superior to the knowledge of the companions, hence the companions must follow and adhere to the teachings of the Ahlulbayt. Furthermore, he forbids the companions from teaching the Ahlulbayt because he considered the Ahlulbayt to be the custodian of his knowledge and Sunnah.

The head of the Ahlulbayt after Prophet Muhammad was Ali, who was brought up in the house of the Prophet. In other words, Ali was brought up in the house of knowledge and wisdom, unlike any other companion. Ali had acquired his knowledge, his merits, his traits and his wisdom from the prolonged company and the training of the Prophet.

It is for this reason that Prophet was commanding the companions to recognize the knowledge of the Ahlulbayt, as he had considered his Ahlulbayt to be the custodian of his knowledge and Sunnah, and he expected them to lead the Muslims after his death.

This tradition of the Prophet is another testament to the fact that the Prophet of Allah had not left the Ummah without guidance regarding the future leadership of the Muslims. He explicitly declares that the leadership of the Muslims was in the hands of the Ahlulbayt, and he not only instructs the companions to follow them, but he also forbids them from leading the Ahlulbayt.

5.5. The Reward of the Prophet

As we have seen earlier that the Ahlulbayt were made righteous and noble as a result of Prophets prayers through divine guidance, so that they could lead the Muslims in his absence. Similarly, Allah has also made the love of Ahlulbayt compulsory and an Islamic duty as a reward for the fulfilment of Prophet's mission.

We read the verse of Affection (Mawaddah) in Holy Quran:

> "...Say (O' Muhammad unto mankind): I do not ask of you any reward for it (preaching the message), but love for my relatives (Ahlulbayt)..."
>
> - *Quran (42:23)*

The famous commentators of the Holy Quran such as Fakhr al-Din al-Razi, al-Tabari, Musnad Ahmad Ibn Hanbal, al-Qurtubi and many others have mentioned the following tradition of the Prophet while explaining the above verse.

The tradition is narrated by Ibn Abbas:

> When the above verse (42:23) was revealed, the companions asked: "O' the Messenger of Allah! Who are those near kin whose love Allah has made obligatory for us?"
> Upon that the Prophet (S) said: "'Ali, Fatimah, and their two sons." He (S) repeated this sentence thrice.
>
> - *Tafsir al-Kabir, by Fakhr al-Din al-Razi, Part 27, pp 165-166*
> - *Tafsir al-Tha'labi, under the commentary of verse 42:23 of Qur'an*
> - *Tafsir al-Tabari, by Ibn Jarir al-Tabari, under verse 42:23*

- *Tafsir al-Qurtubi, under commentary of verse 42:23 of Qur'an*
- *Tafsir al-Kashshaf, by al-Zamakhshari, under commentary of verse 42:23*
- *Tafsir al-Baidhawi, under the commentary of verse 42:23 of Qur'an*
- *Tafsir al-Kalbi, under commentary of verse 42:23 of Qur'an*
- *al-Madarik, in connection with verse 42:23*
- *Dhakha'ir al-Uqba, by Muhibbuddin al-Tabari, p25*
- *Musnad Ahmad Ibn Hanbal,*
- *al-Sawa'iq al-Muhriqah, by Ibn Hajar Haythami, Ch. 11, section 1, p259*
- *Shawahid al-Tanzeel, Hakim Hasakani, al-Hanafi, v2, p132*
- *Many others such as Ibn Abi Hatam, al-Tabarani, etc.*

The verse of the Holy Quran commands the Prophet to inform the Muslims that the only reward that Allah seeks for the fulfilment of Prophet's mission is the love of his Ahlulbayt. So, according to the Holy Quran the reward for the efforts, the endeavour, and the sacrifice that Prophet had made in spreading the Message of Islam is for the Muslims to love his progeny (Ahlulbayt).

In other words, Allah is telling the believers that in order to show their gratitude to the Prophet for fulfilling his mission, and for bringing them to the right path, is to love his Ahlulbayt. The verse in fact makes the Ahlulbayt an integral part of the mission of the Prophet, since the only reward that Allah seeks for the completion of Prophet's mission is the love of his Ahlulbayt.

Ahlulbayt were indeed part of the mission of the prophet throughout his life. It was the sword of Ali that had defended the Prophet at every step of the way and had turned the tables in favour of Islam and Muslims in every decisive battle against the enemies of Islam.

The Prophet had also made the Ahlulbayt to be a part of his mission by instructing the companions and the Muslims to follow and adhere to their leadership in his absence, as we saw in previous sections.

> *"O people I am leaving in you two elements if you follow you shall not go astray. They are the Book of God and the members of my House."*
> - *Al-Hakim Al-Mustadrak part 3 p. 109.*

The verse of Mawaddah further confirms and validates the strategy adopted by the Prophet for the continuity and the success of the Islamic movement both during his lifetime and after his death. The Holy Prophet had personally commented on the above verse (Quran 42:23) and said:

> *"Verily Allah has dedicated my wage (of Prophethood) to love of my Ahlulbayt, and I shall question you about it on the day of judgment."*
> - *Dhakha'ir al-Uqba, by Muhibbuddin al-Tabari, p26*
> - *al-Sirah, by al-Mala*

The Prophet essentially reiterates the words of the Holy Quran but adds that he would in fact question the believers if they had actually loved his Ahlulbayt.

The question now arises as to what "love" actually means?

In the Islamic context the word "love" symbolizes obedience and compliance. Love in Islamic thought advocates following in the footsteps of the person that one chooses to love. For instance, all Muslims are instructed by Allah to love the Holy Prophet. But mere love of the Holy Prophet without following his Sunnah and without following the path laid out by the Prophet has no meaning or value in the eyes of Islam.

True Love in the Islamic sense can only be expressed by following in the footsteps of the individual or the personalities that one claims to love. A Muslim who goes against the clear teachings of the Holy Prophet cannot claim to love the Prophet of Allah. Their claim of the love of the Prophet would have no substance or value and would not be rewarded on the Day of Judgment.

The only way a Muslim can show his true love for the Prophet is to submit to the Sunnah of the Prophet, and to comply with his teachings and to obey the commands of the Prophet in his daily life, otherwise his claim of love for the Prophet is a mere deception.

This is exactly what the verse of Mawaddah is demanding from the companions and the Muslims, that they should follow in the path and the footsteps the Ahlulbayt. They should submit to the teachings of the Ahlulbayt and comply with their commands, as simply loving them without accepting their authority or following in their footsteps serves no purpose and nor does it have any value.

The Holy Quran would not simply ask the Muslims to love the progeny (Ahlulbayt) of the Prophet, unless the Ahlulbayt were viewed by Allah as role models who were worthy enough to be followed. The words of the Holy Quran are not without wisdom or a sense of purpose.

The true love, which the verse of Mawaddah refers to is in fact the obedience and submission to the authority of the Ahlulbayt, since love without compliance is worthless in the eyes of Islam. The only reason why the Holy Quran is demanding the Muslims to love the Ahlulbayt is because Allah wants the Muslims to follow and adhere to the path and the teachings of the Ahlulbayt.

The verse of Mawaddah in other words instructs the Muslims to accept the authority and the leadership of Ahlulbayt, as a reward for the service of the Prophet in the path of Allah.

This notion is indeed confirmed by another saying of the Prophet:

> *"Acknowledgment of Aale-Muhammad (the family of Muhammad) means salvation from the fire, and love for them is a passport for crossing the bridge of the Siraat, and obedience to them is a protection from divine wrath."*
> - *Kitab al-Shafa, by Qadhi 'Ayadh, published in 1328 AH, v2, p40*
> - *Yanabi al-Mawaddah, al-Qundoozi al-Hanafi, section 65, p370*

The Prophet is instructing the believers that the love and the obedience of Ahlulbayt would keep them on the path of Salvation and would allow them to cross the bridge of Siraat on the Day of Judgment.

The Prophet states that the acknowledgement of the Ahlulbayt means salvation from hell fire. However, simply acknowledging the Ahlulbayt as the family of the Prophet could not possibly save anybody from hell fire, since all Muslims were already aware that Ali, Fatima, Hasan and Hussain were the family of the Prophet.

The acknowledgement of the Ahlulbayt actually means to recognize the true position of the Ahlulbayt in relation to the Prophet, and to accept their authority and leadership in the absence of the Prophet, as that is the only way to truly acknowledge the Ahlulbayt.

And in the last part of the hadith the Prophet again reminded the Muslims that they were meant to obey the Ahlulbayt, since it was the obedience of the Ahlulbayt which is a protection from divine wrath. When the Prophet was alive the protection from divine wrath was achieved by obedience to the Holy Prophet, but when the Holy Prophet was no longer present that protection was offered by obedience to the Ahlulbayt.

In another famous tradition the Prophet of Allah further clarifies the status and the stature of the Ahlulbayt to his companions. The Prophet looked towards Ali, Hasan, Hussain, and Fatimah and then said:

> "I am in war with those who will fight you, and in peace with those who are peaceful to you."

- Sahih al-Tirmidhi, v5, p699
- Sunan Ibn Majah, v1, p52
- Fadha'il al-Companions, by Ahmad Ibn Hanbal, v2, p767, Tradition #1350
- al-Mustadrak, by al-Hakim, v3, p149
- Majma' al-Zawa'id, by al-Haythami, v9, p169
- al-Kabir, by al-Tabarani, v3, p30, also in al-Awsat
- Jami' al-Saghir, by al-IBanu, v2, p17
- Tarikh, by al-Khateeb al-Baghdadi, v7, p137
- Sawaiq al-Muhriqah, by Ibn Hajar al-Haythami, p144
- Talkhis, by al-Dhahabi, v3, p149
- Dhakha'ir al-Uqba, by al-Muhib al-Tabari, p25
- Mishkat al-Masabih, by Khatib al-Tabrizi, English Version, Tradition #6145

The Prophet of Allah had prayed for the righteousness and the purification of his Ahlulbayt, to ensure that the Ahlulbayt always remained on the path of truth. The Prophet had covered the Ahlulbayt with a cloak and prayed to Allah for their righteousness. He also went to the door of Ahlulbayt every day for at least six months and supplicated to Allah to purify them from sins and misguidance.

The Prophet was now telling the companions that if they fight the Ahlulbayt or make war with them, then it is like as if they have made war with him. In other words, the Prophet is telling the companions that the Ahlulbayt are the righteous group, and they should not be challenged or disputed with or fought against. Because the authority that the Ahlulbayt command is similar to the authority of the Prophet, and if the companions would challenge the authority of the Ahlulbayt, then it is like as if they have challenged the authority of the Prophet itself.

In the second part of the hadith the Prophet is telling the companions that he is at peace with those who are at peace with the Ahlulbayt. Being at peace with the Ahlulbayt has a deeper meaning. It does not simply mean to remain peaceful with the Ahlulbayt which of course is a must, but the peace that the Prophet is actually referring to in relation to the Ahlulbayt is to be at peace with the authority of the Ahlulbayt.

It is a peace where one accepts the statements, the deeds and the actions of the Ahlulbayt as righteous and worthy of being followed, because it was the Prophet who had established the authority and the leadership of Ahlulbayt over the Muslims.

It is for this reason that Prophet of Allah had also said about the Ahlulbayt that:

> "Regard the Ahlul-Bayt among you as the head to the body, or the eyes to the face, for the face is only guided by the eyes."

- Is'af al-Raghibeen, by al-Saban
- al-Sharaf al-Mua'abbad, by Shaikh Yusuf al-Nabahani, p31, by more than one authority

The beautiful analogy of the Prophet once again confirms the leadership credentials of the Ahlulbayt. The head guides the body as we move, and the eyes guide the face. The Prophet of Allah wanted the Ahlulbayt to guide the Muslims in a similar way. The Prophet wanted the Ahlulbayt to be the head of the Islamic movement in his absence. The Prophet wanted the Ahlulbayt to lead the Islamic nation after his demise and hence he made this amazing analogy which needs no explanation.

5.6. The Blessings and Salutations on the Ahlulbayt in Daily Prayer

The Prophet of Allah has asked Muslims to send blessing and salutations on the Ahlulbayt in the five daily prayers. Many Muslim scholars consider sending blessing on the Prophet and his family as a pillar of the prayer i.e., an integral part of the prayer, without which the prayer is considered invalid. However, some scholars consider it to be obligatory, but they do not consider it as a pillar of prayer, while some scholars consider it to be the Sunnah of the Prophet.

The words which are used to say the blessing and the salutations to the Prophet and his Ahlulbayt are:

> "O Allah bestow Your favour on Muhammad and on the family of Muhammad as You have bestowed Your favour on Ibrahim and on the family of Ibrahim, You are Praiseworthy, Most Glorious. O Allah, bless Muhammad and the family of Muhammad as You have blessed Ibrahim and the family of Ibrahim, You are Praiseworthy, Most Glorious."

The importance of prayer in Islam cannot be overstated. The Prophet of Allah has said regarding the prayer:

> "The first thing that will be judged among a person's deeds on the Day of Resurrection is the prayer. If that is in good order, he will pass the test and prosper, and if that is defective, he will fail the test and will be a loser.
> - *Sunan Al-Tirmidhi*

Prayer is considered as one of the pillars of Islam. It has been made obligatory on every Muslim to pray five times a day. The prayer is a means by which a Muslim establishes a connection with its creator. A prayer is considered to be the shield of a believer as it brings a believer closer to Allah. And a prayer is also a way of keeping a Muslim on the path of truth and righteousness.

By asking the Muslims to give blessings and salutations to the Ahlulbayt in every prayer, the Prophet of Allah is emphasizing the pivotal role that the Ahlulbayt should enjoy in the eyes of the believers. By exalting the Ahlulbayt in every prayer the Prophet is reminding the Muslims of their duty, which is to follow and adhere to the path of the Ahlulbayt.

Just as the prayer is meant to keep a Muslim on the straight path, the path of Ahlulbayt will lead a Muslim to the path of righteousness. Just as prayer is a shield against sins and temptations, the path of Ahlulbayt is a shield against misguidance and ignorance. Just as a prayer will bring a believer closer to Allah, the path of the Ahlulbayt will keep a believer on the path of Allah. It is for this reason that Prophet had asked Muslims to be mindful of Ahlulbayt in their daily prayers, because the Ahlulbayt are like the ark of the Noah, whoever embarked on it was saved and whoever turned away from it was drowned.

The Holy Quran has commanded the Muslims to send salutations and blessings to the Prophet.

The Holy Quran states:

> "Allah and His angels send blessings on the Prophet. O ye who believe! you also should invoke blessings on him and salute him with the salutation of peace"
> - *(Quran 33:57)*

When this verse was revealed, many companions asked the Holy Prophet as to how should they comply with the command of Allah. The Holy Prophet responded to the companions with the following tradition which is reported in al-Bukhari and is narrated by Ka'b bin Ujra.

> *It was said, "O Allah's Apostle! We know how to greet you, but how to invoke Allah for you?" The Prophet said, "Say: O Allah! Send your blessings/greetings (Salawat) on Muhammad and his family, the same way as You sent Your blessings/greetings on Abraham's family. You are indeed worthy of all praise, full of glory.'"*

- Sahih al-Bukhari Hadith: 6.320

Abu Said al-Khudri also narrated as to how should one send salutations on the Prophet.

> *We said, "O Allah's Apostle! (We know) this greeting (to you) but how shall we invoke Allah for you?" He said, "Say: O Allah! Send your greetings on Muhammad who is Your servant and Your Messenger, the same way as You sent Your greetings on Abraham's family. And send Your blessings on Muhammad and on Muhammad's family, the same way as You sent Your blessings on Abraham's family."*

- Sahih al-Bukhari Hadith: 6.322

In similar tradition the Prophet again taught his companions on how to send blessings and salutations on him.

> *The Messenger of Allah said: "Do not salute for me in short!"*
> *The companions asked, "What is saluting in short?"*
> *The Prophet replied, "Saying that Blessing of Allah be upon Muhammad."*
> *They asked, "what should we say?"*
> *The Prophet (S) answered, "Say: Blessing of Allah be upon Muhammad and his Ahlulbayt."*
> *In another wording the Prophet replied: "Say: O Allah bless Muhammad and his household the same way as you blessed Abraham and his household. Verily you are worthy of all praise full of all glory!".*

- al-Sawa'iq al-Muhriqah, by Ibn Hajar, Ch. 11, section 1, p225

Allah commanded the Muslims to send salutations to the Prophet in the Holy Quran. The companions asked the Prophet as to how should they send salutations on him. The response of the Prophet is full of wisdom and insight. He informed the companions that whenever they send blessings and salutations on him, they should also send blessings and salutations on his Ahlulbayt too.

The Prophet of Allah is instructing the companions to simultaneously pray for his Ahlulbayt whenever they pray for him, clearly giving the Ahlulbayt a position next to his own position. By doing so, the Prophet is in fact asking the companions and the wider Muslims Ummah to regard the Ahlulbayt as a guide and a role model, just as they regard him as a guide and a role mode.

As we go through the various traditions and sayings of the Prophet it becomes apparent and clear that Prophet had given the Ahlulbayt a unique and an exalted position, a position that he had not given to any other Muslim group. The reason for this unique and the distinct position of the Ahlulbayt was obvious. As part of the strategy that Prophet had devised for the future of the Islamic movement, his Ahlulbayt were to play a pivotal role in guiding and keeping the rest of the Muslims on the right path.

Just as the Prophet was the leader of all the Muslims and the head of the Islamic State, he wanted that position of leadership to belong to the Ahlulbayt in his absence. That is why he was asking the companions to exalt the Ahlulbayt and to send blessing and salutations on them even in the five daily prayers, to constantly remind the Muslims about the actual status and the position of the Ahlulbayt in Islam.

In another famous tradition of the Prophet, he again confirms the exalted status and the stature of the Ahlulbayt.

The Messenger of Allah said:

> "My Ahlulbayt are like the Gate of Repentance of the Children of Israel; whoever entered therein was forgiven."
>
> - Majma' al-Zawa'id, by al-Haythami, v9, p168
> - al-Awsat, by al-Tabarani, Tradition #18
> - Arba'in, by al-Nabahani, p216
> - al-Sawa'iq al-Muhriqah, by Ibn Hajar al-Haythami, Ch. 11, section 1, pp 230,234

The Prophet of Allah is comparing the Ahlulbayt to the Gate of Repentance for the Children of Israel. The Prophet is telling the companions that if they follow and accept the path of the Ahlulbayt, they would be forgiven and they would find salvation. Just as he had earlier told them that the Ahlulbayt were like the ark of the Noah, and whoever embarked on it was forgiven and saved.

Again, we witness that the Prophet of Allah was reminding the companions time after time about the Status and the position of the Ahlulbayt, to make it clear to them and to the wider Muslims as to how he had envisaged the future of Islam in his absence, and how he had considered his Ahlulbayt to be the custodian of his Sunnah.

5.7. The Challenge from the People of Book (Mubahila)

In the ninth year after the Hijrah a Christian delegation came to Madinah from Nijran to inquire about Islam, and to debate with the Prophet about the new faith that he was propagating. A dialogue took place between the Messenger and the delegation in which the Prophet of Allah stated the positive position of Islam towards the teachings of Jesus (Prophet Isa). However, the delegation persisted in their negative attitude towards the message of Islam and the Prophet of Allah.

A revelation came to the Prophet commanding him to invite the delegation to a prayer which would be offered by both sides, asking the God to bring down His punishment on the party which was on the path of falsehood.

The revelation of the Holy Quran stated:

> "Then whoever disputes with you concerning him ['Isa (Jesus)] after (all this) knowledge that has come to you, [i.e. 'Isa (Jesus)] being a slave of Allah, and having no share in Divinity) say: (O Muhammad SAW) "Come, let us call our sons and your sons, our women and your women, ourselves and yourselves - then we pray and invoke (sincerely) the Curse of Allah upon those who lie."
>
> - Quran 3:61

The Messenger was commanded by Allah to invite the Christian delegation for a confrontational prayer, where each side would invoke the curse of God on the other, and whoever was on falsehood would be perished. Once the date and the time of the confrontation was set, the Holy Prophet took his Ahlulbayt i.e., Ali, Hasan, Hussain, and Lady Fatima from the Muslim side to challenge the Christians. This event is famously known as the event of Mubahila (Malediction).

This milestone event in the Islamic history has been documented by almost all the historians, narrators, and commentators. Zamakhshari, in his Tafsir al-Kashshaf, narrates the event in the following way:

> When this verse (Quran 3:61) was revealed, the Prophet invited the Christians to the malediction, to invoke the curse of Allah upon the liars. The Christians held a discourse among themselves that night in which their leader, 'Abd al-Masih stated his views. He said, "O Christians, know that Muhammad is a God-sent Prophet who has brought you the final message from your Lord. By God, no nation ever dared to challenge a Prophet with malediction ....
>
> The next day, the Prophet, carrying Hussain in his arms, leading Hassan by the hand, followed by his daughter Lady Fatima, behind whom came Ali, entered the appointed place and the Prophet was heard saying to his family, "When I invoke Allah, second the invocation."
>
> The pontiff of Najran, upon seeing the Prophet and his family addressed the Christians:
>
> "O Christians! I am witnessing such faces that if God wishes, for their sake, He would move mountains for them. Do not accept their challenge for malediction, for if you do, you would all perish and there will not remain any Christians on the face of the earth till the Day of Resurrection."
>
> Heeding his advice, the Christians said to the Prophet, "O Abul-Qasim, we have decided not to hold malediction with you. You keep your religion, and we will keep ours."

- Musnad Ahmad Ibn Hanbal, Vol. 1, 185;
- Tabari, Tafsir, Vol. 3, 192;
- al-Hakim, al-Mustadrak, Vol. 3, 150;
- al-Hafiz Abu Nu'aym, Dala'il al-Nubuwwah, 297;
- al-Naysaburi, Asbab al-Nuzul, 74;
- Abu Bakr Ibn al-'Arabi, Ahkam al-Qur'an, Vol. 1, 115;
- al-Fakhr al-Razi, Tafsir al-Kabir, Vol. 8, 85;
- al-Juzri, Usd al-Ghabah, Vol. 4, 25;
- Ibn al-Jawzi, Tadhkira Sibt, 17;
- Qurtubi, al-Jami' li-Ahkam al-Qur'an, Vol. 3, 104;
- Tafsir Ibn Kathir, Vol. 1, 370;
- Ibn Kathir, al-Bidayah wal-Nihayah, Vol. 5, 52;
- Ibn Hajar al-Asqalani, al-Isabah, Vol. 2, 503;
- Ibn al-Sabbagh al-Maliki, al-Fusul al-Muhimmah, 108;
- Jalal al-Din al-Suyuti, al-Durr al-Manthur, Vol. 4, 38;
- Jalal al-Din al-Suyuti, Tarikh al-Khulafa', 115;
- Ibn Hajar, al-Sawa'iq al-Muhriqa

The unique and the indisputable event of Mubahilah reaffirms the unequivocal position that the Ahlulbayt held in the eyes of the Prophet and in the eyes of Allah. When a challenge was made to the truthfulness of the message of Islam, and to the Prophethood of Prophet Muhammad, Allah commanded the Prophet to take his Ahlulbayt with him as a sign and a proof for the truthfulness of his message.

When the Christian delegation saw the blessed faces of the Ahlulbayt, they lost their nerve to confront them and accepted defeat. The Christian leaders stated that we have witnessed such faces that if they invoke a prayer, even the mountains would move.

Let's briefly analyse the event of Mubahilah. The verse of the Holy Quran asks the Prophet:

> "Come, let us call our sons and your sons, our women and your women, ourselves and yourselves"

- Quran ch3, verse 61

The Quran says to the Prophet to bring his sons, but he takes the sons of his daughter Fatima. This is because the Prophet had considered Hasan and Hussain to be like his own sons. When the Holy Quran asks the Prophet to bring his women, he only takes his daughter Fatima, even though Prophet had other women in the family including his wives. This further confirms that the Ahlulbayt were the chosen members of Prophet's family, the members that Prophet himself had handpicked to be the Ahlulbayt. They were those individuals from his family whom Prophet had prayed for, so that they would be purified and be righteous as we have seen in the previous traditions of the Prophet.

However, a question arises as to why would Allah ask the Prophet to take his Ahlulbayt with him in the first place? Isn't the testimony of the Prophet alone good enough?

The testimony of the Prophet alone is of course good enough. Even before announcing the message of Islam one of the titles that Arabs had given the Prophet was "al-Sadiq", meaning, "the truthful one". The Holy Quran has also testified the truthfulness of the Prophet on many occasions. The testimony of the Prophet alone against the Christians of Nijran would have been more than enough to prove the righteousness of the message of Islam.

But it seems that the reason why Allah had instructed the Prophet to take his Ahlulbayt with him was to show the position and the standing of the Ahlulbayt, in terms of their righteousness, in terms of their virtues, and in terms of the authority that they enjoyed in relation to the Prophet. It was Allah's way of showing to the companions and the rest of the Muslims the unique and the distinct position which the Ahlulbayt commanded in his eyes.

Allah had clearly demonstrated through the event of Mubahilah that when the actual message of Islam was being challenged, it was the leadership of the Prophet alongside his Ahlulbayt was chosen by Allah to repulse the ideological attack of the Christians.

The Prophet of Allah had himself informed us in one of his traditions as to why he chose the Ahlulbayt for Mubahilah. The Prophet of Allah said:

> *"Had there been any soul on the whole earth better than Ali, Fatimah, al-Hasan and al-Husain, Allah would have commanded me to take them along with me to Mubahila. But as they were superior in dignity and respect to all human beings, Allah confined His choice on them only for participation in Mubahila."*
>
> - *narrated by Abdullah Ibn Umar - Tafsir al-Baidhawi, under the commentary of Verse 3:61*

The above tradition of the Prophet confirms beyond any doubt that the reason why the Ahlulbayt were chosen to represent the Muslim Ummah against the Christians was not because of their blood relation to the Prophet, but because of their merits and virtues and because of their distinct stature and position in the eyes of Allah. There was nobody superior to the Ahlulbayt to represent the Muslims in Mubahilah and hence they were chosen by Allah for this unique role.

Allah indeed wanted the Ahlulbayt to represent the Muslim nation alongside the Prophet, to show the Muslim Ummah of the exalted status of the Ahlulbayt, and to demonstrate the actual position of Ahlulbayt in relation to the Prophet, so that the rest of the Muslims could clearly see and follow their lead and authority when the time arises.

The Ahlulbayt were chosen by the Prophet to be the guiding minaret for the companions and the rest of the Muslims, as clearly demonstrated by the event of Mubahilah and various other traditions of the Prophet.

Here is another tradition of the Prophet which would further explain as to why the Prophet had chosen the Ahlulbayt for Mubahilah. The Messenger of Allah said:

> "As the stars protect mankind from losing its way in travel, so are my Ahlulbayt; they are the safeguard against discord in matters of religion"
> - al-Mustadrak, al-Hakim (quoting Ibn 'Abbas), 3:149

The Prophet says that the Ahlulbayt are a safeguard against discord in the religion, which is why when the Christians tried to create discord against the Islamic ideology, the Prophet choose the Ahlulbayt to represent the Muslim nation, and successfully defeated their challenge, proving the distinct and the exalted position of the Ahlulbayt in the religion of Islam.

It is imperative on Muslims that if they want to avoid discord in religion, they must follow the teachings and the lead of the Ahlulbayt, as ordained by the Prophet in this tradition.

Before I conclude the discussion of Mubahilah, an interesting point that comes out from the event of Mubahila, is the fact that as to why did the Prophet take Ali with him?

If we read the verse of the Holy Quran again, it says:

> "Come, let us call our sons and your sons, our women and your women, ourselves and yourselves"
> - Quran 3:61

For his sons the Prophet took Hasan and Hussain, for his women he took his daughter Fatima, but Quran did not explicitly ask the Prophet to take Ali, so why did the Prophet take Ali with him?

The only place in the verse where Prophet could take Ali was when the verse mentions "ourselves".

The Arabic word used in the verse for "ourselves" is "anfusana". The word "anfusana" is a plural of the Arabic word "nafs", which means one's own self. Hence, the only way that Prophet could take Ali with him was if he had thought of Ali as an extension of his own self, meaning that Prophet had considered Ali to be so similar and so close to him that he took him as a representative of his own self.

The above notion that Prophet had taken Ali as an extension of his own self may appear as bit of an exaggeration for the readers, who perhaps are not familiar with the closeness of Ali with the Prophet. However, this notion is completely in line with another famous tradition of the Prophet, where regarding his relationship with Ali the Prophet of Allah had said:

> "Ali is from me and I am from Ali"
> - Al-Tirmidhi, Hadith no 3719
> - Imam Ahmad in his Musnad (part 4 page 437)
> - Sunnan Ibn Majah Hadith No. 119 (Narrated by Hubshi ibn Junadah)
> - Imam al Nasai: al Sunan al Kubra, Hadith no. 8091 / Khasa'is Ali, Hadith no. 69

The reason why Prophet could say that Ali is from him, and he is from Ali was because the Prophet had adopted Ali as little boy and brought him up in his own house. He trained and groomed Ali from a small age to be his closest associate and his ideological representative. Ali resembled the Prophet in his traits, in his character, in his manners, and above all in his wisdom and in his intellect. That is why in Mubahilah Prophet takes Ali as a representation of his own self, to prove that if there was anybody who could represent the Prophet in its true sense, then that individual was none other than Ali.

The event of Mubahila took place towards the end of Prophet's mission i.e., a year before his death. There were many prominent companions around at the time. Anyone of them could have been chosen by the Prophet as part his delegation to take on the Christians of Nijran. But Prophet specifically chose Ali to emphasize the position that Ali held in relation to the Prophet. The Prophet wanted to prepare the companions and the wider Muslim Ummah for the leadership of Ali that he had envisaged after his death.

6. THE LEADERSHIP OF ALI

As we have seen in the previous chapter that Prophet of Allah had chosen and selected the Ahlulbayt to lead and guide the Muslim Ummah in his absence. The various sayings and numerous traditions of the Prophet one after the other clearly exalt the status and the stature of the Ahlulbayt and justify their authority over the Muslim Ummah.

In the light of the many traditions of the Prophet discussed in the previous chapter, the Ahlulbayt comprised of five individuals namely Prophet Muhammad, Ali, Lady Fatima, Hasan and Hussain. Lady Fatima being a woman, and Hasan and Hussain being children were not in a position to take on the leadership of the Muslim Ummah at the time of the death of the Prophet. This only left Ali from the Ahlulbayt to carry the mantle of the Islamic leadership after the demise of the Prophet.

In this section I will discuss the numerous traditions of the Prophet which declare and give Ali the unique honour of being the successor and the nominee of the Prophet.

6.1. The Home Conference (Dawat-Dhul-Ashira)

I have briefly mentioned the home conference in chapter two.

The Home Conference took place at the very onset of the Islamic movement when the message of Islam had just begun. The invitation to Islam at the time was confined to the inner circle of the Prophet. Nobody even knew what Islam was at that time. Only Ali and lady Khadija were seen praying behind the Prophet as reported by Ibn Abbas.

> *"One day Ibn Abbas, the uncle of the Prophet was sitting on a hill near the Kaaba. A trader from Yemen was sitting with him. He asked Ibn Abbas who these three persons were, praying in such a strange manner. Ibn Abbas said that the man was his nephew Mohammad , the woman was Mohammad's wife Khadija, and the boy was Abu Talib's son Ali. Ibn Abbas further adds that they follow some strange religion which we are not familiar with yet"*
> - *Ibn Hisham, al-Sirah.*

The situation in Makkah was extremely hostile to any new religion or ideology which might threaten or challenge the status quo of the Arabs. The Qurayshite tribes of Makkah were in no mood to relinquish power or adopt a new faith which might bring down their corrupt business empires. The Quraysh of Makkah were more than willing to take out and physically annihilate anyone who would dare to confront their way of life.

In this deeply tribal and violent society the Prophet of Allah needed some protection and support before he could publicly challenge the Qurayshite way of life. The Prophet came from the Banu Hashim clan of Quraysh. It made perfect sense that Prophet invites his own clan first to the path of Allah and see if he could get the kind of protection and support that he was looking for to carry forward his mission. The plan and the strategy of the Prophet was endorsed by the revelations of the Holy Quran too:

> *"And warn thy nearest kinsmen........"*
> - Quran (26:214)

It was in this context that the above Quranic verse was revealed to the Prophet for him to invite his clan to the path of Islam, so that he could gain the support of his own family first, and to see if he could find among them a group of people or an individual who was willing to work alongside him in his mission, and who would support him on the difficult road ahead. Allah wanted the Prophet to start his first public call to Islam from his own family and from his own clan.

As mentioned previously the Prophet of Allah had a plan and a strategy for the expansion of the Islamic movement that he had started in Makkah. At this stage the Prophet was not only looking for protection from his own clan by inviting them to the path of Allah, but he was also looking for a fearless soul who was going to support and help him in his mission against the Quraysh of Makkah.

The Prophet was specifically looking for someone who was willing to sacrifice his life for the revolution of Islam, someone who would endure and face the hardships and sufferings with him, someone who was not only capable of physically defending the Prophet but was also capable of defending the ideological message of Islam. And above all, the Prophet was looking for someone who could be trusted and relied upon in the most difficult of circumstances.

Prophet gathered forty influential members of his clan, the Banu Hashim, and held a feast inside the house of his uncle Abu Talib. This was the very first public invitation to Islam by the Prophet of Allah. The aim and the goal of the Prophet would be clearly evident from the following words.

> *"O children of 'Abd al-Mutallib! By Allah, I don't know any young person from among the Arabs who has brought his people something better than that which I am bringing you. I have brought you the best of this world and the next, and Allah has commanded me to invite you to it.*
>
> *So, who will be my supporter/minister in this endeavour, to be my brother, my successor, and executer?"*
> *No one stood up to accept this invitation except Ali Ibn Abi Talib, who was only about 13 years old at the time, said, "I will be your supporter/minister in this endeavour."*
>
> *The Prophet requested him to sit down and then repeated his question a second time. Again, only Ali stood up, and again the Prophet asked him to sit.*
>
> *When even on the third occasion, the Prophet heard no answer from the other family members; again, Ali stood up and repeated his support.*
>
> *The Prophet then put his hand on Ali and said:*
>
> *"This is my brother, my executer, and my successor over you, so listen to him and obey him."*

- Ihqaq al-Haqq, Vol. 4, 62;
- Tarikh al-Tabari, Vol. 2, 117 and in the English translation by W.M.Watt, Vol 6 pp 90-91
- Tafsir, by al Tabari, Vol 19, p 121;
- Kanz al Ummal, by al Muttaqi al hindi Vol 15, p 15

- *Musnad Ahmad ibn Hanbal, Vol. 1, 159;*
- *Tarikh Abul Fida, Vol. 1, 116;*
- *Nadhm Durar al-Simtayn, 82;*
- *Kifayat al-Talib, 205;*
- *Tarikh Madinat Dimishq, Vol.1, Hadith 87, 139 and 143;*
- *al-Hasakani, Shawahid al-Tanzil, Vol. 1, 420;*
- *Muhammad ibn Jarir al-Tabari, Jami' al-Bayan, Vol. 19, 131;*
- *Jalal al-Din al-Suyuti, al-Durr al-Manthur, Vol. 5, 97;*
- *Tafsir ibn Kathir, Vol. 3, 350;*
- *al-Baghdadi, Tafsir al-Khazin, Vol. 3, 371;*
- *al-Alusi al-Baghdadi,*
- *Ruh al-Ma'ani, Vol. 19, 122;*
- *al-Tantawi, Tafsir al-Jawahir, Vol. 13, 103;*
- *al-Hakim al-Naysaburi, al-Mustadrak 'ala al-Sahihayn, Vol. 3, 135.*
- *Other historical sources, such as Sirat al-Halabi, say that the Prophet added, "And he will be my minister (wazir) and inheritor (warith)."*

The plan and the strategy of the Prophet had borne fruit. The Prophet had not only revealed the message of Islam to his clan, but he was also able to find a person who was willing to help him, who was willing to support him and who was willing work with him to take on the Qurayshite tribes of Makkah. The Prophet needed a courageous and a firm supporter who would help him at every step of the way, and who would not only take on the enemies of Allah but who would also defend the life and the honour of the Prophet.

Prophet was all-alone at that time. He had no supporters or followers even in his own clan. Ali had offered his protection and his services to the Prophet at that critical moment in the life of the Islamic movement. As a reward for Ali's pledge of support for Prophet's mission, the Prophet of Allah chose him to be his brother, his executer, and his successor.

This event also clearly shows how important and critical the issue of leadership was in the eyes of the Prophet that he chooses his successor at the very onset of his mission. Ali became the successor of the Prophet at the very first public invitation to Islam. The invitation to Islam at that time was only confined to Banu Hashim. They were the only clan who had been invited to the path of Allah, and even in that close nit circle the Prophet had endorsed the message of Ali being his brother and his successor.

The Prophet was about to confront the idol-worshippers, the pagans, and the powerful Qurayshite tribes of Makkah. Soon the invitation of Islam would be extended to all the inhabitants of Arabian Peninsula, many of whom would violently and aggressively resist the message of Allah. They would do their upmost to oppose and undermine the Prophet and his message of truth. The Prophet needed a strong and a sincere supporter who would defend him, who would face off the challenges and dangers facing the Islamic movement, and who would work alongside him in establishing the Islamic faith in the Arabian desert.

The enemies of Islam were too many and Prophet could never match them in terms of their numbers. Therefore, the Prophet of Allah at that stage was after quality rather than quantity. The Prophet was after a fearless supporter who would be dedicated to the cause of Islam, and who would support the message of truth, so that it prevails over the majority who were against the Islamic way of life.

In Ali, Prophet found that sincere supporter who was willing to blindly follow the commands of the Prophet, without questioning or criticizing them.

As a reward for the pledge of support by Ali, the Prophet of Allah gave him the honour of being his brother, his executer, and his successor. These were huge and incredible honours which were bestowed by the Prophet of Allah on Ali. Ali had become the brother of the final Messenger of Allah, Ali had become the executer of the best of the creation, Ali had become the successor of the person who was chosen by Allah to be a guide for the entire mankind.

These incredible honours had placed an incredible amount of responsibility on the shoulders of Ali. Ali had to now convert his words of support into deeds and actions, which was no ordinary task. Ali had become the executor of Prophet's vision, which was the establishment of an Islamic State, where the Islamic ideology and the Islamic thought could flourish, and where the Muslims would be free to practice their faith without persecution or intimidation.

Ali had become the successor of the Prophet at a time when the Islamic State was yet to be founded. Ali had pledged his soul and blood to help the Prophet in laying the foundations of the Islamic State, which was only a vision at that time. Ali's mission was to follow the orders of the commander in chief (the Prophet) and ensure that despite the strength of opposition the Islamic way of life prevails in the desert of Arabia.

Ali had put himself at the disposal of the Prophet after his pledge of support in the home conference. History is testament to the incredible support and sacrifice that Ali had given to the Prophet in making the revolution of Islam a success. Ali stepped forward when others stepped back in face of dangers and threats. Ali's father Abu Talib threw a protective ring around the Prophet in the hostile environment of Makkah, and Ali would shadow the Prophet ensuring his safety and well-being at every step of the way.

As a child Ali defended the Prophet against the children of Quraysh who would abuse and attack the Prophet. Ali slept on the bed of the Prophet on the night of Hijrah when assassins from every tribe of Quraysh were chosen to kill the Prophet. Ali accepted the challenge of Amr Ibn Abd Wud in the battle of Moat when the rest of the Muslims were too terrified to take him on. Ali stayed back and protected the Prophet from harm in the battle of Uhud, when the majority of the companions had fled the battlefield. Ali broke the siege of Khaibar and conquered its fortress which had been besieged by the Muslim army for weeks without any success.

The Prophet gave Ali a tremendous honour when Ali had pledged support to the Prophet and his mission. However, the subsequent actions and the deeds of Ali in the service of Islam proved that Ali had also earned these titles of being the brother, the executer, and the successor of the Prophet, by practically supporting the Prophet in turning his vision of the Islamic State into a reality.

Ali was a man of promise and his words in every sense reflected his deeds.

This is why when Prophet declared Ali to be his brother, his executer, and his successor, he also ordered the audience to follow and obey Ali as well. The Prophet had said:

> "This is my brother, my executer, and my successor over you, so listen to him and obey him."

Therefore, to follow and obey Ali is to in fact honour the Sunnah of the Prophet.

6.1.1. The Precedents in History

The wish and the decision of the Prophet to find and look for a helper and a supporter in the divine mission was not unique or unprecedented in the history of the Prophets. There are similar precedents set by previous Prophets where they had asked for a supporter, a helper and a successor who would assist and strengthen them in their mission.

The Prophet Musa had asked Allah to give him a minister and a successor from his own family who would support him and help him, just like the way Prophet had gathered his close family to find among them a supporter and a trustee for his mission.

We read in the Holy Quran that when Musa received the command of Allah to take on the Pharaoh:

> "Go to Pharaoh certainly he has exceeded the limit "
> - Quran (20:24)

Musa asked his Lord to strengthen him through a minister from his own family.

> "He (Musa) said: O my Lord expand my breast. Ease my task for me and remove the impediment from my speech. So they may understand what I say. And give me a minister from my family Harun my brother. Add to my strength through him and make him share my task."
> - Quran (20:25-32)

When Allah commanded Prophet Musa to take on the Pharaoh, Prophet Musa prayed to Allah to grant him a brother and a minister from his own family who would strengthen him and support him and even share his task.

The actions of Prophet Muhammad were similar and in line with the actions of Prophet Musa. The Prophet of Allah had invited his tribe the Banu Hashim for a feast, to find among them a person who would strengthen and support his mission. Just like Prophet Musa, Prophet Muhammad wanted to choose someone from his own family who could strengthen him, support him and work with him to take on the Pharaoh of the time.

Prophet Musa chose Harun who became his brother and his successor and Prophet of Allah chose Ali to be his brother, his executer and his successor for his mission.

Similarly, Prophet Zakariya had also asked Allah for something very similar, he prayed to Allah to grant him a righteous child. We read in the Holy Quran (3:38-39) that Prophet Zakariya prayed to Allah.

> "Thereupon Zakariya prayed to his Rabb saying: "O my Rabb! Grant me a righteous child as Your special favour; surely You hear all prayers."
> - Quran (3:38)

In return for Prophet Zakariya's prayers Allah granted him a righteous child.

> "As he stood praying in the Mahrab (a prayer place in the sanctuary) the angels called out to him saying: "Allah gives you good news of a son to be named Yahya (John), he will confirm the word of Allah, he will be a great leader and chaste, a Prophet and a righteous man."
> - Quran (3:39)

Prophet Zakariya had asked Allah for a child who would follow in his footsteps, and that child (Yahya) became the successor of Prophet Zakariya and a leader of his nation.

The final Messenger of Allah had also taken a similar course. He adopted his cousin Ali as a child, kept him in his home, trained him in the ideals of the Islamic spirit and made him his successor. And just like Prophet Zakariya who wanted a righteous child from his family, the Prophet of Allah invited his family and chose among them a righteous person who was willing to help and support him in his mission, and made that righteous person (Ali) to be his brother, his executer and his successor.

The Prophet of Allah had actually confirmed that he had followed the path of the previous Prophets with these words:

> *"Every prophet has an executor and inheritor, and my executor and inheritor is Ali.*

- *Kanz Al-Omal, 6/158*
- *Tarikh Baghdad of Al-Khateeb Al-Baghdadi, 11/173*
- *Shawahid Al-Tanzil, 2/223;*
- *Yanabi Al-Mawda, 94*

This approach also guarantees and secures the continuity and the future of Prophet's mission, since it ensures that when Prophet passes away and leaves this world, a trained and a trusted deputy of the Prophet is present to take over the reign of the Islamic State, rather than leaving its future to the turn of events, or in the hands of the very people that Prophet had come to guide.

This is why the Prophet of Allah had also said:

> *"He who wishes to live as I have, and die as I will die, and enter the Garden of Eternal Bliss which Allah has promised to me – let him take Ali as his leader (wali), because Ali will never lead you away from the path of truth nor will he take you into error"*

- *al-Mustadrak al-Hakim 3:128*
- *Kanz al-Ummal al-Muttaqi al-Hindi 6:155*

The Prophet said that he who wishes to live as he did should take Ali as the leader, since Ali would keep them on the path of truth. The reason why Prophet could make such a statement about Ali was because Prophet had raised Ali in his own lap, and Ali had not only pledged support to the Prophet in the home conference, but Ali had tirelessly worked alongside the Prophet to practically support the divine mission.

Ali knew the Sunnah of the Prophet more than any other companion because Prophet had chosen Ali to be his successor and his executer from the very first public call to Islam, giving Ali a proximity that he shared with no other companion.

6.1.2. The Negative Attitude Towards the Leadership of Ali

With such a clear and explicit tradition of the Prophet in favour of Ali's leadership, one may wonder as to why Ali is still not accepted as the true successor of the Prophet by many Islamic scholars.

The answer is obvious, these scholars have predominantly grown up in societies which subscribe to the notion that Prophet did not appoint anyone to be his successor, and he left this matter to the Ummah. They have been informed from the very beginning of their Islamic education that Prophet had never chosen anyone to lead the Muslims before his death.

Therefore, when these scholars come across a hadith which favours the leadership of Ali, they either overlook the hadith as irrelevant, or interpret it in a context or a framework that denies the leadership of Ali. I will briefly discuss one of the notions used by these scholars to try and change the context of the hadith of the Home Conference (Dawat-dhul-Ashira).

These scholars would say that the incident of home conference was only meant for the clan of the Prophet i.e., the Banu Hashim. Essentially, they are implying that Ali was only chosen as a leader and a successor of the Prophet for his own tribe, the Banu Hashim, and not for the Muslims in general.

Let us see what Prophet had actually said in the home conference.

> *"O children of 'Abd al-Mutallib! By Allah, I don't know any young person from among the Arabs who has brought his people something better than that which I am bringing you. I have brought you the best of this world and the next, and Allah has commanded me to invite you to it.*
> *So, who will be my supporter/minister in this endeavour, to be my brother, my successor, and executer?"*

The words of the Prophet are clear, he is inviting his nearest kin to the path of Allah and asking for their support in his divine mission, and whoever supports him would be his successor in this mission. The Prophet is clearly not looking to choose a leader to manage the affairs of Banu Hashim. On the contrary, he is looking for a person from Banu Hashim who would support him in the mission of Islam, and whoever supports him in this mission would become his successor.

Since Ali was the only person who pledged support to the Prophet, Ali was chosen as the successor of the Prophet in supporting the mission of Islam. Ali was not chosen to succeed the Prophet as a leader for the clan of Banu Hashim. Prophet was not looking for someone in the home conference to support him in managing the affairs of Banu Hashim. This is completely absurd and illogical.

And the reason why Prophet had invited the clan of Banu Hashim first was because he was ordered by Allah to do so.

> *"And warn thy nearest kinsmen"*
> - *Quran 26:214*

The event of come conference was in fact the initiation of the Message of Islam to the public. It was merely the starting point where Prophet of Allah had begun to spread the ideology of Islam. Allah could not have possibly ordered the Prophet to inform his nearest kin so that the Prophet could find someone who could lead his own clan. Such an interpretation is completely illogical and senseless.

And there was nothing in the words of the Prophet either which would imply that he was looking for a leader of the Banu Hashim, but these are the kind of arguments given by these scholars who had been educated with a mindset that Prophet had left this world without appointing a successor.

Also, Prophet could not just choose a leader for his tribe and leave the rest of the Muslims leaderless. If we assume that Prophet had only chosen Ali as a leader for the Banu Hashim, then surely at some point Prophet would have to appoint other tribal leaders to lead their respective tribes too.

Obviously, nothing like this ever took place because the Prophet had not come to create tribal leaders. The Prophet was chosen by Allah as a leader for all the tribes of Arabia, so when Prophet chooses his successor, it is also meant for all the tribes and not just for the clan of Banu Hashim.

6.2. The Tradition of Analogy

In this famous tradition the Prophet of Allah had compared his relationship with Ali to the relationship of Prophet Musa (Musa) with Harun (Aaron). The Prophet had stated that my relationship with Ali is same as the relationship of Prophet Musa with Harun, except that there would not be a Prophet after me.

> *The Messenger of Allah said to Ali, "Your position to me is like the position of Harun was to Musa except that you are not a Prophet. I should not go unless you are my Khalifah (successor) in every believer after me."*

- *Asim Al-Shaybani in Kitab Al Sunnah. Vol. 2, Pg. 565.*
- *Ibn Abi Hasem in Al-Sunan. Vol. 2, Pg. 799 - 800.*

Harun became the successor of Prophet Musa while Prophet Musa went to the mountains. Prophet Muhammad regarded Ali to be his successor and hence he made the analogy and the comparison. The Prophet of Allah further clarifies that I will not leave this world until I declare you (Ali) to be my successor (Khalifa) over the believers.

Readers would recall that this is exactly what Prophet had earlier said about the Ahlulbayt that they were his successors (Khalifa) alongside the Holy Quran.

> "I will leave among you the two Khalifahs (Successors) after me: The Book of Allah and my Itrah (Ahlulbayt). Both shall never separate until they meet me at the 'lake-fount."

- *Ibn Abi Hasim in Zilal Al-Jannah. Vol. 2, Pg. # 643. H. # 1049.*
- *Musnad Ahmad Ibn Hanbal (Published in 1995) Vol. 35, Pg. 512. H. # 21654.*
- *Musnad Ahmad ibn Hanbal. Pg, # 5065.*

The Prophet now reaffirms the same statement in favour of Ali and declares Ali to be his successor among the Ahlulbayt. The Prophet made the declaration of analogy on several occasions, the first being in Makkah itself i.e., before the migration to Madinah.

The Prophet of Allah said:

> "I swear by He who sent me with the truth, I only left you for myself, your status to me is like the status of Harun to Musa except there is no Prophet after me, you are my brother and my inheritor'. (Ali) said: 'O Allah's messenger, what shall I inherit from you?' (The Prophet) said: 'You shall inherit from me what the prophets used to inherit'. (Ali) said: 'What did the Prophets inherit?' (The Prophet) said: 'The book of Allah and the Sunnah of the Prophet........"

- *Fadhail al-Sahaba, Volume 2, page 638 Tradition 1085*

A similar statement was made by the Prophet in favour of Ali in Madinah too. The Messenger of Allah said to Ali on the day of brotherhood when the fraternity was being declared between the Ansar and the Muhajireen (in the first year after the Hijrah):

> "By the One Who sent me with the truth I only preserved you for myself. You are to me like Harun to Musa except that there shall be no Prophet after me and you are my brother and my heir..."

- *Al-Muttaqi Al-Hindi Kanz Al-Ummal part 5 p.40 (Al-Fairouzabadi Fadha-Il Al-Khamsah part 1 p. 311)*
- *al-Muttaqi al-Hindi, Kanz al-'Ummal, Vol. V, p.31*
- *Al-Mujam al-Kabir, Volume 9, page 287 Hadith 10929*

And on a separate occasion and in the presence of Caliph Abu Bakr, Caliph Umar, and Abu Ubaydah ibn al-Jarrah the Prophet was leaning on Ali and said that your status to me is like the status of Harun to Musa. Ibn Abbas has narrated this tradition from Caliph Umar:

> "Ibn Abbas narrated that Umar said: 'I heard Allah's messenger (pbuh) saying three virtues about Ali, if I had one of these (virtues) it would be more lovable to me than anything else. I was with Abu Ubayda, Abu Bakr and a group of companions, then the Prophet (s) patted Ali's shoulder and said: 'O Ali, you are the strongest amongst the believers in faith, the first Muslim who embraced Islam and your status to me is like the status of Harun to Musa".

- *Tarikh Damishq, Volume 42 page 167:*
- *Kanz al-Umal, Volume 13, page 123 Tradition 36392:*

On another occasion, Umm Saleem, the wife of Abu Ayoub Al-Ansari whom the Holy Prophet used to visit reported that the Messenger told her:

> *"Umm Saleem the flesh of Ali is from my flesh and his blood is from my blood and he is to me like Harun to Musa."*
>
> - Kanz ul Ummal, Volume 11, page 607 Tradition 32936

In another setting, Asma bint Umays who was the wife of Jaafar Al-Tayyar had also said:

> *"I heard the Messenger of God saying to Ali: You are to me like Harun to Musa except that there shall be no Prophet after me."*
>
> - Ibn Ahd Al-Barr Al-Istee-ab part 3 p. 1098.
> - Zakhair al-Uqba, page 120

Similarly, some nineteen years after the home conference, the Holy Prophet made a similar declaration when he was heading to Tabuk with the Islamic army.

Imam Ahmed in his Musnad reports on the authority of Ibn Abbas:

> *When he (i.e., the Messenger of Allah (saw)) went on Tabuk expedition accompanied by many people." Alee asked him: 'May I join you?' The Messenger of Allah (saw) refused, whereupon Alee (a.s) wept. The Prophet (saw) then asked him: Does it not please you that your status to me is similar to that of Harun is to Musa, except there is no Prophet after me? It is not proper for me to leave this place before assigning you as my vicegerent.' The Messenger of Allah (saw) has also said the following to him: "You are my heir among every believer after me."*
>
> - Musnad Ahmad bin Hanbal. Vol. 3, Pg. 331 - 333.

Imam al-Hakim also reports a similar tradition on the authority of Ibn Abbas:

> *"...They are attacking a man (Ali) who has ten EXCLUSIVE merits...the messenger of Allah, peace be upon him, went out for the battle of Tabuk, and the people went out with him. So, Ali said to him, "Let me go out with you." Therefore, the Prophet, peace be upon him, said, "Do not weep, 'Ali. Are you not pleased that you are to me of the status of Harun to Musa, with the exception that there is no prophet after me? Verily, it is not right that I depart except with you as my khalifah (successor)"*
>
> - al-Mustadrak 'ala al-Sahihain, vol. 3, p. 143, #4652 (Beirut: Far al-Kutub al-Illmiyah;1st edition, 1411H)

Imam al-Nasai's also reports this tradition.

> *".... He (the Messenger of Allah) went out with the people for the battle of Tabuk. So, 'Ali said to him, "Let me go out with you." Therefore, he (the Prophet) said, "Do not weep, 'Ali. Are you not pleased that you are to me of the status of Harun to Musa, with the exception that you are not a prophet? You are my khalifah (successor), that is, over every believer after me."*
>
> - al-Nasai's Sunan al-Kubra, vol. 5, p. 112, #8409

Bukhari in his Sahih also recorded a similar hadith on the expedition to Tabuk.

> *Allah's Apostle set out for Tabuk. appointing 'Ali as his deputy (in Madinah). 'Ali said, "Do you want to leave me with the children and women?" The Prophet said, "Will you not be pleased that you will be to me like Harun to Musa? But there will be no prophet after me."*

- *Sahih al Bukhari Volume 5, Book 59, Number 700*

6.2.1. The Reason for the Analogy

The reasons for the analogy are obvious and clear. Harun was made the successor of Prophet Musa when Musa secluded himself for forty nights and went to the mountain to hear the words of Allah. According to the Holy Quran Prophet Musa appointed Harun to be his successor before going to the mountain:

> *"And Musa said unto his brother Harun: "Take thou my place among my people; and act righteously, and follow not the path of the spreaders of corruption."*

- *Quran 7:142*

Prophet Musa told Harun to take his place among the people while he was away. The Prophet of Allah had given the analogy of Musa and Harun because the Prophet wanted Ali to succeed him just like the way Harun succeeded Prophet Musa. Prophet wanted to reinforce and confirm that Ali was his successor just like Harun became the successor of Prophet Musa.

This analogy is further vindicated by the following verse of the Holy Quran which relates to Prophet Musa and Harun.

> *"We will certainly strengthen your arm with your brother and give both of you such authority that they shall not be able to harm you. Now proceed with Our signs. You, and those who follow you, will surely triumph"*

- *Quran (28:35)*

Not only was Harun made the successor of Prophet Musa, but Allah also gave Harun authority over the people just like the authority that Prophet Musa had enjoyed. If we recall the Home Conference this was exactly what Prophet had done when he not only declared Ali to be his successor, but he also asked the audience to follow and obey Ali, giving Ali the authority over the people.

> *"This is my brother, my executer, and my successor over you, so listen to him and obey him."*

Prophet had given Ali the authority over the believers, just like Allah had given Harun the authority over the people in the time of Prophet Musa. Allah made Harun the leader of all the Israelites in the absence of Prophet Musa, and Prophet of Allah had made Ali his successor and the leader of all the Muslims in his absence. The analogy of Harun and Prophet Musa is a logical continuation of the Home Conference.

If we read the above verse of Quran (28:35) again we will see that the wisdom of Prophet's analogy with Harun and Musa does not end there.

> *"…. they shall not be able to harm you. Now proceed with Our signs. You, and those who follow you, will surely triumph"*

- *Quran (28:35):*

In the above verse Allah had promised protection for both Harun and Prophet Musa from their enemies. This is exactly what happened with Prophet and Ali too. Prophet chose Ali to strengthen his mission, and with the will of Allah Ali was able to defend the Prophet and his mission in the most difficult of the circumstances. Despite the overwhelming number of enemies, with the protection given by Allah, Prophet and Ali always remained safe and well.

The Prophet of Allah and Ali lived for twenty-three years surrounded by danger, but the enemies of Islam were not able to harm them. The Messenger of Allah had faced situations where the Muslims had conceded defeat and had left the battlefield (Battle of Uhad). Yet through the steadfastness of the Prophet, the bravery of Ali, and the protection given by Allah, the Islamic camp remained triumphant. Allah had protected both the Prophet and Ali against the opposing forces, and history is a testament to the fact that they prevailed in every single confrontation against the enemies.

That is another reason why Prophet had compared his relationship with Ali to that of Prophet Musa and Harun, because Allah had given them protection just like he had given protection to Prophet Musa and Harun.

The final part of the Quranic verse (28:35) says that those who follow Prophet Musa and Harun would be successful.

> "….. You, and those who follow you, will surely triumph"
> - Quran (28:35)

Based on the tradition of analogy not only would Prophet and Ali be successful but those who follow them would also be successful. That is why towards the end of the tradition of analogy the Prophet of Allah had in fact said:

> "…. You are my khalifah (successor), that is, over every believer after me."
> - al-Nasai's Sunan al-Kubra, vol. 5, p. 112, #8409
> - al-Mustadrak 'ala al-Sahihain, vol. 3, p. 143, #4652 (Beirut: Far al-Kutub al-Illmiyah;1st edition, 1411H)

The Prophet of Allah wanted the believers to follow the Caliphate and the authority of Ali after him, clearly implying that the followers of Ali would be successful. The verse of the Holy Quran (28:35) and the tradition of analogy are completely in line with each other. The Prophet of Allah had explicitly declared Ali to be his successor (Khalifa) over every believer after his demise.

The Prophet of Allah had made such statements about the leadership of Ali on numerous occasions. The Prophet had informed the Muslims that after his death Ali would lead the nation, ensuring that the future of Islam would not be left to the turn of events.

> "Ali is the Wali (Master) over every believer (mu'min) after me"
> - Al-Suyuti in Jami'ul Ahadeeth. Vol. 16, Pg. # 256
> - Al-Haithami Majma Al-Zawa'id. Vol. 9, Pg. # 109 – 111

Again, the Prophet of Allah is explicitly stating that Ali is the master of every believer after him.

Another interesting point that comes out of the tradition of Analogy is the fact that Harun was the real brother of Prophet Musa. Their brotherhood was through birth, when Prophet Musa prayed to Allah to give him a brother who could strengthen him. Ali was not the real brother of the Prophet. He was Prophet's first cousin. However, the Prophet of Allah had declared Ali to be his brother in many of his traditions. The brotherhood of Ali with the Prophet is more significant, as this brotherhood was not by birth, but Ali had rather earned this brotherhood by supporting the mission of the Prophet at every step of the way.

This far-reaching analogy by the Messenger of Allah had given Ali all the ranks of Harun i.e., the brotherhood of the Prophet, the successorship of the Prophet, and the authority over the Muslims, except the rank of Prophethood. All the ranks which are implied in the hadith of Analogy are also clearly mentioned in the Home Conference when Prophet had said:

"This is my brother, my executer, and my successor over you, so listen to him and obey him."

The Prophet of Allah had made every effort to ensure that he leaves the message of Islam in secure and capable hands, hands that he could trust and rely upon. The hands of Ali had served Islam from its very first public call through to all of its decisive battles, until the Islamic ideology became the dominant force in the Arabian Peninsula.

The Prophet of Allah was the visionary, and the architect of the Islamic State and Ali was the distinguished force which destroyed its advisories and secured the vision of the Prophet. Hence, Prophet had declared Ali to be his successor so that the future of the Islamic movement that he had started could be secured and guaranteed.

6.2.2. The Negative Attitude Towards the Tradition of Analogy

As I have said earlier that the primary reason as to why many scholars deduce a different outcome from the explicit traditions about the leadership of Ali is because the concept that Prophet had chosen a successor to lead the Ummah is an alien one for them. They try and understand all such traditions of the Prophet within the realms and context that Prophet did not appoint a successor in his lifetime. This notion has been ingrained in their minds from the very start of their Islamic education.

On the tradition of Analogy between Ali and Harun these scholars would argue that this hadith came on a specific occasion, namely on the journey to the battle of Tabuk, so Prophet had chosen Ali as a successor just for that occasion. Also, since Musa had gone away for only forty nights when he appointed Harun as his successor, the successorship of Ali was also a temporary one. Ali was not chosen as the permanent successor of the Prophet.

6.2.2.1. Ali's Appointment was for a Specific Occasion

To say that Prophet made the analogy between Ali and Harun on a specific occasion is contradicting the facts of history. As we have seen at the start of this section that Prophet of Allah had made this analogy on many different occasions. The battle of Tabuk was one of those instances where the Prophet had also made this analogy, but it wasn't the only one.

The first instance where Prophet had made the analogy was in fact in Makkah when Prophet had declared fraternity among the Muhajireen (immigrants). The second occasion where Prophet had made the analogy was in Madinah after the Hijrah (migration), when Prophet had declared fraternity and brotherhood between the Ansar and the Muhajireen. The third occasion where Prophet had made the analogy was again in Madinah, this time in the presence of Caliph Abu Bakr, Caliph Umar and Abu Ubaydah ibn al-Jarrah.

Asma bint Umays, the wife of Jaafar Al-Tayyar had also reported the tradition of Analogy. Asma Bint Umays was not in the army that was heading to Tabuk with the Prophet. She had obviously reported the saying of the Prophet from another occasion where Prophet had repeated the analogy in front of her. Similarly, Umm Saleem, the wife of Abu Ayoub Al-Ansari had also reported that she had heard the tradition of Analogy from the Prophet. Again, she was not part of the army going to Tabuk. She had also heard the tradition of Analogy on a completely different occasion.

The Prophet of Allah had given the analogy between Ali and Harun on many occasions, not just on the occasion of Tabuk. To say that Prophet had given the analogy between Ali and Harun only on the occasion of the battle of Tabuk is untrue and contradicts the clear facts of history.

The famous history book Tarikh Damishq by Ibn Asakir has numerous other instances where Prophet had made this analogy. These can be seen in the following references.

- *Tarikh Damishq, Volume 41 page 18*
- *Tarikh Damishq, Volume 42 page 169*
- *Tarikh Damishq, Volume 42 page 179*
- *Tarikh Damishq, Volume 42 page 140*

The aim of these scholars is to diminish the significance of the tradition of Analogy by claiming that it was only mentioned on a specific occasion in Madinah when Prophet was leaving for the battle of Tabuk. And in doing so they ignore and overlook all the other occasions where Prophet had made such a declaration. Because the aim is to in fact understand everything with the realm that Prophet had never chosen anyone to be his successor.

Unfortunately, this approach results in denying the clear Sunnah of the prophet which was in favour of Ali's right to the leadership of the Muslim Ummah.

6.2.2.2. *Ali was a Temporary Successor of the Prophet*

These scholars would further argue that since Musa had gone away for only forty nights when he appointed Harun as his successor, the successorship of Ali was a temporary one too while Ali was left behind by the Prophet in Madinah.

It is true that Ali became the temporary successor of the Prophet on the occasion of Tabuk, but since this tradition is mentioned on numerous other occasions, the implications of this tradition could not be confined or restricted to the occasion of Tabuk alone. The Prophet had mentioned the tradition of Analogy on various instances, but he did not appoint Ali as temporary successor on any of those occasions. This is because the tradition of Analogy is not linked to the temporary successorship of Ali. The Prophet was simply reiterating the tradition of Analogy on the occasion of Tabuk to console Ali, as Prophet was not taking Ali on the military expedition which was upsetting Ali.

If Prophet had only mentioned the tradition of Analogy on the occasion of Tabuk, then there was a possibility that Prophet was only referring to Ali as a temporary successor. However, when we read the actual words of the Prophet even this possibility is negated in a profound manner.

To clarify this point, I will assume that Prophet had only mentioned the tradition of Analogy during the battle of Tabuk. Let's revisit the words of the Prophet.

> *When he (i.e. the Messenger of Allah (saw)) went on Tabuk expedition accompanied by many people." Ali asked him: 'May I join you?' The Messenger of Allah (saw) refused, whereupon Alee (a.s) wept. The Prophet (saw) then asked him: Does it not please you that your status to me is similar to that of Haroon is to Musa, except there is no Prophet after me? It is not proper for me to leave this place before assigning you as my vicegerent.' The Messenger of Allah (saw) has also said the following to him: "You are my heir among every believer after me."*
>
> - *Musnad Ahmad bin Hanbal. Vol. 3, Pg. 331 - 333.*

The Prophet had said "your status to me is similar to that of Harun is to Musa, except there is no Prophet after me". When Prophet uses the term "after me", the Prophet is clearly saying to Ali that you will be my successor after me, except that you will not be a Prophet. If Ali was only a temporary successor of the Prophet, then Prophet would not have used the term "after me". The term "after me" clarifies that Ali was meant to be the successor of the Prophet after his death too, and not just for the expedition of Tabuk.

Also, the scholars who have taken such an attitude towards the tradition of Analogy have forgotten that Prophet of Allah had appointed temporary successors on many occasions. For instance, the Prophet had chosen the following temporary successors at different times.

- Abu Lubabah was chosen to succeed the Prophet in Madinah when he left for the Battle of Badr.
- Ibn Arfatah when the Prophet left to Doumat Al-Jandal.
- Ibn Om Maktoum during the military operations against Banu Quraidah and Banu Lihyanand Thee Qirad.
- Abu Dhar when Prophet left to Banu Al-Mustalaq.
- Numeila during the time of Khaibar.
- Ibn Al-Adbat during Omrat Al-Qada.
- Abu Raham during the time of his military journey to Makkah.
- Abu Dujanah during the Valedictory Pilgrimage.
    - *(Ibn Husahm Biography of the Prophet – Journeys of the Prophet)*

But the Prophet of Allah had never said to any one of his temporary deputies (successors) what he had said to Ali. It was exclusively in case of Ali that Prophet had said that you are to me like Harun was to Musa, except that there would be no Prophets after me. He only ever used those words for Ali and not for any of his other temporary deputies, because Ali was not a temporary deputy of the Prophet. These words of the Prophet had a specific meaning in relation to Ali, and they could not possibly be used for his temporary successors.

Furthermore, by excluding the rank of Prophethood in the tradition of Analogy, the Prophet had clearly indicated that Ali is similar to Harun in every sense except that he was not a Prophet, ensuring that all the other ranks of Harun like brotherhood and successorship were permanently bestowed upon Ali.

It is not possible that Prophet would simply give all these ranks to Ali on a temporary basis, and he will somehow revoke these ranks after the military campaign of Tabuk was over. Such a notion is absurd and illogical.

However, as these scholars do not subscribe to the theory of Ali's leadership, they try and muddle the waters by calling it a position of temporary leadership, since it suits their non-appointment mindset i.e., the Prophet did not appoint anybody to be his successor.

6.3. Ali the Heir of the Prophet's Knowledge

The Prophet of Allah had said:

> *"I am the City of Knowledge, and Ali is its Gate. So, whoever intends to enter the City and the Wisdom, he should enter from its Gate."*

- *Sahih al-Tirmidhi, v5, pp 201,637*
- *al-Mustadrak, by al-Hakim, v3, pp 126-127,226, Chapter of the Virtues of Ali, narrated on the authority of two reliable reporters: one, Ibn Abbas, whose report has been transmitted through two different chain of authorities, and the other, Jabir Ibn Abdullah al-Ansari. He said this tradition is Authentic (Sahih).*
- *Fadha'il al-Companions, by Ahmad Ibn Hanbal, v2, p635, Tradition #1081*
- *Jami' al-Saghir, by Jalaluddin al-Suyuti, v1, pp 107,374; Also, in Jami' al-Jawami'; Also, in Tarikh al-Khulafaa, p171. He said this tradition is accepted (Hasan).*
- *al-Kabir, by al-Tabarani (d. 360); Also, in al-Awsat*

- *Ma'rifah al-Companions, by al-Hafidh Abu Nu'aym al-Isbahani*
- *Ihyaa al-Ululm, by al-Ghazzali*
- *History of Ibn Kathir, v7, p358*
- *History of Ibn Asakir*
- *Tarikh, by al-Khateeb al-Baghdadi, v2, p337; v4, p348; v7, p173; v11, pp 48-50; v13, p204*
- *al-Isti'ab, by Ibn Abd al-Barr, v3, p38; v2, p461*
- *Usdul Ghabah, by Ibn al-Athir, v4, p22*
- *Tahdhib al-Athar, by Ibn Jarir al-Tabari*
- *Majma' al-Zawa'id, by al-Haythami, v9, p114*
- *Yanabi' al-Mawaddah, by al-Qundoozi-al-Hanafi, in Chapter 14*
- *Tadhkirat al-Khawas al-Ummah, by Sibt Ibn al-Jawzi (d. 654), p29*
- *Kanz al-Ummal, by al-Muttaqi al-Hindi, part 15, p13, Traditions #348- 379*
- *al-Sawa'iq al-Muhriqah, by Ibn Hajar al-Haythami, Ch. 9, section 2, p189*

The Prophet is informing the companions that Ali is the treasurer of his knowledge, and if they want to acquire the knowledge of the Prophet they must come to the door of Ali.

The words of the Prophet are full of enlightenment and wisdom. There are two clear and explicit points that Prophet had made in this tradition.

- The most knowledgeable person after the Prophet is Ali.
- And Muslims should come to the door of Ali to seek the knowledge of the Prophet.

6.3.1. The Most Knowledgeable After the Prophet

The hadith is clearly informing the companions that the most knowledgeable person in the eyes of the Prophet was Ali.

As mentioned previously Islam consisted of two distinct sets of knowledge and guidance, one was the book of Allah and the other was the Sunnah of the Prophet. These two invaluable sources of knowledge and wisdom together form the basis of the Islamic law and the Islamic faith. Ali had acquired both these sets of knowledge from the blessed company of the Prophet.

Ali had witnessed the revelations of the Holy Quran to the Prophet. Ali was with the Prophet on many occasions when the Holy Quran was being revealed by Allah. The Prophet had explained the meaning of the verses of Quran to Ali since he was a little boy. Ali grew up in the house of the Prophet witnessing the revelations of the Quran and acquiring the knowledge of the Book of Allah directly from the Prophet.

That is why Prophet had also said:

> *"Ali is with Quran, and Quran is with Ali. They shall not separate from each other till they both return to me by the Pool (of Paradise)."*

- *Al-Mustadrak, by al-Hakim, v3, p124 on the authority of Umm Salama*
- *Al-Sawa'iq al-Muhriqah, by Ibn Hajar, Ch. 9, section 2, pp 191,194*
- *Al-Awsat, by al-Tabarani; also, in al-Saghir*
- *Tarikh al-Khulafa, by Jalaluddin al-Suyuti, p173*

Similarly, Ali had the unique honour of being in the company of the Prophet while Prophet was at home and while Prophet was out in the public. No other companion had the privilege and the honour of witnessing the Sunnah of the Prophet in his house. Ali had acquired the knowledge of Prophet's Sunnah from the prolonged company of the Prophet, which began when he adopted Ali as a child and ended with the death of the Prophet.

For this very reason the Prophet had famously said that if there was a difference of opinion after me then Ali would be the one who would clarify it.

The Prophet said to Ali:

> "You explain to my Ummah after me what they differ about."
> - Al-Hakim in Al-Mustadrak ala As-Sahihain. Vol. 3, Pg. # 132, H. # 218 / 4621.

The Prophet of Allah had also stated in another of his traditions that Ali was the most knowledgeable after him.

> "The most knowledgeable person in my nation after me is Ali.
> - Manaqib Al-Imam Ali Ibn Abi Talib of Ibn Al-Maghazeli Al-Shafii.

This is why Prophet had designated Ali to lead the Muslims in his absence because Ali was the most knowledgeable of the companions, since Ali had acquired that knowledge from the house of the Prophet, an honour which no other companion shared with Ali.

Ali himself has said:

> "Whenever I asked the Messenger of Allah a question, he replied, and when I was silent he would speak to me"
> - Al-Nisai and Al-Hakim in his Mustadrak

This is how Prophet had imparted his knowledge to Ali. Ali would ask the Prophet questions to increase his knowledge, and when Ali was quiet the Prophet would still speak and impart his knowledge to Ali. The Prophet had to ensure that Ali acquires the knowledge of the Quran and the Sunnah which was essential for him to lead and guide the Muslim Ummah in Prophet's absence.

6.3.2. Muslims Should Come to the Door of Ali

Muslims should come to the door of Ali to seek the knowledge of the Prophet.

I will reproduce the tradition of the Prophet to clarify the above statement. The hadith of the Prophet states:

> "I am the City of Knowledge, and Ali is its Gate. So, whoever intends to enter the City and the Wisdom, he should enter from its Gate."

As per the above tradition the Prophet is the city of knowledge and wisdom, so whoever wants to seek the knowledge and the wisdom of the Prophet they should enter the city from its gate, which was Ali. In other words, Muslims should come to the door of Ali to seek the knowledge and the wisdom of the Prophet.

This tradition is clearly implied for a time when the Prophet is no longer around. Because, when the Prophet is alive there is no need for anyone to seek the knowledge of the Prophet from Ali, since the fountain and the city of knowledge i.e., the Prophet of Allah is available to guide the mankind.

This tradition of the Prophet comes into limelight when the Prophet of Allah had passed away. The tradition is telling the companions that if they want to acquire the knowledge of the Prophet, and if they seek to learn the Sunnah of the Prophet when he is no longer present, then they must come to the door of Ali, clearly implying that Ali was the heir of Prophet's knowledge.

This notion is confirmed by another tradition of the Prophet, where Prophet had again stated that Ali is the door to his knowledge and Ali would in fact explain to the Ummah what was been sent to the Prophet. The Prophet said:

> *"Ali is the doorway to my knowledge, and after me he will explain to my followers what has been sent to me."*
> - *Kanz al-Ummal, al-Muttaqi al-Hindi, Vol. 6, 170*
> - *Tafsir Al-Tabari, 3/171*
> - *Shawahid Al-Tanzil, 2/356*
> - *Al-Darr Al-Manthour, 6/379*
> - *Yanabi Al-Mawda, 61*

The Prophet explicitly makes Ali the doorway to his knowledge and says that after him Ali will explain his knowledge to the Ummah. In other words, Prophet has stated that after him Ali will be the heir of his knowledge, and Ali will impart his knowledge to the Ummah. It becomes abundantly clear that these traditions were meant for a time when the Prophet was no longer present among the companions.

The Prophet of Allah had given Ali the authority over his knowledge, and he advises the companions that if they desire to seek his knowledge in his absence then they should turn to the door of Ali, putting Ali in a position where the companions had no choice but to follow the lead of Ali.

Islam is an ideological movement which constituted both divine commands from the Holy Quran, and the instructions from the Sunnah of the Prophet. The Prophet of Allah was the head of this ideological movement, but after his death the Prophet wanted Ali who had the knowledge and the understanding of both the divine commands and his Sunnah to carry that mantle forward and guide the Islamic movement.

In the era of the Prophet there were no schools, colleges, or universities where people could go and acquire knowledge. There were no readily available means for the people to seek and gain knowledge. The companions and the ordinary Muslims did not just see the Holy Prophet as the Prophet of Allah, but they saw him as a teacher, as a guide and as a mentor, who would lead and advise them on all aspects of their lives.

By making Ali the doorway to his knowledge, the Prophet gave the companions a guide and a mentor who they could turn to in his absence and acquire his knowledge even after his death.

As stated previously, the Sunnah of the Prophet was not documented during his lifetime, the Prophet had to leave behind a definite means by which the companions could access his Sunnah. By making Ali the gateway to his knowledge, the Prophet had given the companions a clear and a definite source to his Sunnah.

The Prophet gave Ali the knowledge of his Sunnah and made him his successor, so that he could guide and lead the Islamic movement according to the teachings of the Prophet. The successor of the Prophet could only be a person who was able to impart Prophet's knowledge to others in Prophet's absence. Unless a leader had that ability, he could not command the title of being the "Successor of the Prophet".

6.4. Ali is the Mawla (Guardian) of the Muslims

Islam is a complete system of guidance that governs all aspects of one's life, from the moment a child is born to the moment that person is laid to rest, Islam has a set of rules and regulations that administer the entire lifespan of an individual. Islam controls all aspects of a person's life, their interactions with God, their interactions with people around them, and their interactions with the society at large. Islam stipulates guidelines and rules to manage the affairs of people both in private and in public.

The Prophet of Allah had initiated a thorough and a comprehensive system of governance for the primitive society of Arabia. The Arabs prior to the coming of the Prophet were not used to such an organized way of life, which comprised of rules and regulations that would govern all aspects of their behaviour and interaction with others and with the wider society.

Islam was a new ideological phenomenon for the Arabian Peninsula and was barely two decades old. The organized structure of life that Islam proposed and expected its followers to adhere to, demanded that the head of the Islamic movement is clear and mindful of its future leadership, which would keep that system and that structure intact in his absence.

A system such as Islam which is so comprehensive that it entails rules, regulations and commands for each and every aspect of a person's life, could not possibly ignore the issue of future Islamic leadership, which would affect the life of every single Muslim living under the Islamic State.

It is for this reason that Prophet of Allah with all his wisdom had adopted Ali at the age of four or five and trained him for over twenty years in his own house, so that one day Ali could take on the mantle of the Islamic governance.

6.4.1. The Tradition of Ghadeer

The Prophet of Allah was in the final months of his life. He was returning from his last Pilgrimage and was on his way back to Madinah, when he stopped all the pilgrims at a place called Ghadeer Khum, and there he gave a sermon, which has been narrated by around one hundred companions and has been recorded in almost all the prominent books of hadith and history that we know off.

He ordered Salman, one of his companions to use rocks and camel tooling's to make a pulpit (mimbar), so that he could deliver his sermon and make an announcement. He waited for everybody to gather around before he would deliver his message. Several thousand pilgrims who were with the Prophet gathered around him to listen to his announcement.

The Prophet ascended the pulpit and delivered a sermon, he began by praising Allah and recited around one hundred verses of the Holy Quran. He reminded the people about their responsibility towards Allah and to the religion of Islam.

The Prophet then declared the following to the audience:

> *"It seems the time approached when I shall be called away (by Allah) and I shall answer that call. I am leaving for you two precious things and if you adhere to both of them, you will never go astray after me. They are the Book of Allah and my progeny, that is my Ahlulbayt. The two shall never separate from each other until they come to me by the Pool (of Paradise)."*

Then the Messenger of Allah continued:

"Do I not have more authority over the believers than what they have over themselves? "People cried and answered: "Yes, O' Messenger of God. "Then Prophet (S) held up the hand of 'Ali and said: "Whoever I am his Mawla (Guardian), 'Ali is his Mawla (Guardian). O' God, love those who love him, and be hostile to those who are hostile to him."

- *Sahih Tirmidhi, v2, p298, v5, p63*
- *Sunan Ibn Maja, v1, pp 12,43*
- *Khasa'is, by al-Nisa'i, pp 4,21*
- *al-Mustadrak, by al-Hakim, v2, p129, v3, pp 109-110,116,371*
- *Musnad Ahmad Ibn Hanbal, v1, pp 84,118,119,152,330, v4, pp 281,368,370, 372,378, v5, pp 35,347,358,361,366,419 (from 40 chains of narrators)*
- *Fada'il al-Companions, by Ahmad Hanbal, v2, pp 563,572*
- *Majma' al-Zawa'id, by al-Haythami, v9, p103 (from several transmitters)*
- *Tafsir al-Kabir, by Fakhr al-Razi, v12, pp 49-50*
- *Tafsir al-Durr al-Manthur, by al-Hafiz Jalaluddin al-Suyuti, v3, p19*
- *Tarikh al-Khulafa, by al-Suyuti, pp 169,173*
- *al-Bidayah wal-Nihayah, by Ibn Kathir, v3, p213, v5, p208*
- *Usdul Ghabah, by Ibn Athir, v4, p114*
- *Mushkil al-Athar, by al-Tahawi, v2, pp 307-308*
- *Habib al-Siyar, by Mir Khand, v1, part 3, p144*
- *Sawaiq al-Muhriqah, by Ibn Hajar al-Haythami, p26*
- *al-Isabah, by Ibn Hajar al-Asqalani, v2, p509; v1, part1, p319, v2, part1, p57, v3, part1, p29, v4, part 1, pp 14,16,143*
- *Tabarani, who narrated from companions such as Ibn Umar, Malik Ibn al-Hawirath, Habashi Ibn Junadah, Jari, Sa'd Ibn Abi Waqqas, Anas Ibn Malik, Ibn Abbas, Amarah, Buraydah, ...*
- *Tarikh, by al-Khatib Baghdadi, v8, p290*
- *Hilyatul Awliya', by al-Hafiz Abu Nu'aym, v4, p23, v5, pp26-27*
- *al-Istiab, by Ibn Abd al-Barr, Chapter of word "ayn"('Ali), v2, p462*
- *Kanzul Ummal, by al-Muttaqi al-Hindi, v6, pp 154,397*
- *al-Mirqat, v5, p568*
- *al-Riyad al-Nadirah, by al-Muhib al-Tabari, v2, p172*
- *Dhaka'ir al-Uqba, by al-Muhib al-Tabari, p68*
- *Faydh al-Qadir, by al-Manawi, v6, p217*
- *(Yanabi' al-Mawaddah, by al-Qudoozi al-Hanafi, p297*

Before I discuss this hadith in detail, I will give a few variations of the above hadith to clarify how some of the companions have narrated this hadith.

Al-Hakim in his Mustadrak reported from Zaid Ibn Arqam, that Prophet had said:

"... O people I am leaving in you two elements you will never go astray if you follow them. They are the Book of God and the members of my House my Itrah.' Then he said: Do you know that I have more authority over the believers than they have over themselves (repeating that three times)? They said: Yes. The Messenger of God said: Whoever I am his Mawla this 'Ali is his Mawla."

- *Al-Hakim Al-Mustadrak Part 3 pp. 109-110*

Umm Selemah, the wife of the Prophet had narrated:

"The Messenger held the hand of Ali at Ghadeer Khum. He raised it until we witnessed the whiteness of his armpit and said: Whoever I am his Moula Ali is his 'Moula'. Then he said: 'O people I am leaving in you 'Al- Thaqalain' (The Two Valuables): 'Kitabullah' (the Book of God) and my Itrah (my Ahlulbayt). And they will not part with each other until they join me at the Basin (on the Day of Judgment)."

- *Al-Muttaqi Al-Hindi Kanz Al- Umal part 5 p. 23 hadith no.356.*

The following companions Abu Sa-eed Al-Khidri, Abu Qudamah Al-Arani, Hutheifah Ibn Osaid, Amir Ibn Dhumrah, Zaid Ibn Arqam and Al-Bura Ibn Azib narrated this hadith, according to Imam Ahmad in his Musnad, and Ibn Majah in his authentic Sunan, in the following way:

> "We came with the Messenger of God in his Valedictory Pilgrimage, and he stopped at the road and called for a congregational prayer. Then he took the hand of Ali and said: Am I not the Guardian who has more authority over the believers than they have over themselves? They said: Yes. He said: Do I not have more authority over every believer than he has over himself? They said: Yes. He said:
> This is the 'Wali' (Guardian) of whoever I am his Mowla (Guardian). God love whoever loves him and be hostile to whoever is hostile to him."
>
> - Imam Ahmad Al-Musnad part 4 p. 281
> - Ibn Majah in his authentic Sunan part 1 p. 45.

The last narration that I am going to quote was narrated some 27 years after the event of Ghadeer Khum. Ali was in Kufa which is a city in Iraq today. There remained a few companions of the Prophet who were still living in Kufa at that time. Ali asked the companions to see if they could remember the event of Ghadeer.

The companions could only remember part of the Prophet's sermon from Ghadeer. So, Ali asked the companions to narrate whatever they could remember, but only those companions should narrate who had directly heard from the Prophet, rather than those who were informed by other companions about the event of Ghadeer.

Seventeen companions stood up and testified that they had heard the Prophet declaring Ali to be the Mawla (Guardian) of the believers. Some of the companions who testified were Khuzeimah Ibn Thabit, Sahl Ibn Saad, Oday Ibn Hatam, Aqabah Ibn Amir, Abu Ayoub Al-Ansari, Abu Leila (or Abu Yaala), Abu Al-Haitham Ibn Al-Teihan and some men from Quraysh also testified about the incident of Ghadeer.

Abu Al-Tufail reports this incident.

> "Ali said to the companions who were at that gathering: I ask you in the name of God whoever was present on the Day of Ghadeer Khum to stand up and no one should stand to say: I was informed, or I heard. I only ask a man who directly heard by his own ear and memorized by his heart the words of the Messenger.
> "Seventeen men including Khuzeimah Ibn Thabit, Sahl Ibn Saad, Oday Ibn Hatam, Aqabah Ibn Amir, Abu Ayoub Al-Ansari, Abu Leila (or Abu Yaala), Abu Al-Haitham Ibn Al-Teihan and men from Quraysh stood up and Ali said to them: Tell us what you heard.
> They said: "We testify that we came with the Messenger of God from his Valedictory Pilgrimage. When the noon time came the Messenger of God came out. He ordered that some trees in that place be pruned; a cloth was put above those trees. He called for the prayer and we came out. He said: What shall you say?
> We said: You have delivered the Message. He said: God bear witness repeating that (three times). Then he said: I am about to be summoned (by God and I shall respond to His call). I shall be questioned, and you will be questioned.
> Then he said: "Certainly God is my 'Mawla' (Guardian) and I am the Guardian of the believers. Do you not know that I have more authority over you than you have over yourselves? We said: Yes. He said this three times. Then he held your hand Commander of Believers (Ali) and lifted it and said: 'Whoever I am his Mowla (Guardian) this is his 'Mawla'.
> God love whoever loves him and be hostile to whoever is hostile to him.' Ali said to the testifying companions: You have told the truth and I am among those who bear witness to that."

- *Imam Ahmad Al-Musnad part 4 p. 370.*
- *Al-Oundouzi Yanabi-a-Al-Mawaddah p.42. He recorded that Imam Samhoodi (nor Al-Deen Ali Ibn Abdullah Al-Shafi-i reported that Abu Na-eem in his Hilyat Al- Ouliyah) recorded it.*

I have only given four variations of this amazing tradition of the Prophet to give the readers a gist of what the Prophet had said regarding Ali at Ghadeer Khum. There are so many variations of the tradition of Ghadeer that it would be impractical to give any more variations of this hadith, as it was narrated by so many companions.

6.4.2. Analysing the Tradition of Ghadeer

On the day of Ghadeer the Prophet had essentially summarized the position and the stature of the Ahlulbayt to the masses. The Prophet had given a synopsis of what he had been saying all along about the role that Ahlulbayt and specifically Ali would play in leading the Muslims after his death.

In the presence of several thousand companions the Prophet of Allah reaffirms his vision for the future leadership of the Islamic movement. The Prophet informs the audience as to how he envisages the Muslims to follow the lead and the authority of the Ahlulbayt, especially the authority of Ali. The Prophet of Allah explicitly gives the leadership of the Muslims to Ali and expects Ali to lead the Ummah after his death.

The Prophet begins by announcing that his death was near, and he was expected to meet his creator soon, clearly implying that the speech was meant for a time after his demise.

The Prophet then informs the audience that he was leaving behind two precious things, one was the book of Allah and the other was his Ahlulbayt. The Prophet further says that both these sources of knowledge and guidance will not separate until they meet him in Paradise. The Prophet is clearly telling the audience that they must follow the book of Allah and his Ahlulbayt, as both these jewels will keep them on the path of truth.

The Prophet continues his sermon and asks the audience:

> "Do I not have more authority over the believers than what they have over themselves?"

The audience respond:

> "Yes, O' Messenger of God."

Then Prophet holds the hand of Ali and says:

> "Whoever I am his Mawla (Guardian), 'Ali is his Mawla (Guardian). O' God, love those who love him, and be hostile to those who are hostile to him."

The first thing that Prophet had asked the audience in Ghadeer Khum was to confirm that he had more authority over them then they had over themselves. This is because the Prophet wanted to clarify and drum into the audience the understanding that the declaration he was about to make was regarding the issue of authority and leadership. The Prophet wanted to use this opportunity to make the context of his speech absolutely clear to the audience, so that nobody could doubt that the Prophet was indeed speaking about the issue of authority and leadership.

Once the audience responded in affirmative, that they agree that the Prophet of Allah had more authority over them, only then the Prophet continued with his announcement. The Prophet waited for the positive response of the audience before moving on, to make sure that everybody was on the same page.

The Prophet deliberately made this part of the speech interactive, to ensure that the audience would be completely clear on the context of the speech which was about to follow.

The Prophet then held the hand of Ali and declares to the audience that whoever accepts him (the Prophet) as the Guardian, should also accept Ali as his Guardian. Again, to remove any confusion and to make it absolutely clear the Prophet of Allah held the hand of Ali, to ensure that the audience could clearly see and witness that Prophet was referring to Ali as the Guardian of the Muslims.

The Prophet of Allah as the head of the Islamic State was not just a political figure or simply a Statesman, but he was also a teacher, a mentor, a guide, and a source of knowledge and guidance for the Muslims.

When Prophet of Allah states that whoever accepts him as their guardian should now accept Ali as their guardian is in fact commanding the Muslims and the companions to accept Ali as their leader and their guide. In other words, Ali would not only be the Head of the Islamic State after the demise of the Prophet, but he would also be responsible for teaching and guiding the Muslim Ummah according to the Book of Allah and the Sunnah of the Prophet.

The Prophet was indeed telling the companions that he had vested his authority and his Guardianship in Ali, and he is the one who would lead the movement of Islam in his absence. Just as Prophet had previously stated that he was the city of knowledge and Ali was the gate, the Prophet now endorses Ali as the Guardian of his mandate and authority too.

The Prophet continues his speech and now he prays to Allah and says:

> *"O' God, love those who love him (Ali), and be hostile to those who are hostile to him (Ali)."*

As I have mentioned previously that love in Islam implies obedience, as love for the sake of love has no meaning or relevance in the Quran or the Sunnah of the Prophet. For instance, if a person claims to love Allah, then they must obey the commands of Allah, otherwise their love for Allah has no relevance in the Islamic context, as love without obedience is pointless in Islamic terminology. Allah will not be pleased with someone who simply claims to love Allah but does not follow his commands.

When Prophet says: "O' God, love those who love him (Ali), and be hostile to those who are hostile to him (Ali).", what the Prophet is saying to the audience is that Allah will love those who would follow and accept the authority and the Guardianship of Ali, and Allah will not be pleased with those who would challenge and be hostile to the authority and the leadership of Ali.

The Prophet had gone to the door Ali and the Ahlulbayt and prayed for many months for their purification and righteousness (Chapter five), because the Prophet had wanted Ali and the Ahlulbayt to be the Guardian of his message after his demise. The words of the Prophet in Ghadeer Khum could not be clearer, the Prophet had categorically stated that the Guardianship of the Muslims rests with Ali.

The Prophet had made a similar pronouncement about Ali on a previous occasion too.

The Prophet had said:

> *"Ali holds a right over this nation like the right of a father over his son."*

- *Muslim, 2/361*
- *Al-Tirmidhi, 2/299*
- *Al-Hakim, 3/130*
- *Musnad Ahmad, 3/198*
- *Al-Nisa'i, 7;*
- *Usad Al Ghaba, 3/40*

The Prophet states that the right of Ali over this nation is like the right of a father over his son. A father is a guardian and a protector of his children. A father is meant to guide his children in all spheres of their life. He is meant give them an upbringing and nurture them in a way that they become a productive member of the society. A father is meant to teach his children right from wrong, and to ensure that they make the right choices in their lives. A father is meant to be a role model for his children, so that his children could look up to him and follow his lead and example when they grow up.

This is exactly what Prophet had said about Ali. Prophet wanted Ali to be the Guardian of the Muslims, he wanted Ali to guard and protect the ideological message of Islam against deviation and distortion. He wanted Ali to guide and nurture the movement of Islam in the ideals that he had laid down for his followers. He wanted Ali to keep the Muslim nation on the right path, by guiding the Muslims according to his Sunnah.

He wanted Ali to be role model for his nation, so that his nation could follow the lead and the example of Ali when he was no longer around. After all it was the training and the upbringing of the Prophet that had made Ali the role model that he was.

As on previous occasions, on the day of Ghadeer, Ali was again declared as the Guardian of the Muslims and the Successor of the Prophet of Allah.

6.4.3. The Meaning of the Word Mawla (Guardian)

It would not be out of place here to clarify and discuss the meaning of the word "Mawla", as this word has been used in the hadith of Ghadeer and often there is a confusion and debate about its actual meaning.

If one opens the Arabic dictionary, the word "Mawla" has over twenty meanings. It can mean anything from "Owner", "Guardian", "Leader", "Guide", "Friend", "Helper", "Guest", "Neighbour", "Benefactor", "Son", "Partner" to even "Servant".

When a word has multiple meanings, the only way to understand the meaning of the word is to see the context in which the word is being used. Let's look at the context of the Ghadeer speech.

Before actually declaring Ali to be the "Mawla", the Prophet asked:

> *"Do I not have more authority (Awla bi kum) over the believers than what they have over themselves?"*

The Prophet here used the word "Awla" which means "having more authority".

The people then responded:

> *"Yes, O' Messenger of God."*
> Then Prophet (S) held up the hand of 'Ali and said: *"Whoever I am his Mawla (Guardian), 'Ali is his Mawla (Guardian)."*

The word "Mawla", in this context has the same meaning as the word "Awla", which means "having more authority". Those who try and interpret the word "Mawla" as a "Friend" have either not paid attention to the setting and the context in which this tradition was mentioned, or they are deliberately trying to distort its meaning.

The word "Mawla", in this hadith can only refer to the issue of authority and leadership, as the Prophet had begun the declaration by establishing and confirming his own authority over the audience. The word "Mawla" can only mean "Guardian", or a "Leader" or it can have any other similar meaning which is in line with the context of the hadith.

There was no reason for the Prophet to declare Ali as a friend, especially towards the end of his life, when in fact he had brought Ali up in his own house since Ali was child. It would have been a little late for the Prophet to call Ali just a friend after all these years. Also, calling Ali a friend adds no value as the audience was already aware that Ali and the Prophet were not just friends, but they were in fact cousins and brothers. The Prophet had already declared Ali to be his brother in this world and in hereafter on previous occasions.

The event of Ghadeer took place in the last three months of Prophet's life. So, calling Ali just a friend makes no sense and serves no purpose at this late hour.

Even before posing the question to the audience about his own authority over them, the Prophet had in fact mentioned the authority and the leadership of the Ahlulbayt, and he commanded the Muslims to follow them and accept their lead.

At the very beginning of the speech the Prophet had said:

> *"I am leaving for you two precious things and if you adhere to both of them, you will never go astray after me. They are the Book of Allah and my progeny, that is my Ahlulbayt"*

Unmistakably, each and every aspect of the speech of Ghadeer is set in the context of authority and leadership, and it is specifically linked to the leadership and the authority of the Ahlulbayt.

Even the physical actions of the Prophet on the day of Ghadeer testify that this event was only linked to the issue of authority and leadership. When Prophet arrived in Ghadeer the first thing he did was to ask his companions to construct a pulpit (mimbar) for him, so that everybody could clearly see him and witness his actions. Then when he made the declaration of Ali being the Mawla (Guardian) of the Muslims, he raised the hand of Ali which was a clear sign of the authority that he was vesting in Ali.

6.4.4. The Word "Mawla" and "Wali" in Quran

The words "Mawla", "Awla", "Wali", "Wilayat", all come from the root word "Wali" in Arabic. To further clarify its meaning, we will see how the Holy Quran uses the word "Wali" and "Mawla".

In Surat Al-Maidah, Allah states:

> *Your Guardian (Wali) can be only Allah; and His messenger and those who believe, who establish worship and pay the poor due, and bow down (in prayer).*
>
> - Quran (5:55) (Pickthall Translation)

The Holy Quran states that Allah is your Guardian (Wali), the Prophet is your Guardian (Wali) and those who believe and establish the prayer and pay their due i.e., Allah's righteous men can also be your Guardian (Wali).

Allah has complete authority over all his creation. He lays down the rules as to how they should act and live their lives. Allah's commands and his authority are supreme, and that is why Allah is being referred to as the Guardian (Wali) of the believers. Similarly, the Prophet has authority over the believers, he has a right to manage the affairs of the Muslims and decide for them a path which they must follow and adhere to, so the Prophet is also being referred to as the Guardian (Wali).

The verse towards the end further states that the righteous men can also be your Guardian (Wali) i.e., the righteous men can also have authority over you. Again, the word "Wali" for righteous men is being used in the context of leadership and authority.

The Prophet of Allah used the word "Mawla" for Ali in the tradition of Ghadeer. Both "Mawla" and "Wali" have the same meaning, the only difference is how one would use them in a sentence. For example, you could say "Wali" (Guardian) of the mosque, but you cannot say "Mawla" of the mosque, that is why in certain circumstances the word "Wali" is used and in others the word "Mawla" is used, but their meaning is the same, as the root word itself is "Wali".

For example, we read in Surat Al-Anfal that Allah says:

> *What (plea) have they that Allah should not punish them, when they debar (His servants) from the Inviolable Place of Worship, though they are not its fitting Guardians (Wali). Its fitting Guardians (Wali) are those only who keep their duty to Allah. But most of them know not.*
>
> - *Quran (8:34) (Pickthall Translation)*

The word "Wali" here is being used to address the Guardian of the mosque (Masjid al-Haram). The "Wali" (Guardian) of the mosque is someone who has authority over the mosque and is responsible for managing the affairs of the mosque. The word "Wali" is being used in the sense of having authority over something, and in this case, it is the authority over a mosque which is being referred to with the word "Wali" in Quran.

Similarly in Surat Al-Baqarah Allah states:

> *"Allah is the Protecting Guardian (Wali) of those who believe. He bringeth them out of darkness into light."*
>
> - *Quran (2:257) (Pickthall Translation)*

The word "Wali" in Surat Al-Baqarah is again being used as a Protector or a Guardian. The verse is saying that if you believe in Allah, then he will be your Protector and Guardian, and he will bring you out from darkness into light i.e., he will guide you to the right path. The word "Wali" in this verse is again being used to refer to the authority that Allah commands over the believers.

Along similar lines the word "Wali" is being used for Guardianship in another verse.

> *But if he who oweth the debt is of low understanding, or weak, or unable himself to dictate, then let the Guardian (Wali) of his interests dictate in (terms of) equity.*
>
> - *Quran (2:282) (Pickthall Translation)*

Allah is saying that a person who is weak and is of low understanding, his Guardian is meant to guard his interest and guide that person to make a right choice. This is exactly what Prophet had envisaged for Ali, that he would guard the interest of the believers after him and guide them to the right path.

Similarly, in the below verse the word "Mawla" itself is being used with the same meaning that we saw in above verses.

> *Impose not on us that which we have not the strength to bear! Pardon us, absolve us and have mercy on us, Thou, our Protector (Mawla), and give us victory over the disbelieving folk.*
>
> - *Quran (2:286) (Pickthall Translation)*

The Holy Quran says that Allah is the Protector (Mawla), who would give victory over the disbelievers. The word "Mawla" here is again being used in the context of authority i.e., it is being used as the Protector and the Guardian of the believers.

In Surat Al-Imarn Allah says:

> *Lo! those of mankind who have the best claim to Abraham are those who followed him, and this Prophet and those who believe (with him); and Allah is the Protecting Guardian (Wali) of the believers.*
>
> - *Quran (3:68) (Pickthall Translation)*

Similarly, in Surah Al-Imran Allah is saying that the people who have the best claim to Abraham are the ones who have followed him as a Prophet, and Allah is the Protecting Guardian (Wali) of the believers. The word "Wali" is once more being used in the sense of Guardianship and authority.

Again, in Surat Al-Imarn the word "Mawla" is being used to describe the authority of Allah.

> *But Allah is your Protector (Mawla), and He is the Best of Helpers.*
>
> - *Quran (3:150) (Pickthall Translation)*

The word "Mawla" here refers to being a Protector, Patron or Guardian. The meaning of "Mawla" again is in the sense of someone being in charge and someone who is acting as a Protector.

In Surat Muhammad Allah states:

> *That is because Allah is the patron (Mawla) of those who believe, and the disbelievers have no Patron (Mawla).*
>
> - *Quran (47:11) (Pickthall Translation)*

Again, Quran uses the word "Mawla" to describe the authority of Allah. The word "Mawla" refers to Lord, Master, Helper, Protector, Patron etc. Since Allah is the master of the universe, he has authority over all his creation and is considered to be the Mawla of the believers.

As we have seen that when the Quran uses the word "Mawla" or "Wali" it is generally used in the sense of authority and leadership.

In Surat Al Tahrim Allah says:

> *Allah hath made lawful for you (Muslims) absolution from your oaths (of such a kind), and Allah is your Protector (Mawla). He is the Knower, the Wise.*
>
> - *Quran (47:11) (Pickthall Translation)*

Again, the word "Mawla" is being used as Protector, Lord, Master and as someone who is all knowing and wise, and someone who has authority over others.

Similarly in Surat An-Nisa Allah says:

> *Allah knoweth best (who are) your enemies. Allah is sufficient as a Guardian (Wali), and Allah is sufficient as a Supporter.*
>
> - *Quran (4:45) (Pickthall Translation)*

The Quran has again used the word "Wali" to refer to the authority of Allah, Quran is saying that Allah is sufficient as your Guardian (Wali) and your Protector.

As we can clearly see that the word "Wali' and "Mawla" in Quran are primarily being used in the context of authority and leadership. Allah is the ultimate authority and Guardian (Wali) of the believers, and in Quran Allah is being referred to as both the "Wali" or "Mawla" of the believers.

This is why Prophet had used the word "Mawla" on the Day of Ghadeer, to ensure that Muslims understood the authority that he was vesting in Ali. The Prophet had said:

> *"Whoever I am his Mawla (Guardian), 'Ali is his Mawla (Guardian)."*

After the authority of Allah, the authority of the Prophet is supreme, as it is obligatory on every Muslim to follow and accept the authority of the Prophet. As Prophet was about to depart this world, he had to address the issue of authority and leadership clearly and explicitly, to make sure that he left no doubt as to who should have the authority over his nation after his demise.

This is exactly what Prophet had done on the day of Ghadeer. Firstly, he established his own authority over the Muslims, and then he gave the leadership of the nation into the hands of Ali, by declaring him as the Mawla (Guardian) of the Muslims.

6.4.5. The Meaning of "Mawla" and "Wali" as Explained by the Prophet

The meaning of the word "Mawla" and "Wali" could also be understood through various traditions (hadith) of the Prophet. I will quote some of those traditions in this section to further clarify the meaning of "Mawla" and "Wali" to the readers. I believe this is essential because many scholars who oppose the very concept that Prophet had ever chosen Ali to be his successor, base their argument on the fact that the meaning of the word "Mawla" and "Wali" is "Friend", rather than "Guardian" or a "Leader".

Let's see how Prophet had used the word "Mawla" and "Wali" in many of his other traditions.

We read in Sahih Muslim that Prophet of Allah said:

> *"...... I am, according to the Book of Allah, the Exalted and Majestic, nearest to the believers of all the human beings. So whoever amongst you dies in debt or leaves behind destitute children, you should call me (for help), for I am his Guardian (Wali).........."*
>
> - *Sahih Muslim Vol. 4, Book 11, Hadith 3947*

The Prophet says that if a person dies and leaves behind some debt or destitute children then he (Prophet) is their Guardian (Wali). This means that Prophet would become the Guardian of that person's children i.e., the Prophet would be in-charge of his children and would have authority over them. The meaning of "Wali" is to have Guardianship and authority over someone, or something as clarified by the Prophet.

A similar tradition is found in Sahih Bukhari with the words of "Mawla" instead of "Wali".

> *The Prophet said, "I am closer to the believers than their selves .... So, if a true believer dies and leaves behind some property, it will be for his inheritors (from the father's side), and if he leaves behind some debt to be paid or needy offspring, then they should come to me as I am the Guardian (Mawla) of the deceased."*
>
> - Sahih al-Bukhari Vol. 3, Book 41, Hadith 584

This time Prophet uses the word "Mawla" instead of "Wali", but the meaning is the same i.e., to have authority and Guardianship over something. In this case the Prophet is assuming the Guardianship over the children of the deceased or the authority to pay his debt.

Another tradition of the Prophet along similar lines would further cement the meaning of "Wali". The Prophet of Allah said:

> *.......... "I am more rightful than other believers to be the Guardian (Wali) of the believers, so if a Muslim dies while in debt, I am responsible for the repayment of his debt, and whoever leaves wealth (after his death) it will belong to his heirs."*
>
> - Sahih al-Bukhari Vol. 3, Book 37, Hadith 495

The Prophet is saying that he has more right to be the Guardian (Wali) of the believers, and he would be responsible for paying their debt after they die. Again, the Prophet uses the word "Wali" in the sense of authority and Guardianship over something. In this case the Prophet is referring to himself as being the Guardian of the believers i.e., having authority over the believers. The Prophet, as the head of the Islamic State of Madinah was the Guardian (Wali) and the leader of all the Muslims.

It was in the same context of being the Guardian of the believers that Prophet of Allah had said about Ali:

> *"You are the Wali (Guardian) of every believer after me."*
>
> - Al-Tayalisi in Musnad Abi Dawood. Vol. 4, Pg. # 469 / 470

Again, the word "Wali" is being used in the context of authority and Guardianship. The Prophet of Allah explicitly declares Ali to be the Guardian (Wali) of every believer. The words "after me" further clarify that Prophet wanted Ali to be the Guardian (Wali) of every believer after him, ensuring that the leadership of the Islamic State rests with Ali after his death.

A similar tradition of the Prophet in favour of Ali is also recorded by Al-Dhahabi.

> *"You are the Wali (Guardian) of every believer both men and women after me."*
>
> - Al-Dhahabi in Al-Mustadrak alaa Al-Sahihain. Vol. 3, Pg. # 134.

In this instance the Prophet has said that Ali is the Guardian of every man and woman after him, again giving Ali the explicit right of leadership over the Muslim Ummah after his (Prophet's) death.

With a slight variation in the meaning, other scholars have also mentioned a similar tradition of the Prophet.

> "You are my Heir (Wali) among every believer after me."
> - Ahmad ibn Hanbal in Musnad Ahmad bin Hanbal. Vol. 3, Pg. # 331 – 333
> - bn Kathir in Al-Bidaya Wa'l-Nihaya. Vol. 11, Pg. # 42 - 45

Ali was indeed the heir and the inheritor of Prophet's knowledge and Sunnah. The Prophet of Allah could not possibly leave his Sunnah undocumented or without a guide. The Prophet had made Ali the custodian of his Sunnah as per the above tradition and many other such traditions. In fact, the entire upbringing of Ali in the house of the Prophet itself is undeniable evidence that no one other than Ali could have been the custodian of Prophet's Sunnah.

6.4.6. The Meaning of "Mawla" and "Wali" as Understood by the Companions

In this section we will see how the companions understood the meaning of "Wali" and "Mawla" in the light of the various traditions (hadith) of the Prophet.

Imam Malik reports a hadith concerning the issue of Zakat where the companions are saying:

> "………… The position with us concerning the dividing up of zakat is that it is up to the individual judgment of the man In Charge (Wali). Whichever categories of people are in most need and are most numerous are given preference, according to how the man In Charge (Wali) sees fit…………"
> - Muwatta Imam Malik Book 17 Hadith 30

The word "Wali" is being used by the companions for a man who is "In-Charge" and is in a position of authority. In this case the companions are referring to a man who is the "Wali" (In-Charge) of dividing up and distributing Zakat. The companions indeed understood the meaning of "Wali" in the context of authority and of someone being in charge.

In Sahih Bukhari Lady Aisha clarifies her understanding of the meaning of "Wali".

> " ……. 'Whoever amongst the guardians is rich, he should take no wages (from the property of the orphans) but If he is poor, let him have for himself what is just and reasonable (according to his labours)' (4.6) was revealed concerning the Guardian (Wali) of the orphans who looks after them and manages favourably their financial affairs………
> - Sahih al-Bukhari Vol. 3, Book 34, Hadith 414

Lady Aisha understood the meaning of "Wali" as someone who is a "Guardian", and who manages the financial affairs of others, clearly referring to "Wali" as a person who is In Charge and is in a position of authority, where they have authority to manage someone's affairs. In this case Lady Aisha is referring to the Guardianship and the authority of a person over the orphans.

Similarly, in Sahih Muslim Lady Aisha clarifies her understanding of the meaning of "Mawla".

> "……. I asked Allah's Messenger (Peace be upon him) about a virgin whose marriage is solemnized by her Guardian (Mawla), whether it was necessary or not to consult her. Allah's Messenger (Peace be upon him) said: Yes, she must be consulted…………"
> - Sahih Muslim Vol. 3, Book 8, Hadith 3305

The word "Mawla" is also being understood by the companions as Guardian, or as having authority over something. The father of a virgin girl is her Guardian, and he has authority over her affairs, and this is how the companions understood the meaning of "Mawla", as someone having authority and Guardianship over something.

In the below tradition both lady Aisha and Ibn Abbas confirm their understanding of the meaning of "Wali" as not just Guardian but a Ruler too. Lady Aisha and Ibn Abbas narrate the following tradition:

> *"The Messenger of Allah said: 'There is no marriage except with a Guardian (Wali).'* *"According to the Hadith of Aishah: "And the ruler (Sultan) is the Guardian (Wali) of the one who does not have a Guardian (Wali). "*
> - Sunan Ibn Majah Vol. 3, Book 9, Hadith 1880
> - Sunan Ibn Majah Vol. 3, Book 9, Hadith 1879

The companions clearly understood that a person who does not have a "Wali" (Guardian), their "Wali" is the ruler of the time i.e., the head of the Islamic State. This tradition of the Prophet explicitly makes the ruler (Sultan) or the head of the State, or the Caliph of the time as the "Wali" (Guardian) of a person who does not have a "Wali" (Guardian).

A similar tradition in Abu Dawood further confirms the understanding of the companions about "Wali" as being a Guardian and a ruler (Sultan or head of the State). Lady Aisha says that it is narrated from the Prophet:

> *"………. The marriage of a woman who marries without the consent of her Guardians (Wali) is void. (He said these words) three times………… If there is a dispute, the Sultan (man in authority) is the Guardian (Wali) of one who has none."*
> - Sunan Abu Dawood Vol. 2, Book 12, Hadith 2078

The meaning of "Wali" in the eyes of the companions was certainly in the context of leadership and authority, where they would refer to the ruler of the time as their "Wali" (Guardian).

This is why when Prophet refers to Ali as the Guardian of the believers after him, he is in fact referring to Ali as the ruler (Sultan) and the head of the Islamic State after him. The Prophet of Allah had said:

> *"You are the Wali (Guardian) of every believer after me."*
> - Al-Haithami in Majma Al-Zawa'id. Vol. 9, Pg. # 109 - 111

The Prophet is essentially saying that Ali would be the "Wali" (Guardian) of the believers, the ruler (Sultan) and the head of the Islamic State after him, and this is how the companions had in fact understood the meaning of "Wali", and not as a friend as propagated by some scholars.

6.4.7. The Meaning of "Mawla" and "Wali" as Understood by Caliph Abu Bakr and Umar

Historically, Caliph Abu Bakr became the ruler (Sultan) and the head of the Islamic State after the death of the Prophet. After Caliph Abu Bakr's death Caliph Umar became the ruler (Sultan) and the head of the Islamic State. In this context let us see how the first two Caliphs themselves understood the meaning of "Wali" and "Mawla".

We read the words of Caliph Abu Bakr and Caliph Umar in Sahih Bukhari, which would confirm exactly as to how they understood the meaning of "Wali".

> "………Allah's Apostle kept on acting like that during all his life, Then he died, and Abu Bakr said, 'I am the Successor (Wali) of Allah's Apostle.' So he (i.e. Abu Bakr) took charge of this property and disposed of it in the same manner as Allah's Apostle used to do………. Then Allah caused Abu Bakr to die and I (Umar) said, 'I am the Successor (Wali) of Allah's Apostle and Abu Bakr.' So I kept this property in my possession for the first two years of my rule (i.e. Caliphate and I used to dispose of it in the same way as Allah's Apostle and Abu Bakr used to do……."

- Sahih al-Bukhari Vol. 5, Book 59, Hadith 367
- Sahih al-Bukhari Vol. 9, Book 92, Hadith 408
- Sahih al-Bukhari Vol. 7, Book 64, Hadith 271
- Sahih al-Bukhari Vol. 4, Book 53, Hadith 326

As Caliph Abu Bakr became the first Caliph and a ruler of the Muslims after Prophet's death, he said: "I am the "Wali" (Successor) of the Prophet". Caliph Abu Bakr clearly understood the meaning of "Wali" as being the ruler (Sultan) and the head of the Islamic State. He used the word "Wali" for his own position in relation to the Prophet, since historically he did succeed the Prophet as the first Caliph and the ruler of the Muslims.

After Caliph Abu Bakr's death Caliph Umar became the second Caliph and the ruler over the Muslims. So, keeping in line with the understanding of Caliph Abu Bakr about the meaning of "Wali", Caliph Umar said: "I am the Successor (Wali) of the Prophet and Abu Bakr". Caliph Umar called himself the "Wali" (Successor) of both the Prophet and Caliph Abu Bakr.

This leaves no doubt that both Caliph Abu Bakr and Caliph Umar had clearly understood the meaning of "Wali" as being the ruler (Sultan) and the head of the Islamic State, and hence they had used the word "Wali" to define their own positions in relation to the Prophet. Caliph Abu Bakr and Caliph Umar had certainly not understood the meaning of "Wali" as a friend, as propagated by some scholars of today.

A similar tradition is also found in Sahih Muslim where both Caliph Abu Bakr and Caliph Umar endorse their understanding of "Wali" as a ruler and as a leader of the Muslims. Again, they both call themselves the "Wali" (Successor) of the Prophet i.e., rulers after the Prophet.

> "………… When the Messenger of Allah (Peace be upon him) passed away, Abu Bakr said:" I am the successor (Wali) of the Messenger of Allah (Peace be upon him)." Both of you (Ali and Ibn Abbas) came to demand your shares from the property………… When Abu Bakr passed away and I (Umar) have become the successor (Wali) of the Messenger of Allah (Peace be upon him) and Abu Bakr (Allah be pleased with him), …….. I (Umar) became the guardian of this property…………"

- Sahih Muslim Vol. 4, Book 19, Hadith 4349

Caliph Abu Bakr and Caliph Umar not only understood the meaning of "Wali" as a ruler and as the head of the State, but they in fact called themselves the "Wali" (Successor) of the Prophet, because they became the rulers and the head of the Islamic State after the death of the Prophet. So, when Prophet said about Ali that "You are the Wali of every believer after me", Prophet wanted Ali to become the ruler and the head of the Islamic State after him, just as Caliph Abu Bakr and Caliph Umar had become the rulers and the head of the Islamic State.

The above traditions without a shadow of a doubt confirm that the meaning of "Wali" as understood by Caliph Abu Bakr and Caliph Umar was in the context of being a ruler and the leader of the Muslims.

Another narration in the Muwatta of Imam Malik would further confirm the meaning of "Wali" as understood by Caliph Umar.

> "........ Umar ibn al-Khattab said, "A woman is only married with the consent of her Guardian (Wali), someone of her family with sound judgment or the Sultan (ruler).""

- Muwatta Imam Malik Book 28 Hadith 5

Caliph Umar again confirms his understanding of the meaning of "Wali", by saying that a woman can only be married with the consent of her "Wali" (Guardian), and if she does not have a "Wali" (Guardian), then the ruler (Sultan) of the State can become her "Wali". The meaning of "Wali" understood by Caliph Umar is clearly for someone who is in charge or is in a position of authority (Ruler).

Finally, Caliph Umar also confirms the meaning of "Mawla" as Guardian, thorough a narration in Ibn Majah.

> ".........Umar wrote back to him saying that the Prophet (Peace be upon him) said: Allah and His Messenger are the guardians (Mawla) of the one who has no guardian (Mawla), and the maternal uncle is the heir of one who has no other heir."

- Sunan Ibn Majah Vol. 4, Book 23, Hadith 2737

Caliph Umar reiterates that a person who has no "Mawla" (Guardian), his "Mawla" (Guardian) would be Allah and the Prophet, clearly showing that in his mind the meaning of "Mawla" was in the sense of Guardianship and authority, and not as a friend.

That is why the Prophet had also used the word "Mawla" and "Wali for defining the Guardianship of Ali, because the companions understood those words in the sense of authority and leadership.

The Holy Prophet had also famously said:

> "Verily, Ali and I are inseparable, and he is the Guardian (Wali) of every believer after me."

- Al Tirmidhi, in his Sahih, ii, 297,
- Ahmad Ibn Hanbal in his Musnad, iv, 437, v, 356;
- Abu Dawud al Tayalisi in his Musnad, iii, 111, xi, 360;
- al Haythami, Majma al Zawaid, ix, 109, 127, 128, 199;
- al Khatib al Baghdadi, Tarikh Baghdad, iv, 339;
- al Muhibb al Tabari, al Riyad al Nadirah, ii, 203, 171;
- al Muttaqi al Hindi, Kanz al Ummal, vi, 154, 155, 396, 401;
- Ibn al Athir in Usd al Ghabah, v, 94;
- Abu Nuaym in Hilyat al Awliya, vi, 294;
- al Nasa'i, Khasais, 19, 23;
- as well as Ibn Abi Shaybah, al Tabari, al Tabarani, al ?Daylami, Ibn Mardawayh, Ibn al Jawzi, al Rafii, and Ibn Hajar.

The Prophet of Allah not only stated that Ali is the Guardian (Wali) of every believer after him, but he also stated that Ali is inseparable from him. These words of the Prophet have a huge implication for the position and the status of Ali. The Prophet is essentially saying that Ali in his character, in his manner, in his personality, in his approach, in his knowledge and in his wisdom had resembled him (Prophet) to such a degree that he (Prophet) and Ali are inseparable.

This is why in Mubahilah (Chapter 5), when the Christians had challenged the Muslims, Prophet took Ali as an extension of his own self. Since Prophet and Ali were inseparable in their character, hence the authority of Ali was inevitably similar to the authority of the Prophet.

When Prophet declared Ali to be the "Mawla" and "Wali" (Guardian) of the believers, he wanted Ali to have the same authority over the Muslims that he had over them, so that Ali could guide and lead the Muslim Ummah after his demise.

In Surat Al-Ahzab Allah States:

> "The Prophet has more authority (is Wali) over the believers than they have over themselves"
> - (Quran 33:6)

Again, we can see that the word "Wali" in Quran is being used to refer to the authority of the Prophet, which he enjoyed over the believers. The Holy Quran states that the Prophet has more authority over the believers than they have over themselves. This is exactly what Prophet had asked the audience in Ghadeer to confirm before he made Ali the Mawla (Guardian) of the believers.

The Prophet asked the audience in Ghadeer.

> "Do I not have more authority over the believers than what they have over themselves?"

People cried and answered:

> "Yes, O' Messenger of God.
> "Then Prophet (S) held up the hand of 'Ali and said: "Whoever I am his Mawla (Guardian), 'Ali is his Mawla (Guardian)."

The words of the Prophet were completely in line with the words of the Holy Quran.

Allah had given Prophet the authority over the believers and on the day of Ghadeer Prophet gave that authority to Ali, by declaring him the Mawla (Guardian) of the believers, so that he could guide and lead the Muslims in his absence.

6.4.8. When the Authority of Ali was Challenged

This incident took place almost one year before the event of Ghadeer. The Prophet of Allah had appointed Ali as the leader of an expedition to Yemen, and he placed around three hundred troops under Ali's command. The army led by Ali was victorious and they captured a lot of war booty including many camels.

A dispute began between Ali and some of his soldiers over war booty and female captives. As the leader of the expedition and as the commander in chief of the army, Ali made some strict rules about the distribution of the spoils of war for the soldiers under his command. When the army reached Makkah, some of the troops under Ali's command complained to the Prophet about the leadership of Ali and about the way Ali had handled the spoils of war.

Buraidah al-Aslami was a companion of the Prophet who was under Ali's command, and he complained to the Prophet about Ali. Some narrations suggest that there were four people who complained about Ali.

On hearing the complains about Ali the Prophet said:

> "………… Do not produce falsehoods about Ali, he is from me and I am (saw) from him, and he is your Wali (Guardian) after me………."

- Ahmad ibn Hanbal in Musnad Ahmad. Vol. 16, Pg. # 497, H # 22908.
- Al-Manawi in Faidhul Qadir Sharh Al-Jami' Al-Saghir. Vol. 4, Pg. # 357

In another version of the narration the Prophet had said to the people who were complaining about Ali:

"………… What do you want from Ali? Ali is from me (saw) and I (saw) am from him and he is the Wali (Guardian) of every believer after me (saw)."

- Ibn Hajar in Al-Isaba. Vol. 7, Pg. # 282.
- Muttaqi Al-Hindi in Kanz Al-Ummal. Vol. 13, Pg. # 142.
- Al-Suyuti in Jami'ul Ahadeeth. Vol. 16, Pg. # 256.
- Al-Museli in Musnad Abi Ya'la. Vol. 1, Pg. # 293.

In another variation the Prophet said to the people who were complaining:

"……….Allah's Messenger (saw) turned to him and anger was obvious on his face. He said, "What do you want from Ali? What do you want from Ali? Ali is from me (saw) and I from him and he is the Guardian (Wali) of every believer after me (saw)."

- Al-Tirmidhi in Sunan Al-Tirmidhi. Pg. # 842, H # 3712.
- Ibn Hibban in Saheeh Ibn Hibban. Vol. 15, Pg. # 373.

The response of the Prophet in defence of Ali was swift and unequivocal. Prophet not only stopped the companions who were speaking ill about Ali and who were challenging his authority, but he also clarifies to them the position and the stature of Ali, so that they understand and realize that Ali was not just leading the expedition to Yemen but one day he would lead the entire Muslim nation.

Prophet reminded the companions that Ali is from him, and he is from Ali, establishing the authority of Ali over the companions just like his own authority. In other words, Prophet told the companions that the decisions made by Ali were like his own decisions, and that they should not challenge or question the authority of Ali because the authority of Ali was like his own authority, since Ali is from him, and he is from Ali.

Another key point that comes out from this incident is that the companions had only complained to the Prophet about the leadership of Ali in relation to the expedition of Yemen. However, in response Prophet had said:

"…. Ali is the Wali (Guardian) of every believer after me (saw)."

Why is the Prophet mentioning that Ali is the "Wali" (Guardian) of every believer after him? The reason why Prophet had deliberately brought up the issue of Ali's Guardianship after him, was to show that not only had he made Ali in charge of the expedition to Yemen, but one day Ali's authority would expand to all the believers, so it would be better for them to accept and recognize the leadership of Ali now, instead of questioning it.

Not only did the Prophet endorse the leadership of Ali in relation to the expedition of Yemen, but he also declared Ali as Guardian (Wali) of the believers to the companions who had lodged a complaint against Ali. The Prophet wanted the companions to clearly understand the position and the rank of Ali within the Muslim Ummah.

This incident also confirms that Prophet had declared Ali to be the Guardian (Wali) of the Muslims on other occasions as well, especially when he had felt the need to do so. This incident took place in Makkah one year before the event of Ghadeer Khum, when the army lead by Ali had returned from Yemen.

The event of Ghadeer took place in the last months of Prophet's life when he was returning to Madinah after his final pilgrimage.

Note:- Some scholars deliberately try to mix this event with the event of Ghadeer by claiming that the announcement that Prophet made on the event of Ghadeer was in response to the dispute that Ali had with his comrades on the expedition to Yemen. This is a complete fabrication since the event of Ghadeer was a completely separate event and had nothing to do with the expedition to Yemen, which took place a year before the event of Ghadeer.

6.4.9. The Prophet Keeps Ali in Madinah

Ali has always been Prophet's first choice for leading any expeditions or military detachments. In the final days of Prophet's life i.e., two or three days before the Prophet was about to die, he sent an army under the leadership of a young commander called Usama to Syria, which was part of the Byzantine Empire at the time.

He ordered other prominent companions like Caliph Abu Bakr and Caliph Umar to join the military campaign under the command of Usama. But Prophet kept Ali in Madinah, he neither asked Ali to lead the army and nor did he ask him to join the army as a combatant.

Ibn Sa'd writes in his book Tabaqat Al-Kubra:

> *Narrated Abdul-Wahab ibn Ata Al-Ijli from Al-Umari from Nafi' from ibn Umar who said: 'The Prophet equipped an army that Abu Bakr and Umar were in and he appointed Usama ibn Zayd as their commander, …………"*

- Source: Tabaqat Al-Kubra. Vol. 2, Pg. # 219.

Ali has always been a man of battlefield. Ali's sword and bravery has never been matched by any of his advisories. Ali had brought countless victories to the camp of the Prophet. Ali had never been hesitant to go into a battlefield. Ali had fearlessly taken on the most feared and ferocious warriors that the Quraysh of Makkah and the pagans had thrown at him. Ali had always been the top lieutenant and the commander in chief of Prophet's army. Even when Ali was unwell during the battle of Khaibar, Prophet specifically called Ali and cured his eyes, so that he could bring victory to the camp of the Muslims.

But this time Prophet completely ignores Ali and chooses young Usama to lead the military campaign against the Byzantine Empire. He orders other well-known companions like Caliph Abu Bakr and Caliph Umar to join the Muslim army under the command of Usama.

The reason for ignoring Ali is clear. After the announcement of Ali as the Guardian and the leader of the Muslims in Ghadeer, Prophet did not want to expose Ali to unnecessary risks and dangers. He wanted to keep Ali alive for the position that he had chosen for him. The Prophet of Allah knew that his death was near, he had already given hints about his demise. If Prophet sends Ali on a military expedition at this stage, then it was possible that Ali could have been killed and would never return.

Also, the military campaign against the Byzantine Empire could last for many months. If Prophet sends Ali as part of the military campaign heading to Syria, then Ali won't be around to take on the mantle of the Islamic leadership which Prophet had planned for him.

That is why Prophet keeps Ali in Madinah because he wanted Ali to be around when he passes away, so that Ali could take over the role of the Guardianship of the Muslims. A role for which the Prophet had trained Ali for twenty-five years.

On the other hand, Prophet instructs Caliph Abu Bakr and Caliph Umar to join Usama's army, as he sees no role for them in Madinah around the time of his death.

6.4.10. An Observation

The journey of Ali to be declared the Mawla (Guardian) of the Muslims began when Prophet adopted his little cousin at the age of four or five. Prophet raised the little boy in his own house and shielded him from the Jahiliya traditions which were prevalent in the society at the time.

The Prophet of Allah trained, taught, and groomed the bright little boy in the house of knowledge and piety, where he even witnesses the revelations of Quran. The little boy would ask Prophet questions and the Messenger of Allah would satisfy his curiosity, and when the little boy was quiet, the Prophet of Allah would speak to him and would still impart his knowledge.

When the children of Quraysh would attack and abuse the Prophet, the young boy would step forward and defend the Prophet. When the Prophet announced his first public call to Islam and invited his clan, the little boy is the only one who offers his unconditional support to the Messenger of Allah, whereas others stay silent.

As the young boy grows up in the company and under the immaculate guidance of the Prophet, he not only becomes a fearless warrior, but he also becomes a symbol of knowledge and piety.

As the enemies of Allah threaten the life of the Prophet, the young brave warrior would often sleep in Prophet's bed. He is happy to sacrifice his own life to save the life of his mentor. The habit of sleeping in the bed of the Prophet comes in handy when the Quraysh of Makkah planned to end the life of the Prophet. The young brave Ali would sleep on the bed of the Prophet on a night when an assassin is chosen from every tribe to kill the Prophet. The courage and the bravery of Ali would foil the assassination attempt on the life of the Prophet.

The Prophet moves to a new land called Madinah. The Prophet had a vision to establish a base for the Muslims in this new city. This is where the bravery and the skill of this fearless warrior would become a clear differentiating factor between him and the rest of the companions, who haven't had the upbringing that he had.

The Prophet was the architect and the founder of the Islamic State of Madinah, whereas Ali was the eliminator of the obstructive forces which stood in the way of its establishment and survival. In the battle of Badr, this young warrior had killed almost 40% of the enemy combatants and secured a tremendous victory for the Muslims. In the battle of Uhud, he killed almost all the flag bearers and saved the life of the Prophet from certain death, when the other companions had fled the battlefield.

In the battle of Moat when Amr Ibn Abd Wud crossed over and challenged the Muslims, nobody had the courage to accept his challenge or take him on. It was only this young brave warrior who accepted his dwell and killed him instantly. In the battle of Khaibar, when none of the other companions were able to conquer the forts occupied by the Jewish army, Prophet gave his flag to this young fearsome warrior who once again brought smiles to the face of the Prophet.

This young and brave warrior became the star performer of Prophet's army who would always lead from the front. He participated in eighteen battles and countless expeditions, but he never let the Prophet of Allah down in any of those battles.

Prophet gave this young fearless warrior the title of Assadullah, which means the Lion of God. It would not be an exaggeration to say that without the sword of Ali the Islamic State of Madinah would not have survived.

The unique thing about this gallant warrior was that his distinctions were not only limited to the battlefield. When the Christians of Nijran threw a challenge to the ideological message of Islam, the Prophet of Allah took Ali and his family as a symbol of righteousness and piety. When the Christian priests saw those blessed faces, they withdrew their challenge and accepted defeat.

The Prophet himself had guaranteed the righteousness and piety of Ali by constantly going to his house and praying for his purification. Just as nobody could challenge the sword of Ali on the battlefield, the Prophet had made sure that nobody could be compared to Ali in terms of righteousness and piety either. Since Prophet was the master, the teacher, and the mentor of Ali, he also made him the gateway to his knowledge.

Ali had made a promise to the Prophet in his very first public call to Islam, and as a result Prophet had chosen Ali to be his successor in that very meeting. But Ali through his subsequent actions not only justified the honour that Prophet had bestowed upon him, but he also proved beyond any doubt that he had in fact earned that position.

The successor of the Prophet had to be chosen on merit, it had to be based on achievements in the service of Islam. As an acknowledgement and a reward for the service of Ali, the Prophet of Allah declares him to be the Mawla (Guardian) and the leader of the Muslims in Ghadeer.

The Prophet of Allah chooses the best and the most deserving companion for the ultimate position of being his successor.

And that is why the Prophet of Allah had also said:

> *"Ali holds the position of the Kaaba."*
> - *Mustadrak Al-Sahihain of Al-Hakim Al-Nisapuri, 3/122;*
> - *Musnad Ahmad, 3/82;*
> - *Al-Tabarani, 6/155;*
> - *Kanz Al-Umal*

Just as Muslims flock to Kaaba, Prophet wanted the Muslims to flock to Ali after his death.

The context of the above tradition clarifies that it is meant for a time when Prophet is no longer present, since in the presence of the Prophet there was no need for people to flock to Ali, as Prophet of Allah was the source of knowledge and guidance for the entire mankind.

7. WHY WAS ALI NOT CHOSEN?

Despite the fact that Prophet had ideologically trained and groomed Ali since he was a child to lead the revolutionary movement of Islam, Ali is not chosen as the leader of the Muslims after the death of the Prophet. Despite the fact that Ali was deeply involved in the Islamic movement from its very beginning until the demise of the Prophet, Ali is ignored from the leadership of the Islamic State. Despite the fact that Ali was the differentiating factor in almost all the battles between the Muslims and the Kuffar, and it was the sword of Ali that had saved the Islamic movement from defeat in the key battles of Badr, Uhud, Moat and Khyber, Ali is completely side lined from the Caliphate of the Muslims after the death of the Prophet.

Despite all the traits and merits that Ali had acquired through the unique and the prolonged companionship of the Prophet such as knowledge, wisdom, piety, bravery, humbleness, judgment, patience etc, Ali is not chosen to lead the Islamic movement after the demise of the Prophet.

In spite of the presence of countless traditions of the Prophet in favour of Ali such as the tradition of the Home Conference, the tradition of Analogy, the tradition of the Two Weighty Things and the tradition of Ghadeer Khum, Ali is completely disregarded from the leadership of the Muslim Ummah.

The question now arises as to why was Ali not chosen? And why was he ignored from the leadership of the Muslims? And why did the Caliphate go to Abu Bakr and not to Ali?

To answer this key question, one must look at the mentality and the trends which were affecting the prominent companions and the wider Muslim society at the time of the death of the Prophet.

7.1. The Two Trends

When one analyses and looks at the Islamic society during the lifetime of the Prophet i.e., before his death, one finds that there were two principal trends that accompanied the development of the Muslim society form its very beginning.

- A trend, which strictly follows and submits to the instructions of the Prophet and the Quranic text in all aspects and spheres of life. This trend does not challenge or questions the authority and the decisions of the Prophet, even though at times they may seem unfavourable.
- And a second trend, which believes and observes the basic tenants and rituals of the Islamic faith, but also believes in the possibility of ijtihad (independent judgment), even on clear instructions and orders of the Prophet. This trend takes into account its interests, and looks at the circumstances surrounding an instruction, and based on these considerations it permits the use of

ijtihad (independent judgment), even though it may lead to challenging or questioning the authority of the Prophet.

Although, the companions as a whole were an enlightened vanguard of Islam, who had sacrificed a great deal in the path of Allah, it is important and necessary to accept the existence of a trend, which was inclined towards the use of ijtihad (independent judgment) and circumstantial considerations in determining their interests, as opposed to strict adherence to the commands of the Prophet.

7.2. The Trend of Al-Ijtihad (Independent Judgment)

The existence of the trend of al-ijtihad (independent judgment) among the companions was not completely unexpected or totally surprising. This is because Islam was a completely new way of life for the companions, and it was a complete new ideological system for them, which had challenged and uprooted all the previous customs and traditions that the companions were used to. In this context the reminiscence of some of the previous ideologies and traditions which the companions were exposed to, prior to the coming of Islam was not uncommon or illogical.

Also, each companion's level of understanding of the message of Islam varied significantly. Their understanding of the new faith was dependent upon their own intellectual, spiritual, and previous religious experiences, and their own ability to fully grasp the new ideological message. It was also dependent on how close that companion was to the ideology of the new faith, and their proximity to the Prophet of Allah, and the time that they had spent and dedicated in practicing the new faith. All these factors had affected the individual understanding of the companions to varying degrees in terms of their grasp of the message of Islam.

One of the key factors that had contributed to the spread of the second trend (al-ijtihad) among the companions, was its coherence with man's natural tendency towards making judgments according to his own interests, instead of basing his decisions on a command or an instruction whose significance he does not fully understand. As a result, a person would tend to follow his own instincts and natural inclinations in cases where he fails to fully understand the importance of a command, or where he feels that the circumstances are no longer conducive for him to follow those commands.

The second trend was a minority among the companions of the Prophet, but nevertheless it was represented by a daring group of prominent companions like Caliph Umar. Caliph Umar had disputed with the Prophet and challenged his authority on several occasions and made judgments contradicting the clear instructions of the Prophet, believing that he (Umar) had a right to do so, based on the circumstances around him.

I will clarify the issue of the second trend (al-ijtihad) among the companions with a few examples.

7.2.1. Example 1: The Treaty of Hudaybiyya

The attitude and objections of Caliph Umar against the Treaty of Hudaybiyya are well documented in the books of history. The Treaty of Hudaybiyya was a pact that Prophet of Allah had signed with the Quraysh of Makkah. But Caliph Umar and a few other companions were not happy with the decision of the Prophet to have a truce with the Quraysh. Caliph Umar felt that the terms and the conditions of the Hudaybiyya truce were unfavourable for the Muslims.

On this basis he challenged and criticized the decision of the Prophet, to the extent that he even questions the Prophet hood of the Prophet of Allah. We find the following narration in many books of hadith and history including Sahih Bukhari, Sahih Muslim, al-Tabari and others.

After Prophet had signed the Hudaybiyya treaty Caliph Umar approached the Prophet and said:

> Umar said, "I went to the Prophet and said, 'Aren't you truly the Apostle of Allah?'
> Prophet said, 'Yes, indeed.'
> Umar said, 'Isn't our Cause just and the cause of the enemy unjust?'
> Prophet said, 'Yes.'
> Umar said, 'Then why should we be humble in our religion?'
> Prophet said, 'I am Allah's Apostle and I do not disobey Him, and He will make me victorious.'
> Umar said, 'Didn't you tell us that we would go to the Kaaba and perform Tawaf around it?'
> Prophet said, 'Yes, but did I tell you that we would visit the Ka'ba this year?'
> Umar said, 'No.'
> Prophet said, 'So you will visit it and perform Tawaf around it?'
> Umar further said, "I went to Abu Bakr and said, 'O Abu Bakr! Isn't he truly Allah's Prophet?'
> Abu Bakr replied, 'Yes.'
> Umar said, 'Then why should we be humble in our religion?'
> Abu Bakr said, 'Indeed, he is Allah's Apostle, and he does not disobey his Lord, and He will make him victorious. Adhere to him as, by Allah, he is on the right.'
>
> - Sahih Bukhari vol. 9 pg. 256
> - Sahih Muslim vol. 9 pg. 259
> - Sahih Muslim. Vol. 2, Pg. # 859.
> - Sahih Ibn Hibban. Vol. 11, Pg. # 224
> - Al-Durr al-Manthur, vol. 9 pg. 225
> - Tafsir Tabari, vol. 22 pg. 246

As evident from the above conversation, Caliph Umar questions and challenges the decision of the Prophet regarding the Treaty of Hudaybiyya. He asks the Prophet "Aren't you truly the Apostle of Allah?" Implying that if Prophet was truly the Prophet of Allah, then how could he sign such an unfavourable treaty with the Quraysh of Makkah? Caliph Umar directly questions and challenges the decision and the actions of the Prophet.

However, the response of the Prophet is full of enlightenment. The Prophet says, "I am Allah's Apostle and I do not disobey Him, and He will make me victorious". The Prophet implies that the decision to have the treaty with the Quraysh was the decision of Allah, and that he (the Prophet) does not disobey Allah, further implying to Caliph Umar that he should also fall in line and obey this decision.

However, Caliph Umar was not convinced, he was still not satisfied with the response of the Prophet. He then approaches Caliph Abu Bakr and again questions the Prophethood of Prophet Mohammad. He asks Caliph Abu Bakr: "Isn't he truly Allah's Prophet?" Caliph Abu Bakr gives him the same response as the Prophet, and also tells him to obey the decision of the Prophet.

The reason why Caliph Umar questions and challenges the decision of the Prophet was because he did not believe that every decision and the instruction of the Prophet was correct or had to be followed. He believed that in certain circumstances the decision or the instruction of the Prophet could be flawed, and he (Umar) had a right to challenge it and pass his own judgment on it.

For instance, Caliph Umar did not realize, or he was not able to comprehend that the Prophet does not speak or act without the commands of Allah. Any actions, decisions or speech of the Prophet is with the will of Allah. Hence, disagreeing, questioning, or challenging the authority of the Prophet would be tantamount to challenging the commands of Allah, even though a decision may seem unfavourable.

The Hudaybiyya truce on the face of it seemed harsh against the Muslims, but it brought many benefits to the Muslims.

As a result of the treaty the Quraysh for the very first time had acknowledged the existence of an Islamic government and an Islamic community, something that they had been trying to destroy at all costs. The Quraysh had agreed to stop incursions into Madinah which was the hub and the bastion of the Muslims. The Muslim converts in Makkah were now free to practice their faith openly, something that they could not do previously. The treaty allowed the Prophet to concentrate on the propagation of Islam beyond Makkah and Madinah. Envoys were sent to various countries such as Rome, Persia, Ethiopia, Egypt, Yemen, Syria, and Byzantine empires, and they were invited to the path of Islam.

However, Caliph Umar was simply looking at the covenants of the Hudaybiyya treaty at face value. He did not have the foresight that Prophet had, he did not have the vision that Prophet had, and he did not have the divine link that Prophet of Allah had. Nevertheless, he used his own independent judgment (al-ijtihad) to challenge and criticize the decision of the Prophet, without realizing the significance of what Prophet had achieved.

As we can see from this incident that the trend of al-ijtihad was present in some companions during the very lifetime of the Prophet. These companions would challenge and question the decisions of the Prophet in his presence, since they believed that a decision of the Prophet was not always correct. They believed that if an instruction of the Prophet contradicts their own understanding of the circumstances, then they had a right to question it and even challenge it.

This attitude and approach of the companions is known as the trend of al-ijtihad (independent judgment).

7.2.2. Example 2: The Incident of the Pen and Paper

This incident took place some three or four days before the death of the Prophet. The Prophet was unwell and was surrounded by some of his companions including Caliph Umar. The Prophet asked his companions to bring him some writing material so that he could write something, which would keep them on the path of truth, and which would stop them from going astray. This was going to be a key document that Prophet had wished to right just before his death, to keep the Muslims on the path of truth.

However, after hearing the words of the Prophet Caliph Umar flatly refused to bring the writing material. He said to the companions in the room that Prophet was unwell and that the book of Allah was sufficient for their guidance. On hearing the response of Caliph Umar some companions sided with him, while others wanted to follow the instructions of the Prophet. This caused an argument and a dispute among the companions which quickly turned noisy and unruly.

On seeing the companions squabbling and arguing with each other in loud voices, the Prophet of Allah got upset and told all the companions to leave his room. As a result of the actions of Caliph Umar the Prophet was not able to write those golden words which he had wished to write for the Ummah.

This incident is reported in Bukhari and Muslim in the following way:

> "When Allah's Apostle was on his death-bed and in the house, there were some people among whom was 'Umar bin Al-Khattab, the Prophet said, "Come, let me write for you a statement after which you will not go astray." 'Umar said, "The Prophet is seriously ill, and you have the Qur'an; so the Book of Allah is enough for us." The people present in the house differed and quarrelled. Some said, "Go near so that the Prophet may write for you a statement after which you will not go astray," while the others said as Umar said. When they caused a hue and cry before the Prophet, Allah's Apostle said, "Go away!" Narrated 'Ubaidullah: Ibn 'Abbas used to say, "It was very unfortunate that Allah's Apostle was prevented from writing that statement for them because of their disagreement and noise."

- *Sahih al-Bukhari, 7:70:573*
- *Sahih Muslim, Book 013, Number 4016*

Again, we witness the trend of al-ijtihad (independent judgment) in full swing.

Caliph Umar refuses to follow a simple instruction of the Prophet. All Prophet wanted to do was to write some instructions for the Muslims which would keep them on the path of truth. But Caliph Umar insists that since Prophet was now unwell, the only thing that the Muslims needed was the Book of Allah. Caliph Umar uses his ijtihad and his own judgment to assume that since Prophet was unwell (ill), he was not capable of writing anything wise or useful for the Muslim Ummah, hence he refuses to bring the writing material to the Prophet.

This incident took place right at the end of Prophet's life, which shows that Caliph Umar had still not grasped the fact that the words that come out from the mouth of the Prophet were with the will and the consent of Allah. It did not matter if Prophet was unwell or not. All actions and speech of the Prophet are considered as Sunnah at all times, regardless of the fact that Prophet was well or not.

Unfortunately, the actions of Caliph Umar in this incident further reveal his lack of understanding towards the Sunnah of the Prophet. Caliph Umar says to the other companions: "You have the Quran with you. The Book of Allah is sufficient for us".

Any student of Islamic sciences knows that Quran alone is not enough for the Muslims. Without the Sunnah of the Prophet the religion of Islam is incomplete. The method of prayer, the laws of fasting and the rituals of Haj are all derived from the Sunnah of the Prophet. The Holy Quran primarily gives us guidelines whereas the details and the instructions regarding the tenants of Islam are found in the Sunnah of the Prophet.

It seems from the above incident that Caliph Umar had primarily considered the Holy Quran as a source of guidance, as opposed to both the Quran and the Sunnah of the Prophet.

Another interesting point that comes out this incident is that the Prophet had never specifically asked Caliph Umar to bring him the writing material. It was a general order which any of the other companions could have easily fulfilled. But Caliph Umar intervened unnecessarily, and even prevented the other companions from fulfilling the wish of the Prophet which was indeed really unfortunate.

This was because Caliph Umar believed that not every single instruction of the Prophet had to be followed to the letter. He believed that in certain circumstances the companions also had a right to pass their own judgment, and even ignore the commands of the Prophet.

This incident alone proves the deep-seated attitude of the trend of al-ijtihad (independent judgment) among the companions. This trend had always existed within the ranks of the companions, but it became even more pronounced and open towards the end of Prophet's life.

The next example will further clarify the above statement.

7.2.3. Example 3: The Military Detachment Under Usama

As mentioned briefly in the previous chapter that Prophet of Allah had kept Ali in Madinah during the final days of his life. The Prophet had organized an army to be sent to Syria (the Byzantine Empire) two or three days before his death, while he was in his final illness. He appointed Usama Ibn Zayd ibn Haritha, who was just eighteen years of age as the commander in chief of this army.

The Prophet then asked some of his prominent companions both from the Muhajireen and the Ansar to join this expedition. They included companions like Caliph Abu Bakr, Caliph Umar, Abu Ubaydah and other well-known companions. However, instead of joining the army the companions began to criticize the decision of the Prophet for appointing Usama as the commander of the army. They complained that Usama was too young and inexperienced to lead an army. The companions in the past had also criticized the Prophet for appointing Usama's father as an army commander too, since they were not happy with his leadership either.

This incident is narrated in the famous books of history in the following way:

Ibn Sa'd in his book Tabaqat Al-Kubra and ibn Hajar in his Sharh of Sahih Bukhari writes:

> *'The Prophet equipped an army that Abu Bakr and Umar were in and he appointed Usama ibn Zayd as their commander, then people criticized him about his age, this news reached the Messenger of Allah, so he climbed the Mimbar and praised God and said: "People criticized the leadership of Usama and in the past, they have criticized his father's leadership too. Even though they both are worthy of leadership, and he is the dearest of people to now, I recommend you to be good to him."*
>
> - Tabaqat Al-Kubra. Vol. 2, Pg. # 219.
> - Fathul Bari Sharh Saheeh Al-Bukhari. Vol. 8, Pg. # 445.
> - Al-Muntazam Fi Tarikh Al-Muluk Wa Al-Umam. Vol. 5, Pg. # 306-307.
> - Tarikh Madinatul Damishq. Vol. 8, Pg. # 60.

Bukhari narrates the incident in the following way:

> *"You object to the command of Usama bin Zaid as you had objected before to the command of his father (Zaid). By Allah, he was most competent for it and, by Allah, he was dearest to me amongst people and, by Allah, the same is the case with Usama bin Zaid. He is most dear to me after him and I advise you to treat him well for he is pious amongst you."*
>
> - Bukhari Volume 5, Book 59, Number 552,

Again, we witness the presence of the trend of al-ijtihad among the companions during the very last days of Prophet's life.

The Prophet of Allah had chosen Usama, a very young companion as commander of the Muslim army, to lead an expedition against the Byzantine Empire. But the companions refused to follow the commands of the Prophet and disagreed with the decision made by the Prophet. The companions felt that they were more experienced than Usama, they were older than him and they deserved more to lead the army than the young Usama.

These companions challenged the decision of the Prophet and refused to follow his orders, on the pretext that they had more of a right to lead the expedition than Usama, since they felt that they were better suited for the job.

This incident happened right towards the end of Prophet's life. It clearly illustrates the strength of the trend of al-ijtihad which existed among the companions. These companions believed in their own independent judgment, in spite of the fact that there was a clear instruction from the Prophet to join the army of Usama.

This controversy continued and eventually the Prophet came out and spoke to the companions directly:

> "You object to the command of Usama as you had objected before to the command of his father …. he was dearest to me ….by Allah, the same is the case with Usama"

The companions had not only objected to Usama's appointment, but in the past, they had also objected and challenged his father's appointment by the Prophet too. It wasn't the first time that the authority or the decision of the Prophet was being challenged.

This clearly shows that the trend of al-ijtihad had been present in the approach and the attitude of the companions for a while, but became even more pronounced with the passage of time, to the extent that some of the companions would actually refuse to follow the clear and the simple instructions of the Prophet.

The army of Usama never left the outskirts of Madinah because the companions refused to join him, despite the fact that Prophet had come out and directly spoken to the companions. Like the rest of the companions, both Caliph Abu Bakr and Caliph Umar also refused to join the army of Usama and remained in Madinah until the death of the Prophet.

So, the trend of al-ijtihad (independent judgment) had manifested itself in both the ordinary and the prominent companions alike.

7.2.4. Example 4: The Burning of the Sunnah of the Prophet

Readers would recall that we had discussed this topic in Chapter 4, but for the sake of completeness of this chapter I will briefly discuss it here too.

The Prophet of Allah had made it compulsory for the companions and the ordinary Muslims to follow the Book of Allah and his Sunnah. The famous tradition below confirms this approach. The Prophet of Allah had said:

> "I have left among you two matters by holding fast to which, you shall never be misguided: the Book of God and my Sunnah"

- Dar Al-Hijra Malik ibn Anas in Al-Muwatta. Vol. 2, Pg. # 480, H # 2618.
- Al-Hakim Al-Nishaburi in Al-Mustadrak Alaa Al-Sahihain. Vol. 1, Pg. # 160 - 161, H. # 318.

However, during his reign as the second Caliph, Caliph Umar decided to burn the entire documented Sunnah of the Prophet that existed during his time. This was done because in the judgment of Caliph Umar if the Sunnah of the Prophet was preserved and documented than the Muslims would ignore the Book of Allah!

Contrary to the views of the Prophet, Caliph Umar had declared the following:

> "My intention was to record hadith but then I realized that some people (nations) before you kept writing down the sayings of their Prophets, and kept reading them, as a result, they forgot the book of Allah (their scriptures). I fear that same will happen If I order you to document the sayings of the Prophet, or if I do it myself. I do not want to make the book of Allah a victim here because of the hadith, nothing has precedence over the book of Allah"

- (Kanzl Ummal, 10, hadith 29474)

He then wrote to the Ansar and asked them to erase any traditions of the Prophet that they had written down.

> "Whoever has anything should erase it"
>
> - *(Taqiad ali-Ilm, 49, hujjiyat al-Sunnah, 3:95)*

Caliph Umar further decreed:

> "These (the hadith of the Prophet) are just like the Jewish scripts (mushnat), and they must be burnt"
>
> - *(Ibn Sa'd, Tabaqat al-Kubra, 1:140)*
>
> He then gathered all of the hadith written on leather, tablets, and pieces of wood and ordered them to be burnt.
>
> - *(Kanzl Ummal, 5:239)*

The Prophet had categorically instructed the Muslims to follow both the Holy Quran and his Sunnah, but in Caliph Umar's opinion the companions and the ordinary Muslims would get confused between the Book of Allah and the Sunnah of the Prophet!

Hence, he made a judgment (al-ijtihad) to erase various documented collections of Prophet's Sunnah during his Caliphate, clearly proving that the trend of al-ijtihad had remained present among the companions well after the death of the Prophet.

Keeping in mind the strength of the trend of al-ijtihad (independent Judgement), let's see what actually took place right after the demise of the Prophet.

7.3. After the Prophet's Death

As evident from the previous section that the trend of al-ijtihad was not only visible during the lifetime of the Prophet, but it was also reflected in the approach of the companions after his death. The most glaring example of the trend of al-ijtihad (independent judgment) happened in the meeting of Saqifah, which took place immediately after the death of the Prophet.

The Prophet of Allah had nominated Ali to be his successor on many occasions during his lifetime. The Prophet's stipulation in favour of Ali began with the Home Conference, which took place at the very start of Prophet's mission. The last stipulation of the Prophet in favour of Ali happened in the event of Ghadeer Khum, which took place right towards the end of Prophet's life.

Despite the presence of many clear and explicit traditions of the Prophet declaring Ali to be his successor, the trend of al-ijtihad takes over the meeting of Saqifah, and the commands and the instructions of the Prophet in favour of Ali were completely ignored and bypassed. The trend of al-ijtihad, which was present among the companions during the lifetime of the Prophet, continued to undermine the Sunnah of the Prophet after his death too.

Just as the companions had refused to bring the writing material to the Prophet in the final days of his life, and just as the companions had refused to join the army of Usama because they felt that he was too young to lead them, the companions also ignored the clear instructions of the Prophet in favour of Ali, because they felt that the political situation at the time was not conducive for Ali to take on the mantle of the Islamic leadership.

In this next section I will clarify exactly what happened after the death of the Prophet, and the approach that was taken by the key players in the Muslim Ummah which resulted in Ali being side lined from the leadership of the Islamic State. I will discuss the position and the approach taken by the Ansar (companions from Madinah), the Muhajireen (companions from Makkah) and the Ahlulbayt (the family of the Prophet).

Before I discuss the actions of each group it would make sense to briefly revisit the divisive event of Saqifah, as this event gives an in-depth insight into the actions and the actual decisions that were made by the companions, right after the death of the Prophet.

7.4. The Meeting of Saqifah

Saqifah is an area which is about two or three miles from Madinah. This is where the meeting to choose the new Caliph for the Muslims took place after the death of the Prophet, and hence it is known as the Shura or the meeting of Saqifah.

The news of Prophet's death spread in Madinah and its surroundings like jungle fire. The Ahlulbayt including Ali and Fatima had already been with the Prophet ever since he had been unwell and were beside the Prophet as he passed away. Amidst their sorrow and grief, the Ahlulbayt and the Banu Hashim which included personalities like Ali and Ibn Abbas began the arrangements for Prophet's burial.

As soon as the Ansar (companions from Madinah) heard the tragic news of Prophet's death, they started gathering in Saqifah with the intention of selecting the new Caliph. The Ansar were concerned that after the demise of the Prophet the leadership of the Muslim Ummah might be taken over by the Muhajireen. Despite having welcomed Muhajireen into their city the Ansar had been fearful and cautious about their domination in Madinah. The aim of the meeting was to take a pre-emptive measure and to prevent the leadership of the Muslims from falling into the hands of the Muhajireen.

The Ansar were divided into two tribes Al-Aws and Al-Khazraj. Saad Ibn Ubaadah who was from the al-Khazraj tribe of the Ansar was hoping to be the new leader of the Muslims. Although, he was unwell at the time, but he gave a fiery speech in which he recounted the virtues of the Ansar and told the attendants to take over the Caliphate (leadership) before anybody else could do so. However, some Ansar remembered the words of the Prophet and mentioned that they would only give allegiance to Ali. But there was nobody from Ali's camp to support his right and the meeting swiftly moved on.

The Ansar without wasting much time selected Saad ibn Ubaadah as the future leader of Muslims, and almost finalized him as the new Caliph to rule over the entire Muslim Ummah. The Ansar even declared that in case the Muhajireen refused to accept their choice, they would drive the Muhajireen out of Madinah on the point of their swords.

However, some companions who were present in Saqifah and were observing its proceedings left the meeting, and informed Caliph Umar about the pre-emptive move of the Ansar for the Caliphate of the Muslims. On hearing the news of the meeting of Ansar in Saqifah Caliph Umar immediately informs Caliph Abu Bakr as to what was happening in Saqifah. Caliph Abu Bakr at the time was present in the house of the Prophet where the Ahlulbayt (family of the Prophet) were busy in preparing the Prophet's body for burial.

Once Caliph Abu Bakr is informed as to what was taking place in Saqifah, both Caliph Umar and Caliph Abu Bakr alongside Abu Ubaydah al-Jarrah (who they met on the way) rushed towards Saqifah, to stop the Ansar from acquiring the leadership of the Muslim Ummah.

When the three Muhajireen i.e., Caliph Umar, Caliph Abu Bakr and Abu Ubaydah al-Jarrah arrive in Saqifah, the Ansar were surprised and were taken back as they were not expecting any outsiders in this meeting. The meeting of Saqifah was in full swing and both Caliph Umar and Caliph Abu Bakr realize that the Ansar had almost finalized Saad ibn Ubaadah as the new Caliph. The Ansar were remunerating their merits and were claiming that since they had given refuge and protection to the Prophet, and since Madinah was their city the future Caliph should be from the Ansar.

Once seated, Caliph Abu Bakr intervenes in the meeting and acknowledges the merits of the Ansar, but says that the leadership of the Muslim Ummah is only the right of the Muhajireen, since they were the first to accept Islam, and since they have sacrificed more in the path of Allah, and because the Quraysh would not accept the leadership of the Ansar, so it was essential that the new Caliph must be chosen from the Muhajireen.

The Ansar disagreed and insisted that the Caliph must be from one of them, as they deserved the Caliphate more than the Muhajireen. An intense argument broke out between the Ansar and the Muhajireen especially between Caliph Umar and al-Ḥubab Ibn al-Mundhir, an Ansar from the al-Khazraj tribe. Al-Hubab challenged the Muhajireen that the Ansar would not allow anyone to rule over them. He spoke with passion and pleaded with the Ansar to stay united against the Muhajireen. A serious discord and dispute began to emerge between the Ansar and the Muhajireen, to the extent that it seemed that the meeting of Saqifah might lead to an open war between the two groups.

Despite the extremely serious and the tense situation with the Ansar, Caliph Abu Bakr and Caliph Umar refused to budge and did not give into the demands of the Ansar. They kept insisting that the Caliph must be from the Muhajireen, since the Quraysh would only accept the leadership of the Muhajireen.

As the meeting of Saqifah reached a stalemate the Ansar proposed a compromise. They offered the Muhajireen to have one ruler from the Ansar and one from the Muhajireen. The Muhajireen i.e., Caliph Abu Bakr and Caliph Umar declined the offer of the Ansar and said that there could only be one leader, and that leader must be from the Muhajireen i.e., the leader has to be from the Quraysh, and Quraysh would not accept an Ansar as the new Caliph.

There was a lot of commotion, dispute, disagreement, and turmoil in the meeting of Saqifah and threats are openly flying. On seeing the situation Caliph Abu Bakr proposed a compromise. He said to the Ansar that we the Muhajireen should become the rulers and you the Ansar should become our advisors, essentially offering Ansar the position of the advisory to the Caliph. Caliph Abu Bakr further stated that the Muhajireen would not make any decisions without consulting the Ansar, giving the Ansar a further incentive to accept his offer.

The Ansar at this stage had suffered a setback, they had lost unity within their own ranks. The old rivalry between the two tribes of the Ansar i.e., Al-Aws and Al-Khazraj began to resurface. These tribes were bitter enemies in the pre-Islamic days and had fought many battles with each other. As the internal rivalry and bickering between the two tribes of Ansar began to emerge, the political advantage started to shift to the Muhajireen, who were now leading the proceedings of Saqifah.

The Ansar now began to contemplate the offer of Caliph Abu Bakr.

Despite the offer of Caliph Abu Bakr, the arguments, and the wrangling between the Ansar and the Muhajireen continued unabated, where each side was still vying for power. However, the Ansar could feel that the balance of power was shifting to the Muhajireen, who were in the ascendency and were now dictating the proceedings and the terms of the Shura.

On seeing that the Caliphate was slipping away from them and into the hands of the Muhajireen, the Ansar shifted their position and reluctantly accepted the offer of Caliph Abu Bakr to become the advisors to the Caliph.

The Ansar at that stage realized that the topmost position that they could possibly acquire in the presence of the Muhajireen was the position offered by Caliph Abu Bakr. The position of being the advisors (vazirs) would give them a say in the decision-making process of the State, something that the Ansar had always desired and wished for, and hence they eventually accepted the offer of being the advisors (vazirs) to the Caliph.

As soon as Caliph Umar sensed that the Ansar had conceded and some sort of an agreement was in the making, he seized the moment and asked Caliph Abu Bakr to stretch out his hand. As Caliph Abu Bakr stretched out his hand Caliph Umar immediately paid allegiance to him, so as not to allow any more discourse or wrangling between the Ansar and the Muhajireen.

The impromptu allegiance of Caliph Umar on the hand of Caliph Abu Bakr sealed the Caliphate for the Muhajireen. This was followed by the allegiance from Abu Ubaydah Ibn al-Jarrah who was the other Muhajir (immigrant from Makkah) present in the meeting of Saqifah.

On seeing that the key Muhajireen present in Saqifah had paid allegiance to Abu Bakr, Bashir ibn Saad from the al-Khazraj tribe of Ansar paid allegiance to Abu Bakr, in order not to lose out on the position of being the advisor (vazir). On witnessing that members of al-Khazraj have paid allegiance to Abu Bakr, the leaders of al-Aws also paid allegiance to Abu Bakr, so as not to lose favour in the eyes of the new Caliph, and also to acquire the promised position of being the advisors (vazirs).

A few people from al-Khazraj resist the allegiance and took out their swords but were restrained by others. However, Saad Ibn Ubaadah from al-Khazraj who was initially chosen by the Ansar as their potential Caliph refused to pay allegiance to Abu Bakr. But the other leaders and elders of his tribe agreed to pay allegiance to Abu Bakr, who had also promised them the position of being the advisors (vazir).

Saad Ibn Ubaadah had been extremely unwell on the day the event of Saqifah took place. He had very high fever on that day. At the end of the meeting of Saqifah, he told Caliph Umar that if he had been well, then he would have taken on the Muhajireen with full force which would have been very painful for Caliph Umar and his supporters. On hearing these comments Caliph Umar assaulted Saad Ibn Ubaadah and accused him of hypocrisy and wanting the Caliphate for himself. Saad Ibn Ubaadah fell to the ground and was then trampled upon. Caliph Umar wanted to kill Saad Ibn Ubaadah, but he was restrained by Caliph Abu Bakr from doing so.

This was how the meeting of Saqifah ended with Abu Bakr becoming the first Caliph and the leader of the entire Muslim Ummah.

Based on the event of Saqifah I will analyse and discuss in depth the position and the approach adopted by each faction, which had a stake in the future leadership of the Muslim Ummah.

7.5. The Approach of the Ansar

As soon as the Prophet passes away, the Ansar (companions from Madinah) assemble at Saqifah to choose the new leader of the Muslims. The companions from Madinah were fearful that after the demise of the Prophet the Muhajireen might take over the reins of power and would rule them for good. Based on this fear they made their own judgment (al-ijtihad), that the leadership of the Muslims should be confined to them, even if it was against the commands and the wishes of the Prophet, and the interest of the Muhajireen, or the interest of the rest of the Muslim Ummah.

The approach and the attitude of the Ansar towards the Islamic leadership proved that the trend of al-ijtihad had gained a serious foothold among the companions. The Ansar were willing to disregard the interests of all the other stakeholders to achieve their goals. They had shown no consideration for any other group in the Muslim Ummah. They had simply decided to acquire the Caliphate for their own tribe.

7.5.1. An Unannounced Meeting

The Ansar who were the companions of the Prophet from Madinah had gathered in Saqifah without informing anybody else about their plans or motives. If a meeting is to be conducted which is going to decide the successor of the Prophet, then surely the time when it is going to take place and the location where it is going to be held should be made public to all the concerned parties.

The Ansar had not only kept the timing and the location of the Shura a secret, but they ignored and side-lined all the other stake holders who had a say in that matter. The Ansar had ignored the Ahlulbayt (the family of the Prophet) and the Muhajireen (immigrants from Makkah). They included companions like Ibn Abbas, Caliph Abu Bakr, Caliph Umar, Caliph Uthman, Talha, Zubair and Ali.

By not informing anybody about the timing and the location of the meeting of Saqifah, the Ansar had completely contradicted the spirit of justice and fair play. A meeting such as Saqifah, which was going to select the future leader of the Muslims must consult with all the relevant groups and personalities, who had a stake in this matter. This is a basic and a fundamental principle of justice and fair play. One group cannot just decide to hold a meeting among themselves and then impose its decision on the rest of the Muslims. This kind of a meeting or gathering has no validity in the eyes of Islam.

By taking this course of action the Ansar had clearly shown that the concept of selecting the new leader of the Muslim Ummah, which they had in mind could not have been taught or advocated by the Prophet of Allah. The Prophet would have never advocated such a meeting for his successor where nobody is informed about its timing or location, and where the relevant parties are not even represented.

7.5.2. A Dubious location

The location of Saqifah was just as dubious as its timing.

Saqifah is a place which is around three miles from Madinah. During the lifetime of the Holy Prophet, the Mosque of the Prophet was the centre of all Islamic activities. It was the mosque of the Prophet where the decisions of war and peace were made. It was in Prophet's Mosque where foreign deputations were received, sermons were delivered, and cases were discussed. Hence, when the news spread about the death of the Prophet the Muslims naturally assembled in that very mosque.

It would have made perfect sense to hold that meeting in the mosque of the Prophet, rather than in Saqifah. This would have allowed all the eminent Islamic personalities and tribes to take part in the meeting. The proceedings of the meeting would have been open and transparent for all to see.

If Prophet of Allah had wanted his successor to be chosen by such a meeting (Shura), then surely, he would have instructed the Muslims to carry out its proceedings in his mosque. The Prophet's Mosque would have been the most appropriate and suitable location for this kind of a meeting.

But as one can clearly see that even the location of the meeting of Saqifah shows that it was based on the trend of al-ijtihad (independent judgment), rather than any instructions or guidelines given by the Prophet.

7.5.3. The Ansar were Willing to Wage War

The Ansar had adopted an extremely belligerent approach towards the leadership of the Muslims, and they were even prepared to declare war if necessary. We read in Tareekh Al-Islam:

> "(The) Ansar said: 'In case they reject our Caliph, we shall drive them out from Al-Medinah at the point of our swords.' However, the few Muhajirs in the assembly protested against this attitude and this led to a dispute and disorder of a serious nature and a war between the Muhajirs and Ansars seemed possible."

- Tareekh Al-Islam Vol.1, p.273-274

The Ansar had almost finalized Saad Ibn Ubaadah as their Caliph over Muslims who was from the tribe of al-Khazraj. After being nominated as the new leader of the Muslims Saad ibn Ubaadah conveyed the following message to his fellow Ansar:

> "You have precedence in religion and merit in Islam that no other tribe of the Arabs can claim. Muhammad remained ten-odd years in his tribe, calling them to worship the Merciful and to cast off idols and graven images, but only a few men of his tribe believed in him, and they were able neither to protect the Apostle of Allah, nor to render his religion strong ,....... He (Mohammad) intended excellence for you (O Ansar); He sent nobility to you and distinguished you with grace .... You (O Ansar) were the most severe people against his enemies .... When Allah took (the Prophet) to Himself, he was pleased with you (O Ansar) .... "So, keep control of this matter (i.e., the Caliphate) to yourselves, to the exclusion of others, for it is yours and yours alone."

- The History of al-Tabari, Vol.10, p.2

The above statements of the Ansar confirmed that they were willing to side-line and ignore all the other Muslim groups like the Ahlulbayt and the Muhajireen, because they felt that they were the most deserving group for the role of the Caliphate. They believed that since they had given protection to the Prophet, helped the Muhajireen to settle down in Madinah, and they had fought alongside the Prophet against Quraysh, it was their exclusive right to rule over the Muslims, clearly showing the trend of al-ijtihad (independent judgment) which had plagued their ranks.

They were even willing to kill and wage war against the other companions and Muslims and drive them out of Madinah on the point of their swords, if their man wasn't chosen. Such was the strength of the trend of al-ijtihad that the companions of the Prophet were willing to even shed the blood of fellow companions if their decision would be challenged.

For many companions of Madinah, the statements of their leaders like Saad Ibn Ubaadah where he says:

> "So, keep control of this matter (i.e., the Caliphate) to yourselves, to the exclusion of others, for it is yours and yours alone."

- The History of al-Tabari, Vol.10, p.2

took precedence over the commands and wishes of the Prophet. The reason why these companions would give more importance to the instructions of their leaders rather than to the commands of the Prophet was because the Prophet had passed away, but their tribal leaders were still alive. It made more sense to follow a leader who was alive rather than the one who was dead. Unfortunately, after the death of the Prophet this was the reality on the ground in Madinah.

7.5.4. Ali Does Get Mentioned

In the initial stages of the meeting of Saqifah some of the companions of Madinah (Ansar) remembered the words of Prophet and stipulated that they would only pay allegiance to Ali. These companions stated:

> *"We will never pay allegiance to anyone except Ali Ibn abi Talib"*
> - Tarikh al-Tabari 3:198
> - Ibn al-Atheer 5:157

Unfortunately, Ali was not present in Saqifah to support his nomination. He was busy preparing the body of the Prophet for burial. There was nobody from the Ahlulbayt or Banu Hashim in the meeting either who could support Ali's case. Although Ali does get mentioned by some of the Ansar in the meeting of Saqifah, but due to the lack of support for him the meeting moves on, and the nominee of the Prophet is disregarded.

The merits of Ali, the training of Ali at the hands of the Prophet, the selection of Ali in Ghadeer Khum, the nomination of Ali in the Home Conference and the hadith of the Two Weighty things were a non-issue for the majority of the Ansar in Saqifah. The Ansar who were present in Saqifah felt that their interests would be best served by someone who was from their own clan, rather than somebody who was an outsider like Ali. So, even though Ali is mentioned, the meeting overall follows the trend of al-ijtihad and does not support the nomination of Ali as the future Caliph.

It also shows that the leaders of the Ansar had failed to realize that when Prophet of Allah had nominated Ali, it was not done for tribal reasons. Prophet chose Ali because Prophet had ideologically nurtured Ali in the ideals of the Islamic thought. The sole reason why Prophet had nominated Ali as his successor was because Ali had been specifically trained and groomed by the Prophet for this role, since he was a child. The merits and distinctions of Ali were unique, as he had acquired those merits through the prolonged company of the Prophet.

However, the majority of the Ansar present in Saqifah were looking at Ali's successorship to the Prophet in a tribal sense, because they themselves were still controlled and dominated by the tribal allegiances, but this was not how Prophet had envisaged Ali's successorship.

Hence, as soon as they find out that the Messenger of Allah had passed away, the first thing they did was to quickly rush to Saqifah and select their own candidate to rule over the Muslims, knowing very well that Ali at the time would be busy with the funeral proceedings of the Prophet.

7.5.5. The Interest of the Ansar Came First

The meeting of Saqifah was a pre-emptive attempt by the companions of Madinah (Ansar) to primarily side-line the Muhajireen and the Quraysh of Makkah, and in the process they had also side-lined Ali and the Ahlulbayt. The Ansar had fought many battles against the Quraysh of Makkah. Although, the Quraysh had now accepted Islam after the conquest of Makkah but there was a lot of blood that had been spilt on both sides, and the wounds were still fresh. The Prophet of Allah was a unifying figure but after his death the old rivalries resurfaced, and the Ansar had no intention of being ruled by their traditional foes.

Also, Madinah was the hub of the Islamic State. Prophet ruled over the Islamic State from the city of Madinah. Ansar were the majority inhabitants of Madinah, and it was their city. Although, they had given refuge to the Muslims of Makkah and to the Prophet, but after the death of the Prophet they themselves wanted to rule the Islamic State from Madinah. They were not prepared to allow any other group especially the Muhajireen to dominate them in their own city. They were prepared to use force, if necessary, to defend their interests.

There were historical reasons as well as to why the Ansar felt that they would lose out if the Caliphate went to another group. Ansar had not forgotten that after the Battle of Hunayn the Prophet had showered the Quraysh and all the other tribes of Arabia with gifts of war booty, but he left out the Ansar. This action of the Prophet at the time had really infuriated the Ansar and they were determined that something like this should not happen again.

We read in Ibn Ishaq, Seerah Rasool-Allah that Abu Sa'id Al-Khudri said:

> "When Allah's Messenger had given the Quraysh and Arab tribes those gifts and allotted nothing to the Ansar, a group of the Ansar felt so uneasy about it that a lot of ill-statements against the Prophet were spread amongst them to an extent that one of them said: 'By Allah, Allah's Messenger is ill-spoken of by his folk's men!'"

On the issue of war booty, Saad Ibn Ubaadah who was almost finalized by the Ansar as their Caliph had earlier said to the Prophet:

> "O Messenger of Allah, the group of Ansar is furious at you about the distribution of the booty that you had won. You have allotted shares to your own (Quraysh) kinsmen and forwarded lots of gifts to the (other) Arab tribes, but this group (of Ansar) has obtained nothing."

- *(Ar-Raheequl Makhtum, p.485)*

The Prophet then reassured Saad Ibn Ubaadah and the Ansar by saying:

> "You Ansar, do you feel eager for the things of this world where with I have sought to incline these people (i.e., the Quraysh and Arab tribes) into the Faith (of Islam) in which you (Ansar) are already (firmly) established?"

- *(Ar-Raheequl Makhtum, p.486)*

The Ansar felt that if the new leader of the Muslims was from Quraysh, then they could again be sidelined, especially when it came to getting the war booty of the future wars. Some of the Ansar were so angry with the Prophet of Allah on the issue of war booty that they had spread false statements about the Prophet and had even slandered the Prophet.

One of the companions from Madinah had said about the Prophet:

> "By Allah, Allah's Messenger is ill-spoken of by his folk's men!"

These were some of the limits which certain companions were willing to cross when they felt that their interest was threatened or when the decision of the Prophet went against their will or wishes.

The reason why Prophet had given majority of the war booty to the Quraysh was because the vast majority of Quraysh were recent converts, who had converted to Islam after the conquest of Makkah. The war booty was an incentive form the Prophet to keep these newly converted tribes on the path of Islam.

The messenger of Allah had tried his level best to reassure the Ansar and to alleviate their fears of discrimination. He had advised them that they should not worry about the material wealth of this world, which has been given to Quraysh, since what mattered more was their faith in Islam which they already had. But it seemed that there were other influences and motivations which were affecting these companions from Madinah.

This incident also highlights the lack of ideological attachment that many of the companions had with the message of Islam. For these companions the war booty or lack of it in this case, were the main driving factors, rather than the love of Allah or adherence to the commands of the Prophet.

This was indeed the mindset that was operating in the meeting of Saqifah, where the future leader of the Muslims was going to be chosen.

7.5.6. Ignoring the Funeral of the Prophet

It was ironic that that the leaders of the Ansar could not even wait for the burial of the Prophet before initiating the meeting of Saqifah. The Ansar began the proceedings for choosing the next Caliph as soon as they heard the news of Prophet's death. Instead of assembling at the mosque of the Prophet or visiting the house of the Prophet for condolences, they started assembling in Saqifah to select their new leader. It seems as if there was no grief or sense of loss among them at the passing away of the Prophet.

The actions of these companions clearly demonstrate their lack of attachment to the Prophet and his mission. The majority of the companions present in Saqifah were Ansar i.e., the companions from Madinah, who had gathered there to select their new leader rather than participate in the funeral proceedings of the Prophet.

It is then not too difficult to deduce that when the majority of the participants of Saqifah were not even that emotionally attached to the Prophet, then why would they follow his commands and his instructions for choosing the next caliph, especially when they also perceived that those commands and instructions went against their personal and tribal interests.

When Ansar, being the companions of the Prophet from Madinah, were capable of ignoring the funeral of the Prophet, then they would also be capable of ignoring the traditions of the Prophet in favour of Ali, which had given Ali the leadership of the Muslim Ummah.

It was indeed the perceived threat from the Muhajireen which had made the Ansar insular to the interest of the wider Muslim Ummah, and they chose to act in a way which would only preserve their own tribal interests, even if that meant ignoring the clear traditions of the Prophet.

It was in this context that the Ansar had side-lined Ali who was indeed chosen by the Prophet to lead the Muslims after his death.

7.5.7. Our Approach

The leaders of the Ansar had made a decision based on the circumstances and the political situation of the time that it wasn't in their best interest to recognize Ali as the successor of the Prophet. If the companions of Madinah had made a mistake based on their ijtihad (independent judgment), then their decisions and their actions are between them and Allah. It is for Allah to judge their deeds and intentions.

But researchers like us who have a wealth of evidence in front of our eyes, can make a much more informed choice today, and recognize that although the Ansar had nominated Saad Ibn Ubaadah as the successor of the Prophet, but Prophet himself had only nominated Ali to be his successor.

If Ansar had side-lined and disregarded Ali for certain reasons, then that was their decision and choice. Fortunately, there is no Ansar or Muhajireen divide in the Muslim Ummah today, so there is no reason for us to fall in the same trap that the Ansar did after the death of the Prophet.

On the Day of Judgment, we will not be questioned or asked about the choice that Ansar made some fourteen centuries ago in Saqifah. But we will be held accountable for the choice that we make in our lifetimes. We are not bound to follow the nominee of the Ansar, but we are obliged to follow the nominee of the Messenger of Allah.

Today we can do justice to the nominee of the Prophet, by giving Ali the status and the stature that Prophet had given him, and that he indeed deserves, which is to recognize Ali as the rightful successor of the Prophet.

7.6. The Approach of the Muhajireen

The approach of the Muhajireen was unfortunately a continuation of the trend of al-ijtihad that we had observed in the actions of Ansar. On witnessing the pre-emptive move of the Ansar in Saqifah for the leadership of the Islamic State, the Muhajireen also acted in way that would only protect their own personal and tribal interests, instead of following the commands of the Prophet.

7.6.1. Both Caliph Abu Bakr and Caliph Umar Did Not Inform Others

A person came and informed Caliph Umar about the pre-emptive move of the Ansar in Saqifah. When Caliph Umar finds out that the Ansar were gathering in Saqifah to choose the future leader of the Muslims, he decides to only inform Caliph Abu Bakr. Caliph Abu Bakr at the time was present in house of the Prophet alongside many key personalities of the Muslim Ummah, which included the Ahlulbayt i.e., Ali, the notables of Banu Hashim such as Ibn Abbas and many other prominent companions like al-Zubair, Talha, Ammar, Salman who had all come to pay their respects to the Prophet and were present in Prophet's house at the time.

> *"Umar learned of this (i.e., the meeting of Ansar in Saqifah) and went to the Prophet's house and sent (a message) to Abu Bakr, who was in the building.... Something (terrible) has happened that you must attend to personally. So, he (Abu Bakr) came out to him...."*
>
> - The History of al-Tabari, Vol.10, p.3

However, Caliph Umar uses his personal judgment (al-ijtihad) and chooses not to inform anybody else except Caliph Abu Bakr. It was not a personal or a private issue that could be restricted to one individual. The meeting of Saqifah was an issue for the entire Muslim Ummah. This was where the companions of Madinah were about to choose the future Caliph of the Muslims. As per the words of Caliph Umar:

> *"Something (terrible) has happened that you must attend to personally. So, he (Abu Bakr) came out to him...."*
>
> - The History of al-Tabari, Vol.10, p.3

Caliph Umar knew exactly what the Ansar were up to, and that is why he had sent an urgent message to Caliph Abu Bakr, but he chooses not to inform others about the pre-emptive move of the Ansar.

When Caliph Abu Bakr finds out about the meeting of Ansar in Saqifah he also chooses not to inform anybody around him, even though he had just come out of the Prophet's house where all the other stakeholders were still present.

Both Caliph Abu Bakr and Caliph Umar leave for Saqifah alongside Abu Ubaydah al-Jarrah, who they met on the way. As they arrived in Saqifah they immediately found themselves in the midst of a power struggle, which was being orchestrated by the Ansar. The Ansar had almost finalized Saad Ibn Ubaadah as their candidate for the Caliphate. The Ansar were stipulating their merits and virtues to justify their claim for the leadership of the Muslims.

If there was any doubt about the intentions of the Ansar initially i.e., when Caliph Umar and Caliph Abu Bakr had received the news about the meeting of Saqifah, then certainly those doubts were removed once they had arrived in Saqifah. Now, the intentions of the Ansar were absolutely clear, they were going for the leadership of the Muslims. But still both the prominent companions choose not to inform anybody else especially the people who had assembled at the house of the Prophet.

They could have easily sent someone like Abu Ubaydah al-Jarrah (who they met on the way), or another companion who was present in the meeting, to inform the rest of the Muslims about the proceedings of Saqifah, but unfortunately, they choose not to do so.

The reason why Caliph Abu Bakr and Caliph Umar had not informed others was because in their judgment (al-ijtihad), they felt that they were the best-suited people to handle the situation. The political scenario in Madinah had suddenly changed. The Ansar had made the first move to acquire the leadership of the Muslims, in complete contradiction to the wishes of the Prophet. But both Caliph Abu Bakr and Caliph Umar still felt that they did not need to inform others, and that they were the right people to handle the affair.

Both Caliph Abu Bakr and Caliph Umar were well aware of the commands and the instructions of the Prophet regarding the leadership of Ali. However, as the circumstances and the political scene changes in Madinah, they do their own ijtihad (judgment), and keep the news of Saqifah to themselves.

Unfortunately, as a result of the trend of al-ijtihad the people who had assembled at the house of the Prophet for his burial were kept in the dark about the proceedings of Saqifah.

7.6.2. The Core of Caliph Abu Bakr's Argument

On arriving in Saqifah Caliph Abu Bakr and Caliph Umar found that the Ansar had almost finalized Saad Ibn Ubaadah as the new Caliph, and the leaders of the Ansar were remunerating their merits to justify their claim. After hearing the arguments of the Ansar Caliph Abu Bakr intervenes in the proceedings of Saqifah and advocates the right of the Muhajireen to rule over the Muslims.

Following are some of the statements of Caliph Abu Bakr justifying his stance:

> *"However, it is a fact that we the Muhajireen were the first to accept the din of Islam. The Prophet of Islam was from our tribe. We are the relatives of the Prophet ... and therefore we are the people who are entitled to the Caliphate...."*

- Al-Ḥalabi - As-Sirat al- Ḥalabiyyah, vol. 3, p. 357

> *"(We were) the first on earth to worship Allah (in Islam) and we were the patrons (of the Prophet) and the supporting group of the Prophet. (It is we) who tolerated (great suffering) and suffered with him (through many) adversities..."*

- *(History of al-Tabari, Volume 3, p.219)*

> "(O Ansar) you are our brethren in Islam and our partners in religion...but the Arabs will not submit themselves except to this clan of Quraysh...we (the Quraysh) are in the centre among the Muslims with respect to our position..."

- *(The History of al-Tabari, Volume 9, p.193)*

> "O Ansar! You deserve all the qualities that you have attributed to yourselves, but this question (of Caliphate) is only for the Quraysh"

- *(Sahih Bukhari, Volume 8, Book 82, Number 817)*

> "O Saad (Ibn Ubaadah)! You know very well that the Prophet had said in your presence that the Quraysh shall be given the Caliphate because the noble among the Arab (masses) follow their (Quraysh) nobles and their ignobles follow their (Quraysh) ignobles."

- *(Musnad Ahmad, vol. 1, p.5)*

The above statements formed the core argument that was used by Caliph Abu Bakr to substantiate his claim against the Ansar, which eventually resulted in him being selected as the Caliph over the Muslims.

Just like the Ansar who had earlier said they were the most deserving group to attain the leadership of the Muslims, Caliph Abu Bakr makes a similar case for the Muhajireen. The key points of Caliph Abu Bakr argument were that the Muhajireen were the first to embrace Islam, they had endured great sufferings in this path, they were also the relatives of the Prophet, and that the Arabs would only accept the leadership of the Quraysh, and the Prophet had said that the Caliphate should only stay in the Quraysh.

Let's look at the justifications that Caliph Abu Bakr had given from the side of Muhajireen to support their claim for the Caliphate. I will analyse and discuss in detail the key justifications that Caliph Abu Bakr had given in Saqifah to support his position.

7.6.3. The Merits of a Group

The key theme that comes out from the meeting Saqifah is the fact that each group was trying to justify their claim to the Caliphate based on the merits of an entire group.

For instance, Saad ibn Ubaadah justified his stance in favour of the Ansar with the following words:

> "Company of the Ansar! You have precedence in religion and merit in Islam that no other tribe of the Arabs can claim.... So, keep control of this matter (i.e. the Caliphate) to yourselves, to the exclusion of others, for it is yours and yours alone."

- *(The History of al-Tabari, Vol.10, p.2)*

On the other hand, Caliph Abu Bakr justified his stance for the Muhajireen with these words:

> "However, it is a fact that we the Muhajireen were the first to accept the din of Islam. The Prophet of Islam was from our tribe. We are the relatives of the Prophet ... and therefore we are the people who are entitled to the Caliphate...."

- Al-Ḥalabi - As-Sirat al-Ḥalabiyyah, vol. 3, p. 357

The main flaw in this line of argument is that both the Ansar and the Muhajireen were trying to justify their claim to the Caliphate based on the merits of an entire group, as opposed to the merits of an individual.

The successorship of the Prophet was not meant for an entire group of people such as the Ansar or the Muhajireen, or the entire tribe of Quraysh. The successor of the Prophet was going to be an individual who had the right credentials. The successorship of the Prophet was not going to be for the whole of the Ansar, or for all the Muhajireen or for all the Quraysh.

The successorship of the Prophet was meant for one person based on his merits, rather than the collective merits of an entire segment of the society.

The successor of the Prophet was going to be someone who was the most distinguished companion in terms of his achievements during the lifetime of the Prophet, regardless of the collective achievements or the merits of the group he belonged to.

The reason why the participants of Saqifah were advocating the merits of an entire group, rather than the merits of an individual, was because there was nothing that really separated these candidates from each other.

For instance, the calibre and the stature of Caliph Abu Bakr was similar to the calibre and the stature of Saad Ibn Ubaadah. Saad Ibn Ubaadah was a prominent companion from Madinah, whereas Caliph Abu Bakr was a prominent companion from Makkah. Their service and achievements in the path of Islam were similar and comparable.

There was nothing that truly distinguished these companions from each other. Hence, they tried to claim an edge over each other by stating the merits of their respective groups.

7.6.4. The First to Embrace Islam

Caliph Abu Bakr had stated in Saqifah that Muhajireen were the first to embrace Islam and worship Allah.

> *"(We were) the first on earth to worship Allah (in Islam) ......"*
- *(History of al-Tabari, Volume 3, p.219)*

The statement of Caliph Abu Bakr was certainly true in comparison with the Ansar, but not if one brings Ali into the picture.

Ali had opened his eyes in lap of the Prophet. Ali was raised and brought up in the house of the Prophet since the age of four or five. Ali had only ever followed the monolithic faith, which the Prophet and his family were on, even before the announcement of the Prophethood.

When Prophet informed Ali about the revelations, Ali immediately accepted his status as the Prophet of Allah, since Ali himself had witnessed the revelations coming to the Prophet on many occasions. That is why many scholars don't even call the acceptance of Islam by Ali as a conversion, because Ali had always been on the path of Muhammad from the very start of his life.

In fact, among the Muhajireen Ali was the first person who had worshipped Allah. Ali was the first person who prayed behind the Prophet alongside Khadija, the wife of the Prophet. Nobody even knew what Islam was at that time when Ali and Khadija were praying behind the Prophet.

> *"Ali b. Abi Talib was the first man to believe in the Prophet, ... to pray together with him, and to affirm the veracity of that which God gave him......."*
- *Ibn Hisham, al-Sirah, Vol. I, p.245.*

Also, the Home Conference was the very first occasion when the Prophet had publicly invited his clan Banu Hashim to the path of Islam. No one from the general public became a Muslim before this feast, except Ali and Khadija. Ali was indeed on the path of Islam even before the event of the Home Conference. Ali was not one of the invitees in the Home Conference, but Ali was the host alongside the Prophet.

Caliph Abu Bakr became a Muslim after the event of the Home Conference. He was around the age of forty when he accepted Islam. Caliph Abu Bakr had spent some forty years in the pre-Islamic (Jahiliya) traditions. Ali on the other hand had not only accepted Islam before Caliph Abu Bakr, but Prophet had also shielded Ali away from the pre-Islamic (Jahiliya) customs, since Prophet had brought Ali up in his own house.

Caliph Abu Bakr certainly had precedence over Saad Ibn Ubaadah on this issue, but his argument would not hold ground in the presence of Ali.

7.6.5. We Suffered and Supported the Prophet More

Caliph Abu Bakr states in Saqifah that we have suffered more in the path of Allah and we have sacrificed and supported the cause of Islam more than the Ansar.

> "………. we were the patrons (of the Prophet) and the supporting group of the Prophet. (It is we) who tolerated (great suffering) and suffered with him (through many) adversities…"
>
> - *(History of al-Tabari, Volume 3, p.219)*

The argument of Caliph Abu Bakr could possibly hold against the Ansar, but this argument would lose its merit once the service of Ali in the path of Islam is brought into the frame. There was only one person who had suffered, sacrificed, and supported the cause of Islam more than any other companion, and that person was none other than Ali. The Chapter 3 of this book "Ali and the Establishment of the Islamic State" is a small testament to the service of Ali in the path of Islam.

Let's analyse the assertion of Caliph Abu Bakr in the light of Islamic history.

There were two individuals who were instrumental and indispensable in protecting and defending the Prophet and his mission, and in the establishment of the Islamic state, which allowed the Muslims to expand and flourish. These two individuals were Ali and his father Abu Talib.

Abu Talib was the guardian of the Prophet from childhood, and he became Prophet's main defender and protector after Prophet announced his mission. It was the protection offered by Abu Talib which allowed the Prophet to spread the message of Islam in an extremely hostile environment of Makkah. The only reason why Prophet was not killed by the Quraysh in Makkah, and why he was able to continue his mission was because of the protection given to the Prophet by Abu Talib. The Quraysh of Makkah had given Abu Talib many warnings and ultimatums to stop the mission of the Prophet, but Abu Talib refused to budge and carried on supporting the Prophet against all odds.

Ali carried on the mission of sacrifice, defence, and the protection of the Prophet after the demise of his father Abu Talib. In fact, Ali had worked alongside his father in Makkah to secure the life and the honour of the Prophet. When Prophet would walk on the streets of Makkah the children of Quraysh would abuse and attack the Prophet, it was Ali who would come to the defence of the Prophet and disperse the little Qurayshites. Abu Talib would make Ali sleep on Prophet's bed to save Prophet's life from the clans of Quraysh who were always looking for an opportunity to kill the Prophet.

7.6.5.1. The Night of the Hijrah

The first big sacrifice came in Makkah on the night of the Hijrah when Ali slept on Prophet's bed to save his life.

There were around 150 to 200 Muslims in Makkah at the time. But only the bravest of them all would be sleeping alone on Prophet's bed that night to face the assassins of Makkah. Not only was Ali facing certain death, but he also had to withhold Prophet's whereabouts under potential torture. On top of this if somehow Ali makes it, he would now have to risk his life again in the hostile environment of Makkah and returns the trusts of the people that Prophet had given him. Only a man of Ali's courage, sacrifice and bravery could have risen to the occasion, and that is why Prophet had urged other companions to leave for Madinah, but he gave Ali this unique responsibility.

The argument of Caliph Abu Bakr against the Ansar that the Muhajireen had sacrificed more in the path of Islam holds no value when the service of Ali is brought into the picture.

7.6.5.2. The Battle of Badr

Ali had sacrificed and supported the Prophet more than any other companion in the defence and the establishment of the Islamic State of Madinah. The first challenge to the Islamic State came from the Quraysh in the crucial battle of Badr.

The battle of Badr was the first key battle for the defence of the Islamic State. The Prophet had said special prayers at the beginning of the battle for a Muslim victory because Prophet knew that if Muslims would lose this battle, it would be the end of the newly established Islamic State in Madinah. Ali killed al-Waleed who had challenged Muslims for a duel. He was one of the most feared warriors of Quraysh. When the general offensive began, Ali killed almost 40% of the enemy soldiers, whereas the rest of the companions killed the remaining 60% of the enemy combatants. The contribution of Ali in the battle had tipped the scales in favour of Islam and Muslims.

Again, the effort and the support of Ali in defence of the Islamic faith was unique and distinct and was unmatched by anyone either from the Ansar or from the Muhajireen.

7.6.5.3. The Battle of Uhud

The battle of Uhad would again tell a similar story of Ali's sacrifice and supremacy over the other companions whether they were from the Ansar or the Muhajireen.

The Qurayshites regrouped for the battle of Uhud with three thousand fighters to avenge their defeat in the battle of Badr. Once again Ali stepped forward and single headedly killed most of the flag bearers of the enemy in Uhud, and as a result the moral of the Muslims heightened, and they launched a general offensive and forced the enemy to flee from their camps. However, some companions left their positions against the advice of the Prophet and started collecting spoils of war. The enemy regrouped and launched a counter offensive, forcing the majority of the Muslims including the prominent companions like Caliph Umar to flee the battlefield. The near Muslim victory was turned into a defeat.

As majority of the companions fled, the life of the Prophet itself was endangered. But Ali stayed back and ensured that no harm would come to the Prophet. He killed a number of Qurayshite fighters who saw an opportunity to attack the Prophet, before any harm could be inflicted on the Messenger of Allah. If Prophet would have been killed on that day, not only would the Islamic State of Madinah be finished, but the religion of Islam itself would have come to an end with the death of the Prophet. Ali became the saviour of Islam and the Prophet in the battle of Uhud.

Ibn Abbas has said that Ali has four unique distinctions that he shares with no other companion.

> "Ali has four distinctions no one shares with him: He was the first male who prayed with the Messenger of God. He was the bearer of his banner in every battle and he was the one who stayed with the Prophet at the Battle of Uhud and he is the one who washed his blessed body and laid him in his tomb."

- Al-Hakim recorded in his Al-Mustadrak, Part 3, p.111

The argument of Caliph Abu Bakr against Ansar once again holds no merit when the effort and the sacrifice of Ali is highlighted in the battle of Uhud.

7.6.5.4. The Battle of Khandaq (Moat)

The battle of Moat followed the same pattern as the battle of Badr and Uhud as far as the effort and endeavour of Ali was concerned.

In the battle of Moat, the Qurayshites and their pagan supporters massed an army of 10,000 to take on the Muslims. On the advice of Salam al-Farsi, the Prophet ordered the Muslims to dig a moat around the city of Madinah. As part of the physiological warfare the hypocrites were circulating frightening rumours to harm the morale of the Muslims. On the other hand, the moral of the enemy increased further when a Jewish tribe around Madinah sided with them. Amr Ibn Abd Wud who was the most dreaded warrior of Makkah crossed the moat with his soldiers and challenged the Muslims for a duel. He repeated his challenge several times but none of the companions stepped forward. Only Ali accepted the challenge and a very short and a violent confrontation took place, resulting in the death of Amr Ibn Abd Wud.

If Ali hadn't stepped up to the mark and killed Amr Ibn Abd Wud, the rest of the enemy soldiers would have also crossed the moat and the city of Madinah would have been invaded, destroying the Islamic State in the process. The role of the rest of the companions in the battle of Moat was negligible, as they only stood behind the Moat and never actually faced the enemy, even when they were challenged. The distinguished performance of Ali not only stopped the invasion of Madinah, but it was recognized by the Prophet with these words:

> "The duel of Ali Ibn Abu Talib against Amr Ibn Abd Wud at the Battle of the Moat outweighs the good deeds of my whole nation until the Day of Judgment."

- Al-Mustadrak, Part 3, p. 32.

So, once again the argument of Caliph Abu Bakr against the Ansar would be futile in the presence of Ali.

7.6.5.5. The Battle of Khaibar

The battle of Khaibar was no different as far as the distinction of Ali was concerned.

The Jews of Khaibar had become a real threat and a danger to the Islamic State. The Prophet had decided to subdue the Khaibarites for the safety and the security of Madinah. Prophet laid a siege of Khaibar and its fortresses with an army of around sixteen hundred companions. Even after several days of the siege not a single Jewish fortress had been captured. Prophet gave the banner of the army to Caliph Abu Bakr and then to Caliph Umar, but both of them failed to conquer any of its fortresses.

Even though Ali was unwell and exempt from jihad, Prophet was obliged to call upon his most trusted lieutenant to deliver the victory, which had been eluding the other companions. Ali literally led from the front and killed the renowned Jewish warrior Marhab in a duel, which frightened the Khaibarites who fled the battlefield and started taking refuge inside the fortresses. Ali and his men followed the retreating army into the fortress, which the enemy were unable to defend, as none of them had the courage to take on Ali. The Jewish fortresses started falling one after the other to the Muslim army, until the Muslims conquered the entire region of Khaibar.

The whole of the Muslim army for days was unable to conquer any of the fortress in Ali's absence. The presence of Ali alone was the difference between victory and defeat in the battle of Khaibar.

7.6.5.6. The Support and Sacrifice of Ali was Unique

The support and sacrifice of Ali in the service of Islam was unique and distinct. All the key events which were critical for the destiny of Islam during the lifetime of the Prophet, are strongly linked to the effort and endeavours of Ali.

Whether it was the battle of Badr, the battle of Uhud, the battle of Moat or the battle of Khaibar, it was the amazing courage, bravery, and skill of Ali, which had given the Muslims victory over their enemies. Ali was the main contributor after the Prophet in founding and defending the Islamic State of Madinah. Ali was the implementer of Prophet's strategy and the eliminator of his adversaries.

The establishment of the Islamic State of Madinah was probably the single biggest achievement of the Prophet during his lifetime, as it secured the future of Muslims for good. Muslims were a very small minority before the Islamic State of Madinah came into existence. It was the State of Madinah which allowed the Muslims to flourish and expand the message of Allah and increase their numbers many folds.

In Prophet's biggest achievement and in his most important and critical project, Ali's support and sacrifice was unique and distinguished. Ali was that unique hero who tipped the balance in favour of Islam and Muslims at every critical juncture. Ali was that amazing individual who ensured that Prophet's vision would in fact become a reality.

The argument between Caliph Abu Bakr and Saad Ibn Ubaadah in Saqifah, where both of them were trying to justify their claim to the Caliphate based on the achievements of each group, would have been futile if Ali had been present in Saqifah. The effort, the endeavour and the achievement of Ali in supporting and changing the destiny of Islam would have dwarfed the efforts of any other companion, including Caliph Abu Bakr, Caliph Umar or Saad Ibn Ubaadah.

It was possible that Caliph Abu Bakr was worthier to be the Caliph than Saad Ibn Ubaadah, but that was only the case as long as Ali stays out of the picture. As soon as Ali comes into the frame, the comparison between Ali and the rest of the candidates of Saqifah becomes an unfair contest.

But unfortunately, Ali is neither present in Saqifah and nor there was anyone else to support his case.

7.6.6. We are the Relatives of the Prophet

One of the key arguments that Caliph Abu Bakr had used against the Ansar to justify his claim was his closeness to the Prophet, in the sense that being from Quraysh he was a relative of the Prophet. Since Ansar were the companions from Madinah, they did not share this privilege with Abu Bakr, so he had an edge over the Ansar on this issue.

> "..........The Prophet of Islam was from our tribe. We are the relatives of the Prophet ... and therefore we are the people who are entitled to the Caliphate... It will be advisable to have the leadership among us...."

- Al-Ḥalabi - As-Sirat al- Ḥalabiyyah, vol. 3, p. 357

Quraysh had many clans, Abu Bakr belonged to the Banu Taym clan of the Quraysh. He was the 8th or the 9th cousin of the Prophet. The argument of Caliph Abu Bakr certainly holds in front of the Ansar.

However, again if one brings Ali into the fold, the edge is inevitably with Ali. Prophet belonged to the clan of Banu Hashim and so did Ali. Ali's father Abu Talib was Prophet's real uncle who had brought the Prophet up in his own house. Ali and the Prophet shared the same grandfather, which meant that Ali was Prophet's first cousin.

Leaving all the other merits and traits a side like knowledge, bravery, piety, service in the path of Islam etc. Simply on the basis of lineage Ali was unique and distinguished among all the companions. No other companion shared the lineage that Ali shared with the Prophet.

Caliph Abu Bakr could certainly win this argument against the Ansar in the absence of Ali. But if the gathering of Saqifah had taken place in the presence of all the stakeholders, then Ali would once again be on top even on the issue of lineage.

7.6.7. The Caliph should be from the Quraysh

During his argument against the Ansar Caliph Abu Bakr narrated a hadith of the Prophet, which states that the Caliph after the Prophet should be from Quraysh. This hadith of the Prophet which Caliph Abu Bakr had quoted in Saqifah is absolutely authentic and correct. In fact, there are many such hadiths where the Prophet of Allah had mentioned that the Caliphate after him should remain in Quraysh, and that the number of Caliphs after him would be twelve.

> "O Saad (Ibn Ubaadah)! You know very well that the Prophet had said in your presence that the Quraysh shall be given the Caliphate........"

- *(Musnad Ahmad, vol. 1, p.5)*

By narrating this hadith of the Prophet Caliph Abu Bakr had at least accepted the fact that Prophet did not leave the entire choice of his successor in the hands of the Muslims. The companions could not just choose anybody to be the successor of the Prophet. The Prophet had decreed that the person who succeeds him must be from the tribe of Quraysh.

It is then inconceivable to think that Prophet would name the tribe to which his successor would belong to but would not actually name his successor. Prophet would not simply choose the tribe of his successor and leave the selection of the individual to the companions. It makes no sense and serves no purpose.

There was no point or benefit in simply specifying the tribe, without actually specifying the individual who would succeed the Prophet. The tribe of Quraysh was divided into many clans, each clan having hundreds or potentially thousands of members. There was no added benefit in simply specifying the tribe of the successor. It would not make the choice of the successor of the Prophet any easier or simpler for the companions.

I have already given numerous traditions of the Prophet in the Chapter 6 "The Leadership of Ali" to prove that Prophet had indeed chosen Ali to be his successor on many occasions during his lifetime. But let's analyse this issue in the context of the tradition that Caliph Abu Bakr had mentioned to the Ansar in Saqifah.

Caliph Abu Bakr said to Saad Ibn Ubaadah that Prophet had mentioned that the Caliphate should belong to someone from the Quraysh. These were the words of Caliph Abu Bakr to the Ansar in the meeting of Saqifah. Let's see in a historical context who could have actually been the successor of the Prophet from the Quraysh.

The tribe of Quraysh comprised of many clans. It is a historical fact that only a very small segment of the Quraysh were loyal Muslims, whereas the vast majority of Quraysh were recent converts who had accepted the faith of Islam after the conquest of Makkah. The overwhelming majority of the Quraysh had been the biggest enemy of the Prophet and the Muslims, until Makkah had been conquered. The majority of the battles like Badr, Uhud and the Moat were all fought against the Quraysh of Makkah.

After the conquest of Makkah, Prophet had showered Quraysh with gifts and vast amounts of war booty to entice them, and to keep them on the path of Islam. Despite this many new converts apostatized and slipped back into disbelief, who then had to be fought and brought back into the fold of Islam.

In contrast to all of this, there was one clan of the Quraysh which had sided with the Prophet from the very beginning of his mission. This clan was the clan of the Prophet itself i.e., the clan of Banu Hashim. The head of the Clan of Banu Hashim was Abu Talib who was the uncle of the Prophet and the father of Ali. Under the leadership of Abu Talib, the Banu Hashim had given shelter and protection to the Prophet and the Muslims, while all the other clans of Quraysh were determined to annihilate Islam at any cost.

It was only due to the support of Banu Hashim that Prophet had managed to survive the hostile and the extremely violent society of Makkah. The role of Banu Hashim was indispensable in protecting the Prophet and the small number of Muslims who lived in Makkah. It was the clan of Banu Hashim who had given protection to the Prophet and the Muslims when all the other clans of Quraysh had imposed an economic boycott on the Muslims. Due to the support offered by Banu Hashim the Quraysh also imposed a complete economic boycott of the clan of Banu Hashim too.

Despite suffering economically and physically at the hands of the Quraysh, the clan of Banu Hashim refused to budge in their support of the Prophet and his mission. Under the leadership of Abu Talib, the Banu Hashim had supported the Prophet and the Muslims at a time when Muslims were extremely vulnerable and were a small minority in Makkah.

If Prophet had mentioned that his successor would be from the Quraysh then surely, he must be from the clan of Banu Hashim, since it was this clan that had ensured the continuity of Prophet's mission in Makkah, despite the opposition from all the other clans of Quraysh. The successor of the Prophet could not possibly be from a clan of Quraysh which was hostile to the Muslims. The successor of the Prophet could only be from the clan of Quraysh that was supporting the Muslims i.e., the clan of Banu Hashim.

In the clan of Banu Hashim, the person who had distinguished himself in support of Prophet's mission from the very beginning of his life to the very end was inevitably Ali. If there was anybody in the clan of Banu Hashim who was worthy of becoming the successor of the Prophet, then surely that person was only Ali.

The argument of Caliph Abu Bakr against the Ansar had credibility in the sense that Caliph Abu Bakr belonged to the Banu Taym clan of Quraysh. However, his argument completely loses its validity if Ali from the Banu Hashim clan of Quraysh had been present in Saqifah.

7.6.8. The Offer of Ministry and a Political Adjustment

As the argument and the disagreement between the Ansar and the Muhajireen continued the Ansar proposed a compromise. The Ansar stated that there should be two leaders one from the Ansar and one from the Muhajireen.

> *"O Quraysh. There should be one ruler from us and one from you."*
> - Sahih Bukhari, Volume 8, Book 82, Number 817

Caliph Umar opposes this move of Ansar by saying that we cannot have two swords in one sheath.

> *"How preposterous! Two swords cannot be accommodated in one sheath. By Allah, the Arabs will never accept your rule..."*
> - (History of al-Tabari, p.194)

This led to an intense argument and caused a lot of commotion, confusion, disorder, and anger between the Ansar and the Muhajireen. It was possible that a war might ensue between the two groups. On seeing the situation deteriorate Caliph Abu Bakr proposed a compromise to the Ansar. He offers the Ansar the position of being the advisors to the Caliph.

> *".... We (the Muhajirs) are the leaders, and you (Ansars) are the helpers; matters shall not be settled without consultation, nor shall we decide on them without you."*
> - (The History of al-Tabari, Vol.10, pp.4-5)

Caliph Abu Bakr says to the Ansar that although the caliphate is for us, but we will make you our advisors or ministers and we will not make decisions without consulting you. Caliph Abu Bakr offers this incentive to the Ansar to pacify them and to gain their support for a candidate from the Muhajireen.

Although, the Ansar were arguing against the Muhajireen, but they had also suffered an internal setback. Their own unity had disappeared and the old rivalry between the two clans of Ansar i.e., Al-Aws and Al-Khazraj had resurfaced. The Ansar at this stage had lost the political advantage. The Ansar could see the resurgence of Muhajireen in Saqifah.

The offer of Caliph Abu Bakr gave them a say in the decision-making process of the State by becoming advisors to the Caliph. It was something that they had always desired and aspired to, and hence they reluctantly conceded to the Muhajireen and accepted the offer of Caliph Abu Bakr.

> *"What you say is correct: we are your advisors, and you are our rulers."*
> - Musnad Ahmad, Vol.1, p.5

This is how the meeting of Saqifah ended with Caliph Abu Bakr who was from the Muhajireen becoming the first Caliph and the leader of the Muslims. The Caliphate of Abu Bakr came because of a deal and a political adjustment which took place between the Ansar and the Muhajireen, where the former agreed to become the advisors and the later agreed to become the rulers.

However, the offer of becoming the advisors or the ministers to the Caliph never materialized for the Ansar, as Caliph Abu Bakr never created such a position for the Ansar once he acquired the Caliphate. The Ansar were never made advisors or ministers to the Caliph. There is no historical evidence to suggest that after the inauguration of Caliph Abu Bakr he appointed an Ansar as one of his advisors. The chief advisor and tactician in Caliph Abu Bakr's administration remained his closest friend and ally Caliph Umar.

The offer of ministry and the incentive of becoming the advisors to the Caliph was simply a tactics used by Caliph Abu Bakr to pacify the Ansar at the time.

7.6.9. The Proposal of the Candidates

In Saqifah the Ansar had proposed Saad Ibn Ubaadah as their nominee for the leadership of the Muslims. After justifying the leadership for the Muhajireen, Caliph Abu Bakr proposed Caliph Umar and Abu Ubaydah al-Jarrah as the future Caliphs of the Muslims. Caliph Umar in turn proposed Caliph Abu Bakr as the future leader of the Muslims.

The only candidates that are nominated in Saqifah were the candidates who managed to get there in time, and who were physically present in that meeting, a meeting whose location and timing was unknown to the rest of the candidates, who also had a stake in that matter.

Ali at the time was busy with the burial of the Prophet, but he was not proposed by either Caliph Abu Bakr or Caliph Umar, even though they were well aware of the position of Ali in relation to the Prophet. They also knew fully well that Ali was not aware of the meeting of Saqifah, as nobody had informed him about the pre-emptive move of the Ansar. Despite this, Caliph Abu Bakr only proposes Caliph Umar and Abu Ubaydah al-Jarrah as potential candidates for the Caliphate.

Leaving the status of Caliph Abu Bakr and Caliph Umar aside, surely the status and the position of Ali in the eyes of the Prophet was higher than that of Abu Ubaydah al-Jarrah! But he gets proposed for the caliphate and Ali doesn't. The contribution and the service of Ali in support of Islam and the mission of the Prophet was surely more than the service of Abu Ubaydah al-Jarrah.

If there was any fairness in the process of Saqifah then at least Ali should have been proposed as one of the potential candidates, whether he actually gets selected would have been a different matter. Proposing Abu Ubaydah al-Jarrah, who just happen to have met Caliph Abu Bakr on the way to Saqifah, but not proposing Ali who was the nominee of the Prophet was a travesty to say the least.

7.6.10. Leading the Prayer and Companion of the Cave

After an understanding was reached between the Ansar and the Muhajireen that the Muhajireen would become the rulers and the Ansar would become the advisors, Caliph Abu Bakr proposes Caliph Umar and Abu Ubaydah al-Jarrah for the position of the Caliphate. Caliph Umar refuses to accept the proposal of Caliph Abu Bakr and in turn proposes Caliph Abu Bakr as the new Caliph, and immediately pays allegiance to him.

> *Abu Bakr said: "Umar and Abu Ubaydah are here: choose any one of them."*
> *Umar said: "No! Abu Bakr is the most excellent amongst the Muhajirs. He has been the Companion of the Prophet in the cave; the Prophet asked him to be the Imam to lead the prayers, ...Umar stretched his hand first of all to take Baya'ah (oath of allegiance) at the hand of Abu Bakr ...."*
> - *(Tareekh al-Islam, Vol.1, p.275)*

Caliph Umar justifies his proposal of Caliph Abu Bakr in Saqifah with the following words, and almost simultaneously pays allegiance to him.

- Abu Bakr had led the prayers in Prophet's absence.
- Abu Bakr had been the companion of the Prophet in the cave.

Some scholars today assert that the reason why Caliph Abu Bakr was chosen as the leader of the Muslims in Saqifah was because Prophet had asked him to lead the Prayers. They insist that this was the reason why Muslims choose Caliph Abu Bakr as the first caliph.

Let's see if the Ansar who were the majority in Saqifah had in fact accepted the Caliphate of Abu Bakr for the above two reasons, and if Caliph Abu Bakr was chosen in Saqifah based on the above statements of Caliph Umar.

7.6.10.1. It wasn't the Deciding Factor

Leading the prayers or being the companion of the cave weren't the issue at stake in Saqifah. They were not the deciding factors or the reasons as to why Abu Bakr was chosen as the first caliph. The Ansar did not agree to the Caliphate of Abu Bakr because he had led the prayers, or because he had been the companion of the cave.

The Ansar had in fact made a pre-emptive move to take over the leadership of the Muslims. Caliph Abu Bakr and Caliph Umar were not even invited to the meeting of Saqifah. The Ansar had no intention of choosing Caliph Abu Bakr or Caliph Umar as the leaders of the Muslims. The fact that Caliph Abu Bakr had led the prayers or had been a companion of the cave were irrelevant to the Ansar.

In reality, both Caliph Abu Bakr and Caliph Umar simply managed to find out about the pre-emptive move of the Ansar, and managed to get to Saqifah in time to thwart their plans.

And the reason why Ansar in the end accepted the leadership of the Muhajireen was because first of all they were not able to stay united. The old rivalry between the two clans of the Ansar i.e., Al-Awas and Al-Kazraj resurfaced, giving Muhajireen a political advantage in Saqifah. And secondly Caliph Abu Bakr had offered them the position of being the advisors (vazirs) to the Caliph.

It was the offer of being the Vazirs (advisors) which eventually persuaded the Ansar to accept the leadership of the Muhajireen. It was the highest position that the Ansar could hope for once the Muhajireen began to dominate the proceedings of Saqifah. The position of being the advisors to the Caliph would give Ansar a say in running the affairs of the Muslim Ummah, something that they had always desired.

Caliph Abu Bakr said to the Ansar:

> We (the Muhajirs) are the leaders, and you (Ansars) are the advisors/ministers; matters shall not be settled without consultation, nor shall we decide on them without you."
>
> • *(The History of al-Tabari, Vol.10, pp.4-5)*

Ansar finally accepted the offer of Abu Bakr and said:

> "What you say is correct: we are your advisors, and you are our rulers."
>
> • Musnad Ahmad, Vol.1, p.5

It was in this context that the leadership of the Muhajireen was accepted by the Ansar, and not in the context of Caliph Abu Bakr leading the prayers or being the companion of the cave.

In fact, Caliph Abu Bakr had proposed Caliph Umar and Abu Ubaydah as potential candidates for the position of the Caliphate, even though they had not led the prayers or been companions of the cave, which in itself clearly shows that leading the prayers or being the companion of the cave wasn't the issue, otherwise Caliph Abu Bakr would not have proposed Caliph Umar and Abu Ubaydah ibn Al-Jarrah in Saqifah.

> *Abu Bakr said, "Umar and Abu Ubaydah are here: choose any one of them."*
> - Tareekh al-Islam, Vol.1, p.275

The reason why Caliph Abu Bakr proposed Caliph Umar and Abu Ubaydah ibn Al-Jarrah was because they were both fellow Muhajireen, and they would be acceptable to the wider Quraysh clans as the new Caliphs.

The consensus that was reached in Saqifah between the Ansar and Muhajireen was not based on the grounds that Caliph Abu Bakr had led the prayers or had been a companion of the cave. The consensus was reached on the grounds that Muhajireen would become the rulers and Ansar would become the advisors. Once the consensus had been reached, at that point Caliph Umar said that between him, Caliph Abu Bakr and Abu Ubaydah ibn Al-Jarrah, Caliph Abu Bakr took precedence because he had led the prayers and had been a companion of the cave.

Leading the prayers and being the companion of the cave were simply the comments of Caliph Umar as he paid allegiance to Caliph Abu Bakr. It wasn't something that was debated or even discussed in the meeting of Saqifah.

However, for the sake of completeness I will discuss these topics as many supporters of Saqifah still justify the Caliphate of Abu Bakr on these grounds.

7.6.10.2. Caliph Abu Bakr had Led the Prayers

As mentioned above after an agreement had been reached between the Ansar and the Muhajireen that Muhajireen would become the rulers and Ansar would become the advisors, Caliph Umar paid allegiance to Abu Bakr by saying that among the three Muhajireen present Caliph Abu Bakr was most deserving, since he had led the prayers and been a companion of the cave.

Leading prayers in the absence of the Prophet was certainly an honour that Caliph Abu Bakr had. However, the conditions and the qualifications required to be the Imam of the mosque and the conditions, qualification and traits required to become the successor of the Prophet, and the Imam (leader) of the entire Muslim Ummah are very different.

Any good Muslim can lead the prayers and become an Imam (leader) of a congregation of Muslims. But that cannot be used as a justification for being the Imam and the leader of the entire Muslim Ummah.

If the Imam of the mosque is unwell or away, then any other Muslim from the congregation can stand up and lead the prayers and become the Imam (leader) temporarily. This temporary leadership of the congregation cannot become the basis of being the successor of the Prophet or being the leader of the entire Muslim Ummah.

When Prophet left for the battle of Badr, Prophet appointed Abu Lubabah to manage the affairs of the Muslims in Madinah. When Prophet left for the battle of Khaibar he appointed Abu Rahman to oversee the affairs of the Muslims in Madinah. When Prophet went for the final pilgrimage to Makkah, he left Abu Dujana in charge of Madinah.

This temporary leadership that Prophet had given to many of his companions, cannot be used as a justification for being the successor of the Prophet, or leader of the entire Muslim Ummah, otherwise any of the above-mentioned companions could claim to have a right of being the successor of the Prophet. And these companions were not simply in charge of leading the prayers, they were left in charge of the entire city of Madinah in Prophet's absence, which was the hub and the bastion of the Muslims.

Also, the destiny of Islam and Muslims or the destiny of the Islamic movement was not affected by the person who leads the congregational prayer in the absence of the Prophet. For instance, if Caliph Umar instead of Caliph Abu Bakr had led the congregational prayers, the status quo of the Muslims at that time would not have changed by this exchange.

Similarly, when Prophet went to the battle of Badr and left Abu Lubabah to manage the affairs of the Muslims in Madinah, it wasn't the presence of Abu Lubabah in Madinah which had changed the destiny of the Islamic movement. Instead, it was the sword of Ali in the battle of Badr which had brought victory to the Muslims and changed the destiny of the Islamic movement.

The successor of the Prophet was someone whose contribution had been distinguished and unique in changing the course of history in favour of Islam and the Muslims. Leading congregational prayers in the absence of the Prophet was certainly an honour, but it is not a contribution that could justify the claim of being the successor of the Prophet.

It was possible that between the three Muhajireen i.e., Caliph Abu Bakr, Caliph Umar and Abu Ubaydah ibn Al-Jarrah, Caliph Abu Bakr took precedence for leading the prayers and being the companion of the cave. But this certainly wasn't the case when one brings Ali into the picture. The merits and the role of Ali in the service of Islam was far superior to any of the three Muhajireen present in Saqifah.

7.6.10.3. Caliph Abu Bakr is the Companion of the Cave

Being the companion of the cave on the night of the Hijrah was another honour that Caliph Abu Bakr had, which was not shared by Caliph Umar or Abu Ubaydah ibn Al-Jarrah. But this isn't the case if one begins to compare the companionship of Ali with the Prophet.

The companionship of Ali with the Prophet was unique and unrivalled. It began with the birth of Ali and ended with Ali lowering the Prophet's body into the grave.

It is said that after Ali was born, he did not open his eyes for three days until the Prophet of Allah had arrived. When Prophet held the little boy in his lap, Ali opened his eyes. The first thing that Ali saw was the blessed face of the Prophet. The Prophet held Ali in his arms, and he puts his tongue in Ali's mouth who exuberantly starts sucking it. This was how the companionship of Ali began with the Prophet.

After Prophet's marriage with lady Khadija, Prophet formally adopts Ali who was only four or five at the time. The Prophet of Allah brought Ali up in his own house. Prophet's lap is the school of Ali, Prophet's house is the fountain of knowledge which nurtures Ali. The Prophet of Allah himself became Ali's guide, his teacher, and his mentor.

Ali had always been with the Prophet, and he used to accompany the Prophet everywhere. Even when Prophet goes for meditation in the cave of Hira, he often used to take Ali with him. This was the cave where Prophet had received the first revelations from Allah. Ali was a companion of the Prophet in the cave of Hira. This was another unique distinction and honour of Ali that he was the companion of the Prophet in the cave where the message of Islam was first revealed.

On many occasions Ali is present in the cave when Quran was being revealed to the Prophet. Ali became a witness to the revelations that came to the Prophet of Allah. Ali was not only a companion of the cave (cave of Hira), but he was also a witness to the revelations of the Holy Quran.

On the night of the Hijrah when Caliph Abu Bakr had become the companion of the cave, Ali was sleeping alone on the bed of the Prophet, sacrificing his life in order to save the life of the Prophet. Ten of the most renowned warriors from the various clans of Quraysh were chosen to ambush the Prophet on that night. Only the bravest of the companions would dare to sleep in Prophet's bed on that night. This is another unique distinction of Ali that he saved the life of the Prophet on the night of the Hijrah by putting his own life at risk.

Even at the time when Caliph Umar was paying allegiance to Caliph Abu Bakr in Saqifah and stating that he was the companion of the cave, Ali was still with the Prophet! Ali was busy preparing the body of the Prophet for burial, while the meeting of Saqifah was in full swing where Caliph Abu Bakr and Caliph Umar were justifying their claim to the Caliphate.

The companionship of Ali and the Prophet was unlike the companionship of the Prophet with any of his other companions. It began with the birth of Ali and ended with the lowering of the Prophet's body into the grave. Ali's entire life, until the death of the Prophet was spent in the company of the Prophet.

It was possible that being the companion of the cave, Caliph Abu Bakr in comparison to Caliph Umar and Abu Ubaydah ibn Al-Jarrah was more worthy to be the Caliph, but in comparison to the companionship of Ali with the Prophet this wasn't the case.

7.6.11. The Real Reason

Caliph Abu Bakr later tried to justify his stance in Saqifah by giving the following reason to Ali. Caliph Abu Bakr said to Ali:

> *"Had I delayed the matter, it would have posed a greater danger to the unity, integrity, and solidarity of Islam. How could I send for you when there was no time?"*
>
> - *(Tareekh al-Islam, Vol.1, p.276)*

First of all, the justification given by Caliph Abu Bakr makes it clear that in the eyes of Caliph Abu Bakr, Ali had a claim to the Caliphate and hence he thought it was necessary to justify his stance in Saqifah.

When Caliph Abu Bakr found out about the meeting of Saqifah, he was present at the house of the Prophet alongside Ali. Just as Caliph Abu Bakr had reached Saqifah in time to thwart the ambitions of the Ansar, Ali would have also got there to justify his position as the successor of the Prophet.

In case Caliph Abu Bakr had no idea as to what was happening in Saqifah until he got there, even in that case he could have sent someone like Abu Ubaydah al-Jarrah or another companion to inform Ali about the motives of the Ansar.

Saqifah was about 2 to 3 miles from Madinah. The average speed of a horse is around 15mph to 20mph. let's assume that the horse could only gallop at 15 mph (miles per hour) and Saqifah was 3 miles from Madinah. It would take Ali at most 12 minutes to get to Saqifah. The meeting of Saqifah lasted for many hours, Ali alongside the rest of the Banu Hashim would have easily reached Saqifah in minutes.

Also, Caliph Abu Bakr did not require Ali to be physically present in Saqifah, in order to nominate or propose him as one of the candidates. Surely, there was enough time to at least propose and nominate Ali in the meeting of Saqifah. The time excuse cannot be used for not even proposing Ali as one of the candidates in Saqifah.

The reason given by Caliph Abu Bakr was simply to pacify the emotions of Ali and his supporters. It was similar to the incentive given to the Ansar where they were promised to be the advisors to the Caliph, but in reality, they were never given that position.

7.6.11.1. Many Years Later

The real reason why Ali was not informed about the meeting of Saqifah and the real reason why Ali was not even nominated in Saqifah by Caliph Abu Bakr or Caliph Umar, came out many years later. During the reign of Caliph Umar, he had a conversation with Ibn Abbas, who was the uncle of the Prophet. The conversation goes like this:

> *Caliph Umar: "Do you know why the people did not elect you (the family of the Prophet) to the Caliphate?"*
> *Ibn Abbas: "No, I do not know."*
> *Caliph Umar: "I know what the reason was."*
> *Ibn Abbas: "What was it?"*
> *Caliph Umar: "The Quraysh was unwilling to let you (the Hashemites) have the honour of both Prophethood and Caliphate. If that would have happened, you would have wronged the people! Quraysh chose for itself; it succeeded and made the right decision."*

- *Tarikh al-Tabari, 5:30*
- *Qasas al-Arab, 2:263*
- *Ibn al-Atheer al-Kamal fil-Tarikh, 3:63*
- *Tarikh-e-Islam: 481-482, by Akbar Shah Najibabadi*

This was the crux of the matter! The reason why Ali was not informed about the meeting of Saqifah and the reason why Ali is not even nominated in Saqifah, was because the Quraysh would not accept the Prophethood and the Caliphate to be in the same clan i.e., in the clan of Banu Hashim, and Ali happened to be from the clan of Banu Hashim just like the Prophet.

The demand of the Quraysh was the exact opposite of what the Prophet had commanded, wished, and hoped for. But unfortunately, Caliph Abu Bakr and Umar advocated the views and the wishes of the Quraysh in Saqifah.

Prophet had nominated Ali to be his successor because Prophet had specifically prepared and trained Ali for this role, and not because he belonged the clan of Banu Hashim. But the participants of Saqifah had denied Ali this right because he belonged to the same clan as the Prophet. These companions unfortunately still had the reminisce of the pre-Islamic mentality, where they viewed both the Prophethood and the Caliphate in a tribal sense.

The Prophet to them was not simply the Prophet of Allah, but he was also a leader of Banu Hashim. So, the next leader of the Muslims could not possibly be from the same clan as the Prophet i.e., the successor of the Prophet could not be from Banu Hashim!

It was for this reason that Caliph Abu Bakr and Umar did not nominate Ali in Saqifah and sided with the view of Quraysh with respect to the Caliphate, because both of them were also the leaders of the Quraysh, and they knew the feelings and the sentiments of their tribe.

Unfortunately, in doing so they went against the clear Sunnah of the Prophet, and the trend of al-ijtihad (independent judgement) which had plagued the companions, managed to change the course of Islamic history forever!

7.6.11.2. Ali and the Quraysh

The majority of the Quraysh hated the Prophet, they hated Ali, and they hated the Clan of Banu Hashim as well.

The tribe of Quraysh consisted of many clans. For instance, Prophet and Ali belonged to the Banu Hashim clan, Caliph Abu Bakr belonged to the Banu Taym clan and Caliph Umar belonged to the Banu Adi clan of Quraysh. Although, individuals from the various clans of Quraysh had accepted Islam like Caliph Abu Bakr and Caliph Umar, but the vast majority of the Quraysh had only accepted Islam after the conquest of Makkah.

The majority of the clans of Quraysh had fought the Prophet from the very beginning of his mission until the conquest of Makkah, with the exception of the clan of Banu Hashim. The Banu Hashim under the leadership of Abu Talib, who was the father of Ali and the uncle of the Prophet, had given refuge to the Muslims and supported the path of Islam in Makkah, against the most intense opposition from the rest of the clans of Quraysh.

As Islam began to grow in Makkah the Quraysh felt that since the Prophet was from Banu Hashim, the clan of Banu Hashim would become way too powerful if the message of Islam succeeds, and the Banu Hashim could use Islam as a means to rule over them. Hence, they opposed both Islam and the clan of Banu Hashim.

To add to this Ali had been a thorn against the Quraysh, as he had been the biggest contributor and supporter of Prophet's mission. Ali had killed hundreds of Qurayshites in various expeditions and battles that he undertook against them. In the battle of Badr alone Ali had killed over 20 Qurayshites including their top warrior al-Waleed. In the battle of Uhud Ali had killed Tallah Ibn Abu Tallah, Abu Saad Ibn Abu Tallah and the majority of the Qurayshite flag bearers. In the battle of Moat Ali had killed Amr Ibn Wud, who was one of the greatest warriors of Quraysh.

Ali had not killed the Qurayshites for personal or tribal reasons. They were killed in defending the religion of Allah, but nevertheless Ali had a lot of Qurayshite blood on his hands, and the memory of their family members being killed by Ali was still fresh in the minds of the Quraysh.

Although, the Quraysh had now accepted Islam, but this had only happened after the conquest of Makkah. They were new converts to Islam, and they had only accepted Islam after it had become the most powerful force in the Arabian Peninsula. Also, the majority of the Quraysh were being kept on the path of Islam with the incentives of gifts and war booty.

The last thing that the Quraysh wanted to see was the leadership of the Muslims to be given to Ali, and the clan of Banu Hashim. This was the man and the clan that they had fought for almost two decades. So, Quraysh had no desire to see Ali as the head of the Islamic State.

But the wish and the desire of the Prophet was the exact opposite of what the Quraysh had wished and desired for.

7.6.11.3. Caliph Abu Bakr, Caliph Umar and the Quraysh

As mentioned earlier both Caliph Abu Bakr and Caliph Umar were leaders of Quraysh. They were well aware of the feelings and the mentality of the Quraysh towards Ali and Banu Hashim. That is why if one looks at the speech of Caliph Abu Bakr in Saqifah, it becomes obvious that on more than one occasion he had insisted on the right of the Quraysh to rule over the Muslims. Caliph Abu Bakr made the following assertions in Saqifah:

> "All the good that you have said about yourselves (O Ansar) is deserved. But the Arabs will recognize authority only in this clan of Quraysh..."

- *(Ibn Ishaq, Seerah Rasool-Allah)*

> "(O Ansar) you are our brethren in Islam and our partners in religion...but the Arabs will not submit themselves except to this clan of Quraysh...we (the Quraysh) are in the centre among the Muslims with respect to our position..."

- *(The History of al-Tabari, Volume 9, p.193)*

Caliph Abu Bakr kept insisting to the Ansar that the right of leadership only belonged to the Quraysh, as Arabs would not submit to anyone else's rule except the rule of the Quraysh. Essentially in Saqifah, Caliph Abu Bakr and Umar had sided with the view of Quraysh regarding the Caliphate, rather than the view of the Prophet, which indeed was most unfortunate.

The word "Quraysh" that Caliph Abu Bakr uses in Saqifah did not include the clan of Banu Hashim. It included all the clans of Quraysh minus the clan of Banu Hashim, and Caliph Umar later confirmed this in his conversation with Ibn Abbas, when he admitted that the reason why Ali was not chosen in Saqifah was because the Quraysh did not want the leadership of the Muslims to stay in the clan of Banu Hashim.

7.6.11.4. The Irony

This reason why Ali was not proposed in Saqifah was because he belonged to the clan of Banu Hashim, and because of what he had done to the Quraysh in support of the Islamic movement. In other words, the service, and the sacrifice of Ali in support of Prophet's mission had in fact become the main reason as to why Ali was not even nominated in Saqifah. The efforts, the contribution, and the endeavour of Ali in support of Islam and Muslims had in fact become his nemesis in Saqifah.

This indeed was most unfortunate and unfair to say the least, but unfortunately this is exactly what happened in the meeting of Saqifah.

Ali was denied the Caliphate in Saqifah because of his closeness to the Prophet, in the sense that he was from the same clan as the Prophet i.e., the clan of Banu Hashim, and hence the Quraysh would not accept him as the new Caliph. But Caliph Abu Bakr had justified his Caliphate to the Ansar on the basis of his closeness to the Prophet, in the sense that he was from the same tribe as the Prophet i.e., he was from the tribe of Quraysh just like the Prophet!

The irony and the injustice against Ali in Saqifah knew no bounds.

7.6.12. Our Approach

Our approach and responsibility in this day and age is to follow the course of history which the Prophet had wished and hoped for, rather than the course of history which was made in Saqifah.

Prophet had nominated and appointed Ali to be his successor, while Caliph Umar had nominated Caliph Abu Bakr to be the Caliph in Saqifah. Today, we can please the Prophet of Allah by recognizing and accepting his Sunnah, rather than the verdict of Saqifah.

The event of Saqifah took place some fourteen centuries ago. On the Day of Judgment, we will not be questioned about the gathering of Saqifah. However, we will be asked if we had followed the Sunnah of the Prophet.

If some prominent companions had adopted the path of Saqifah to justify their Caliphate, and sided with the view of Quraysh, then we leave their judgment, their decisions, and their intentions with Allah. We will not be questioned about the decisions or the choices that Caliph Abu Bakr or Caliph Umar made in Saqifah.

However, we will be asked about the choice and the decisions that we make in our lifetimes. If Saqifah had done injustice to Ali, then today we can remove that injustice by recognizing and accepting him as the true successor of the Prophet.

The real lovers of the Prophet who are willing to lay down their lives in the defence and the honour of the Prophet, should honour the Sunnah of the Prophet by accepting Ali as the rightful successor of the Prophet. Muslims who are proud to be called the Ahle-Sunnah, the followers of the Sunnah, have no option but to follow the nominee of the Prophet rather than the nominee of Saqifah.

Ali was the choice of the Prophet and Caliph Abu Bakr was the choice of Saqifah. We cannot change the course of history or turn back the clock, however, in this age of freedom and choice we can choose to follow the nominee of the Prophet rather than the nominee of Saqifah.

8. DEFIANCE OF THE PROPHET AND THE LEGALITY OF SAQIFAH

The meeting of Saqifah took place in clear defiance of the numerous traditions of the Prophet in favour of Ali. The question now arises as to how the companions could possibly defy the Sunnah of the Prophet and side with the view of the Quraysh with respect to the Caliphate.

8.1. How could the Companions Defy the Prophet?

How could the companions especially Caliph Abu Bakr and Caliph Umar let this happen? They were both present in Saqifah, they both managed to get there in time before the Ansar could finalize their candidate. They knew exactly what Prophet had said about Ali. They were both the key companions of the Prophet. Caliph Abu Bakr was one of the first Muslims and so was Caliph Umar. They both had been the companions of the Prophet from the very early days of Islam. They had both played their part in supporting the Prophet and the cause of Islam. How could the companions of their stature defy the commands and the wish of the Prophet after his death?

8.1.1. The Trend of Al-Ijtihad (Independent Judgment)

The answer to this key question lies in the trend of al-ijtihad (independent judgment), which I had explained in the previous chapter.

When Caliph Abu Bakr and Caliph Umar reached Saqifah they saw that the Ansar had almost finalized their candidate Saad ibn Ubaadah as the new Caliph. They knew that Quraysh would find it difficult to accept an Ansar as their new leader, since the Ansar had been an enemy of the Quraysh for many decades, especially since the establishment of the Islamic State of Madinah. Hence they opposed the Ansar in Saqifah and argued for the right of the Quraysh to lead the Muslim Ummah.

Caliph Abu Bakr and Umar also knew that Prophet on many occasions had announced the leadership of Ali, including on the event of Ghadeer Khum. However, they themselves were also the leaders of Quraysh, and they also knew the sentiments and the feelings of Quraysh towards Ali. They knew that the Quraysh had a grudge against Ali for what he had done to them. They knew that Ali had killed some of their finest warriors, and Ali had been a prime enemy of the Quraysh for over two decades.

On top of this they also knew that Quraysh did not want to see the Caliphate and the Prophethood to stay in the same clan i.e., the clan of Banu Hashim, and Ali happened to be from the clan of Banu Hashim as well, so Ali had a black mark against his name on the issue of lineage too.

Then there was also a pre-Islamic Arab tradition where the Arabs preferred the leadership of older men as opposed to the younger ones. We saw clear evidence of this tradition when the companions refused to join the army of Usama because he was only 18 years of age, even though Prophet had insisted that Usama would lead that army. Caliph Abu Bakr and Umar were much older that Ali. Caliph Abu Bakr was almost the same age as the Prophet, so Ali had a disadvantage based on his age as well.

On the other hand, both Caliph Abu Bakr and Umar had no Qurayshite blood on their hands. The Quraysh did not have any animosity or grudge against them. They were non-controversial figures as far as the Quraysh of Makkah were concerned. They had not killed anyone from the Quraysh in any of the battles. At the same time Caliph Abu Bakr and Caliph Umar did not belong to the clan of the Prophet i.e., Banu Hashim, so they had a green tick against their names in this box too. Their age was also more appropriate than Ali to take over the mantle of the leadership, as per the pre-Islamic Arab tradition.

Hence, in the gathering of Saqifah they made a judgment (al-ijtihad), that under the current circumstances they were the most appropriate candidates to lead the Muslims. They believed that the decision of the Prophet to choose Ali was not justified under the current climate, and they were better suited than Ali to lead the Muslims in the current political scenario.

Also, Ali was not present in Saqifah, and nor was there anybody else present from the Banu Hashim to support Ali's case, so there was no pressure on Caliph Abu Bakr or Umar to choose Ali either, and that is why they only proposed each other in Saqifah for the position of the Caliphate.

However, in this process they defied the clear commands and the instructions of the Prophet by using their ijtihad (independent judgment), based on the circumstances around them.

8.1.2. Not the First Time

This unfortunately was not the first time where they had used their judgment against the clear traditions of the Prophet. Criticism of the Treaty of al-Hudaybiyya, refusal to join the army of Usama, not bringing pen and paper to the Prophet, and burning the Sunnah of the Prophet were all evidence of the trend of al-ijtihad. The trend of al-ijtihad had taken root in some key companions, which resulted in them challenging the authority of the Prophet, based on their own understanding of the circumstances that surrounded them.

The reason they would defy the Prophet was because they wrongly believed that in certain matters, they had the right to disagree with the Prophet, especially in matters which in their opinion concerned the affairs of the Muslims. In the matters of prayer, fasting, zakat etc, they would accept the Prophet's instructions, but when it came to the instructions of the Prophet in relation to the affairs of the Muslims, they would question, criticize, and even refuse to follow his instructions.

8.1.3. They Believed they were Right

Caliph Abu Bakr and Caliph Umar also believed that the decision of not choosing Ali and siding with the Quraysh was a correct one. They believed that the decision of the Prophet to have both the Prophethood and the Caliphate in one clan was wrong.

Caliph Umar had categorically stated that if the Prophethood and the Caliphate had stayed in the clan of Banu Hashim, they would have wronged the people, implying that Banu Hashim would have become too powerful and arrogant, and would have interfered in the rights of other clans.

Caliph Umar: "The Quraysh was unwilling to let you (the Hashemites) have the honour of both Prophethood and Caliphate. If that would have happened, you would have wronged the people! Quraysh chose for itself; it succeeded and made the right decision."

- *Tarikh al-Tabari, 5:30*
- *Qasas al-Arab, 2:263*
- *Ibn al-Atheer al-Kamal fil-Tarikh, 3:63*
- *Tarikh-e-Islam: 481-482, by Akbar Shah Najibabadi*

Caliph Umar confirmed his view that Quraysh had done the right thing by moving the Caliphate away from the Banu Hashim.

The Quraysh actually wanted the Caliphate to be shared among its various clans, and not just be confined to one clan. The Quraysh wanted to rotate the leadership of the Muslims in different clans, so as to please all of its clans. The Quraysh's idea of the leadership of the Muslim Ummah was a purely tribal one. They were simply looking at the leadership of the Islamic State on a tribal basis, since they had always been governed by the tribal norms.

And as the two prominent leaders of Quraysh, Caliph Abu Bakr and Caliph Umar did exactly what Quraysh had desired and hoped for. The first Caliphate went to the Banu Taym clan of Quraysh in the form of Caliph Abu Bakr. The second Caliphate went to Banu Adi clan of Quraysh in the form of Caliph Umar, and the third Caliphate went to Banu Ummayad clan of Quraysh in the form Caliph Uthman. However, the Banu Ummayad was a very big and a powerful clan of Quraysh. Once they had acquired power, they never wanted to let go off it, and they kept the Caliphate in their own clan for around a century.

Unfortunately, as a result of all of this, the Quraysh whom the Prophet and the Muslims had fought for over twenty years, had in fact become the key factor in deciding the future leadership of the Muslims, whereas the person who had fought the Quraysh for over two decades was completely ignored and side-lined.

This undoubtedly was the biggest injustice and travesty of Saqifah.

8.2. Why did the Majority Accept the Mandate of Saqifah?

To answer this key question, we need to look at the composition of the Muslim Ummah at the time of the death of the Prophet, and we also need to understand the view and the mentality of the various groups that formed the Islamic nation at the time of the demise of the Prophet.

8.2.1. The Quraysh of Makkah

The Quraysh of Makkah were a large section of the Muslim Ummah at the time of the death of the Prophet. These Qurayshite clans were the primary reason as to why Ali was not even nominated in Saqifah. They were more than happy to see that the leadership of the Muslims had been taken away from the clan of the Prophet i.e., the Banu Hashim, and that their eternal nemesis Ali had been side-lined. There was no reason for them to challenge the verdict of Saqifah. As long as they were getting their share of the gifts and the war booty, they were happy to stay on the path of Islam.

Also, after the death of the Prophet many new converts to Islam had apostatized both in Makkah and around Madinah too. They had assumed that Islam would end with the death of the Prophet, and as soon as they heard the news of Prophet's death, they went back to their pagan ways. As a result, entire tribes had renounced Islam and slipped back into disbelief (Kufr). This section of the population obviously did not care about the nominee of the Prophet or his Sunnah, as they had decided to leave Islam all together.

8.2.2. The Key Companions in Madinah

The question now arises as to why did the key companions in Madinah accept the verdict of Saqifah?

As mentioned previously, the inhabitants of Madinah were divided in to two tribes i.e., al-Aws and al-Khazraj. The prominent companions from these tribes were Saad Ibn Ubaadah, al-Ḥubab Ibn al-Mundhir, Bashir ibn Saad etc. They were not only the key companions of the Prophet from Madinah, but they were also the leaders and elders of their tribes too.

Unfortunately, these were the very companions who had made the first move in Saqifah after the death of the Prophet, fearing domination from the Muhajireen. They were the founders and the architects of Saqifah. They had decided to side-line not just the Muhajireen but all the other stakeholders too. They had almost finalized their candidate Saad Ibn Ubaadah when Caliph Abu Bakr and Caliph Umar reached Saqifah. As the meeting of Saqifah progressed they could not stay united, and their own tribal rivalries resurfaced. The Ansar wavered and this allowed the Muhajireen to take advantage of the situation and turn the decision in their favour.

So, unfortunately most of the key companions from Madinah were part and parcel of the Saqifah proceedings. However, as they lost out to the Muhajireen on the day, they ended up paying allegiance to the nominee of the Muhajireen i.e., Caliph Abu Bakr. Although, they had no intention of selecting Caliph Abu Bakr initially, and indeed the whole move of the Ansar in Saqifah was against the Muhajireen in the first place, but Caliph Abu Bakr managed to get there in time, and with the incentive of the advisory role to the Caliph, he won the day against the Ansar.

Hence, due to the victory of the Muhajireen in Saqifah the prominent companions from Madinah (Ansar) ended up paying allegiance to Caliph Abu Bakr and accepted the verdict of Saqifah.

However, the question still remains as to how did the thousands of other ordinary companions and Muslims who were living in Madinah accepted the mandate of Saqifah?

8.2.3. The Tribal Vote

At the time of the death of the Prophet the Islamic community of Madinah and indeed the wider Muslim Ummah was formed from a confederation of tribes, clans, and families. Although Islamic in nature, the Muslim Ummah was essentially a primitive tribal society where tribal allegiances and links were just as dominant as the Islamic thought.

The pre-emptive move of the Ansar in Saqifah to out manoeuvre the Muhajireen was a classic example and a clear reflection of the dominance of the tribal system prevalent within the Muslim Ummah, alongside the newly established Islamic way of life.

It wasn't a society where every individual represented an independent vote. There was no electoral concept at the time where each individual represented a single vote. Instead, if the tribal chief decided to pay allegiance to a leader the entire tribe will follow suit. In a tribe of 2000 people, all of the votes would belong to one person i.e., the tribal chief. When Bashir ibn Saad, the head of the al-Khazraj tribe of the Ansar paid allegiance to Caliph Abu Bakr, it meant that the entire tribe of al-Khazraj would pay allegiance to Abu Bakr, simply because the tribal chief had done so.

Alongside the Islamic system the tribal system was just as prevalent. This is why the Ansar kept insisting to have the Caliph from their tribe and the Muhajireen wanted someone from their clan. When Caliph Umar paid allegiance to Caliph Abu Bakr, it meant that the entire tribe of Banu Adi would also pay allegiance to Caliph Abu Bakr, because the vote of Caliph Umar commanded the votes of all his tribesmen too.

The vast majority of the companions and the ordinary Muslims were looking up to their tribal leaders, and if the leaders had been swayed by the events of Saqifah, then there was no reason or justification for them to oppose the verdict of Saqifah. They had been following the Islamic way of life alongside the tribal customs, which also used to govern their lives.

Once the tribal chiefs of Al-Khazraj and Al-Aws had decided to pay allegiance to Caliph Abu Bakr, after they had reached the political adjustment with the Muhajireen in Saqifah, it meant that almost the entire Muslim population of Madinah would end up paying allegiance to Caliph Abu Bakr.

The strong tribal system that existed among the Arabs at the time was a key factor in persuading the majority of the Muslims to accept the verdict of Saqifah.

8.2.4. Caliph Umar's Speech at Prophet's Mosque

The other key factor which led the companions to accept the verdict of Saqifah was the speech of Caliph Umar at the mosque of the Prophet.

It was ironic that the meeting to choose the successor of the Prophet was conducted in Saqifah, a place which is some three miles away from Madinah, without inviting or informing any of the stakeholders. But the outcome of the meeting of Saqifah was publicly announced in the mosque of the Prophet, where thousands of companions had gathered to receive the news and information about the current political situation.

Caliph Umar came to the mosque of the Prophet a day after the event of Saqifah, and addressed thousands of companions who had gathered there with these words:

> *"God has enabled you to agree on the best of the companions of the Prophet who accompanied him at the Cave (of Thour at the time of the Hijrah). Rise up and give your allegiance to him."*
> - *Ibn Husham in his Biography of the Prophet Part 2 pp. 659-660.*

Caliph Umar said to the audience that an agreement had been reached on the best of the companions i.e., Caliph Abu Bakr, because he was the companion of the cave, and then he urges all the companions who had gathered at the mosque of the Prophet to stand up and give allegiance to Caliph Abu Bakr.

Caliph Umar did not elaborate on the intricate details of how this agreement was reached. The actual details of the proceedings of Saqifah at the time were only known to its participants, or perhaps a few other companions who were in touch with the main players of Saqifah. The agreement on the Caliphate of Abu Bakr was not reached because he was the companion of the cave. The agreement between the Muhajireen and the Ansar was reached because Caliph Abu Bakr had offered the Ansar to become the advisors to the Caliph.

Nevertheless, that was the news which was fed to the companions who had gathered at the mosque of the Prophet. It wasn't the age of information where news from any corner of the globe would be readily available on one's smart phone. And that is why thousands of companions and ordinary Muslims had gathered at the mosque of the Prophet to receive news and information about the new leader of the Muslim Ummah.

The vast majority of the companions and Muslims had no knowledge about the proceedings of Saqifah, or what had actually taken place in that meeting. When a prominent and a well know companion like Caliph Umar stands up in the mosque of the Prophet, and informs the companions that an agreement had been reached on the Caliphate of Abu Bakr, and he is also urging them to pay allegiance to the new Caliph, then there was no reason for these companions and ordinary Muslims not to believe or accept his statement.

As far as the companions and the Muslims who had gathered at the mosque of the Prophet were concerned, an agreement had been reached among all the Muslim leaders on the Caliphate of Abu Bakr. Also, most of their tribal leaders and elders had already paid allegiance to Abu Bakr either in Saqifah or just after it, hence they also paid allegiance to the new Caliph without questioning it.

This was how the majority of the companions and Muslims had come to accept the Caliphate of Abu Bakr, and this is how he became the head of the Islamic State after the death of the Prophet.

8.3. The Legality of Saqifah

In this section I will discuss the legality of Saqifah from an Islamic and a legal point of view to see if the meeting of Saqifah could be justified on these grounds.

8.3.1. The influence of Quraysh

As mentioned previously, the real reason why Ali is not even nominated in Saqifah was because Quraysh were unwilling to have the Prophethood and the Caliphate confined to the clan of Banu Hashim.

The reality was that the Quraysh of Makkah had never really accepted the Prophet as the Prophet of Allah either, so why would they accept his nominee? They had fought and opposed the Prophet from the very beginning of his mission. They had only accepted Islam after Muslims had conquered Makkah, and after Muslims had become the strongest and the most powerful force in Arabia. There was no way that they would accept the choice of the Prophet when they had never truly accepted the Prophet in the first place.

The Quraysh had been against the Prophet from the very start of his mission. They had done everything possible to stop and destroy the Islamic movement from its inception. But Prophet never compromised, or accepted the demands of the Quraysh, or got influenced by their views. The feelings, the sentiments and the plans of Quraysh had always been hostile towards Muslims, but the Prophet of Allah kept fighting them in every possible way.

The Prophet never changed his strategy just because the majority of the Qurayshite clans were not willing to allow the expansion of Islam. If Prophet had changed his strategy or given in to the wishes of Quraysh, or accommodated their sentiments in his decision-making process, then Islam would have never flourished and there would have been no Muslims in the world today.

In fact, the opposition from Quraysh for the leadership of Ali should have been seen as a clear sign for its legitimacy, since Quraysh had opposed the Prophet, they would oppose his nominee too. But unfortunately, rather than supporting the nominee of the Prophet, both Caliph Abu Bakr and Caliph Umar choose to be influenced by the view of the Quraysh, against Ali and Banu Hashim.

It is a historical fact after the conquest of Makkah most of the Qurayshite clans were being kept on the path of Islam through the incentives of gifts and war booty. Giving preference to the feelings and sentiments of a group whose faith in Islam was still in limbo, and ignoring the group that had fought for the supremacy of Islam, cannot become the basis of the Islamic Caliphate.

The Prophet knew the sentiments and feelings of Quraysh more than Caliph Abu Bakr and Caliph Umar. Prophet had faced the Quraysh and had fought them from the very beginning of his mission. He knew that they were the real enemies of the Muslims, even though on the face of it they had now accepted Islam.

Prophet had chosen Ali to be his successor for good reasons. Ali also knew the dark past of the Quraysh, and he knew their plans against Islam and Muslims. The aim of the Prophet was to keep the influence of groups like Quraysh, who had been hostile to the Muslims and who were still being kept on the path of Islam by the way of incentives to a minimum. But unfortunately, due to the ijtihad of Caliph Abu Bakr and Caliph Umar, they managed to do the exact opposite of what the Prophet had planned and hoped for, which cannot be called anything other than a tragedy.

In fact, after the conquest of Makkah the authority and the power of the Quraysh had diminished significantly. The pre-Islamic leaders of Quraysh like Abu Sufyan had been defeated and had lost their influence and significance. Caliph Abu Bakr and Caliph Umar had a golden opportunity in Saqifah to uphold the commands of the Prophet, but instead they choose to support the view of the Quraysh. They allowed their decision to be influenced by the sentiments and the feelings of Quraysh towards Ali and the Banu Hashim. This unfortunately was a clear breach of the Sunnah of the Prophet.

If Caliph Abu Bakr and Caliph Umar had simply proposed or nominated Ali in Saqifah, their position would have been vindicated.

They would have done their duty and would have followed the Sunnah of the Prophet. Now whether Ali would actually get selected in Saqifah would be a different story. Caliph Abu Bakr and Caliph Umar would not be responsible for the outcome of Saqifah, since they would have done their bit in supporting the Sunnah of the Prophet, by simply nominating Ali. But unfortunately, they choose to follow the trend of al-ijtihad against the clear instructions of the Prophet.

The outcome of such a meeting which is based on the sentiments and feelings of group that had been the biggest enemy of Islam, cannot possibly become binding on the Muslims, and Muslims are not obliged to follow the person who is selected in this manner.

8.3.2. The Quran and the Sunnah

The religion of Islam comprises of two sources of knowledge and guidance i.e., the Holy Quran, which is the book of Allah and the Sunnah (traditions) of the Prophet.

There is no verse in the Holy Quran which mentions or even hints at the Caliphate of Abu Bakr. Also, there are no traditions of the Prophet which claim that Caliph Abu Bakr should have been the successor of the Prophet. The Caliphate of Abu Bakr only came about as a result of the gathering of Saqifah.

If a Muslim does not pay allegiance to Caliph Abu Bakr or refuses to follow his Caliphate, then he or she would not be sinful, because neither Allah nor the Prophet of Allah had appointed him as the first Caliph. On the other hand, to insist and force people to follow the Caliphate of Abu Bakr would indeed be an innovation (bidah), because there is no justification from the Holy Quran or the Sunnah of the Prophet to prove his Caliphate.

This would have been the case for the Muslims who were contemporary to Caliph Abu Bakr.

Muslims who came in later generations would have even more right not to accept the Caliphate of Abu Bakr, because first of all his Caliphate has already ended, and secondly it was never established on the basis of Quran or the Sunnah of the Prophet.

It was simply established on the basis of the meeting of Saqifah.

8.3.3. The Prophet's Nominee

Caliph Umar had informed Caliph Abu Bakr about the meeting of Saqifah. Caliph Umar was also the person who proposed Caliph Abu Bakr in Saqifah, and he was also the first person to have paid allegiance to Abu Bakr in Saqifah. Finally, he also urged the Muslims who had gathered at the mosque of the Prophet to accept the Caliphate of Abu Bakr and give him allegiance as the first Caliph. Hence, Caliph Abu Bakr was the nominee and the choice of Caliph Umar.

The verdicts and the deeds of a Caliph who is chosen by someone other than the Prophet are not binding on the Muslims, and Muslims are not required to follow his words and actions. The Caliph may have the political and the administrative authority over the Muslims who were his contemporary, but following his Sunnah would not be obligatory on them, because he was not chosen by the Prophet.

On the other hand, the verdicts, the deeds, and the actions of a person who is appointed by the Prophet would become obligatory on all Muslims to follow, even though he may not have the political or the administrative authority. This is because the person who is chosen by the Prophet is indeed his representative, and Prophet had chosen that individual based on his merits and knowledge in Islam. His words, his verdicts, his deeds, and his actions would become obligatory for all the Muslims to follow, and that would be the case for Muslims who came in later generations too, because a Caliph appointed by the Prophet represents the Sunnah of the Prophet which is indeed eternal.

Paying allegiance to the nominee of the Prophet would be like paying allegiance to the Prophet himself, because Prophet had appointed him to lead the Ummah. And paying allegiance to the Prophet is like paying allegiance to Allah.

The Holy Quran declares that paying allegiance to the Prophet is same as paying allegiance to Allah.

> "Indeed, those who pledge allegiance to you, [O Muhammad] - they are actually pledging allegiance to Allah
> - Quran 48:10

Paying allegiance to Prophet's nominee is also not restricted to the Muslims who were contemporary to the Prophet. Just like following the Sunnah of the Prophet is obligatory on Muslims of all generations to come, similarly paying allegiance to Prophet's nominee is also obligatory on all the Muslim generations to come, until the Day of Judgment.

8.3.4. The Process of Fairness

Leaving aside the fact that Prophet had chosen Ali to lead the Ummah, simply based on the principles of justice and fair play the meeting of Saqifah had no legality.

The timing and the location of Saqifah was only known to a few companions from the Ansar, who choose not to inform others about this gathering. The key stakeholders who had a right in the Caliphate were not even made aware of this gathering. As a result, there was no presence of Ali or the Ahlulbayt in Saqifah, which meant that there was nobody in this gathering to support their position either. This approach breaks the very basic rules of an Islamic Shura (consultation). A Shura, which is conducted without the participation of all the stakeholders has no validity.

A meeting where all the candidates for the Caliphate are not even present, because they have not been informed about its timing and its location, cannot be used to justify the Caliphate of any Muslim, let alone the Caliphate of the successor of the Prophet. A consultation (Shura), which is conducted in this fashion has no legal value in the eyes of Islam or even in the commonly accepted principles of justice and fair play. The Caliphate of a person who is chosen in this way cannot become legally binding, even on Muslims who were contemporary to the Caliph, let alone on Muslims who came in later generations.

8.3.5. A Key Point

We read in Sahih Bukhari that Prophet had informed his daughter Fatima that he would not survive his present ailment and would not recover from it.

> *"The first time he disclosed to me that he would not recover from his illness and I wept. Then he told me that I would be the first of his family to join him, so I laughed."*
>
> • Sahih Al-Bukhari, 2/638

Prophet knew that this would be his final illness and he would meet his creator after this.

As I have mentioned previously that Prophet had organized an army in his final ailment to be sent to Syria (the Byzantine Empire). This army was organized two or three days before the death of the Prophet. He appointed Usama Ibn Zayd ibn Haritha, who was just eighteen years of age as its commander in chief. The Prophet then asked Caliph Abu Bakr, Caliph Umar, Abu Ubaydah and other prominent companions to join Usama's army. However, the companions refused to join his army and criticized the Prophet for choosing such a young commander.

> *"The Prophet equipped an army that Abu Bakr and Umar were in and he appointed Usama ibn Zayd as their commander, then people criticized him about his age.........."*
>
> • Tabaqat Al-Kubra. Vol. 2, Pg. # 219.
> • Fathul Bari Sharh Saheeh Al-Bukhari. Vol. 8, Pg. # 445.

If Caliph Abu Bakr and Caliph Umar had followed the commands and the instructions of the Prophet, then they would not even be present in Madinah when the Prophet had died. The only reason why they were present in Madinah at the time of the death of the Prophet was because they had used their own ijtihad (judgment) against the clear instructions of the Prophet, and they had refused to join the expedition under the command of Usama.

The events of Saqifah would have been very different in the absence of either Caliph Abu Bakr or Caliph Umar.

There was no way that Caliph Abu Bakr would have been chosen as the first Caliph over the Muslims if he or Caliph Umar were not present in Madinah at the time of the death of the Prophet. Nobody would have even nominated them if they were absent from the meeting of Saqifah.

This clearly shows that Prophet had not envisaged Caliph Abu Bakr or Caliph Umar to play any part in the leadership of the Muslim Ummah after his death, otherwise he would not have sent them away from Madinah, when he was about to die. He was expecting Caliph Abu Bakr and Caliph Umar to be fighting the Byzantine Empire at the time of his death.

It is true that when Caliph Abu Bakr became the first Caliph, he sent the army under Usama's command to fight the Byzantine Empire. But that was not the command or the instruction of the Prophet. Prophet had asked Caliph Abu Bakr and Caliph Umar to fight the Byzantines under the command of Usama!

If either Caliph Abu Bakr or Caliph Umar had left Madinah and had gone away with Usama to fight the Byzantines, as per the commands of the Prophet, the outcome of Saqifah would be completely different. Neither Caliph Abu Bakr nor Caliph Umar would have acquired the Caliphate of the Muslims if either one of them was not present in Saqifah.

On the other hand, Prophet had kept Ali in Madinah, to ensure that Ali takes over the leadership of the Islamic State after his death. Ali was a man of battlefield and a star warrior in Prophet's army. The only reason why Prophet keeps Ali in Madinah was because Prophet was expected to die, and he wanted Ali to take over the leadership of Muslims after his death.

But unfortunately, the destiny was not in favour of Ali.

9. THE APPROACH OF ALI

The approach of Ali to the verdict of Saqifah was unique and distinct just like his character and merits were unique and distinct among all the companions.

When the prophet was in his final ailment the Ahlulbayt i.e., the family of the Prophet were by his side throughout this critical time. Both Ali and Fatima were nursing and looking after the Prophet in the last few days of his life.

Lady Fatimah, the daughter of the Prophet was sitting beside her father's bed and was looking at his blessed face and could see the perspiration of death flowing down his forehead. With a heavy heart, tearful eyes, and a choked throat she was reciting the following words:

> *"The luminous face in whose honour rains are sought from the clouds. The person who is the asylum for the orphans and the guardian of the widows".*

Prophet asked Fatimah to bring his grandsons Hasan and Hussain to him so that he could bid a final farewell to them.

> *"Bring your sons to me. Fatimah brought Hasan and Husain to the Prophet. Both of them greeted the Prophet, they sat by his side and wept at witnessing the agony of the Prophet in such a manner that the people who saw them weeping could not hold their tears. Hasan rested his face upon the Prophet's face and Hussain rested his head upon the Prophet's chest. The Prophet opened his eyes and kissed his grandsons lovingly"*
> - Rawdatul-ahbab

Hasan puts his face on Prophet's face and Hussain puts his head on Prophet's chest, as a gesture of final farewell to their beloved grandfather, the Prophet of Allah. Both Hasan and Hussain start crying on seeing the Prophet in such a state. On witnessing Hasan and Hussain cry the few companions who were around the Prophet could not hold back tears and started crying too.

The Prophet opened his eyes for a final moment and said to his daughter in a low voice to recite the following verse of the Holy Quran:

> *Muhammad is but a messenger. The messengers have already passed away before him. Will it be that, when he dies or is slain, you will turn back on your heels? He who turns back does no hurt to Allah, and Allah will reward the thankful.*
> - Quran 3:144

The best of the creation ever had left this temporary world and gone to meet Allah the creator and the sustainer of the Universe. The grief and sorrow which had befallen on the family of the Prophet is difficult to put into words. The Prophet was the head and the guardian of the Ahlulbayt, and with his death the Ahlulbayt had lost their father their protector and their defender.

9.1. The Funeral of the Prophet

Amidst their grief and sorrow the Ahlulbayt and the Banu Hashim, which included personalities like Ali and Ibn Abbas began the arrangements for Prophet's funeral.

Ali, in his own words describes the final moments of Prophet's life and his funeral proceedings.

> *"I never disobeyed Allah or His Messenger at all, and by virtue of the courage with which Allah honoured me I supported him with my life on occasions when even the brave turned away and feet remained behind (instead of proceeding forward).*
> *When the Prophet died his head was on my chest, and his (last) breath blew over my palms and I passed it over my face. I performed his (funeral) ablution, and the angels helped me. The house and the courtyard were full of them.*
> *One party of them was descending and the other was ascending. My ears continually caught their humming voice, as they invoked Allah's blessing on him, till we buried him in his grave."*

- Nahjul Balagha (Sermon 195)

The Prophet's head was resting on Ali's chest as Prophet took his final breath.

Readers would recall from Chapter 2 that after the birth of Ali he did not open his eyes until he saw the blessed face of the Prophet, and it seems that the Prophet also did not close his eyes until his head was lying on Ali's chest. The companionship of Ali with the Prophet was unique and distinct. It began with the birth of Ali and ended with the death of the Prophet.

Ali washes and baths the blessed body of the Prophet. Ali then performs the funeral prayers for the Prophet, alongside the Ahlulbayt and some of the companions who had gathered at the house of the Prophet. The Prophet of Allah had ordered Muslims to bury their dead as soon as possible and this is exactly what Ali did after the death of the Prophet.

The angles were coming in groups to pay their respects and recite salutations on the Messenger of Allah. Ali was a witness to this unique and amazing spiritual experience, which took place after the death of the Prophet. Just like the way Ali was a witness to the revelations that Angle Gabriel had brought to the Prophet in the cave of Hira, Ali again became a witness to the decent of the angels on the Prophet after his death.

9.2. Saqifah took Precedence over the Prophet's Funeral

While Ali was busy with the funeral proceedings of the Prophet, the meeting of Saqifah not only took place right at that moment, but it also concluded with the allegiance given to Caliph Abu Bakr even before the Prophet could be buried.

We read in al-Tabari:

> *Amir asked: "When was the oath of allegiance given to Abu Bakr?"*
> *"The very day the Messenger of Allah died,"*
>
> - al-Tabari, Vol.1, p.195

Both famous historians Abul-Fida and Ibn al-Wardi reported that the Prophet died on Monday and was buried the next day i.e., Tuesday. And in one of the traditions, it is said that he was buried in the night between Tuesday and Wednesday, and this tradition appears to be more authentic. The oath of allegiance to Abu Bakr in Saqifah was given before the burial of the Prophet.

Leaving aside the issue of whether the Prophet had chosen Ali to be his successor, or whether he had left the matter of the Caliphate to the Ummah, the very first duty of the prominent companions was to be with the Prophet after his death, before contemplating or addressing any other issue. The Prophet of Allah could not have possibly wished that his prominent companions would finalize their new leader even before his burial.

The traditions of the Prophet in fact completely negate the assembly of the companions in Saqifah. The Prophet had commanded the Muslims to bury their dead as soon as possible.

> *"Hurry up with the dead body (for its burial), for if it is pious, you are speeding it to goodness....."*
>
> - Al-Bukhari Vol. 2, Book 23, Hadith 401

There was nobody more pious than the Prophet of Allah. Participating in the funeral of the Prophet and burying him was the very first duty and responsibility of every companion as per the above tradition of the Prophet.

It is a very well-known Islamic practice that Muslims bury their dead as soon as possible, unlike some of the other religions where the dead are kept for days before the burial takes place. This in fact is a key difference that Islam has with the other major faiths like Christianity and Judaism, where the dead can be buried many days after their death.

Even if we assume that the primary responsibility of Prophet's funeral lied with his family, and the companions were not strictly required to be there, but simply based on the logic of love and respect for the Prophet of Allah, who had been a beacon of light for the entire mankind, one cannot imagine that on hearing the news of Prophet's death, the first thing that some of the companions would do was to choose their new leader!

The gathering of Saqifah does not look right even on these grounds.

A contemporary historian Sir John Glubb says:

> *"Mohammed was not dead an hour before the struggle for power threatened to rend Islam into rival factions."*

Such words from a non-Muslim historian about the meeting of Saqifah are a little uncomfortable to say the least, for a Muslim who has grown up to love and respect the Prophet all his life.

9.3. The News from Saqifah Reaches Ali

The news from Saqifah started to spread and it reached Ali and the family of the Prophet, who were in a state of grieving and mourning and were still preparing his body for burial. They could not believe or comprehend as to what had suddenly taken place in Saqifah. The death of the Prophet was expected, but the news that came from Saqifah was not. It came as a complete shock to Ali and the family of the Prophet (Ahlulbayt) that a new leader of the Muslim Ummah had already been chosen. They were completely taken back by the sequence of events that took place in Saqifah.

Despite hearing the news that Abu Bakr had been given allegiance as the new Caliph, Ali kept himself busy with the funeral proceedings of the Prophet. Ali could not contemplate leaving the body of the Prophet before it was buried.

Ali had planned to go to the Mosque of the Prophet after his burial, and he had planned to address the thousands of companions who had gathered there, to formally take over the proceedings of the Islamic State.

However, after the verdict of Saqifah, Ali's plans lie in ruins, and instead of going to the Prophet's Mosque where Caliph Umar had been urging the Muslims to pay allegiance to Caliph Abu Bakr, Ali heads back to his house where the daughter of the Prophet lady Fatima was grieving for her father.

The manner in which Ali conducts himself on hearing the verdict of Saqifah, is in itself a testament to the unique and the distinguished character of Ali.

9.4. The Demand of Allegiance

Caliph Umar had been urging the companions who had gathered at the mosque of the Prophet to pay allegiance to Caliph Abu Bakr, but Ali wasn't present there, instead Ali had gone back to his house after the burial of the Prophet, and after hearing the news of Caliph Abu Bakr's appointment as the new leader of the Muslim Ummah.

Caliph Abu Bakr had already received allegiance from both the key tribes of Madinah, and from the companions who had gathered at the mosque of the Prophet. The only exception was Ali, the family of the Prophet and a few companions who were supporting Ali. These companions had distanced themselves from the outcome of Saqifah and had refrained from pledging allegiance to Caliph Abu Bakr.

We read the account of Caliph Umar in Bukhari:

> Umar said: "And no doubt after the death of the Prophet we were informed that the Ansar disagreed with us and gathered in the shed of Bani Sa'da. 'Ali and Zubair and whoever was with them, opposed us, while the emigrants gathered with Abu Bakr."
>
> - Sahih al-Bukhari, Arabic-English, v8, Tradition #817

A similar account is also found in Musnad of Ahmad Ibn Hanbal, and Sirah al-Nabawiyyah:

> Umar said: "Ali Ibn Abi Talib, Zubair Ibn Awwam and those who were with them separated from us (and gathered) in the house of Fatimah, the daughter of the messenger of Allah."
>
> - Ahmad Ibn Hanbal, v1, p55
> - Sirah al-Nabawiyyah, by Ibn Hisham, v4, p309

The position of Caliph Abu Bakr had become very strong after he had received the allegiance from the various tribes and segments of the Islamic world. Caliph Abu Bakr was now the head of the Islamic State and the Caliph of the entire Muslim Ummah.

Apart from Ali, the family of the Prophet and few companions who were supporting Ali, everybody else was inline and had accepted the verdict of Saqifah. Caliph Abu Bakr now sends Caliph Umar with a few other companions to demand allegiance from Ali and the family of the Prophet.

We read in Al-Aqd al Farid by Ibn Abd Rabbah al-Andalusi

> "Those who refrained from giving the bayah (allegiance) to Abu Bakr were Ali, Abbas (the uncle of the Prophet), Zubayr bin al-Awan (cousin of the Prophet) and Saad bin Ibadah (who was the nominee of Ansar in Saqifah). As for Ali and Abbas they sat in the house of Fatima until Abu Bakr sent Umar to take them out of the house of Fatima and he (Abu Bakr) said to him (Umar), "If they refuse, then fight them." Thus he (Umar) came with a torch of fire to engulf the house on them and upon arriving, he encountered Fatima. She said, O Ibn al-Khattab, did you come to burn our house?" He said, " Yes, unless you enter what the Ummah entered into."

- Ibn Abd Rabbah al-Andalusi, Al-Aqd al-Farid, 4:259

The above incident is also reported in a similar fashion by the famous historian al-Baldari in his book Ansab al-Ashraf:

> Abu Bakr sent for Ali, asking him to pay allegiance. He didn't pay allegiance and thus Umar came with a torch to the house of Fatima. He came face to face with Fatima and she said to him, "Are you really going to burn the door of the house?" Umar answered, "Yes indeed."

- Al-Baladri, Ansab al-Ashraf, 1:586

Al-Tabari also relates the same story, however, he says that Talha, Zubayr and some other men from Muhajireen were also present in the house of Ali.

> Umar Ibn al-Khattab came to the house of Ali. Talha and Zubair and some of the immigrants were also in the house. Umar cried out: "By God, either you come out to render the oath of allegiance, or I will set the house on fire." al-Zubair came out with his sword drawn. As he stumbled (upon something), the sword fell from his hand so they jumped over him and seized"

- Tarikh al-Tabari, 2:198
- Tarikh al-Tabari (Arabic), v1, pp 1118-1120
- Tarikh al-Tabari, English version, v9, pp 186-187

Other historians have also reported this incident in a slightly shorter version:

> When Umar came to the door of the house of Fatimah, he said: "By Allah, I shall burn down (the house) over you unless you come out and give the oath of allegiance (to Abu Bakr)."

- Ibn Abe Shaiba 38200
- History of Ibn Athir, v2, p325
- al-Isti'ab, by Ibn Abd al-Barr, v3, p975
- Tarikh al-Kulafa, by Ibn Qutaybah, v1, p20
- Tarikh Abul Fida, 1:156

There was no need for any of this on part of Caliph Abu Bakr and Caliph Umar. Ali had not challenged the authority of Caliph Abu Bakr, despite the fact that Prophet had nominated him as his successor. Ali had not gone to the mosque of the Prophet with a sword and challenged the Caliphate of Abu Bakr, which he was very much capable of doing.

On the contrary, on hearing the verdict of Saqifah Ali went back to his house and in fact dropped his plans, which he had made to formally take over the leadership of the Muslims.

However, the only thing that Ali had not done was to pay allegiance to Caliph Abu Bakr. The demand of Caliph Abu Bakr to give him allegiance despite the fact that Ali had not even challenged his authority, proved beyond any doubt that in the eyes of Caliph Abu Bakr Ali also had a claim to the Caliphate, and hence Caliph Abu Bakr wanted Ali to pay him allegiance to settle that matter.

It was extremely unfair and unreasonable to demand allegiance from the very person who also had a claim to the Caliphate, and while that person was not even challenging or opposing the Caliph.

The demand of allegiance also had no justification from the Holy Quran or the Sunnah of the Prophet. The Caliphate of Abu Bakr had not come as a result of a verse from the Book of Allah or as a result of a tradition of the Prophet. It had come as a result of the meeting of Saqifah, a meeting where Caliph Abu Bakr was not even invited.

Caliph Abu Bakr had simply managed to get to the meeting of Saqifah in time, and managed to stop the Ansar in their tracks, and acquired the leadership of the Muslim Ummah as a result of a political deal, but that does not make Caliph Abu Bakr the choice of Allah or a nominee of the Prophet.

9.5. Threatening the Ahlulbayt

It would not be out of place to mention that the method employed for demanding the allegiance from Ali was extremely harsh, unethical, and unwarranted. This was a time when the family of the Prophet was grieving and were in a state of mourning. If anything, this was a time to console and support the family of the Prophet, who had just lost their most loving, kind and precious member.

Its common courtesy that when someone has passed away their friends would come to the bereaved family and offer condolences and would try and support the family as much as they can, in order to help them get over the mourning phase. And this was the family of the Prophet, and the person who had just passed away was none other than the Prophet of Allah himself.

The verses of the Holy Quran instruct us to love the family of the Prophet.

> "...Say (O' Muhammad unto mankind): I do not ask of you any reward for it (preaching the message), but love for my near relatives Ahlulbayt'; and whoever earns good, we give him more of good therein,.."
> - Qur'an 42:23

Threatening the family of the Prophet who had gathered in the house of Ali and Fatima, where even the Prophet used to seek permission before entering, as a sign of respect for his daughter, cannot be justified under any circumstances, especially after his death.

The Prophet had said about Fatima:

> *"Fatima is a part of me, and whoever makes her angry, makes me angry."*
> - *(Sahih Bukhari: Volume 5, Book 57, Number 111)*

It was most unfortunate that a prominent companion like Caliph Umar could threaten the daughter of the Prophet soon after the death of her father. It was a time of immense loss for this noble family, and it was a time of compassion and kindness towards the family of the Prophet.

The Prophet of Allah who was a mercy for the mankind had just passed away. One cannot imagine burning the house of the Prophet down under any circumstance, especially after his death and especially when his family were in fact grieving in that very house.

Regardless of the political scenario in Madinah, and regardless of whether Ali had given the oath of allegiance to Abu Bakr or not, threatening to burn down the house of the beloved daughter of the Prophet is a completely unjustifiable act.

These sentiments had a pre-Islamic tone, when in the days of Jahilliyah (pre-Islamic times), Arabs would burn down the houses and properties of their opponents and rivals as a show of victory over them.

9.6. Enforcing the Verdict of Saqifah

Even the rulings of the Holy Quran or the Sunnah of the Prophet cannot be forced upon people.

If someone does not follow the Holy Quran or the Sunnah of the Prophet then obviously, they would be sinful, and one should guide them and try and persuade them to follow the path of Islam, but the use of force is not allowed in the religion of Allah.

The Holy Quran states:

> *"There is no compulsion in religion"*
> - Quran 2:256

And forcing the view of Saqifah on the very person who was in fact its biggest victim, cannot be classed as anything other than a travesty.

Caliph Abu Bakr had tasked Caliph Umar to enforce the outcome of Saqifah. In fact, forcing the verdict of Saqifah was another clear evidence of the trend of al-ijtihad (independent judgment), which had become even more pronounced after the death of the Prophet.

Ali refused to budge and told Caliph Abu Bakr that he would not pay allegiance to him. I will reproduce the answer that Ali gave to Caliph Abu Bakr after refusing to give him allegiance.

> *"I am more worthy of this position than you. You all should swear allegiance to me. You have sought allegiance from the Ansar on the basis of your proximity to the Holy Prophet and now you wish to snatch this right from us, Ahlulbayt? Did you not offer this argument that on account of your closeness to the Holy Prophet you are more eligible for the caliphate than them? Surely it is on this account that they handed over this position to you.*
>
> *I now offer you the same argument – I am the one who was the closest to the Holy Prophet in his life and even after this death. I am his rightful successor and trustee. I am the keeper of his secrets and the protector of his knowledge."*
>
> - Abdul Fattah Abdul Maksoud Al-Imam Ali Ibn Abu Talib Part 1 p. 179.

Ali not only justified his position as the successor of the Prophet to Caliph Abu Bakr, but he also demanded allegiance from Abu Bakr. He gave the same argument to Caliph Abu Bakr which Caliph Abu Bakr had given to the Ansar, that he (Ali) should get the Caliphate because he was closer to the Prophet than Abu Bakr. He also told Caliph Abu Bakr that he was the keeper of Prophet's knowledge and secrets, and that he was his rightful successor and trustee.

9.7. The Issue of Fadak

The issue of Fadak was one of the most contentious issues during the Caliphate of Abu Bakr. The issue of Fadak was about the right of inheritance of lady Fatima, the daughter of the Prophet.

Fadak was a well-developed and a productive farmland which was owned by the Prophet of Allah. The land of Fadak came into the ownership of the Prophet after the Jews were defeated in the battle of Khaibar at the hands of Ali. The Jewish tribes struck a settlement with the Prophet, where the Jews were offered protection under the Islamic State and Prophet took over the ownership of half of Fadak. The land of Fadak became a source of revenue and income for the Prophet and his family (Ahlulbayt).

After taking over the Caliphate, Caliph Abu Bakr ousted Lady Fatima's hired residents from Fadak, and confiscated the land from her. When lady Fatima found out, she immediately protested to Caliph Abu Bakr and demanded the return of the land of Fadak. Caliph Abu Bakr refused and rejected her demands and cited a hadith (tradition) of the Prophet to justify his stance.

Caliph Abu Bakr said to Lady Fatima that I have heard from the Prophet that a Prophet does not leave inheritance and he only leaves behind charity.

> *"We do not leave inheritance, what we leave behind is charity."*
>
> - *(Sahih al-Muslim, jitab al-Jihad Was Siyar, no 49)*

He used the above hadith as a justification for confiscation of the land of Fadak from the family of the Prophet. He claimed that since the Prophet owned this land, and as Prophets do not leave behind inheritance and they only leave behind charity, everything that was owned by the Prophet would now be owned by the State.

The daughter of the Prophet tried to justify her claim to Fadak by showing various forms of evidence, but Caliph Abu Bakr turned all of those down on one ground or the other. Lady Fatima told Caliph Abu Bakr that Fadak was actually a gift that Prophet of Allah had given to her four years before his death, so it was in fact her property rather than the property of the Prophet.

Caliph Abu Bakr then asked her to bring witnesses to substantiate and justify her claim. The four witnesses that Lady Fatima brought forward were Ali, Hasan, Hussain and Umme Ayman, the wife of the Prophet. However, Caliph Abu Bakr rejected the testimony of all the witnesses on various accounts, like being the members of the same family etc.

The Prophet had said the following about lady Fatima.

> *"Fatima is the leader of the women of Paradise."*
>
> - *Sahih Al-Bukhari volume 3, Kitab Al-Fadha'il, p. 1374*

Being the leader of the women of Paradise, the testimony of Lady Fatima alone should have been good enough to substantiate her claim, and there should have been no reason to have any other witnesses once the daughter of the Prophet had testified that Fadak had been gifted to her.

The daughter of the Prophet was not a greedy lady. When she got married to Ali, Prophet gave her some very basic items for starting her new life, which are listed below.

- A sheepskin to sleep on
- A pillow of leather stuffed with palm-tree fibres
- A bed made of palm-tree branches
- A quern
- A water skin
- Two jars
- Some pottery vessels

The daughter of the Prophet thanked her father and never asked for anything more, such was the character and the personality of Fatima. She was only demanding what had been given to her by her father.

Without getting into the legality of Fadak, despite Fatima's claim, Caliph Abu Bakr confiscated Fadak and refused to give it back to her and made it into a state property. Ironically, the hadith that Caliph Abu Bakr used where he had stated that prophets do not leave behind inheritance and they only leave behind charity, is only narrated by Abu Bakr himself. It is a Shaz (a rare/unusual) hadith which no other individual other than Caliph Abu Bakar had narrated from the Prophet!

9.8. The Rift Between the Ahlulbayt and Caliph Abu Bakr and Umar

Before the death of the Prophet, the Prophet of Allah was the head of the Islamic State and the leadership of the Muslim Ummah rested with the Prophet. After the death of the Prophet, not only was the leadership of the Muslims taken away from the family of the Prophet, but they were also deprived of their main source of income, which was the land of Fadak. The family of the Prophet had suffered, sacrificed, and contributed more than the family of any other companion, but this noble family which had given everything in the path of Islam now finds itself on the wrong side of the law.

Firstly, the State tried to force them to pledge allegiance to the newly elected Caliph, by threatening to burn down their house, even though it was their right to lead the Muslim Ummah. Secondly, the State confiscates most of their wealth and deprives them of their main source of income. And when they try to justify their claim, their own testimony is not accepted, and as they put forward witnesses to substantiate their case, the witnesses are also rejected for not being sound.

This indeed was most unfortunate and tragic.

As a result of Saqifah and the subsequent confiscation of Fadak, a huge rift and a gulf had opened up between the family of the Prophet and both Caliph Abu Bakr and Caliph Umar. The daughter of the Prophet was no longer on speaking terms with either Caliph Abu Bakr or Caliph Umar, and she died without ever speaking to them again.

We read in Sahih Bukhari.

> *After the death of Allah's Apostle Fatima the daughter of Allah's Apostle asked Abu Bakr As-Siddiq to give her, her share of inheritance from what Allah's Apostle had left of the Fai (i.e. booty gained without fighting) which Allah had given him. Abu Bakr said to her, "Allah's Apostle*

said, 'Our property will not be inherited, whatever we (i.e. prophets) leave is Sadaqah (to be used for charity)." Fatima, the daughter of Allah's Apostle got angry and stopped speaking to Abu Bakr, and continued assuming that attitude till she died. Fatima remained alive for six months after the death of Allah's Apostle.*

- Sahih Bukhari Volume 4, Book 53, Number 325

A similar tradition is also found in other books of history.

Fatimah and al Abbas came to Abu Bakr demanding their [share of] inheritance of the Messenger of God. They were demanding the Messenger of God's land in Fadak and his share of Khaybar ['s tribute]. Abu Bakr replied, "I have heard the Messenger of God say: 'Our [i.e the prophet's property] cannot be inherited and whatever we leave behinds is alms [i.e to be given in charity]. The family of Muhammad will eat from it. ' By God, I will not abandon a course which I saw the Messenger of God practicing, but will continue doing it accordingly." Fatimah shunned him and did not speak to him about it until she died. Ali buried her at night and did not permit Abu Bakr to attend [her burial].

- Tabari, vol IX p 196
- Tabaqat of Ibne Sad, vol VIII p 29,
- Yaqubi History, vol II p 117,
- Masudi in his Tanbih, p 250

As a result of the rift between lady Fatima and Caliph Abu Bakr, Ali buried her in the night without informing either Caliph Abu Bakr or Caliph Umar about her funeral. Some historians narrate that it was in fact the will of lady Fatima that Caliph Abu Bakr and Umar should be barred from her funeral, and that is why Ali quietly buried her in the night.

The Prophet had deemed the Ahlulbayt to be a source of knowledge and guidance for the companions and for the rest of the Muslim Ummah.

"....'O people I have left in you that which if you adhere to you will never go astray: The Book of God and the members of my House."

- Sunan Al-Tirmidhi. Vol. 3, Pg. # 543 - 544, H. # 3786 – 3788
- Sunan Al -Tirmidhi. Vol. 6, Pg. # 335

Caliph Abu Bakr had acquired the political and the administrative authority of the Muslim Ummah as a result of the meeting of Saqifah. But the mandate of the Prophet remained with the Ahlulbayt, as per the above tradition of the Prophet. To challenge and to threaten the Ahlulbayt was to challenge and to threaten the mandate and the clear Sunnah of the Prophet, which indeed was an unjustifiable act to say the least.

9.9. Why did Ali not Raise his Sword?

Ali was a man of the battlefield. Ali had killed some of the most feared warriors of Quraysh in the path of Allah. In every battle that Ali had taken part he came on top against the enemy. There was no other warrior who could match the bravery, the courage, and the skill of Ali in the Arabian Peninsula.

As Prophet had nominated Ali to be his successor, it was Ali's right to take over the leadership of the Muslim Ummah, then why did Ali not raise his sword to claim his right? A right that was indeed given to him by the Prophet.

Ali answers this key question in his own words:

> "O' my Allah! I beseech Thee to take revenge on the Quraysh and those who are assisting them, for they have cut asunder my kinship and over-turned my cup and have joined together to contest a right to which I was entitled more than anyone else. They said to me: "If you get your right, that will be just, but if you are denied the right, that too will be just. Endure it with sadness or kill yourself in grief." I looked around but found no one to shield me, protect me or help me except the members of my family. I refrained from flinging them into death and therefore closed my eyes despite the dust, kept swallowing saliva despite (the suffocation of) grief and endured pangs of anger although it was more bitter than colocynth and more grievous than the bite of knives."

- *(Nahjul Balaghah sermon 217)*

I will discuss in depth the circumstances to which Ali had alluded in his sermon, and the reason why he chose not to raise his sword.

9.9.1. The Ground Reality

The meeting of Saqifah had ended with a political deal between the Ansar and the Muhajireen, that the Muhajireen would become the leaders of the Islamic State and the Ansar would become their advisors. As a result of this political deal, the two biggest tribes of Madinah i.e., Al-Aws and Al-Khazraj had given their allegiance to Abu Bakr.

As mentioned previously, the vast majority of the Muslims had accepted the mandate of Saqifah, primarily due to the tribal vote and the speech of Caliph Umar at the mosque of the Prophet, where many companions had gathered to receive information about the new leader of the Muslims. These two factors, especially the tribal vote had immensely helped in solidifying the support for Caliph Abu Bakr.

As a result, most of the tribes, clans, and factions in and around Madinah had pledged allegiance to Abu Bakr and had accepted him as the new head of the Islamic State.

The Quraysh of Makkah, who were the main reason why Ali was denied Caliphate in the first place had also happily pledged allegiance to the central government, as long as they were getting their fair share of gifts and income. The Quraysh had no qualms about the Caliphate of Abu Bakr as they were more than happy to see one of their men lead the Muslims, rather than somebody from the Banu Hashim.

Once Caliph Abu Bakr acquired the Caliphate, the entire Islamic State came under his control. Caliph Abu Bakr had become extremely powerful both politically and militarily because of his newly acquired status. Caliph Abu Bakr was no longer just a prominent companion, he was now the head of the entire Muslim Ummah.

Ali had support from his family and from some prominent companions of the Prophet, like Ammar bin Yasir, al-Miqdad bin al-Aswad, Salma al-Farsi, Abu Dharr al Ghifari and others, but these were mostly poor individuals who lacked influence and prestige in an era of tribal dominance. These companions were not the leaders of their tribes, they did not have the political clout or the following that was needed to mount a challenge to the authority of Caliph Abu Bakr.

Also, the land of Fadak had been confiscated and turned into state property, denying the family of the Prophet any economic power, or any economic means that they could potentially use to take on the State authority.

This was the ground reality that Ali faced after Caliph Abu Bakr had become the head of the Islamic State.

9.9.2. The Frightening Prospect of Multiple Civil Wars

If Ali picks up his sword and assassinates Caliph Abu Bakr, which he had the courage and the capacity to do so, the entire Islamic State would be completely thrown into anarchy and turmoil. Apart from being the Caliph, Abu Bakr was also the head of Bani Taym clan, which was a very big and an influential clan of the Quraysh. First of all, the clan of Bani Taym would immediately launch a war against the Banu Hashim, the clan of the Prophet to avenge Abu Bakr's death.

Caliph Umar, who was the main architect of Abu Bakr's Caliphate, was also the head of Bani Adi clan, which was another notable clan of the Quraysh. Caliph Umar's clan would not stay quiet either, they would also join the war alongside the Banu Taym against the Banu Hashim. The rest of the Qurayshite clans who were dead against Ali and the Banu Hashim would certainly not stay on the side lines, they would not only try to kill Ali and attack the Banu Hashim, but they would in fact try and destroy the Islamic State itself, which they had never really accepted in the first place.

The situation in Madinah would not be too different either. Although, among the companions of Madinah, there was some support for Ali, and we saw in Saqifah that some Ansar did nominate Ali, but their tribal allegiances were far stronger than any support they had for Ali, and they had already pledged allegiance to Abu Bakr. After the assassination of Abu Bakr, it would be extremely unlikely that they would support Ali. They would undoubtedly support one of their own tribal leaders like Saad Ibn Ubaadah, and the friction between the al-Aws and al-Kazraj tribe would re-surface again, initiating another war in Madinah.

A number of civil wars would immediately break out in the Islamic State after the assassination of Caliph Abu Bakr, and the Islamic State itself would have been completely destroyed.

Also, many companions who had pledged allegiance to Abu Bakr after hearing the speech of Caliph Umar at the mosque of the Prophet, had absolutely no idea as to what had actually taken place in Saqifah. They would see Caliph Abu Bakr as a victim and regard Ali as an aggressor, if Ali had killed Caliph Abu Bakr. This would have seriously weakened Ali's case and destroyed his reputation too.

Then there were outside powers, who were looking to ambush the Muslims at the slightest opportunity. They saw the newly established Islamic State as threat to their very existence. If a civil war broke out in the Islamic State these outside forces would certainly make most of it and would leave no stone unturned in destroying the dream of the Prophet, i.e. The Islamic State itself.

After the verdict of Saqifah, Ali could have never gained his right by raising his sword against Abu Bakr. It had become practically impossible to acquire the Caliphate by the use of force at that point. Assassination of Caliph Abu Bakr alone would not enable Ali to come to power, Ali would have to kill a lot more companions and Muslims who had pledged allegiance to Abu Bakr, and in the civil war that would ensue there was no guarantee that Ali would come on top.

Ali, more than anybody else understood the ground reality of the time. It is for this reason Ali says that he swallowed the grief and the anger, which was more painful than the bites of the knife.

Ali was far too pious and righteous to allow such bloodletting of the Muslims, in order to claim his right of the Caliphate.

9.9.3. The Offer of Abu Sufyan

Abu Sufyan was the most renowned leader of the Quraysh, who had been the biggest enemy of the Prophet and the Muslims for almost two decades. He had fought the Prophet and the Muslims until he was defeated at the conquest of Makkah. He had fought the Muslims in the battle of Badr, in the battle of Uhud, in the battle of Moat, and he was also responsible for countless other expeditions against the Muslims in both Makkah and Madinah. At the conquest of Makkah when he saw the Muslim army approaching his heart sank, and to save his life he finally accepted Islam.

After Caliph Abu Bakr had taken over the reins of Caliphate, Abu Sufyan saw an opportunity to do damage and to cause trouble within the Islamic State, since he knew that it was in fact Ali's right to lead the Muslim Ummah. Abu Sufyan approached Ali and offered to give him allegiance as the new leader of the Muslims. He also offered to fill the streets of Madinah with cavalrymen, in order to forcefully remove Abu Bakr from the office of the Caliphate.

Abu Sufyan essentially offered Ali to take his right by force, here is what Abu Sufyan said to Ali:

> *The people have entrusted the caliphate to Taym (Abu-Bakr's family) neglectfully and they have deprived the Hashemites (the Prophet's family) of their right and then Umar, this hot-tempered of Adiy (Umar's family) will rule over us. Let us go to Ali and ask him to come out and get his legal right."*
>
> *They came to Ali. Abu-Sufyan said to him: "Give me your hand to pay homage to you and if anyone disagrees, I will fill all the streets of Medina with cavalrymen."*

- al-Tabari, 198-199
- al-Tabari vol. 3, p 202

Here is the response that Ali gave to Abu Sufyan.

> *Ali replied: "By God, you do not intend to do anything but stir up dissension. For long you have desired evil for Islam. We do not need your advice."*

- al-Tabari, 198-199
- al-Tabari vol. 3, p 202

The offer of Abu Sufyan to pay allegiance to Ali, and to fill the streets of Madinah with cavalrymen was not born out of his love for Ali, or his acceptance of Ali's position as the rightful successor of the Prophet. Abu Sufyan had never even accepted the Prophet as truly the Prophet of Allah. So why would he accept Ali as the rightful successor of the Prophet. Abu Sufyan had only accepted Islam after Islam had become the strongest force in Arabia, and he felt that there was no other option left for him other than becoming a Muslim.

The offer of Abu Sufyan was born out of jealousy for the clan of Caliph Abu Bakr, as he would rather see power in his own Umayyad clan then in the clan of Banu Taym, to which Caliph Abu Bakr belonged.

Also, Abu Sufyan saw an opportunity to initiate a civil war that would engulf the entire Muslim Ummah. His offer had grave consequences, thousands of Muslims would be killed and the Islamic State that Prophet had worked so hard to establish would cease to exist.

This is why Ali immediately turned down the opportunistic and the poisonous offer of Abu Sufyan.

Also, for the sake of argument, let's say if Ali had accepted the offer of Abu Sufyan, and Ali was somehow successful in dislodging the administration of Caliph Abu Bakr, without too much bloodshed.

Then afterwards, Abu Sufyan would want to share power with Ali, since the aim of Abu Sufyan was to get to the helm of the Islamic State in the guise of supporting Ali. Ali could not possibly use force against Caliph Abu Bakr to share power with the Umayyad's, the clan of Abu Sufyan, a clan which had been the biggest enemy of the Prophet since the birth of Islam. This would have been another wrong just like the wrong of Saqifah.

Ali categorically rejects the politically ambitious offer of Abu Sufyan. Ali says to Abu Sufyan that your intention is to stir-up dissension, and you only have evil designs for the religion of Allah, a statement which could not be truer and more accurate.

A lesser man than Ali, who had seen his right taken away, would have probably accepted the lucrative offer of filling the streets of Madinah with cavalrymen to take back their right. But Ali was the choice of the Prophet, and Ali's decisions and Ali's actions at every step of the way after the debacle of Saqifah, reflected the time that Prophet had taken to make Ali the man he was.

If Ali had accepted the offer of Abu Sufyan, it meant that Ali had accepted the offer of a known enemy of the Prophet. Ali could not possibly justify his stance to the Prophet on the Day of Judgment, and Ali would have placed himself in an indefensible position in the eyes of Prophet.

Prophet had given Ali his companionship since he was a child, Ali's decisions had to reflect his unique and distinct position. Ali was not just the custodian of Prophet's knowledge and wisdom, but Ali was the custodian of Prophet's patience and forbearance too.

9.9.4. The Testimony of History

If Ali had raised his sword against Caliph Abu Bakr, then history would have never forgiven Ali. The testimony of history would be along the following lines.

After the death of the Prophet the Ansar had gathered in Saqifah to choose a Caliph over the Muslims. When the Muhajireen found out they also reached Saqifah. In the meeting of Saqifah a political agreement was reached between the Muhajireen and the Ansar, whereby it was agreed that Abu Bakr would become the first Caliph and the leader of the Muslim Ummah. However, when Ali found out about the Caliphate of Abu Bakr, he took out his sword and killed Abu Bakr, and took over the Caliphate of the Muslims by force.

In the eyes of history Ali would have become the aggressor and Abu Bakr would have become the victim. Ali could not possibly take a step that would damage his status and his stature as the true successor of the Prophet.

History would also write that Abu Bakr had acquired his Caliphate through a Shura (consultation), but Ali had acquired the Caliphate by shedding the blood of the Muslims. History would have never forgiven Ali.

Ali had the title of being the commander of the faithful, as per many traditions of the Prophet. Ali could not possibly place himself in such an indefensible position in the eyes of the history.

9.9.5. The Prophet is a Mercy for Mankind

One of the titles of the Prophet was "Rahmatul-lil-Alameen", which means that he was a mercy for all the mankind. Ali being the true successor of the Prophet also has to show the same mercy and kindness in his actions and in his deeds, despite the unfair event of Saqifah.

We read in Chapter 7 that the companions had disobeyed the Prophet on number of occasions. The incident of pen and paper where Caliph Umar had refused to bring the writing material for the Prophet, the issue of Usama where both Caliph Abu Bakr and Umar had refused to join his army, are clear examples where companions had disobeyed the Prophet.

But there is no evidence from the life of the Prophet which would suggest that prophet had ever ordered the killing of a companion or a Muslim or anyone else for refusing to follow his commands. If Prophet had taken such a stance, then many of the key players of Saqifah would not have lived to participate in that gathering!

Prophet had chosen Ali to be his successor and the leader of the Muslims after his death. If some prominent companions had gone against the Sunnah of the Prophet, then Ali cannot make the same mistake and also go against the Sunnah of the Prophet by killing those companions. If Ali also transgresses the Sunnah of the Prophet, then there would be no difference between Ali and those companions.

Ali was not only the successor of the Prophet, but Ali was the custodian of Prophet's Sunnah too. Ali's actions had to be a reflection of Prophet's Sunnah regardless of the politics of the time.

If Ali kills the main players of Saqifah, the civil war that would be initiated as a result of the killing of the key companions, would engulf many ordinary and pious companions too. Ali being the successor of the person who had come as a mercy for the entire humanity, could not possibly take such a callus action.

If Caliph Abu Bakr had sent Caliph Umar to forcefully take allegiance from Ali, then we leave their actions with Allah. But Ali, being the inheritor of Prophet's Sunnah could not have gone against the very traditions in which Ali was ingrained in.

9.9.6. The Ruling of the Quran

There is no testimony bigger than the testimony of the Holy Quran. The holy Quran states:

> *"Let there be no compulsion in religion"*
> - *Quran 2:256*

The Holy Quran does not permit a Muslim to use force for implementing the laws of Allah or the Sunnah of the Prophet. Prophet had never killed a non-Muslim for refusing to accept the message of Islam.

When Prophet had never killed anybody for refusing to accept his Prophethood, then Ali being the nominee of the Prophet also cannot use force against the companions, who had refused to accept him as the successor of the Prophet.

When Prophet had not raised his sword against anyone who had refused to accept him as the Prophet of Allah, then Ali would not be able to give a justification for raising his sword against the people, who had refused to accept him as the successor of the Prophet.

Prophet had famously said about Ali that you are to me like Harun was to Musa, except that there would be no Prophets after me. Ali was the inheritor of Prophet's traditions, without being a Prophet.

Ali, of all people had to follow the verses of the Quran and the traditions of the Prophet to the letter.

9.9.7. The Progeny of the Prophet

I will reproduce the words of Ali that I had mentioned earlier at the beginning of this section.

> *"I looked around but found no one to shield me, protect me or help me except the members of my family. I refrained from flinging them into death and therefore closed my eyes despite the dust, kept swallowing saliva despite (the suffocation of) grief"*
>
> - *(Nahjul Balagha sermon 217)*

Another key reason as to why Ali did not raise his sword was because if Ali had killed some of the key companions, then in retaliation their supporters could have killed his children al-Hasan and al-Hussain, who at the time were only eight years and six years old respectively. Apart from being Ali's children they were also part of the Ahlulbayt. The Prophet's descendants had to come from these noble children.

God forbid, if they were killed at those tender ages then not only the family of the Prophet would have been wiped out, but also there would have been no descendants of the Prophet (Syeds) to come. Ali's sons were the sons of the Prophet too, through his daughter Fatima. They were not just Ali's children, they were the children of the Prophet too.

Ali could not put the lives of Prophet's children at risk at that young age. This was another reason why Ali endured the pain and the grief silently but did not raise his sword.

9.9.8. Last but not least, the Mandate of the Prophet

Many years after the meeting of Saqifah, when Ali was inducted in the six-member committee to choose the third Caliph, Ali gave an explicit answer as to why he did not raise his sword. I will briefly mention Ali's words as this point will also be discussed in Chapter 11 "Ali is Denied Caliphate for the Third Time".

Ali addressed the committee and the convention that Caliph Umar had setup with these words:

> *"...We have a right. If we are given it we will take it; if we are deprived of it we will take the back seat even if the journey will be long. Had the Messenger given us a directive we would have fulfilled his directive. Had he told us to take an action we would have fought for it until we died...."*
>
> - *Ibn Al-Atheer Al-Kamil Part 3 p. 37.*

Ali clarifies exactly as to why he did not pick the sword against Caliph Abu Bakr. Ali says: "We have a right", implying that Ahlulbayt had a right to lead the Muslim Ummah, and if they were given this right, they would have taken it, but if they are denied their right, they would take a back seat.

Ali then clarifies as to why the Ahlulbayt would take a back seat. Ali said:

> *"Had the Messenger given us a directive we would have fulfilled his directive. Had he told us to take an action we would have fought for it until we died."*

The Prophet had given Ali and the Ahlulbayt the right to lead the Muslim Ummah, but Prophet had not given them the right to take that right by force.

That is the reason why Ali did not raise his sword, and that is why Ali had said that if the Prophet had given them a directive to take an action, the Ahlulbayt would have fought for their right until they died. But since the Prophet had not given them the mandate to take their right by force, Ali and the Ahlulbayt took a back seat and did not use force.

By not picking his sword against Caliph Abu Bakr, Ali had testified from his actions and not just from his words that Ali was indeed the custodian of Prophet's Sunnah. Ali did not transgress the mandate that Prophet had given him, and Ali did not try to acquire his right by force.

The immaculate upbringing and the training of the Prophet was evident from every action that Ali took after the death of the Prophet. Ali completely works within the boundaries laid out by the Prophet of Allah, despite the fact that his right of leadership was interfered with.

It was for this reason that the Prophet had said to Ali that you are my brother in this world and in hereafter.

> *"You are my brother in this life and the Hereafter."*
> - *Al-Khasa'is of Al-Nisa'i, 5.*
> - *Al-Tirmidhi.*
> - *Yanabi Al-Mawda, 61.*
> - *Ibn Al-Maghazeli, 37.*
> - *Ibn Husham Part 1 p.505*

9.10. The Acceptance of Political Authority

Before I delve into this key topic, it would be worth explaining and clarifying exactly in what sense was Ali the successor of the Prophet.

9.10.1. The Spiritual Leadership and Political Authority

In broad terms, being the successor of the Prophet entails of three parts.

Spiritual Leadership (Imamat)

Spiritual leadership means that a person is able to lead and guide the people in all matters. The Prophet had trained and given Ali the knowledge and the wisdom that was required to lead the Muslims spiritually. Ali was the custodian of the Prophet's knowledge and his spiritual leadership.

Spiritual Authority (Wilayat)

This means that a person who has spiritual leadership, his words and commands are binding on the Muslims, and therefore Muslims are obliged to accept him as a spiritual authority. Ali was the spiritual leader appointed by the Prophet of Allah, and hence he had the spiritual authority in the absence of the Prophet, as per many of the Prophet's traditions.

Political and Social leadership (Mulukiyat)

This is the political and the social leadership of the Muslims. This is like being the head of the State or being like the prime minister or the president in this day and age. Ali being the successor of the Prophet should also be the head of the Islamic State in Prophet's absence.

Before the establishment of the Islamic State of Madinah and during Prophet's life in Makkah, Prophet had the spiritual leadership (Imamat) and the spiritual authority (wilayat) over the Muslims, but he did not have the political and the social leadership (Mulukiyat) over the Muslims. The Prophet only acquired the political and the social leadership of the Muslims after the establishment of the Islamic State of Madinah.

However, even in Makkah, before the establishment of the Islamic State of Madinah, the Prophet was still the Prophet of Allah, even though he did not have the Political and the social leadership (Mulukiyat) of the Muslims.

9.10.2. Ali had Refused to Pay Allegiance to Abu Bakr

As mentioned previously, a huge gulf and a rift had been opened between the family of the Prophet and the establishment of Caliph Abu Bakr. This happened because of Saqifah and the subsequent events which followed, namely the demand of allegiance from Ali, threatening to burn down the house of Lady Fatima, and the confiscation of the land of Fadak. All these events contributed to a serious discord and a dispute which took place between the Ahlulbayt and Caliph Abu Bakr.

Abu Bakr had been the Caliph for over six months, but Ali had not given him the allegiance or accepted his Caliphate. Even when Abu Bakr had forcefully demanded allegiance from Ali on the first or the second day of his Caliphate, Ali not only refused to give allegiance to Abu Bakr, but instead Ali demanded that Abu Bakr should give him the allegiance.

We read in Abdul Fattah Abdul Maksoud Al-Imam Ali Ibn Abu Talib.

> *"I am more worthy of this position than you. You all should swear allegiance to me. You have sought allegiance from the Ansar on the basis of your proximity to the Holy Prophet and now you wish to snatch this right from us, Ahlulbayt? Did you not offer this argument that on account of your closeness to the Holy Prophet you are more eligible for the caliphate than them? Surely it is on this account that they handed over this position to you.*
> *I now offer you the same argument – I am the one who was the closest to the Holy Prophet in his life and even after this death. I am his rightful successor and trustee. I am the keeper of his secrets and the protector of his knowledge."*
>
> - Abdul Fattah Abdul Maksoud Al-Imam Ali Ibn Abu Talib Part 1 p. 179.

Ali could have easily continued the path of not giving allegiance to Abu Bakr until the end of Abu Bakr's Caliphate, because if Ali had regarded Abu Bakr as the spiritual leader and the spiritual authority after the death of the Prophet, then Ali would have accepted Abu Bakr's political and social leadership on the very first day when he became the Caliph.

And there was no reason for Ali to change his mind now and give allegiance to Abu Bakr when he hadn't done so at the time of Abu Bakr's inauguration as the first Caliph.

9.10.3. The Movement of Apostasy and the False Prophets

However, as time moved on things began to change around Madinah. The people who were deserting the faith of Islam after the death of the Prophet had now morphed into a very strong movement of apostasy. Entire tribes around Madinah had completely left Islam, and large-scale apostasy flared across most of the region. The rebels against the Islamic State took a position that they had submitted to the Prophet, and they had an agreement with him, but they will not submit to the new head of the Islamic State, as they had no covenant with him. This movement began to tear down the Muslim Ummah around Madinah.

On top of the movement of apostasy, some rebels like Tulayhah al-Azdi, Musaylimah bin Habib, Sajjah bint Harith and Al-Aswad al-Ansi were also claiming to be the Prophets. They thought that they could also start a new religion and establish their own authority on the back of the idea of Prophethood. This was an extremely dangerous movement for the future of Islam, where any individual could simply get up and claim to be a new Prophet.

The authority of the Islamic State around Madinah began to diminish, and many regions became devoid of any authority from the central government. Many false Prophets were popping up all over the region, and the movement of the desertion of faith had become a strong rebellion, which could potentially consume the city of Madinah and the wider Islamic State too.

In these circumstances Ali reversed his position and accepted the political authority of Caliph Abu Bakr, because the State had decided to fight the rebels, and regardless of how Abu Bakr had got to that position, Abu Bakr at that point happen to be the head of the Islamic State.

Ali, in his own words explained his decision in one of the letters he wrote to Malik al-Ashtar, who was the governor of Egypt during Ali's Caliphate.

> *"... And I withheld my hand until I found the deserters of the faith of Islam calling for the destruction of the religion of Mohammad. (As this danger emerged I reversed my position) and decided to aid Islam and its followers lest I witness a total or partial destruction in Islam then the tragedy to me becomes greater than losing your leadership..."*

- Nahjul-Balagha Part 3 pp. 198-199.

When the movement of the desertion of faith began to rock the very foundations of the Islamic society, and when the entire sections of the Muslim Ummah apostatized, and started denying the Tauheed (oneness of Allah) and the Prophethood of Prophet Mohammad, and false Prophet's began to raise their heads, it was at that point in history that Ali conceded his political leadership to Caliph Abu Bakr, in order to aid the Islamic State against the rebels.

Because now the issue was not about whether Ali was the rightful successorship of the Prophet, the issue now was about the oneness of Allah and the Prophethood of Prophet Mohammad, and these issues were superior to the issue of Ali being the successor of the Prophet. And Ali could not possibly put his right of Successorship above the Prophethood of the Prophet, and the Tauheed of Allah, otherwise Ali would not be able to justify his claim of being the true successor of the Prophet.

Although Caliph Abu Bakr was politically in charge of the Islamic State, but Ali and the Ahlulbayt also commanded a lot of respect and love as far as the city of Madinah was concerned. The Muslims of Madinah had primarily given allegiance to Caliph Abu Bakr on the basis of the tribal vote, because the leaders of their two main tribes i.e., al-Aws and al-Khazraj had accepted the political leadership of Caliph Abu Bakr in Saqifah, so the ordinary Muslims of Madinah also had to accept the Caliphate of Abu Bakr, as per their tribal customs.

However, as Ali and the Ahlulbayt had not accepted the political leadership of Caliph Abu Bakr, there was a lot of unease and apprehension in Madinah about this fact. And as the movement of apostasy began to grow this issue was also causing disunity and dissension among the Muslim ranks, hence Ali decided to reverse his position towards the political authority of the Islamic State in the wider interest of the Muslim Ummah.

If Ali at that point had not aided the Islamic leadership, regardless of how they got to that position and regardless of Ali's right in that matter, the Islamic State itself could have easily been destroyed, something which Ali could never bear to watch, since Ali had been one of the founders of the Islamic State alongside the Prophet.

9.10.4. Ali had no Personal or Political Ambition

The acceptance of Caliph Abu Bakr's political authority also clearly demonstrates that Ali had no personal ambition in this matter. Ali's opposition to Abu Bakr was based on the fact that Prophet had chosen him for the leadership of the Muslims. And Ali had considered all three parts of his successorship to be his exclusive right i.e., the spiritual leadership (Imamat), the spiritual authority (Wilayat) and the political leadership (Mulukiyat). However, when the entire Islamic doctrine itself was being destroyed, and when Muslims started deserting the faith in droves, Ali decided to concede his political leadership to aid the war against the apostates, and the false Prophets who were popping up in the Islamic State.

The successor of the Prophet does not have to acquire the political authority to justify his position as the true successor of the Prophet. It is not mandatory to have the political authority to be a successor of the Prophet, because the Prophet cannot guarantee that his successor would always acquire the political leadership that he deserves. Since the Prophet himself cannot guarantee that he would always have the political authority that he desires.

For instance, the Prophet of Allah had only acquired the political authority after the establishment of the Islamic State of Madinah, before that Prophet had no political authority (Mulukiyat) over the people, but he was still the Prophet of Allah, and he still had the spiritual leadership (Imamat) and spiritual authority (Wilayat) over the Muslims.

Many Prophets before Prophet Mohammad had never acquired any political leadership, but they remained Prophets of Allah. Similarly, the successor of the Prophet can remain his successor even if he gives up and forgoes his political authority.

9.10.5. Abu Bakr Happened to be the Caliph

Ali had in fact accepted the authority of the Islamic State rather than the authority of Abu Bakr as an individual. It just happened to be the case that when the movement of the desertion of the faith became a rebellion, Caliph Abu Bakr had the political authority over the Islamic State. It was highly probable that instead of Caliph Abu Bakr someone else could have been the head of the Islamic State at that time.

To prove this point, I will briefly revisit Saqifah.

When the Ansar decided to gather in Saqifah, they had no intention of either informing or inviting the Muhajireen. It was just by chance that someone had informed Caliph Umar, who then informed Caliph Abu Bakr about the meeting of Saqifah. When Caliph Abu Bakr got to Saqifah, the Ansar had almost finalized Saad Ibn Ubaadah as the new Caliph. If Caliph Abu Bakr had not received the news about Saqifah, and had not been present in that meeting, then it was extremely unlikely that he would have ever become the first Caliph.

In the meeting itself, Caliph Abu Bakr had nominated Caliph Umar and Abu Ubaydah al-Jarrah as the new heads of the Islamic State. It was possible that one of these candidates could have also become the first Caliph. Hence there were four potential candidates for the slot of the first Caliphate i.e., Caliph Abu Bakr, Caliph Umar, Abu Ubaydah al-Jarrah and Saad Ibn Ubaadah (from the Ansar). It just happened to be the case that as a result of the political manoeuvring in Saqifah, Caliph Abu Bakr had won the day and he became the first Caliph.

At the time of the rebellion, the head of the Islamic State could have easily been Caliph Umar or Saad Ibn Ubaadah or Abu Ubaydah al-Jarrah, instead of Caliph Abu Bakr, and Ali would have made the same decision. However, when the rebellion of the desertion of faith took place, Caliph Abu Bakr happened to have the political authority, and hence Ali had to concede his political authority to Caliph Abu Bakr.

The acceptance of the political authority of Abu Bakr was never an endorsement of his Sunnah or the approval of his actions after the death of the Prophet. The spiritual authority and the spiritual leadership of the Muslims had always been with Ali, regardless of who enjoyed the political leadership.

Even if Ali wanted to, he could not impart his knowledge and wisdom to Caliph Abu Bakr that he had acquired as a result of Prophet's company. Ali could never forsake his spiritual authority (Imamat) or his spiritual leadership (Wilayat) to Abu Bakr or any other companion for that matter.

9.10.6. Not an Acceptance of Abu Bakr's Sunnah

The acceptance of the Political authority of Caliph Abu Bakr was not an acceptance of his Sunnah. In fact, Ali chose to lose his political authority rather than follow the Sunnah and the path of Caliph Abu Bakr or Caliph Umar. Ali had declined the third Caliphate on this very basis, because he was asked to follow the Sunnah (path) set by Caliph Abu Bakr and Caliph Umar.

Before his death, Caliph Umar formed a committee to choose his successor. He made Abdur Rahman bin Auf in charge of this committee. Abdur Rahman bin Auf offers the third Caliphates to Ali on the following three conditions:

> *"Will you pledge to God and covenant Him that you will follow the Book of God the teachings of the Messenger and the precepts of the two caliphs (Abu Bakr and Omar) after him?"*
> - Ibn Al-Atheer in his Al-Kamil Part 3 pp. 32-35
> - Al-Tabari Vol. 1 pp. 63-65

Ali's response is as follows:

> *Ali replied: "I shall follow the Book of God the teachings of the Prophet and I shall follow my best knowledge and endeavour to the maximum of my ability."*
> - Ibn Al-Atheer in his Al-Kamil Part 3 pp. 32-35
> - Al-Tabari Vol. 1 pp. 63-65

Ali told Abdur Rahman bin Auf that he would follow the Book of Allah, the Sunnah of the Prophet and he would follow his own knowledge and judgment, rather than the path of Caliph Abu Bakr and Umar.

Ali could not possibly follow the precedents set by Caliph Abu Bakr or Caliph Umar. Ali could not under any circumstances follow the trend of al-ijtihad (independent judgment), which was the basis of the meeting of Saqifah. Ali could not accept the rulings made in the case of Fadak, and Ali could not accept the tradition of using force to acquire the allegiance from the Ahlulbayt. Ali preferred to lose his political authority rather than accept the judgments and the Sunnah of Caliph Abu Bakr or Caliph Umar.

If Ali had accepted what Abdur Rahman bin Auf had offered as conditions for the third Caliphate, then Ali would have compromised his spiritual authority, because Ali would have gone against the Sunnah of the Prophet, and hence Ali turned down the third Caliphate on this very basis.

Caliph Uthman happily accepted all the three conditions set by Abdur Rahman bin Auf, and he became the third Caliph and acquired the political authority over the Muslims.

9.10.7. A Man of Character

The rebellion by the deserters of the faith had severely weakened the central government. The establishment of Caliph Abu Bakr had suffered a major setback, as thousands of Muslims had started to leave the faith of Islam. The threat coming from the people claiming to be the false Prophets was equally damaging and destructive to the ideological base of the Islamic State.

A lesser man than Ali could have easily seen this as a golden opportunity to take advantage of the political situation and destroy the Caliphate of Abu Bakr. As a rival of Abu Bakr for the Caliphate this was the ideal time to strike. Ali could have easily used the issue of the Muslims deserting their faith and the issue of the false Prophets appearing in the midst of the Islamic State, as a basis for discrediting and challenging the Caliphate of Abu Bakr. And this is exactly what many other companions did when they saw their political rivals in disarray, as we will see in later chapters.

But Ali was a man of unique character and piety. Even when his rivals were struggling politically to maintain their grip on power, Ali looks at the bigger picture and the wider interests of the Muslim Ummah, and he prefers to concede his own right rather than manipulate the circumstances in his favour.

Ali declines every single unscrupulous opportunity that came his way to regain power, because Ali had no personal desire for power, his only aim was to keep the Muslims on the path of the Prophet, a path that Ali was more familiar with than any other companion, because it was the Prophet who had trained Ali on this path for twenty-five years.

Despite his personal feelings towards Caliph Abu Bakr and Caliph Umar when he said that he:

> *"kept swallowing saliva despite (the suffocation of) grief and endured pangs of anger although it was more bitter than colocynth and more grievous than the bite of knives."*

- *(Nahjul Balagha sermon 217)*

He did not let his personal feelings affect his professional judgment, which in this case was the survival of the Islamic State. Ali did everything he could to safeguard the destiny of the Islamic State despite the fact that it was in the hands of his political rivals.

The training of the Prophet was evident from every step that Ali took in the interest of the Muslim Ummah, and undoubtably the Prophet of Allah had chosen a man of unique character to lead the Muslims after his death.

9.10.8. Ali Establishes his Spiritual Authority

As a result of Ali conceding his political authority, Caliph Abu Bakr softens his approach towards Ali, because now Caliph Abu Bakr no longer saw Ali as a rival and a contender for the political leadership of the Muslims. The spiritual authority of Ali was never really an issue for either Caliph Abu Bakr or Caliph Umar. They knew exactly where Ali stood in relation to the Prophet. It was the political authority of Ali which they had a problem with!

Ali, by conceding his political authority allowed both Caliph Abu Bakr and Caliph Umar to come to his door, seeking answers on issues which they could not resolve on their own. As the tensions eased between the establishment of Caliph Abu Bakr and Ali, Caliph Abu Bakr started consulting Ali and taking his advice on Islamic matters, which he was unable to address on his own. And Caliph Umar followed the same approach as Caliph Abu Bakr during his reign too, where he would also come to Ali for advice on issues and problems that he was not able to resolve on his own.

That is why both Caliph Abu Bakr and Caliph Umar had said during their reigns:

> *Abu Bakr said:* "*May Allah never put me in a situation where I cannot have access to Abul Hasan (i.e., 'Ali) to solve a problem.*"
>
> *Sa'id al-Musayyib said:* "*Umar Ibn al-Khattab used to beg God to preserve him from a perplexing case which the father of al-Hasan (Ali) was not present to decide.*"
>
> *Umar also said:* "*If there was not 'Ali, Umar would have perished (spiritually)*"
>
> - Fadha'il al-Sahaba, by Ahmad Ibn Hanbal, v2, p647, Tradition #1100
> - al-Isti'ab, by Ibn Abd al-Barr, v3, p39
> - Manaqib, by al-Khawarizmi, p48
> - al-Tabaqat, by Ibn Sa'd, v2, p338
> - al-Riyadh al-Nadhirah, by Muhibbuddin al-Tabari, v2, p194
> - Tarikh al-Khulafaa, by Jalaluddin al-Suyuti, p171

Often cases would be brought to Caliph Umar during his Caliphate, and he would struggle to find the correct Islamic ruling on them. He would then ask Ali for advice and Ali would come and judge those cases based on the Holy Quran and the Sunnah of the Prophet, and he would give the correct ruling to Caliph Umar.

For instance, Ali advised Caliph Umar to set the Hijra i.e., the emigration of the Prophet from Makkah to Madinah as the beginning of the Islamic lunar calendar.

The knowledge and the spiritual authority of Ali was for the benefit of all, it could not be restricted to the circle of friends alone.

That is why Caliph Umar had also said:

> "*The best judge among us is Ali*"
>
> - Abu 'Abd Allah Ahmad b. Hanbal al-Shaybani, Musnad (Cairo: Muasassat Qurtubah) [annotator: Shu'ayb al-Arnaut], vol. 5, p. 113, # 21122
> - Abu 'Abd Allah Muhammad b. Isma'il b. Ibrahim b. Mughirah al-Bukhari al-J'ufi, al-Jami' al-Ṣahih al-Mukhtasar (Beirut: Dar Ibn Kathir; 3rd edition, 1407 H) [annotator: Dr. Mustafa Dib al-Bagha], vol. 4, p. 1628, # 4211
> - Abu 'Abd Allah Muhammad b. 'Abd Allah al-Hakim al-Naysaburi, al-Mustadrak 'ala al-Ṣahihayn (Beirut: Dar al-Kutub al-'Ilmiyyah; 1st edition, 1411 H) [annotator: Mustafa 'Abd al-Qadir 'Ata], vol. 3, p. 145, # 4656

By conceding his political right, Ali not only saved the Islamic State from destruction, but he also established his spiritual authority (Imamat) on the very people who had interfered in his right.

Such was the patience and the wisdom of Ali, which could have only come from the lap of the Prophet.

And that is why Caliph Abu Bakr had famously said in the last days of his life that:

> "*To look at the face of Ali is ibadah (worship)*"
>
> - Al-Mustadrak al Hakim, vol 3, pg 152-153
> - Manaqeb Ibn Maghazeli, pg 207, Hadith no. 245
> - Riyaazun Nazrah, vol.2, pg. 219
> - al-Tabarani

Implying that the reflection of Prophet's training and closeness was so evident on Ali's face, that by simply looking at Ali it reminded the companions about the religion of Allah.

9.11. Our Approach

Our approach should exactly be the approach of Ali.

We recognize that Caliph Abu Bakr had the political and the administrative authority over the Muslims after the death of the Prophet, and he became Khalifatul-Muslimeen, i.e., he became the Caliph of the Muslims for two and a half years.

But Ali was Khalifatul-Rasool, Ali was the Caliph appointed by the Prophet. The Prophet had given Ali both the political and the spiritual authority over the Muslims.

However, Caliph Abu Bakr managed to acquire the political authority of the Muslims in Saqifah and as a result he became the first Caliph. Although Ali eventually accepted the political and the administrative authority of Caliph Abu Bakr, but Ali refused to follow his Sunnah. Ali had in fact preferred to lose the third Caliphate on this basis, when he declined to follow the Sunnah of Caliph Abu Bakr. Our position should exactly be the position taken by Ali.

We accept that Caliph Abu Bakr had the political authority over the Muslims while he was alive, and he became the first Caliph of the Muslims. However, the political and the administrative authority (Mulukiyat) of Caliph Abu Bakr came from the gathering of Saqifah, which inevitably ended with the death of Caliph Abu Bakr. But the spiritual authority (Imamat) and the spiritual leadership (Wilayat) of Ali had come from the traditions of the Prophet, and hence it is valid until the Day of Judgment.

With the passage of time, the Caliphate of all the Caliphs has long gone, but the love and the authority of Ali still lives in the hearts of the believers, because the authority of Ali represents the Sunnah of the Prophet which indeed is valid until the end of time.

10. ALI IS DENIED THE CALIPHATE FOR THE SECOND TIME

As the death of Caliph Abu Bakr nears and he comes towards the end of his life, there was still hope among the followers and the supporters of Ali that the first Caliph might just honour the wish and the Sunnah of the Prophet, and he might choose Ali to be the next leader of the Muslims.

It was still not too late to reverse the path of Saqifah. It had only been two and a half years since the death of the Prophet. Ali was still young and eager to take on the mantle of the Islamic leadership. The event of Ghadeer was still fresh in the minds of the Muslims. Ali had even reversed his position towards the political authority of Caliph Abu Bakr. In fact, Ali had aided the administration of Caliph Abu Bakr against the deserters of the faith, and the false Prophets who were seeking to destroy the Islamic State from within.

The Qurayshite influence within the Islamic establishment had certainly grown, but it was still in its early days, and it could still be curtailed if the right person was put at the helm. It was still possible to put things right and follow the vision that Prophet had envisaged for the future of the Muslims.

It was still possible to establish the tradition of Thaqalayn (the Two Weighty Things) where the Prophet had said:

> *"....'O people I have left in you that which if you adhere to you will never go astray: The Book of God and the members of my House."*
>
> - *Sunan Al-Tirmidhi. Vol. 3, Pg. # 543 - 544, H. # 3786 – 3788*
> - *Sunan Al -Tirmidhi. Vol. 6, Pg. # 335*

It was still possible to give Ali the right, which was denied to him in Saqifah, and honour the tradition of the Prophet where he had said:

> *"Verily, Ali and I are inseparable, and he is the Guardian (wali) of every believer after me."*
>
> - *Al Tirmidhi, in his Sahih, ii, 297,*
> - *Ahmad Ibn Hanbal in his Musnad, iv, 437, v, 356.*
> - *Abu Dawud al Tayalisi in his Musnad, iii, 111, xi, 360.*
> - *al Haythami, Majma al Zawaid, ix, 109, 127, 128, 199.*
> - *al Khatib al Baghdadi, Tarikh Baghdad, iv, 339.*
> - *al Muhibb al Tabari, al Riyad al Nadirah, ii, 203, 171.*
> - *al Muttaqi al Hindi, Kanz al Ummal, vi, 154, 155, 396, 401.*
> - *Ibn al Athir in Usd al Ghabah, v, 94.*
> - *Abu Nuaym in Hilyat al Awliya, vi, 294.*
> - *al Nasa'i, Khasais, 19, 23.*

- as well as Ibn Abi Shaybah, al Tabari, al Tabarani, al Daylami, Ibn Mardawayh, Ibn al Jawzi, al Rafii, and Ibn Hajar.

Caliph Abu Bakr was in complete control of the Islamic State as his death approaches. The deserters of the faith had been subdued and the false Prophets had also been eliminated, which was the reason why Ali chose to support the central government. The withholders of Zakat had been forced to pay their due and their movement had also been crushed.

Caliph Abu Bakr was in a very strong position as his tenure was about to come to an end.

10.1. No Seeming Emergency Now

There was no seeming emergency now which some historians claim was declared at the death of the Prophet. The Ansar were also inline, and they had made no pre-emptive moves this time round to take over the leadership of the Muslims. They were no longer threatening to drive the Muhajireen out of Madinah at the point of their swords. There was no impeding threat of a civil war between the Ansar and the Muhajireen on the issue of the Caliphate anymore.

These were some of the reasons given for the impetuous and the spontaneous meeting of Saqifah, soon after the death of the Prophet.

Caliph Umar had Stated:

> "The pledge of allegiance given to Abu Bakr was an un-premeditated spontaneous affair……."
- (Sahih Bukhari, Volume 8, Book 82, Number 817)

Caliph Umar had also said that because of the seeming emergency at the time of the death of the Prophet, the proceedings of the Saqifah could not have been delayed, and the leader of the Muslims had to be chosen there and then.

Caliph Umar explained the reasons:

> "…because we were afraid that if we left the people (without rendering the oath of allegiance), they might (in our absence) give the pledge of allegiance after us to one of their men (someone from Ansar)…"
- (Sahih Bukhari, Volume 8, Book 82, Number 817)

> "We feared that if we left (without getting the oath of allegiance), no agreement would be hammered out (with the Ansar) later. (And if they then elected one of their own men) it was either to follow the Ansar in what we did not approve of, or else oppose them (with the sword)"
- (History of al-Tabari, Vol. 9, p.194)

Caliph Umar had stated that if we (the Muhajireen) did not get the oath of allegiance in Saqifah, then the Ansar would have chosen someone from their side to lead the Ummah, which we (the Muhajireen) did not approve off, and then we would have to fight them with our swords. That is why we had to get the oath of allegiance in the meeting of Saqifah, and hence issue of the Caliphate could not have been delayed.

There were no such circumstances plaguing the issue of the Islamic leadership now.

It was hoped that with everything else settled, Caliph Abu Bakr would either nominate the choice of the Prophet as his successor, or he would establish a fairer way of choosing his own successor, so that the Ahlulbayt and the Banu Hashim who were completely left out of the decision-making process in Saqifah, could also have a say in choosing the future leader of the Muslims.

10.2. Time Constraint

Readers would recall that after the meeting of Saqifah, Caliph Abu Bakr had said to Ali that the reason why he could not invite Ali to the meeting was because there was no time to reach out to Ali.

> *"Had I delayed the matter, it would have posed a greater danger to the unity, integrity, and solidarity of Islam. How could I send for you when there was no time?"*
>
> - *(Tareekh al-Islam, Vol.1, p.276)*

There was plenty of time now to invite Ali to the position of leadership. The time factor could not be used as an excuse anymore. Caliph Abu Bakr had ample time on his hands to choose whoever he wanted as the new head of the Islamic State, or perhaps construct a fairer system of Shura, which gave all the potential candidates an equal shot at the leadership of the Muslims.

It was expected that with all his maturity and wisdom and as the head of the Islamic State, Caliph Abu Bakr would ratify the failings and the unfairness of Saqifah, by either nominating Ali as the new Caliph, or at least ensuring that Ali is on equal footing with the rest of the candidates for the position of the Caliphate.

After all, it was Caliph Abu Bakr who had previously said to Ali that the reason why he could not invite Ali to Saqifah was because he had no time to do so.

Despite of what Caliph Abu Bakr had said to Ali after Saqifah, when the actual opportunity came to choose his successor, he nominated Caliph Umar for that role. The hopes of the followers and supporters of the Ali were dashed once again, and the trend of al-ijtihad (independent judgment) continued unabated.

The Quraysh once again stood between Ali and the second Caliphate. Although Ali had accepted the political authority of Caliph Abu Bakr, and the tensions between his administration and the Ahlulbayt had eased, but as far as the issue of Caliphate was concerned, Caliph Abu Bakr's views were exactly the same as they were in Saqifah.

He chose someone from a non-Hashimite clan of Quraysh, just as the Quraysh had wished and hoped for. Caliph Umar belonged to the Banu Adi clan of Quraysh, and Quraysh were happy to rotate the Caliphate in of its other clans, as long as it was not the clan of Banu Hashim.

Despite the unique and the distinguished position of Ali in the eyes of the Prophet, despite Ali's unrivalled contribution in the service of Islam, despite Ali being the differentiating factor in the establishment and the defence of the Islamic State of Madinah, despite Ali being the custodian of Prophet's knowledge and Sunnah, Ali was once again side lined and ignored from the leadership of the Muslim Ummah.

This indeed was most unfortunate and tragic to say the least.

10.3. Caliph Abu Bakr Dictates his Will

Once again history by-passes and overlooks the nominee of the Prophet, and once again Ali stays patient and shows the true calibre of his upbringing by not challenging the order of the day.

Caliph Abu Bakr dictates his will to Caliph Uthman as reported in al-Tabari and Ibn al-Athir.

> When Abu Bakr called 'Uthman to write his last testament, he lost consciousness while he was dictating and 'Uthman wrote the name of 'Umar b. al-Khattab. When he regained consciousness, he said: "Read what you have written! So, he read it and mentioned 'Umar's name. Abu Bakr asked him: "From where did you get this?" He answered: "You were never wont to oppose him". Abu Bakr replied: "You are right".
>
> When he finished his will, some of the companions, Talha among them, called upon him. Talha said to him: "What will you say to your Lord tomorrow? You have chosen a severe, harsh man to govern us. People run away from him and their hearts beat because of him".
>
> Abu Bakr said: "You all helped me, and he was my support. So now support him". He said to Talha: "Do you try to scare me with Allah? If I am asked about it tomorrow, I will say: 'I selected the best of your people to rule them".

- *History of the Prophets and Kings al-Tabari pp. 2138-9*
- *Ibn al-Athir*

Here is another variation of Caliph Abu Bakr's will by Ibn Qutayba

> "Then he summoned 'Uthman b. 'Affan and said: 'Write my will'. So, Abu Bakr dictated and 'Uthman wrote thus: 'In the name of Allah, the Beneficent the Merciful. This is what Abu Bakr b. Quhafa does decide as his last will and testament in this world that he is about to leave, and the first testament to the hereafter that he is about to enter.
>
> I appoint 'Umar b. al-Khattab as my successor, if you perceive him as a just man among you, and this is my opinion of him and hope in him. If he distorts and changes, I only wish for [your] good, and I do not have knowledge of the unseen. And those who do wrong will soon know their fate". He then put his seal upon the document and gave it to 'Uthman.
>
> When the news that he had named 'Umar as his successor reached the Muhajirs and the Ansar, they entered and said: "We see that you have placed 'Umar as the Caliph over us. You know and are aware of his severity with us even while you are among us, how about when you leave us? Now you are going to meet Allah, the Most High and Majestic, and He will ask you about it, what will you say?"
>
> Whereupon Abu Bakr replied: "If Allah asks me, I will most certainly say: 'I appointed as Caliph over them he who seemed to me to be the best of them".

- *Ibn Qutayba reported in his History of the Caliphs (Ta'rikh al-Khulafa'), in "The Chapter of Abu Bakr's illness and his Designation of 'Umar (R) as his successor":*

When Caliph Abu Bakr was dictating his will, he became unconscious, while he was unconscious Caliph Uthman inserted the name of Caliph Umar in the will, knowing very well what Caliph Abu Bakr had on his mind. When Caliph Abu Bakr regained consciousness, he dually approved the insertion of Caliph Umar's name in his will.

Caliph Abu Bakr nominated Caliph Umar in his final will as the new leader of the Muslim Ummah.

10.4. Companions Complain about Caliph Abu Bakr's Nominee

When the news reached the masses that Caliph Abu Bakr had appointed Caliph Umar as the new head of the Islamic State, many companions came to the house of Caliph Abu Bakr and complained about his nominee. Even his own cousin (Tallha) complained about his choice since Caliph Umar was well known for his harsh and abrasive personality.

Tallha said to Caliph Abu Bakr:

> "What will you say to your Lord tomorrow? You have chosen a severe, harsh man to govern us. People run away from him and their hearts beat because of him".
> - History of the Prophets and Kings pp. 2138-9 al-Tabari

Caliph Abu Bakr replied:

> "You all helped me, and he was my support. So now support him". He said to Talha: "Do you try to scare me with Allah? If I am asked about it tomorrow, I will say: 'I selected the best of your people to rule them".
> - History of the Prophets and Kings pp. 2138-9 al-Tabari

Tallha and other companions refuted the choice of Caliph Abu Bakr on the grounds of Caliph Umar's harsh personality and style of governance, but Caliph Abu Bakr refused to budge. They even questioned Caliph Abu Bakr as to how he was going to justify his choice to Allah, as they strongly felt that Caliph Abu Bakr had made a wrong decision.

The response of Caliph Abu Bakr was to categorically support his nominee. Caliph Abu Bakr said to them that Caliph Umar had his full support, and hence they should also support him, and he would tell Allah that he had chosen the best of the companions to lead them. Caliph Abu Bakr gave his unequivocal support to Caliph Umar and rejected the pleas and the arguments against the caliphate of Umar.

Once the opposition to Caliph Umar's appointment was pacified, Caliph Abu Bakr addressed the audience and commanded them to obey and follow his successor.

> Abu Bakr Stood up before the people and said to them, 'Are you pleased with the person that I have appointed over you? Verily, I have thought long and hard before making this decision, and I did not appoint a relative; instead, I appointed over you Umar Ibn Al-Khattab, so listen to him and obey him.' They said, 'We hear, and we obey.'
> - al-Tabari (4/248)

If we go back two and half years ago to the mosque of the Prophet, just after the meeting of Saqifah, Caliph Umar had said something very similar in favour of Caliph Abu Bakr.

Caliph Umar had said:

> "God has enabled you to agree on the best of the companions of the Prophet who accompanied him at the Cave (of Thour at the time of the Hijrah). Rise up and give your allegiance to him."
> - Ibn Husham in his Biography of the Prophet Part 2 pp. 659-660.

Just as Caliph Umar had urged the Muslims to give allegiance to Caliph Abu Bakr in the mosque of the Prophet, now Caliph Abu Bakr writes a will in favour of Caliph Umar and urges the Muslims to listen to him and obey him. Just as Caliph Umar had called Caliph Abu Bakr the best of the companions, Caliph Abu Bakr now calls Caliph Umar the best of the companions. And just as the majority had accepted the call of Caliph Umar after Saqifah, the majority again accepts the nominee of Caliph Abu Bakr.

10.5. Another Peculiar Shura (Consultation)

After the experience of Saqifah, it was expected that Caliph Abu Bakr would put forward a fairer way of choosing his own successor.

Caliph Abu Bakr had not only witnessed the proceedings of Saqifah, but he was a key participant in that meeting. It was expected that Caliph Abu Bakr would perhaps organize a proper and a transparent Shura (consultation), where he would invite all the stakeholders and interested parties to the table. It was expected that all the candidates for the position of Caliphate would be allowed to put their names forward, and the Shura would deliberate in a fair and a transparent way, and at the end of the consultation the best and the most deserving candidate would be picked.

But unfortunately, Caliph Abu Bakr chose his own peculiar style of Shura, if it could be called a Shura at all. He met some of the companions on an individual basis i.e., he met them separately, one by one, not together as a group, which is what a Shura is all about, and then he only puts forward one candidate i.e., Caliph Umar for the role of the Caliphate. There was no other candidate whose name was put forward for the position of the second Caliph, except Umar.

Even in the debacle of Saqifah there was at least more than one nominee. There was a choice between Caliph Abu Bakr, Caliph Umar, Saad Ibn Ubaadah and Abu Ubaydah al-Jarrah, but this time round there is only one candidate for the top job, and that was Caliph Umar. There were no other candidates that Caliph Abu Bakr had discussed when he met some of the companion's individually regarding his successor.

As an outcome of this unique Shura, Caliph Abu Bakr writes a will in which he nominated Caliph Umar as his successor and the head of the Islamic State.

Caliph Umar had informed Caliph Abu Bakr about the meeting of Saqifah, and Caliph Umar was the one who had proposed Caliph Abu Bakr in the gathering of Saqifah, and he was also the first person to give allegiance to Caliph Abu Bakr in Saqifah, and again Caliph Umar was the one who had urged the Muslims in the mosque of the Prophet to accept the Caliphate of Abu Bakr.

Caliph Umar was the main pillar and the architect of Caliph Abu Bakr's Caliphate, and Caliph Abu Bakr had owed his caliphate to Caliph Umar, since without the presence of Caliph Umar in Saqifah, Caliph Abu Bakr would have never acquired the leadership of the Muslims.

That is why when Caliph Abu Bakr became the first Caliph, he made Caliph Umar his right-hand man and his closest advisor. And that is why when Caliph Abu Bakr chose his successor, he chose Caliph Umar, as if to return the favour.

10.6. The Choice of the Successor is not Left to the Ummah

A key point that comes out of the above discussion is the unequivocal fact that Caliph Abu Bakr did not leave anything to a chance, and he certainly wasn't passive about the future leadership of the Muslims.

He did not leave the choice of his successor to the Ummah, as some scholars claim was the Sunnah of the Prophet. He made sure that he appoints his successor during his lifetime. He said to the audience that he had thought long and hard about this issue, and once he had chosen his nominee, he also urged the Muslims to follow and obey his successor.

Apart from being an Islamic issue, it was an Arab tradition not to leave the issue of leadership unresolved. We read in the History of al-Tabari.

> *"Amir asked: "When was the oath of allegiance given to Abu Bakr?"*
> *"The very day the Messenger of Allah died," he (Saeed) replied. "People disliked to be left even part of the day without being organized into a community (jama'ah)."*
>
> - al-Tabari, Vol.1, p.195

The Arabs did not like to be left without a leader even for half a day. With such strong tradition of leadership among the Arabs, to then say that Prophet had remained passive about the issue of future Islamic leadership, and that he did not directly appoint a successor, is not only a denial of the traditions (Sunnah) of the Prophet, but a denial of his wisdom too.

When Caliph Abu Bakr was challenged about his nomination of Caliph Umar as his successor, he said:

> *"If Allah asks me, I will most certainly say: 'I appointed as Caliph over them he who seemed to me to be the best of them".*
>
> - History of the Prophets and Kings al-Tabari pp. 2138-9
> - Ibn Qutayba reported in his History of the Caliphs (Ta'rikh al-Khulafa'), in "The Chapter of Abu Bakr's illness and his Designation of 'Umar (R) as his successor"

Caliph Abu Bakr stated that he would tell Allah that he had appointed the best man for the job. For this very reason we leave the case of Caliph Abu Bakr with Allah.

On the Day of Judgment, we will not be asked about the choice that Caliph Abu Bakr had made, but we will be asked about the choice that Prophet had made. The choice and the nominee of the Prophet represents his Sunnah, which is eternal and valid for all the generations to come.

Muslims who are proud to follow the Sunnah of the Prophet can today decide to honour his Sunnah and recognize Ali as the rightful successor of the Prophet. If history had done injustice to this fearless and distinguished warrior, then the followers of the Sunnah can today do justice to the traditions and the Sunnah of the Prophet, by paying allegiance to Ali, the nominee of the Prophet.

11. ALI IS DENIED THE CALIPHATE FOR THE THIRD TIME

The reign of Caliph Umar lasted for almost ten years. One of his slaves by the name of Abu Lulu stabbed the Second Caliph which eventually resulted in his death. The issue of Caliphate was once again on the cards.

The followers and the supporters of Ali saw a glimmer of hope. They had seen that Ali had been denied the Caliphate on two previous occasions. Just as there were hopes when Caliph Abu Bakr was in his final days, there was again hope that the second Caliph might just honour the Sunnah of the Prophet and give Ali the right that he had deserved.

After all it was Caliph Umar who had nominated Caliph Abu Bakr in Saqifah, and he was the main force and influence which had brought Caliph Abu Bakr to power. As his own reign was coming to an end there was hope and expectation that he might distance himself from the views of Quraysh, which had plagued the gathering of Saqifah.

Although Caliph Umar had agreed with the outcome of Saqifah, but in later life when Caliph Umar had time to think about the proceedings of Saqifah he called it a 'falta', which means an unexpected event, a mistake or an error.

> *Caliph Umar said: "Abu-Bakr's bay`ah was a 'falta' or something done without thinking about it. Even then, Allah spared us from His anger. Again, if someone follows this method, he must be killed."*
> - *Treekh-Al-khulafa p 51,*
> - *Al-Bidaya wal-Nihaya by ibn Katheer 5/215*
> - *Musnad Ahmad Bin Hanbal 1/323*

The supporters of Ali were hoping that since Caliph Umar had finally recognized the frailties of Saqifah, he would also reconsider his position on its outcome, and give the nominee of the Prophet the leadership of the Muslim Ummah which he had deserved.

Also, during Caliph Umar's reign Ali had advised him on various Islamic issues, which he was not able to resolve on his own. To acknowledge and accept the authority of Ali's knowledge Caliph Umar had famously said:

> *"Umar Ibn al-Khattab used to beg God to preserve him from a perplexing case which the father of al-Hasan (Ali) was not present to decide."*

Umar also said: "If there was not 'Ali, Umar would have perished (spiritually)"

- *Fadha'il al-Sahaba, by Ahmad Ibn Hanbal, v2, p647, Tradition #1100*
- *al-Isti'ab, by Ibn Abd al-Barr, v3, p39*
- *Manaqib, by al-Khawarizmi, p48*
- *al-Tabaqat, by Ibn Sa'd, v2, p338*
- *al-Riyadh al-Nadhirah, by Muhibbuddin al-Tabari, v2, p194*
- *Tarikh al-Khulafaa, by Jalaluddin al-Suyuti, p171*

Since Caliph Umar had accepted the supremacy and the authority of Ali's knowledge during his own Caliphate, there was hope that he might recognize the political authority of Ali too, especially when his own rule was coming to an end. The supporters of Ali were hopeful that Caliph Umar might just use his influence and his position as the head of the Islamic State to put things right and nominate Ali as his successor.

Both Caliph Abu Bakr and Caliph Umar had nominated each other for the Caliphate on the pretext of being the best of the companions. Caliph Umar had urged the Muslims who had gathered at the mosque of the Prophet after Prophet's death to pay allegiance to Abu Bakr because he was the best of the companions. Similarly, when Caliph Abu Bakr was about to die, he had nominated Umar for the Caliphate on the grounds that he was the best of the companions.

As the reigns of both Caliph Abu Bakr and Umar had come to an end, the supporters of Ali were hoping that at least now Ali could be recognized as the best of the companions and would be given the leadership of the Muslim Ummah, which had by-passed him on the previous two occasions.

But unfortunately, the trend of al-ijtihad (independent judgment) which had taken root among the prominent companions would dash any such hopes and expectations. The influence of Quraysh had grown rapidly during the reign of Caliph Umar. The growth of Qurayshite influence was only going to increase the distance between Ali and the Caliphate.

When Caliph Umar was urged to appoint a successor, at first, he refused to appoint anybody as his successor and said:

> *"Had Abu Ubaydah al-Jarrah been alive I would have appointed him. If God questions me, I will say: 'I heard Thy Prophet saying: "Abu Ubaydah is the trustworthy of this nation.".*
> *"Had Salim slave of Abu Hutheifa been alive I would have appointed him. If God questions me, I shall tell Him: 'I heard Thy Prophet saying: "Salim is a strong lover of God."*

- *Ibn Sa'd, al-Tabaqat al-Kubra, Vol. 3*
- *Tarikh Medina, Kamil Ibn Atheer vol.3 p.74*

It is astonishing that Caliph Umar had remembered such words of the Prophet for these two companions, but he could not remember any of the sayings of the Prophet regarding Ali and the Ahlulbayt. He was willing to appoint Abu Ubaydah al-Jarrah and even Salim the slave of Abu Hutheifa to the position of the Caliphate, but he was not willing to appoint Ali, the nominee of the Prophet as his successor. Even though there was no comparison of any sorts between Ali and Abu Ubaydah al-Jarrah or Ali and Salim the slave of Abu Hutheifa.

It is difficult to ascertain as to why Caliph Umar wanted to choose Abu Ubaydah al-Jarrah or Salim as the next Caliphs. Even if we leave Ali out of the picture, there were many other companions who were far more worthy of being the next Caliphs than Abu Ubaydah al-Jarrah or Salim.

It also shows that Caliph Umar did not really believe in the institution of Shura (Consultation), as his preferred method was to select his own successor. If Caliph Umar had an option, he would not have invoked a Shura at all, instead he would have chosen his own successor.

In any case people were still urging Caliph Umar to appoint a successor, or at least leave some instructions behind as to how they should choose his successor. It is said that initially he refused to appoint anyone to be his successor, but then he fell asleep or became unconscious, while he was unconscious, he had a dream, where he saw a man picking some fresh and ripe fruit, and he was keeping those fruits for himself.

Caliph Umar interpreted this dream in the sense that he does not want to share the responsibility of appointing his own successor, as that would become a burden for him even after his death. So, instead he decided to setup a committee of six men and gave them the responsibility for choosing his successor.

11.1. The Proceedings of the Shura

Caliph Umar created a six-member Shura to select the new Caliph. He named the six men as Ali, Uthman, Abdul Rahman Ibn Auf, Saad Ibn Abi Waqqas, Al-Zubeir Ibn Al-Awam and Talhah Ibn Ubaydullah. The next day Caliph Umar came out and defined some really strict and harsh rules for the committee or the Shura (Consultation), which would be responsible for choosing his successor.

Caliph Umar stated:

> *O group of Muhajireen! Verily, the Apostle of God died, and he was pleased with all six of you. I have, therefore, decided to make it (the selection of khalifa) a matter of consultation among you, so that you may select one of yourselves as khalifa.*
> *If five of you agree upon one man, and there is one who is opposed to the five, kill him. If four are one side and two on the other, kill the two. And if three on one side and three on the other, then Abdur Rahman ibn Auf will have the casting vote, and the khalifa will be selected from his party. In that case, kill the three men on the opposing side.*
> *You may, if you wish, invite some of the chief men of the Ansar as observers but the khalifa must be one of you Muhajireen, and not any of them. They have no share in the khilafat. And your selection of the new khalifa must be made within three days.*
> - *Tarikh Tabari Volume 3 Page 294*
> - *Kamil Ibn Atheer vol. 3 p.35*
> - *Tabaqat Ibn Saad volume 3 pg 342*

Caliph Umar further stated:

> *"If three days pass before they decide on a leader kill them all and let the Muslims choose for themselves."*
> - *Ibn Saad Al-Tabaqat Part 3 p. 342*

Caliph Umar also made his son Abdullah Ibn Omar an arbitrator and an advisor to the Shura but said that he would have no part in the Caliphate itself.

After the burial of Caliph Umar, the Shura began its deliberations. There were heated discussions and arguments among its participants. It is reported that Talhah withdrew from the race in favour of Uthman, Al-Zubeir withdrew in favour of Ali and Saad Ibn Abi Waqqas withdrew for his cousin Abdul Rahman ibn Auf. This left three men behind in the race i.e., Ali, Uthman and Abdul Rahman ibn Auf.

Abdul Rahman Ibn Auf suggested that he would take himself out of the race, but in return he would be authorized to choose between the remaining two candidates i.e., Ali and Uthman. Uthman authorized him without hesitation, but Ali did not authorize him until he made Abdul Rahman take an oath. Abdul Rahman was Uthman's brother-in-law and was married to Uthman's sister Um Kulthoum.

Ali took an oath from Abdul Rahman ibn Auf to say that he would only side with the truth, and he would not follow any personal desire, and he would not give preference to his relative (Uthman) over the interest of the nation.

After giving the oath to Ali, Abdul Rahman met other companions and Muslims to see who should be chosen as the new Caliph. He also met with Ali and Uthman separately to discuss the Caliphate with them. As expected, the majority of the Qurayshites were in favour of Uthman to be the next Caliph. On the other hand, the supporters of Ali which included companions like Ammar and Miqdad wanted the nominee of the Prophet to win the day.

As per instructions of Caliph Umar, the matter had to be settled within three days. On the third day the mosque of the Prophet was full, and Abdul Rahman was determined to bring the issue to a close.

Following is an extract from the discussion which that took place between the supporters of Ali and the Qurayshites who were supporting Uthman.

> *Abdul Rahman stood up and said: "People the visitors have to go to their own towns. Counsel me.*
> *Ammar Ibn Yasir stood up and said to him: 'If you want to avoid the Muslims division select Ali."*
> *Al-Miqdad Ibn Al-Aswad another companion seconded Ammar saying: "Ammar told the truth. If you select Ali we say: We listen and obey."*
>
> - *(The History of al-Tabari, Vol.14, p.152)*

These two companions were contradicted by Abdullah Ibn Abu Sarh who said to Abdul Rahman:

> *"If you want to avoid the Qurayshites division select Uthman."*
> *Abdullah Ibn Abu Rabi-ah from the clan of Makhzoom seconded him saying: "You told the truth. Should Abdul Rahman select Uthman we say: We heard and will obey."*
>
> - *(The History of al-Tabari, Vol.14, p.152)*

Ammar said to Ibn Abu Sarh:

> *"When were you sincere to the Muslims?"* (Ibn Abu Sarh embraced Islam during the time of the Prophet. Then he deserted the faith. The Messenger ordered the Muslims to kill him wherever they found him.)
>
> - *(The History of al-Tabari, Vol.14, p.152)*

The Hashimites spoke and so did the Umayyads. Ammar then addressed the people by saying:

> *"O people certainly God has honoured us with His Prophet and strengthened us with His religion. Where do you divert the caliphate from the members of the House of your Prophet?"*
>
> - *(The History of al-Tabari, Vol.14, p.152)*

A man from Makhzoom contradicted him by saying:

> "Son of Sumayah who are you to tell Quraysh what to do for themselves?"
>
> Saad Ibn Abi Waqqas said to his cousin Abdul Rahman: "Finish it before people fall into dissension."
>
> - (The History of al-Tabari, Vol.14, p.152)

After witnessing the above commotion, Abdul Rahman invited Ali and offered him the caliphate, but he added a condition. He offered the Caliphate to Ali on three grounds.

> "Will you pledge to God and covenant Him that you will follow the Book of God the teachings of the Messenger and the precepts of the two caliphs (Abu Bakr and Omar) after him?"
> Ali replied: "I shall follow the Book of God the teachings of the Prophet and I shall follow my best knowledge and endeavour to the maximum of my ability."
>
> - Ibn Al-Atheer in his Al-Kamil Part 3 pp. 32-35
> - Al-Tabari Vol. 1 pp. 63-65

As Ali did not accept all the three conditions put to him, and only accepted the first two i.e., he accepted to follow the book of Allah and the Sunnah of the Prophet, but he refused to follow the precepts of the first two Caliphs. Abdul Rahman turned to Uthman with the same offer and Uthman accepted the offer immediately. It is said that Abdul Rahman made the offer three times to each of the men, and each time Ali refused to accept the third condition, and each time Uthman accepted all the three conditions.

At this point Abdul Rahman lifted his head towards the ceiling of the Mosque and said:

> "God be my witness I have transferred the responsibility from my neck to the neck of Uthman. Then he pledged his allegiance to Uthman.
>
> - Ibn Al-Atheer in his Al-Kamil Part 3 pp. 32-35
> - Al-Tabari Vol. 1 pp. 63-65

Ali commented on what took place and said:

> "This is not the first day you have collaborated against us (members of the House of the Prophet) . . . By God you gave him the leadership only to return it to you later. God is able to change the situation." Then he turned to both Abdul Rahman and Uthman saying: "May God plight you with a mutual and lasting hostility."
> Abdul Rahman retorted saying: "Ali do not incur trouble upon yourself (reminding him that the Second Caliph ordered them to kill any dissenter)."
>
> - Ibn Al-Atheer in his Al-Kamil Part 3 pp. 32-35
> - Al-Tabari Vol. 1 pp. 63-65

Ali then left the convention after he gave his pledge to Uthman and said:

> "What is written of timed events will reach its maturity."
>
> - Ibn Al-Atheer in his Al-Kamil Part 3 pp. 32-35
> - Al-Tabari Vol. 1 pp. 63-65

Then the supporters of Ali namely Ammar and Miqdad argued with Abdul Rahman:

> Ammar said to Abdul Rahman: "By God you have left out the man of truth and correct judgment!"

> *Al-Miqdad Ibn Al-Aswad joined Ammar saying: "By God I have never witnessed anything similar to what has been done to the members of the House of the Prophet after his death. I am amazed at Quraysh who left out a man unequaled in knowledge piety and justice. If I have supporters I will fight the Qurayshites now as I fought them in the battles of Badr and Uhud."*
> *Abdul Rahman replied: "Miqdad fear God. I am afraid that you will bring about divisions among Muslims."*
> *Al-Miqdad retorted angrily saying: "The one who creates division is the one who follows his own selfish interest."*

- Ibn Al-Atheer in his Al-Kamil Part 3 pp. 32-35
- Al-Tabari Vol. 1 pp. 63-65

The injustice of history against Ali continued unabated and Uthman bin Affan from the Banu Ummayad clan of Quraysh was chosen as the third Caliph of the Muslim Ummah.

11.2. The Rules of the Shura

Initially Caliph Umar wanted to appoint Abu Ubaydah al-Jarrah or Salim the slave of Abu Hutheifa as his successors. But since none of them were alive he decided to form a Shura (Consultation) and defined a very strict code for the proceedings of the Shura.

Caliph Umar came up with some really astonishing rules for the Shura.

> *If five of you agree upon one man, and there is one who is opposed to the five, kill him. If four are one side and two on the other, kill the two. And if three are on one side and three on the other, then Abdur Rahman ibn Auf will have the casting vote, and the khalifa will be selected from his party. In that case, kill the three men on the opposing side. If three days pass before they decide on a leader kill them all and let the Muslims choose for themselves."*

- Tarikh Tabari Volume 3 Page 294
- Kamil Ibn Atheer vol. 3 p.35,
- Tabaqat Ibn Saad volume 3 Page 342

11.2.1. The Killing of the Companions and the Ahlulbayt

Caliph Umar had sanctioned the killing of the companions and the Ahlulbayt (Ali), simply because they might be in the minority group within the Shura, or simply because they might be in the group opposed to Abdul Rahman ibn Auf. Furthermore, he ordered the killing of every single Shura member if they had failed to appoint someone within three days.

Such a verdict has no basis from the Holy Quran or the Sunnah of the Prophet. Islam sanctifies life and life is considered sacred in Islam. The Holy Quran states:

> *But whoever kills a believer intentionally - his recompense is Hell, wherein he will abide eternally, and Allah has become angry with him and has cursed him and has prepared for him a great punishment.*

- (Quran 4:93)

The Holy Quran states that if one kills a believer intentionally their abide is eternal hell. Islam does not permit killing of a believer just because they disagree with the majority, or just because they disagree with the group represented by Abdul Rahman ibn Auf. It is true that the majority view should prevail, but that does not mean that one would kill the people who hold the minority view. There is absolutely on justification or grounds for such a decree, and it has no standing in the eyes of Islam.

Also, at the beginning of his speech Caliph Umar had stated that he was choosing these six men because the Prophet of Allah was pleased with them.

> *O group of Muhajireen! Verily, the Apostle of God died, and he was pleased with all six of you. I have, therefore, decided to make it (the selection of khalifa) a matter of consultation among you"*
> - Tarikh Tabari Volume 3 Page 294
> - Kamil Ibn Atheer vol. 3 p.35
> - Tabaqat Ibn Saad volume 3 Page 342

But then at the same time he orders the killing of these very people. Surely if Prophet was indeed pleased with them all, then killing them would be an even bigger crime and a complete breach and a negation of the Sunnah of the Prophet. The dichotomy of Caliph Umar's statements is perplexing!

A Caliph just like any other Muslim has to work within the parameters set out by the Holy Quran and the Sunnah of the Prophet. He cannot make lawful what has been forbidden by Allah and his Prophet. Many companions had disagreed with the Prophet, but he never sanctioned the killing of any of those companions. Islam as an ideology does not follow such logic.

As we saw in Chapter 7, at the time of the Hudaybiyya Pact Caliph Umar himself had disagreed with the Prophet and even questioned his Prophethood, but the Prophet of Allah never took such an action. In the final days of Prophet's illness, he asked if someone could bring him a pen and a paper, so he could write something which would keep the Muslims on the right path. Again, Caliph Umar refused to fulfil the request of the Prophet and said that Book of Allah was enough for the Muslims. Even then the Prophet did not adopt such a path, he simply asked Caliph Umar and the other companions to leave his room.

With such harsh rules about the killing of Shura members, the Shura would never be able to choose the best man for the job, as everybody would be fearful of ending up in the minority group and getting killed. Also, Caliph Umar had stated that if the Shura was evenly divided then the group with Abdul Rahman would prevail, and the three members opposing his group would be killed, which basically means that nobody would dare to oppose Abdul Rahman, as your chances of getting killed would increase significantly, essentially making Abdul Rahman the kingmaker.

Also, it would be needless to say that the rules laid out by Caliph Umar could never be used again as an example for any other Shura.

It is clear from the rules set out by Caliph Umar that he had no understanding of the principles governing the proceedings of a Shura. This indeed was not surprising given the fact that Prophet had never trained any of his companions on the modalities of a Shura, since Prophet had never envisaged a Shura as a means of selecting his successors.

The rules that Caliph Umar had set out for the Shura would probably have worked in the pre-Islamic times, but they certainly had no reflection from the Holy Quran or the Sunnah of the Prophet.

11.3. The Ansar are Barred from the Shura

Another clear and noteworthy guideline that Caliph Umar had given to the Shura was to completely bar the Ansar from having any share in the Caliphate.

> "You may, if you wish, invite some of the chief men of the Ansar as observers but the khalifa must be one of you Muhajireen, and not any of them. They have no share in the khilafat"

- Tarikh Tabari Volume 3 Page 294
- Kamil Ibn Atheer vol. 3 p.35
- Tabaqat Ibn Saad volume 3 Page 342

Caliph Umar categorically bars the Ansar from having any say in the Caliphate. He neither admits them in the decision-making process (Shura) and nor does he allow an Ansar to become the next Caliph. The Ansar according to Caliph Umar should not have any say whatsoever in the Caliphate, they can only be present as observers.

If we turn back the clock twelve years ago, readers will recall that during the meeting of Saqifah Caliph Abu Bakr had said to the Ansar:

> ...Oh company of the Ansar, your superiority in religion and great precedence in Islam are undeniable. May Allah be satisfied with you as helpers (Ansar) for His religion and His Apostle. He made his Hijrah to you...so after the Muhajirs there is no one among us who is in your station.
>
> We (the Muhajirs) are the leaders, and you (Ansars) are the helpers; matters shall not be settled without consultation, nor shall we decide on them without you."

- The History of al-Tabari, Vol.10, pp.4-5

We can witness how Caliph Abu Bakr was enticing the Ansar in accepting the leadership of the Muhajireen in Saqifah. He said to the Ansar that your superiority and precedence in Islam is undeniable. Allah was satisfied with you as helpers and Prophet had made migration to your land, and after the Muhajireen there was no one who has the stature and the status that you have.

After praising the Ansar Caliph Abu Bakr also offers them to become the advisors to the Caliph, and in fact it was this offer which had formed the basis of Abu Bakr's Caliphate. In contrast one can observe the approach of Caliph Umar, who does not mince his words and categorically bars the Ansar from any kind of role in the Caliphate.

By Simply looking at the words of Caliph Abu Bakr and Caliph Umar, one might think that their words were diametrically opposed to each other. However, when one digs a little deeper and analyses the context and the setting in which these words were said, then one would realize that there was in fact very little difference in these words.

Caliph Abu Bakr had said all those flowery words for the Ansar in Saqifah, but there was no substance behind those admirable words. He never backed his words with the promise that he had actually made to the Ansar. His promise remained unfulfilled, and the Ansar were never given the position of being the Caliph's advisors, because the Muhajireen and the Quraysh had no intention of sharing the Caliphate with anybody else.

Those beautiful words of Caliph Abu Bakr for the Ansar were a political manoeuvre to win over the leadership of the Ansar in the meeting of Saqifah. At the time of Saqifah the Ansar were a very strong political force who had pre-empted the Muhajireen for the position of the Caliphate. They had threatened to drive the Muhajireen out of Madinah on the point of their swords.

> "(The) Ansar said: 'In case they (Muhajireen) reject our Caliph, we shall drive them out from Al-Medinah at the point of our swords."

- *Tareekh Al-Islam, Vol.1, p.273-274*

The Muhajireen had to play diplomatically and hence the flowery words of Caliph Abu Bakr.

But after twelve years of Muhajireen and the Qurayshite rule the Ansar had been completely marginalized and side lined. There was no need for any political or diplomatic niceness, and hence one sees the harsh words of Caliph Umar for the Ansar. The Muhajireen were now the dominant force in Madinah and Caliph Umar could set out his rules as he wished.

In any case let us see if it was appropriate to side-line the Ansar who were the majority inhabitants of Madinah in such a callus way.

As far as the rights of the Ansar were concerned for the position of the Caliphate there can be two logical approaches on this issue.

- Either one chooses the nominee of the Prophet and gives him the allegiance and accepts him as the rightful candidate for the Caliphate and honours the Sunnah of the Prophet.

Or

- If for whatever reason one is not willing to accept the choice of the Prophet or believes that Prophet never made such a choice in the first place, then surely every other group and party has an equal right to the Caliphate.

To bar a group as big as the Ansar from the Caliphate, and to announce that they have no share in the Caliphate is a complete breach of the principles of justice and fair play.

Ansar were the companions from Madinah, they were the ones who had welcomed the Prophet and the Muhajirs into their city. They had opened their houses to the Muhajireen when they migrated from Makkah. They gave Muhajireen food, shelter, clothing, and everything else that they needed in the time of their need. It was their hospitality and generosity which had strengthened the Islamic movement in its early days. They had given protection to the Prophet and the Muslims when they were in desperate need. The Prophet of Allah had made the brotherhood between the Ansar and the Muhajireen.

The Prophet of Allah had stated the following about the Ansar:

> *"None loves the Ansar but a believer, and none hates them but a hypocrite. So Allah will love him who loves them, and He will hate him who hates them."*

- *Sahih al-Bukhari 3783*
- *Sahih Book 63, Hadith 8*
- *Sahih Vol. 5, Book 58, Hadith 127*

The barring of Ansar from having any share or say in the matter of Caliphate was a complete breach and a negation of the Sunnah of the Prophet.

Madinah was the capital of the Islamic State, the Ansar were the majority inhabitants of Madinah, it was their city after all, and the previous two Caliphs had already been from the Muhajireen. It was only fair that they are at least given some say and representation in the Shura now, so that they at least feel part of the process for selecting the new Caliph.

The Ansar were well aware of the position of Muhajireen towards the Caliphate, they knew exactly what Caliphate meant for the Muhajireen and how eager and keen some of the Muhajireen were for this position. It was for this reason that as soon as Prophet had passed away, they had pre-empted the Caliphate in Saqifah and tried to secure it for themselves, as they were fearful that if they didn't secure the Caliphate the Muhajireen would rule over them for good.

Unfortunately, this is exactly what happened to the Ansar. Their plans got thwarted in Saqifah as Caliph Abu Bakr and Caliph Umar found out about their meeting and managed to get there in time to stop the Ansar from reaching the Caliphate.

11.4. The Choice of the Shura members

As stated above, Caliph Umar did not choose any companions from Madinah for the Shura that he had setup to select the next Caliph. Many companions from Madinah (Ansar) were now inclined towards Ali, especially after the rule of the first two Caliphs, because they had seen the influence of Quraysh increase rapidly during the reigns of the first two Caliphs. They saw Ali as the only person who could curtail the influence of Quraysh in the Islamic State and give the Ansar a voice among the political elites of the Muslim Ummah. Unfortunately, Caliph Umar only chose the companions from the Muhajireen to form the Shura, denying Ali any support that he could have had from the Ansar.

Also, the companions that Caliph Umar chose had their own inclinations and aspirations, and most of them were averse to Ali being the next Caliph.

Just like Ali, Uthman was hoping to be the next leader, so he wasn't going to favour Ali. Abdul Rahman Ibn Auf was Uthman's brother-in-law. Saad Ibn Abi Waqqas was Abdul Rahman's cousin and he had already pulled out of the race in favour of Abdul Rahman. So, Both Abdul Rahman and Saad Ibn Abi Waqqas were in the camp of Uthman. All three men i.e. Uthman, Abdul Rahman Ibn Auf and Saad Ibn Abi Waqqas were from the Umayyad clan of Quraysh. These men were not going to compete with each other, and Uthman being the most senior in terms of age, they were always going to support his candidacy.

Talhah Ibn Ubaydullah was from the clan of Abu Bakr. Because of Ali's rivalry with Abu Bakr for the first Caliphate, he was opposed to Ali's nomination, and hence he withdrew his candidacy in favour of Uthman. Out of the six Shura members only Al-Zubeir Ibn Al-Awam supported Ali. Thus, the majority of the Shura members were unfavourable or oppose to Ali's nomination as the third Caliph.

On top of this Caliph Umar had given Abdul Rahman the casting vote i.e. if the Shura was evenly divided then Abdul Rahman's camp would win the day, this left Ali with virtually no chance of success, as the odds were heavily stacked against him.

Also, the choice of Abdullah Ibn Umar as the advisor and an arbitrator for the Shura would further steer the Caliphate away from Ali. Although Caliph Umar had said that his son Abdullah Ibn Umar would have no part in the Caliphate, but he was well known for his hostility towards Ali. Abdullah Ibn Umar hostility towards Ali became evident when Ali actually became the fourth Caliph, as he was one of the companions who never paid allegiance to Ali throughout the duration of Ali's Caliphate, which lasted for around four and a half years.

After Caliph Umar had announced the Shura and its rules, Ali virtually had no chance of becoming the third Caliph. Ali informed the members of Banu Hashim and his Uncle Abdullah Ibn Abbas about his feelings:

> "If the people (the Qurayshites) are obeyed we will never reach the leadership."
> "Uncle the leadership has already been diverted away from us... Umar equalized Uthman with me and ordered the people to follow the majority of the six members. If the members are divided

equally he told the Muslims to side with Abdul Rahman and Abdul Rahman is a brother-in-law of Uthman. Saad is Abdul Rahman's cousin and they will not disagree with each other. If the other two are with me they will not avail me."

- Ibn Al-Atheer Al-Kamil Part 3 p. 33.

Leaving all the other companions aside, surely between Ali and Abdul Rahman, Ali deserved more to have the casting vote than Abdul Rahman. Ali's upbringing in the house of the Prophet, his unique companionship with the Prophet, his knowledge of Quran and Sunnah, his service in the establishment of the Islamic State and his unique honour of being the brother of the Prophet had set him apart from the rest of the companions.

There was no comparison of any sorts between Ali and Abdul Rahman, but still Abdul Rahman takes precedence over Ali, because it was the trend of al-ijtihad (independent judgment), and the Qurayshite view of the Caliphate, which had overshadowed the clear Sunnah of the Prophet. Abdul Rahman being from the Umayyad clan of Quraysh took precedence over Ali who belonged to the Banu Hashim clan of Quraysh.

Also, Caliph Umar could have easily inducted Ibn Abbas in the Shura. Ibn Abbas was one of the senior most companions of the Prophet at the time, he was well known for his knowledge, prudence and judgment. He was far more reputable than Abdul Rahman who was given the casting vote. Ibn Abbas was also the uncle of the Prophet and from the clan of Banu Hashim, his induction would have given the Shura the much-needed balance that it required.

Caliph Umar knew exactly the position of Ali in relation to the Prophet, he had heard countless sayings of the Prophet in favour of Ali, he could have easily steered the Caliphate in the direction of the nominee of the Prophet. He could have had the privilege of honouring the Sunnah of the Prophet, but he chose to do exactly the opposite. He chose to give precedence to the Umayyad's over the nominee of the Prophet. He chose companions of average stature and standing and made them competitors of Ali for the position of the Caliphate.

Caliph Umar chose the path that Quraysh wanted him to choose.

Caliph Umar knew very well the inclinations of each of the Shura members that he had chosen. He knew that Quraysh were firmly standing against Ali, and he knew that Quraysh wanted their man for the job, so he chose members who were inclined to give the Caliphate to the Quraysh rather than to Ali, deliberately tipping the balance of the Shura in favour of Uthman, which indeed was most unfortunate.

11.5. Head-to-Head

Once the proceedings of the Shura began the two trends would be clearly visible going head-to-head. A trend, which believed in adhering to the Sunnah of the Prophet, and a trend that believed in its own independent judgment, based on the circumstances of the time.

The mosque of the Prophet was full, and although Ali did not have much support in the Shura, but there were companions in the audience who believe that Ali was the rightful successor of the Prophet, and should now be given the third Caliphate as he had already been by-passed on the first two occasions.

The supporters of Ali namely Ammar Ibn Yasir and Al-Miqdad Ibn Al-Aswad make their case to the Shura in the following words:

Ammar Ibn Yasir stood up and said to him: 'If you want to avoid the Muslims division select Ali."

> *Al-Miqdad Ibn Al-Aswad another companion seconded Ammar saying: "Ammar told the truth. If you select Ali we say: We listen and obey."*
>
> *Ammar further said: "O people certainly God has honoured us with His Prophet and strengthened us with His religion. Where do you divert the caliphate from the members of the House of your Prophet?"*
>
> - *(The History of al-Tabari, Vol.14, p.152)*

Although, it was only from the Public gallery, but this was the first time that the supporters of Ali had a chance to support the nominee of the Prophet, and at least make the Shura members aware of the position and the stature of Ali, so nobody has any doubt as to who was the actual nominee of the Prophet. On the previous two occasions the supporters of Ali were denied even this basic right.

Ammar tells the Shura members and the audience that if they want to avoid divisions within the Ummah, then they should choose Ali. He further asks them not to divert the Caliphate away from the members of the house of the Prophet i.e. the Ahlulbayt. Al-Miqdad seconds whatever Ammar had said as these companions believed that Prophet had nominated the Ahlulbayt for leading the Ummah after his death. They argue their case publicly as they believe that Ali was the man that Prophet had chosen to lead the Muslims in his absence.

The supporters of Quraysh inevitably contradicted the supporters of Ali:

> *Abdullah Ibn Abu Sarh tells Abdul Rahman: "If you want to avoid the Qurayshites division select Uthman."*
>
> *Abdullah Ibn Abu Rabi-ah from the clan of Makhzoom seconded him saying: "You told the truth. Should Abdul Rahman select Uthman we say: We heard and will obey."*
>
> - *(The History of al-Tabari, Vol.14, p.152)*

The Quraysh were not willing to accept Ali at any cost. The Quraysh could not accept the fact that the Caliphate and the Prophethood could stay in the same clan i.e. the clan of Banu Hashim.

The Quraysh never really considered the Prophet as simply the Prophet of Allah, they had always thought of him as the head of the Banu Hashim clan and a tribal leader. They had seen that Prophet had ruled the Islamic State for over ten years. They could not accept the prospect of another member of Banu Hashim ruling over them, especially when that person was so close to the Prophet in lineage like Ali was. Ali was not just from the same clan as the Prophet, but he was from the same family as the Prophet, he was part of the Ahlulbayt, the people of the house of the Prophet.

On top of this Ali had a lot of Qurayshite blood on his hands from the battles of Badr, Uhud and Moat. Ali had killed some of their most well-known warriors and leaders of Quraysh in these battles. The memory of their loved ones being killed by Ali was still fresh in their minds.

This is why as soon as the supporters of Ali try and convince the Shura to vote for him, the Quraysh immediately intervened, and stipulate to the Shura that if they wanted to avoid Qurayshite division, they should choose Uthman who was from the Umayyad clan of Quraysh, and if the Shura chooses Uthman they would be willing to listen to him and obey him.

Just as in Saqifah Caliph Abu Bakr had argued the case for Quraysh against the Ansar, twelve years later, the supporters of Quraysh are again supporting their candidate against Ali, and just as Caliph Abu Bakr had won the day against the Ansar, the Quraysh were confident of winning here too. The history was about to repeat itself.

Caliph Abu Bakr made the following statements in support of Quraysh in Saqifah to pacify the Ansar:

> "All the good that you have said about yourselves (O Ansar) is deserved. But the Arabs will recognize authority only in this clan of Quraysh,…"

- *(Ibn Ishaq, Seerah Rasool-Allah)*

> "(O Ansar) you are our brethren in Islam and our partners in religion…but the Arabs will not submit themselves except to this clan of Quraysh…we (the Quraysh) are in the center among the Muslims with respect to our position…"

- *(The History of al-Tabari, Volume 9, p.193)*

Just as Caliph Abu Bakr had told the Ansar that the Arabs would only submit to the leadership of the Quraysh, Abu Sarh tells the Shura appointed by Caliph Umar that unless they choose Uthman, the Quraysh would not submit to the new Caliph.

Essentially, after the death of the Prophet, the Quraysh only wanted to have the Caliphate in non-Hashimite clans i.e., they were happy to rotate the Caliphate in other clans of Quraysh, but not in the clan of the Prophet i.e., the clan of Banu Hashim. For instance, giving the Caliphate to Abu Bakr was fine as he was from the Banu Taym clan of Quraysh. Giving the Caliphate to Umar was acceptable too since he was from the Banu Adi clan of Quraysh. And giving the Caliphate to Uthman was also ok as he belonged to the Banu Umayyad clan, which was one of the biggest and the most influential clans of Quraysh.

But giving the Caliphate to Ali was not acceptable as he belonged to the clan of the Prophet. Unfortunately, this was the irony and the reality of politics which had plagued the Caliphate after the death of the Prophet. The person who was closest to the Prophet in every sense including lineage is side-lined, while others are given precedence over him to please the Quraysh and to ensure that their feelings and their influence is dually acknowledged. The nominee of the Prophet is ignored but the candidate of the Quraysh is given the Caliphate.

The person who was by the side of the Prophet all his life, and who had been the differentiating factor in every decisive battle against the enemies of Islam is cast aside, whereas the Quraysh who were the biggest enemy of the Prophet and his mission, from the moment he announced his Prophethood until the conquest of Makkah, were given precedence in the Caliphate.

The injustice of history against Ali was simply incredible.

11.6. Ammar Ibn Yasir and Abdullah Ibn Abu Sarh

A simple comparison between Ammar Ibn Yasir who was supporting the nomination of Ali, and Abdullah Ibn Abu Sarh who was supporting Caliphate of Uthman, would give an invaluable insight into the kind of people that each camp had attracted.

11.6.1. Ammar Ibn Yasir

Ammar's father Yasir was a poor man who came from Yemen and settled in Makkah. It is unclear from history if Ammar's father Yasir became a slave of Abu Huthaifah who was from a powerful clan of Quraysh known as Makhzum, or if he was simply sponsored by Abu Huthaifah, as it was a custom in those days to sponsor people and keep slaves. Nevertheless, Yasir stayed under the patronage of Abu Huthaifah, who also had a very intelligent and a smart slave girl known as Sumayyah. She was later given into marriage to Yasir, and Ammar was born from this marriage and was commonly known as Ammar Ibn Yasir.

The family and the tribal background of Ammar Ibn Yasir was unimpressive in a society which valued wealth and tribal power. As the message of Islam spread, all three family members embraced Islam and became one of the earliest Muslims. Ammar Ibn Yasir and his mother Sumayyah were among the first ten people who were enlightened by Islam, and they had the privilege of swearing allegiance to the Prophet and his mission in its very early days. Sumayyah became one of the foremost women companions of the Prophet, and Ammar including both his parents became staunch supporters of Prophet and his mission.

Although Yasir and his family i.e. his wife Sumayyah and his son Ammar were no longer in slavery, but when the Makhzum clan of Quraysh found out that they had accepted Islam, they decided to confront the family and challenged them on their new found faith. The family refused to budge and refused to leave the path shown by the Prophet of Allah

This infuriated the Makhzum clan, and as a punishment they plundered Yasir's house, set fire to all their goods and started torturing the whole family. This noble family was chained and was taken outside of Makkah where slaves were normally punished and beaten. They were stretched across the desert in the burning sun, and heavy stones were put on top of them to increase their suffering. Their howls of pain could be heard inside Makkah, and the torture would go on for days to discourage anyone else from giving allegiance to the Prophet. Despite such horrible torture the family refused to go back to the pagan ways and remained steadfast on the path of Islam.

Prophet's heart went out to Yasir and his family when he saw the pain that the Quraysh were inflicting on them. At the time Muslims were very weak and small in number, and the Prophet of Allah was unable to physically stop the torture. In order to console the family, and to ease their pain and to give them strength the Prophet would continuously say to them:

> *"Patience oh family of Yassir, for you are destined for Paradise."*
> - *(Sahih al-Tirmidhi, v5, p233)*

The torture of the family carried on unabated, and one day the leader of the Banu Makhzum clan who was known as Abu Jahl stabbed Sumayyah and killed her, and later her husband Yasir was also killed while being tortured.

Sumayyah became the first martyr of Islam, an honour that went to the mother of Ammar Ibn Yasir.

Both the parents of Ammar were killed by Quraysh in the very early days of the Islamic movement. Because of the sacrifice of his family and the torture that Ammar himself endured, he had a special place in the heart of the Prophet. The Prophet became very close to Ammar and used to lovingly call him by the name of his mother, Ibn Sumayyah, the son of Sumayyah i.e. the son of the first martyr of Islam.

Ammar later became one of the intermediaries in Prophet's marriage to Lady Khadijah. He was also one of the few companions who had the honour of building the very first mosque for the Muslims in Madinah.

On one hand, there was Ammar Ibn Yasir who was supporting the nomination of Ali for the third Caliphate, whose entire family had been tortured and killed in the path of Allah, and who himself had endured enormous sufferings, but remained steadfast on the path of truth.

11.6.2. Abdullah Ibn Abu Sarh

On the other hand, there was Abdullah Ibn Abu Sarh who was supporting the nomination of Uthman for the third Caliphate. Abdullah Ibn Abu Sarh had apostatized and had become such an enemy of the Prophet that Prophet had ordered him to be killed, even if he was to be found under the curtain of Kaaba.

> *"When Muhammad had gathered enough troops to besiege Mecca, he issued an order to his followers that Abd Allah ibn Sa'd would be one of those who had to be killed even though he was hiding beneath the curtain of the Kaaba But Abd Allah then went to his adopted brother, Uthman ibn Affan asking for help. Then together they went to Muhammad to beg for forgiveness. When he met the two of them, Muhammad, who was accompanied by some of his companions, was silent for a long time until he said yes. But after the two of them left, Muhammad said to his followers, "I kept silent so that one of you might get up and strike off his head!" One of the Ansar said, "Then why didn't you give me a sign, O apostle of God?" He answered that a prophet does not kill by pointing"*
>
> - Ibn Ishaq. The Life of Muhammad - Sirat Rasul Allah. p. 550
> - Hadith 2683 Sunan Abu-Dawud
> - Al-Tabari, "History of al-Tabari Vol. 9 - The Last Years of the Prophet", transl. Ismail K. Poonawala, p.148

As his name Abdullah Ibn Sad Ibn Abi Sarh is quite long, for the purpose of our discussion we will refer to him as Abu Sarh.

The Prophet of Allah throughout his Prophethood had only ordered the killing of a handful of individuals. The people that Prophet had ordered to be killed were the true enemies of Allah and the Prophet, and Abu Sarh was one of them. The reason why Prophet was so upset and angry with him was because he used to lie upon the Holy Quran and the Prophet after he had apostatized.

Ibn al-Athir in his book Usud Ulghabah fi Marifat Is-Sahabah writes:

> *He converted to Islam before the conquest of Makkah and immigrated to the Prophet [i.e. in Medina]. He used to record the revelation for the Prophet before he apostatized and went back to Makkah. Then he told Quraysh: 'I used to orient Muhammad wherever I willed, he dictated to me "All-Powerful All-Wise" and I suggest "All Knowing All-Wise" so he would say: "Yes, it is all the same."*
>
> - Ibn al-Athir, Usud Ulghabah fi Marifat Is-Sahabah, 1995, Dar al-Fikr, Beirut (Lebanon), Volume 3, p. 154.

Prophet at one point had appointed Abu Sarh as a scriber of the Holy Quran. However later on Abu Sarh apostatised and went back to Makkah, where he used to discredit the Holy Quran by claiming that he used to change the words of the Quran at will, and that the Prophet was ok with what he did. Essentially Abu Sarh not only discredited the Holy Quran after apostatizing, but he discredited the Prophet too, by fabricating and inventing lies against both the Quran and the Prophet of Allah.

This really infuriated the Prophet, who ordered the companions to kill him even if he was seen hiding under the curtain of Kaaba. When the Muslim army conquered Makkah, Abu Sarh knew he would be killed so he hid himself under the protection of Caliph Uthman, who was his foster brother. The initial few days of the conquest of Makkah were critical for the enemies of Islam. They knew that if they could survive the initial onslaught of the first few days, then as the dust would settle, they would have more chance of making it through, since Muslims would feel less threatened by these enemies as Makkah would have been secured by then.

This was exactly what Abu Sarh was hoping for, and he needed someone to give him that protection initially. Caliph Uthman being his foster brother obliged, and instead of carrying out the orders of the Prophet he did exactly the opposite. Caliph Uthman hid Abu Sarh in his home against the clear instructions of the Prophet and saved him from being killed.

After a few days into the conquest of Makkah, and once things had settled down, Caliph Uthman brought Abu Sarh to the Prophet pleading for his life. Even at that point Prophet stayed silent for a long time, hoping that one of his companions around him would kill Abu Sarh based on his previous commands. But nobody killed Abu Sarh, so after waiting for a while the Prophet reluctantly forgave him. Even when Caliph Uthman left after securing immunity for Abu Sarh, Prophet asked his companions as to why had nobody killed Abu Sarh when he (Prophet) stayed silent. Such was the depth of hatred that Prophet had for Abu Sarh.

So, Caliph Uthman managed to save his foster brother Abu Sarh after the conquest of Makkah, and now Abu Sarh was repaying his debt to Caliph Uthman, by supporting his nomination for the third Caliphate.

11.6.3. The Difference in the Two Camps

The camp of Ali was supported by companions like Ammar Ibn Yasir, who was tortured in the path of Allah, and who had lost his entire family in the path of Islam, and as a result Prophet had promised paradise for him and his family.

On the other hand, we have Abu Sarh who was supporting the camp of Caliph Uthman. Abu Sarh was a known enemy of the Prophet and the Holy Quran, a person who invented lies against the Prophet and the Book of Allah, and a person who was only reluctantly forgiven by the Prophet as nobody had killed him after the conquest of Makkah, despite the ruling of the Prophet.

The difference in the two camps could not be starker. Ammar was testifying that Ali was the nominee of the Prophet so he should be given the third Caliphate. Abu Sarh was supporting his foster brother Caliph Uthman for the position of the third Caliphate, as Caliph Uthman had earlier saved Abu Sarh from certain death in Makkah. However, there is no doubt that if Prophet was alive on that day, he would have certainly accepted the testimony of Ammar Ibn Yasir over the testimony of Abu Sarh!

Unfortunately for Ali, Ammar Ibn Yasir came from a Yemeni family of slaves, whereas Abu Sarh was from the prestigious Umayyad clan of Quraysh. The testimony of Abu Sarh carries the weight and the influence of his powerful Qurayshite clan. The testimony of Ammar Ibn Yasir from the public gallery in support of Ali carries no weight in the eyes of the pro-Qurayshite Shura appointed by Caliph Umar.

And the Quraysh dually reminded Ammar Ibn Yasir of his status.

> *A man from Makhzum contradicted him by saying: "Son of Sumayah who are you to tell Quraysh what to do for themselves?"*
> - *(The History of al-Tabari, Vol.14, p.152)*

A man from the Makhzum clan of Quraysh calls Ammar by the name of his mother Sumayyah, in a derogatory manner, since she was once a slave of the Makhzum clan. They remind Ammar that a son of slave does not have a right to challenge the authority and the ways of the Quraysh. They remind Ammar that he could not possibly tell Quraysh what to do, as he was only a son of a slave. Their arrogance had a reminisce of the pre-Islamic era, and they were advocating tribal superiority as if the revolution of Islam had never taken place.

The Makhzum clan was the same clan that had tortured and killed the family of Ammar Ibn Yasir and other early Muslims. It was their leader Abu Jahl who had killed Sumayyah the mother of Ammar. But now the members of this clan have become so strong that they have a say and an influence in deciding the leadership of the very faith that they had sought to destroy. And the very people who had sought to preserve the faith, suffered, tortured, and sacrificed their entire family in its path are side lined and cast a side like Ammar Ibn Yasir.

Not only would the testimony of Abu Sarh be accepted in favour of Caliph Uthman, but the support of Makhzum clan would further ensure that Ali is once again by-passed for the Caliphate. The biggest supporter of the Prophet in the establishment and the subsequent defence of the Islamic State is castaway, and the very people who were the biggest enemy of the Islamic State, who had tortured early Muslims, and who had launched numerous wars against it, would not only be given a say in the future leadership of the Islamic State, but they would in fact become the deciding party as to who should lead that State.

The injustice against Ali and his supporters could not be more obvious and glaring.

It seems that after the death of the Prophet the issue of Caliphate was all about the Quraysh. The Caliphate could only be given to a person who was approved and sanctioned by the clan of Quraysh.

11.7. An Unwarranted Stipulation

As the Shura dragged on with both sides putting statements in support of their candidates, Saad Ibn Abi Waqqas advised his cousin Abdul Rahman to close the matter.

> *Saad Ibn Abi Waqqas said to his cousin Abdul Rahman: "Finish it before people fall into dissension."*.

- *(The History of al-Tabari, Vol.14, p.152)*

Abdul Rahman now has the responsibility of choosing between Ali and Uthman for the position of the third Caliphate. Abdul Rahman turns towards Ali and offers him the Caliphate on three conditions.

> *"Will you pledge to God and covenant Him that you will follow the Book of God the teachings of the Messenger and the precepts of the two caliphs (Abu Bakr and Omar) after him?"*
> *Ali replied: "I shall follow the Book of God the teachings of the Prophet and I shall follow my best knowledge and endeavour to the maximum of my ability."*

- *Ibn Al-Atheer in his Al-Kamil Part 3 pp. 32-35*
- *Al-Tabari Vol. 1 pp. 63-65*

Abdul Rahman offers the Caliphate to Ali with and unjustifiable addition. Abdul Rahman had put a clause out of the blue, that the third Caliph has to follow the precepts of the first two Caliphs, i.e. to become the third Caliph Ali had to agree to follow the traditions of Caliph Abu Bakr and Caliph Umar, alongside the book of Allah and the Sunnah of the Prophet.

This was something which was unexpected and something that the camp of Ali had not anticipated. The cunning political move of Abdul Rahman ibn Auf had taken everybody by surprise.

11.7.1. Elevating the Traditions of the First Two Caliphs

Abdul Rahman had suddenly elevated the traditions and the precepts of the first two Caliphs and had put them at the same level as the Sunnah of the Prophet and the book of Allah, which was not only a grave error but indeed a heresy. The book of Allah and the Sunnah of the Prophet are flawless and immune from error, whereas the precepts and the traditions of the first two Caliphs are not immune from error. The words and the deeds of the first two Caliphs cannot be equated with the book of Allah or the Sunnah of the Prophet, as it would be tantamount to a clear innovation in the religion of Allah.

Abdul Rahman was asking Ali to follow the traditions and the precepts of Caliph Abu Bakr and Caliph Umar, in order for Ali to become the third Caliph. But neither Caliph Abu Bakr nor Caliph Umar were appointed by the Prophet to lead the Muslim Ummah. Their traditions could not become a standard for the subsequent Caliphs. The Caliphate of Abu Bakr came through the meeting of Saqifah, and the Caliphate of Umar came through appointment by Caliph Abu Bakr, hence, neither one of them were appointed by the Prophet of Allah.

The Caliphate which has come through Shura or by appointment of the previous Caliph does not make the Caliph more sacred, more knowledgeable, or more worthy in the eyes of the Prophet or Allah, and nor does it increase his closeness with the Prophet or Allah. By simply acquiring the political position of the Caliphate, the words and the actions of a Caliph does not become mandatory on Muslims or the subsequent Caliphs.

At best, the words, and the deeds of the first two Caliphs can be seen in the light of them being a mujtahid (an Islamic scholar). Their words and deeds cannot be classed as sacred law that had to be followed by the later Caliphs. Their traditions cannot become obligatory and cannot be put at par with the book of Allah or the Sunnah of the Prophet, but that is exactly what Abdul Rahman did to side-line Ali.

11.7.2. Their Traditions were Not in Line in the First Place

The absurdness of Abdul Rahman's innovation falls flat on its face when one actually looks at the traditions and the precepts of Caliph Abu Bakr and Caliph Umar during their respective Caliphates. Since in many cases the traditions of Caliph Abu Bakr differed vastly from the traditions and the ways of Caliph Umar. So, it was in fact impossible to follow the precepts of both the previous Caliphs simultaneously, as they were not in line with each other in the first place.

For instance, the method of distribution of public funds during the Caliphate of Abu Bakr was different from the era of Caliph Umar. Caliph Abu Bakr had followed the method of the Prophet and he distributed the funds equally among all the companions. However, Caliph Umar had classed companions into categories, the companions who belonged to the preferred categories would get more money than others.

This created a great imbalance in the wealth of many companions, and by the end of Caliph Umar's rule which lasted for almost ten years a whole new wealthy class of companions was created, which did not exist at the time of the Prophet or the time of Caliph Abu Bakr.

The illogical and the meaningless condition imposed by Abdul Rahman for the third Caliphate was practically impossible to be followed, even if one was willing to accept it, since the traditions of the first two Caliphs were not always in line with each other to begin with. That is why Ali immediately rejected this senseless and ludicrous innovation of Abdul Rahman and said that he would follow his own knowledge and judgment rather than the precepts of the previous two Caliphs.

11.7.3. The Authority of Ali's Knowledge

Although the first two Caliphs had not recognized the political authority of Ali, but they had both accepted the authority of Ali's knowledge in Islamic jurisprudence, especially on issues which they were unable to resolve on their own. They would often seek Ali's advice on such matters and as a result both of them had accepted the supremacy of Ali's knowledge and wisdom. As mentioned previously both Caliph Abu Bakr and Caliph Umar had said:

> *Abu Bakr had said: "May Allah never put me in a situation where I cannot have access to Abul Hasan (i.e., 'Ali) to solve a problem."*
>
> *Sa'id al-Musayyib said: "Umar Ibn al-Khattab used to beg God to preserve him from a perplexing case which the father of al-Hasan (Ali) was not present to decide."*
>
> *Umar also said: "If there was not 'Ali, Umar would have perished (spiritually)"*
> - *Fadha'il al-Sahaba, by Ahmad Ibn Hanbal, v2, p647, Tradition #1100*
> - *al-Isti'ab, by Ibn Abd al-Barr, v3, p39*
> - *Manaqib, by al-Khawarizmi, p48*
> - *al-Tabaqat, by Ibn Sa'd, v2, p338*
> - *al-Riyadh al-Nadhirah, by Muhibbuddin al-Tabari, v2, p194*
> - *Tarikh al-Khulafaa, by Jalaluddin al-Suyuti, p171*

When Ali's knowledge and authority in Islamic law had already been recognized by the first two Caliphs, then on what grounds could Ali be forced to follow their traditions and judgements. The condition imposed by Abdul Rahman becomes even more irrelevant, because the knowledge and the authority of Ali in Islamic jurisprudence was superior to his predecessors, hence it made no sense and served no purpose to follow in the footsteps of Caliph Abu Bakr and Caliph Umar.

11.7.4. A Self Contradiction

In fact, the condition imposed by Abdul Rahman contradicts the precepts and the traditions of the first two Caliphs, since they themselves had never imposed such a condition. For instance, Caliph Abu Bakr had nominated Caliph Umar as the second Caliph, but he never imposed his traditions on him, he never asked Caliph Umar to follow in his footsteps. Similarly, Caliph Umar appointed a Shura which was no doubt pro-Uthman, but even he did not stipulate that the following Caliph has to follow in his footsteps or the footsteps of his predecessor.

The condition imposed by Abdul Rahman was self-contradictory, and clearly goes against the traditions of the first two Caliphs themselves, as they had never imposed such a condition for the subsequent Caliphs.

Abdul Rahman was not naive, he was a prominent companion of the Prophet, he was well aware of all the contradictions and the unjustifiable nature of the condition that he had imposed, but he had good reasons for this smart political move.

11.7.5. Abdul Rahman was not Naive

The reality facing Abdul Rahman was quite tricky. He wanted to choose Uthman over Ali, without damaging his own reputation for impartiality and fairness. All the powerful Qurayshite clans were vying for Uthman to be the next Caliph, who also happened to be his brother-in-law and a fellow Umayyad. If the Caliphate goes to Uthman there is good chance that it will stay within the Umayyad clan, and could even come to Abdul Rahman himself one day, as he also had aspirations for the Caliphate, just like the other six committee members who were appointed by Caliph Umar.

In the presence of Uthman, Abdul Rahman does not have chance, as Caliph Uthman was lot older and senior, so he pulls out of the race to become the adjudicator, knowing very well that if Caliphate goes to Uthman there is a possible opening for him later on.

At the same time, for Abdul Rahman to choose Caliph Uthman over Ali was not easy. Ali was the nominee of the Prophet, and Ali had already been by-passed twice for the Caliphate. Ali's distinctions in terms of knowledge, bravery, closeness to the Prophet and service in the path of Islam were unique and remarkable. Ali stood head and shoulders above the rest of the companions including Caliph Uthman.

Abdul Rahman faced a real dilemma, he has to somehow go with the choice of the Quraysh which could also bring him to power one day, but he also needs to maintain his own credibility as a reputable companion, without appearing biased or openly siding with Caliph Uthman.

Abdul Rahman invents an alibi, he offers the Caliphate to Ali first rather than to Caliph Uthman, with a condition that he knows Ali would never agree to. As Ali rejects the offer, he turns to Caliph Uthman and offers him the same conditions, knowing very well that Caliph Uthman would immediately accept those conditions.

As Caliph Uthman accepts all three conditions and gets the Caliphate, Ali turns to Abdul Rahman and says to him:

> "This is not the first day you have collaborated against us (members of the House of the Prophet). . . By God you gave him the leadership only to return it to you later. God is able to change the situation."
> - Ibn Al-Atheer in his Al-Kamil Part 3 pp. 32-35
> - Al-Tabari Vol. 1 pp. 63-65

The words of Ali confirmed the alibi of Abdul Rahman. The veil that Abdul Rahman tried to put over his ploy was too thin. Ali immediately recognizes it and confronts Abdul Rahman with the truth. Ali tells Abdul Rahman that it is not the first time that you (i.e., the Quraysh) have collaborated against us (i.e. the Ahlulbayt), and Ali further says to Abdul Rahman that you have done this so that the Caliphate could one day come back to you.

The words of Ali sum up the stance that Quraysh had taken against the Ahlulbayt after the death of the Prophet. The Ahlulbayt were chosen by the Prophet to lead the Muslim Ummah. The Prophet had said:

> 'O people I have left in you that which if you adhere to you will never go astray: The Book of God and the members of my House."
> - Sunan Al-Tirmidhi. Vol. 3, Pg. # 543 - 544, H. # 3786 – 3788
> - Sunan Al -Tirmidhi. Vol. 6, Pg. # 335

But Quraysh did exactly the opposite of what Prophet had instructed and hoped for. They choose to side-line the Ahlulbayt every time there was an opportunity to give them the Caliphate.

Caliph Uthman became the Caliph on three conditions i.e., he would follow the book of Allah, the Sunnah of the Prophet and the precepts of the first two Caliphs. But history is a testament to the fact that after Caliph Uthman became the third Caliph, he neither followed the Book of Allah, or the Sunnah of the

Prophet, and nor did he follow the traditions of the first two Caliphs. He only followed his chief advisor Marwan ibn al-Hakam.

And once again history was also testament to the injustice that the Ahlulbayt and Ali had faced at the hands of Quraysh.

11.8. Ali's Exemplary Character

Rarely has history witnessed a man of such unique character and principles as Ali, especially in societies which are primarily driven by tribal or ethnic allegiances and loyalty.

The reason why Ali's character stood out from the rest of the companions was because the Prophet of Allah had shielded Ali since he was a child from the pre-Islamic traditions which had dominated the Arabian society. The upbringing of the Prophet was evident from every step that Ali had taken after the death of the Prophet.

The only thing that stood between Ali and the third Caliphate was a promise that Ali would follow the traditions of the first two Caliphs. Ali was offered the Caliphate first, Ali could have easily accepted all the three conditions and become the third Caliph, just like Caliph Uthman. But Ali was the nominee of the Prophet, his refusal to accept an unjust condition reflected the training and the discipline of Prophet's upbringing.

No temptation of any magnitude could entice or lure Ali into accepting something which he believed was fundamentally against the Sunnah of the Prophet.

Unlike the Quraysh, acquiring Caliphate by any means was neither the aim nor the goal of the successor of the Prophet. If Ali was simply after the Caliphate in a political sense, or if Ali simply wanted to take the Caliphate by hook or crook, then history had presented Ali with many opportunities which he could have easily availed.

For instance, the first opportunity came soon after Abu Bakr became the first Caliph. Abu Sufyan who had been the biggest enemy of the Prophet and the head of the Umayyad clan of Quraysh, had offered to fill the streets of Madinah with cavalrymen, in support of Ali's right for the Caliphate against Caliph Abu Bakr. The lucrative offer of Abu Sufyan was not born out of love for the nominee the Prophet. On the contrary, it was born out of jealousy towards Abu Bakr, and at the same time the intention was to destroy the Islamic State altogether, through a civil war which would be initiated in the guise of supporting Ali's right.

Ali immediately rejected the poisonous offer of Abu Sufyan, just as Ali had rejected the unjustifiable condition of Abdul Rahman for the third Caliphate. Ali was not after power for the sake of it, unlike many others, where the goal was to simply get to the helm of the Islamic State by whatever means possible.

History had presented Ali with another great opportunity to ambush and destroy the Caliphate of Abu Bakr. But again, Ali chose the path which would ensure the continuation of the Islamic State, rather than selfishly pursue his own right to the Caliphate and destroy the very State that he had helped to establish under the leadership of the Prophet.

In a big set back to the administration of Caliph Abu Bakr, during the early days of his Caliphate, entire tribes had decided to leave the faith of Islam. A huge new movement of apostasy began to flare around Madinah, severely weakening the hold of Caliph Abu Bakr on the Islamic State. At the same time, false Prophets were popping up, creating further havoc for the establishment of the Islamic State. A lesser man than Ali could have easily viewed this as an ideal opportunity to settle scores and go after the Caliphate of Abu Bakr.

This is something that is commonly witnessed in politics that when you see your political rivals or opponents in trouble, you make your move to further weaken them or completely remove them from power. But Ali was not trained to play politics with the Islamic state.

Despite Ali's own right to the Caliphate, when the Islamic State faced a crisis, Ali chose to strengthen the hand of the Islamic State, by reversing his position towards the political leadership of Abu Bakr. In a move which is unrivalled in the history of Caliphate, and a move which could have only come from the pure upbringing of the Prophet.

The unselfish attitude of Ali towards power and political authority was in complete contrast to the selfish and the self-seeking approach that Quraysh had adopted towards the Caliphate. The Quraysh had used every possible opportunity to increase their influence over the Caliphate, and they had side-lined Ali on every possible occasion, as they considered him to be their main rival and political opponent for the leadership of the Muslim Ummah.

As followers of the Sunnah of the Prophet, it becomes obligatory on us to recognize and pay allegiance to the exemplary character of Ali, and distance ourselves from the unjust approach that Quraysh had taken towards the leadership of the Muslims.

If Quraysh had decided to side-line Ali and if they had refused to accept the Sunnah of the Prophet, then on the Day of Judgment they will be held accountable for their actions and deeds. We will not be asked about the decisions and the choices that Quraysh had made, but we will be held accountable for the decisions and the choices that we make in our lifetimes.

We as Muslims have no choice but to accept the exemplary character of Ali and move away from the path that history had taken against the Sunnah of the Prophet. The successor of the Prophet could only be an individual whose character had a reflection of the character of the Prophet. The allegiance to Ali is allegiance to the Sunnah of the Prophet, and accepting the status quo established by Quraysh is a clear negation of the Sunnah of the Prophet.

Despite the course that history had taken against Ali, we can today honour him, by giving allegiance to this remarkable individual who never placed his own right above the rights of the Muslim Ummah.

11.9. Ali in his Own Words

During the course of the convention Ali had made some vital statements and observations, which informed us as to what Ali actually thought about the whole process and the Shura that was setup by Caliph Umar.

Ali makes his feelings known to the members of Banu Hashim and his Uncle Abdullah Ibn Abbas:

> "If the people (the Qurayshites) are obeyed we will never reach the leadership."
> "Uncle the leadership has already been diverted away from us. . . Omar equalized Uthman with me and ordered the people to follow the majority of the six members. If the members are divided equally he told the Muslims to side with Abdul Rahman and Abdul-Rahman is a brother-in-law of Uthman. Saad is Abdul Rahman's cousin and they will not disagree with each other. If the other two are with me they will not avail me."

- Ibn Al-Atheer Al-Kamil Part 3 p. 33.

After seeing the makeup of the Shura Ali immediately predicted its outcome. Ali was under no illusions as to who was the favourite candidate to get the Caliphate. Ali was well aware of the politics that Quraysh were playing against him. He knew exactly how they had consistently worked against his right of the Caliphate.

But Ali was the custodian of Prophet's Sunnah, he could not possibly play the same sort of dirty politics that his rivals were conducting. Ali had to face the Prophet on the Day of Judgment. Ali was not prepared to lose his dignity and compromise his principles to simply acquire the political office of the Caliphate.

After all, there had to be some difference between the choice of the Prophet and the choice of the Shura.

11.9.1. Ali's Participation was Essential

Despite the makeup of the Shura Ali was also obliged to take part in its proceedings, because if Ali completely shies away from the Shura, then it would give the impression that either Ali had no right in the Caliphate, or Ali had no interest in the Caliphate. Both of these notions would have put Ali in an indefensible position in the eyes of the history.

Ali's supporters would have been gutted to see that even when Ali was given a shot at the Caliphate, he had refused to participate. And Ali's rivals would argue that when Ali was given a chance to become the Caliph, he declined it, because he never had a right in the Caliphate in the first place. Ali's rivals would use Ali's absence from the Shura as a means of denying Ali's right to the Caliphate altogether.

That is why it was critical that Ali took part in the Shura, regardless of its biased makeup.

Furthermore, Ali's participation openly exposes the hypocrisy of Quraysh against the family of the Prophet (the Ahlulbayt) and the Banu Hashim. It highlighted the fact that Quraysh had to come up with an innovation to stop Ali from getting to the Caliphate.

It showed that Quraysh had to resort to confining the Caliphate to the traditions of the first two Caliphs, in order to side-line the nominee of the Prophet. It unmasked the intentions of the Quraysh towards both Ali and the Sunnah of the Prophet, since Quraysh had to equate the traditions of the first two Caliphs with the Sunnah of the Prophet to get their man selected.

The participation of Ali publicly exhibits the struggle and the dichotomy between the two trends that had set foot among the companions of the Prophet. A trend, which believed in strict adherence to the Sunnah of the Prophet, and a trend which believed in its own judgment (al-ijtihad), especially when it came to the leadership of the Islamic State.

Unfortunately, it was the trend of al-ijtihad among the companions which denied Ali his right, and also contradicted the clear Sunnah of the Prophet.

It is our responsibility today to adhere to the trend which believed in following the Sunnah of the Prophet, and distance ourselves from the trend which used its own independent thought. There is no doubt that on the Day of Judgment we would not be judged on the actions and choices made by the first generation of Muslims, but we would be judged on the choice and the path that we adopt in the course of our lives.

The path of Ali is the path designated by the Prophet of Allah, and the path adopted by the history is the path chosen by the supporters of Quraysh. As Muslims of 21st Century we are not obliged to follow the path set by history, but we are obliged to follow the path established by the Prophet of Allah.

11.9.2. The Dignified Path Adopted by Ali and the Ahlulbayt

The following words of Ali during the convention which I had briefly mentioned in Chapter 9 give us a complete synopsis of the path that Prophet had set for the Ummah, and the course that the Ahlulbayt had adopted after the demise of the Prophet.

Ali addressed and advised the convention with these words:

> *"Praise be to God who from us has chosen the Prophet Mohammad and sent him to us as a Messenger. We are the members of the House of the Prophet the source of wisdom the security of the people of the earth and the haven to the seekers of security (against deviation)*
> *We have a right. If we are given it we will take it; if we are deprived of it we will take the back seat even if the journey will be long. Had the Messenger given us a directive we would have fulfilled his directive. Had he told us to take an action we would have fought for it until we died. No one will be faster than I in response to a righteous invitation or kindness to a kin.*
> *Listen to my word and comprehend my presentation.*
> *Your leadership after this Convention (if you fail to select the qualified leader) will be violently contended. Covenants will be breached and swords will be drawn until your unity will come to an end. Some of you will be imams of revisions some will be followers of men of ignorance."*
>
> - Ibn Al-Atheer Al-Kamil Part 3 p. 37.

The words of Ali not only confirmed the Sunnah of the Prophet, but they also showed the dignified stance that the Ahlulbayt had adopted towards the Caliphate.

Ali informed the electoral convention that the Ahlulbayt were a security against deviation, just as Prophet had stipulated that if the Muslims would follow the Ahlulbayt they would never go astray.

> *'O people I have left in you that which if you adhere to you will never go astray: The Book of God and the members of my House."*
>
> - Sunan Al-Tirmidhi. Vol. 3, Pg. # 543 - 544, H. # 3786 – 3788
> - Sunan Al -Tirmidhi. Vol. 6, Pg. # 335

Ali repeats the words of the Prophet to the electoral convention. Ali informs the convention that "We have a right" i.e. the Ahlulbayt have a right to the Caliphate. He says to the convention that if the Ahlulbayt were given the right they would take it. And If they were denied their right then they would be patient even if the journey was long. The magnanimity of the words of Ali were a proof of his distinct upbringing and his remarkable character.

Ali further clarifies to the convention that if Prophet had commanded the Ahlulbayt to take their right by force, then they would have fought for their right until they died, implying that Ahlulbayt strictly followed the Sunnah of the Prophet, unlike others.

The words of Ali not only clarify the mandate that Prophet had given to the Ahlulbayt, but it also answers the critics who insist that if it was Ali's right to become the Caliph then why did he not take his right by force? or if it was the Sunnah of the Prophet that Ali was meant to be the leader after the Prophet, then why did Ali not establish the Sunnah of the Prophet by force?

The fact was that although Prophet had given the Ahlulbayt the mandate to lead the Muslim Ummah, and he had chosen Ali to lead the Muslims after his demise, but he had not given Ali or the Ahlulbayt the mandate to take that right by force. The use of force was never part of the mandate of the Prophet. It is for this reason that Ali stayed patient, because if Ali uses force to take his right, he transgresses the Sunnah of the Prophet.

Ali was the custodian of the Sunnah of the Prophet, he could not possibly become part of the trend of al-ijtihad (independent judgment), just because his right was being trampled upon.

Ali was a man of the battlefield, Ali was the star performer of Prophet's army, Ali had subdued some of the most feared and audacious fighters of Quraysh, during the defence of the Islamic State of Madinah. Both friends and enemies a like were aware of Ali's fearsome warrior character. The first three Caliphs i.e. Caliph Abu Bakr, Caliph Umar and Caliph Uthman were not men of battlefield. History does not record any battlefield significance or success for the first three Caliphs.

If Prophet had given Ali the mandate to take his right by force, then there was little that would have stood between the sword of Ali and the Caliphate!

But at the same time if Ali takes the Caliphate by the virtue of his sword it would ensue a civil war that would eventually destroy the Islamic State itself, especially if Ali had raised his sword against Caliph Abu Bakr. That is why Prophet had never given Ali the mandate to take his right by force, as Prophet understood the politics that Quraysh might play after his death, and Ali proved his worth by following the words of the Prophet to the letter.

Also, Islam as an ideology does not believe in the use of force to enforce its message. The Prophet had never used force to convince anybody to accept him as the Prophet of Allah. Even the institution of Prophethood cannot not be enforced by the use of force. Prophet had of course invited people to the path of Allah and to his Prophethood, but Prophet had never used force to subdue anybody to accept his status as the Prophet of Allah. It was left up to the individual to accept and recognize the message of truth and to accept the authority of the Prophet.

Similarly, the mandate and the authority of Ali could not be enforced by the use of force. Such an approach completely goes against the very ethos of Islam. If the institution of Prophethood could not be imposed by the use of force, then how could the Prophet allow the authority of Ali to be enforced by the use of force. The Sunnah of the Prophet is not meant to be enforced on the point of a sword.

However, there is no reason as to why we cannot voluntarily accept the mandate and the authority of Ali, which was given to him by the Prophet of Allah, and which was rejected by the supporters of Quraysh, and in doing so we would honour the traditions and the Sunnah of the Prophet.

Ali further says to the convention that "No one will be faster than I in response to a righteous invitation or kindness to a kin", implying that if there was a genuine and a just invitation to the leadership of the Islamic State, Ali would immediately accept the offer. The Prophet of Allah had given Ali the right to the leadership of the Muslims. There was absolutely no reason as to why Ali would not accept the Caliphate, if it was given to him without any of the unfair and the unjustified conditions attached to it.

Ali was more than happy to honour the Sunnah of the Prophet and take the leadership of the Muslim Ummah, but Ali was not prepared to accept any scrupulous offers, or unfair conditions which were attached to the offer.

The final words of Ali where he says "Listen to my word and comprehend my presentation……." will be discussed in the next Chapter.

12. THE LEGACY OF SAQIFAH

Ali was the nominee of the Prophet whereas the first three Caliphs were the legacy of Saqifah. They had come to the helm of the Islamic State because of what took place in the gathering of Saqifah. Abu Bakr was chosen in Saqifah as the first Caliph and in the final moments of his life he appointed Caliph Umar to succeed him. Caliph Umar in turn formed a committee which selected Caliph Uthman as the leader of the Muslims, hence all the three Caliphs had acquired power because of the initial meeting of Saqifah.

The Caliphate of Abu Bakr had laid the foundations for the trend of al-ijtihad (independent judgment) to become the dominant opinion in the choice of the subsequent Caliphs too. As the leadership of the Islamic State went to the Umayyad clan of Quraysh in the form of Caliph Uthman, it brought an unprecedented number of innovations and changes to the institution of Caliphate itself.

The words of Ali during the electoral convention would practically resonate during and after the reign of Caliph Uthman. Ali had advised the convention with the following words:

> *Listen to my word and comprehend my presentation.*
> *Your leadership after this Convention (if you fail to select the qualified leader) will be violently contended. Covenants will be breached, and swords will be drawn until your unity will come to an end. Some of you will be imams of revisions some will be followers of men of ignorance."*
>
> - Ibn Al-Atheer Al-Kamil Part 3 p. 37.

The warning given by Ali could not be more clear or stark. Ali stipulated that if the convention made a wrong choice, swords would be drawn, covenants would be broken and the unity of the Islamic State would be shattered, and this is exactly what took place towards the end of Uthman's Caliphate. The leadership of the Islamic State was violently contested, and Caliph Uthman was murdered. Thousands of companions were killed in many wars and battles which followed the death of Caliph Uthman. Leaders of deviation and ignorance emerged, and masses of Muslims became their followers.

Despite the warnings and advise of Ali, the electoral convention brought the star of the Umayyads Uthman bin Affan to the seat of power.

12.1. The Caliphate of Uthman

We saw earlier that Caliph Uthman had won the day against Ali for the position of the third Caliphate.

When the news of Uthman's success reached Abu Sufyan who was now over ninety years old, he could not contain his elation. He asked one of the men to take him to the grave of Al-Hamzah, the uncle of the

Prophet who was martyred in the battle of Uhud. Once Abu Sufyan reached the grave of AL-Hamza, he stood at the grave and addressed him with the following words:

> "Abu Imarah (a nick name of Al-Hamzah) the matter for which we fought with each other has become a play in the hands of our youth." Then he kicked the grave with his foot.
>
> - Obd Al-Fattah Abd Al-Masqood Al-Imam Ali Part 1 p. 287.

Abu Sufyan taunted Al-Hamza in his grave by stating that what they had fought over has now become a toy in the hands of the Umayyads, implying that Umayyads had won the war against Banu Hashim for the leadership of the Arabs, since the Caliphate was now in the hands of the Umayyads. The words of Abu Sufyan in fact reflected the mentality of the Umayyads in general. Abu Sufyan and the majority of the Umayyad's had never really considered the Prophet as simply the Prophet of Allah. They had always thought of him as the head of the Banu Hashim clan who was trying to use Islam as a means of controlling the Arabs and their way of life.

Abu Sufyan was the biggest enemy of the Prophet and was the most prominent Umayyad leader of his time. He had fought the Prophet and the Muslims at every step of the way. He only reluctantly accepted Islam at the conquest of Makkah. It is reported that when he saw the Muslim army approaching Makkah his heart sank, and he unwillingly accepted Islam as he had no other option left.

On the other hand, Al-Hamza, the uncle of the Prophet was one of the bravest Muslim warriors who was killed in the battle of Uhud. The Prophet of Allah was very close to his uncle as his own father had died when he was very young.

It is narrated by Ibn Masud:

> "Prophet Muhammad cried over Hamza so much so that it was unprecedented ... and he was nearly unconscious ..."
>
> - (Dhakha'ir al-Uqba, p.181)

After killing Al-Hamza in the battle of Uhud, Hind bin Utbah who was the wife of Abu Sufyan ripped open the liver of Al-Hamza and chewed it, finding it unpleasant she spat it out. However, she carried on mutilating the body of Al-Hamza and made anklets, necklaces, and pendants from his body, and brought them to Makkah as a show of victory over the Muslims and the Banu Hashim.

Halabi writes in his Sira

> "When Prophet Muhammad found Hamza martyred he cried and when he realized that he had been mutilated he cried out loud".
>
> - Halabi Sira (vol. 2, p. 247)

Prophet had cried and mourned the death of his Uncle Al-Hamza whereas Abu Sufyan went and kicked his grave.

As a result of what took place in the meeting of Saqifah where the nominee of the Prophet was side-lined, eventually the clan which had been the staunchest enemy of the Prophet and the Muslims had acquired the leadership of the Islamic State.

The above words of Abu Sufyan where he said that the leadership of the Muslims had become a toy (play) in the hands of the Umayyads would in fact set the scene for the Caliphate of Uthman.

Caliph Uthman had two aspects to his personality. On one hand he was one of the earliest companions who had accepted Islam even before Caliph Umar. But on the other hand, his love for his clan had no bounds, despite their dark past and despite their enmity towards the Prophet and the faith of Islam.

It wasn't long before the assertions of Abu Sufyan became a reality under Caliph Uthman's rule. The Umayyad clan exploited and abused the third Caliphate as far as they possibly could, and Caliph Uthman allowed it to happen under his leadership without taking any measures or steps to stop the Umayyads. In fact, he played right into their hands and simply became a tool of the Umayyads.

In a matter of few years under the Caliphate of Uthman the Umayyads had put their hands on the two key sources of power within the Islamic State i.e.

- The authority of the key provinces.
- And their Treasuries.

12.2. The Authority of the Key Provinces

The main power and wealth of the Islamic state was concentrated in the three provinces i.e., Syria, Iraq, and Egypt. During the first few years of the reign of Caliph Uthman these vast provinces became Umayyad Kingdoms.

12.2.1. Syria

Caliph Umar had appointed Muawiyah as the governor of Damascus during his reign and later he added Jordan to his authority too. Muawiyah was the son of Abu Sufyan and Hind bin Utbah, who were the biggest enemies of the Prophet and Muslims as mentioned earlier. Unfortunately, Muawiyah was no different from his Umayyad parents either in his character or in his ways, nevertheless Caliph Umar appointed him as the governor of Syria.

Although, the influence of Muawiyah had started to grow during the Caliphate of Umar, but it remained relatively limited, and Muawiyah was not able to challenge the central authority of the Islamic State.

However, instead of properly supervising or checking the influence of Muawiyah, Caliph Uthman added Palestine, Homs and Qinnisrine to his authority too (Ibn Al-Atheer in Al-Kamil, Part 3 p. 57). Thus, just within two years of Caliph Uthman's reign, Muawiyah became the governor of what can be termed today as greater Syria. The area under the authority of Muawiyah more than doubled during the Caliphate of Uthman. Muawiyah's influence and authority in Syria became almost absolute and free of any supervision from the central government.

Within a space of few years Syria almost became an autonomous state within the Islamic State itself, and Muawiyah became a political powerhouse of the Muslim world. Muawiyah's authority and influence had grown so much that he was able to muster an army of around one hundred thousand (100,000) men into the battlefield.

12.2.2. Egypt

Amr Ibn Al-Auss was the governor of Egypt when Caliph Umar died. During the first two years of his reign Caliph Uthman dismissed Amr Ibn Al-Auss and replaced him with his foster brother Abu Sarh. Readers will remember from the previous Chapter that Abu Sarh had supported the nomination of Caliph

Uthman against Ali during the electoral convention. He had challenged Ammar bin Yasir who was supporting the camp of Ali.

Abu Sarh had said to Abdul Rahman:

> "If you want to avoid the Qurayshites division select Uthman."
> - (The History of al-Tabari, Vol.14, p.152)

Caliph Uthman rewarded the loyalty and support of his foster brother with the governorship of Egypt. As discussed previously Abu Sarh was a known enemy of the Prophet, who had embraced Islam and then apostatized. He used to ridicule and discredit the Holy Quran and lie upon the Prophet.

At the conquest of Makkah, Prophet had ordered Abu Sarh to be killed even if he was found hiding under the curtain of Kaaba. It was Caliph Uthman who had saved the life of his foster brother by hiding him in his house and pleading for his life. Even then, the Prophet was hoping that somebody from his companions would kill him. As nobody stood up and killed Abu Sarh Prophet reluctantly forgave him.

A person who used to ridicule the holy Quran, lie upon the Prophet, and was only reluctantly forgiven by the Prophet was made the governor of one of the Key provinces within the Islamic State, simply because he was the foster brother of the Caliph, and because he had supported the Caliph during the electoral process.

There were scores of good companions and other leading Muslim figures who could have been chosen for this position, but unfortunately Caliph Uthman chooses to ignore them all.

12.2.3. Iraq (Kufa)

During that era Iraq had two important cities Kufa and Basra.

On Caliph Umar's recommendation Caliph Uthman had appointed Saad Ibn Abi Waqqas as the governor of Kufa. However, within one year of his rule Caliph Uthman replaced him with Waleed Ibn Uqba who was Caliph Uthman's cousin and half-brother. According to the testimony of Holy Quran Waleed was a hypocrite and a transgressor.

Waleed embraced Islam after the Hudaybiyya Pact. The Prophet of Allah had sent him to the tribe of Banu Al-Mustaliq to collect Zakat. Expecting his arrival Banu Al-Mustaliq rode their horses to receive him. On seeing Banu Al-Mustaliq approaching him he got frightened. He went back to the Prophet without meeting them and said that Banu Al-Mustaliq wanted to kill him. Relying upon what Waleed had said Muslims considered a punitive action against Banu Al-Mustaliq. However, Banu Al-Mustaliq came to Prophet and informed him that their intention was to receive and honour Waleed rather than to kill him.

Allah revealed the following verse regarding the incident of Waleed and Banu Al-Mustaliq where Waleed was described as a wicked and an evildoer, and Muslims were warned not to rely on the testimony of such people.

The Holy Quran stated:

> "O you who believe, if a wicked (evildoer) person brings any news to you, you shall first investigate, lest you commit injustice towards some people, out of ignorance, then become sorry and remorseful for what you have done"

- Quran 46:9

The following Tafseers of Quran confirms the above incident.

- Tafsir Tabari, v26, p159
- Tafsir al-Thalabi, v9, p77
- Tafsir al-Dur al-Manthur, v6, p88
- Tafsir al-Baghawi, v4, p212
- Tafsir al-Qurtubi, v16, p311

The most unfortunate thing here is that Caliph Uthman had ordered the compilation of the Holy Quran during his reign, and he was well-aware of the above verse and its relation to Waleed. In fact, one of the promises that Caliph Uthman had made to acquire the Caliphate was to follow the Book of Allah. But unfortunately, despite Waleed's past and despite the testimony of the Holy Quran, Caliph Uthman still chose his half-brother as the governor of Kufa which was one of the key cities in the Islamic State at the time.

It is reported that when Waleed came to replace Saad Ibn Abi Waqqas, Saad asked Waleed:

> "Have you become wise, or have we become fools?"
> Waleed replied: "Abu Is-Haq (nick name of Saad) neither of this is the case. It is the royal authority which some people take as lunch and then others take it as supper."
> Saad replied: "You (Umayyad) evidently have made the caliphate a kingdom."

- Ibn Al-Atheer in Al-Kamil Part 3. p. 40.

Abdullah Ibn Masud also made a similar comment to Waleed:

> "I do not know whether you have become good or people have became bad."

- Ibn Al-Atheer in Al-Kamil Part 3. p. 40.

Waleed did not change his ways after becoming the governor either, he kept his pre-Islamic mentality and his old way of life. He remained the governor of Kufa for five years and he used to openly consume alcohol and take intoxicants. The tipping point came when Waleed was so intoxicated that he led the morning prayer and recited four rakats instead of two, and asked the congregation if he should continue. Waleed's actions became the talk of the town and enraged many Muslims. Finally, Waleed was given the prescribed punishment and dismissed from his position.

It was expected that Caliph Uthman would replace Waleed with a righteous Muslim, but instead Caliph Uthman replaced him with another Umayyad by the name of Saeed Ibn Al-Auss. Although Saeed was not as bad as Waleed, but he did not have the qualifications, or the inspiring personality needed for being the governor of a bustling city like Kufa. He was unable to rectify the mess left by Waleed and the events which later unfolded in Kufa took a turn for the worse under the leadership of Saeed.

12.2.4. Iraq (Basra)

When Caliph Umar died Abu Musa Al-Ashari was the governor of Basra, he remained in this position for the first few years of Caliph Uthman's rule. A delegation from Basra came to Caliph Uthman complaining about Abu Musa's misuse of public funds. Abu Musa Al-Ashari was no saint, during the reign of Caliph Umar he was also accused of taking money from the public exchequer. At that time Caliph Umar took the surplus money from Abu Musa and put it back into the Islamic treasury. However, Caliph Umar did not dismiss him and kept him as the governor of Basra due to his loyalty and support for his Caliphate.

When the delegation from Basra made the complaint about Abu Musa, it was expected that Caliph Uthman would replace Abu Musa Al-Ashari with a leading companion, considering the importance of Basra to the Islamic State at the time. Instead, Abu Musa Al-Ashari was replaced with another Umayyad youth by the name of Abdullah ibn Amir.

Thus within a few years of Caliph Uthman's rule the three key provinces of the Islamic State i.e., Syria, Egypt and Iraq became Umayyad kingdoms. Most of these rulers were either enemies of the Prophet like Abu Sarh in Egypt, or they had been condemned by the Holy Quran like Waleed Ibn Uqba in Kufa.

To add to this Caliph Uthman virtually had no supervision or checks on these governors, and they were free to act as they pleased. For instance, Muawiyah had carved out his own state in Syria which was devoid of any authority from the central government, since supervision from the Caliph's office was almost non-existent.

Islam is not opposed to the idea of appointing one's relatives to positions of authority, as long as they have the right credentials and as long as they deserve those positions. Unfortunately, in case of Caliph Uthman many righteous and deserving companions were overlooked, and he chose his relatives over them even though his relatives were far from being righteous and did not deserve those positions.

It is for this reason that the unfortunate words of nepotism and cronyism are associated with the Caliphate of Uthman.

12.3. Loose Monetary Policy

Just as Caliph Uthman had preferred his relatives over others when it came to appointing the governors for the key provinces in the Islamic State, his monetary policy towards his relatives was extremely loose and controversial too. Caliph Uthman showered his Umayyad relatives with huge sums of money and gifts from the Islamic treasury, even though they were least adherent to the path of Islam, and despite the fact that they had not done anything to deserve such reward.

12.3.1. Al-Hakam Ibn Al-Auss

Al-Hakam Ibn Al-Auss was the uncle of Caliph Uthman and was one of the worst enemies of the Prophet. Like the majority of the Umayyads he only became a Muslim after the conquest of Makkah i.e., after Islam had become the dominant force in the Arabian Peninsula. For many Qurayshites it now made more sense to become part of the Muslim ranks rather than openly oppose the Islamic movement.

Despite accepting Islam Al-Hakam kept harassing the Messenger of Allah. He used to imitate and ridicule the Prophet in the way he walked. Once Prophet caught him while he was being imitated and said:

> "This way you will be"

al-Hakam started shaking immediately and continued that way until he died.

It is also reported that al-Hakam used to hide and listen to Prophet's conversations as he spoke to the companions, and then he used to circulate what he had heard. This used to really infuriate the Prophet. One day while sitting with some of his companions the Messenger of Allah said:

> *"A cursed man will enter the room."* Shortly thereafter, Al-Hakam entered the room, he was the cursed man.
>
> - *(Yusuf Ibn Abd Al-Barr, Al-Istiab, part one, pages 359-360)*

Once Prophet of Allah was sitting in his room, he saw someone peeping through a slit in the door. The Prophet of Allah immediately came out of his room and saw al-Hakam standing at the door. The Prophet of Allah said:

> *"Should anyone blame me for punishing this cursed man?"*
>
> - Al-Istiyaab Page 359 and 360

For his constant harassment and intimidation, the Prophet finally exiled him and his family to Taif and forbade him from dwelling in Medina.

In a clear contradiction to the Sunnah of the Prophet, Caliph Uthman not only brought al-Hakam back to Madinah, but he also gave him three hundred thousand (300,000) Dirhams from the Islamic treasury, simply because he was his uncle (Al-Balathori, Ansab Al-Ashraf, Part 4 p. 28).

The readers may remember that Caliph Uthman had acquired the Caliphate on the promise that he would uphold the Sunnah of the Prophet. However, his actions did not match his words, and unfortunately, he broke his earlier covenant that he had made to the six member Shura setup by Caliph Umar.

12.3.2. Marwan bin al-Hakam

Marwan bin al-Hakam was the son of Al-Hakam Ibn Al-Auss and Caliph Uthman's first cousin. He was also married to Uthman's daughter Um Aban, so he was Uthman's son in law as well. Caliph Uthman appointed Marwan to be his right-hand man and his closest advisor during his Caliphate.

In fact, when one reads Islamic history, it becomes evident that Marwan was the most powerful man in Caliph Uthman's cabinet. Caliph Uthman allowed Marwan to make all the key decisions in his government and followed his advice as if it was the word of Allah. It would not be an exaggeration to state that Marwan was the actual decision maker and Caliph Uthman was simply a figurehead. Marwan would take and distribute money from the Islamic treasury as and when he pleased, and Caliph Uthman allowed him to do this.

When the Muslim army conducted their second expedition to North Africa, they sent one fifth of the spoils of war back to Madinah. Marwan decided to purchase these spoils of war for five hundred thousand Dirhams (500,000). However, when the time came to pay the money Marwan did not pay a single dirham into the Islamic treasury, despite this fact Caliph Uthman allowed him to keep the spoils of war. Essentially, the spoils of war which were meant for the Islamic treasury ended up in Marwan's pocket (Ibn Al-Atheer in Al-Kamil Part 3 p. 49).

The readers would recall from Chapter 9 that the issue of Fadak had caused a huge rift between the Ahlulbayt and Caliph Abu Bakr. Fadak was a well-developed and productive farmland owned by Prophet of Allah. According to lady Fatima, the daughter of the Prophet, her father had gifted her Fadak four years before his death. However, Caliph Abu Bakr overruled the testimony of Lady Fatima on the grounds that

Prophets do not leave behind inheritance. This caused a huge discord between Caliph Abu Bakr and Lady Fatima and she never spoke to him again, and she was buried in the night without allowing him to even attend her funeral.

Caliph Abu Bakr had confiscated Fadak from Lady Fatima and made it a state property, so the land of Fadak was owned by the Islamic State. However, to the shock and dismay of the Ahlulbayt Caliph Uthman gave the land of Fadak to Marwan, his chief advisor and son-in-law which indeed was most unfortunate and regrettable. Confiscating something from the Ahlulbayt and making it a state property was bad enough, but then to give it to one of your Umayyad cousins was completely unwarranted (Sunan Abu Dawood Part 2 p. 127, Ma'arif of ibn Qutayba, p. 84, Tarikh Abul Fida, vol. 1, p. 168).

The Umayyads had opposed the Islamic movement for almost two decades. To give something which Ahlulbayt claimed was theirs to a clan which had been the biggest enemy of the Muslims cannot be called anything other than a travesty.

Unfortunately, these decisions reflected the reality of corruption and nepotism which had plagued the administration of Caliph Uthman.

Caliph Uthman had accepted the third Caliphate on three conditions i.e., he will follow the Book of Allah, the Sunnah of the Prophet and the Sunnah of Caliph Abu Bakr and Caliph Umar. Both Caliph Abu Bakr and Caliph Umar had kept Fadak as the state property, but Caliph Uthman gave it to his cousin and son-in-law, Marwan bin al-Hakam, clearly going against the Sunnah of both Caliph Abu Bakr and Caliph Umar, and hence breaking the pledge that he took under oath to become the third Caliph.

Also, if we accept that the hadith narrated by Caliph Abu Bakr is correct where the Prophet had stated:

> *"We do not leave inheritance, what we leave behind is charity."*
> - *(Sahih al-Muslim, jitab al-Jihad Was Siyar, no 49)*

Then in that case Caliph Uthman had also gone against the Sunnah of the Prophet, since he gave Prophet's inheritance to his cousin Marwan bin al-Hakam, rather than leaving it as charity for all the Muslims.

Those Muslims who argue that Caliph Abu Bakr was correct in taking the land of Fadak away from Lady Fatima, surely, must accept that Caliph Uthman was then wrong in gifting it to his cousin and son-in-law, because they both can't be right!

12.3.3. Al-Harith Ibn Al-Hakam

Al-Harith was the younger brother of Marwan. He was married to Uthman's second daughter, so he was also Caliph Uthman's cousin and son in 3law.

Caliph Uthman gave al-Harith three hundred thousand (300,000) Dirhams from the Islamic treasury for no reason other than the fact that he was his cousin and son in law.

Just as he had given the land of Fadak to Marwan, he gave a similar estate in Madinah known as the Mahzur valley to al-Harith.

Also, Caliph Uthman had appointed Al-Harith as a Zakat collector for Qudah. When he collected the Zakat and brought it to the Caliph, instead of putting the money into the Islamic treasury, Caliph Uthman allowed al-Harith to keep all the Zakat money (Dr. Taha Hussein in his Al-Fitnatul-Kubra Part 2 p. 193).

12.3.4. Abdullah bin Khalid

Abdullah bin Khalid was another son-in-law of Caliph Uthman. Readers would remember from the previous section that Caliph Uthman had appointed Abdullah bin Amir as the governor of Basra, replacing Abu Musa Al-Ashari who was accused of misusing the public funds. When Caliph Uthman gave his daughter to Abdullah bin Khalid, he ordered Abdullah bin Amir the governor of Basra to give Khalid six hundred thousand (600,0000) dirhams from the Islamic treasury.

On another occasion Khalid visited the Caliph with a delegation, Caliph Uthman ordered his treasurer to pay three hundred thousand (300,000) dirhams to Khalid and one hundred thousand (100,000) dirhams to each member of the delegation.

The treasurer at the time was Abdullah Ibn Arqam who refused to comply with the orders of Caliph Uthman and refused to pay such huge amounts to Khalid and his delegation. When Caliph Uthman heard that Abdullah Ibn Arqam was refusing to pay the money, he challenged Abdullah Ibn Arqam by saying:

> *"Who are you to interfere with my order? You are my treasurer".*
> - Taha Hussein Al-Fitnat Al-Kubra Part 1 p. 193.

Abdullah Ibn Arqam responded by saying:

> *"I did not believe that I was your treasurer. Your treasurer is one of your servants. I am the treasurer of the Muslims."*
> - Taha Hussein Al-Fitnat Al-Kubra Part 1 p. 193.

Abdullah Ibn Arqam then came with the keys of the treasury, resigned from his post, and hung the keys on the pulpit of the Prophet in the mosque of Madinah.

12.3.5. Waleed Ibn Uqba

The governors of various provinces in the Islamic State followed the lead of Caliph Uthman in misusing public funds. A similar situation arose with Waleed who was appointed by Caliph Uthman as the governor of Kufa.

Waleed took a loan from the Islamic treasury of Kufa while he was the governor. At the time the treasurer in Kufa was Abdullah Ibn Masud. When the loan matured Abdullah Ibn Masud demanded Waleed to pay back the loan. However, rather than paying back the loan, Waleed wrote to Caliph Uthman complaining about Abdullah Ibn Masud.

Instead of supporting Abdullah Ibn Masud, Caliph Uthman sided with Waleed and asked Abdullah Ibn Masud to leave Waleed alone. Caliph Uthman also wrote to Abdullah Ibn Masud telling him that he was the treasurer of the Caliph i.e., he was a treasurer of Caliph Uthman. On receiving the letter Abdullah Ibn Masud angrily resigned from his post as the treasurer (Al-Balathori, in Ansab Al-Ashraf, Part 4, p. 31).

It is difficult to ascertain that a person who was one of the earliest companions, and who had ordered the compilation of the Holy Quran, and who had vowed to uphold the Book of Allah and the Sunnah of the Prophet, would take part in such misuse of the Islamic treasury and public funds.

Unfortunately, the love of Caliph Uthman for his clan had blinded him to the earlier pledge that he had made to uphold the Book of Allah and the Sunnah of the Prophet.

The rise of the Umayyad clan into the corridors of power was a direct consequence of what had taken place in the meeting of Saqifah, where the rightful successor of the Prophet was side lined in favour of a candidate who would be acceptable to the wider Quraysh (i.e., Caliph Abu Bakr).

The corruption and nepotism which had seeped into the institution of Caliphate was in fact the tragic legacy of Saqifah.

12.3.6. Muawiyah

The Muslims of Kufa were lucky to have a treasurer like Abdullah Ibn Masud, who had the courage to stand up to Waleed, the governor of the city. The Muslims of Syria were not so fortunate. Muawiyah had an absolute authority in Syria with no limits to his power. History is a testament to the fact that Muawiyah lived like a king, and he handled the public treasury of Syria as if it was his personal wealth. There were no checks or supervision on Muawiyah from the central government in Madinah either.

Muawiyah used the Islamic treasury of Syria for purchasing loyalty and support from men of influence, and from various tribal chiefs in Syria who otherwise would not have supported him. Muawiyah was preparing himself to succeed Caliph Uthman and he had sufficient time to do so. As a matter of fact, Muawiyah had started his preparations during the days of Caliph Umar.

Caliph Umar himself had witnessed the extravagance and the lavish way of life that Muawiyah was leading when he visited the Syrian front during his own reign. Caliph Umar was angered by Muawiyah's luxurious lifestyle, but Muawiyah managed to justify his actions using his proximity with the Roman Empire as an excuse for his extravagance.

Although Caliph Umar was generally very strict with his governors, but surprisingly he gave Muawiyah a lot of leeway, and allowed him to continue his extravagant and lavish way of life. Caliph Umar said about Muawiyah:

> *"By no means do I enjoin him nor prohibit him"*
> - *(Mukhtasar Tarikh Dimashq, vol. XXV, p.18)*

Caliph Umar neither endorsed nor stopped Muawiyah's grandeur which essentially gave Muawiyah a free hand in Syria. As a result, Muawiyah did whatever he pleased without any challenge or questions from the Caliphs in Madinah.

When Caliph Uthman took office, he more than doubled the area under the jurisdiction of Muawiyah, and during his reign there was absolutely no supervision of Muawiyah from the central government in Madinah. It would not be an exaggeration to state that Muawiyah became the absolute ruler of Syria with nobody to challenge his authority or criticize his misuse of public funds.

Muawiyah in fact became the king (Caesar) of Syria.

12.3.7. Abu Sufyan

The readers would recall that Abu Sufyan was the father of Muawiyah and was the worst enemy of the Prophet. Abu Sufyan had fought the Prophet and the Muslims at every step of the way for almost two decades. Abu Sufyan had launched countless raids and expeditions against the Muslims and was the biggest tormentor of the Prophet. He had fought the Muslims in almost every single battle including the battle of Badr, Uhad and Moat. His wife Hind bin Utbah had chewed the lever of Prophet's beloved uncle al-Hamza.

Despite such an ugly past and despite the fact that he had been the worst enemy of the Prophet, Caliph Uthman gave Abu Sufyan two hundred thousand (200,000) dirhams from the Islamic treasury. It was incredible that even an individual like Abu Sufyan got funds from the Islamic treasury, simply because he belonged to the Umayyad clan (Dr. Taha Hussain, Al-Fitnah Al-Kubra, Ali wa Banuh, Pg. 94).

Unfortunately, such was the level nepotism and corruption during the reign of Caliph Uthman.

12.3.8. When Challenged on Corruption and Nepotism

As the corruption and nepotism reached new heights, some of the prominent companions including Ali approached Caliph Uthman and challenged him on his loose monetary policy towards his Umayyad relatives. History has preserved the response that Caliph Uthman gave to these companions.

Caliph Uthman said:

> *"Abu Bakr and Umar sought reward in the hereafter by withholding from their kin, and I seek reward by giving to my kin'*
>
> - *(Ansab al-Ashraf V.28)*

The response of Caliph Uthman was simply astonishing. He stated that he gave money to his relatives in order to seek Allah's reward in hereafter. If this was truly the understanding of Caliph Uthman about the religion of Islam, then surely the choice made by the six-member Shura setup by Caliph Umar was indeed questionable. A person who has such a view of the Islamic treasury which belongs to all the Muslims surely does not deserve to be a Caliph.

There is no doubt that Islam advocates love and kindness to one's relatives and Islam encourages every Muslim to help their relatives, especially if they are in need. Helping relatives from one's personal money and wealth is indeed rewarded in hereafter. But this cannot be done at the expense of public funds which belong to the entire Muslim Ummah. One cannot hope to seek Allah's reward by opening the doors of the Islamic treasury to their family members and kin. This is completely absurd and has no justification from the Book of Allah or the Sunnah of the Prophet.

It was for this reason that Prophet had not left the choice of his successor to the Ummah, since the Ummah could easily make a wrong choice and appoint someone who lacked the true spirit and understanding of Islam.

But the event of Saqifah had overruled the choice of the Prophet and Muslims had to endure the legacy left by the debacle of Saqifah.

12.4. The Consequences

As a result of Caliph Uthman's attitude towards the Islamic treasury, the majority of the officials appointed by him also misused public funds in proportion to the level of authority that they enjoyed. The Islamic Caliphate indeed became an Umayyad dynasty under his reign.

This unscrupulous policy had many repercussions for the Muslim Ummah.

12.4.1. The Wealthy Class

The lucky individuals who had received huge sums of money from the Islamic treasury and the government officials who had misused public funds invested their surplus wealth into real estate and businesses, yielding them enormous profits and making them extremely rich. On top of this Caliph Uthman gave many of his relatives, friends, and supporters vast pieces of public land in and around Hijaz, turning the Islamic State established by the Prophet into an Umayyad State.

Apart from his relatives, the generosity of Caliph Uthman was also extended to certain individuals as a reward for their loyalty or as an appeasement to his potential opponents. Caliph Uthman gave Zaid Ibn Thabit one hundred thousand (100,000) dirhams. He gave Al-Zubeir six hundred thousand (600,000) dirhams, and he gifted Talhah Ibn Ubaydullah two hundred thousand (200,000) dirhams from the Islamic treasury (Taha Hussein Al-Fitnat Al-Kubra Part 1 p. 77).

Al-Zubeir and Talhah were members of the electoral convention which had brought Caliph Uthman to power. Neither of these two companions needed any financial assistance. Both were wealthy individuals with big holdings and big businesses. They already had a great deal of real estate and liquid funds at their disposal but were given thousands of dirhams additionally at the expense of the public treasury.

The readers would recall that Caliph Umar had changed the method of distribution of public funds during his reign. In the time of the Prophet and during the rule of Caliph Abu Bakr all the companions would get an equal amount of money from the Islamic treasury. However, Caliph Umar had classed companions into categories, the companions who belonged to the preferred categories would get more money than others. This method of distribution of public funds continued under the leadership of Caliph Uthman too.

This new policy established by Caliph Umar eventually resulted in the creation of a group of rich and wealthy companions which did not exist at the time of the death of the Prophet.

Thus, there were rich and prosperous Umayyads who had massed huge amounts of wealth because of Caliph Uthman's rule, and then there were also the preferred companions who had become rich and successful because of Caliph Umar's method of distributing the funds, which continued during the days of Caliph Uthman too. Hence, an entirely new wealthy class of Muslims was created which never existed during the time of the Prophet.

Furthermore, Caliph Uthman allowed the companions to live outside Medina, ending the ban which was imposed by Caliph Umar. Many of the prosperous Umayyads and rich companions found new ways and avenues of multiplying their fortunes. They purchased real estate, orchards and lands in Iraq, Yemen and other provinces of the Islamic State, and Caliph Uthman encouraged these transactions. Thus, many deals were made, and the fortunes of these individuals increased rapidly. (Ibn Al-Atheer in Al-Kamil Part 3 p. 52)

As a result, many prominent companions became multi-millionaires. The fortune of Al-Zubeir amounted to around forty million dirhams (Ibn Saad in his Al-Tabaqat Part 3 p. 110), and the wealth of Talhah was around thirty million dirhams (Ibn Saad Al-Tabaqat Part 3 p. 222), whereas the worth of Abdul Rahman Ibn Auf was estimated to be around three million dirhams (Ibn Saad Al-Tabaqat Part 3 p. 126).

12.4.2. Over Taxation

The generosity of Caliph Uthman and his appointed officials required liquid capital from the Islamic treasury. The only way this could be achieved was through over taxation of the newly conquered lands and nations who had no political power or voice at the time.

A dialogue took place between Caliph Uthman and Amr Ibn Al-Auss which vindicates the above assertion. Amr Ibn Al-Auss was the governor of Egypt when Caliph Uthman took office. Caliph Uthman dismissed Amr Ibn Al-Auss and replaced him with his foster brother Abu Sarh.

Sometime after his dismissal Caliph Uthman said to Amr:

> *Caliph Uthman: "The camels are giving much more milk after you left."*
> *Amr replied: "yes but their babies have perished!"*
>
> - Al-Fitnah Al-Kubra Part 1

Caliph Uthman said to Amr that after he was dismissed that the camels were giving lot more milk, implying that after Amr was dismissed as the governor more funds were coming from Egypt. Amr responded to the Caliph by stating that although more funds were coming, but the babies of the camels had perished, implying that Egyptians had become more impoverished and poorer because of sending more money to the Islamic treasury, since the money was coming from over taxing the local population.

12.4.3. Misinformation by the Umayyads

As the grip of the Umayyads consolidated over the Islamic State they advocated the superiority of Qurayshites over the rest of the Arabs, and the superiority of the Umayyad clan over the other Qurayshite clans. They imposed a complete ban on narrating the merits and distinctions of the Ahlulbayt in general and Ali in particular. They wrongly informed their subjects and the new Muslims of their close relationship with the Prophet, and they deliberately kept them in the dark about their historic hostility towards the Prophet and the Muslims.

The new converts to Islam had no idea as to how the Umayyads had come to power or what had taken place in the meeting of Saqifah. They had no knowledge of the endless wars that the Umayyads had waged against the Prophet and the early Muslims.

As far as the new Muslim converts were concerned and for many ordinary Muslims Umayyads were the legitimate rulers of the Muslim world, since they were not aware of the history of the Umayyads or how they had acquired power. And they were certainly not aware of the role that Ali had played in establishing the Islamic State of Madinah, and nor were they aware of the close relationship between the Prophet and Ali. To them Umayyads were the people who had brought them to the path of Islam, and they were the undisputed rulers of the Muslim Ummah.

Once Muawiyah met Ammar ibn Yasir in Madinah and had a heated argument with him where he said to Ammar:

> *"There are in Damascus one hundred thousands plus an equal number of their sons and servants. They receive their annual salaries and they do not know Ali and his kinship (to the Prophet) or Ammar and his early Islam nor Al-Zubeir and his companionship."*
>
> - (Abdul-Fattah Abd Al-Maqsoud in Al-Imam Ali Ibn Abu Tilab Part 2 p. 120)

Muawiyah taunted Ammar that there were thousands of Muslims living in Syria who receive their salary from the Islamic treasury, but these Muslims had no knowledge of the kinship of Ali with the Prophet, nor did they know about the companionship of Ammar and Al-Zubeir with the Prophet.

This is why when Ali was killed in the mosque of Kufa and the news reached Syria, many Syrian Muslims were puzzled as to how was it be possible that Ali was killed in a mosque, since they were led to believe that Ali was an enemy of Allah. They could not comprehend the fact that Ali could have been killed in a mosque!

Over time the decision to side-line Ali in Saqifah had created such a legacy that many Muslims in the Islamic State were not even aware of who Ali was, let alone be aware of the fact that he was the rightful successor of the Prophet. In fact, due to the influence and the absolute power of Muawiyah in Syria, many Syrian Muslims considered Ali to be an enemy of Allah, and they fought against Ali in many battles.

12.4.4. Inflamed Ambitions

Readers would recall that Caliph Umar had setup the six-member Shura (Consultation Body) to select the third Caliph. This political move of Caliph Umar had huge ramifications for the leadership of the Muslim Ummah in the long run. The companions who were inducted in the Shura by Caliph Umar felt that they belonged to a higher class of companions, since they were chosen to elect the next caliph, and since they were also made candidates for the position of the new Caliph. This inflamed the passion and the personal ambitions of these companions for the leadership of the Muslim Ummah.

By admitting these companions to the Shura Caliph Umar made them feel as if they were equals of Ali, and as if they were his competitors for the leadership of the Muslims, even though there was no comparison between these companions and the service of Ali in the path of Islam. Both Talha and al-Zubair became part of this elite group of companions with aspirations for the top position in the Islamic State. At the same time these two companions had massed huge amounts wealth as explained earlier. Talha's fortune was around thirty million dirhams and al-Zubair's fortune was around forty million dirhams.

With inflamed ambitions for the leadership of the Islamic State and with so much wealth at their disposal, they conspired against Caliph Uthman and tried to hasten his death, even though they had earlier pledged their loyalty to him, and both of them became aspirants to succeed him.

The same ambition for the leadership of the Islamic State motivated Talha and al-Zubair to challenge Ali's authority when Ali became the fourth Caliph. They also breached their covenant with Ali where they had pledged their loyalty and support to him after he had taken over the reins of the Caliphate.

12.5. The Start of the Opposition

As a result of the policies of Caliph Uthman opposition against his rule and his Caliphate began to surface in the Muslim Ummah. Caliph Uthman tried to stifle the opposition to his rule either by exiling his opponents or by using violence to subdue them.

12.5.1. Abu Dhar

When Caliph Uthman gave Marwan bin al-Hakam five million (5,000,000) dirhams, Zaid Ibn Thabit one hundred thousand (100,000) dirhams and Harith ibn al-Hakam three hundred thousand (300,000) dirhams, Abu Dhar who was a companion of the Prophet raised his voice against the Caliph for the misuse of public funds.

Abu Dhar repeatedly recited the following verse of Quran:

> *"Give the news of a painful punishment to those who treasure gold and silver and do not spend them in the way of God."*

- Ibn Abu Al-Hadeed Commentaries on Nahjul-Balaghah Vol. 1 p. 240.

Caliph Uthman sent one of his men to stop Abu Dhar from reciting the above verse, but Abu Dhar would not budge and responded by saying:

> "Does Uthman want to prevent me from reciting the Book of God and denouncing those who disobey the commandment of God? By God it is more desirable to me and better for me to please God by displeasing Uthman rather than displeasing God by pleasing Uthman."

- Ibn Abu Al-Hadeed Commentaries on Nahjul-Balaghah Vol. 1 p. 240.

The opposition by Abu Dhar infuriated Caliph Uthman. As a punishment, Caliph Uthman exiled Abu Dhar to Syria and placed him under the authority of Muawiyah. Later, Muawiyah threw him out of Syria, and he was sent back to Madinah in a pretty uncivil manner. After coming back to Madinah, he was again exiled, this time he was sent to Rabathah where he lived in intolerable poverty until he died.

Readers would recall that in a clear breach of the Sunnah of the Prophet, Caliph Uthman had brought his uncle Al-Hakam Ibn Al-Auss back to Madinah who was an enemy of the Prophet. On the other hand, Caliph Uthman exiled Abu Dhar a companion of the Prophet from the city of Madinah, simply because he had criticized the mishandling of public funds.

Apart from being extremely cruel the actions of Caliph Uthman angered many Muslims who believed that there was no justification in exiling Abu Dhar, a punishment which was only reserved for the enemies of Islam.

12.5.2. Abdullah Ibn Masud

Another companion of the Prophet Abdullah ibn Masud also joined the opposition against Caliph Uthman. As mentioned previously Abdullah ibn Masud had resigned as the treasurer of Kufa, after Caliph Uthman allowed Waleed, the governor of Kufa to keep the loan he took from the treasury.

Abdullah Ibn Masud used to deliver a weekly sermon in which he would criticize Caliph Uthman with the following words:

> "Certainly, the trust is the Book of God and the best guidance is the guidance of Mohammad. And the worst deed is that which does not conform with the teaching of God and His Messenger. For every such deed is an innovation and every innovation is a heresy and every heresy leads to Hell."

- Dr. Taha Hussein Al-Fitnat Al-Kubra Part 1 p. 160

Waleed who was now the governor of Kufa informed Caliph Uthman about Ibn Masud's insinuating speeches. Caliph Uthman summoned Ibn Masud and when he entered the Mosque of the Prophet Caliph Uthman said to the congregation:

> "The one that entered the Mosque is an evil insect which causes a person to vomit and secrete when it walks on its food."
> Ibn Masud said: "I am not so but I was a companion of the Prophet at Badr, Uhud, Hudaybiyya the Moat and Hunayn."
> Caliph Uthman ordered one of his servants to throw Ibn Masud out of the Mosque. The servant carried him on his shoulders and violently threw him outside the Mosque.

- Dr. Taha Hussein Al-Fitnat Al-Kubra Part 1 pp. 160-161

As a result, Abdullah Ibn Masud suffered broken ribs, but Caliph Uthman did not stop there, he also withheld Abdullah Ibn Masud salary from the Islamic treasury. Despite the actions of Caliph Uthman, Abdullah Ibn Masud continued his opposition until he died, and he wrote in his will that Caliph Uthman would not attend his funeral.

Violence against your political opponents and calling them names like "evil insect" and withholding their salaries from the public treasury were all practices of the pre-Islamic era. It is not something that one would expect from the Caliph of the Muslims, especially when that Caliph sat on the same pulpit where the Prophet of Allah once sat.

12.5.3. Ammar Ibn Yasir

Just like Abdullah Ibn Masud, Ammar Ibn Yasir also became a key critic of the government of Caliph Uthman. Ammar was not a man who would stay silent when the Sunnah of the Prophet was being breached and the Book of Allah was being violated.

There were some stones and gems of great value in the Islamic treasury, Caliph Uthman gifted those gems to the ladies of his family. People started talking about this event and it angered Caliph Uthman. Caliph Uthman then gave a sermon and said:

> *"We shall take what we need from the treasury even if some people would be displeased."*
> *Ali replied: "Then you shall be prevented and stopped."*
> *And Ammar said: "I make God my witness that I am one of the first people who are displeased."*
> *Caliph Uthman retorted angrily: "Do you dare say that to me? Take him."*

- Dr. Taha Hussein Al-Fitnat Al-Kubra Part 1 p. 167

Ammar was taken by the authorities and Caliph Uthman went to see where Ammar was confined. Caliph Uthman started beating Ammar until Ammar fainted. When Ammar regained his senses, he said:

> *"Praise be to God. This is not the first time I was tortured for my endeavours in the way of God."*

- Dr. Taha Hussein Al-Fitnat Al-Kubra Part 1 p. 167

Caliph Uthman not only tortured Ammar but Caliph Uthman also wanted to exile Ammar just like he had exiled Abu Dhar, however, Ali and other companions raised strong objections and prevented the exile of Ammar.

Readers would recall that in the early days of Islam Ammar ibn Yasir and his family were tortured by the Makhzoom clan of Quraysh, and because of the torture both his parents were martyred. After witnessing the torture and the pain that the family of Ammar went through the Prophet of Allah praised and consoled the family with these words:

> *"Patience oh family of Yassir, for you are destined for Paradise."*

- (Sahih al-Tirmidhi, v5, p233)

It was most unfortunate and regrettable that a Muslim who was tortured at the hands of the pagans in the early days of Islam was again being tortured, but this time the torture was at the hands of a Muslim Caliph. It was for this reason that Prophet of Allah had not left the issue of his successor in the hands of the Ummah, since the Ummah could easily select a ruler who could violate the book of Allah and the Sunnah of the Prophet.

12.5.4. Malik al-Ashtar

The opposition to Caliph Uthman rule began to expand to other cities such as Kufa where the notables of the city would challenge and criticize both Caliph Uthman and his appointed governor. One such key opposition figure in Kufa was Malik al-Ashtar.

Readers would recall that the aristocracy of the Quraysh over the other Arabs was established in Saqifah, when Caliph Abu Bakr won the day against the Ansar on the basis that the right of the leadership only belonged to the Quraysh. The same theme continued when Caliph Umar had step up the Shura for his successor and stated that the leadership of the Muslim Ummah should only stay within the Qurayshite clans. This notion of Qurayshite supremacy peaked under the reign of Caliph Uthman when the Islamic State in fact became a Qurayshite kingdom of the Umayyad clan.

This caused a lot of resentment among other ethnic groups who felt left out and marginalized. Also, many ordinary Muslims were dismayed and unhappy about advocating the supremacy of Quraysh over other groups as they considered it to be a pre-Islamic practice.

An argument took place between the residents of Kufa led by Malik al-Ashtar and its governor Saeed Ibn Al-Auss who was appointed by Caliph Uthman. The argument was about some orchards in Kufa which the governor and his supporters wished were owned by Caliph Uthman, so that the governor and his supporters could take over those orchards. Malik al-Ashtar and the other residents of Kufa disagreed with the views of the governor and his supporters. They argued that these orchards should remain public property and the establishment should not touch them (Ibn Al-Atheer, Al-Kamil, Vol.3 pp. 71-72).

The argument between the two sides quickly flared up and turned violent. This incident became the spark that began to challenge the authority of Caliph Uthman and his governor, and it also showed the lava that was building up against the administration of Caliph Uthman among the ordinary citizens of the Islamic State. This event was the tip of the iceberg in terms of the frustration that was simmering against the rule of Caliph Uthman, and it confirmed that the people were truly fed up with the overarching hands of the Umayyads.

Malik al-Ashtar and other opponents in Kufa met the same fate as Abu Dhar at the hands of Caliph Uthman. Caliph Uthman again tried to stifle his opponents by exiling them. The exiling of opposition became the punishment of choice and Syria became the destination of the exiled critics.

In Syria the opponents of Caliph Uthman would be disciplined at the hands of Muawiyah, the de facto ruler of Syria. Muawiyah would lecture them on the merits and the distinctions of Quraysh over others, and he would claim how God had protected Quraysh even when they were unbelievers. He would also praise his father Abu Sufyan, the arch enemy of the Prophet, as one of the most honourable men of the Muslim Ummah (Ibn Al-Atheer, Al-Kamil, Vol.3 pp. 70-71).

The bitterness and the resentment that the exiled Muslims felt is evident from the following letter that was sent by Malik al-Ashtar to Caliph Uthman, after he reprimanded the opposition in Kufa and exiled Malik al-Ashtar.

> *"From Malik Ibn Al-Harth to the tested and sinful Caliph who is deviating from the precepts of his Prophet and turning his back on the rule of the Holy Qur'an.*
> *We have read your message. You ought to prohibit yourself and your officers from injustice aggression and exiling our righteous men. This will make us content to obey you. You alleged that we have wronged ourselves. This is your conjecture, which caused you to perish (spiritually) and made you consider inequity a justice and the wrong right. As to what we desire we want you*

to change and repent and to ask God His forgiveness for incriminating our righteous men exiling our good people driving us out of our homes and ruling us by our youth. We desire that you appoint Abdullah Ibn Qais Abu Musa governor of our city. We ask you to keep your Waleed and Sa-eed away from us".

- Al-Balathori Ansabul-Ashraf Part 4 p. 46.

The above passage needs no explanation. It reflected the true sentiments of many ordinary Muslims towards the regime of Caliph Uthman. People clearly believed that Caliph Uthman had breached the covenants of the Book of Allah and the Sunnah of the Prophet, and they felt a great deal of resentment and injustice at the exiling of the righteous Muslims. They accused Caliph Uthman of spiritual downfall and asked him to repent to Allah for his crimes of driving good Muslims out of their homes. The also demanded that he changes his governors and put righteous Muslims at the helm of the Islamic State, instead of his undeserving relatives.

The stifling of the opposition became counterproductive, and in fact had the opposite effect to what Caliph Uthman had desired. It resulted in hasting the end of Caliph Uthman's rule rather than prolonging it.

12.6. The Opposition Grows

The opposition against Caliph Uthman's rule began to grow and he became the first high-ranking victim of the path that was established in Saqifah.

The meeting of Saqifah had brought Abu Bakr to the seat of the Caliphate. Abu Bakr nominated Caliph Umar to be his successor during the last days of his life. Caliph Umar in turn formed a committee to choose his successor which brought Caliph Uthman to power. Thus, the Caliphate of Uthman came as a result of what took place in the meeting of Saqifah. But unfortunately, he became the first victim of the path that was established against the wish of the Prophet in Saqifah.

The policies of misusing public funds and appointing unqualified relatives to the top positions finally came to haunt Caliph Uthman. The opposition to Caliph Uthman's rule came from many quarters within the Muslim Ummah. The most decisive opposition against the rule of Caliph Uthman began in Madinah itself, and it was led by some of the most influential and renowned personalities of the Muslim world. The most prominent and outspoken critics of Caliph Uthman were Abdur Rahman ibn Auf, Talhah, Zubair, Lady Aisha, Amr Ibn Al-Auss and Ammar Ibn Yasir.

12.6.1. Abdul Rahman Ibn Auf

Readers would recall that it was Abdul Rahman Ibn Auf who had used the unfair condition of following the precepts of the first two caliphs to select Caliph Uthman ahead of Ali for the third Caliphate. Many companions and ordinary Muslims were now blaming Abdul Rahman for the bad governance and policies of Caliph Uthman. They held Abdul Rahman responsible for bringing the institution of the Caliphate into disrepute and for imposing the authority of the Umayyads on the Muslims.

Also, at the time of selecting Caliph Uthman, Abdul Rahman was hopeful that the Caliphate might come to his own door one day. However, during the reign of Caliph Uthman the way Marwan and Muawiyah had consolidated their power base, Abdul Rahman realized that his own chances of reaching the top spot had significantly faded.

As a result, Abdul Rahman did a U-turn and changed his heart towards the Caliph and became one of Caliph Uthman's most vocal and hostile critics. The criticism of Caliph Uthman by Abdul Rahman was political in nature as Abdul Rahman had lost any hope of becoming the next caliph, and it was also due to the severe criticism being levelled against him by the ordinary Muslims for making the wrong choice of the Caliph in the first place.

12.6.2. Talhah and Al-Zubair

Talhah and Al-Zubair were members of the Shura which had brought Caliph Uthman to power. They also joined the ranks of the opposition against Caliph Uthman. Although, on the face of it they opposed Caliph Uthman due to his wrong policies but in reality, their opposition was political in nature. It was unlikely that these two companions were opposed to Caliph Uthman due to his misuse of public funds, since they themselves had received huge sums of money from the Islamic treasury during the reign of Caliph Uthman. Al-Zubair had received six hundred thousand (600,000) dirhams and Talhah had received two hundred thousand (200,000) dirhams.

Both Talhah and Al-Zubair were politically ambitious and were aspiring to succeed Caliph Uthman. As mentioned previously, Caliph Umar had not only inducted both Talhah and Al-Zubair into the committee for choosing the third Caliph, but he also made them candidates for the post of the Caliphate. This inflamed their own ambitions for the leadership of the Islamic State. Also, both these companions had massed enormous amounts of wealth which further enhanced their status and importance in their own eyes and in the eyes of many Muslims too.

Talhah gained numerous supporters in Basra and Al-Zubair had a big following in Kufa. Both Talhah and al-Zubair were extremely concerned and worried by the rapid growth of the Umayyad power. It was disturbing for them to see how the key provinces in the Islamic State had fallen into the hands of the Umayyads. It became apparent to them that the Umayyads would keep the Caliphate in their own clan, and they would block others from reaching the seat of power. For this reason, these two companions decided to end the reign of Caliph Uthman before he could choose an Umayyad successor.

Although both these companions opposed Caliph Uthman, but the role of Talhah against Caliph Uthman was more violent and pronounced.

Al-Tabari reported in his history that when Caliph Uthman was besieged in his house, Ibn Abbas came to see him.

> *Uthman said: "Ibn Abbas, come with me." He made him listen to some of the conversations among the besiegers outside the house. They witnessed Talhah pass and ask the people: "Where is Ibn Udays (the leader of the Egyptian revolters)?"*
> *Ibn Udays came and conferred secretly with Talhah. Ibn Udays then returned to his group and said: "Do not let anyone enter or leave 'Uthman's house."*
> *Uthman said to Ibn Abbas: "This is an order from Talhah. God, I ask Thee to take care of Talhah Ibn Ubaydullah. He instigated these people against me. By God, I hope his share of the caliphate is zero and that his blood is shed."*
> - *(Al-Tabari, part 4, page 379)*

The above report shows how Talhah instigated revolters against Caliph Uthman. Talhah stopped anyone from entering or leaving the house of Caliph Uthman, ensuring that the siege of Caliph Uthman's house was watertight. Caliph Uthman was well aware of Talhah's motives. He knew that Talhah was after the Caliphate. Caliph Uthman told Ibn Abbas that Talhah had instigated the revolters against him, and he hoped that Talhah would have no share in the Caliphate, and that Talhah's blood would be shed.

12.6.3. Lady Aisha

One of the most influential and high-profile agitators against Caliph Uthman was none other than Lady Aisha, the wife of the Holy Prophet and the daughter of Caliph Abu Bakr. She became an open critic of Caliph Uthman accusing him of abandoning the Sunnah of the Prophet. She would occasionally display a garment of the Prophet saying that the garment of the Prophet had not yet deteriorated but Caliph Uthman had brought the Sunnah of the Prophet into disrepute.

She used to call Caliph Uthman a Naathal, which means a heavily bearded Jew. Historian have recorded that she used to say:

> "Kill Naathal because he deserted the faith."
> - Al-Tabari History of Messengers and Kings about the events of the year 36 p. 3112
> - Ibn Al-Atheer in Al-Kamil Part 3 p. 102.

Lady Aisha not only called Caliph Uthman a Jew who had deserted the faith of Islam, but she also advocated his killing. Although the tone of some of her opposition seemed genuine, but her motives were merely political, and were identical to the motives of Talhah and al-Zubair. Talhah was Lady Aisha's cousin and al-Zubair was her brother-in-law, and she wanted one of them to succeed Caliph Uthman. This became clear in a conversation that she had with Ibn Abbas.

Lady Aisha said to ibn Abbas:

> *"Ibn Abbas, you are endowed with an effective tongue. I ask you in the name of God not to try to scatter people away from Talhah by putting doubt in their minds. The situation of Uthman has become obvious. People have come from many locations for something big that is about to happen. I know that Talhah Ibn Ubaydullah has acquired the keys of the treasury houses. If Talhah succeeds Uthman, he will follow the path of his cousin Abu Bakr . . ."*
> - Al-Tabari, page 407
> - Al-Balathori Ansab Al-Ashraf part 1 of volume 4 p.75

Lady Aisha was openly supporting Talhah in his opposition to Caliph Uthman. She was asking other influential Islamic personalities like Ibn Abbas not to deter people from joining the opposition movement against the Caliph. She was hopeful that her cousin Talhah would succeed Caliph Uthman and he would follow the path of her father Caliph Abu Bakr.

Just like Talhah and al-Zubair she was also worried and disturbed by the expansion of the Umayyad's power base. It was evident to her that Caliph Uthman would not go against the advice and wishes of people like Marwan and Muawiyah, who would make sure that Caliph Uthman chooses an Umayyad successor before his Caliphate ends.

With this in mind Lady Aisha did all she could to end the Caliphate of Uthman. It is reported that when the situation in Madinah became extremely grave and the life of Caliph Uthman was being threatened, Caliph Uthman asked Marwan to persuade Lady Aisha from campaigning against him.

Marwan went to Lady Aisha while she was preparing to leave for pilgrimage. Marwan said to Lady Aisha:

> *"We pray that you stay in Medina and that Allah may through you save this man (Uthman)."*
> *Lady Aishah said: "I have prepared my means of transportation and vowed to perform the pilgrimage. By God, I shall not honour your request."*
> *Lady Aisha further said to Marwan:*

> "Marwan, I wish that he (Uthman) was in one of my sacks, and that I could carry him. I would then throw him into the sea."
>
> - (Al-Baladhuri, part 1 of Vol.4, page 75)

Caliph Uthman even sent his top advisor Marwan to lady Aisha to see if she would change her mind and to see if she could be subdued, but she refused to budge. She told Marwan that if it was in her hands, she would put Uthman in one of her sacks and throw him into the sea, implying that if it was up to her she would not hesitate to kill Caliph Uthman.

12.6.4. Amr Ibn al-Auss

As mentioned previously Caliph Umar had appointed Amr Ibn al-Auss as the governor of Egypt. When Caliph Uthman came to power he dismissed Amr Ibn Al-Auss and replaced him with his foster brother Abu Sarh. This left Amr ibn al-Auss with a lot of bitterness and resentment against Caliph Uthman. Amr ibn al-Auss became extremely hostile towards Caliph Uthman and carried a grudge against him after his dismissal.

When Lady Aisha, Talhah and al-Zubair launched their campaign against Caliph Uthman, Amr Ibn al-Auss also joined the opposition. He saw this as a perfect opportunity to ambush Caliph Uthman and avenge his earlier dismissal as the governor of Egypt. Amr Ibn al-Auss used to meet Talhah and al-Zubair and accused Caliph Uthman of many wrong doings. He also used to instigate the pilgrims and shepherds against the Caliph and would inform them about numerous deviations of Caliph Uthman.

Amr Ibn al-Auss was a cunning and a shrewd man and he became one of the most dangerous agitators and conspirators against the Caliphate of Uthman. It is reported that when Caliph Uthman was besieged by the revolters, Amr Ibn al-Auss had moved to a place called al-Ajlan, and he was observing the end of the Caliphate from a distance.

Al-Tabari reported that Amr Ibn al-Auss asked a traveller who came from Madinah:

> "How is Uthman doing?"
> The man replied: "He has been killed."
> Amr then said: I am Abu Abdullah. When I scratch an ulcer, I cut it. I used to campaign against him vehemently. I even instigated the shepherds at the top of the mountains to revolt against him."
>
> - (Al-Tabari, part 4, pages 356-57)

Amr Ibn al-Auss compared Caliph Uthman to an ulcer, and at the same time he confirmed his own involvement in ending the Caliphate of Uthman, and it seems as if he was quite pleased with the eventual outcome.

12.7. Ali's Role in the Crisis

Just as Ali was unique and distinguished on the battlefield among all the companions his role in the crisis facing the Muslim Ummah was unmistakably distinct and admirable.

If there was anybody who should have held a grudge against Caliph Uthman, then it should have been Ali. After all it was Ali who lost out to Caliph Uthman for the top position when Abdul Rahman choose Caliph Uthman a head of Ali for refusing to follow the precepts of the first two Caliphs. So, if there was anybody who should have pulled the rug under the feet of Caliph Uthman then it should have really been Ali.

This was another perfect opportunity that history had presented Ali to take out his political rival and avenge his earlier disappointments. After all, this was exactly what the other politically ambitious companions like Talhah and al-Zubair were doing, even though they really had no claim to the Caliphate. They were using the mismanagement of Caliph Uthman's administration as an excuse to take him out altogether and to further their own political goals.

But Ali's character was unlike the character of any other companion. Ali was the choice of the Prophet, his character and his actions had always reflected his pure upbringing at the hands of the Messenger of Allah. The sanctity and the preservation of the Islamic State had always been a red line for Ali, regardless of who was at the helm of the affairs.

Ali had never adopted a path which would further his own claim to the Caliphate and would be at the detriment of the wider Muslim Ummah. Ali had never manipulated any political or social events in his favour at the expense of the Islamic State. Readers would remember that when the Caliphate of Abu Bakr was in trouble due to the movement of apostasy, Ali choose to strengthen the hand of the Islamic State. Similarly, when Abu Sufyan had offered his men to Ali to take out the caliphate of Abu Bakr, Ali refused the unscrupulous offer of Abu Sufyan.

Under the leadership of Caliph Uthman, the Muslim Ummah was facing its biggest crisis. But once again the role of Ali reflected the traditional dignity and unselfishness of his Character. Ali refused to be sucked into a war that would destroy the very fabric of the Islamic State, even though if Ali really wanted, he could have easily manipulated the events in his own favour.

Ali tried his level best to end the crisis through dialogue and mediation rather than taking sides or joining the opposing parties. Ali could clearly see that the root cause of all the problems was the outlandish nepotism and corruption of Caliph Uthman's administration. The misuse of public funds and the appointment of undeserving Umayyad relatives by Caliph Uthman was the source of all the instability and chaos in the Muslim Ummah.

Ali tried to guide Caliph Uthman so that he could mend his ways and change his policies, in order to subdue the opposition and bring back the unity of the Muslim Ummah. But unfortunately, Caliph Uthman's advisors had other ideas. They would not let Caliph Uthman mend fences with the opposition or change his policies.

As far as the opposition to Caliph Uthman's rule was concerned it came in three different forms.

12.7.1. The Genuine Opposition

This kind of opposition was led by companions and individuals like Ammar ibn Yasir, Abdullah Ibn Masud, Abu Dhar and Malik al Ashtar. These people were genuinely opposed to the administration of Caliph Uthman for its breach of the Sunnah of the Prophet and for its violation of the Book of Allah. These individuals had no ulterior motives or personal ambitions in the Caliphate. Their aim was to rectify the flaws and the un-Islamic nature of the Caliphate by forcing Caliph Uthman to change his ways.

Caliph Uthman had tried to subdue such opponents by exiling them or thorough the use of force, but all those methods severely backfired and the genuine opposition grew even stronger, as many of the exiles eventually returned to their lands and continued the opposition. Most of the Muslims who opposed Caliph Uthman were part of the genuine opposition who were looking to re-establish the Islamic character of the Caliphate.

12.7.2. The Politically Motivated Opposition

This form of opposition was led by prominent companions like Talhah, al-Zubair and the wife of the Prophet Lady Aisha. Although these personalities were also using the policies of Caliph Uthman as a pretext for opposing him, but their motives were not genuine. In fact, their motives were merely political and were based on their own ambition for acquiring the top position. They were concerned and anxious about the rapid growth of the Umayyad influence in the Islamic State, and they wanted to end the Caliphate of Uthman before he could nominate a fellow Umayyad as his successor, as it would end their own hopes of acquiring the next Caliphate.

Up until now the Caliphate had been alternating in the various clans of Quraysh such as the Banu Taym (clan of Caliph Abu Bakr), Banu Adi (clan of Caliph Umar) and Banu Umayyad (clan of Caliph Uthman). However, under the leadership of Caliph Uthman the Banu Umayyads had not only taken over the Caliphate, but they had also taken over the leadership of all the key provinces and their wealth. The Umayyads had no intention of relinquishing power as they were gradually taking over the entire Islamic State.

Talhah, al-Zubair and Lady Aisha realized that unless the Umayyads were stopped, they would make the Caliphate an Umayyad dynasty, and the previous path of alternating the Caliphate in different clans of Quraysh would end, as the Umayyads would not allow any other clan of Quraysh to acquire the Caliphate.

Hence, all three of them opposed Caliph Uthman and worked for the downfall of his Caliphate in the most aggressive manner possible.

12.7.3. The Opportunistic Opposition

This form of opposition was led by companions like Amr Ibn al-Auss. Amr Ibn al-Auss held a grudge against Caliph Uthman after he was dismissed as the governor of Egypt. Such individuals were simply looking for the right opportunity to jump on the Caliph, and the policies of Caliph Uthman gave them ample opportunity to avenge their earlier treatment. Their motives were neither genuine nor political and were purely based on vengeance and hatred towards the Caliph.

12.7.4. Ali's Strategy to Defuse the Crisis

The aim and the strategy of Ali was to remove the source of the problem through dialogue and mediation. Ali was trying his level best to get Caliph Uthman to change his policies. In Ali's view if the source of the problem could be removed then the genuine and the opportunistic opposition would fade away on its own.

Ali wanted Caliph Uthman to drastically change his lose monetary policy and tame his advisors and governors like Marwan and Muawiyah. This would not only meet the demands of the genuine opposition, but it would also bring stability and calm to the Islamic State. Ali neither called for the resignation of Caliph Uthman nor did he advocate his killing as Ali believed that both those measures would be counterproductive.

Umayyad's had become way too powerful after twelve years of Caliph Uthman's rule. The Umayyad governors were in charge of all the key provinces, and they had infiltrated the very fabric of the Islamic State. The killing of an Umayyad Caliph would certainly result in revenge wars and forcing the Caliph to resign would be seen as taking the power away from the Umayyads. Both options were fraught with dangers and risks, hence Ali tried to avoid these two options.

If an Umayyad Caliph was either killed or forced out of the office the Umayyad's would then try to regain power by all possible means including war. For this reason, Ali was treading very carefully. Ali was well-aware of the characteristics and the intentions of the Umayyad clan. Ali had fought against the Umayyads since he was a child. Ali had faced the wrath of the Umayyad's in the battles of Badr, Uhud and Moat. Ali also knew that if Umayyad's kept the authority they would devour public funds, enslave righteous Muslims, and corrupt the religion of Allah.

Although the real solution was to completely remove the Umayyad's from power but that needed to be done over a period of time.

Ali's aim was to first contain and then reverse the Umayyad influence with prudence. It wasn't just a matter of killing or simply removing the Umayyad Caliph from the office. The tentacles of the Umayyads had become deeply entrenched in the Islamic State after a decade of Caliph Uthman's rule. The Umayyad governors and ministers were controlling almost all the resources of the Islamic State. As far as Ali was concerned, a knee jerk reaction against the powerful Umayyad Caliph would be disastrous for the Muslim Ummah, and for this reason Ali resorted to the path of dialogue and mediation.

In Ali's view the most pragmatic approach at that time was to allow Caliph Uthman to continue, but with a drastically revised and a completely new set of policies. Ali wanted the Umayyad Caliph to subdue his fellow Umayyad governors and advisors so that the sanctity of the Islamic State could be preserved.

Ali wanted Caliph Uthman as the head of the Umayyads to put things right, because if an outsider forced Caliph Uthman out of the office, it would be seen as a stance against the entire Umayyad clan which they would inevitably try to avenge. Ali wanted to save the Muslim Ummah from a civil war as he was well-aware of the mentality of the Umayyads.

Being the Umayyad Caliph, Uthman was the best placed individual to reduce and curtail the powers that he had given to his Umayyad governors, and that is exactly what Ali wanted Caliph Uthman to do.

12.7.5. Ali Advises the Caliph and the Opposition

Ali sincerely tried to resolve the crisis by advising both Caliph Uthman and his opponents. Though, the solution of the crisis primarily lied with Caliph Uthman because if he could mend his ways then most of the opposition would melt away anyway.

Ali advised Caliph Uthman with the following words:

> *By God I don't know what to tell you......You have seen heard and accompanied the Messenger of God ...... I ask you in the name of God to be merciful to yourself. You are not suffering blindness nor ignorance. The right road is clear and obvious and the demarcation of religion is standing. Uthman remember that the best of the servants of God In the eyes of God is a just Imam who is led to the truth and leads to the truth.*
>
> - Ibn Al-Atheer Al-Kamil Part 3 p. 76.

Ali Further said:

> "I have heard the Messenger of God saying: 'An unjust Imam will be brought on the Day of Judgment while he has no helper nor a vindicator. He will be thrown into hell. . . . I warn you of the wrath of God and His smite and chastisement...... I warn you not to be the murdered imam of this nation. It is said that an imam will be killed and his death will open on the nation the door of killing and wars until the Day of Judgment. He will confuse the affairs of the nation and throw

> the Muslims into divisions that they will not be able to see the truth because of the height of the falsehood. . . .'"
>
> - Ibn Al-Atheer Al-Kamil Part 3 p. 76.

In another dialogue Ali told Caliph Uthman:

> ".....You are weakened because you are too lenient on your relatives.....Muawiyah makes his decisions without consulting you then he tells people that this is the order of Uthman. You know it and you do not change anything. Nor do you stop him from doing what he is doing."
>
> - Ibn Al-Atheer Al-Kamil Part 3 p. 76.

Ali tried to advice and put sense into Caliph Uthman. Ali reminded Caliph Uthman that he was a companion of the Prophet, and his actions should reflect his stature. Ali reminded him about the demarcations of the religion of Allah and warned him not to become an unjust leader as that would inevitably lead to hell fire. Ali specifically warned Caliph Uthman not to follow the policies which could lead to his own killing, as it would open the door to civil wars and divisions in the Muslim Ummah.

Ali also advises Caliph Uthman against his lenient approach towards his relatives. For instance, Muawiyah would make a decision without consulting Caliph Uthman, but then he would announce it to the public as if it was the decision of the Caliph, and Caliph Uthman was aware of this phenomenon, but still, he would not do anything about it. It was this policy of Caliph Uthman that allowed Muawiyah to carve out his own autonomous Syrian empire within the borders of the Islamic State. Essentially Caliph Uthman had given Muawiyah a free hand in Syria which had allowed Muawiyah to become the powerhouse of the Muslim world.

Unfortunately, the advice of Ali fell on deaf ears and despite Ali's sincere advice Caliph Uthman refused to change his policy. The crux of the problem lied in the fact that Caliph Uthman was not the decision maker, he was simply a figurehead, and it was his governors and advisors like Muawiyah and Marwan who devised his policies. These individuals would not allow Caliph Uthman to change his policies as it would be at the detriment of their own interests.

Similarly, Ali tried to deter the politically motivated opposition to defuse the crisis. Talhah was one of the biggest and the most dangerous agitators against Caliph Uthman and he was at the forefront of the opposition against the administration of Uthman.

Ali said to Talhah:

> "I ask you in the name of Allah to deter people from attacking 'Uthman."
> Talhah responded: "No, by God, until the Umayyad returns to the people their rights."
>
> - (Al-Tabari, page 405)

Talhah rejected the advice of Ali on the basis that since the Umayyad's were abusing power and since they had trampled upon people's rights, his opposition would continue until they change their ways. As mentioned previously the basis of Talhah's opposition was genuine but his motives were political. The aim of the political opposition was to manipulate the events in their own favour to get to the helm of the Islamic State.

Readers would recall that Caliph Uthman had punished and exiled many members of the genuine opposition like Abu Dhar, Abdullah ibn Masud, Malik al-Ashtar etc. These companions did not have the backing of powerful tribes. They were neither wealthy nor were they well-connected, hence Caliph Uthman was able to punish and exile them as and when he felt it was necessary.

The story with the political opposition was a little different. Talhah was not somebody who Caliph Uthman could simply punish or exile. Talhah was a well-connected individual who belonged to the powerful Qurayshite tribe of Taym. Talhah had also massed huge amounts of wealth and his status and clout had grown significantly, and as a result he was able to command influence and following in the society.

Also, Caliph Umar inducted him in the six member Shura as a candidate for the third Caliphate. This move further raised his political profile within the Muslim ranks, and Talhah made most of his newfound standing and stature. On top of this he had the backing of his powerful cousin Lady Aisha. Being the wife of the Prophet and the daughter of Caliph Abu Bakr, she also commanded a lot of influence and clout among the Muslims. As mentioned previously Lady Aisha had thrown her weight behind Talhah.

Lady Aisha said to Ibn Abbas

> "……I ask you in the name of God not to try to scatter people away from Talhah ……….I know that Talhah Ibn Ubaydullah has acquired the keys of the treasury houses. If Talhah succeeds Uthman, he will follow the path of his cousin Abu Bakr . . ."
>
> - (Al- Tabari, page 407)

Lady Aisha specifically told Ibn Abbas not to drive people away from Talhah, implying that the opposition against Caliph Uthman must continue. Talhah was a key opposition figure against the administration of Caliph Uthman, and he had already acquired the keys to the treasury. Lady Aisha wanted Talhah to succeed Caliph Uthman and rule like her father Caliph Abu Bakr.

With such powerful backers, Caliph Uthman was unable to subdue Talhah who unabatedly carried on his opposition against the Caliph. Talhah felt that his ambitions were in line with his current standing in the Muslim Ummah, plus he also had the support of leading Islamic personalities like Lady Aisha, hence, he refused to heed the advice of Ali to stop the opposition against Caliph Uthman.

Despite Ali's best and sincere efforts, he failed to convince either Caliph Uthman or the politically motivated opposition to back off from their extreme positions.

12.8. The End Game

As Caliph Uthman refused to budge the end game began to take shape. All three forms of opposition i.e., genuine opposition, politically motivated opposition and the opportunistic opposition grew louder and closer to Madinah.

The companions living in Madinah wrote to the companions in other provinces inviting them to rectify the un-Islamic nature of Caliph Uthman's administration.

The companions in Madinah wrote to others:

> "You have left Medina to endeavour in the way of God and promote the religion of Muhammad. The religion of Muhammad has been corrupted. Come back and straighten the religion of Muhammad."
>
> - (Al-Tabari, al-Ta'rikh, part 4, page 367)

The message of invitation by the companions living in Madinah had the desired effect. Groups of Muslims came to Madinah from other provinces such as Egypt, Basra and Kufa, asking Caliph Uthman to either dismiss his ruling relatives or resign from his post, otherwise they were ready to kill him.

Caliph Uthman was disturbed by the arrival of protestors from all over the Muslim world. It was not something that he was expecting, or he had envisaged. When Caliph Uthman realized the seriousness of the situation, he could not turn to anybody except Ali, even though previously he had refused to heed Ali's advice on many occasions.

Caliph Uthman asked Ali to mediate between him and his adversaries. Despite previous misgivings Ali accepted the offer of acting as a peacemaker to try and resolve the crisis and save the Ummah from chaos and anarchy. Ali asked Caliph Uthman for his terms of reconciliation.

> *Ali asked him: "What are your terms for reconciliation?"*
> *Caliph Uthman replied: "You are fully authorized to pledge to them whatever you choose. I shall do whatever you propose."*
>
> - Ibn Al-Atheer Al-Kamil Parr 3 p. 82.

Ali reminded Caliph Uthman once again that he had repeatedly asked him to take corrective steps, but due to the influence of Marwan, Muawiyah, Ibn Amir and Abu Sarh, the promises made by Caliph Uthman had always remained unfulfilled. Caliph Uthman pleaded with Ali that he would not fall in the same trap again and he would disobey his advisors and would only follow Ali's advice.

> *Caliph Uthman replied: "I will disobey them and obey you."*
>
> - Ibn Al-Atheer Al-Kamil Parr 3 p. 82.

Based on the positive response of Caliph Uthman there was still hope that the crisis could potentially be resolved through dialogue and rapprochement.

12.8.1. A Glimmer of Hope

A glimmer of hope was raised that even at this last hour violence and anarchy could be averted and an amicable solution could possibly be reached between Caliph Uthman and his opponents.

As mentioned previously groups of Muslims had come from Egypt, Basra and Kufa to protest against the policies of Caliph Uthman. The Egyptian group was leading the pack and they were most forceful in their opposition against the Caliph. Readers would recall that Caliph Uthman had replaced Amr Ibn Al-Auss with his foster brother Abu Sarh as the governor of Egypt. The Egyptian group was not only protesting against Caliph Uthman, but they were also protesting against their provincial governor Abu Sarh. They wanted Caliph Uthman to replace their Umayyad governor with a righteous Muslim.

Ali led a delegation of thirty men which comprised of Qurayshite companions and companions from Madinah. Ali met with the Egyptian protestors and managed to convince them to stay peaceful and not to resort to violence. As Caliph Uthman had given Ali complete authority to negotiate on his behalf, Ali promised the protestors on behalf of Caliph Uthman that the Caliph's ruling Umayyad relatives would be dismissed, and he would also drastically change his lose monetary policy.

Ali went back to Caliph Uthman and advised him to go to the mosque of the Prophet and publicly pledge that he was going to make the reforms to subdue and calm the opposition. Caliph Uthman responded positively to the efforts of Ali. He went to the mosque of the Prophet and addressed the congregation with these words:

> "I am the first one that should obey God. I ask God to forgive me for what I did. I shall repent to him. A man like me is expected to change and repent. When I come down let your leaders come and make a decision about me. By God if justice reduces me to a slave I shall do what a slave does and I shall be as humble as a slave. There is no escape from the anger of God but through Him. By God I shall give you the satisfaction and I will keep Marwan and my relatives away from me. I shall not seclude myself from you."

- Ibn Al-Atheer Al-Kamil Parr 3 p. 82.

Caliph Uthman asked Allah to forgive him for what he had done. Caliph Uthman publicly accepted his mistakes and asked for forgiveness. He also pledged to satisfy the demands of the opposition and to keep Marwan and his relatives away from his administration.

The words of Caliph Uthman had moved the audience and they wept until the tears moistened their beards. Caliph Uthman wept too, and everybody hoped that a new chapter would begin in the Muslim Ummah.

12.8.2. A Colossal Disappointment

Marwan had also heard the speech of Caliph Uthman. He was furious and livid with the words of the Caliph. Marwan could not believe what he had heard, since Caliph Uthman had specifically mentioned Marwan's name in his speech. Caliph Uthman had mentioned that he would keep Marwan and his relatives away from his administration.

Marwan waited patiently for Caliph Uthman to get back home. Once Marwan was alone with the Caliph, he completely derailed the rapprochement process that both Ali and Caliph Uthman had embarked upon. He persuaded and talked Caliph Uthman into going back to his old Umayyad ways. He convinced and swayed Caliph Uthman not to give into the demands of the opposition, since according to Marwan the opposition members were simply looking to take the leadership of the Muslims away from the Umayyads.

An opposition crowd had gathered outside Caliph Uthman's house and was waiting for an announcement for the reforms to start, which had been promised in Caliph Uthman's speech earlier. However, events took a turn for the worst. After convincing Caliph Uthman back to his old ways and taking him into confidence, Marwan came out of Caliph Uthman's house and reprimanded the opposition crowd with some harsh words.

Marwan rebuked the opposition and said:

> "... *You have come to rob us of the authority, which is in our hands. Go away. By God if you challenge us you will see what will displease you ...*".

- Ibn Al-Atheer Al-Kamil Parr 3 p. 82.

Marwan completely thwarted the reconciliation efforts that Ali had set in motion. Marwan refused to give into the demands of the opposition and refused to make any reforms in the Umayyad policy. He rebuffed the opposition and accused them of trying to rob the Umayyad's of the authority of the Islamic State. Furthermore, Marwan threatened the opposition with dire consequences if they kept challenging the authority of Caliph Uthman.

The words of Marwan infuriated the opposition, they were inflamed by what they had just heard. When the news reached Ali of what Marwan had done, Ali spoke to the people around him with the following words:

> "......If I try to help him (Uthman) and a good comes out of my effort Marwan dissuades him and deceives him. He (Uthman) has become an obedient tool in the hands of Marwan after having been the companion of the Prophet."
>
> • Ibn Al-Atheer Al-Kamil Part 3 p. 82.

Ali then went to Caliph Uthman and spoke to him angrily:

> "You couldn't satisfy Marwan but by your deviation from your religion and wisdom. You have become like a ridden camel led by his rider to wherever he pleases. By God, I foresee that he (Marwan) will bring you danger but he (Marwan) will not be able to take you out of it. I will not come back to you after this. You have ruined your honour and lost the power of judgment."
>
> • Ibn Al-Atheer Al-Kamil Part 3 p. 82.

The words of Ali could not be sharper or clearer. Ali scolds off at Caliph Uthman and tells him that despite being a companion of the Prophet, Caliph Uthman had become a tool in the hands of Marwan. Ali further rebuked Caliph Uthman and stated that he had not only deviated from Islam, but he had also gone against wisdom and common sense. Ali warned Caliph Uthman that the policies of Marwan would endanger his life, and then Marwan would not be able to take him out of that danger. Finally, Ali rebuffs Caliph Uthman and states that he had ruined his honour and had lost the power of judgment by accepting the advice of Marwan.

The speech that Caliph Uthman had given earlier which had moved the audience to tears was now a distant memory. Those words which had given all the Muslims a glimmer of hope, unfortunately remained mere words, since Marwan would not allow the Caliph to put those words into meaningful actions. Marwan knew that accepting the demands of the opposition would not only go against the larger interest of the Umayyad clan, but it would also go against his own personal interests, since the opposition was asking Caliph Uthman to remove Marwan from his advisory position too.

12.8.3. An Inevitable End

The blatant intervention of Marwan in the reconciliation process inflamed the opposition and increased their momentum against Caliph Uthman. The opposition was incensed by the approach of the Umayyad leadership and the speech of Marwan became a final nail in the coffin of Caliph Uthman. The protestors who had come from various provinces had started to besiege the house of Caliph Uthman, and Talhah was strongly supporting the opposition movement from inside Madinah.

Despite Ali's harsh words earlier, Caliph Uthman again approached Ali to try and save him. Caliph Uthman pleads with Ali to stop Talhah, the leading opposition figure from his activities.

Caliph Uthman said to Ali:

> "You owe me my Islamic right and the right of brotherhood and relationship. If I have none of these rights and if I were in the pre-Islamic era, it would still be a shame for a descendant of Abd-Manaf (both Ali and Uthman are descendants of Abd-Manaf) to let a man of Taym (Talhah's clan) rob us of our authority."

The desperate words of Caliph Uthman had a pre-Islamic tribal tone, but they also had a subtle truth in them. Caliph Uthman recognizes that Talhah from the Taym clan was politically motivated to take the leadership away from the Umayyads. Caliph Uthman was certainly right in his assessment of Talhah.

As mentioned previously Talhah was using the mismanagement of Caliph Uthman's administration as an excuse to acquire power, and he also had the backing of the powerful wife of the Prophet Lady Aisha.

Regardless of the power play, which was taking place in the Islamic State, Ali being Ali (Ali literally means most high), again accepts the plea of Caliph Uthman and tries to save the unity of the Islamic State for the very last time. Ali goes to the house of Talhah where a large number of Talhah's supporters had gathered. This was also the hub of the politically motivated opposition in Madinah against Caliph Uthman.

> *Ali asked Talhah: "What are you involving yourself in?"*
> *Talhah replied: "It is too late." (He meant that Caliph Uthman's rule was coming to an end.)*

Ali tried to stop Talhah from his activities, but Talhah refused to heed Ali's advice. Talhah said to Ali that it was too late, implying that Caliph Uthman's days were numbered, and it was futile for Ali to try and stop the opposition now.

Ali could see the political and the materialistic nature of Talhah's opposition. To subdue Talhah's supporters Ali went to the Islamic treasury and asked for it to be opened. When the keys of the treasury could not be found Ali broke the door and distributed some money from the treasury among the people who had gathered around Talhah. As expected, on receiving the funds some of the supporters of Talhah deserted him.

Ali tried to do whatever he could to stop the politically motivated opposition as there was nobody who cared more about the sanctity of the Islamic State than Ali. Ali had spent a lifetime in the establishment and the defence of the Islamic State that Prophet of Allah had founded. Regardless of who was leading the Islamic State and regardless of who was opposing the order of the day, Ali could not possibly see the Islamic State being destroyed in front of his eyes.

But there was very little that Ali could do about the protestors who had besieged the house of Caliph Uthman. They were demanding serious reforms from the administration of Caliph Uthman, and if Caliph Uthman was not able to meet their demands, they wanted him to resign from his position and leave the office of Caliphate. The protestors had not come with a pre-planned mindset of Killing the Caliph. The main demand of the protestors was to get Caliph Uthman to change his monetary policy and to remove his Umayyad relatives from his administration.

The siege of Caliph Uthman's house continued for forty days. Caliph Uthman had ample time to at least start some reforms during this period. If Caliph Uthman had initiated the reforms, met some of the demands of the protestors, and changed his monetary policy, the protests against his administration would have subsided. The majority of the opposition was genuine, and they were simply looking for a change of heart from the leadership of the Umayyads. They were not necessarily looking to take out Caliph Uthman from the office. They were primarily asking Caliph Uthman to change his policies.

Unfortunately, Caliph Uthman was under the thumb of Marwan and Caliph Uthman had completely lost his decision-making powers. If Caliph Uthman had fixed his own house, the genuine opposition would have fizzled out. It would then become easier to tackle the non-genuine opposition too. But Caliph Uthman failed to deliver any reforms, even though he was besieged for forty days. Caliph Uthman had plenty to time to think about the crisis and resolve it amicably.

As Caliph Uthman had failed to meet any of the demands of the opposition, some of the protestors now began to get violent. They cut off his water supply to try and pressurize him into meeting their demands. Even in these last stages Ali intervened and asked his two sons al-Hasan and al-Hussain to take the water to the Caliph. Ali was still trying to get Caliph Uthman to change his policies to preserve the unity of the Muslim Ummah.

But unfortunately, in the end all the sincere and reconciliatory efforts of Ali did not materialize.

The protestors were informed that armies from various cities were on their way to Madinah to rescue Caliph Uthman. On hearing this announcement some of the protestors felt that the only solution now was to kill Caliph Uthman, because if he lives on, he wouldn't change his policies and the approaching armies would save him. They decided to scale the walls of Caliph Uthman's house, entered his room, and killed him. The doors of Caliph Uthman's house were still being guarded but the guards did not know what had taken place until it was too late.

The killing of Caliph Uthman was a sad and a tragic day for the Muslim Ummah. It ended the unity of the Muslims once and for all. It was an event that Ali had tried his level best to prevent through his sincere advice and practical efforts, but unfortunately, he did not succeed.

Readers would recall that when the six-member Shura setup by Caliph Umar was choosing the third Caliph, Ali had addressed and advised the Shura with these words:

Listen to my words and comprehend my presentation.

> *Your leadership after this Convention (if you fail to select the qualified leader) will be violently contended. Covenants will be breached and swords will be drawn until your unity will come to an end. Some of you will be imams of revisions some will be followers of men of ignorance."*
>
> - Ibn Al-Atheer Al-Kamil Part 3 p. 37.

Despite the warning of Ali, the Shura made the wrong choice, and the prediction of Ali became a reality. The killing of Caliph Uthman had opened the doors to endless civil wars within the Muslim Ummah, and these wars took the lives of thousands of companions and ordinary Muslims.

12.9. A few Observations

12.9.1. Preventing the Killing of Caliph Uthman

The Killing of Caliph Uthman could have easily been prevented if he had heeded the advice of Ali. Ali had been advocating reforms in the administration of Caliph Uthman for a very long time, way before any of the opposition against his rule had ever surfaced. But Caliph Uthman never had the courage or the wisdom to go against the words of his Umayyad advisors like Marwan.

Even after pledging reforms in a speech at the mosque of the Prophet, where the audience was reduced to tears, he backtracked his pledges on the behest of Marwan and did not deliver what he had earlier promised.

Also, when the protestors came from other provinces to Madinah, it wasn't as if they came and immediately killed Caliph Uthman. They protested peacefully against Caliph Uthman's administration for forty days before the protests turned violent. Even in the last stages of the crisis Caliph Uthman had ample time to resolve this issue amicably and save his life.

It was in the hands of Caliph Uthman to meet the demands of the protestors and to fix the corruption and nepotism in his government. But his Umayyad advisors like Marwan would not let him budge as it went against their tribal and personal interest.

In the end the advice and the policy devised by Marwan cost Caliph Uthman his life.

12.9.2. The Inhabitants of Madinah

Another key point that comes out from the killing of Caliph Uthman is the fact that there was no resistance offered by the inhabitants of Madinah against his killing. Even though the inhabitants of Madinah were way more in numbers than the invading protestors, but they chose to stay on the side lines. If the inhabitants of Madinah wanted to, they could have easily ended the siege of Caliph Uthman's house by the protestors, but they chose not to act and allowed the protestors to take over the residence of Caliph Uthman.

The reason was obvious, most of the inhabitants of Madinah were Ansar i.e., companions from Madinah, and they had no qualms about ending the caliphate of Uthman, since they saw him as an Umayyad caliph who was simply enriching his own clan.

Readers would recall that in the meeting of Saqifah, Caliph Abu Bakr had justified his Caliphate to the Ansar on the pretext that the right of leadership only belonged to the Quraysh, hence there cannot be a Caliph from the Ansar. Similarly, Caliph Umar had said to his six-member Shura that the Caliphate would only stay in the Qurayshite clans and Ansar would have no say in it.

Caliph Uthman took the notion of Qurayshite leadership to new heights. During Caliph Uthman's reign the Islamic State became a Qurayshite Kingdom of the Umayyad clan, with all the key provinces being ruled by the Umayyad governors.

The inhabitants of Madinah felt frustrated and marginalized at the hands of the Quraysh. That is why when Caliph Uthman was besieged the Ansar did not intervene or supported the Caliph as they felt no obligation to save an Umayyad Caliph.

12.9.3. The Incredible Choices

Caliph Uthman made two astonishing choices which in the end cost him his life. One of them was the appointment of Abu Sarh as the governor of Egypt, and the other one was to choose Marwan bin al-Hakam as his closest advisor.

When Caliph Uthman was besieged, it was the group of protestors from Egypt who were most vocal in their opposition against the Caliph. The reason why there was so much opposition in Egypt against Caliph Uthman was because he had chosen his foster brother Abu Sarh as the governor of Egypt.

Caliph Uthman had boasted how the camels were giving more milk in Egypt after Abu Sarh's appointment. Essentially under the governorship of Abu Sarh the province of Egypt was sending more money to the Islamic treasury of the central government since Egyptians were being overtaxed. This made ordinary Egyptians poorer and impoverished, hence they came in droves to protest against the Caliph and his governor.

Readers would also recall that Abu Sarh was a known enemy of the Prophet who had embraced Islam and then apostatized. At the conquest of Makkah, Prophet had ordered Abu Sarh to be killed even if he was found hiding under the curtain of Kaaba. However, later Prophet reluctantly forgave Abu Sarh as Caliph Uthman pleaded for his life and none of the companions followed Prophet's orders of killing Abu Sarh.

The choice of Abu Sarh, a known enemy of the Prophet as the governor of Egypt was incredible and flawed and in the end cost Caliph Uthman his life.

Similarly, the choice of Marwan bin al-Hakam as his top advisor was a huge blunder by Caliph Uthman. Marwan was the son of al-Hakam, who was again a well-known enemy of the Prophet. The Prophet of Allah had exiled the entire family of al-Hakam from Madinah for his constant harassment and intimidation.

Al-Hakam was also Caliph Uthman's uncle. In a clear breach of the Sunnah of the Prophet, Caliph Uthman not only brought the entire family of al-Hakam back to Madinah, but he also chose his son Marwan to be his top advisor.

On the advice of Ali when Caliph Uthman had finally agreed to start the process of reforms in a speech at the mosque of the Prophet, it was Marwan who made him backtrack on his promises. Marwan at that time came out and reprimanded the opposition which thwarted the reconciliatory efforts of Ali. Even when Caliph Uthman was besieged for forty days, Marwan did not allow the Caliph to change his policies, as the demands of the opposition went against the Umayyad tribal and Marwan's personal interests.

It was the advice and the decisions of Marwan which in the end destroyed the Caliphate of Uthman and cost him his life.

12.9.4. The Character of Ali

During the establishment of the Islamic State of Madinah the sword of Ali was the differentiating factor on the battlefield among all the companions. Similarly, after the death of the Prophet and during the biggest crisis facing the Muslim Ummah it was the character of Ali which became the differentiating feature of the crisis.

The training and the upbringing of Ali at the hands of the Prophet was visible from every unselfish step that Ali took in the interest of the Islamic State during the crisis.

No temptation or political opportunity of any magnitude could sway Ali into manipulating the events in his favour. Unlike other opportunistic and politically minded companions who used a genuine grievance to further their own political aims, or to settle their scores with Caliph Uthman, Ali chose a path which confirmed his status as the true successor of the Prophet. Because a person who was chosen by the Prophet could have never taken advantage of a political situation at the expense of the Islamic State.

The legacy of Saqifah had brought upon a crisis on the Muslim Ummah which in fact became a true test of everyone's character. The Prophet was no longer there to guide and steer the ship, or to keep a lid and a check on the actions of the companions. Everyone was free to act in a way which reflected their own inner feelings and temptations. At that critical juncture where others seem to fail the test, the character of Ali comes out in shining armour.

In the absence of the Prophet when other companions felt that there was everything to play for, Ali passes the true test of character with flying colours. The events of history itself testify that Ali never took a step which breached the Sunnah of the Prophet, despite the fact that Ali had the strongest claim to the Caliphate. He tried his best to guide both Caliph Uthman and the opposition according to the path laid out by the Prophet, in order to defuse the crisis and preserve the unity of the Muslim Ummah.

Throughout the course of the crisis Ali upheld the Sunnah of the Prophet to the letter. The actions of Ali proved beyond any doubt that Ali was in fact the custodian of the Sunnah of the Prophet, an honour that could only belong to the rightful successor of the Prophet.

Ali was indeed that unique and distinct companion of the Prophet whose merits are proven by the actual events of history, unlike the academic merits of many companions which are mentioned in the books but have no relevance or bearing on the historical events which shaped the early history of Islam.

12.9.5. The Vindication of the Prophet's Strategy

In the meeting of Saqifah where the choice of the Prophet was ignored in favour of Caliph Abu Bakr, resulted in a progressive downfall of the institution of the Caliphate, to the extent that the Caliphate ended up into the hands of the Umayyads, a clan which had been the biggest enemy of the Prophet and the Muslims. The Umayyads had fought the Muslims for almost two decades, and they had only accepted Islam after they were completely defeated by the Muslims at the conquest of Makkah.

The simple fact that a clan like the Umayyads had manage to acquire the leadership of the Islamic State, testifies that the decision made in Saqifah to side-line the nominee of the Prophet was a catastrophe that was waiting to happen. The events of history which took place in the aftermath of Saqifah bear witness to the fact that the Islamic leadership had lost its spiritual and moral direction, and the Islamic State had in fact become a toy in the hands of the Umayyad leaders like Marwan and Muawiyah.

Readers would recall that the reason why Ali was not chosen in Saqifah was because the non-Hashimite clans of Quraysh did not want to see the leadership of the Muslim Ummah to remain in the clan of Banu Hashim. And both Caliph Abu Bakr and Caliph Umar advocated and represented this view and the sentiments of Quraysh in Saqifah.

As Ali belonged to the clan of Banu Hashim just like the Prophet, Ali was bypassed in Saqifah, even though Ali was chosen by the Prophet to lead the Muslim Ummah. The tribal tone of Saqifah where Ali was ignored simply because of his lineage could never do justice to the leadership of the Muslims, and this fact eventually became evident from the events of history itself.

The dominance of the trend of al-ijtihad (independent judgment) in the meeting of Saqifah, where the clear Sunnah of the Prophet was breached in favour of a Qurayshite candidate, eventually resulted in ending the unity of the Muslim Ummah once and for all, and opened the doors to civil wars which would cost the lives of thousands companions and ordinary Muslims.

12.9.5.1. Shura was not Part of the Prophet's Strategy

The process of Shura was never part of Prophet's plan for choosing his successor.

Readers would recall that the Shura of Saqifah did not include Ali and did not represent all the key Muslim factions that existed at the time of the death of the Prophet. The clan of Banu Hashim and the Ahlulbayt were missing from the gathering of Saqifah. But even if the Shura of Saqifah was done fairly with the participation of all the Muslim groups, even then there was no guarantee that Ali would come on top, and he would have been chosen as the leader of the Muslim Ummah.

For instance, the Shura setup by Caliph Umar to choose the third Caliph did include Ali, but still Ali was not chosen as the Shura was biased towards Caliph Uthman.

The process of Shura or elections by their very nature cannot guarantee that the best and the most able individual would always win the day. A Shura or elections, even if they are done sincerely, could potentially bring the best, the second best, an average person, or even a person who does not deserve to be chosen as the leader of the nation, as we saw was the case with Shura that was established by Caliph Umar where Caliph Uthman was chosen.

It was for this reason that Prophet had not envisaged the process of Shura or elections as a method for choosing his successor.

12.9.5.2. *The Prophet's Plan*

The Prophet's plan was to ensure that the spiritual and the ideological message of Islam stays in the right hands.

Islam was not simply a set of beliefs that were kept in one's heart. Islam at its core was a completely new system of governance for the Arabs that had come to eradicate their previous customs and their old way of life, which had had been entrenched among their midst for centuries.

The reformatory movement of Islam was driven by a brand-new ideology that Prophet of Allah had introduced into the Arabian Peninsula. The Islamic framework comprised of a complete new set of rules and instructions which were extracted from the Book of Allah and the Sunnah (traditions) of the Prophet.

The successor of the Prophet was responsible for upholding and defending the ideological message of Islam, alongside implementing the system of governance that was devised by the Prophet. For this very reason the Prophet had to ensure that the person who succeeds him had the right credentials, in order to ideologically lead the newly established Islamic State, without jeopardizing its future and without bringing the Sunnah of the Prophet into disrepute.

The only way that Prophet could ensure and guarantee that the best and the most able candidate is chosen to lead the ideological movement of Islam was to hand pick someone himself. Any other system of appointment or selection could not guarantee the desired outcome.

It was for this reason that Prophet had not left the issue of his successor to the Ummah, as the Ummah could not possibly decide as to who should have been the ideological successor of the Prophet.

Also, the person who could hold such a position would not simply appear on the horizon near the time of the death of the Prophet. The Prophet would have to train and groom this person from an early age, and ingrain into him the ideals of Islamic thought and spirit, to ensure that one day he could truly represent the Prophet in his absence.

This was exactly the plan and the strategy of the Prophet when he adopted Ali as a child. Prophet trained and worked on Ali for almost twenty-five years before Ali was ready to take over the mantle of the Islamic leadership. The events which unfolded immediately after the death of the Prophet in the form of Saqifah side-lined Ali, but the history itself in the end vindicated the plan and the strategy of the Prophet.

If Ali had taken over the reign of the Muslim world as planned by the Prophet, the Muslim Ummah would have been saved from the disastrous legacy of Saqifah. The Umayyad's who had been the biggest enemy of the Prophet would have never been able to acquire the leadership of the Islamic world. The likes of Marwan and Muawiyah would have never had the privilege of interfering in the destiny of the Muslims.

12.9.5.3. Our Responsibility

Unfortunately, history took a wrong turn after the death of the Prophet, but fortunately as Muslims we are not bound by the turns of history or the legacy of Saqifah. Our responsibility in this life is to simply follow the Sunnah of the Prophet, which inevitably forces us to follow the plan and the strategy laid out by the Prophet, instead of following the path laid out by the events of history.

We leave the case of Caliph Abu Bakr, Caliph Umar, and Caliph Uthman with Allah, as on the Day of Judgment we will not be held accountable for their actions or decisions. At the same time, on the Day of Judgment we will be held accountable for our own actions and decisions that we make in our lifetime.

As Ahle Sunnah, the followers of the Sunnah, we have no choice but to follow the Sunnah of the Prophet. The Ahle Sunnah, more than any other group have an obligation to recognize the clear Sunnah of the Prophet, and to give allegiance to the person whom Prophet had chosen to lead the Muslims.

The allegiance to Ali is allegiance to the Sunnah of the Prophet and the allegiance to Saqifah is a clear negation of the Sunnah of the Prophet.

13. THE MAKINGS OF THE TRAGEDY

The most disastrous consequence of the Umayyads coming to power was felt some two decades after the death of Caliph Uthman, when Yazid the Umayyad Caliph of the time murdered the entire family of the Prophet on the plains of Karbala which is a city in southern Iraq today.

The makings of this tragedy which is known as the tragedy of Karbala was undoubtedly manifested in the fateful meeting of Saqifah when the choice of the Prophet was ignored in favour of the trend of al-ijtihad (independent judgment). The prominent companions chose a leader who would suffice the political will of the Quraysh, rather than to choose the most able person who was trained and nominated by the Prophet to lead the Ummah.

Both Caliph Abu Bakr and Caliph Umar during their respective reigns as Caliphs had a golden opportunity to return the Caliphate to its rightful successor. They were fully aware of Ali's relation to the Prophet and Ali's indisputable claim to the Caliphate. However, just as Ali was side-lined in Saqifah they both chose to bypass Ali too. Caliph Abu Bakr nominated Caliph Umar on his deathbed to be the next caliph, whereas Caliph Umar tipped the balance in favour of the Umayyads by admitting Caliph Uthman to the six-member Shura which gave him the caliphate.

Caliph Umar was well-aware of the mentality of the Umayyads, he had seen how Umayyad influence had started to grow under Muawiyah's rule in Syria during his own reign. Looking at the lifestyle of Muawiya, Caliph Umar once compared him to Kasra (Sassanian King), yet he did nothing to stop the grandeur of Muawiyah in Syria (Ansab al Ashraf, vol. IV, p550). Despite knowing these facts about the Umayyads, Caliph Umar formed a Shura which had no political will to choose Ali and had all the makings of bringing the Umayyads to the seat of power.

Even if Ali would have taken office as the third Caliph it still wasn't too late. Muawiyah had not come of age at the death of Caliph Umar. Ali could have removed the Umayyad plant in its infancy. But the trend of al-ijtihad stopped Caliph Umar from choosing the nominee of the Prophet and tipping the balance of the Shura in favour of Ali.

By the time Caliph Uthman was killed the Umayyads were well entrenched in the fabric of the Islamic State. They had already laid their hands on all the key provinces of the Muslim world such as Kufa, Basra, Egypt, and Syria. In the case of Syria, they had made it into a de facto Umayyad State where Muawiyah had absolute power, without any supervision or checks from the central government in Madinah.

The killing of Caliph Uthman in Madinah had caught the Umayyad's off guard. It was a huge shock and a setback for them as they were not expecting the murder of their top man. They did not envisage that the protestors who had gathered in Madinah could kill the Caliph.

The killing of Caliph Uthman had completely changed the political scene in the Islamic State. As a result of Caliph Uthman's killing the Umayyads had temporarily lost the political initiative especially in the city of Madinah. The Umayyads were in shock and disarray after the murder of Caliph Uthman. They struggled to regroup and remained in a limbo for a few days. This gave the natives of Madinah an opportunity to assert themselves politically, something that they had been denied since the debacle of Saqifah.

Both Caliph Abu Bakr and Caliph Umar had opposed the Ansar (companions of Madinah) from acquiring the leadership of the Islamic State. For instance, Caliph Abu Bakr had argued against the Ansar in Saqifah and had thwarted their plans of taking over the leadership of the Muslim Ummah. Similarly, when Caliph Umar formed a committee (Shura) to choose the next ruler he categorically stated that the Ansar could observe the proceedings of the Shura, but they had no right to the leadership of the Islamic State.

After the demise of the first three Caliphs the Ansar had realized that the only person who could serve and defend their interests was indeed Ali, the nominee of the Prophet, and someone who they had side-lined in Saqifah. However, times had changed, and now they flock to the door of Ali insisting and pleading that he takes over the reins of the Islamic State.

13.1. The Caliphate of Ali

The Caliphate of Ali came out of the blue. It certainly wasn't part of the Umayyad plan. After twenty-three years of non-Hashimite rule there was very little chance that the Caliphate would ever come back to the clan of Banu Hashim or to the door of Ali. If it were up to the Umayyads then Ali would have never even sniffed the fragrance of the Caliphate.

As mentioned above the killing of Caliph Uthman had stunned the Umayyads and they were struggling to cope with the political fallout. This allowed the inhabitants of Madinah (Ansar) to rally in favour of Ali. It was simply by chance that Ali found himself as a candidate for the fourth Caliphate.

After the corruption and nepotism of Caliph Uthman people had finally realized the strategic mistake that they had made in accepting the path of Saqifah. Apart from the Ansar many prominent companions and many ordinary Muslims were now standing behind Ali to be the next Caliph.

The people now turn to Ali in droves with the following words and insisted that he takes on the mantle of the Islamic leadership.

> "We shall choose none but you……We know of no one who has more right or precedence in Islam or closer relation to the Prophet than you."

- Al-Tabari his History part 4 p. 427

> "No man has given more distinguished service to Islam, nor is anyone closer to Muhammad than you. We consider you to be the worthiest of all men to be our Khalifa."

- Tarikh Kamil, Vol. III, p. 98, Ibn Atheer

Ali however was now reluctant to take on the reins of power of the Muslim Ummah. The political scene and the dynamics of the Islamic State had completely changed after two decades of Qurayshite rule. The ways and the trends of the Umayyads were well entrenched in the Islamic diaspora. The corruption, nepotism, and the exploitation of public wealth by Muslim elites was no longer taboo, but it had in fact become a norm for many privileged individuals in the Islamic State.

Ali was not after a ceremonial position where he simply becomes the figurehead of the Islamic State for the sake of acquiring the political office of the Caliphate, while the corruption and the nepotism continued unabated under his nose. Ali was not looking to fill the political vacuum left by the killing of Caliph Uthman, while the Umayyads bided their time to regroup and plan their next move. Simply acquiring the political office of the Caliphate had never been the aim or the approach of Ali, and that wasn't going to change now.

Ali's sole ambition was to bring the Ummah back to the path of the Prophet without compromising on the principles of Islam. After the rule of the first three Caliphs the only way Ali could achieve this goal was to get the people to support and accept his agenda of reforms and change. For this very reason Ali was initially reluctant to take over the reins of power because Ali wanted the people to accept his terms and conditions first before he takes their pledges of allegiance.

Ali wanted to transform the Islamic State back to the times of the Prophet, and he wanted to make sure that the people who pledge allegiance to him understood his priorities and would support his agenda of reforms.

Ali laid out his terms to the people for becoming their Caliph. He informed the masses that if they choose him, he will strictly rule according to the Holy Quran and the Sunnah of the Prophet.

> *"If you want me for your worldly desires, leave me alone and choose another one who may realize your wishes. I will not give up the principles of Islam to secure neither my authority nor the interests of the others. With regard to the subject of the rights and privileges enjoyed by every one, I do not care for the influential people because all the peoples are equal before God. If you have decided to pay homage to me, think it over and over because after the homage if you protest against me or put obstructions in my way, I will force you to come back to the right path. Bear in mind these conditions, and then you can reach your heart's desires."*
>
> - *Nahjul Balagha*
> - *Kitab-ul-Imamah was-Siyasah*

The words of Ali sum up the corruption and nepotism that had plagued the institution of Caliphate, where worldly desires and personal interests had overshadowed the sublime principles of Islam.

Ali clarified to the people that if they were after material wealth then he wasn't their man. Ali states that he would not protect the interests of a privileged few at the expense of others. Ali also reassures people that he would not use his position as a means of securing or extending his own authority. Ali reminds all his subjects that the elite class and the people of influence would be treated just like everybody else, as all Muslims are equal in the eyes of Allah. Ali warns his subjects that if they chose him as their leader then they would not be allowed to put obstructions in his way, as he intends to bring them back to the path of Allah.

The people of Madinah and the majority of the Muslims accepted the conditions laid out by Ali, and with the support of the people of Madinah behind him Ali finally accepts the will of the people and becomes the fourth Caliph.

Once Ali takes over the reins of power, he issues a strict decree:

> *"The public are hereby notified that a decree will be issued against those who have made money in unlawful ways and their monies will be requisitioned. The offenders will be soon prosecuted..."*
>
> - *Nahjul Balagha*

From the very onset of his Caliphate Ali lays out the new rules of governance, which would inevitably collide with the interests of many influential groups that had been privileged in the previous administrations.

Ali argued that prior to the murder of Caliph Uthman the demands of the protestors were legitimate. The corruption, extortion, nepotism, monopolies, and autocracies were deeply embedded in the core of the state. Ali stated that he would seek to end the economic exploitation and corruption within the state, and he would put an end to the extravagant materialism that was being displayed in the name of Islam.

The purging of the state from corruption required reversing the policies of Caliph Uthman. This was where the troubles began for Ali's administration. As Ali sought to change the course of the Caliphate after his inauguration the opposition to his rule began in earnest.

The Caliphate was diverted away from Ali when the Muslim Ummah was strong and united, and unfortunately it was given to Ali when the Islamic nation had been divided and the Caliphate itself had become a bloody affair.

13.1.1. The Elite Class and the Privileged Companions

As readers would recall that Caliph Umar had classed the companions into categories. The companions who belonged to the preferred categories would get more money than others. This method of distribution of public funds continued under the leadership of Caliph Uthman too, and it resulted in the creation of a completely new rich and wealthy class of companions which had never existed at the time of the Prophet. This new elite group of companions had no wish to lose their power, wealth, privileges, and social status that they had acquired over time.

Then there were rich and prosperous Umayyads who had massed huge amounts of wealth because of Caliph Uthman's rule. Many of Caliph Uthman's appointed governors also had huge sums of money and owned vast pieces of land. This also created an entirely new wealthy class of Muslims which never existed at the time of the Prophet. They also saw Ali as a serious threat to their lifestyle and the status quo.

Ali dissolved the preferred class of companions and went back to distributing the funds equally among all the companions as was done during the time of the Prophet. This caused a huge backlash against the administration of Ali from the preferred companions.

Ali also intended to recover the vast amounts of money and land that the Umayyad's had acquired, and he wanted to put it back into the Islamic treasury. This also resulted in massive opposition from the officials of the previous administration who had no intention of relinquishing their newfound wealth.

Ali further proceeded with his plans to reform the administration of the Islamic State by dismissing the governors that Caliph Uthman had appointed. However, the governors refused to step down and challenged Ali's authority making the transition extremely difficult for Ali and his new administration.

13.1.2. The Politically Ambitious Companions

As mentioned previously Caliph Umar had included Talha and al-Zubair in the six-member Shura which had brought Caliph Uthman to power. This move in itself had inflamed the political ambitions of the Shura members, since they were not only chosen to elect the next caliph, but they were also made candidates for the position of the Caliphate. Both Talha and al-Zubair did all they could to bring down the Caliphate of Uthman, hoping that they could replace Caliph Uthman as the new Caliph.

Unfortunately for Talha and al-Zubair the Caliphate had ended up in the hands of Ali and all their efforts against Caliph Uthman had gone to waste. They did not bring the administration of Caliph Uthman down for Ali to be at the helm of the Islamic State. As Ali took over the mantle of the Islamic government, they realized that their best hope now was to possibly acquire the governorship of one of the provinces within the Islamic State. They both approached Ali seeking the governorship of a province in the Islamic State.

However, Ali did not entertain their request and gave them the cold shoulder. Ali could not possibly give them the governorship of a province when Ali had witnessed their political ambitions at first hand. Ali had seen with his own eyes how Talha and al-Zubair had used a genuine grievance against Caliph Uthman to further their own political careers. The governorship that they were seeking was purely for the purpose of advancing their own political ambitions rather than to serve the Islamic nation. Ali could not possibly allow such a move in his administration.

Disappointed with the response of Ali, Talha and al-Zubair followed the same approach towards the Caliphate of Ali as they did towards the Caliphate of Uthman. They joined the ranks of the opposition and did everything they could to discredit Ali and bring down his government.

Both Talha and al-Zubair were extremely powerful. Their fortunes alone were in millions of dirhams (Al-Tabaqat, Part3, p.110, p122). They also had the support of the Qurayshite clans including large number of people from Basra and Kufa. And above all they had the support of the powerful wife of the Prophet Lady Aisha. Lady Aisha, being the wife of the Prophet and daughter of the first Caliph commanded huge influence and prestige. She was instrumental in fermenting the revolt against Caliph Uthman as she wanted to replace him with her cousin Talha or her brother-in-law Al-Zubair.

Lady Aisha had called for the head of Caliph Uthman, but she was even more hostile to Ali. She was one of the biggest obstacles that Ali had to face and overcome during his reign. She used all her influence and sway to stir people against Ali, which eventually resulted in her leading an army against Ali in a battle famously known as the battle of Camel (Jamal).

Lady Aisha was one of the most outspoken critics of Caliph Uthman's administration. It was her propaganda and agitation against Caliph Uthman that became a key factor in bringing the rebels to Madinah and besieging the Caliph, which eventually resulted in his murder. However, her attitude towards Caliph Uthman immediately reversed when she received the news that Ali had been chosen as the new Caliph.

Here reversal could be witnessed in the following dialogue that she had with Obeid Ibn Abu Salema. The dialogue took place while lady Aisha was returning from the pilgrimage.

> *Aisha: What do you know?*
> *Obeid: Uthman was killed and the people remained eight days without a caliph.*
> *Aisha: Then what did they do? Obeid: They elected Ali.*
> *Aisha: May Heaven fall on earth if your man succeeds. Return me to Makkah.*
> *She turned her face towards Makkah saying "By God Uthman was killed unjustly. By God I shall avenge for his blood.".*
> *Obeid: By God you are the first one who discredited him. You used to say about him: Kill Naathal (likening Uthman to a heavily bearded Arab Jew named Naathal) because he deserted the faith.*
> *Aisha: They made him repent then they killed him. They said and I said and my last saying is better than my first saying.*
>
> - *(Abn Al-Atheer Al-Kamil part 3 p. 106)*

After hearing the news of Ali's Caliphate, Lady Aisha had a sudden change of heart towards Caliph Uthman. She made a complete U turn and started calling for avenging the death of Uthman, even though she was one of the key perpetrators advocating for his murder, alongside Talha and Al-Zubair. She justified her new stance in a peculiar way by stating that her last saying (i.e. avenging the death of Uthman) was better than her first saying (i.e. advocating the killing of Caliph Uthman).

Her change of heart towards Caliph Uthman was purely political as she was stunned by the news of Ali's Caliphate. She had not imagined that after twenty-five years of Qurayshite rule, Ali could possibly get a shot at the leadership of the Islamic State. She could not stand the fact that Ali had acquired the top position as she was hoping that either Talha or Al-Zubair would succeed Uthman.

13.1.3. Lady Aisha Starts a Ferocious Campaign Against Ali

Almost as soon as Ali took over the reins of the Caliphate Lady Aisha started a ferocious campaign against Ali and his government.

She went to the sacred mosque in Makkah and gave a fiery speech urging people to avenge the blood of Caliph Uthman. Her audience in Makkah were the Qurayshites tribes who shared her dislike and hatred of Ali since the days of the Prophet. Ali had killed some of the finest Qurayshite warriors in the defence and the establishment of the Islamic State. They could not stand the sight of Ali let alone accept him as their leader. They had made continuous efforts for the last twenty-five years to keep Ali away from the Caliphate. They knew that Makkah was a sacred city and Ali would not violate the sanctity of Makkah, so it was an ideal place for the conspirators to gather and work against Ali and his government.

As mentioned previously both Talha and Al-Zubair were aspirants to be the next Caliphs after Uthman. However, their dreams were shattered when the Ansar rallied behind Ali and gave him the Caliphate. They were now hoping that Ali might give them the governorship of one the provinces in the Islamic State. However, Ali chose not to give them any positions in his administration. Keeping in line with their political ambitions both Talha and Al-Zubair joined the call of Lady Aisha and mobilized their supporters to take on the Caliphate of Ali.

Lady Aisha, Talha and Al-Zubair used the excuse that Caliph Uthman was innocently killed, and Ali was not bringing his killers to justice, hence, to seek justice Ali must be fought and removed from the office. The irony of their call against Ali could not be more unjust and illegitimate, since these three individuals were in fact the key players who had advocated the killing of Caliph Uthman (Al-Tabari his History part 4 p. 459). Ali on the other hand was the only person who had tried his upmost to save both the life and the Caliphate of Uthman.

The actual killers of Caliph Uthman had since runaway and their whereabouts were unknown. Some reports had suggested that they were killed after killing Caliph Uthman, while others suggested that they had escaped from Madinah altogether. Ali also said that he could not possibly punish the rest of the protestors as they had no actual part in the killing itself, and the protestors had since disappeared and many of them had gone back to their hometowns such as Egypt, Basra, Kufa etc.

History has recorded five names who could potentially have been the killers of Caliph Uthman. They were Soudan Ibn Hamran, Al-Gahafiqi, Qutairah, Kinannah Ibn Bashir and Amr ibn Al-Hamiq (Al-Tabari, part 4, p. 391-394). History also recorded that Soudan Ibn Hamran, Qutairah and Kinannah Ibn Bashir were killed at the same time when Caliph Uthman was killed (Ibn Al-Atheer Al-Kamil part 3 pp. 89-90, Al-Tabari part 4 p. 431, Ibn Al-Atheer Al-Kamil part 3 p. 102).

Thus, only two of the actual killers of Caliph Uthman had survived, but Lady Aisha, Talha and Al-Zubair did not go after the actual killers, as it did not serve their political interests. Instead, they went after Ali and his administration. They used the pretext of avenging Caliph Uthman's murder to further their own political aims and bring down the Caliphate of Ali. They had previously taken a similar approach towards Caliph Uthman and had succeeded in bringing down his government. They were now determined to do the same to Ali and his establishment.

13.1.4. Lady Aisha, Talha and Al-Zubair Launch a War Against Ali

Lady Aisha, Talha and Al-Zubair went to Basra and mobilized a huge army against Ali. Despite the fact that Lady Aisha was the wife of the Holy Prophet and carried his honour, she led an entire army of men against Ali on a Camel. This is something which was unheard of in that era. Even now in 21st century for a pious Muslim lady to lead an army of men would be a rare phenomenon.

In any case as most of the fighting took place around the camel of Lady Aisha the battle is famously known as the "Battle of Camel (Jamal)".

Ali tried his level best to avoid this war. When Lady Aisha reached the battlefield, Ali sends his son al-Hasan to try and convince her against instigating the war, but she turned down Ali's request in those final moments. Ali then sends her own brother Muhammad bin Abu Bakr to try and persuade her away from the path of violence, but she did not heed his advice either and refused to budge. She was determined to defeat and kill Ali and take the Caliphate away from him.

The battle finally commences, and the army of Ali eventually wins the battle. Talha is killed on the battlefield. Al-Zubair did not join the battle but remained in the camp of Lady Aisha. Even though Lady Aisha had led the army against Ali, and despite all her actions and hostility towards Ali, Ali did not harm or hurt her. Instead, he sends her back to Madinah with her brother Muhammad bin Abu Bakr.

A lesser man than Ali would have certainly taken a different course of action after overpowering the enemy, but such was the magnanimous character of Ali!

It is reported that almost 10,000 companions of the Prophet and ordinary Muslims were killed in this battle (Al-Tabari his History part 4 p. 539). The only reason why such a tragedy fell on the Muslim Ummah was because Lady Aisha, Talha and Al-Zubair had refused to accept the authority of Ali, for no reason other than the fact that they had their own personal and political ambitions to acquire the Caliphate of the Muslims.

Also, Ali's Caliphate was unlike the Caliphate of the previous caliphs. Ali was not only the choice of the Prophet, but he was also the choice of the people too. The previous three caliphs were either chosen through the Shura or through direct nomination. For instance, Caliph Abu Bakr was chosen through the Shura of Saqifah (if it could be called a Shura), and Caliph Umar was nominated by Caliph Abu Bakr to be the next Caliph. But Ali was not chosen by either of these methods, he was chosen by the people of Madinah who rallied behind him after the killing of Caliph Uthman.

Despite all these facts and realities Lady Aisha and her group simply used the excuse of avenging the killing of Caliph Uthman to bring down the administration of Ali, so that they could further their own narrow and selfish political ambitions. These three leaders took the law into their hands which caused the deaths of thousands of Muslims. They were neither the heirs nor the relatives of the murdered Caliph, and nor were they elected or appointed by the Muslim Ummah to avenge the blood of Caliph Uthman.

Their actions unfortunately represented their personal ambitions and political aspirations. And they used their influence to convince thousands of ordinary companions and Muslims to fight against a just Caliph, who had both been nominated by the Prophet of Allah and was also chosen by the people of the Ummah.

Also, despite the fact that as the wife of the Holy Prophet Lady Aisha was commanded by Allah to stay in her home, lady Aisha in her hostility towards Ali even transgresses the verses of the Holy Quran, and not only leaves her house but in fact ends up leading an army against the Caliph of the time.

> *"Wives of the Prophet, you are not like other women.....And stay in your homes and do not go about displaying your allurements as in the former time of Ignorance"*

- *Quran (33:32)*
- *Quran (33:33)*

Also, launching wars to avenge the killing of an individual was a pre-Islamic custom, where these wars of revenge would last for decades and would cost the lives of hundreds or thousands of people. Islam had come to put an end to all these Jahiliya (pre-Islamic) traditions which were re-established by Lady Aisha, Talha and al-Zubair in their quest for power.

Unfortunately, in her hostility towards Ali Lady Aisha had crossed all the lines. She even ignored the verses of the Quran and numerous traditions of the Prophet which were in favour of Ali, and she decided to fight the very person who was the flag bearer of Prophet's army.

The Prophet had famously said:

> *"The carrier of my flag in this life and the Hereafter is Ali."*

- *Kanz Al-Umal, 6/122*
- *Al-Tabari, 2/201*
- *Al-Khawarizmi, 250*
- *Al-Fada'il of Ahmad, 253*
- *Ibn Al-Maghazeli, 42/200*

Ali was indeed the flag bearer of Prophet's army in countless battles and expeditions, and still lady Aisha chose to fight Ali. The Prophet had in fact stated that Ali was not just his flag bearer in this world, but he was also his flag bearer in hereafter. Despite such clear words of the Prophet, Ali was not even allowed to settle down as the fourth Caliph while Lady Aisha began her opposition to the rule of Ali.

13.1.5. Talha and Al-Zubair's Revolt Against Ali

Talha and Al-Zubair had no legitimate excuse for their revolt against Ali. Talha and Al-Zubair were one of the first people to give allegiance to Ali when he became the fourth Caliph. Both these companions had a brilliant past during the time of the Prophet, but they broke their covenant with Ali after pledging allegiance to him. In fact, Al Zubair was one of the few companions who stood up for Ali against Caliph Abu Bakr when Ali was denied the first Caliphate.

When Caliph Umar came with his group of men to take allegiance from Ali, Al-Zubair challenged Caliph Umar and said:

> *"I shall not sheathe my sword until Ali is elected." Umar said to companions who were with him: Take his sword and hit the rock with it"*

- *Ibn Al-Atheer Al-Kamil part 3 p. 120*

At that time Al-Zubair was ready to fight for Ali's Caliphate with his sword. So, what had changed after twenty-five years that now al-Zubair was ready to fight against Ali, when Ali had in fact become the Caliph of the Muslims.

In twenty-five years, the world of both Talha and AL-Zubair had moved on. They were now rich and prosperous individuals with millions of dirhams of wealth and assets, thanks to the decree of Caliph Umar which resulted in creating an entirely wealthy class of companions. Furthermore, Caliph Umar made them think that they were equals of Ali, by making them candidates for the third Caliphate, alongside Ali. This inflamed their own political ambitions and they both became aspirants to be the next Caliphs.

Ali spoke to Talha and Al-Zubair before the battle of Jamal began. The words of Ali and the response of Talha and Al-Zubair are self–explanatory.

> *Ali: "Certainly you have prepared arms horses and men …. I do not know whether you have prepared an excuse when you meet your Lord on the Day of Judgment. Fear God and be not like a woman who unspun her strands after she had strongly spun it. Was I not your brother and you used to believe in the sanctity of my blood and I believed in the sanctity of your blood? Did I do anything that makes it legitimate for you to shed my blood? Then he said to Al-Zubeir: What brought you here?*
>
> *Al-Zubeir: You have brought me here and I do not believe that you are qualified to be caliph. You have no more right than we have to be caliphs. And you killed Uthman.*
>
> *Ali: … Zubeir do you hold me responsible for the blood of Uthman while you were his killer? May God punish today our harshest to Uthman"*
> - Al-Tabari his History part 4 p.501
> - Al-Tabari his History part 4 p.511

Ali reminded Talha and Al-Zubair about the past that once they were brothers and were on the same side, and that they should not embark upon shedding his blood and they should fear Allah. However, al-Zubair's response clarifies as to why these two companions were fighting Ali. Al-Zubair said to Ali that he was not qualified to be the Caliph and that they had as much right to be the Caliphs as Ali did, and that Ali had killed Uthman which indeed was not true.

Al-Zubair who was ready to fight with his sword for Ali's right of Caliphate some twenty-five years ago, now does not even consider Ali qualified enough to be a Caliph, and states that he had as much right to be a Caliph as Ali had, and hence he had come to fight Ali.

It is indeed sad to witness that how companions who were once righteous and had even supported the nominee of the Prophet (i.e., Ali), had now become his enemies and rivals!

Prophet had in fact predicted such a scenario. Prophet had informed the companions that a day would come when they would fight each other for worldly gains.

> *"….By Allah! I am not afraid that you will worship others along with Allah after my death, but I am afraid that you will fight with one another for the worldly things."*
> - al-Bukhari 1344, al-Bukhari Vol. 2, Book 23, Hadith 428
> - al-Bukhari 3596, al-Bukhari Vol. 4, Book 56, Hadith 795
> - al-Bukhari 6426, al-Bukhari Vol. 8, Book 76, Hadith 434

In a similar tradition the Prophet had said:

> *I am not afraid that you would associate anything with Allah after me, but I am afraid that you may be (allured) by the world and (vie) with one another (in possessing material wealth) and begin killing one another, and you would be destroyed as were destroyed those who had gone before you. 'Uqba said that that was the last occasion that he saw Allah's Messenger on the pulpit.*

- Sahih Muslim 2296 b, Sahih Muslim Vol. 6, Book 30, Hadith 5689

The prophecy of the Prophet had indeed come true. The companions were fighting for the material wealth of this world, killing each other, and destroying the unity of the Muslim Ummah once and for all.

It was for this very reason that Prophet had not envisaged his companions to be the custodian of his Sunnah. He knew through the light of Allah that a day would come when the companions would go against his Sunnah, and they would fight each other for material and worldly gains.

We saw how lady Aisha, Talha and Al-Zubair first led a rebellion against Caliph Uthman, with the sole aim of acquiring the Caliphate from him. Unfortunately for them the Caliphate came to the door of Ali, so now they launched a war against Ali to bring down his administration.

13.1.6. The Responsibility of Lady Aisha

Lady Aisha, being the wife of the Prophet should have been a role model for the Muslim Ummah. It was expected that a personality like lady Aisha would work for the unity and the stability of the Islamic State. Because of her position and standing among the Muslims she carried immense responsibility on her shoulders. She was meant to ensure that the newly established nation of Islam stayed firm and united.

Unfortunately, after the death of the Prophet she chose a path which did not do justice to her status and her stature.

Lady Aisha instigated thousands companions and ordinary Muslims against Ali, for a crime that she had indeed committed herself against Caliph Uthman. It was Lady Aisha and her group that had led the agitation against Caliph Uthman which eventually resulted in his killing, but she blamed Ali for it.

After twenty-five years of non-Hashimite rule many ordinary Muslims were not fully aware of the merits and the distinctions of Ali, and she was easily able to convince and persuade them to fight Ali. However, being the wife of the Prophet, she herself was fully aware of the unique position that Ali held in relation to the Prophet, but she chose to hide those merits from her supporters, and because of her actions against Ali thousands of ordinary Muslims and companions were innocently killed in the battle of Jamal.

The blood of these innocent Muslims will no doubt remain a question mark for her on the Day of Judgment.

The Prophet had indeed warned Lady Aisha from adopting such a path. Prophet had informed Lady Aisha that when she hears the barking of dogs around the well of Hawab, she should realize that she was on the wrong path.

> *Qays said: 'When Ayesha reached Bani Amer's well at night, some dogs barked at her. She asked: 'What is the name of this well?' They replied: 'This is Hawab's well'. She replied: 'I have to return'. Some of those who were with her said: 'Nay you shall go forward so that the Muslims shall see you and Allah makes peace'. She replied: 'Allah's messenger (pbuh) once said: 'Then what would you (the wives of the prophet) do when you hear the barking of Al-Hawab dogs?'*

- *Musnad Ahmed bin Hanbal, Volume 6 Pg 52 Tradition 24299*
- *Musanaf ibn Aby Shayba, Volume 8 page 708*

As lady Aisha reached the well of Hawab she heard the barking of the dogs and realized that she was in the wrong, but people around her convinced her to go forward and said to her that she might be able to bring peace. But when she moved forward, instead of bringing peace she refused all the offers of Ali not to start the war, and she turned down the mediation requests of al-Hasan and her own brother Muhammad bin Abu Bakr, and she chose to fight against Ali!

A similar warning to Lady Aisha is also found in other traditions of the Prophet.

> *Ibn Abbas narrated that Allah's messenger (S) said to his wives: 'Who amongst you would be the rider of the camel, she would march until the dogs of Hawab barked at her, many people shall be killed to the right and left of her. She would subsequently survive after which she would be made to feel guilty'*

- *Fatah ul Bari, Volume 13 page 55*
- *Majma al-Zawaed, Volume 7 page 474 Tradition 12026*

The Prophet had warned Lady Aisha that don't be the one who would ride the camel and beware when the dogs of Hawab would bark at her. He informed Lady Aisha that many people would be killed around her, but she would survive, and this is exactly what happened in the battle of Jamal. Thousands of Muslims were killed around Lady Aisha as she rode her camel into the battlefield.

There is no doubt that Ali was on the path of truth against Lady Aisha and her group. The following tradition of the Prophet confirms this notion. A person came to Umm Salama who was also the wife of the Prophet and asked her as to which side should he had taken in the battle of Jamal.

> *"...... I told her my story and she said: Where were you when the hearts flew away? I said to her: During that day Allah had relieved the doubt in me and I adopted the same stand (i.e. I was on the side of Ali).*
>
> *She said: Good on you. I once heard the Messenger of Allah (saw) say, Ali is with the Quran and the Quran is with Ali. They will never separate until they reach me at the lake-fount".*

- *al-Mustadrak 'Ala al-Sahihayn, al-Hakim al-Nisaburi, Volume 3, page 134, Hadeeth 4628*

Another tradition again confirms that in the battle of Jamal Muslims were either obeying Allah i.e., they were on the side of Ali, or they were on the side of Lady Aisha.

> *When Talha, al-Zubair and Aisha moved to Basra, Ali sent Ammar bin Yasir and Hasan bin Ali who came to us at Kufa and ascended the pulpit. Al-Hasan bin Ali was at the top of the pulpit and Ammar was below Al-Hasan. We all gathered before him. I heard Ammar saying, "Aisha has moved to Al-Basra. By Allah! She is the wife of your Prophet in this world and in the Hereafter. But Allah has put you to test whether you obey Him (Allah) or her (Aisha)."*

- *al-Bukhari 7100, al-Bukhari Vol. 9, Book 88, Hadith 220*

Lady Aisha was a scholar of her time. She knew many traditions of the Prophet by heart. She had spent almost fourteen years in the blessed company of the Prophet. Despite knowing all the traditions of Prophet in favour of Ali she still chose to fight him simply because of her political ambitions and her dislike of Ali.

Being the wife of the Prophet, Lady Aisha also had a lot of clout and following among the Muslim masses. But instead of supporting the administration of Ali to rectify the failings of the previous Umayyad government, she chose to launch a war against Ali which can only be described as a travesty.

Lady Aisha had launched the very first civil war in the Muslim Ummah which was immensely destructive and an extremely bloody affair for the Muslims. It destroyed the unity of the Muslims once and for all, and it opened the doors to many other wars which would soon follow the war of Jamal.

Needless to say, that the civil war that Lady Aisha had launched created a huge division and gulf among the Muslims, and the ramifications of those divisions unfortunately can still be felt in the Muslim Ummah.

13.1.7. Muawiyah and the Umayyad Clan

With the assassination of Caliph Uthman, the Umayyad's had lost the political clout in Madinah. However, the Umayyad's were way to smart and cunning to allow the Caliphate to slip away from them for too long. They immediately started working on getting their hands on the leadership of the Islamic State.

Their strong man Muawiyah was the defector ruler of greater Syria, who not only commanded a huge army but also had access to huge sums of money and wealth which he would use to buy loyalty and support from the tribal chiefs.

The Umayyad's were masters in exploiting the Arab tribal system where the tribesmen had to be in line with the decisions of their tribal chiefs, regardless of their own personal views. With all the money and wealth from the Islamic treasury at their disposal, the Umayyads were easily able to buy the loyalty of the tribal chiefs and entice them in supporting their candidate for the ultimate position of being the Caliph of the Muslims.

13.1.8. The Umayyad's Used Lady Aisha and her Group

The aim of the Umayyad's was also to dislodge the Caliphate of Ali, and their aim was in line with the aim of Lady Aisha, Talha and al-Zubair too. However, the Umayyads did not share their ultimate goal. The ultimate goal of the Umayyads was to have an Umayyad Caliph, whereas Lady Aisha's group was vying for Talha or al-Zubair to be the next Caliphs. While Umayyads had a common interest with Lady Aisha's group up to a certain point, which was to dislodge the Caliphate of Ali, but they also saw Lady Aisha, Talha and al-Zubair as dangerous political rivals.

They had witnessed at first-hand how these towering personalities had instigated the killing of an Umayyad Caliph. It was not something that they would forget or forgive easily. They were not fooled by the political slogans of avenging Caliph Uthman's death, as they knew exactly who the culprits were. They considered both Ali and Lady Aisha's group as their rivals, who had to be eliminated.

The war between lady Aisha's group and Ali was a blessing in disguise for the Umayyads. They saw it as a perfect opportunity to sow discord and disunity among the Muslims, and they used Lady Aisha's group to eliminate one of their main adversaries i.e., Ali. They worked behind the scenes to support her. The Umayyads were far more shrewd and cunning than Lady Aisha and her group. To the Umayyads it was an ideal proposition, even if Ali wins and comes on top, it means Lady Aisha's group would be eliminated, which would still be a win for the Umayyads, since they saw Lady Aisha, Talha and Al-Zubair as their rivals too.

And this is exactly what happened. Lady Aisha's group was defeated, Talha was killed and Al-Zubair withdrew from the scene, and only Ali was left to face the wrath of the Umayyads. The Umayyad's achieved their first goal pretty swiftly without even participating in the battle.

That is why once Lady Aisha's group had lost the battle against Ali and her army was retrieving, Marwan Ibn al-Hakam who was fighting against Ali on the side of Lady Aisha killed his own comrade Talha. The Umayyads saw no use for Lady Aisha's group anymore. Lady Aisha, Talha and Al-Zubair had already done the dirty work for the Umayyads by catastrophically damaging the Caliphate of Ali.

It was a perfect opportunity for them to avenge the killing of their Umayyad Caliph Uthman. They were not deceived by the slogans of Talha and Al-Zubair who were fighting Ali on the pretext of avenging the blood of Caliph Uthman.

As soon as Marwan saw an opportunity, he killed Talha and told Aban (Son of Caliph Uthman) that I have avenged the blood of your father.

> *"Talha was killed in the battle of Jamal by the arrow of Marwan, who then told Aban (son of Uthman) that I have taken the revenge for the blood of your father Uthman"*
>
> - *Siyar alam al-Nubala, Volume 1 page 36*
> - *Riyahul Nudhra, v 4, p 34*

Another report also confirms the above assertion.

> *Marwan Ibn-Hakam, who was in the ranks of Talha, saw Talha who was retreating (when his army was being defeated in the battlefield). Marwan and all Bani Umayyah considered him as the killer of Uthman. Marwan shot an arrow at him and severely wounded him. He then said to Aban, the son of Uthman, that: "I have spared you from one of your father's murderers." Talha was taken to a ruined house in Basra where he died.*
>
> - *Tabaqat, by Ibn Sa'ad, v3, part 1, p159*
> - *al-Isabah, by Ibn Hajar al-Asqalani, v3, pp 532-533*
> - *Tarikh Ibn al-Athir, v3, p244*
> - *Usdul Ghabah, v3, pp 87-88*
> - *al-Isti'ab, Ibn Abd al-Barr, v2, p766*
> - *A similar report is given in al-Mustadrak, by al-Hakim, v3, pp 169,37*

Readers would recall that Marwan was the chief advisor to Caliph Uthman. Lady Aisha, Talha and Al-Zubair had destroyed the Caliphate of Uthman, and Marwan saw that happen in front of his eyes. Marwan could not possibly forgive the killers of Caliph Uthman, and he also knew exactly who they were!

After the elimination of Lady Aisha's group, the Umayyad's had set their sights on bringing down the Caliphate of Ali. The top Umayyad leader at the time was none other than Muawiyah who had been the governor of Syria for over two decades. Marwan had now become a confidant of Muawiyah.

As mentioned previously Muawiyah had carved out an autonomous Syrian empire within the Islamic State, and was hoping to succeed Caliph Uthman, but the turn of events had gone against the Umayyads in Madinah, and they lost the political edge in the heart of the Islamic State temporarily.

13.1.9. Muawiyah Refused to Accept Ali and Launches a War

Unsurprisingly, Muawiyah the governor-cum-emperor of Syria refuses to recognize Ali as the new Caliph and challenges Ali's authority as the leader of the Muslims. Ali on his part intends to bring Syria back into the Islamic fold and remove Muawiyah from power. Ali orders Muawiyah to step down as the governor of

Syria and relinquish his authority. Muawiyah refuses to comply with the orders of Ali and instead starts a campaign in Syria to discredit Ali.

Muawiyah tells his supporters in Syria that since Ali was not bringing the killers of Caliph Uthman to justice, he must be fought and removed from the office.

In fact, this whole idea and notion that Ali must be fought to bring the killers of Caliph Uthman to justice had indeed come from Muawiyah in the first place. Muawiyah was the first person to suggest such a notion and instigated people against Ali, and Lady Aisha had simply jumped on the bandwagon that Muawiyah had started, because of her animosity towards Ali.

Muawiyah with all his cunningness would often display the blood-soaked shirt of Caliph Uthman to arouse people against Ali. Muawiyah used such tactics to get the sympathy of the Syrian Muslims for his cause, and to constantly remind his supporters about the murder of Caliph Uthman, a fellow Umayyad.

Muawiyah was a master politician. He would use such devious tricks to stir up hostility towards Ali and the central government. It was a classic political ploy by Muawiyah, where you make a reasonable but an unattainable demand from your opponent, with the sole purpose of discrediting him in the eyes of the public.

Muawiyah knew perfectly well that the demand for the vengeance of Caliph Uthman's blood was a mere deception. One of the key instigators against Caliph Uthman was Talha, who had already been killed by Marwan. The other two main agitators against Caliph Uthman were Lady Aisha and al-Zubair who had now withdrawn from the political scene. The actual killers of Caliph Uthman were allegedly five men, three of those men had already been killed and the whereabouts of the other two were unknown.

Also, the demand for the vengeance of Caliph Uthman's blood from Ali had no justification whatsoever. Ali was not in charge of the Islamic State when Caliph Uthman was killed. Ali was an ordinary citizen of the Islamic State when the killing of Caliph Uthman took place. It was Caliph Uthman and his administration who were running the show at the time, and they were tasked to protect the Caliph and not Ali.

The demand for the vengeance of Caliph Uthman's blood from Ali was completely unjustifiable, as Ali was neither responsible for protecting the life of Caliph Uthman, and nor was he responsible for bringing the killers to justice, since the killing was done before Ali took over the office of the Caliphate. It was the administration of Caliph Uthman who should have been held accountable for the killing of their own Caliph and not Ali.

Furthermore, if Muawiyah was indeed sincere in finding the killers of Caliph Uthman, then he should have first accepted the Caliphate of Ali, before demanding vengeance for the killing of Uthman. If you don't even accept someone as your leader, then you have no right to demand anything from them either. You cannot make a demand from someone whom you haven't even accepted as your Caliph. First, you must accept them as your leader and then by all means you can make a demand.

Muawiyah had never accepted Ali as the Caliph, he never paid allegiance to Ali, and he never accepted the authority of Ali. Hence, Muawiyah had no right to ask Ali for anything, let alone make a demand that Ali should bring the killers of Caliph Uthman to justice.

Despite these facts Muawiyah stuck to his guns and demanded that Ali should find the killers of Caliph Uthman. As Muawiyah increased his hostility towards Ali tensions reached a new height, and Muawiyah finally launched a war against Ali. He led an army from Syria to confront Ali who was a legitimate Caliph of the Muslims at the time.

Ali was left with no choice and had to lead an army from Kufa to take on the forces of Muawiyah. The two armies met at a place called Siffin which was just outside the Syrian border. The battle was hence named as the battle of Siffin.

This was the second civil war that Ali had to deal with in a very short span of time. The battle ends in a stalemate with no decisive victor. A reconciliation agreement (arbitration) is reached between the two warring parties to avoid further war and bloodshed. However, Muawiyah kept on with his malicious campaign against Ali in Syria and never recognized the legitimacy of Ali's Caliphate.

13.1.10. An Observation

The three leaders Lady Aisha, Talha and Al-Zubair had opened the doors to civil wars for mere political gains, even though they were some of the most renowned companions of the Prophet, especially Lady Aisha, who being the wife of the Prophet enjoyed a unique position. Had these prominent personalities supported the hand of Ali instead of instigating people against him, Muawiyah would have never had the courage to take on the authority of Ali.

When Muawiyah saw that a huge army rose against Ali on the behest Lady Aisha and her group, he felt emboldened in Syria and thought that he could do the same against Ali. Had Lady Aisha's group supported the caliphate of Ali, he would have removed the Umayyad sedation from the Ummah and he would have brought back the righteous Caliphate as ordained by the Prophet. The battle of Jamal was a key factor in Muawiyah's continued defiance against the Caliphate of Ali.

Although Ali's army had won against Lady Aisha, but both sides had been seriously weakened as thousands of Muslims had been killed on each side. The tribes of the defeated camp remained unfriendly and carried a grudge against Ali. The tribes in the camp of Ali were severely weakened by their losses and as a result lost the determination to wage a decisive war against Muawiyah, the Syrian King. This emboldened Muawiyah and allowed him to flourish in Syria, and Ali was unable to bring Syria back into the Islamic fold.

The three leaders i.e., Lady Aisha, Talha, Al-Zubair had successfully eliminated Caliph Uthman, but were unable to acquire the political position that they were hoping for. Instead, the circumstances somehow became in favour of Ali and people voluntarily accepted him as the new Caliph. The three leaders waged a war against Ali to bring down his Caliphate too. However, in the end they achieved absolutely nothing, except the fact that they managed to severely weaken the central government of Ali, to the extent that it was unable to control the Umayyad power base in Syria.

It would not be an exaggeration at all to say that because of the actions of these three prominent companions, the hands of the unrighteous Umayyad's such as Muawiyah were greatly strengthen against Ali, and it eventually allowed the Umayyads to take over the Islamic Caliphate for good.

This indeed was most tragic and disastrous for the Muslim Ummah.

13.1.11. The Khawarij

Another opposition to Ali's rule came from the Khawarij (the seceders), a breakaway group. They were a group of soldiers from Ali's army who were not happy with the arbitration that was achieved between Ali and Muawiyah in the battle of Siffin. As a result, they became an enemy of both Ali and Muawiyah.

They also engaged in a fierce battle with Ali's army outside the city of Kufa at a place called Naharwan. The battle was hence dubbed as the battle of Naharwan. Although Ali won the battle, but Khawarij later regrouped and continued to cause unrest, constantly challenging the authority of Ali.

Two years after the battle of Naharwan the Khawarij decided to kill Ali, Muawiyah and Amr Ibn Al-Auss at the same time. Muawiyah and Amr Ibn Al-Auss survived the assassination attempt, however Ali was not so lucky and was killed.

13.1.12. The Assassination of Ali

On the morning of the 19th of Ramadan 40 A.H., Ali came to the Great Mosque of Kufa to lead the morning prayers. He took his place in the alcove and the worshippers stood behind him. As the prayer began, standing in the front row with other worshippers was Abdur Rahman bin Muljam, a Khawarij who had come to kill Ali. He had hidden a sword in the folds of his cloak. Just as Ali touched the ground with his forehead for prostration (Sajda), Abdur Rahman bin Muljam stepped out of his row and crept into the alcove. As Ali lifted his head from the ground ibn Muljam struck the fatal blow on his forehead with such deadly force that it split open.

The words that Ali uttered when he was struck by the sword were remarkable, just as his life was. Ali said:

> "By the Lord of the Kaaba, I am successful!"
> - Nahjul Balagha

Ali had never made such a statement throughout his entire life. In the battle of Moat when Ali had killed Amr Ibn Abd Wudd who had crossed the moat into Madinah, Ali never said that he was successful. In the battle of Badr when Ali had disposed off almost 40% of the enemy soldiers, he never stated that he was successful. Similarly, when Ali conquered the Jewish fort of Khaibar where other companions like Caliph Abu Bakr and Caliph Umar had failed, Ali never claimed that he was successful. Even when Ali went to Mubahila alongside the Prophet and defeated the Christians of Najran, Ali never said that he was successful.

But when Ali was hit with a sword and was about to die, he said he had been successful.

The reason why Ali made such a statement when he was about to die was because his entire life was spent in the service of Islam. Ali had opened his eyes in the lap of the Prophet, and he was martyred in a mosque, prostrating in prayers, while he was fasting, an honour that very few individuals acquire in this world.

Ali was completely satisfied with his life and had no regrets about the path he had chosen. Ali had been a defender of the Prophet and his Sunnah since he was child. He had never placed his own interests above the interests of the Muslim Ummah. Even when his own right was being usurped, he remained patient and worked in the interest of the Islamic State. He never took a single selfish step that would harm the interests of the Muslims or the Islamic nation to further his own political career.

History had presented Ali with ample opportunities to take back his right, but he never manipulated any such events in his favour. Ali had declined the unscrupulous offer of Abu Sufyan to take out the Caliphate of Abu Bakr, which he had made soon after the inauguration of the first Caliph. Similarly, when the movement of desertion began to harm the very foundations of the Islamic State, Ali conceded his political authority to Caliph Abu Bakr, to aid the Islamic State against the rebels.

It was most unfortunate that although Ali had strengthened the hand of Caliph Abu Bakr and aided his administration against the rebels, but his daughter Lady Aisha choose to launch a war against Ali, especially when he needed some support to take on the Umayyad strong man Muawiyah. She chose not to return the favour that Ali had offered her father, and instead she instigated people to fight him, which indeed was most tragic and catastrophic for the Muslim Ummah.

Ali was indeed successful in this world and in hereafter, as Prophet had famously said:

> "O Ali! You are my brother in this world and in the Hereafter."
> - Al-Tirmidhi, Vol 2, Page 143

The meaning of the Arabic word Ali is "Most High". The life of Ali itself testifies that he was indeed the "Most High" after the Prophet.

13.2. The Caliphate of Hasan

After the Martyrdom of Ali his elder son Hasan takes the seat of the Caliphate in Kufa which was unanimously agreed upon by all the Muslims. Unfortunately, the Umayyad ascendency in the form of Muawiyah was in full swing. Muawiyah had been hoping to be the leader of the Muslims since the time of Caliph Uthman. Muawiyah's power base in Syria was now stronger than ever. He not only commanded the loyalty of almost all the Syrian tribes, but he also had a huge army which he could use to subdue his enemies.

13.2.1. Muawiyah Refuses to Accept the Caliphate of Hasan

Not surprisingly, Muawiyah refuses to recognize Imam Hasan as the legitimate Caliph, just as he had refused to recognize the Caliphate of Ali. Muawiyah being one of the most cunning and shrewd politicians of his time embarks on a mission to weaken the government of Imam Hasan. He starts a campaign to discredit Imam Hasan and undermines his authority by the following means:

- He uses the media of the time i.e., Friday sermons to spread propaganda about the character of Imam Hasan. He then ensures that the propaganda filters through from Syria to Iraq and Madinah through a network of his spies and informants.
- Muawiyah infiltrates Imam Hasan's power base in Kufa by sending spies and informants from Syria to find jobs in the government departments in Kufa. This keeps Muawiyah abreast of all the government activities in Kufa and gives him a huge edge in planning his moves accordingly.
- Muawiyah also infiltrates Imam Hasan's army, first at the lower ranks, but then he also recruits high ranking officers with a promise of large amounts of money to defect to him when called upon.

Muawiyah uses all the wealth and resources from the Islamic treasury in Syria to fulfil his dream of becoming the leader of the Muslim world.

His bribery and promises of money pay off. As Muawiyah's army of 60,000 men faces Imam Hasan's army of around 12,000 men, the commander of Imam Hasan's army Ubaydullah defects to Muawiyah. Muawiyah offered him 1 million dirhams, some reports suggest that he was offered 100,000 dirhams. Either way it was a huge sum of money even by today's standards.

Ubaydullah betrays Imam Hasan, and he switches allegiances in the middle of the night. By the time Imam Hasan's army realizes what has happened, Muawiyah plays another trump card the following morning. He falsely tells Imam Hasan's army that Imam Hasan has agreed to a peace arrangement (which was not true), and that he would also pay them money to come over to his side. The devious trick of Muawiyah worked perfectly, and around 8,000 soldiers out of 12,000 defected to Muawiyah, even though there was no peace agreement at that time. This completely destroyed the effectiveness and cohesion of Imam Hasan's army.

Having won over most of Imam Hasan's army through trickery and bribes, Muawiyah now offers Imam Hasan a peace treaty with the condition that the office of Caliphate should be handed over to him.

13.2.2. The Reasons for the Peace Treaty

Imam Hasan now considers his options of whether to go into battle against Muawiyah with his remaining army, which is completely demoralized and in absolute disarray, or take up the offer of Muawiyah for a peace treaty.

Peace treaties are always done with enemies where instead of using military force diplomatic means are used to overcome differences and end wars. In case of Imam Hasan there wasn't much of a military left to take on the might of Muawiyah's army. Imam Hasan contemplates his next move. He has the example of his grandfather Prophet Muhammad, where the Prophet of Allah had signed the peace treaty of Hudaybiyya with the pagans of Makkah, who were the worst enemy of Islam and Muslims at the time. That treaty also had some very harsh and unfavourable conditions for the Muslims.

Keeping the treaty of Hudaybiyya in mind, Imam Hasan decides to take the offer of Muawiyah and explains to his supporters as to why he has chosen this path:

> *'People of Allah! You know that Allah (swt) guided the people through my grandfather, and saved you from error and took you out of Jahiliya. Muawiyah has fought me over that matter which is my right not Muawiyah's. I was worried about protecting the Ummah, and you gave me bayah on the condition that you make peace with whoever I make peace with and fight whoever I fight. I looked at the problems and made peace with Muawiyah and put an end to war.*
> - *(Shaykh Mufti Kamaluddin Ibn Talha Shafiyee recorded in Matalib al Seul)*

Imam Hasan clarifies that Caliphate was his right rather than Muawiyah's, and Muawiyah had fought him to acquire the Caliphate, and he was finally making peace because he wanted to protect the Ummah from bloodshed and he wanted to put an end to the war.

Both Imam Hasan and Muawiyah have now decided to sign the peace agreement, but the reasons for signing the peace treaty for both parties are very different.

Imam Hasan wanted to sign the peace agreement for the following reasons:

- Imam Hasan wanted to expose the hypocrisy and the two-faced character of Muawiyah to the entire Muslim Ummah. Muawiyah had already won militarily as most of Imam Hasan's army had defected, and Muawiyah could take the Caliphate by force if he wanted to. But through the terms and the conditions of the agreement Imam Hasan wanted to expose the true character of Muawiyah and win the hearts and minds of the Muslims.
- Imam Hasan wanted to show and expose how desperate and hungry Muawiyah was for power.
- The fact that Muawiyah had given Imam Hasan a blank piece of paper to sign, with any conditions that Imam Hasan wanted to put on it, except that in return Muawiyah would get the Caliphate, completely proved that Muawiyah had no interest in actually abiding by the terms of the agreement, and he was only after getting his hands on the Caliphate.

- Imam Hasan also wanted to avoid the complete destruction and inhalation of his remaining army at the hands of Muawiyah's forces. Since the remaining army was from his loyal supporters who were still standing with him despite all the odds.

Muawiyah also wanted the peace treaty but for different reasons:

- Firstly, by not engaging in the battle Muawiyah wanted to be seen as someone who had not acquired the Caliphate by force, and as someone who avoids spilling the blood of the Muslims, thereby increasing his stature and leadership credibility in the Muslim Ummah.
- Secondly, Muawiyah knew that the right of the leadership belongs to the Ahlulbayt (family of the Prophet) as per many traditions of the Prophet. By signing the peace treaty with Imam Hasan, he stands to legitimize his bid for the leadership of the Muslim Ummah.
- Last but not least, Muawiyah does not intend to abide by the peace agreement, so signing a piece of paper does not mean much to him.

13.2.3. The Peace Treaty is Signed on Six Points

The peace treaty is finally signed between Muawiyah and Imam Hasan on the following six points.

- Muawiyah must rule according to the book of Allah and the Sunnah of the Prophet.
- Muawiyah would take over the political administration, but he has no right to appoint a successor, and the Caliphate would return to Imam Hasan on Muawiyah's death.
- All the people living under the Islamic State are to be protected regardless of their ethnic or political affiliations.
- Life, honour, and the properties of the Shias of Ali would be safeguarded.
- Muawiyah will not directly or indirectly harm, threaten or attempt to kill any of the members of the Prophet's family.
- Muawiyah will stop the practice of cursing Ali which he had started in Syria.

I will briefly discuss each one of these points.

13.2.4. Muawiyah must Rule by the Quran and the Sunnah

Muawiyah must rule according to the book of Allah and the Sunnah of the Prophet.

The reason why Imam Hasan puts this point in the agreement is to ensure that Muawiyah is fully exposed as an un-Islamic ruler. Since Muawiyah was not ruling Syria according to the Book of Allah or the Sunnah of the Prophet, Imam Hasan deemed it necessary to mention this point in the agreement, to at least put some pressure on Muawiyah to change his un-Islamic ways, and to unmask the real character of Muawiyah to the entire Muslim Ummah.

Does Muawiyah abide by his commitment of ruling by the Islamic principles? His practices and actions tell a different story.

- During his rule Muawiyah introduces a tax which went straight into his own pocket. It is reported that when he died he had a personal fortune of about 10 million dirhams.
- Muawiyah removes the recitation of Quran in court assemblies and introduces singing instead.
- Shockingly Muawiyah also introduces lap dancing by girls in the court assemblies.
- Muawiyah changes the order of the Eid sermon from being given after the prayers to be given before the prayers, contrary to the Sunnah of the Prophet.

- Muawiyah purposely wears silk garments, contrary to Islamic law which forbids men from wearing silk.
- Worst of all, Muawiyah distorts Islamic history and manipulates the traditions of the Prophet to suit his agenda. He paid people to fabricate and modify events of history and the traditions of the Prophet in his favour and in the favour of the companions who were rivals of Ali, in order to diminish the status and the stature of Ali in the eyes of the ordinary Muslims.

13.2.5. Muawiyah would not Appoint a Successor

Muawiyah would take over the political administration of the Caliphate, but he has no right to appoint a successor and the Caliphate would return to Imam Hasan on Muawiyah's death.

As part of the agreement Imam Hasan had temporarily given the political office of the Caliphate to Muawiyah, since Muawiyah had managed to get most of Imam Hasan's army on his side, leaving Imam Hasan with very few options. However, Imam Hasan makes it clear that the political office of the Caliphate would return to the Ahlulbayt on Muawiyah's death. As Imam Hasan was twenty years younger than Muawiyah, it was expected that Muawiyah would die before him and the Ahlulbayt would retain the Caliphate on Muawiyah's death.

> *"Hasan said:' I placed a condition on Mu'awiya that I will become leader after Mu'awiya"*
> - *Fathul Bari Sharh Bukhari, Volume 13 page 65 Kitab al Fitan*

Also included in this point was a strict condition that Muawiyah had no right to appoint a successor.

> *"When Mu'awiya made peace with Hasan, he made a promise that leadership would go to Hasan after him"*
> - *al Bidayah wa al Nihaya, Volume 8 Pg 80 Dhikr 57 Hijri*

Contrary to his pledge Muawiyah appointed his son Yazid as the new Caliph before his death, breaking the promise that he had made in the peace treaty. By including this point in the agreement Imam Hasan had exposed Muawiyah as a true hypocrite, who could not be trusted to keep his word, even though he had personally signed the treaty.

13.2.6. Protection for All

All the people living under the Islamic State are to be protected.

The fact that this had to be mentioned proved that Muawiyah had only protected his own supporters and sympathizers, with a complete disregard for the life and honour of the people who were not in his camp. Despite this pledge Muawiyah did not abide by his word, he harassed, tortured, and killed his political opponents especially in Basra and Kufa.

By adding this condition to the peace treaty with Muawiyah who was claiming to be the saviour of all the Muslims, Imam Hasan exposed Muawiyah as a ruthless ruler who was merely after the political office of the Caliphate.

13.2.7. The Life and Honour of Shias to be Protected

Life, honour, and the properties of the Shias of Ali must be safeguarded.

The word Shia here should not be confused with the present-day Shia/Sunni division or conflict that we see in some parts of the Muslim world today. The word Shia in the peace treaty refers to the group of companions and Muslims who considered Ali to be the rightful successor of the Prophet, as per many traditions of the Prophet.

Muawiyah had considered Ali and his Shia (supporters) to be his prime enemy, since he saw them as his main political rivals for the office of the Caliphate.

Imam Hasan wanted to ensure that the life and the honour of the Shias was protected, and that they are not discriminated against when Muawiyah takes over the political office of the Caliphate. The actions and practices of Muawiyah again show a complete disregard for his promises.

Any individual who was known to be a Shia was exiled to Northern Syria. The Shias were also denied government allowances which were given to other Muslims. The Shias were allocated lower quality housing and were not allowed to work in any government departments including the army, the judiciary, or the civil service. These measures were particularly harsh as the government employees were the most well-paid individuals at the time.

The aim of Muawiyah, contrary to the agreement that he had signed was to keep the Shias on the back foot. This was done through depriving them from both the economic and the social privileges that others enjoyed. Muawiyah's strategy was to ensure that the Shias could never build a power base to challenge his rule or authority. Imam Hasan by mentioning this point in the treaty again exposed Muawiyah's true face as a pre-Islamic power-hungry Arab leader.

13.2.8. Muawiyah would not Kill Members of the Ahlulbayt

Muawiyah would not directly or indirectly harm, threaten or attempt to kill any of the members of Prophet's family.

Muawiyah was well known for killing his political opponents and rivals. Despite signing the agreement, he did exactly the opposite of what he had promised. Muawiyah successfully planed and financed the killing of Imam Hasan, the very person who he had signed the peace treaty with. He used Joda Ashath, the wife of Imam Hasan to put poison in his food in return for money and a promise for her to be married to his son Yazid, whom he had planned to be the next caliph.

After poisoning and killing Imam Hasan, Muawiyah pays Joda but did not allow the promised marriage to take place. Muawiyah told Joda that if she was willing to kill one husband, she could do the same to his son Yazid too.

The account of above events can be seen in Tadkhirat au Khawwas with these words:

> "Sho'ubi states that Muawiyah sent a message to Jada bint al-Ash'ath bin al Qays that if you poison Hasan then I shall marry you to Yazid and in addition to this I shall give 100,000 dirhams. When Hasan was martyred Judh sent a message to Muawiyah asking that he fulfil his side of the deal. Muawiyah sent the money but said "I reject that matter of Yazid since I want him to remain alive, had this matter not occurred then I would have married you to Yazid".

- *(Tadkhirat au Khawwas, page 192)*

We read a similar story in Sirrul Awliya.

> "Imam Hassan (ra)'s wife Ja'da bint Ash'ath Kindi somehow managed to poisoned him on the orders of Mu'awiya".
>
> - (Sirrul Awliya by S.M. Mubarak Alawi Karmani (Urdu translation by Ijaz ul Haqq Quddoosi) page 81)

Again, we see that Imam Hasan achieves his objective by exposing Muawiyah as an enemy and a killer of the Ahlulbayt (family of the Prophet), rather than as the pious and a devout Muslim that he portrayed himself to be.

Abu Sa'id al-Khudri reported that the Prophet of Allah had said:

> 'Hasan and Hussain are the leaders of the youth in Paradise...'
>
> - (Sunan al-Tirmidhi. Hadith no. 3701. Book of Superiorities. Chapter; the Superiority of Imam Hasan and Hussain)

And Muawiyah ended up poisoning a leader of the Paradise, such was Muawiyah's hatred towards the Prophet and his family. Instead of following in the footsteps of the person that Prophet had called the leader of the paradise, Muawiyah poisons him to death, simply to ensure that the next Caliph would come from his own clan. This was the extent of the lust that Muawiyah had for the leadership of the Muslim Ummah.

13.2.9. Muawiyah would Stop the Practice of Cursing Ali

Muawiyah had started an abhorrent practice of cursing Ali, especially in Friday sermons in all the major cities of Syria. For instance, we read in Sahih Muslim that Muawiyah questions one of his governors as to why he did not curse Ali.

> "....Muawiya b. Abi Sufyan appointed Sa'd as the Governor and said: What prevents you from abusing Abu Turab (Ali), whereupon be said : It is because of three things which I remember Allah's Messenger having said about him that I would not abuse him (Ali)...... I heard Allah's Messenger say about 'Ali ..... Aren't you satisfied with being unto me what Harun was unto Musa but with this exception that there is no Prophethood after me. And I heard him say on the Day of Khaibar: I would certainly give this standard to a person who loves Allah and his Messenger and Allah ..... and Allah gave him victory. (The third occasion is this) when the (following) verse was revealed: "Let us summon our children and your children." Allah's Messenger called 'Ali, Fatima, Hasan and Husain and said: O Allah, they are my family.
>
> - (Sahih Muslim, Chapter of Virtues of Companions, Section of Virtues of Ali, Book 31, Number 5915)

Also, we read in Musanaf Ibn Abi Shayba and Sunan Ibn Majah the following tradition:

> "On his way to Hajj, Sa'd met Muawiyah and his companions mentioned Ali upon which Muawiyah cursed him, Sa'd got angry and asked 'why do you say such things?'"
>
> - (Musanaf Ibn Abi Shayba, volume 7 page 496 as well as in Sunan Ibn Majah, Volume 1 page 45)

Instead of stopping the practice of cursing Ali, on acquiring the Caliphate Muawiyah spreads the practice to other parts of the Islamic State, yet again breaching the contract that he had signed with Imam Hasan. And once again the peace treaty exposes Muawiyah for what he really was, an unprincipled man and an arch enemy of Ali and the Ahlulbayt, contrary to what he had claimed to be.

Despite losing militarily to Muawiyah, Imam Hasan being a true representative of the Prophet signs an agreement that exposes Muawiyah for centuries to come. The character of Muawiyah was unmasked in such a profound manner that even the supporters of Saqifah do not consider Muawiyah to be a rightly guided Caliph.

13.3. The Caliphate of Muawiyah

After the peace treaty was signed the dreams of the Umayyad's to regain the control of the Caliphate became a reality. Muawiyah became the second Umayyad Caliph after Uthman. In fact, since the killing of Caliph Uthman the entire focus of the Umayyad's had only been on regaining the Caliphate. Muawiyah had used every possible trick in his arsenal to achieve this objective.

Muawiyah had first used Lady Aisha's group to severely weaken the Caliphate of Ali. He then challenged and fought Ali in the battle of Siffin, using the same argument that Ali had not found the killers of Caliph Uthman. Muawiyah used to display the blood-soaked shirt of Caliph Uthman to stir people against Ali. He had used all the cunning tactics that he possibly could to whip up hatred and animosity among ordinary Muslims against Ali and his government.

However, when Muawiyah becomes the Caliph, he does absolutely nothing to find the killers of Caliph Uthman, contrary to his earlier demands. In fact, the actions of Muawiyah during his Caliphate of almost twenty years would prove beyond any doubt that he could not care less about avenging the killing of Caliph Uthman. It was simply a ploy and an excuse that he had used to harm and bring down the government of Ali.

The Chief Mufti of Madinah Imam al-Barzanji gave the following account of Muawiyah in his famed book Ishrat al-Sa'a:

> *"It was a false pretext of Muawiya to justify his fight with Ali under the guise of revenge for the murder of Uthman because when he completely attained the power and became ruler of the whole State, he never opened the case of the murder of Uthman and did not arrest the murderers though he claimed earlier that the killers were still around. This proves that all his fight was for worldly rule under the deceit of revenge for the murder."*

- *Ishrat al-Sa'a*

Once Muawiyah had acquired the Caliphate there was little chance that Muawiyah and his Umayyad clan were now going to relinquish power, even though they had signed a deal with Imam Hasan to give the Caliphate back to him. In fact, during his rule Muawiyah did everything that he possibly could to further consolidate his hold on the Caliphate. Just as Muawiyah had used every possible trick to acquire power, he would use every possible trick to hold on to power too.

Ibn Kathir confirmed the above account in his famous book al-Bidaya wan Nihaya:

> *Muawiya was not appointed with the consensus of Muslims at large as was the case with his predecessors. Despite this Muawiya wanted to be the Khalifa and he fought for this position and became ruler by force. When he imposed his Caliphate on people, they had no choice but to give him bay'ah (allegiance). If people did not give him bay'ah (allegiance), they would not only lose their positions/jobs but also would have lost their lives. It would have been a catastrophe for them. People would rather give bay'ah (allegiance) than confront these consequences. That is why Imam Hassan stepped down and other Sahaba joined him so as to avoid the risk of civil War amongst Muslims. Muawiyah was well aware of this strategy. He himself confessed, "I was absolutely aware of nation's discontent with my caliphate; however, I secured it by sword"*

- *Al-Bidaya wan-Nihaya, Vol 8, Page 132*

As confirmed by Muawiyah himself, he knew that the majority of the Muslims were against his rule, but he ensured by the way of his sword that the masses stayed inline and accepted his authority. People were forced to give allegiance to Muawiyah because if they didn't approve Muawiyah as the new Caliph, they risked losing their livelihoods and even their lives.

And it was for this reason that Imam Hasan had signed the peace treaty with Muawiyah and had stepped down from his position to avoid the civil war which would have claimed the lives of thousands of ordinary y Muslims.

13.3.1. The Character of Muawiyah

Muslims who have not read the Islamic history objectively would perhaps fail to understand the significance of Muawiyah's influence in shaping the early history of Islam. Muawiyah was no ordinary personality in the Islamic history. Muawiyah was one of the most extraordinary characters in the history of Islam, but for all the wrong reasons. Muawiyah did what no other Caliph had done before him. Muawiyah destroyed the Islamic system of governance that Prophet had established and changed it into a pre-Islamic hereditary system which was governed by his Umayyad clan.

Muawiyah essentially undid the revolution of the Prophet which was probably his biggest crime, and in his own mind it was probably his biggest achievement. But Muawiyah did this in a subtle way, where the overall grandeur of the Islamic State was maintained, but its soul was destroyed from within.

Muawiyah was an intelligent man but with an extremely devious mind. He simply used Islam as a tool to expand his powerbase and to ensure that the Caliphate would stay in his Umayyad clan. On one hand Muawiyah conquered territory and expanded the borders of the Islamic State, while at the same time he poisoned and killed the family of the Prophet and many of Prophet's companions, for no reason other than the fact that he saw them as his political rivals. Muawiyah really had no regard for Islam as a way of life or as a system of governance. He simply used Islam as a means to further his own political ambitions.

To understand Muawiyah, one really has to understand the background and the mind-set that Muawiyah had grown up in. Muawiyah's father was Abu Sufyan who was the head of the Umayyad clan was the biggest enemy of the Prophet and the Muslims. Abu Sufyan had fought the Prophet for almost two decades and was responsible for the deaths of thousands of Muslims. Abu Sufyan only accepted Islam after the conquest of Makkah when the Qurayshite tribes were completely defeated by the Muslims, and when he felt that there was no option left other than becoming a Muslim. Muawiyah's mother was Hind who had mutilated the body of Prophet's beloved uncle Hamza, after he was killed in the battle of Uhud. So, Muawiyah had grown up in an extremely anti-Islamic and an anti-Muslim household.

The loss of Makkah to the Prophet and the Muslims was a very big blow to the Umayyads. Abu Sufyan and his Umayyad clan had essentially lost their monopoly in trade and business in the heart of Arabia since Makkah was the trading capital of the Arab world at the time. The Umayyads were not simply against the Muslims because Muslims were inviting them to worship one God. The Umayyads were against the Muslims because the Islamic system of governance would annihilate their wealth, power, their way of life and the monopoly that they had enjoyed among the Arabs. This was the kind of environment which had cultivated the character and the personality of Muawiyah as a young man.

Abu Sufyan and his family felt dejected and dispirited after their defeat in Makkah, as their family and their Umayyad clan had lost everything to the Muslims, including the leadership of the Arabs. So once Muawiyah acquired power, he wanted to bring back the lost glory of his family and the Umayyads, he wanted to regain the lost honour and the respect that his family and his clan had enjoyed among the Arabs, and everything that he did during his Caliphate would go to prove this fact.

Muawiyah started working on this plan from the time of Caliph Umar when he appointed Muawiyah as the Governor of Syria.

> Al-Hassan al-Basri said: "Muawiya had been preparing himself for Caliphate since Umar' tenure"
> - Mukhtsar Tarikh Damishq, Vol 25, Page 24
> - Tathbit Dala'il al-Nubuwwa, Page 593

Muawiyah was smart enough to know that Islam as a religion was now here to stay, and he could not possibly remove the Islamic beliefs from the hearts of the Muslims, so once he acquired the Caliphate, he used his position to undermine the Islamic system of governance and destroy its soul.

Muawiyah being a shrewd politician kept the outer shell of the Islamic State intact, to ensure that on the face of it Islam could be seen as the dominant force, but at the heart of the Islamic State he established an Umayyad dynasty which was corrupt to the core, which would undermine the Islamic values, which would change the Sunnah of the Prophet, and which would rule the Muslim Ummah for the next one hundred years to come.

Under the guise of his Caliphate, Muawiyah brought back the Umayyads to the helm of the Islamic State, a State that the Umayyads had opposed with all their might. The historic enemies of the Prophet and the Islamic State would in fact become its undisputed rulers under Muawiyah's tenure. The Umayyads who had lost the leadership of the Arabs as result of their defeat at the conquest of Makkah, would now regain their past glory, but this time as leaders of the Islamic State and the Muslim Ummah.

That is why Ammar bin Yasir, just before the battle of Siffin summed up the feelings of ordinary Muslims towards Muawiyah and his Umayyad supporters:

> Ammar (on the eve of the Battle of Siffin) said: "By Allah, they (Muawiyah and the Umayyads) did not convert to Islam (fully), but they surrendered (reluctantly at the fall of Makkah) and veiled their (partial) disbelief until they found support so they unveiled it"
> - (Tarikh Ibn Abi Khaythama, Vol 2, Page 991)

The companions of the Prophet like Ammar bin Yasir were well-aware of the fact that Muawiyah and his Umayyad clan had reluctantly converted to Islam. The Umayyads had kept their animosity and hatred towards Islam under the wraps, until they found the right opportunity and support for their agenda, and then they unveiled their true face to the Muslim Ummah.

The Umayyad powerplay had initially begun with the Caliphate of Uthman when he began to appoint his fellow Umayyads to all the key positions within the Islamic State, but unfortunately for the Umayyads Caliph Uthman was killed and their plans lay in ruins, but Muawiyah being one of the most skilful politicians brought back the Umayyad glory. Muawiyah did not achieve this overnight. Muawiyah ruled the Islamic Caliphate for nearly two decades which gave him ample time to change the course of history in favour of his Umayyad dynasty.

Muawiyah achieved this goal through a variety of clever, cunning, and brutal means. Where possible Muawiyah would bribe individuals and buy them out and bring them to his side. Bribing people was Muawiyah's preferred way of doing business. Muawiyah bribed most of the army of Imam Hasan and made them defect to his side. He even bribed the wife of Imam Hasan to poison him.

If Muawiyah could not buy someone out with money he would try and use the Arab tribal system to pressurize them and to bring them in line. The Arab tribal system is even intact to this day in many parts of the Muslim world and was far more stronger and effective back in those times. Muawiyah would buy out or threaten the tribal leaders, ensuring that the ordinary tribesmen toed the government line.

And if bribery and the tribal system would fail to bring an individual inline, then Muawiyah would use brute force to ensure that the person stayed on the right track, and in case they persisted in their opposition to Muawiyah, then Muawiyah would physically take them out and orchestrate their killing. These three key techniques of bribery, tribal lineage and brute force ensured that no opposition to Muawiyah's rule was ever successful, and Muawiyah kept the internal peace in the Islamic State through these cunning methods.

Muawiyah essentially began a counter-revolution against the revolution of the Prophet, by devising rules and policies which would contradict the teachings of the Quran and the Sunnah of the Prophet, but which would be in his personal interest and in the interest of his Umayyad clan.

The counter-revolution started by Muawiyah specifically targeted the people who were at the forefront of Prophet's revolution. This clever strategy of Muawiyah served two key goals. Firstly, it established Muawiyah's own credentials as a top Umayyad leader within his clan, since Muawiyah was seen as someone who was willing to take revenge for the defeat of the Umayyads in Makkah. Secondly, the people who Muawiyah primary targeted were the true representatives of the Prophet, and by targeting these people Muawiyah sought to dilute and destroy the Sunnah and the message of the Prophet itself.

The three key individuals who formed the basis of Prophet's revolution were Abu Talib who was Prophet's uncle and Ali's father, the Prophet of Allah himself, and Prophet's right hand man Ali. These three individuals were at the forefront of the Islamic revolution. The Prophet of Allah was the architect of the revolution, whereas Abu Talib was the main defender of the Prophet in Makkah, and Ali was the flag bearer and commander in chief of Prophet's army in all the key battles against the Qurayshite clans, including the clan of the Umayyads.

Muawiyah and the Umayyads as a whole had a grudge against all these three individuals i.e., the Prophet, Abu Talib and Ali, since they were the main characters responsible for defeating the Umayyads and the other Qurayshite clans in Arabia. However, both Prophet and Abu Talib had passed away before Muawiyah came of age. Hence the wrath of the Umayyads was directed against Ali and his progeny who were still alive.

The progeny of Ali was also the progeny of the Prophet as Ali was married to Prophet's daughter Fatima. Hence the revenge against the Prophet and Abu Talib was also taken from Ali and his children, as they were the children and the grand children of Prophet and Abu Talib too. Essentially, after the establishment of the Umayyad dynasty by Muawiyah, the progeny of the Prophet became the prime target of the Umayyads.

The family of the Prophet also happened to be the flag bearer of Prophet's Sunnah, so targeting them meant targeting the Sunnah of the Prophet too, which unfortunately was also the goal of the Umayyads. The Prophet had placed the leadership of the Muslim Ummah into the hands of his family, as per many of his traditions.

> "...... 'O people I have left in you that which if you adhere to you will never go astray: The Book of God and the members of my House."
> - Sunan Al-Tirmidhi. Vol. 3, Pg. # 543 - 544, H. # 3786 – 3788
> - Sunan Al-Tirmidhi. Vol. 6, Pg. # 335

Muawiyah was well-aware of the above facts, and by targeting the Ahlulbayt Muawiyah was removing the biggest hurdle from his path that would stop him from turning the Islamic State into an Umayyad dynasty. Muawiyah had a calculated plan and a strategy to take over the Islamic State, and everything that he did during his Caliphate revolved around his political ambitions.

The Caliphate of Muawiyah was signified by many crimes against the Muslim Ummah. I will list some of those crimes to show how Muawiyah had indeed destroyed the soul of the Islamic State during his corrupt rule.

13.3.1.1. The Killing of the Ahlulbayt (Family of the Prophet)

It was in this context that Muawiyah had killed Imam Hasan the beloved grandson of the Prophet. Imam Hasan was one of the last members of the Prophet's family who was still alive when Muawiyah came of age.

A peace treaty had been signed between Imam Hasan and Muawiyah which had stated that the Caliphate would go back to Imam Hasan on Muawiyah's death, so Muawiyah's first plan of action was to remove Imam Hasan from his path, in order to keep the Caliphate in his Umayyad clan.

Muawiyah achieves this objective by bribing Imam Hasan's wife Joda, with a promise of money and with a promise to marry her to his son Yazid. Joda poisons Imam Hasan and Muawiyah rewards her handsomely, but he does not marry her to Yazid, since he tells Joda that if she could kill Imam Hasan, she could kill his son Yazid too.

To see the hatred that Muawiyah had for the family of the Prophet one simply has to revisit the conversation that Muawiyah had with Miqdam, a companion of the Prophet who lived during the time of Muawiyah. After the death of Imam Hasan, Miqdam came to see Muawiyah for a personal matter. The conversation that they had gives us a clear picture of the feelings that Muawiyah had towards the Ahlulbayt.

The conversation goes like this:

> *Mu'awiyah said to al-Miqdam: Do you know that al-Hasan ibn Ali has died?*
> *Al-Miqdam recited the Qur'anic verse "We belong to Allah and to Him we shall return."*
> *A man (Mu'awiyah) asked him: Do you think of it (i.e the death of Hasan) as a calamity?*
> *He (Miqdam) replied: Why should I not consider it a calamity when it is a fact that the Messenger of Allah used to take him on his lap, saying: This belongs to me and Husayn belongs to Ali?*
> *The man of Banu Asad said: (He was) a live coal which Allah has extinguished*
> *Al-Miqdam said: Today I shall continue to make you angry and make you hear what you dislike......*
> - Abu Dawood 4131, Abu Dawood Vol. 4, Book 34, Hadith 4119

A similar conversation is also found in Musnad of Ahmad bin Hanbal.

> *Miqdam and Amr bin Aswad came to meet Muawiyah.*
> *Muawiyah said to Miqdam: Do you know that Hasan bin Ali has died?*
> *Miqdam recited the Qur'anic verse: "We belong to Allah and to Him we shall return."*
> *Muawiyah said to Miqdam: Do you regard it (the death of Hasan) as a calamity?*

> *Miqdam Replied: Why shouldn't I regard it (the death of Hasan) as a calamity?, while I myself had seen that the Prophet of Allah used to take Hasan in his lap and say: He (Hasan) is from me (Mohammad), and Hussain is from Ali.*

- *Musnad Ahmad 17228 (Vol. 4 Page-132)*

Muawiyah informed Miqdam that Imam Hasan had died. On hearing the news of Imam Hasan's death, like any good Muslim Miqdam recited the verse of the Holy Quran that we belong to Allah and to him we shall return. But Muawiyah did not like the response of Miqdam and said to him as to why did he (Miqdam) thought that the death of Imam Hasan was a calamity. Miqdam responds and says to Muawiyah that why shouldn't he consider the death of Imam Hasan a calamity, when Prophet himself had stated that Hasan was from him.

Muawiyah had considered Imam Hasan to be a roadblock in his ambitions of turning the Islamic State into an Umayyad kingdom. The supporters of Muawiyah were just as bad in their view of the Ahlulbayt. One of the supporters of Muawiyah who was witnessing this conversation said to Miqdam that Imam Hasan was a fireball and a live coal, implying that Imam Hasan was threat and an obstacle to the rule of Muawiyah, and it was good that the obstacle had now been removed.

Muawiyah had considered the Ahlulbayt to be his biggest enemy, as they were the custodians of Prophet's Sunnah, and Muawiyah had to eliminate them in order for him to consolidate his rule over the Islamic State. Muawiyah and his supporters were relieved and happy at the death of Imam Hasan, since they considered Imam Hasan to be a fireball and a live coal which had to be extinguished.

Miqdam was not aware at the time that it was in fact Muawiyah who had poisoned and killed Imam Hasan. Contrary to the sentiments of Muawiyah and his supporters towards Imam Hasan, the Prophet of Allah had said to Ali, Fatima, Hasan and Hussain:

> *'I oppose those who oppose you, and I am peaceful to those who are peaceful to you.'*

- *Sunan al-Tirmidhi. Hadith no. 3705*

Muawiyah had not only opposed Imam Hasan, but Muawiyah had indeed poisoned him to death. On the Day of Judgement, the Prophet of Allah will no doubt question Muawiyah on the killing of his grandson, and Muawiyah will have to justify his actions in the highest of the courts.

13.3.1.2. The Killing of the Companions and the Ordinary Muslims

Just as Muawiyah had killed the members of the Ahlulbayt (family of the Prophet), he also killed many companions of the Prophet and ordinary Muslims. Anybody whom Muawiyah suspected of being a supporter of Ali, or anyone who was considered a political threat would become a target of Muawiyah's tyranny. One such unfortunate companion was Hujr bin Adi, who was brutally murdered on the orders of Muawiyah.

Muawiyah's appointed governor Ibn Ziyad had delayed the Friday prayer to such an extent that even the time for the Assar prayer was about to end. Hujr bin Adi along with a few other Muslims complained to Ibn Ziyad that the prayers must be done at their proper times, in accordance with the Sunnah of the Prophet, and delaying the prayers tantamount to breaching the Sunnah of the Prophet.

Instead of correcting his mistake and ensuring that the Friday prayers should be done at their specified times, Ibn Ziyad gave orders to arrest Hujr bin Adi and his fellow associates, and then implicated Hujr and his men in a false case, stating that Hujr and his associates had attacked him while he was giving the

Friday sermon which was a completely untrue. Hujr and his men had only complained about the timings of the Friday prayer, and they had neither verbally or physically attacked or abused Ibn Ziyad.

Nevertheless, Ibn Ziyad sends Hujr bin Adi and the arrested men to Syria to face the justice of Muawiyah. Hujr bin Adi and his men pleaded with Muawiyah that they were innocent and that they had not attacked the governor and nor were they looking to challenge Muawiyah. Hujr bin Adi was a supporter and a lover of Ali. But since the peace treaty between Imam Hasan and Muawiyah had been signed all these followers of Ali had also accepted the Caliphate of Muawiyah.

Hujr bin Adi and his men desperately plead with Muawiyah that they are abiding by the peace treaty of Imam Hasan, and that they were not looking to create any problems for the Caliph.

Muawiyah being a ruthless dictator paid no heed to the pleas of Hujr and his men and sentenced all of them to death. A ditch was dug up in a village near Damascus where Hujr and his men were taken, and then one by one each one of them were beheaded by Muawiyah's soldiers.

It is reported that just before Hujr bin Adhi was about to be beheaded, the soldiers of Muawiyah offered Hujr amnesty. They said to Hujr that if you do lanath on Ali i.e., if you curse Ali your life would be spared. Hujr being a true lover of the Prophet and the Ahlulbayt refused to curse Ali and said that how could he possibly curse a person whom he had loved all his life, and how could he possibly utter such words that would displease Allah.

Here is how history has recorded the killing of Hujr bin Adi and his men.

> *"Hujr was amongst the virtuous Sahaba (Companions)"*
> - *Istiab, Volume 1 page 97 – Hujr bin Adi al-Kindi*
> - *Asadul Ghaba fi Ma'rafat Sahabah, Volume 1 page 244*

> *He (Hujr bin Adhi) was killed upon the orders of Mu'awiya in a village called Mriaj Adra near Damascus. At the time of his execution he requested: 'Do not remove these chains after I am killed, nor clean the blood. We will meet again with Mu'awiya and I shall petition my case against him'.*
> - *al Isaba, Volume 1 page 313 Dhikr Hujr ibn Adi*

> *"Hujr and his associates were arrested and taken to a ditch in Adra which was near Damascus. Mu'awiya ordered that Hujr and his associates be executed in this ditch"*
> - *Asad'ul Ghaba, Volume 1 page 244 Dhikr Hujr ibn Adi*

> *Abi al-Aswad reported that Mu'awya went to Aysha, and she asked him: 'Why did you kill the people of Adra, Hujr and his companions?'. He replied: 'Oh mother of believers! I saw that their death was referring to the good for the nation and their lives referring to the corruption of nation.' She said: 'I heard the messenger of Allah (pbuh) saying: 'Some people will be killed in Adra, Allah and the people of heaven will become angry over that"*
> - *Kanz ul Ummal, Volume 13 page 556 Tradition 37510*

> *Prior to their murder, the executors put some conditions before them which were: 'We have been instructed to pardon you on a condition if you disassociate yourselves from Ali (ra) and curse him otherwise you are to be murdered'. They refused to accept that offer and Hujr said: 'I cannot not say that thing from my tongue that displease Allah'. Finally he and his seven companions were murdered. From amongst them, Abdur Rahman bin Hasaan was sent back to Ziyad with a*

written instruction that he be murdered in the worst possible manner, hence Ziyad buried him alive.

- Tarikh al Tabari, Volume 4 page 190 – 208
- al Istiab by Ibn `Abdul Barr Vol I page 135
- Tarikh by Ibn Athir Volume 3 page 234 – 242,
- al Bidayah al Nihaya by Ibn Kathir, Volume 8 page 50 -55j,
- Ibn Khaldoon Volume 3 page 13

Many Muslims were shocked at the callous killing of Hujr bin Adi, even Lady Aisha condemned Muawiyah for innocently murdering Hujr and his men. One of the associates of Hujr, Abdur Rahman bin Hasaan was not killed on the same day. He was taken back to Ibn Ziyad who instead of beheading him buried him alive.

As Hujr bin Adi said just before he was beheaded:

'Do not remove these chains after I am killed, nor clean the blood. We will meet again with Mu'awiya and I shall petition my case against him'.

- al Isaba, Volume 1 page 313 Dhikr Hujr ibn Adi

No doubt on the Day of Judgment Hujr will be standing in shackles with his blood-stained clothes, and Muawiyah will have to face the justice of Allah.

Hujr bin Adi was not the only companion who was killed by Muawiyah. Muawiyah had killed many other companions and ordinary Muslims. Muawiyah also killed Malik bin Ashtar who was a close confidant of Ali. Ali had appointed Malik bin Ashtar as the governor of Egypt during his Caliphate. Malik bin Ashtar was a true lover and supporter of Ali. Muawiyah ordered his killing and then gave a sermon confirming his death.

"……Mu'awiyah stood among the people and delivered a khutbah (sermon). He praised God and extolled Him and then said "Ali b. Abi Talib had two right hands; one of them was cut off on the day of Siffin (meaning Ammar b. Yasir) and the other today (meaning Al-Asthar)"

- History of Tabari, Volume 18 pages 144-146

Anybody who was close to Ali or the Ahlulbayt was considered a threat and was either bribed or physically eliminated by Muawiyah.

Muawiyah's brutality did not stop there, he killed another companion of the Prophet called Amr bin Hamiq. Amr was first beheaded on Muawiyah's orders and then his head was thrown into the lap of his wife, who was held in a dungeon by Muawiyah's soldiers.

"Amr Ibn Al Hamiq, Ibn Kahil and they also call him Ibn Kuhin, Ibn Habeeb Al Khuzai, a companion who lived in Kufa then in Egypt, he was killed during the caliphate of Muawiya"

- Taqreeb al Tahdeeb, page 420 Translation No. 5017

"Amr was hence arrested and murdered, and his head was sent to Muawiyah in Syria."

- Asadul Ghaba, Volume 1 page 846, Amr bin al-Hamiq al-Khazai

The tyranny of Muawiyah continued unabated. Muawiyah killed the grandsons of Ibn Abbas who was the uncle of the Prophet and a great scholar of his time. Ali had appointed Ubaydullah bin Abbas who was the son of Ibn Abbas as be governor of Yemen during his Caliphate. Ubaydullah bin Abbas was not only the cousin of Ali, but he was also a close friend and a loyal supporter of Ali.

Muawiyah sent Busar bin Irtat who was a ruthless killer to Yemen and Hijaz, in order to remove any support that Ali and the Ahlulbayt enjoyed in these lands. As a deterrent to the supporters of Ali, Busar bin Irtat killed the two young sons of Ubaydullah bin Abbas, to install fear and terror among the followers of Ali and the Ahlulbayt, and to ensure that any possible opposition to Muawiyah's rule was crushed.

Here is how history has recorded the killing of the two young sons of Ubaydullah bin Abbas.

> "Busar bin Irtat was a bad person... He slit the throats of the two children of Ubadullah ibn Abbas bin Abdul Mutalib in the presence of their mother, Mua'waiya had sent him to Yemen during the days of Sifeen"
>
> - al Istiab, Volume 1 page 49, Chapter: Busar

> "Muawiya sent him (Busar) to Yemen, so he killed the two sons of Ubaydullah bin Al Abbas, and he remained Muawiya's companion till he died."
>
> - Tarikh ibn Asakir, Volume 10 page 146

Muawiyah did not just randomly order the killing of these companions and Muslims. Muawiyah would pick and select his targets extremely carefully. He would ensure that anybody who was a threat to his rule and to his ultimate ambition of an Umayyad dynasty was eliminated and neutralized.

13.3.2. Muawiyah Changed the Sunnah of the Prophet

Just as Muawiyah had killed the members of the Ahlulbayt and the companions of the Prophet, he also embarked upon destroying the basic rituals of Islam by changing the Sunnah of the Prophet. He changed number of Islam practices which no other Muslim would even dare to question, as he had no real value or respect for the Islamic way of thinking.

He changed aspects of daily prayers, Eid prayers, Haj rituals and many other established Islamic practices by giving adhoc rulings which openly contradicted the traditions of the Prophet.

13.3.2.1. Muawiyah Changed the Talbya Practice in Haj

One of the key practices for any Muslim in Haj is to loudly recite the Talbya i.e., to say in Arabic "Labbaik Allahumma Labbaik", which means "I respond to your call O Allah". Reciting the Talbya is a cornerstone during the practice of Tawaf i.e., when Muslims are circling the Holy Kaaba itself. Anyone who has performed the Haj would confirm the practice of reciting the Talbya as it is deemed to be a Sunnah of the Prophet.

However, during Muawiyah's reign he stopped the practice of reciting the Talbya, because of his hatred for Ali. It is reported that Ali used to recite the Talbya loudly as per the Sunnah of the Prophet, but because Muawiya hated Ali he stopped this practice altogether in defiance of Ali.

Saeed bin Jubair said:

> 'We were with ibn Abbas in Arafa and he said to me: 'Oh Saeed, why don't I hear the people performing talbya?' I replied: 'They are afraid of Muawiya'. Then ibn Abbas went out from his cottage and said: 'I respond to your call, Oh Allah I respond to your call, they abandon the Sunnah for their hate towards Ali (ra).
>
> - Sunan Nasai, Volume 5 page 253 Tradition 3019
> - Sahih Ibn Khuzaima, Volume 4 page 260 Tradition 2830

- *Mustadrak al-Hakim, Volume 1 pages 364-365*

Anyone who abandons the Sunnah of the Prophet would be held accountable for their actions. But a person who not only abandons the Sunnah of the Prophet but also forces others to abandon it, would really have to come up with a pretty special alibi on the Day of Judgement!

13.3.2.2. Muawiyah Changed the Eid Prayer

Every Muslim is aware of the fact that Eid prayers take place before the sermon, and this is indeed the Sunnah of the Prophet. However, during Muawiyah's reign he ordered the Imams of the mosques to do the Eid sermon before the prayers.

There was a very good reason for making this change. Muawiyah began the abhorrent practice of cursing Ali in the Eid and the Friday prayers. Many Muslims began to leave the mosque as soon as the prayers would finish and would not stay on to listen to the insults and curses being levelled against Ali. So, Muawiyah changed the order of the sermon and instructed all the Imams of the mosques to have the sermon before the prayers, making sure that everybody listened to the horrible content of the sermon before they did their prayers.

> *Imam Shafii stated that Abdullah bin Yazid al-Khutmi said: The Prophet, and all Khulafa e Rashideen used to start by praying before the Sermon on Eid till Muawiya came and made the sermon before the Prayer.*

- *(Al-Uam, Vol. 1, Page 329 by Imam Shafii).*

13.3.2.3. Muawiyah Made Changes to the Daily Prayers

Muawiyah even made changes to the daily prayers, something which is unthinkable for any Muslim. He reduced the number of Takbeers i.e., the number of times one would say "Allah hu Akbar" (God is Great) in the daily prayers.

> *Muawiya not only made changes to the Eid prayers, but he also had the audacity to make changes in the daily prayers by reducing the takbir.*

- *Umadatul Qari, (Sharah Sahih Bukhari) by Imam Badruddin al-Aini volume 8, page 58*

"The first person who reduced Takbir was Muawiya"

- *al-Wasael ela al-Musamerah, page 164 by Imam Jalaluddin Syuti*

It is not clear from the historical accounts as to why Muawiyah actually made this change. Perhaps it was to assert his authority on the Ummah, to show that he was powerful enough to even change the basic tenants of Islam, so that nobody would dare challenge his authority.

13.3.2.4. Muawiyah Blurred the Islamic Concept of Legitimacy

In the eyes of Islam, a child born through a marriage is considered legitimate and a child born outside of the Islamic marriage is considered illegitimate. Muawiyah's father Abu Sufyan had an illegitimate son called Ziyad bin Abih. Only Muawiyah and a handful of people knew about the fact that Ziyad bin Abih was an illegitimate son of Abu Sufyan.

Ziyad bin Abih also happened to be a strong leader and was a supporter of Ali. Ali had made Ziyad bin Abih the governor of Estkhar province in Persia (Iran) during his Caliphate, and Ziyad bin Abih remained the governor of Estkhar province during the brief reign of Imam Hasan too. Muawiyah had tried to lure Ziyad bin Abih to his side on many occasions while Ali was alive, but Ziyad bin Abih did not oblige and remained in the camp of Ali.

However, after Muawiyah took over the Caliphate, he recalled Ziyad bin Abih to Damascus and made him an offer which he could not refuse. Muawiyah officially declared Ziyad bin Abih to be the son of Abu Sufyan i.e., Muawiyah declared Ziyad bin Abih to be his real brother. Ziyad bin Abih's name was changed to Ziyad bin Abu Sufyan in the official records, and Muawiyah also made him a beneficiary of Abu Sufyan's inheritance. Muawiyah then lavishly rewarded Ziyad and made him the governor of Basra and later gave him the charge of Kufa too, which were the two key cities of Iraq at the time.

Becoming the brother of the Caliph who was the head of the entire Muslim Ummah, was a temptation that finally broke the loyalty that Ziyad had for Ali. This was Muawiyah at his very best, where he finally managed to buy out Ziyad bin Abih who was a governor of Ali when Ali was the Caliph. The same Ziyad who was once on the side of Ali would now oversee the public cursing of Ali in Basra and Kufa, ensuring that the decree issued by Muawiyah to curse Ali was followed to the letter. The public cursing of Ali by Muawiyah would be discussed in the next section.

Later on, Muawiyah also used Ziyad to brutalise the people of Basra and Kufa, especially the supporters of Ali, to make sure that they toed the government line.

Muawiyah had little love or care for the laws laid out by the Prophet, and it is for this reason that the scholars of Fiqh and Hadith have said that Muawiyah blurred the concept of legitimacy of marriage in Islam by this act, where he declared an illegitimate son to be a legitimate child. A child born under a legitimate marriage was put on par with a child who was born outside the wedlock. By this decree, Muawiyah introduced the law of the pagans and opened the doors to adultery which were closed by the Prophet.

Imam Suyuti wrote:

> *"When Ziyad was attributed, as Mu'awiya attributed him to his father Abu Sufyan while he (Ziyad) was known as Ziyad bin Abih ….. this was the first Sharia law that was changed in Islamic State by Muawiya"*
>
> - *(Al-Debaj ala Muslim, Volume 1 page 84)*

Imam Ahmad bin Hanbal also wrote:

> *"The first law of the Holy Prophet that was rejected is the case of Ziyad"*
>
> - *(Masa'el ahmed bin Hanbal, Page 89)*

13.3.3. The Cursing of Ali and Instigating People Against the Ahlulbayt

The Islamic revolution that had swept Arabia was essentially an ideological revolution started by the Prophet of Allah, which was against the Jahilliyah traditions and customs that were prevalent among the Arabs. Muawiyah on the other hand had started a counter-revolution against the ideological revolution of the Prophet, by undermining the very principles of Quran and the Sunnah which the revolution of the Prophet was based upon.

For the revolution of Muawiyah to succeed, he needed to defeat the ideological flag bearers of the Prophet, who were still around when he came to power. Muawiyah needed to neutralize the people who represented the legacy of the Prophet, in order for his own strategy to be successful. Muawiyah wasn't bothered by the companions or Muslims who were focused on prayer, fasting, Haj, Zakat and other basic Islamic rituals. But he was troubled by individuals who were ideologically committed to Islam as a way of life and as a system of governance. Muawiyah saw such individuals as a threat and a challenge to his rule and future ambitions.

The person who was most dedicated to the ideological revolution of the Prophet was none other than Ali. Muawiyah knew exactly the position of Ali in relation to the Prophet. Muawiyah knew that it was Ali and the Ahlulbayt who were the ideological successors and the representatives of the Prophet in his time.

After all it was Muawiyah's father Abu Sufyan who had come to the door of Ali, offering to fill the streets of Madinah with cavalrymen against Abu Bakr, when Abu Bakr became the first Caliph. Abu Sufyan knew that Ali was the rightful successor of the Prophet, and it was Ali's right to lead the Muslim Ummah after Prophet's death. Ali of course declined the poisonous offer of Abu Sufyan as the intention of Abu Sufyan was to create a civil war within the Islamic State.

Nevertheless, Muawiyah knew that it was Ali and the progeny of the Prophet who represented the ideological message of Islam. He knew that Prophet had instructed the Muslims to follow Ali and the Ahlulbayt. Hence, Muawiyah embarked on a chilling but an extremely clever ploy of cursing Ali and his supporters, and instigating people against the progeny and the family of the Prophet.

The aim and the goal of Muawiyah was to essentially break the link that Prophet had established between Ali and the Muslims, and to drive a wedge between the Ahlulbayt and the ordinary Muslims, in order to keep them away from the ideological message of Islam.

The practice of cursing Ali was part of this strategy. It initially began in Syria where Muawiyah had his powerbase. But as Muawiyah took over the reins of the Caliphate he expanded this practice to all corners of the Islamic State, including Makkah and Madinah.

The irony could not be starker. The person who was at the forefront of establishing the Islamic State, was now being cursed from its pulpits in every Friday sermon! The person who was the flag bearer of Prophet's army in almost all the key battles was now being foul mouthed throughout the Muslim Ummah. The individual who was chosen by the Prophet to lead the Muslims was now being discredited by the enemies of the Prophet, who he had defeated in establishing the Islamic State.

But this strategy was crucial for the success of the counter revolution started by Muawiyah, that the people who represented the true Sunnah of the Prophet were cast out as enemies of the State, and the people who were in power i.e., the Umayyads, were seen as the true leaders of the Muslim Ummah. It was in this context that Muawiyah had begun the practice of cursing Ali and instigating people against the Ahlulbayt.

Even the Devil (Shaitan) was not being cursed in every sermon, but Ali and his supporters were being cursed in every Friday sermon in the Islamic State. Muawiyah ruled for twenty years and in this time a whole new generation of Muslims had grown up cursing and abusing Ali and the Ahlulbayt. They had no idea as to who Ali was, let alone to know what his contribution was in the service of Islam. The only thing that they knew about Ali was that he was an enemy of God and the State, who had to be cursed and kept at a distance. This was indeed the exact opposite of what Prophet had proposed for Ali and the Ahlulbayt.

If this new generation of Muslims which was growing up under Muawiyah was allowed to come close to Ali and the Ahlulbayt, then the ultimate goal of Muawiyah which was to establish a future Umayyad dynasty in the guise of the Islamic Caliphate would be lost. If people were allowed to follow the ideological successors of the Prophet, then the counter-revolution started by Muawiyah would fail to materialize. Hence, Muawiyah did everything he could to turn people against Ali and the progeny of the Prophet.

This is why as soon as Ali became the fourth Caliph Muawiyah used the killing of Uthman as an excuse to instigate people of Syria against Ali. Muawiyah was so successful in his campaign that thousands of Syrian Muslims joined Muawiyah and fought against Ali in the battle of Siffin. Once Muawiyah acquired power and became the head of the Islamic State, he further expanded the practice of inciting people against Ali and the Ahlulbayt, by ordering the Imams of the mosques to curse and abuse Ali and his followers in all the Friday sermons across the Islamic State.

13.3.3.1. Muawiyah Instructs his Governors to Curse Ali

Muawiyah appointed Mughira ibn Shubah as the governor of Kufa and ordered him to curse Ali and his supporters, with the sole aim of inciting people against Ali and the Ahlulbayt.

> *"...I have based your appointment on common sense, give me bayya (allegiance) on the condition that you continue with the practice, that you don't cease to disgrace and curse 'Ali and praise Uthman. Mughira was the Governor of Kufa for some time, during it he cursed and disgraced 'Ali".*

- Tarikh Kamil' Volume 3 page 234

A similar report is also found in Al-Tabari

> *"When Muawiya Ibn Abi Sufyan put al-Mughira Ibn Shubah in charge of Kufah .... he summoned him.... Although I have wanted to advise you about many things, I left them alone......what helps my regime and what sets my subjects [raiyyah] on the right path. I would continue to advise you about a quality of yours - do not refrain from abusing Ali and criticizing him.... Continue to shame the companions of Ali, keep at a distance, and don't listen to them. Praise the faction of Uthman, bring them near, and listen to them."*

- History of Tabari, English version, events of year 51 AH, Execution of Hujr Ibn Adi, v18, pp 122-123

Mughira ibn Shubah remained the governor of Kufa for seven years. As per the instructions of Muawiyah he would insult and abuse Ali and his followers and would blame them for the murder of Uthman, and at the same time he would praise Uthman who was the first Umayyad Caliph. The goal was pretty straight forward, the aim was to generate sympathy for the Umayyads among the general population and create hatred for Ali and his camp by blaming them for killing an Umayyad Caliph.

A similar tradition is also found in Sunan Abi Dawood, in Sunan Nisai and in Musnad of Imam Ahmad ibn Hanbal. Abdullah ibn Zalim narrates:

> *".... When so and so (Muawiyah) came to Kufah, and made so and so (Mughirah bin Shubah) stand to address the people, Sa'id ibn Zayd caught hold of my hand and said: Are you seeing this tyrant (Mughirah bin Shubah cursing and insulting Ali (doing lanat on Ali))? ......"*

- Sunan Abi Dawood 4648/4650
- Sunan Nisai: 8208
- Musnad of Imam Ahmad: 1644 (Vol 1, Page 189) / 1629 (Vol 1, Page 187)

Madinah, which was the city of the Prophet was no different as far as the abuse and the insults against Ali were concerned. Muawiyah had appointed Marwan bin al Hakam as the governor of Madinah. Readers would recall that Marwan was the top advisor of Caliph Uthman, and it was his stubbornness in the end which had cost Caliph Uthman his life. Marwan like the other governors of Muawiyah was under the same instructions to curse and abuse Ali.

> *"When Marwan was a governor of Mu'awiya in Madinah, he would curse Ali every Friday from the pulpit (Minbar)...."*

- *Al Badaya wa Al Nahaya, Volume 8 page 285*
- *Tarikh ul Khulafa, page 199*
- *Tarikh al Islam, by Al-Dhahabi, vol. 2, page 288*

In another report the governor ordered Sahl who was a companion of the Prophet to abuse Ali. On the refusal of Sahl the governor asked him that if he did not want to curse Ali by name then he could curse Ali by his nick name, which was Abu Turab.

> *Sahl b. Sa`d reported that a person from the offspring of Marwan was appointed as the governor of Medina. He called Sahl b. Sa`d and ordered him to abuse `Ali. Sahl refused to do that. He (the governor) said to him: If you do not agree to it (at least) say: May Allah curse Abu Turab. Sahl said: There was no name dearer to `Ali than Abu Turab (for it was given to him by the Prophet himself) and he felt delighted when he was called by this name.*

- *Sahih Muslim 2409, Book 44, Hadith 59*

Abu Turab was a name that was given to Ali by the Prophet of Allah. It was in fact the Sunnah of the Prophet to call Ali by the name of Abu Turab. The governors of Muawiyah were inciting people to curse Ali in the city of the Prophet, a city that Ali had indeed defended against the Umayyads in the battle of Moat, when Umayyads and other Qurayshite clans had laid a siege on the city of Madinah.

This could not be called anything other than a tragedy that Ali was being cursed in the city of the Prophet, a city that he had defended against the very people who were cursing him now.

As a rule of thumb all the governors of Muawiyah would curse and abuse Ali and his followers, and they would incite people against the family of the Prophet in a calculated campaign to discredit the leadership of Ali and the Ahlulbayt, and to ensure that Umayyads were seen as the rightful leaders of the Muslim Ummah.

Many historians have confirmed this strategy of Muawiyah.

> *"Mu'awiya and his Governors during the Friday Sermons would say things in praise of Uthman and would curse Ali".*

- *Tarikh Abul Fida Volume 1 page 120*

Occasionally exceptions would happen when someone would refuse to curse Ali. One such exception was Sad, who was also a governor of Muawiyah, but he refused to curse Ali. Since it was the norm to curse and abuse Ali, Muawiyah was surprised and asked Sad as to what prevents him from cursing Ali?

> *"Muawiya b. Abi Sufyan appointed Sa'd as the Governor and said: What prevents you from abusing Abu Turab (Ali), whereupon be said: It is because of three things which I remember Allah's Messenger having said about him…. Allah's Messenger said to him: Aren't you satisfied with being unto me what Harun was unto Musa but with this exception that there is no prophethood after me. And I (also) heard him say on the Day of Khaibar: I would certainly give this standard to a person who loves Allah and his Messenger and Allah and his Messenger love him too.….(The third occasion is this) when the (following) verse was revealed:" Let us summon*

our children and your children." Allah's Messenger called 'Ali, Fatima, Hasan and Husain and said: O Allah, they are my family."

- Sahih Muslim 6220/2404, Muslim Vol. 6, Book 31, Hadith 5915
- Sunan Nisai: 8439
- Sunan ibn Majah: 121

The response of Sad was unequivocal in support of Ali. He recounted some of the merits of Ali where Prophet had said that Ali's relationship with him was same as the relationship between Harun and Musa, and it was Ali who was given the flag of Prophet's army in the battle of Khaibar, and it was Ali and the rest of the Ahlulbayt whom Prophet took with him when the verse of Mubahila was revealed.

Muawiyah was left speechless by the response of Sad and had no answer for it.

13.3.3.2. Muawiyah Refused to Stop the Cursing of Ali

The cursing of Ali under Muawiyah's rule had reached such proportions that many people thought that the Friday prayers could not be completed without cursing Ali.

> *"This practice (of cursing) reached such a state that the people considered that without cursing Ali their Friday worship was incorrect"*
>
> - al-Nasa'ih al-Kaafiyah, page 77

Muawiyah would also personally abuse and curse Ali just like his governors, and he made the cursing of Ali into a tradition for his future Umayyad dynasty too.

> *"At the end of the Friday sermon Mu'awiya would say 'O Allah, curse Abu Turab, he opposed your Deen and path, curse him and punish him in the fire.' He introduced this bidah during his reign, his Governors acted upon it, this bidah continued until the reign of Umar bin Abdul Aziz"*
>
> - Ibn Abi al Hadeed in his commentary of Nahjul Balagha Volume 1 page 464 states:

Some people from Muawiyah's own clan approached him and tried to stop the practice of cursing and abusing Ali, but Muawiyah refused to budge.

> *Some people from Banu Umayyah approached Mu'awiya and said 'You've attained power so why don't you stop the practice of cursing Ali, he replied "By Allah I wont, not until every child grows up, not until every grown up becomes elderly, not until no one is left to praise him".*
>
> - al-Nasa'ih al-Kaafiyah page 70 by Allamah Muhammad bin Aqeel al-Shafiyee

The response of Muawiyah summed up his plan and strategy for the future. Muawiyah told his people that he would not stop the practice of cursing Ali until every child had grown up, and until every grown up had become elderly, and until no one was left to praise Ali.

Muawiyah wanted to ensure that everybody who was living under his rule, including the children who were growing up in the Islamic State would grow up hating and abusing Ali, so that they could never possibly accept Ali and his progeny as the future leaders of the Muslim Ummah.

Muawiyah knew that the only people who were his contenders and rivals for the leadership of the Islamic State were Ali and his offspring, since they represented the Sunnah of the Prophet and since they were the only people who were chosen by the Prophet to lead the Muslim Ummah. Hence the aim of Muawiyah was to create a distance between the Ahlulbayt and the Muslim masses, by insulting and discrediting them throughout the Islamic State.

Muawiyah was so successful in his ploy that many ordinary Muslims considered Ali to be an enemy of God, and they not only cursed Ali, but they also fought against him in many battles. Even to this day many Muslims are unaware of the actual merits of Ali, or what his contribution really was in the service of Islam. They simply think of Ali as the fourth Caliph and a companion of the Prophet, just like any other companion. This unfortunately is the legacy of Muawiyah.

Even Imam Hasan tried to stop Muawiyah from abusing and cursing Ali. One of the conditions of the peace treaty that Imam Hasan had signed with Muawiyah was to stop the practice of cursing Ali. Imam Hasan reminded Muawiyah about the condition of not cursing Ali, but Muawiyah refused to honour his pledge.

> "The conditions were: To give him what is in Kufa's public treasury, the tax of Darabjird city in Persia, and not to curse Ali. He (Mu'awiya) didn't accept the condition that the cursing of (Ali) be stopped. So, He (al-Hasan) asked them to stop cursing when he (al-Hasan) could hear it. (Mu'awiya) accepted that condition but he didn't fulfil it."

- Tarikh of Al-Wardi, Volume 1 page 251
- Al Bidayah wal Nihayah, Volume 8 page 17
- Tarikh Kamil (Arabic), Volume 3 page 272 (Beirut)

Muawiyah could not possibly stop the cursing of Ali and inciting people against Ali and the Ahlulbayt, as that would threaten his ultimate ambition of establishing an Umayyad Kingdom.

13.3.4. Muawiyah Turns the Islamic Caliphate into an Umayyad Dynasty

Ever since Caliph Umar made Muawiyah the governor of Syria, Muawiyah had been working to re-establish the lost glory of the Umayyads. His first goal was to establish an Umayyad powerbase within the Islamic State which he successfully achieved in the Syrian province. Caliph Uthman who became the first Umayyad Caliph was a huge boost for Muawiyah's ambitions. Caliph Uthman not only kept Muawiyah as the governor of Syria, but he actually doubled the amount of land under Muawiyah's jurisdiction, thus allowing Muawiyah to turn Syria into an Umayyad Kingdom which was devoid of any authority or accountability from the central government in Madinah.

Once Muawiyah acquired the Caliphate his dream of turning the entire Islamic State into an Umayyad Kingdom became a reality. Muawiyah had worked very hard and very smartly to be where he was. He had spent a lifetime in laying the groundwork and in planning and calculating countless political and military moves to become the Caliph of the entire Muslim Ummah.

Muawiyah had spent over two decades in building his empire. He had invested huge amounts of wealth and resources on this project. As Muawiyah approaches the end of his life there was little chance that Muawiyah would relinquish power, and hand over the reins of the Caliphate to someone other than his Umayyad family.

Muawiyah plans for the succession of his son Yazid as the new Caliph. Muawiyah wanted to keep the Caliphate within his immediate family. Muawiyah knew that his plan to appoint Yazid as the new Caliph would meet stiff opposition, as Yazid was well known for his abhorrent character and un-Islamic ways.

Muawiyah being the cunning politician he was, lays out a plan for his son Yazid to succeed him.

- Muawiyah pays poets to compose poetry praising and glorifying Yazid in public. The recitation of poetry was a very effective means of communication at the time.
- Muawiyah pays a lot of money to the influential and prominent people who were resisting his plan and buys out most of them.
- An order goes out to all the governors in the various provinces of the Islamic State that they should publicly support the decree from Syria, for the nomination of Yazid as the new head of the State.
- Muawiyah organizes a huge conference in Syria where delegations from all the provinces are invited. He informs them about the suitability of Yazid as the next caliph. The conference is carefully stage-managed to show support for Yazid. However, some delegates refuse to endorse Yazid and oppose Muawiyah's planned succession.
- Muawiyah stops financial benefits of various individuals, in particular the Hashimites and the Ahlulbayt (family of the Prophet), for their opposition to his plan.
- Muawiyah engineers the murder of other influential Islamic personalities who were opposing his plans. He kills people like Saad ibn abi Waqqas, Abdur Rahman bin Khalid, and many others.
- Muawiyah comes to Madinah on several occasions to drum up support for Yazid's nomination. He has meetings with prominent individuals of Madinah like Imam Hussain, Ibn Abbas and Al-Zubair, who all oppose Yazid's succession but Muawiyah sticks to his guns.
- In conversations with Muawiyah, Imam Hussain leaves Muawiyah in no doubt that he would not pledge allegiance to Yazid.

Muawiyah uses a variety of methods like intimidation, bribery, political manoeuvrings, deceit, oppression, withholding of public allowances and even murder to ensure Yazid is nominated as his successor.

13.3.4.1. Muawiyah Uses Deception to Gather Support for Yazid

Madinah was one of the main hubs of the Islamic State. It was home to many renowned Islamic personalities of the time.

The four key people in Madinah who were opposed to the succession of Yazid were Imam Hussain, Al-Zubair, Abdullah bin Umar (Son of Caliph Umar) and Abdul Rehman bin Abu Bakr (son of Caliph Abu Bakr). All these personalities had vehemently opposed Muawiyah's plan to make Yazid the new Caliph. People of Madinah were well-aware of this fact and had so far not supported Muawiyah's choice of appointing Yazid as his successor.

Muawiyah came up with a devious plan. He invites these four personalities to the grand mosque of Madinah alongside the general public. As these personalities took their seats, Muawiyah puts two guards on each of the four men with instructions to cut their heads off if they utter a single word, while Muawiyah speaks to the people.

Muawiyah then stood up and addressed the huge gathering. Muawiyah says that these four men are the leaders of Muslims and no decision could be taken without their consent, and they are happy for Yazid to become the next Caliph, and in the name of Allah they have already paid the oath of allegiance to Yazid.

This was a complete lie and deception on part of Muawiyah. The four men had swords drawn to their heads, and if they were to speak their throats would have been cut off. The public at large had no idea as to what Muawiyah was up to and the game that he was playing behind the scenes. When the public heard that the four leading personalities of Madinah had paid allegiance to Yazid, they followed suit and also gave their allegiance to Yazid.

Here is how history has recorded this incident.

> "....Thereupon the commander of Mu'awiya's guard ordered two men to stand over each of the nobles of the Hejaz who opposed him and to each he said, "If your man leaves his guards to speak one word, either for me or against me, then let the guards strike off his head with their swords". Then he mounted the pulpit and proclaimed: "These men are the Leaders and the choicest of the Muslims; no matter can be successfully handled without them, nor can any decision be taken without their counsel. They are now satisfied to take the oath to Yazid , and have indeed already taken that oath by the name of Allah". So the people took the oath..."

- Social Justice in Islam, (English translation) pages 209-210

This incident alone shows the true face and character of Muawiyah. He was a master of deception and trickery. To the ordinary public it seemed as if Muawiyah loved and respected these personalities, so much so that he would not take a decision without their consent, but in reality, he was about to slit their throats.

13.3.4.2. Muawiyah Pays People to Support Yazid's Nomination

Mughira bin Shuba who had been cursing and inciting people against Ali in Kufa was still Muawiyah's governor in the city. Muawiyah had now tasked him to gather support for Yazid's succession. In typical Muawiyah style, Mughira bribes the high ups of Kufa to maintain their support for Yazid's nomination.

Mughira then sends his son called Musa to Damascus with the same strategy of securing support for Yazid's nomination. Musa also bribes the people in Damascus and buys them out, who reiterate their support for Yazid.

> "Mu'awiya kept Mughira in his post. Mughira arrived at Kufa and spoke to his close representatives, bribing them with 30,000 dirhams to maintain their support. Mughira sent his son Musa bin Mughira to Head a delegation that visited Damascus, there they [the group] reiterated their support for the nomination of Yazeed as Khalifa. Mu'awiya summoned Musa and asked him how much money his father had spent to buy these individuals, he replied 30,000 dirhams".

- Tarikh al Kamil, Volume 3 page 350:

The money of course came from the Islamic treasury as Muawiyah was using all the State resources to secure Yazid's Caliphate.

13.3.4.3. Muawiyah Killed People to Secure Yazid's Succession

Muawiyah was one of a kind. If he was not able to buy someone with money, he would use all other means available to take that person out. Even the people in his own camp were not immune from his deceit and tyranny.

Abdul Rehman bin Khalid, who was the son of Khalid bin Waleed was killed by Muawiyah for being politically ambitious. Abdul Rehman bin Khalid had fought alongside Muawiyah and against Ali in the battle of Siffin. He was an associate and supporter of Muawiyah and was an enemy of Ali and the Ahlulbayt, but he also had his own ambitions of becoming the Caliph. He commanded a fair bit of support and respect in Syria too.

Muawiyah wanted to test the waters to see whom the Syrian people will support if they were to be given a choice. To Muawiyah's surprise the Syrians opted for Abdul Rehman bin Khalid. Being the cunning individual he was, Muawiyah took no action against Abdul Rehman bin Khalid at the time, since he did not want to be seen as someone who would go against the wishes of his own people. But Muawiyah realized that Abdul Rehman bin Khalid was a political rival and would have to be taken out if the Caliphate was to stay within his immediate family.

Muawiyah bided his time and waited for the right opportunity to take out his rival. Once Abdul Rehman bin Khalid fell ill and needed treatment. Muawiyah saw this as a perfect time to strike. Muawiyah told the doctor to poison Abdul Rehman bin Khalid through the syrup he was being given to get better. The doctor administered the syrup and poisoned Abdul Rehman bin Khalid to death.

Such was the devious mind of Muawiyah, he poisoned his friend and a supporter, just as he had poisoned his enemy Imam Hasan.

> "Abdurrahman was against Ali and Bani Hashim ... he had fought in Sifeen alongside Muawiyah...When Muawiyah decided to take bayah from people for his Yazeed, he gave a sermon to the people of Syria in which he said: 'the time of my death is approaching, I am elderly and I want to make a ruler for you people, what do you people want?'. They said: 'We like Abdurrahman'. Muawiya didn't like it but kept it within him and once Abdurrahman got ill, Muawiya told the doctor to treat him and gave him a syrup that could kill him, the doctor administered it and killed him by giving him poison."

- al Istiab, Volume 1 page 250, Dhikr Abdur Rahman bin Khalid

It was a perfect crime, where the general public assumed that Abdul Rehman bin Khalid had died through an illness, but Muawiyah had taken out another political rival without anyone realizing or knowing as to what had actually taken place.

13.3.4.4. Muawiyah Leaves a Will for Yazid

Before his death Muawiyah writes a will for Yazid, telling him that the allegiance for his leadership has been secured from all the provinces in the Islamic State, barring four people in Madinah i.e. Imam Hussain, Abdullah bin Umar, Abdul Rehman bin Abu Bakr and Al-Zubair.

> "O my son, I have arranged everything for you, and I have made all the Arabs agree to obey you. No one will now oppose you in your title to the caliphate, but I am very much afraid of Husayn b. Ali, Abd Allah b. 'Umar, Abd ar-Rahman b. Abi Bakr, and Abd Allah b. az- Zubayr. Among them Husayn b. Ali commands great love and respect because of his superior rights and close relationship to the Prophet. I do not think that the people of Iraq will abandon him until they have risen in rebellion for him against you. As far as possible, try to deal with him gently. But the man who will attack you with full force, like a lion attacks his prey, and who will pounce upon you, like a fox when it finds an opportunity to pounce, is Abd Allah b. az-Zubayr. Whenever you get a chance, cut him into pieces."

- (Iqd al Fareed, Volume 4 page 226)

Muawiyah ensures before his death that the Caliphate would stay in his Umayyad clan, and that his son Yazid would become the next Caliph. Muawiyah informed Yazid that he had secured allegiance for him from all the quarters of the Muslim Ummah. Muawiyah tells Yazid that all the Arabs will obey him, and no one will oppose his Caliphate except for four individuals. He advises Yazid to treat Imam Hussain gently, not because of his love for Imam Hussain, but because Imam Hussain had a lot of following in Iraq and the rebellion by the Iraqis might hurt Yazid's Caliphate.

At the same time Muawiyah advises Yazid to cut al-Zubair into pieces, since Muawiyah knew the past of al-Zubair more than anyone else. Muawiyah knew how politically ambitious al-Zubair really was. Al-Zubair had relentlessly worked against the governments of both Caliph Uthman and Ali, and there was no reason as to why al-Zubair would not try to bring down the administration of Yazid too. Hence Muawiyah advised Yazid to cut al-Zubair into pieces whenever he gets the opportunity.

The will that Muawiyah wrote to his son had an interesting truth to it. The will was essentially a private document between a father and a son. In this document Muawiyah recognizes the superior merits of Imam Hussain, and also accepts the closeness of Imam Hussain to the Holy Prophet. Despite these facts he deliberately side-lined the true custodian of the Prophet's Sunnah, and he choose his son Yazid who absolutely had no merits to lead the Muslim Ummah.

Muawiyah with all his shrewdness and cunning ploys won in the end, and with the inauguration of his morally corrupt son Yazid he successfully established an Ummayad dynasty in the heart of Arabia. This Umayyad dynasty will now rule in the guise of the Islamic Caliphate for the next one hundred years to come.

The trend of al-ijtihad which began in Saqifah against the wish of the Prophet eventually undid the Islamic system of governance and replaced it with an Umayyad Kingdom!

13.3.5. An Unfortunate Defence

It is most unfortunate and sad to see that even in this day and age we have scholars who would defend the actions and character of a personality like Muawiyah.

Muawiyah was an individual who had made the companions of the Prophet dig their own graves before beheading them. He was an individual who had poisoned the grandson of the Holy Prophet Imam Hasan, after signing a peace treaty with him. Muawiyah was someone who paid and ordered the Imams of the mosques to curse and abuse Ali and the Ahlulbayt in every Friday prayer, a practice which lasted for almost nighty years.

Muawiyah not only cursed and abused Ali to malign his reputation, but he also fought and launched wars against him in order to acquire the leadership of the Muslim Ummah. Contrary to the approach of Muawiyah, the Prophet of Allah had made the love of Ali a sign of being a believer, and the hatred of Ali a sign of being a hypocrite. The Prophet of Allah had famously said to Ali:

> *"None loves you except a believer and none hates you except a hypocrite."*
> - *Sahih Muslim Vol. 1, Book of Faith (Kitab Al-Iman), Hadith 141*
> - *Jami` at-Tirmidhi Vol. 6, Book 46 of Al-Manaqib (Virtues), Hadith 3736*
> - *Sunan Ibn Majah Vol. 1, Book 1 of Purification and its Sunnah, Hadith 114*
> - *Sunan an-Nasaa'i Vol. 6, Book of Faith and its Signs, Hadith 5025*

It is no wonder that the companions of the Prophet used to say:

> *"We recognized the hypocrites by their hatred of Ali."*
> - *Fada'il al-Sahaba, by Ahmad Ibn Hanbal, v2, p639, Tradition 1086*
> - *al-Isti'ab, by Ibn Abd al-Barr, v3, p47*
> - *al-Riyad al-Nadirah, by al-Muhibb al-Tabari, v3, p242*

The love and the hatred of Ali was the litmus test for being a believer or a hypocrite, and Muawiyah certainly did not pass that test. The actions of Muawiyah contradicted countless traditions of the Prophet, in which the Prophet had specifically ordered the companions to love and respect the Ahlulbayt and to follow their lead.

However, the biggest crime of Muawiyah was probably the fact that he changed the system of governance that Prophet had established, and he replaced the Islamic Caliphate with an Umayyad dynasty, which simply used Islam as a tool to expand and consolidate its grip on power.

Muawiyah used every trick under the sun to keep the Caliphate in his Umayyad clan. The words of nepotism and corruption did not exist in Muawiyah's dictionary. He bribed tribal leaders and elders who were refusing to pay allegiance to Yazid from the Islamic treasury. He threatened and physically eliminated any individual who had challenged his decision to forcefully appoint his son Yazid as the new Caliph.

Muawiyah's modus of operandi had always been to first offer money to buy out his opponents, and if that approach failed for any reason and the individual refused to fall in line, then Muawiyah would use brute force to ensure that his decision and choice was respected.

Almost everything that Muawiyah did was for personal and worldly gains and was in complete contradiction to the Book of Allah and the traditions of the Prophet. There is really no need and no point in defending Muawiyah, a character who is indefensible in the eyes of history. Any sane Muslim who has even an ounce of fairness and spirituality in them would not dare to defend the crimes of Muawiyah.

As Ahl-e-Sunnah (followers of the Sunnah) our aim should be to defend the honour and the Sunnah of the Prophet, rather than to defend the actions of an individual who trampled over the Sunnah of the Prophet. Such a defence indeed goes against the very ethos of being an Ahl-e-Sunnah. It would be pretty difficult for us to face the Prophet on the day of Judgement, when we in this lifetime try and defend a person who had changed and destroyed his Sunnah and murdered his family members.

13.3.5.1. The Merits of Muawiyah

Despite such a horrendous track record against Islam and Muslims, Muawiyah to this day commands the love and respect of a large section of Muslim population. Some scholars argue that despite what Muawiyah did he was a companion of the Prophet, and for this fact alone he cannot be criticized and must be respected. Others would argue that since Muawiyah wrote some revelations of the Holy Quran for the Prophet, he is exempt from any criticism. While some scholars would present traditions of the Prophet praising Muawiyah, arguing that merits of Muawiyah are proven from the Sunnah of the Prophet.

The issue of Muawiyah's merits is an interesting one.

Muawiyah accepted Islam at the conquest of Makkah alongside his father Abu Sufyan. They were the enemies of Islam who had fought against the Muslims for nearly two decades. The Prophet finally forgave them for surrendering to the Muslim army as it entered Makkah. Simply based on this historic fact Muawiyah could not possibly have acquired too many merits during the lifetime of the Prophet, as Prophet only lived for one and a half years after the conquest of Makkah.

Also, the conquest of Makkah was the final hurdle in the establishment of the Islamic State in the Arabian Peninsula. The creation of the Islamic State was the biggest and the most important project undertaken by the Prophet in his lifetime, and Muawiyah obviously played no part in this endeavour. Similarly, Muawiyah was missing form all the key battles of Islam such as the Battle of Badr, the Battle of Uhud, the Battle of Moat and the battle of Khaibar. These battles were truly the battles for the destiny of Islam and Muawiyah had no role in any of these battles.

The merits of Muawiyah really began to surface after he took over the office of the Caliphate, and his merits kept coming out of the wood works until the last Umayyad Caliph. This was the golden period of the Umayyads which lasted for around one hundred years when the Umayyad dynasty ruled the Muslim Ummah.

Muawiyah and his Umayyad clan needed to justify their claim to the leadership of the Islamic State. They needed to legitimize their rule in the eyes of the Muslim masses. They knew that the true heirs of the Prophet were Ali and the Ahlulbayt and that they had unfairly taken over the leadership of the Muslim Ummah.

The merits of Ali were unique and distinct and were not matched by any other companion, let alone the likes of Muawiyah. Ali was brought up in the house of the Prophet. Ali was the differentiating factor in the defence and the establishment of the Islamic State. Ali was the flag bearer of the Prophet in all the key battles which changed the destiny of Islam once and for all.

Muawiyah on the other hand had only accepted Islam after the conquest of Makkah when a general amnesty was given to all the Qurayshite tribes, hence Muawiyah really had no merits except for the fact that he had become a Muslim. So, Muawiyah and his Umayyad clan embarked on a two-prong strategy. The first tactics was to curse and belittle Ali and incite ordinary Muslims against him, by blaming him for the murder of Caliph Uthman, in order to create a rift between Ali and the Muslim masses.

The second strategy was to fabricate traditions in favour of Muawiyah, to bring the status of Muawiyah in line with the status of Ali, and to justify Muawiyah's newly found position as the leader of the Muslim Ummah.

Fortunately for Muawiyah and the Umayyads Ali had many enemies and they all joined hands with the Umayyads against him. They looked hard to find faults in Ali, but they couldn't find any, so they started fabricating praises for Muawiyah who had fought against Ali to justify Muawiyah's claim to the Caliphate, and to give the impression that somehow Ali and Muawiyah were equals, and that they both had a right to the leadership of the Muslims.

Imam Ahmed Ibn Hanbal summed up this reality in a beautiful answer that he gave to his son Abdullah.

> "I asked my father (Ahmad Ibn Hanbal) about Ali and Muawiya. He (Ahmad Ibn Hanbal) answered: "Know that Ali had a lot of enemies who tried hard to find a fault in him, but they found it not. As such, they joined a man, (Muawiya) who verily fought him, battled him, and they praised him (Muawiyah) extravagantly setting a trap for themselves for him"

- History of Caliphs by Jalaluddin Suyuti page 202
- Al-Sawa'iq al-Muhriqah, by Ibn Hajar, Ch. 9, section 4, p 197
- Al-Toyuriyyat, by al-Salafi, by Abdullah Ibn Ahmad Hanbal

It was in this context that merits of Muawiyah were fabricated during the time of the Umayyad dynasty. It was in fact part of the counter revolution that Muawiyah had started against the Islamic Caliphate, so that he could justify his position as the true leader of the Muslim Ummah.

And it is for this reason that many classical scholars of Hadith (Traditions of the Prophet) and Fiqh (Jurisprudence) have agreed that are no genuine merits of Muawiyah, and all the traditions of the Prophet in favour of Muawiyah are fabricated and are without any authentic chain of narrators.

> *Jalaluddeen Suyuti wrote: "Imam al- Hakim states that he never came across a single Hadith in praise of Muawiya that was Sahih (Authentic)"*

- La'ali al-Masnu`aa fi ahadith al-Maudu`aa" Volume 1 page 424

> Imam Shawkani said: "Ibn Hibban commented that all Ahadith in praise of Muawiya are fabricated".

- Fawa'id al Mujmu`a fi bay`an al-hadith al-maudu`a page 147

> Shaykh Ismail bin Muhammad stated: 'There exist no Hadith in praise of Muawiya that is Sahih (Authentic)"

- Kashful Khafa Vol. 2 page 420

> Imam Dhahabi States "Ishaaq Ibn Rehwiya said: 'There is not any Sahih (Authentic) hadith from the prophet (pbuh) about the merits of Muawiya'.

- Siyar alam al Nubla' Volume 3 page 132

> Allama al 'Aini commented: "No reports in praise of Muawiya are proven. If many are present, the reply is that no Hadith exists with a Sahih (Authentic) isnaad (Chain of narators) as stated by Isaac bin Rahwayh and Imam Nasai, and that's why Imam Bukhari wrote a Chapter Baab ai Dhikr (Biography) of Muawiya rather than bab ai Fadail (Merits) of Muawiya"

- Ummdat al Qari fi Sharh Sahih al Bukhari P 994, Volume 7

> Ibn Hajr al-Asqalani, in his commentary of Bukhari states "..… Ibn Abi Asim wrote a book about his (Mu'awyia's) merits and so did Umar Ghulam Thalab and Abu Bakr al-Naqash but Ibn Jawzi recorded in (his book) "Mawdu'at" some of the traditions which the previous scholars had recorded in their books and then he quoted from Ishaq ibn Rehwiya that he said: 'Nothing is authentic in praise of Mu'awiya'. And this is the reason which made Bukhari avoid using the word 'virtue' (in chapter name)."

- Ibn Hajr al-Asqalani, Fathul Bari Vol. 7 page 104

As evident from the works of these scholars that Muawiyah really had no merits. His merits were invented after he took over the reins of the Caliphate. This was done as part of a ploy by the enemies of Ali who collaborated with Umayyads to raise the status of Muawiyah to such a level that he would be seen as a rival of Ali for the leadership of the Muslim Ummah.

As a result of this strategy of the Umayyads for almost a century, a whole new generation of Muslims had grown up hating and cursing Ali while praising Muawiyah and the Umayyad rulers.

Once Imam Nasai travelled to Syria (Damascus), he witnessed that many people there hated Ali and regarded Ali as an enemy of God. Syria was of course the power base of the Umayyads. Imam Nasai decided to stay in Syria, so that he could change the view of the people regarding Ali. He opened an Islamic school in Damascus and started teaching there, advocating the love and the respect Ali among the Syrians.

He specifically wrote a book called "Khasais of Ali", which contained many traditions of the Prophet in favour of Ali, in order to bring the Syrian Muslims back to the Sunnah of the Prophet of loving and following in the footsteps of Ali. When the supporters of Muawiyah heard that Imam Nasai had written a book in praise of Ali, they approached him and demanded that he should write a book in praise of Muawiyah too. Imam Nasai refused and quoted a tradition of the Prophet in which Prophet had cursed Muawiyah.

> Imam Nasai said - When he was in Damascus, people asked him to write about the virtues of "Mu'awiya. He replied, what should I write about him? I know his only virtue is Prophet cursed him - May Allah never satiate his stomach.

- *Tarikh Ibn Khalikaan, V 1, P 35; Tadhkiratul Huffaz, 2/194*

The story goes like this. Once Muawiyah was eating food and Prophet called him, but he kept on eating his food and ignored Prophet's call. The Prophet called him again and he again ignored Prophet's request and kept enjoying his food. The Prophet got angry and said that may Allah never fill Muawiyah's belly. Imam Muslim in his Sahih has recorded this tradition in a chapter titled "People who were Cursed by Prophet Mohammad".

> *Ibn Abbas says: … He (the Prophet) came and patted my shoulders and said: Go and call Mu'awiya. I returned and said: He is busy in taking food. He again asked me to go and call Mu'awiya to him. I went (and came back) and said that he was busy in taking food, whereupon he (Prophet) said: May Allah not fill his (Muawiyah's) belly!*

- *Sahih Muslim, Chapter 23 - titled "People who were Cursed by Prophet Mohammad" Hadith # 6298*

As Imam Nasai had refused to write the book in honour of Muawiyah, and instead had given a tradition of the Prophet cursing Muawiyah, the supporters of Muawiyah who approached him became violent. They attacked Imam Nasai in his mosque, they jumped on him and opened his stomach. It is reported that Imam Nasai was then taken to Makkah or Palestine where he died of his injuries.

The Prophet had even prayed for Muawiyah to be in hell.

> *Abi Burza said: 'We were with the Prophet then he heard someone singing (objectionable songs), so the Prophet said: 'Go and see what is going on there'. Thus, I climbed and looked, I saw Muawiya and Amr bin al-Auss singing, then I returned and told (the Prophet) He (the Prophet) said: 'May Allah throw them in fitna and push them towards hell'.*

- *Mizan al-I'tidal, Vol 3 Page 311; (2)*
- *Siyar alam al Nubla, Vol 3, Page 132*

The misguidance of Muawiyah was evident from the time of the Prophet. He had never been sincere to the values of Islam and once he acquired the Caliphate he ruled as if he was a pre-Islamic Arab King.

The merits of Muawiyah are a fabrication of the Umayyad dynasty and have no relevance to the Sunnah of the Prophet.

13.3.5.2. Muawiyah was the Writer of the Revelations

Even after Abu Sufyan's family accepted Islam, Muslims would keep a distance from them, because of their past and because of what they had done to the Muslims. Most Muslims would not even speak to Abu Sufyan or his family. As a result, Abu Sufyan's family felt isolated and unwanted by the Muslims, so Abu Sufyan approached the Prophet and asked for some favours. One of the things he requested from the Prophet was to appoint his son Muawiyah as a scribe (a writer), so that his family could be seen in a positive light among the Muslims.

Prophet was also keen to integrate the new Muslims into the fold of the Islamic nation, so Prophet accepted the request of Abu Sufyan and appointed Muawiyah as a scribe.

> *"……And he (Abu Sufyan) again said: Accept Mu'awiya to serve as your scribe (Writer). He (the Prophet) said: Yes……"*

- *(Muslim, Book 31, Hadith # 6095)*

It is not clear from historical accounts whether Muawiyah was appointed as the scribe for writing the Holy Quran, or whether he was appointed to write some letters and general documents for the Prophet. Nevertheless, the supporters and defenders of Muawiyah claim that he was appointed as a scribe for writing the Holy Quran.

For the purpose of our discussion, I will assume that Muawiyah was appointed as the writer of the revelations, rather than as someone who was writing letters or general documents for the Prophet.

Writing the revelations of the Holy Quran in the presence of the Prophet is a huge honour, which only a handful of individuals ever had on this earth. If Muawiyah indeed had the honour of writing the verses of the Holy Quran, then what he actually did after the death of the Prophet is absolutely unforgivable!

Every honour comes with responsibility and accountability. The higher the honour of an individual the greater will be his accountability, and this is evident both from the Sunnah of the Prophet and from the events of Islamic history.

Readers would recall from Chapter 11 section "Ammar Ibn Yasir and Abdullah Ibn Abu Sarh" that a writer of the Holy Quran named Abu Sarh had gone against the words of Allah, and he had apostatized. The Prophet had ordered his companions to kill Abu Sarh even if he was found hiding under the curtain of Kaaba.

> "…… When the Prophet entered Makkah he ordered him (Abu Sarh)….. to be executed even if they were under the curtains of the Kaaba. ……."
> - *Ibn Husham Biography of the Prophet Part 2 p. 409*
> - *al-Qurtubi, Op.Cit*

The Prophet throughout his lifetime had rarely ordered the killing of any individual, since Prophet was sent as a mercy for the mankind. But he instructed his companions to kill Abu Sarh, because Abu Sarh was the writer of the Holy Quran, and after writing the revelations of the Quran he went against those very revelations, and hence his punishment was so harsh and severe.

The actions of the Prophet clearly reveal two key points. Firstly, It is the Sunnah of the Prophet that if someone has been given an honour then their accountability will also be severe. Secondly, the actions of the Prophet also show that no one is above the law. Even if a person had the honour of writing the Holy Quran and was a companion of the Prophet, but if he breaks Allah's law, he would be punished just like any anyone else, and this indeed is the beauty and the justice of Islam.

And Muawiyah had indeed broken countless Islamic laws, and had gone against numerous commands of Allah, despite being a writer of the Holy Quran. The list of Muawiyah's crimes is long and bloody, and it is documented in many books of Hadith and history. The position of Muawiyah is absolutely untenable as far as the Islamic jurisprudence is concerned.

Just like Abu Sarh, there was another writer of the Holy Quran who also went against the commands of Allah, and his fate was even worse. After being a writer of the Holy Quran he once said that Prophet knows nothing except for what I have written for him. This insult of the Prophet was unforgivable in the eyes of Allah.

When he died his friends buried him but next morning his body had been thrown out of the grave and was lying on the ground. They thought it was Prophet and his companions who had done this as he had gone against Islam, so his friends again buried him but this time in a much deeper grave, however next morning his body was again out of the grave and lying on the ground. They again thought it was the Prophet and his companions who had dug him out, so now they dug the grave as deep as they possibly could and buried him again, but the next day his body was again out of the grave (Sahih al-Bukhari, Volume 4, Book 56, Number 814 / Sahih Bukhari 3421).

They finally realized that it wasn't the Prophet or his companions who were doing this, but it was in fact a punishment from Allah.

It is clear from the above events that being a writer of the Holy Quran gives no immunity or defence in the eyes of Allah or the Prophet. On the contrary, it increases the accountability and the punishment of the individual if they had transgressed the laws of Allah.

If Muawiyah was indeed a writer of the Holy Quran, then he really has no alibi on the Day of Judgment!

13.3.5.3. Muawiyah was a Companion of the Prophet

The scholars of past and present who have tried to defend Muawiyah have failed miserably as there isn't any justifiable excuse that one can really give for the crimes of Muawiyah.

When all the lines of defence fail against Muawiyah and there is no alibi left, as a last resort the defenders of Muawiyah bring up the notion that after all he was a companion of the Prophet, and based on this historical fact Muawiyah cannot be criticized, regardless of what he had done during his lifetime. They say that since Muawiyah once had the honour of Prophet's company, even if he did something wrong afterwards, he is immune from criticism. They further add that it is the belief of the Ahl-e-Sunnah (followers of the Sunnah), that they are not allowed to speak negatively about any of the companions, despite what those companions may have done during their own lifetimes.

These weak and illogical lines of defence have no place in the era of logic and reasoning.

13.3.5.3.1. The Elite Class of Muslims

The religion of Islam does not recognize any elite class of Muslims who are above the law or who are immune from criticism or accountability. Islam does not hold any such notion. The laws of Allah apply equally to all of humanity, irrespective of their colour, creed, race, ethnicity, or their proximity to the Prophet. Just because an individual had seen or met the Prophet and had the honour of his company, does not make that individual any less accountable in the eyes of Allah. The laws of Allah would apply equally to all regardless of their position or status.

The Prophet had famously said that even if my daughter Fatima steals, she would face the same Islamic punishment as any other women.

> *Usama approached the Prophet on behalf of a woman (who had committed theft). The Prophet said, "The people before you were destroyed because they used to inflict the legal punishments on the poor and forgive the rich. By Him in Whose Hand my soul is! If Fatima (the daughter of the Prophet) did that (i.e. stole), I would cut off her hand."*
> - *Sahih al-Bukhari 6787*
> - *Sahih al-Bukhari Book 86, Hadith 16*

This is the beauty of Islam that it treats everyone equally regardless of their status. Even Fatima, the daughter of the Prophet who is the leader of the women in paradise, and who is a member of the Ahlulbayt, and who is also a companion, would face the same punishment as any other Muslim. Whether it's a companion of the Prophet, or whether it is an ordinary Muslim or whether they are the members of the Ahlulbayt, no one is above the law, and they will all face the same justice in the eyes of Allah.

These were pre-Islamic notions where certain elite classes were protected, based on their wealth, tribal lineage, or proximity to the leaders of the time. Islam came to destroy such notions where certain people were above the law and could not be criticized. Islam gave Muslims the freedom of thought and expression to challenge and criticize anyone who would break the Islamic law. These were the key distinctions of the Islamic revolution, that an ordinary citizen of the Islamic State could criticize and challenge the Caliph of the time or a powerful tribal leader, if they had gone against the Islamic law.

And Prophet certainly did not come to create an elite class of Muslims called the companions, who were above the law, and above criticism, and who would not be held accountable for their actions. Such notions are alien to the very ethos of Islam. There is no concept of diplomatic immunity in the Islamic jurisprudence, where some individuals could break the law and would be immune from prosecution or criticism. These are strange thoughts as far as the Islamic system of governance and jurisprudence is concerned.

The companions as a whole are certainly worthy of our respect, since they had the honour of Prophet's blessed company, but that does not mean that there is an elite class of Muslims who are above the rest. The Holy Quran clearly negates this notion.

> "…. Indeed, the most noble of you in the sight of Allah is the most righteous of you……"
> - Quran (49:13)

The most noble in the eyes of Allah is the most righteous among the Muslims regardless of whether that individual is a companion or not. This verse of the Holy Quran beautifully sums up the Islamic concept of eliteness. The eliteness in Islam is not defined by the fact that an individual is a companion of the Prophet, it is defined by the fact that an individual is righteous or not, and Muawiyah certainly was no way close to being righteous, even though he was a companion of the Prophet.

13.3.5.3.2. The Testimony of the Holy Quran

The Prophet of Allah had thousands of companions. The Holy Quran divides these companions into three categories. The three consecutive verses of Surah Tawbah highlights these categories.

> *And the first to lead the way, of the Muhajireen and the Ansar, and those who followed them in goodness – Allah is well pleased with them and they are well pleased with Him, and He hath made ready for them Gardens underneath which rivers flow, wherein they will abide for ever. That is the supreme triumph.*
> - Holy Quran (9:100)

> *And among those Bedouins (wandering Arabs) who are around you there are hypocrites, and among the people of Madinah as well. They are adamant on hypocrisy. You do not know them. We know them. We will chastise them twice, then they shall be driven to a terrible punishment (in the Hereafter).*
> - Holy Quran (9:101)

> *And there are others who admitted their sins while they had mixed a good deed with an evil one. It is likely that Allah will relent towards them. Surely, Allah is Most-Forgiving, Very-Merciful.*
> - Holy Quran (9:102)

The first category are the righteous companions from the early Muhajireen (companions from Makkah) and the Ansar (companions from Madinah), who Allah is pleased with, and they are pleased with Allah. Their destiny is paradise beneath which there are gardens where rivers flow and where they will live for ever.

However, even in this category not every companion is righteous as Allah has put a condition which states: "And the first to lead the way, of the Muhajireen and the Ansar, and those who followed them in goodness". This means that only those companions from the early Muhajireen and the Ansar who had led the way in terms of good deeds and those who have followed them in those deeds are part of this group. So even in this category Allah has set a condition for being a righteous companion.

The next verse defines the second group of the companions who the Holy Quran calls the hypocrites. These were those companions who had accepted Islam outwardly, but their hearts were against the faith of Islam. And these hypocrites were both from the Bedouin (wandering) Arabs and from the people of Madinah. The people of Madinah comprised of both the Muhajireen (companions from Makkah) and the Ansar (companions from Madinah), since both Muhajireen and the Ansar were living together in Madinah after the hijra.

Allah further says that these hypocrites were adamant in hypocrisy and even the Prophet did not know who they were, but Allah knew them, and their destiny would be a terrible punishment in hereafter.

The third group of companions are a mixed bag. Sometimes they do good deeds and sometimes their deeds are evil, and as Allah is all merciful so he may choose to forgive them.

This is the reality of the companions of the Prophet unlike what some of the scholars claim. The companions of the Prophet were not all righteous. There were many hypocrites among them as testified by the Holy Quran.

The defenders of Muawiyah should read the Book of Allah with an open mind before defending his crimes. The Holy Quran reaffirms the notion that not all of the companions of the Prophet are worthy of our respect, since many of them were hypocrites and others had a mixture of both good and evil deeds, and Muawiyah certainly does not fall in the first category of companions.

In Islam respect for any individual is based on their actions and their deeds. It is not based on their ethnicity, their tribal lineage, or their proximity to the Prophet. If an individual had spent time in the company of the Prophet, then that is certainly a huge honour for that individual, but his respect in the eyes of Allah is based on what he actually did during his lifetime, rather than the fact that he had the honour of meeting the Prophet.

And that is why Quran is calling some of the companions as hypocrites as they went against the word of Allah, despite the fact that they were the companions of the Prophet, and despite the fact that they had the honour of his company.

13.3.5.3.3. The Tradition of the Prophet, Do not Abuse my Companions

One of the most common traditions used by the defenders of Muawiyah to stop people from criticising him or any of the other unrighteous companion is to give the following tradition of the Prophet where Prophet had said:

> *"Do not abuse my companions for if any one of you spent gold equal to Uhud (in Allah's Cause) it would not be equal to a Mud or even a half Mud spent by one of them."*

- *Sahih al-Bukhari 3673*
- *Book 62, Hadith 23*

The defenders of Muawiya will quote this hadith without mentioning the context and the circumstances in which Prophet had mentioned these words, and without considering whether these words would also apply to the later generations of Muslims who came after the companions.

The above tradition of the Prophet was mentioned specifically for Khalid Ibn Al-Walid when he had unjustly killed several men from the tribe of Banu Jadhimah. At the time Abdul Rahman Ibn Auf had challenged Khalid on his actions as Khalid had transgressed the commands of the Prophet. In retaliation Khalid verbally abused and cursed Abdul Rahman. So, when Prophet heard as to what had taken place, he said the following:

> "...Khalid, leave my companions alone. By God, should you have a piece of gold the size of Uhud Mountain, and you spend it in the path of God, your charity would not compare to a morning or evening trip in defence of Islam by any one of my companions."

- *(Ibn Hisham, in his Sirat of the Prophet, part 2, page 421)*

A number of points come out from the above tradition of the Prophet.

Firstly, this tradition clarifies that not everyone who had seen the Prophet and was present in his company was considered a companion, unlike the view of many of the scholars today. Prophet tells Khalid to leave his companions alone and do not abuse them, clearly implying that the Prophet did not consider Khalid Ibn Al-Walid to be one of his companions. The Prophet considered Abdul Rahman Ibn Auf to be his companion but not Khalid Ibn Al-Walid, even though both of them had seen the Prophet and were present in his company.

Secondly, the Prophet had stopped Khalid Ibn Al-Walid from verbally abusing Abdul Rahman Ibn Auf because Abdul Rahman was correct on this issue and not because he was a companion of the Prophet. Khalid had killed several men unjustly and when Abdul Rahman criticised him, Khalid started abusing Abdul Rahman, so Prophet was siding with Abdul Rahman because he had taken a correct stance on this matter, and not because he was simply a companion of the Prophet.

The reason why prophet used the word companion for Abdul Rahman Ibn Auf was because he did not consider Khalid Ibn Al-Walid to be his companion, and he only considered Abdul Rahman to be his companion.

Thirdly, since of Abdul Rahman Ibn Auf had taken a correct stance on this issue and Khalid Ibn Al-Walid was abusing him unfairly, the Prophet is telling us that if there is dispute between two parties then we should side with the party which is on the path of truth, and not sweep their differences under the carpet, as some scholars try to do today when it comes to the disputes among the companions or the early Muslims.

Fourthly, this tradition is specifically for the incident of Khalid Ibn Al-Walid and Abdul Rahman Ibn Auf where Prophet is telling Khalid Ibn Al-Walid not to criticize Abdul Rahman Ibn Auf. It does not apply to the later generations of Muslims since we were not a party to that dispute.

In fact, Prophet had considered the later generation of Muslims who had not seen the Prophet like our generation to be superior to the generation of the companions who had seen the Prophet.

The readers may think that the last point has no validity, but I will clarify this point in the next section.

Khalid Ibn Al-Walid had accepted Islam after the treaty of Hudaybiyya and Prophet did not consider him to be his companion, whereas Muawiyah had accepted Islam after the conquest of Makkah well after the treaty of Hudaybiyya. Based on the above tradition of the Prophet the companionship of Muawiyah itself is in doubt, and it is possible that in the eyes of the Prophet Muawiyah may not even be considered a companion, despite what the defenders of Muawiyah may say.

This hadith of the Prophet gives no grounds for shielding Muawiyah as this hadith is specific to the incident of Khalid Ibn Al-Walid and Abdul Rahman Ibn Auf, and also the crimes of Muawiyah were far more severe than the insults that Khalid Ibn Al-Walid had directed towards Abdul Rahman Ibn Auf.

Lastly, let us say for the sake of argument that this tradition of the Prophet bars Muslims from criticising or abusing any of the companions of the Prophet. Then in that case Muawiyah had gone against this very tradition of the Prophet too. Since Muawiyah cursed and abused Ali from every pulpit under his jurisdiction, and Ali was not only a companion of the Prophet, but Ali was a member of the Ahlulbayt too.

Muawiyah not only cursed and abused Ali and the rest of the Ahlulbayt, but he also fought against them and killed the grandson of the Prophet Imam Hasan, and many other pious companions of the Prophet like Hujr bin Adi and Malik bin Ashtar.

Even if we understand this tradition in the context that the defenders of Muawiyah want us to understand, even then Muawiyah had transgressed the Sunnah of the Prophet by abusing and cursing Ali who was both a companion of the Prophet and a member of the Ahlulbayt.

13.3.5.3.4. The Later Generations can be Superior to the Generation of the Companions

This may come as a surprise to some of the readers, but it is actually true that Prophet had considered the Muslims who came in later generations and who had not seen him but believed in him to be superior to the generation of the companions.

Abdullah ibn Muhiriz narrates the famous tradition of the Prophet:

> "...... One day, we were having a meal with the Holy Prophet. Abu Ubaydah ibn Jarrah was present in our company as well. He asked the Holy Prophet, 'Are there any people better than us because we believed in you and fought (jihad) alongside you?' The Holy Prophet answered, 'Yes, after you there will be a group of people from among my Ummah who will believe in me without even having seen me.'"

- *Musnad Imam Ahmed bin Hanbal 17102*
- *Mishkat 6291*

The Prophet of Allah clarifies the actual position of the companions in Islam, and also the position of the later generations of Muslims who had not seen the Prophet but believed in him, like all of us today.

Abu Ubaydah ibn Jarrah was one of the early companions of the Prophet from the emigrants (companions from Makkah). He is also part of the Ashra Mubashara, the ten companions who have apparently been promised paradise by the Holy Prophet. As a companion, Abu Ubaydah ibn Jarrah is one of the foremost companions of the Prophet.

Abu Ubaydah ibn Jarrah is sitting in the company of the Prophet and is having a meal with him. He asks the Prophet of Allah that are we (the companions) the best generation of the Muslims, since we believed in you, and we did jihad (fought) alongside you?

The response of the Prophet is a surprising one. The Prophet says to Abu Ubaydah ibn Jarrah that the best generation is not the generation of the companions, but it is the generation which will believe in him without even seeing him. So, the likes of me and you who believe in the Prophet and follow his Sunnah without seeing him can be superior to the companions, as long as we truly believe in the message of Islam.

And this is the reality and the beauty of Islam. Islam does not create a distinction between a companion and an ordinary Muslim, simply because an ordinary Muslim had not seen or met the Prophet. Islam had not come to create an elite group of Muslims called the companions who were above the rest, and who were free from any criticism despite their actions.

As stated in the Holy Quran the most noble among you is the most righteous of you.

> "…. Indeed, the most noble of you in the sight of Allah is the most righteous of you……"
> - Quran (49:13)

Although we have not seen the Prophet, but if we sincerely believe in the word of Allah and follow the teachings of the Holy Prophet, then we could be superior to the companions who had the honour of Prophet's company and who had done jihad (fought) alongside him in the path of Allah.

The Prophet of Allah does not stop there but in another narration, which is narrated by Abu Amama he further states:

> "Blessed are those who had faith in me and saw me, and blessed seven times are those who had faith in me and never saw me."
> - Musnad Imam Aḥmad 12578 / 22490
> - Mishkat 6290

Again, the Prophet is clarifying the true position of the companions in Islam. A person who has seen the Prophet i.e., a companion of the Prophet is blessed once, but a person who has not seen the Prophet but believed in him is blessed seven times. So, Muslims who came in later generations and are true believers are blessed seven times whereas companions are blessed only once.

In the same context Abu Hurairah has narrated that Prophet of Allah has said:

> *The people most loved by me from amongst my Ummah would be those who would come after me but everyone amongst them would have the keenest desire to catch a glimpse of me even at the cost of his family and wealth.*
> - Sahih Muslim 7145
> - Sahih Muslim 2832, Book 53 Hadith 14
> - Mishkat 6284

The generation that the Prophet of Allah loves the most among his Ummah is not the generation of the companions, but it is the generations which had come after he had left this world.

The Prophet of Allah clarifies that the generations who came after him would have a keen desire to catch his glimpse, even at the expense of their family and wealth, and as a result he loves them the most.

People who defend the actions of certain companions because these individuals had the honour of Prophet's company, should read these traditions of the Prophet with an open mind, and realize that even people like us who live in the 21st century can be better or superior to the companions, as long as we truly believe in the message of Islam.

So, defending a person simply because they had the honour of Prophet's company is futile and it is clearly against the traditions of the Prophet and the ethos of Islam.

Muawiyah certainly had the honour of Prophet's company but did Muawiyah himself honour the Sunnah of the Prophet when he had the opportunity to do so, especially when he became the leader of the Muslim Ummah. Did he actually abide by the Sunnah of the Prophet when he acquired the Caliphate of the Muslims? If Muawiyah had honoured the Sunnah of the Prophet, then he would have commanded the respect of the Muslims, but since he went against the Sunnah of the Prophet and the Book of Allah, there is no justification in defending the honour of Muawiyah, despite the fact that he had the honour of Prophet's company.

The aim of this discussion is not to diminish the honour of the companions but to highlight the true position of the companions as stated by the Prophet of Allah. The goal here is to invite Muslims to distance themselves from the actions of individuals like Muawiyah, who had abused their position and status in the society to consolidate power, in order to further their own narrow political and tribal interests at the expense of the Muslim masses.

13.3.5.3.5. The Highest Honour of a Human Being

The highest honour that a human being can possibly have in the eyes of Allah is to have the honour of being a Prophet. The first Prophet and the first human in this universe was Prophet Adam. Allah tells the angels that I will create a human being called Adam and you will prostrate to him.

> *'I am going to create a human (Adam) from sounding clay ... then you fall down prostrate to him."*
>
> - *(Quran 38:71-72)*

Allah not only gave Prophet Adam the honour of being a Prophet and the first human being, but he also made the angles prostrate to him as a sign of respect, an honour that no other Prophet was given.

Allah then became the teacher of Prophet Adam and taught him everything.

> *"He (Allah) taught Adam all the names of everything."*
>
> - *(Quran 2:31)*

Allah further bestowed his mercy and blessings on Prophet Adam by creating a beautiful wife named Eve for him, and then he gave both Adam and Eve a place in paradise.

> *And We said, "O Adam, dwell, you and your wife, in Paradise and eat therefrom in [ease and] abundance from wherever you will.*
>
> - Quran (2:35)

Allah gave Adam and Eve everything in abundance in paradise for them to enjoy and dwell in tranquillity, but he forbade them from approaching a tree, as it would make them the wrongdoers.

> *But do not approach this tree, lest you be among the wrongdoers."*
>
> - Quran (2:35)

But Adam and Eve could not resist the temptation and approached the forbidden tree.

> "Then they both ate of that tree.... Thus did Adam disobey his Lord, so he went astray......."
- (Quran 20:121-122)

Allah immediately held Prophet Adam accountable for his actions and expelled him from paradise as a punishment for breaking his covenant with Allah.

> "Get you down (upon the earth), all of you together, from Paradise......"
- (Quran 20:123)

Despite the fact that Adam had the honour of being a Prophet, despite the fact that angels were made to prostrate to Adam, an honour that no other Prophet or human being ever had, and despite the fact that Allah had given Prophet Adam a place in paradise, when Prophet Adam went against the commands of Allah, he was punished and held accountable for his actions, and his story was documented by Allah in his blessed Book.

A number of lessons can be drawn from this story. The first lesson that comes from the story of Adam is pretty straight forward that no one is above the law. Anyone who breaks the commands of Allah will be punished and will be held accountable for their actions, even if that person happens to be a Prophet.

The second key lesson that comes from this story is the fact that Allah did not hold back the criticism of Prophet Adam in his Book, even though it gave a negative impression of his very first Prophet. Allah wrote down exactly what he thought of Prophet Adam and what Prophet Adam had actually done. Allah specifically wrote in his supreme book that Prophet Adam disobeyed his Lord and went astray.

Allah said in the Holy Quran:

> "....Thus did Adam disobey his Lord, so he went astray......."
- (Quran 20:121-122)

To say that it is the belief of the Ahl-e-Sunnah (followers of the Sunnah), that they are not allowed to speak negatively about any of the companions, is to have a belief which is in complete contradiction with the Book of Allah. Because when Allah can speak negatively about his prophets and criticise them in his book, then surely the same rules will apply to a companion too, when the status of a companion is way lower than the status of a Prophet!

The beliefs of the Ahl-e-Sunnah cannot go against the Book of Allah. The followers of the Sunnah cannot possibly hold such fallible beliefs which openly negate the verses of the Holy Quran. The beliefs of the Ahl-e-Sunnah must be in line with the Book of Allah.

These beliefs are essentially myths, which were created to protect the likes of Muawiyah and other such companions, who had transgressed the Holy Quran and the Sunnah of the Prophet. These myths surfaced in the Islamic history during the era of the Umayyads, who had to find a way of defending the actions of Muawiyah and other companions who were his complicities in crimes against the Muslim Ummah.

They could not make a rule just to protect Muawiyah, so they made a blanket rule which covered the entire crop of the companions, that one cannot criticize any of the companions since they had the honour of Prophet's company. It was a very convenient way of hiding the mistakes and crimes of any individual who had ever met or seen the Prophet. Blanket immunity was given to all such individuals, even the ones who had never met the Prophet but had only seen him from a distance, even they were classed as companions with complete immunity from any kind of criticism.

The logic of reality is however very different. If a companion of the Prophet breaks the law and goes against the Sunnah of the Prophet, then his offense is far bigger than the offense of an ordinary Muslim, because he had the honour of Prophet's company, and despite such an honour he still chose to dishonour the Sunnah of the Prophet.

And Muawiyah was indeed such an individual, who despite being a companion of the Prophet killed the family of the Prophet and other fellow companions. He destroyed the soul of the Islamic State and replaced the Islamic system of governance with an Umayyad dynasty, which was cruel, corrupt, and unIslamic to the core.

In Islam it is irrelevant as to who breaks the laws of Allah, whether it is an ordinary Muslim, whether it is a companion of the Prophet, or whether it is any other human being, the laws of Allah would equally apply to all of them.

13.3.5.3.6. Some Companions will be driven to Hellfire

The Prophet of Allah had also predicted the deviation of his companions.

The Prophet of Allah had said:

> *"Some men from my companions will come to my Lake-Fount and they will be driven away from it, and I will say, 'O Lord, my companions!' It will be said, 'You have no knowledge of what they innovated after you left: they turned apostate as renegades (reverted from Islam)."*

- *Saheeh Al-Bukhari 8:586*
- *Saheeh Al-Bukhari. Pg. # 20, H. # 3349*
- *Saheeh Al-Bukhari. Pg. # 1747, H. # 7049*
- *Saheeh Al-Bukhari. Pg. # 1634, H. # 6593*

The Prophet is stating that he will meet some of his companions on the Day of Judgement at the Lake-Fount, but they will be taken away from him, and Allah would inform him that he does not know what his companions had innovated after his death, and that they had become apostates and had reverted from Islam.

Again, the key theme that comes out of this tradition is the fact that not all the companions of the Prophet were righteous. Some of them would be residing in Hell because of their actions and deeds after the demise of the Prophet.

The defence of Muawiyah on the basis of him being a companion of the Prophet is pointless and futile. Muawiyah had made numerous innovations in the religion of Islam during his Caliphate and had committed heinous crimes against the Muslim Ummah.

It is an absurd form of logic that the defenders of Muawiyah use, where the people who simply mention the crimes of Muawiyah and other such companions are considered as deviants, and outside the pale of the Ahl-e-Sunnah, but Muawiyah and his complicities who in fact committed those crimes and torn apart the Sunnah of the Prophet, are regarded as righteous and worthy of our respect.

In the eyes of the defenders of Muawiyah, committing a crime or breaking the commands of Allah is not an issue, since those acts were committed by the first generation of Muslims i.e., the companions. But mentioning those acts is a crime and a deviation from the path of Allah!

Islam completely negates such fallacies. On the contrary, the very ethos of Islam dictates that we as Muslims clearly distinguish the right from wrong and truth from falsehood. If we are not even allowed to discuss or mention as to who did what in the Islamic history, then on what grounds are we supposed to distinguish the right from wrong or truth from falsehood.

Such logic would bar any Muslim from ever reading the Islamic history objectively or discussing any of the past events with anyone else, since it might portray the companions in a negative light! Such misleading logic would make all of us completely blind to what really took place in the Islamic history.

Islam fortunately negates this notion in its totality. In fact, Islam as a system of governance and as a way of life gives Muslims the freedom of thought and expression to discuss anything and everything, so that as enlightened Muslims we could make an informed decision and choose the path of the righteous people and distance ourselves from the path of the wrong doers, such as Muawiyah and his Umayyad clan.

13.3.6. The Prophecy of the Prophet

The Prophet of Allah had made many prophecies during his lifetime as a way of guiding the Muslim Ummah after his death. The Prophet's aim was to ensure that when he was no longer around, Muslims would still stay on the right path and associate themselves with leaders and groups which were aligned to his Sunnah, and distance themselves from the groups and personalities who were opposed to his Sunnah.

One such prophecy became a reality in the battle of Siffin which was fought between Ali and Muawiyah. Ammar bin Yasir was the commander in chief of Ali's army in Siffin. The Prophet of Allah had predicted that Ammar would be killed by a rebellious group of Muslims who would be inviting him to hellfire and Ammar would be inviting them to Paradise.

And Ammar was killed by the army of Muawiyah during the battle of Siffin, making the prophecy of the Prophet a reality. The Prophet had made the prophecy while Ammar was helping the Prophet build a mosque in Madinah.

> *".....We were carrying one adobe at a time while 'Ammaar was carrying two. The Prophet saw him and started removing the dust from his body and said, "May Allah be Merciful to 'Ammaar. He will be killed by a rebellious, aggressive group. He will be inviting them to Paradise and they will invite him to Hell-fire....."*
>
> - Sahih Bukhari 447
> - Sahih Muslim 7320

The words of the Prophet are as clear as the difference between day and night. Ali and Ammar were inviting Muawiyah and his group to Paradise, whereas Muawiyah and his group were inviting Ali and Ammar to hell fire.

The words of the Prophet also leave no doubt as to which side was on the path of truth and which side was fighting against the commands of Allah.

Unfortunately, many Muslims did not heed the advice of the Prophet, or perhaps they were unaware of it at the time, and as a result aligned themselves with the likes of Muawiyah and his Umayyad clan. However, we as Muslims of 21st century have a clear choice to make. We can today distance ourselves from the enemies of the Prophet, such as Muawiyah and his Umayyad cronies, and align ourselves with the family of the Prophet, who were fought, cursed, abused, and killed by Muawiyah and his supporters.

Even the Muslims who had heard the words of the Prophet and were aware that Ammar would be killed by a rebellious group, were tricked by Muawiyah into believing that they were on the righteous path, such was the cunning and the deceptive personality of Muawiyah.

Hazm narrated : When 'Ammar bin Yassir was killed (in Siffeen), 'Amr bin Hazm came to 'Amr bin al-'Aas and said: "Ammar has been killed and the Apostle of Allah said: "The rebellious group will kill him". 'Amr bin al-'Aas got up in panic and went to Muawiya.
Muawiya said: 'What happened to you?' He said: 'Ammar has been killed.
Muawiya said: 'Ammar has been killed so why are you like this?'
Amr bin al-'As said: 'I heard the Apostle of Allah say: "The rebellious group will kill him."
Muawiya said: "You fall in your own urine, have we killed him? He was killed by Ali and his companions who brought him and threw him between our spears....."

- Ahmad ibn Hanbal, Musnad Ahmad, vol. 4, p. 199, No. 17813
- Al-Mustadrak al Hakim 5661
- Al-Dhahabi, Tarikh al-Islam, vol. 1, p. 420 & 426
- Al-Bayhaqi, Sunan Al-Bayhaqi Al-Kubra, vol. 8, p. 189.

Muawiyah claimed to his supporters that it was in fact Ali and his group who had killed Ammar, since it was them who had brought Ammar to the battlefield.

When the news of Muawiyah's twisted logic reached Ali, he said to his supporters that if Muawiyah's logic was correct then the killing of Hamza, the uncle of the Prophet would have been blamed on the Prophet, because it was the Prophet who took Hamza to the battle of Uhud against the Kuffar.

The distorted and the misleading logic of Muawiyah would no doubt be verified by Allah on the Day of Judgment, and none of Muawiyah's cunning tricks or tactics are likely to succeed on that day.

13.3.7. A True Talent would Always Shine

Muawiyah tried his level best to incite people to curse and abuse Ali to suppress his merits. He paid people to fabricate traditions of the Prophet in his own favour and in the favour of his Umayyad clan, but despite all the efforts of Muawiyah and despite all the money that Muawiyah had spent against Ali in buying out loyalties, history still managed to preserve certain traditions which were enough to justify Ali's position as the true successor and a representative of the Prophet.

In the time of the Prophet all the wars that were fought were between the Muslims and their non-Muslim enemies. No wars were fought among the Muslims during the time of the Prophet. However, during the Caliphate of Ali every single battle was against a fellow Muslim army, be it the army of Lady Aisha, the army of Muawiyah or the army of the Khawarij.

There were no examples from the lifetime of the Prophet as to how a Muslim rebel who was fighting a legitimate Muslim Caliph would be treated once he was captured. What kind of punishment should be given to the rebels? What should be done with their property? And how should their women and children be treated by the State. This whole area of jurisprudence was missing since the Prophet of Allah never had to deal with such issues.

It was in the time of Ali that this whole area of jurisprudence was established, based on how Ali had dealt with the Muslim rebels who had risen against him. The rulings and the judgments of Ali regarding the rebels became the bedrock of how the future Muslim rebels would be dealt with in an Islamic State.

Scholars such as Imam Shafii, Imam Shaybani and others used the rulings and decrees of Ali as a reference point for deducing rules of jurisprudence in this field.

Imam Shafi'i said:

> "I derived the rulings about Rebels from the battles of Ali with Muawiya"

- Ibn Hajr Makki in Tatheer al-Janan, page 30

Imam Mohammed Shaybani who was a student of Imam Abu Hanifa wrote:

> "If Muawiya had not fought with Ali whilst He (Muawiya) was a Dhalim, Unjust and Rebel, who transgressed, then we would not have known the rulings for fighting with Rebels"

- Hanafi Tabqat, al-Jawahirn al-Mudiya

The knowledge and the wisdom of Ali remained a source of guidance for the Muslim Ummah long after his departure from this world, since the knowledge and the wisdom of Ali were acquired from the prolonged training and the blessed company of the Prophet.

The talents and the merits of Ali could not be suppressed or diluted despite all the efforts of Muawiyah and his Umayyad dynasty. They still shined because the merits of Ali were in fact a reflection of Prophet's Sunnah, and Allah has promised to keep the Sunnah of his Prophet alive until the Day of Judgment.

13.3.8. The Legitimacy of Muawiyah's Caliphate

Muawiyah acquired the Caliphate of the Muslim Ummah through the peace treaty that he had signed with Imam Hasan. The legitimacy of Muawiyah's Caliphate was conditional on him fulfilling the terms of the peace agreement which had brought him to power.

The terms of the peace agreement with Imam Hasan stated the following conditions.

- Muawiyah must rule by the Book of Allah and the Sunnah of the Prophet.
- Muawiyah would protect everyone in the Islamic State.
- Muawiyah would protect the life and honour of Shias of Ali.
- Muawiyah would not kill members of the Ahlulbayt.
- Muawiyah would stop the practice of cursing Ali.
- Muawiyah would not appoint a successor before his death.

Since Muawiyah broke every single one of the above conditions during his Caliphate, the legitimacy of his rule eroded completely, especially after he appointed his son Yazid as the future Caliph, breaching the final condition of the treaty where he had agreed that he will not appoint a successor before his death.

The legitimacy of Muawiyah's Caliphate began to disappear when he started shedding the blood of the innocent Muslims. He killed countless companions, members of the Ahlulbayt and hundreds of ordinary Muslims to secure his rule and to ensure that any opposition to his Umayyad dynasty was immediately crushed.

The defenders of Muawiyah argue that since he conquered land and expanded the borders of the Islamic State, he was a great Muslim leader and a legitimate Caliph.

Unfortunately, in Islam the legitimacy of a ruler is not defined by the fact that he had conquered land or brought territory under their rule. It is defined by the fact that whether the Caliph ruled by the Book of Allah and the Sunnah of the Prophet. History is a testament to the fact that Muawiyah did not rule either by the Book of Allah or the Sunnah of the Prophet.

Muawiyah ruled like a pre-Islamic Arab king and a Monarch, and in the palaces that he built one would find everything that was associated with the lifestyle of an emperor, rather than the humble settings of genuine Muslim Caliph.

One of the companions of the Prophet called Al-Miqdam gave a glimpse of Muawiyah's lifestyle when he visited Muawiyah.

> Al-Miqdam said: Today I shall continue to make you (Muawiyah) angry and make you (Muawiyah) hear what you dislike.
> Al-Miqdam then said: Mu'awiyah, if I speak the truth, declare me true, and if I tell a lie, declare me false.
> Muawiyah said: Do so.
> Al-Miqdam said: I adjure you by Allah, did you hear the Messenger of Allah forbidding use to wear gold?
> Muawiyah replied: Yes.
> Al-Miqdam said: I adjure you by Allah, do you know that the Messenger of Allah prohibited the wearing of silk?
> Muawiyah replied: Yes.
> Al-Miqdam said: I adjure you by Allah, do you know that the Messenger of Allah prohibited the wearing of the skins of beasts of prey and riding on them?
> Muawiyah said: Yes.
> Al-Miqdam said: I swear by Allah, I saw all this in your house, O Mu'awiyah.
> Mu'awiyah said: I know that I cannot be saved from you, O Miqdam.
> ….Mu'awiyah then ordered to give him ……. two hundred (dirhams) ……
>
> - Abu Dawood 4131, Abu Dawood Vol. 4, Book 34, Hadith 4119
> - Musnad Ahmad 17228 (Vol. 4 Page-132)

Muawiyah used to wear silk, gold, and the skins of animals like lions, leopards etc, things that could only be associated with the kings of Roman and Persian empires. A legitimate Caliph of the Muslims was in fact a servant of the Muslim Ummah, whose lifestyle would reflect the lifestyle of an ordinary Muslim citizen.

Muawiyah being a shrewd politician offered Miqdam money, after Miqdam had highlighted the unIslamic nature of Muawiyah's rule. So, Muawiyah straight away tried to pacify Miqdam by offering him a bribe. As mentioned previously, offering money and buying out people was Muawiyah's preferred method of pacifying criticism or opposition to his rule.

We read in Sahih Muslim that a person approached Amr bin al Ass who was a cousin of Muawiyah and said:

> "…..This cousin of yours, Mu'awiya, orders us to unjustly consume our wealth among ourselves and to kill one another, while Allah says:" O ye who believe, do not consume your wealth among yourselves unjustly, unless it be trade based on mutual agreement, and do not kill yourselves. …… The narrator says that (hearing this) Abdullah b. 'Amr b. al-As kept quiet for a while and then said: Obey him (Muawiyah) in so far as he is obedient to God, and disobey him in matters involving disobedience to God."
>
> - Sahih Muslim Vol. 5, Book 20, Hadith 4546
> - Sahih Muslim Vol. 5, Book of Government, Hadith 4546

Muawiyah had made corruption endemic among the Islamic society where he would order other Muslims to misuse the public funds too. He also ordered Muslims to kill one another unjustifiably when it would suit his political ambitions.

Muawiyah certainly conquered land, but he established an Umayyad monarchy rather than a true Islamic Caliphate.

The Prophet of Allah had in fact prophesised that his Ummah would be destroyed by the clan of Banu Umayyad, and Muawiyah was the very first leader who established the Umayyad dynasty.

> "……..Abu Hurairah said: I heard the truthful and trusted by Allah (i.e. the Prophet) saying, The destruction of my followers will be through the hands of young men from Quraish……"
> - Sahih Bukhari: 7058

The young men of Quraysh here refer to the clan of Banu Umayyad. The reason why Abu Hurairah did not explicitly mention the name of Banu Umayyad was out of fear for his own life, because if he had narrated anything against them the Umayyad's would have killed him.

Another tradition from Abu Hurairah on similar lines shows how Banu Umayyad had changed the system of governance established by the Prophet of Allah.

> Abu Hurairah said : "Woe unto the Arabs from a danger that has come near, at the head of (year) sixty. Trust will be treated as booty, charity as a fine, and witness shall be given on the basis of acquaintance , and decisions will be made based on desires."
> - Mustadrak al-Hakim 8489

Year sixty was the year when Muawiyah's Caliphate was coming to an end. The above tradition describes the situation of the Muslim Ummah during the last part of Muawiyah's Caliphate. It points out to the fact that the decisions of the State were based on personal desires and nepotism was rife in this period. The elite class treated the trusts of the Muslims as war booty. This was indeed the true description of Muawiyah's Caliphate which clearly shows how far removed the rule of Muawiyah was from an Islamic perspective.

The Caliphate of Muawiyah really had no legitimacy in the eyes of Islam as Muawiyah had no regard for the Book of Allah or the Sunnah of the Prophet. His only ambition was to establish an Umayyad dynasty and bring back the glory of the Umayyads, which they had lost at the conquest of Makkah.

Unfortunately for the Muslim Ummah, Muawiyah successfully achieved this goal, and it was for this reason the Prophet of Allah had predicted that the first person who would change my Sunnah would be a man from Banu Umayyad.

> "The first one to change my Sunnah will be a man from Banu Umayyah."
> - (Al-Awail by ibn abi Asim: 63; Declared Hasan by Allama Albani in Silsilah As-Saheeha: 1749)

Scholars who have commented on this tradition consider the change in the Sunnah, to mean changing the system of governance that was established by the Prophet of Allah. And it was a man from Banu Umayyah i.e., Muawiyah who had changed the Islamic Caliphate into an Umayyad kingdom.

13.3.9. Imam Hussain Sums up the Caliphate of Muawiyah

Imam Hussain was the younger brother of Imam Hasan. Imam Hasan had signed the peace treaty with Muawiyah which Muawiyah had violated. Since Imam Hasan had already passed away, many Muslims would now look towards Imam Hussain for leadership and guidance. They would visit Imam Hussain and complain to him about the state of the affairs of the Muslims, and the tyrannical leadership of the Umayyads and their destruction of the Islamic way of life.

Imam Hussain was residing in Madinah, the city of the Prophet, and the governor of Madinah at the time was Marwan bin Hakam. Readers would recall that Marwan bin Hakam was the advisor to Caliph Uthman, who had prevented the reconciliation process that Ali had initiated between Uthman and the opposition. This eventually resulted in the killing of Caliph Uthman.

Muawiyah had now appointed Marwan bin Hakam as the governor of Madinah. Marwan observed that many Muslims would come to Imam Hussain seeking advice and guidance, and that Imam Hussain commanded immense love and respect among the people of Madinah, even though he held no official position in the city.

Marwan wrote to Muawiyah that the people of Madinah have a very close relationship with Hussain, and this is extremely dangerous for the future Umayyad leadership which is about to come. So, Muawiyah then wrote a letter to Imam Hussain, warning, and threatening Imam Hussain against causing any problems for his government.

Imam Hussain responds back to Muawiyah with the following words:

> *"After praise to Allah and blessings upon the Prophet of Allah, I wish to inform you that I have received your letter, in which you have mentioned that you have heard some reports about me which you detested. And in your opinion, this was not expected of me. You have also mentioned that it is only Allah Who guides the people towards righteousness. And only He is the Helper and Support of one and all.*
>
> *You should know that reports concerning me have reached you through a sycophant and a backbiter. I do not intend any war or rebellion against you. But, by Allah I am proceeding on a way which is not against your rule. It is not that I consider not confronting you likeable in the eyes of Allah. Neither do I fear divine retribution if I confront you. I fear Allah that He may not accept my excuse of keeping silent against you and your evil friends who are cohorts of the devil.*
>
> *Are you not the murderer of Hujr Ibne Adi and his chaste companions, who opposed injustice and considered innovations to be evil? They did not pay heed to any accusations in the way of Allah. Had you not made promises and oaths to them? Had you not assured them that you will not arrest them? And that you will not trouble them? Despite such oaths and promises, have you not put them to death?*
>
> *Are you not the killer of the righteous companions of the Prophet of Allah, Amr Ibne Humq Khuzaee? One who had become physically frail and pale in complexion due to incessant worship? Had you not promised them safety? Had such an assurance been given to a bird, it would have come down from the mountain peak. But you did not even care to respect this oath of peace. You trampled upon your oath and did not fear Allah. You had him killed as well.*
>
> *Are you not the one who certified Ziyad the son of Sumayya to be the off-spring of Abu Sufyan although he was born on the bed of a slave from Bani Thaqif? You attributed him to your father*

and opposed the explicit order of Allah's Messenger, "A son is related to a father and the adulterer is to be stoned." Have you not obeyed your evil desires? After this you imposed him upon the people of Iraq and Khorasan. You amputated their hands and feet, gouged out their eyes and crucified them on date palms. You behaved as if you are not from the Islamic Ummah and have nothing to do with it.

Are you not the one to whom the son of Sumayya (Ziyad Ibne Abih) wrote that the tribe of Hazrami were upon the religion of Ali Ibne Abi Talib? And you replied that anyone who was on the religion of Ali (A.S) should be put to death. Thereafter, Ziyad had them killed and mutilated their bodies as per your order. By Allah, Ali had fought against you and your father for the sake of Allah. And you are upon this throne due to this very religion. Had it not been for the loftiness of this faith, you, your father and ancestors would still have wandered in the lanes during summer and winter (that is, you people would still be vagabonds).

You have written that I must sit quiet for the sake of my life and the safety of Muhammad's Ummah. And that I must not sow the seeds of dissension and corruption in the society. But I do not consider anything more corrupt for this Ummah than your tyrannical rule. I consider Jihad against you to be the best and most meritorious thing for me and for Muhammad Ummah. If I wage a holy war against you, it shall be the best means of seeking nearness to Allah. If not, then I seek forgiveness from Allah. And I shall pray to Allah for guidance in my affairs.

You have also mentioned that 'if I oppose you, you would oppose me and if I proceed against you, you will proceed against me.' You may take whatever steps you can against me. I am sure that your planning will cause me no harm. The greatest harm shall be to you. For, you are riding the vehicle of ignorance and are apt at breaking oaths and treaties. By my life, you have never considered any point of agreement.

You have killed those with whom you had made treaties, promises and oaths. And you killed them when they had neither any intention of waging a war against you nor had they committed any murder. You shed their blood only because they related our merits and were cognizant of the greatness of our rights. Although it was possible that natural death would have occurred to them or to you even before their uprising to reach to a conclusion.

O Muawiya! Be prepared for divine retribution and be sure of the accounting before Allah. And know that the scroll of deeds has a record of every small and big sin. Nothing is omitted from it. Allah will never excuse your act of arresting people on mere suspicion. You accused wrongly the saintly people with baseless allegations and slaughtered them. You made them abandon their houses to be homeless in strange lands. You forcibly extracted allegiance from the people for your drunkard and dog-loving son.

I see that you are sinking in loss and destroying your faith. You are oppressing your subjects and are degrading the divine trusts. You accept the advice of foolish and ignorant people and for their sake, you are threatening the pious and religious people, Was Salaam"

- Rejaal-e-Kashi, pg.32; Behaarul Anwaar, vol. 44, pg.212;
- Ayaanush Shia by Sayed Mohsin Ameen Aameli, vol. l, pg.582)

The letter of Imam Hussain to Muawiyah needs no explanation. It is abundantly clear from the letter as to what Imam Hussain thought of Muawiyah and his rule. Imam Hussain had considered jihad against Muawiyah to be the most virtuous act, because of the crimes that Muawiyah had committed against the Muslim Ummah.

Despite the fact that Imam Hussain absolutely despised the Caliphate of Muawiyah, he did not raise his sword against Muawiyah, since he was bound by the peace agreement that this elder brother Imam Hasan had signed with Muawiyah.

As the death of Muawiyah approached and he appointed Yazid as his successor, the peace agreement between the two sides came to an end, and this brought a new era of tragedy and suffering for the family of the Prophet.

14. THE TRAGEDY OF KARBALA AND THE STAND OF HUSSAIN

By the time Muawiyah died the Islamic State had expanded far and wide. The flag of Islam flew from the fields of Persia to the shores of North Africa, but despite this physical expansion the soul of the Islamic State had no fire or vigour left in it. As the Umayyads expanded the Islamic State they would often discourage people from even converting to Islam, since it would reduce the taxes that they could levy against the non-Muslim population.

Their expansion was primarily political so that the Umayyad dynasty could be established as far as possible in the guise of the Islamic State. The fundamental principles of Prophet's revolution had been undone by twenty years of Muawiyah's tyrannical rule. There was certainly no expansion of the ideals of Prophets revolution under the Umayyad Caliphate. Islam was confined to the hearts of the believers and the Islamic State established by the Prophet now resembled like a pre-Islamic Persian or the Byzantine Empire.

At this juncture where every single Muslim leader had either been bought or pacified by the fear of the Umayyad sword, Hussain took a stand against the rule of the Umayyads to reignite the ideals of the Prophet's Sunnah, and to rejuvenate the soul of the Islamic State which had lost its zeal and direction under the Umayyad rule.

The reformatory movement of Islam that was started by the Prophet of Allah had lost its way, as the leadership of the Muslim Ummah ended up in the hands of the very people who had fought against the Prophet. The enemies of the Prophet had now become the custodian of Prophet's revolution. The stand of Hussain not only preserved the revolution of Islam and shock the conscious of the believers, but it also gave inspiration to the free men and women of this world, who seek justice and freedom in the face of oppression and tyranny, and who would prefer to die in dignity rather than live a life of a coward.

The stand of Hussain was to challenge the status quo of the Umayyad rule, on the basis that it had not only deviated from the path established by the Prophet of Allah, but it had also taken away the basic freedoms of thought and expression from its subjects which Islam had given to its adherents.

14.1. The Inauguration of Yazid

As per the will of Muawiyah his son Yazid was inaugurated as the new Umayyad Caliph of the Muslim Ummah. With the inauguration of Yazid history takes an unprecedented brutal turn against the family of the Prophet, but despite all the odds Hussain stood as a beacon of hope and resistance for the believers, something which was unprecedented in the history of Islam and the Arabs.

Yazid had all the makings and the character of a pre-Islamic Arab king just like his father Muawiyah. The only difference was that Muawiyah was subtle in his ways, whereas Yazid being young and hot-headed openly flaunted the laws of Allah. Muawiyah of course was well-aware of the abhorrent character of his son, but despite this fact Muawiyah forced Yazid's Caliphate on the Muslim Ummah.

We read in al-Tabari about the character of Yazid:

> *'We have come from a man who has no religion, who drinks wine, who plays lutes, who passes his time with songstresses, who plays with dogs and spends his evenings talking to robbers and young men.'*
>
> - *(p.198. The History of al-Tabari; The Caliphate of Yazid. b. Mu'awiyah. Volume XIX. Translated by I.K.A. Howard. State University of New York Press, USA, 1990.)*
> - *Jalal al-Din al-Suyuti describes the character of Yazid in his book Tarikh al-Khulafa.*

'Yazid indulged in sinful behaviour. He married women along with their mothers, daughters and sisters. He drank alcohol and did not perform Salah.'

- *p. 161, Ibid.*

Yazid had no assemblance of Islam in him, he openly flouted the Islamic law, drank alcohol in public, used to gamble, married women who were forbidden, and lacked any administrative or governmental experience to become a leader of any sorts, let alone become the leader of the entire Muslim Ummah.

Leaving aside the character and the personal sins of Yazid, the bigger and the far more troubling issue for the Ummah was the corrupt and the despotic system of governance established by the Umayyads, which in fact had brought a character like Yazid to the helm of the Islamic State. It was this system which had to be challenged and transformed, so that the Caliphate could once again represent the ideals of the Prophet and the revolution that he had started.

It was in this context that the stand and the sacrifice of Hussain had changed and rewritten the rules of the game. Unlike the character of Yazid, the character of Hussain carried the testimony of the Prophet of Allah. The Prophet had said:

> *'I am from Hussain and Hussain is from me. Allah loves the one who loves Hussain...'*
>
> - *(Sunan al-Tirmidhi. Hadith 3708. Book of Superiorities. Chapter; the Superiority of Imam Hasan and Hussain)*

This amazing tradition of the Prophet affirms both the character and the stand of Hussain.

When Prophet says that Hussain is from me, he is implying that the character and the virtues of Hussain were a reflection of his own character and virtues, and Hussain in fact represented the Sunnah and the traditions of the Prophet just like the other members of the Ahlulbayt.

However, when Prophet says that "I am from Hussain", the meaning here is more deep and profound. This is something that Prophet had never said about anyone else. The Prophet of Allah is in fact prophesizing that in my absence the path that Hussain adopts would indeed be the path that I would have adopted. The stand of Hussain against the Umayyads would indeed have been the stand of the Prophet if he would have been alive. Prophet trusts the personality and the decisions of Hussain to the extent that he is willing to own them as his own.

The ideological revolution started by the Prophet had been undone by the Umayyad rule, but the stand of Hussain rekindled that revolution in the hearts of the believers, and hence Prophet had prophesized that he was from Hussain. Since Hussain would bring back the ideological message of the Prophet at a time when everybody else in the Muslim Ummah had been pacified or coerced, and no one would even dare to speak up let alone have the courage to rise up against the Umayyads.

14.2. Yazid Demands Allegiance

Despite the fact that the character of Hussain carried the testimony of the Prophet, Imam Hussain is not only side-lined in favour of a character like Yazid, but Yazid on becoming the Caliph immediately demands that Hussain gives him the allegiance as the new leader of the Muslim Ummah.

Yazid orders Walid ibn Utbah, his governor in Madinah to forcefully get the oath of allegiance from Imam Hussain.

> *'Seize Hussain, Abd Allah ibn Umar and Abd Allah ibn Zubair to give the oath of allegiance. Act so fiercely that they have no chance to do anything before giving the oath of allegiance…'*

- (p. 146-7, Al-Bidaya wa al-Nihaya. Hafiz ibn Kathir (d. 774 A.H.) Vol. VIII.
- Maktaba al-Ma'arif, Beirut, Lebanon. 1999. See also pp.1-2.
- The History of al-Tabari; The Caliphate of Yazid. b. Mu'awiyah. Volume XIX. Translated by I.K.A. Howard. State University of New York Press, USA, 1990.)

The words of Yazid are unmistakable, he wants allegiance by force, even though his father Muawiyah had advised him to treat Imam Hussain with care. Muawiyah was a very smart politician, he preferred avoiding open confrontation and used to work behind the scenes by bribing people, or buying his opponents out, and if all else fails he would prefer to poison his rivals rather than killing them by his sword. Yazid on the other hand was a crude and an inexperienced man who immediately opted for open confrontation with Imam Hussain.

Imam Hussain was part of the Ahlulbayt and was the grandson of the Prophet through his daughter Fatima. He commanded a huge amount of love and respect among the Muslims. Also, as per many traditions of the Prophet the leadership of the Muslim Ummah should rest with the Ahlulbayt. The Prophet had said:

> *"O people I am leaving in you two elements if you follow you shall not go astray. They are the Book of God and the members of my House."*

- Al-Hakim Al-Mustadrak part 3 p. 109.

Yazid was well-aware of the position of Imam Hussain and the right of the Ahlulbayt to lead the Muslim Ummah. He also knew that the peace treaty with Imam Hasan which had legitimized his father's (Muawiyah's) rule had been broken, since his father had appointed him as the new caliph against the terms of the treaty.

Yazid also knew that his own Caliphate had been acquired through coercion, bribery and by killing the people who stood in his father's path. Yazid needed the allegiance of a personality like Imam Hussain to legitimize his own Caliphate. The allegiance from Imam Hussain would give Yazid's leadership credibility and recognition and an endorsement from the Ahlulbayt. Because if Yazid was good enough to be recognized by Imam Hussain as a legitimate Caliph, then he must be good enough to be a Caliph for the rest of the Muslims too.

Yazid was adamant to get the oath of allegiance from Imam Hussain and he made some serious threats against the life of Imam Hussain if he refused to comply. Walid ibn Utbah, the governor of Madinah invites Imam Hussain to his office and informs him about Yazid's decree, which was to either take the oath of allegiance from Imam Hussain or kill him.

14.3. Hussain Refuses

Imam Hussain was the grandson of the Prophet and the son of Ali. Imam Hussain's father Ali was the most famed warrior among the Arabs. Ali's bravery and valour were second to none. Ali had killed some of the greatest and the finest warriors of his time in the battles of Badr, Uhad, Moat and Khaibar. No one would dare challenge Ali for a duel on the battlefield, and Hussain was the inheritor of Ali's sword and valour.

There was no possibility that Hussain would be intimidated or frightened by the demands of Yazid. Imam Hussain tells Yazid's governor Walid ibn Utbah that giving allegiance is an important matter, which could not be done in private and must be done in public. Walid agrees and allows Imam Hussain to leave, but he asks Imam Hussain to attend the public gathering which would be arranged later for the oath of allegiance to be administered.

However, Marwan bin al-Hakam, the long-term Umayyad advisor was still around, and he advised Walid against this move. Readers would recall that Marwan bin al-Hakam had become the governor of Madinah in the time of Muawiyah, and he was previously the advisor of Caliph Uthman too. He had now been appointed as the advisor to Yazid's governor in Madinah.

Marwan tells Walid that if Hussain was allowed to go free without giving allegiance, then he would not be able to get hold of Hussain again, so Walid should either take the oath of allegiance from Hussain now or kill him. However, Walid is reluctant to kill Imam Hussain as he is aware of the status and stature of Imam Hussain. Also, the youth of Banu Hashim are standing outside Walid's office with their swords drawn, and Walid wants to avoid a bloodbath at this stage.

An argument then breaks out, and Imam Hussain challenges both Walid and Marwan to kill him if they had the guts to do so. Imam Hussain then walks out of Walid's office with the youth of Banu Hashim, who had entered the governor's office after hearing the commotion between Imam Hussain, Walid and Marwan.

The enmity of Marwan towards Imam Hussain was clear. He wanted to kill Imam Hussain in Madinah if Imam Hussain refuses to pledge allegiance to Yazid. Next day Marwan again meets up with Imam Hussain and asks for his decision. Imam Hussain gives him the famous response which has been preserved in the books of history:

Imam Hussain said:

> *"We are the household of the Prophet hood, the source of messenger ship, the descending place of the angels, through us Allah had begun showering His favours, whereas Yazid is a sinful person, a drunkard, the killer of innocent people and one who openly indulges in sinful acts......... A person like me can never do bay'aa (pay allegiance) to a person like him (Yazid). I look upon death as but the felicity of martyrdom and I regard life among oppressors and transgressors as nothing but agony and torture. By God I will never give you my hand like a man who has been defeated; nor will I flee like a slave."*

- *Hadiyyat al-Ahbb, p. 111, where al-Bayhaqi's biography is detailed.*

The defiant words of Imam Hussain were a reflection of his charismatic personality which was undeterred by the might of the Umayyad dynasty. The response of Hussain to Yazid was an unequivocal no. Imam Hussain categorically refuses to pay allegiance to Yazid who had inherited the Caliphate from his father.

In response to the demand of allegiance from Yazid, Imam Hussain first clarifies his own position and stature to Marwan, the all-time loyal advisor of the Umayyads. Imam Hussain tells Marwan that he was a member of the Ahlulbayt, he was from the family of the Prophet, implying that he was a man of piety and principles, whereas Yazid was an open sinner who indulge in the killing of the innocent, and there is no way that a man of his character could ever give allegiance to a man of Yazid's character.

Marwan had threatened to kill Imam Hussain, so Imam Hussain tells Marwan that he was not afraid of death, and in fact he prefers death rather than live a life under tyranny and oppression which the Umayyads had unleashed on the Muslim Ummah.

The bravery and the resolve of Hussain was evident from his unambiguous response to the Umayyad leadership, which had successfully subdued and pacified the entire Muslim population. Hussain was the only individual who had refused to accept Yazid as the rightful Caliph of the Muslims and had openly challenged the Umayyad leadership.

The reason why Imam Hussain had refused to accept Yazid as the legitimate Caliph was because Imam Hussain saw himself as the custodian of Prophet's Sunnah, whereas Yazid represented a system which had diluted and abandoned the Sunnah of the Prophet. Yazid represented the counter-revolution of the Umayyads against the revolution of the Prophet, and Hussain as a representative of the Prophet had to take a stand against this trend.

14.3.1. The Peace Treaty with the Umayyads

The peace treaty with the Umayyads had already been tried. Imam Hussain had already witnessed as to what had happened to the peace treaty that his elder brother Imam Hasan had signed with Muawiyah. The Umayyads broke every single term of that deal. Muawiyah had agreed to rule by the commands of Allah and the Sunnah of the Prophet, but once he acquired the Caliphate he ruled by the virtue of his desires.

Imam Hasan had signed the treaty between the two warring factions to give peace a chance. The wars between Ali and Muawiyah had claimed the lives of thousands of Muslims. In the battle of Siffin alone more than 70,000 companions and Muslims were slaughtered.

The Umayyads had firmly set their sights on the Caliphate and were desperate for power. Every single political and military move of the Umayyads reflected their desire to acquire the leadership of the Muslim Ummah, and every single war that Muawiyah and his Umayyad supporters had waged was ultimately aimed at taking over the Caliphate of the Muslims. So, Imam Hasan finally agreed to hand over the Caliphate to Muawiyah which he so desperately wanted, in order to bring peace and tranquillity to the Muslim lands.

The aim of Imam Hasan with the peace treaty was to avoid further bloodshed, by handing over the Caliphate to the Umayyads temporarily, and by binding them in an agreement which would force them to not only rule by the Book of Allah and the Sunnah of the Prophet, but it would also stop them from appointing a successor i.e. the Umayyads would not be allowed to establish their own dynasty after taking over the Caliphate.

However, by appointing Yazid as his successor Muawiyah established the Umayyad dynasty, contrary to the terms of the agreement, and broke the very last condition of the treaty too. At this point Imam Hussain was left with no option but to take a stand against this new system of governance i.e., the system of monarchy (Malokiyat), which the Umayyads had created in place of the Islamic Caliphate.

The option of a peace treaty between Imam Hussain and Yazid was not possible, since Yazid was looking for total submission from Imam Hussain, and Yazid had no intention of mending the ways of his Umayyad rule, even if it was only on a piece of paper.

14.3.2. In Defence of the Prophet's Revolution

The refusal of Imam Hussain was not an emotional or a spontaneous decision. Imam Hussain had carefully thought and considered his position before refusing to accept the Caliphate of Yazid. Imam Hussain was also fully aware of the consequences of his decision, and he was fully prepared for the trials and tribulations that he and his family would have to suffer.

Imam Hussain had been observing the Umayyads since the time of his father. He had seen how Muawiyah, who was the governor of a single province in the Islamic State had tried to use the killing of Caliph Uthman to unjustly dislodge the government of a legitimate Muslim Caliph i.e., his father Ali.

Imam Hussain had also seen that even when his elder brother Imam Hasan gave the Caliphate to the Umayyads as part of the peace treaty, they did not change or mend their ways. But instead, they slowly began to change the entire system of governance and turned the Islamic Caliphate into an Umayyad dynasty.

The commands of Allah and the Sunnah of the Prophet were put aside, and the interest of the Umayyad clan became the driving force of their government. The people who spoke up to defend the Sunnah of the Prophet were imprisoned or put to the sword. The state of the affairs had reached such a point that even many of the companions and Tabaeen (people who came after the companions) were publicly supporting the Umayyad rule, and had accepted the Caliphate of Yazid out of fear for their lives or for monetary gains, despite knowing exactly what the Umayyads were up to.

The Sunnah of the Prophet was gradually being dismantled by the rule of the Umayyads, and at that critical juncture somebody had to take a stand, and they had to remind the Muslims that what the Umayyads were doing was against the Sunnah of the Prophet, and that the ideology of the Umayyads was contradictory to the ideology of the Prophet.

In that hour of fear and oppression someone had to shake the conscious of the Muslim Ummah, to try and bring the Caliphate back to the traditions of the Prophet, and to side with the forgotten revolution of the Prophet against the revolution of the Umayyads.

And Hussain was that brave individual who stood up and defended the revolution of the Prophet.

After all, Hussain was the grandson of the Prophet. The Prophet used to hold Hussain in his lap and put him on his shoulders, and when Hussain would jump on Prophet's back while Prophet was praying, the Prophet of Allah would extend his prayer in the honour of Hussain, so Hussain had that amazing upbringing in the household of the Prophet.

Hence, Hussain had to take a stand for the honour of the Prophet, especially at time when others had chosen to stay silent out of fear for their lives.

14.3.3. A Protest Against Oppression

Apart from changing the Sunnah of the Prophet and distorting the teachings of Islam to suite their interests and personal desires, the Umayyads had created an oppressive and a tyrannical dictatorship in the guise of the Caliphate, where even the basic freedoms of expression were crushed with an iron fist.

No one was allowed to publicly express a view contrary to view of the Umayyad leadership, without the threat of either being killed or being imprisoned. Any such expressions were seen as dissent and were immediately crushed by the Umayyad sword. The freedom of expression and the freedom of enjoining the good and forbidding the evil (amar bil maroof wa nahi anil munkar), a right which Islam had given to every Muslim was not only denied but was punishable by death.

Muawiyah had killed and imprisoned many innocent Muslims to create the right environment for his son Yazid to take over the reins of the Islamic State. The Caliphate of Yazid had come at the expense of the blood of countless innocent souls, and Hussain as the flag of bearer of Prophet's ideals could not possibly accept the tyrannical and the oppressive rule of the Umayyads.

The refusal of Hussain was also a protest against the oppression and the tyranny which the Umayyads had unleashed on the Muslim Ummah. Hussain could not side with Yazid and ignore the cries of all those innocent and pious Muslims who were put to the sword by Muawiyah. Hussain had to side with the oppressed, as Hussain was the forbearer of "amar bil maroof wa nahi anil munkar" (enjoining the good and forbidding the evil).

The position of Hussain was unique in the Muslim Ummah. It was unlike the position of any other companion or Tabiee at the time. Hussain carried the testimony of the Prophet behind him where Prophet had said that Hussain was from him, and he was from Hussain.

The stand of Hussain had to reflect his unique and distinct position in the Muslim Ummah.

Note: Tabiee – are the generation of Muslims who came after the companions.

14.3.4. Hussain, the Last Man Standing

When Yazid took over the Caliphate almost all the other key leaders and notables of the Muslim Ummah had either been bought, and had already pledged allegiance to Yazid, or they had been pacified by the fear of the Umayyads and had distanced themselves completely from the political events affecting the Muslim nation. There was no one else left to carry the flag of the Prophet forward when Yazid had taken over the leadership of the Islamic state and when he was sitting on the pulpit of the Prophet.

For example, Abdullah ibn Umar who was the son of Caliph Umar, was meant to be an Islamic personality who commanded respect and influence among the Muslims at that time, but out of fear for his own life he sided with the Umayyads and accepted the Caliphate of Yazid.

Abdullah bin Abu Bakr, who was the son of Caliph Abu Bakr had already been subdued. Muawiyah's right-hand man Mugheera bin Shuba had a confrontation with Abdullah bin Abu Bakr regarding the Caliphate of Yazid. Mugheera had threatened Abdullah bin Abu Bakr, so he ran into the house of his sister Lady Aisha and took refuge there. Later, Abdullah bin Abu Bakr travelled to the mountains and secluded himself from everyone to avoid the wrath of the Umayyads.

Al-Zubair was another leading Islamic personality at the time. He was present in Madinah when Yazid was inaugurated as the new Caliph. Yazid was demanding allegiance from him too, but he refused to meet Walid, the governor of Yazid in Madinah, and took a back route and fled to Makkah and hid there.

Hussain was the last man standing, without fear and with conviction, who was ready to confront the Umayyad might regardless of the consequences. No one else had the guts to rise and defend the Sunnah of the Prophet at that time. No one would dare challenge or question the authority of Yazid, except the grandson of the Prophet.

In that dark hour, when the fear of the Umayyad swords had silenced the entire Muslim Ummah, including all the companions of the Prophet and all the Tabaeen (the generation that came after the companions), it was Hussain alone who stood up and spoke the word of truth. It was only Hussain, the son of Ali and Fatima who had the courage and the strength to rise up and was unfazed by the might of the Umayyads.

Just as the sword of Ali was unique and distinct on the battlefield, the stand of Hussain was unique and distinct in the history of Islam.

14.4. Hussain Leaves Madinah and Heads to Makkah

Madinah was the city of the Prophet. This is where Imam Hussain had grown up and had spent his childhood. Imam Hussain is extremely well loved and respected in this city. However, the people of Madinah notice that Imam Hussain is in a sombre mood, and he spends a lot of time by the grave of the Prophet, his mother Lady Fatima, and his elder brother Imam Hasan.

Imam Hussain's mind is occupied in planning his next move. Imam Hussain realizes that the situation is very tense and grave in Madinah. It could easily lead to bloodshed and chaos in the Holy city of the Prophet. To preserve the sanctity and the dignity of this blessed land Imam Hussain decides to leave for Makkah with his family.

Before leaving the city of the Prophet Imam Hussain writes his will, and he clarifies exactly as to why he had chosen to take a stand against the Umayyads.

> "............This movement of mine is not on account of stubbornness, rebellion, worldly passions or instigation by Satan. It is also not my object to create trouble or to oppress anyone. Rather, I marched out seeking to reform my grandfather's nation and eradicate corruption. I desire to enjoin what is right and to forbid what is wrong and to follow the Sunnah of my grandfather the Prophet and my father Ali bin abi Talib. If the people respond to my call, and accept truth from me, well and good; and if they do not accept it, I shall observe patience and am not afraid of unpleasant events, hardships, and sufferings............"

- Abdullah Nur-Allah al-Bahrani, Maqtal al-Awalim, p. 54.
- al-Khawarizmi, Al-Maqtal, Vol. 1, p. 188, chapter 9

The aim of Hussain was to reform the Ummah of his grandfather, and to eradicate the corruption which the Umayyads had sowed in the guise of the Islamic Caliphate. The aim of Hussain was to reignite the fire in the reformatory movement of Islam which was established and nurtured by the Prophet of Allah. The stand of Hussain was to seek justice, enjoin good and forbid evil, traits which had been completely abandoned and ignored under the Umayyad rule.

The stance of Hussain was seeking to end the tyranny and oppression which the Umayyads had unleashed on the ordinary Muslims. The stance of Hussain was to purify the movement of Islam form the innovations that the Umayyads had planted in its foundations. Just as the Prophet of Allah had established the movement of Islam, Hussain being the representative of the Prophet was seeking to reform that very movement which had lost its way as result of the Umayyad rule.

But the stand of Hussain was peaceful in nature, unlike the stand of the Umayyads. People were free to join the path of truth and accept the call of Hussain, but if they refused, Hussain would stay patient, and this was the beauty of Hussain's stance, as it reflected the spirit of freedom and choice which the Prophet of Allah had given to the Muslims.

The small caravan of Hussain leaves the city of the Prophet and arrives in the bustling city of Makkah.

The aim of Imam Hussain was to publicise his stand against the Umayyads as much as possible. Makkah is a busy place, there are pilgrims who come here throughout the year from all over the Muslim world, and hence Imam Hussain chose to move to Makkah to publicize his stand to the widest possible audience.

Imam Hussain informs the pilgrims about his decision of not giving allegiance to Yazid. He invites the people of Makkah to the path of the Prophet and explains the dangers of living under the Umayyad rulers. But at the same time Imam Hussain does not start a rebellion nor does he build an army to fight the Umayyads. His primary objective was to start the process of reforms in the minds of the Muslims, which have been subjected to the corruption of the Umayyads for years.

Imam Hussain remains in Makkah and decides to perform Hajj which was couple of months away.

14.5. The Invitation from Kufa

During Imam Hussain's stay in Makkah the people of Kufa learn that Imam Hussain had refused to accept the leadership of Yazid. They also learn that Imam Hussain had left his home city and was now residing in Makkah. This was welcome news for many of the inhabitants of Kufa, as they were fed up with the Umayyad tyrannical rule. They saw a glimmer of hope that Hussain could come and liberate them from the shackles of the Umayyad slavery.

A significant portion of the population of Kufa was considered to be the followers of Ahlulbayt and the Shias of Ali i.e., the people who regarded Ali as the rightful successor of the Prophet. However, like every other city and province in the Islamic State Kufa was under the control of the Umayyads. A secret meeting was held in the house of Suleman bin Surad al-Khuzai, who was a leading Shia personality in Kufa and a well-known companion of the Prophet. Sulayman Surd al-Khuzai is also a narrator of various traditions of the Prophet which are found in several books of Hadith and history.

It was decided in the meeting that Imam Hussain would be invited to Kufa and the people of Kufa would support the stand of Hussain against the Umayyads. The first letter of invitation to Imam Hussain was written and signed by Sulayman Surd al-Khuzai and other notables of Kufa, who were Al-Musayyab bin Najaba, Rifa bin Shaddad, Habib bin al-Muzahir and Muslim bin Awsaja.

As the word spread that Imam Hussain is being invited to Kufa the ordinary people of Kufa also start writing to Imam Hussain, inviting him to their city and pledging support and allegiance to him in their letters. They were hoping to replace Yazid's appointed Governor Noman Bashir and have Imam Hussain as their leader in Kufa.

Imam Hussain gave the letters that he had received from Kufa a serious consideration. He consults with his family and his close associates of whether to accept the invitation or remain in Makkah.

14.5.1. Hussain Sends his Ambassador to Kufa

Imam Hussain sends his ambassador to assess the situation at first-hand on the ground in Kufa. He chooses Muslim bin Aqeel as his ambassador, and upon Muslim bin Aqeel's assessment of the situation in Kufa Imam Hussain would plan his next move.

As Muslim bin Aqeel is a renowned warrior, Imam Hussain tells Muslim to take his two young sons Ibrahim and Muhammad with him to show the peaceful nature of his mission. Both the sons of Muslim bin Aqeel were under the ages of twelve. Muslim ibn Aqeel with his two young sons reaches Kufa and stays in the house of Mukhtar al-Thaqafi.

As the news of Muslim bin Aqeel's arrival circulates in Kufa the people of Kufa stream out in large numbers and warmly welcome Muslim bin Aqeel, and they assure him of their allegiance and support for Imam Hussain. Muslim bin Aqeel and his deputies (the local leaders) now actively start rallying support for Imam Hussain in Kufa. This process goes on for about two months and about eighteen thousand people pledge their support for Imam Hussain at the end of this period.

The pledge of allegiance by such a large number of supporters raises eyebrows. It wasn't clear at this stage as to whether they were all genuine and truly committed to supporting the cause of Imam Hussain, or if they had other motives.

The supporters of Imam Hussain in Kufa could be divided into three distinct groups.

The first group of Imam Hussain's supporters were made up of the original Shias of Ali. This was the group that considered Ali to be the rightful successor of the Prophet. They were genuine in their invitation to Imam Hussain and were ready to support him as best as they could. They were also the ones who wrote the very first letters of invitation to Imam Hussain when he was in Makkah. For the purpose of this discussion, I will class them as the theological Shias of Ali to keep their identity separate.

The second group of Imam Hussain's supporters were the political Shias of Ali. They had also written letters to Imam Hussain inviting him to their city. However, the political Shias of Ali did not consider Ali to be the rightful successor of the Prophet, but they had whole-heartedly accepted Ali as the fourth Caliph. They had also sided with Ali in the battles of Jamal and Siffin against Lady Aisha and Muawiyah. Hence, they are also referred to as the Shias of Ali, but they are the political Shias of Ali.

The political Shias of Ali were also not happy with the leadership of Yazid. They saw Imam Hussain as a credible person who could help remove Yazid's governor in Kufa, so they also joined the movement of the theological Shias of Ali in Kufa.

The third group of the supporters of Imam Hussain were the mercenaries or the opportunists in Kufa. They were supporting Imam Hussain purely for their own material or political gains. They had seen the trend of support in Kufa rise in favour of Imam Hussain and against the Umayyads, so they also joined the movement of Muslim bin Aqeel to stay on the winning side.

Muslim bin Aqeel was aware of the composition of these three groups. He makes a judgment call, that even after allowing for the different motives of each group, and for some people to withdraw their support when the time comes, Imam Hussain would have enough support to remove Yazid's governor (Noman Bashir) from Kufa and make Kufa his base.

Based on his assessment of the political situation in Kufa, Muslim bin Aqeel writes a letter to Imam Hussain telling him to leave Makkah and to come to Kufa. The letter reaches Imam Hussain and based on the favourable findings of Muslim bin Aqeel, Imam Hussain now seriously considers going to Kufa.

14.5.2. The Situation Deteriorates in Kufa

At almost the same time when Imam Hussain had received the good news from Kufa, the situation in Kufa takes a drastic turn for the worse.

Muslim and his deputies were openly rallying support for Imam Hussain. Noman Bashir, the governor of Kufa was fully aware of the activities of Muslim bin Aqeel and his rallying of support for Imam Hussain, but he does not take any concrete steps to stop Muslim bin Aqeel. The supporters of the Umayyads in Kufa write a letter to Yazid in Damascus and informed him about the activities of Muslim bin Aqeel. They also warn Yazid of the impending danger of allowing Imam Hussain to come to Kufa, and the reluctance of Noman Bashir in putting a stop to the activities of Muslim bin Aqeel.

Yazid is at a loss, he does not know what he should do to stop losing the control of Kufa to Muslim bin Aqeel. He consults his experienced non-Muslim advisor Sir John, who had also been the adviser to Muawiyah when he was the Caliph. Sir John advises Yazid that he should do exactly what his father had done when he was about to lose the control of Basra.

Muawiyah had sent Ziyad bin Abih as the governor to Basra to crush any resistance against the Umayyads, and to impose a strict and oppressive rule on the city, especially on the followers of Ahlulbayt and the Shias of Ali. Ziyad bin Abih was a well-known dictator and was feared for his extreme brutality and oppressive personality. He had cut the hands and legs of the people of Basra, and he had gouged out their eyes when he was the governor there under Muawiyah's rule.

Readers would recall that Ziyad bin Abih was the illegitimate son of Abu Sufyan, and Muawiyah had made him his real brother against the traditions of Islam, and Muawiyah also rewarded him handsomely and gave him the charge of Basra, and then used him to crush any opposition to his rule.

Sir John advises Yazid to appoint Ubaydullah bin Ziyad as the governor of Kufa. Ubaydullah bin Ziyad was the son of Ziyad bin Abih, and just like his father he was also known for his brutality and savagery.

14.5.3. Yazid Appoints a New Governor in Kufa

As per the advice of Sir John, Yazid appoints Ubaydullah bin Ziyad as the new governor of Kufa and orders Noman Bashir to step down. At that time Ubaydullah bin Ziyad was also the governor of Basra and Yazid added Kufa to his authority as well, to stop the movement of Muslim bin Aqeel. Ubaydullah bin Ziyad like his father Ziyad bin Abih was known for his oppressive and brutal rule in Basra. The idea was for Ubaydullah bin Ziyad to repeat his brutality in Kufa, so that the movement of Muslim bin Aqeel in favour of Hussain could be crushed.

Yazid writes to Ubaydullah that he should immediately go to Kufa, replace Noman Bashir as the governor, put an end to the activities of Muslim bin Aqeel by killing him, and under no circumstances should he allow Imam Hussain to enter Kufa.

Here is an extract of Yazid's letter to Ubaydullah bin Ziyad:

> *'...My followers among the people of Kufa have written to me to inform me that Muslim ibn Aqeel is in Kufa gathering units in order to spread rebellion among the Muslims. Therefore, when you read this letter of mine, go to Kufa and search for Muslim ibn Aqeel, as if you were looking for a bead, until you find him. Then bind him in chains, kill him, or expel him. Peace be with you.'*
>
> - *(p.31. The History of al-Tabari; The Caliphate of Yazid. b. Mu'awiyah. Volume XIX. Translated by I.K.A. Howard. State University of New York Press, USA, 1990.)*

The letter of Yazid is clear, he wants the head of Muslim bin Aqeel. As Yazid starts to show his true Umayyad colours the turn of events begin to go against the grandson of the Prophet.

Ubaydullah takes his entourage and leaves for Kufa. Apart from being a cruel oppressor he was an extremely cunning and a very shrewd tactician. He decides to make an unannounced entry into the city of Kufa.

He does this for two reasons.

- Firstly, he wants to gauge at first-hand the level of support that Muslim bin Aqeel has rallied for Imam Hussain.
- Secondly, he fears that the people of Kufa might not let him enter the city if they recognize him.

So, Ubaydullah comes up with a cunning plan. He arrives on the outskirts of Kufa at dusk when people cannot see his face clearly. He puts on a black turban and covers his face with a piece of cloth (this was normal for desert travellers to shield from dust). He then instructs his entourage that on entering the city of Kufa and while he is riding through the streets, they should surround him and shout "Welcome Imam", "Welcome Imam".

As he rides from one district of Kufa to another the locals come out into the streets thinking that Imam Hussain has arrived. He is wearing a black turban like the one that the Imams from the household of the Prophet used to wear. His face is not visible as it is dark and it is partially covered with a piece of cloth, and they hear the shouts of "Welcome Imam" and "Welcome Imam". A huge crowd follows him to the city centre and people are joyful as they think that Imam Hussain has at last come to lead them.

Ubaydullah sees for himself the huge support that Imam Hussain enjoys in Kufa, and how successful Muslim bin Aqeel had been in rallying the people of Kufa to the cause of Hussain. Ubaydullah heads straight to the governor's palace and calls on Noman Bashir, who has no idea that Ubaydullah has come to the city.

As Ubaydullah arrives at governor's palace Noman Bashir thinks that Imam Hussain has arrived. He tells Ubaydullah (thinking its Imam Hussain) that he should not cause any problems for his government, otherwise he (Imam Hussain) would be arrested. Ubaydullah now removes his turban and the face cloth, and he tells Noman Bashir that by the order of Yazid he is removed as the governor of Kufa, and he (Ubaydullah) would now take over as the new governor.

This move of Ubaydullah had shocked the people of Kufa. They were not expecting to be exposed and deceived by Yazid's most brutal governor in Iraq in such a cunning way. Their hopes have been dashed and their hearts have sunk, and they have no idea as to what the cruel Ubaydullah will do next. The people who had come out to welcome Imam Hussain quickly disperse and head to their homes. The mood in Kufa suddenly changes from one of being joyous and jubilant to a mood of extreme fear and apprehension.

14.5.4. Ubaydullah Asserts his Authority

The following morning Ubaydullah holds a meeting with the security forces in his palace. He gives orders that all the tribal chiefs must keep a close watch on their people, and they are to report to the security forces anyone who is any way associated with the movement of Muslim bin Aqeel, and failure to do so would be seen as an act of treason, a crime which would be punishable by death.

Ubaydullah then goes to the grand mosque of Kufa and delivers a speech. He warns the people of Kufa from supporting Muslim bin Aqeel and offers them generous rewards for conforming to the Umayyad rule. He says to the people of Kufa:

> "Anyone found to be sheltering one of those who scheme against the authority of the commander of the faithful (Yazid), and who does not hand him over will be crucified on the door of his own house."

- *al-Mufid, Al-Irshad*

The people of Kufa were threatened with crucifixion on their own doorsteps if they were to support the movement of Muslim bin Aqeel. The people realize that this was not just a scare tactics for they were fully aware of Ubaydullah's tyranny in Basra, and the tyranny of his late father Ziyad bin Abih in Kufa itself.

The army and the security forces were put on full alert to ensure that there were no public meetings, and that Muslim bin Aqeel was tracked down and arrested. Muslim bin Aqeel and his two young boys move from house to house to avoid being arrested by Ubaydullah's men. Muslim bin Aqeel moves from the house of Mukhtar al-Thaqafi to the house of another loyal supporter of Imam Hussain called Hani bin Urwa. The move of Muslim bin Aqeel to the house of Hani is kept a secret and only a selected few knew the actual location of Muslim bin Aqeel.

In a matter of two days the situation in Kufa has turned upside down. Muslim bin Aqeel who was openly rallying support for Imam Hussain is now in hiding, and he is moving from one safe house to another to avoid being arrested by Ubaydullah's men.

The security forces are finding it difficult to track down Muslim bin Aqeel. The supporters of Imam Hussain are determined to protect Muslim bin Aqeel and are not giving anything away to the authorities. They are hoping to keep the support network of Imam Hussain alive, until he arrives in the city of Kufa.

The network of Imam Hussain's supporters has now gone underground, but they haven't lost hope and are still awaiting the arrival of the grandson of the Prophet to their city.

14.5.5. Ubaydullah Hires a Spy

Ubaydullah was a shrewd man. He had been tasked by Yazid to find Muslim bin Aqeel and kill him. He decides to use an experienced spy named Moaqqal. Ubaydullah gives Moaqqal three thousand dirhams to try an infiltrate Muslim bin Aqeel's network, and to gather information about Muslim bin Aqeel's whereabouts and his future plans.

Another key member of Muslim bin Aqeel's network was Muslim bin Awsaja. Muslim bin Awsaja was one of the signatories to the very first letter of invitation which was sent to Imam Hussain by the people of Kufa. Muslim bin Awsaja was acting as an intermediary between the people of Kufa and Muslim bin Aqeel, while Muslim bin Aqeel was in hiding. Moaqqal sees that people usually gather around Muslim bin Awsaja in the mosque, so he approaches him with a story that he has run away from Damascus to escape from the persecution of Yazid, and he wants to support Muslim bin Aqeel and has brought some money that he wants to contribute towards this cause.

After a few meetings, Muslim bin Awsaja is taken in by the stories of Moaqqal. Moaqqal now tells Muslim bin Awsaja that he wants to meet Muslim bin Aqeel in person to hand over the money to him. Muslim bin Awsaja finally agrees, and he arranges a meeting between Muslim bin Aqeel and Moaqqal. Moaqqal now meets Muslim bin Aqeel in the house of Hani bin Urwa where Muslim bin Aqeel had been residing.

Moaqqal has now infiltrated the network of Muslim bin Aqeel and the supporters of Imam Hussain in Kufa, and he reports his finding back to Ubaydullah bin Ziyad.

14.5.6. Muslim bin Aqeel's Network is Compromised

The underground network of Muslim bin Aqeel had now been compromised and this was indeed a death blow to the supporters of Imam Hussain in Kufa.

Ubaydullah now knows everything about Muslim bin Aqeel's network. Ubaydullah has regular meetings with all the tribal chiefs of Kufa to ensure that the tribes are in line with the government policy. Hani bin Urwa, who had been hiding Muslim bin Aqeel in his house was also one of the tribal chiefs of Kufa. Hani bin Urwa had not been attending these meetings for fear of being forced to reveal any information about Muslim bin Aqeel's network.

Ubaydullah knows that Muslim bin Aqeel had been hiding in Hani bin Urwa's house. Ubaydullah calls Hani to the governor's palace and questions him on the whereabouts of Muslim bin Aqeel. Hani bin Urwa denies all knowledge and tells Ubaydullah that he has no idea where Muslim bin Aqeel might be hiding. Ubaydullah then calls in Moaqqal, and Hani bin Urwa immediately realizes that Moaqqal was a spy who was working for Ubaydullah. Ubaydullah tells Hani bin Urwa to send a word to Muslim bin Aqeel to come to the governor's palace voluntarily and hand himself over to the authorities. Hani refuses to do so as he does not want to betray Muslim bin Aqeel.

Ubaydullah then hits Hani bin Urwa on the face with his sword, causing the flesh from his cheeks and forehead to scatter on to his beard. Hani bin Urwa is then taken to the dungeon under the governor's palace and is locked up.

Muslim bin Aqeel hears about Hani's arrest and realizes that their underground network is now compromised.

14.5.7. Muslim bin Aqeel calls upon his Supporters

Muslim bin Aqeel calls upon his supporters to come out on to the streets and march to the governor's palace to get Hani released and to remove Ubaydullah from the office. Out of about eighteen thousand people who had earlier pledged their support for Muslim bin Aqeel, around four thousand of them turned up. The turn out in support of Muslim bin Aqeel's call was still not too bad, considering how drastically things had changed in Kufa since the arrival of Ubaydullah.

There are other genuine reasons for the drop in the numbers too.

- Firstly, this was a sudden and an unplanned mobilization of people and many residents of Kufa were unaware of the call made by Muslim bin Aqeel.
- Secondly, Kufa is a city made up of distinct localities with one main road between these districts. The word had to be sent around to the various districts very quickly to mobilize all the supporters. The main road was now patrolled by the security forces, who were stopping people from getting into these localities.
- Thirdly, some supporters of Imam Hussain had already been arrested and were in the custody of Ubaydullah.

Also, some of the key supporters of Muslim bin Aqeel like Suleman bin Surad al-Khuzai, Al-Musayyab bin Najaba, Rifa bin Shaddad, and Muslim bin Awsaja, who had written the very first letter to Imam Hussain were not able to join the call for one of the three reasons given above.

However, Muslim bin Aqeel with about four thousand supporters march towards the governor's palace. When Ubaydullah gets the news that Muslim and his supporters are coming to the palace, he goes to the central mosque next door and issues a stern warning to the tribal chiefs and to the people at large, and he warns them of dire consequences for supporting Muslim bin Aqeel.

14.5.8. Ubaydullah Pacifies Supporters of Muslim bin Aqeel

Ubaydullah then goes back to the palace, summons all the tribal chiefs of Kufa and then uses them as human shields. The strategy was to stop the supporters of Muslim bin Aqeel from attacking Ubaydullah inside his palace, as the people were unlikely to attack the palace for the fear of hurting their own tribal chiefs. Ubaydullah was an extremely cunning man, and he uses the tribal chiefs of Kufa as human shields and as hostages against their own people.

He then uses three tactics to persuade people to desert Muslim bin Aqeel and return to their homes.

Firstly, he calls upon two of his army officers Muhammad Ashath and Haseen Nameer. Muhammad Ashath was the bother of Joda Ashath, the woman who had poisoned Imam Hasan on the orders of Muawiyah. Haseen Nameer was a ruthless man and the police chief of Kufa. Ubaydullah tells them to spread a rumour that a huge army from Damascus was approaching Kufa, and that the supporters of Muslim bin Aqeel would be crushed in a matter of hours. There was no army coming from Damascus, but the ploy of Ubaydullah worked brilliantly. Many of the supporters of Muslim bin Aqeel got frightened, as they knew the ruthlessness of the Syrian army, plus these were ordinary people of Kufa, who were no match for a regular army. Many supporters of Muslim bin Aqeel abandoned him and returned to their homes out of fear of the approaching Syrian army.

Secondly, Ubaydullah orders the tribal chiefs of Kufa to tell their people that if they continue to support Muslim bin Aqeel their government salaries and housing allowances would be withdrawn. When the womenfolk of Muslim bin Aqeel's supporters hear about this order of Ubaydullah, they came out and pleaded with their men to return to their homes. The women would tell the men that this was not their fight, and they should not risk their lives and homes for a cause that is not a direct concern of theirs. Mothers would come and take their sons away, sisters would come and take their brothers away, and wives would come and take their husbands away. More and more people were now abandoning Muslim bin Aqeel.

Thirdly, Ubaydullah offers Muslim bin Aqeel's supporters an immediate amnesty, and a promise of no further investigations, detention, or execution, should they abandon Muslim at this stage. Even more people now abandon Muslim bin Aqeel and return to their homes.

Ubaydullah was so successful in his tactics that from about four thousand men who joined Muslim bin Aqeel at the start of the day, only about thirty men remained with him by the evening time. When Muslim bin Aqeel comes to the central mosque for the evening prayers there were only ten men with him. As he walks down the streets of Kufa after the evening prayers even those ten men had disappeared.

The ambassador of Imam Hussain, Muslim bin Aqeel is now a lonely man in a strange land.

14.5.9. The Killing off Muslim bin Aqeel

Night has set in, and a curfew is in place by the authorities in Kufa. Muslim bin Aqeel is alone and abandoned. He is thinking about the invitation that he has sent to Imam Hussain. He wants to inform Imam Hussain about the unprecedented change in the situation in Kufa. He also has two young sons who came with him to Kufa. He has no idea about their whereabouts. As a father he is thinking about the safety and the well-being of his sons too.

Ubaydullah's officers are carrying out house-to-house searches looking for Muslim bin Aqeel. They have offered a reward to anyone who would provide information leading to the arrest of Muslim bin Aqeel. As Muslim bin Aqeel walks down the Streets of Kufa, he finds himself in a district inhabited by the tribe of

Kinda. He knocks on a door and asks for some water. The lady who opens the door is a lover of the Ahlulbayt and a supporter of Imam Hussain. She decides to put Muslim bin Aqeel in her house for the night.

However, her son was a greedy individual and when he finds out that Muslim bin Aqeel was sheltering in their house, he informs the authorities to get the reward promised by Ubaydullah. Muhammad Asthath was in charge of the manhunt for Muslim bin Aqeel. On receiving the news of Muslim bin Aqeel's whereabouts, he takes about seventy soldiers and surrounds the house of the lady where Muslim bin Aqeel had spent the night.

Muslim bin Aqeel thanks the lady for her hospitality and he comes out of the house with his sword drawn. Muslim bin Aqeel was brave and a fearsome warrior. He attacks the soldiers of Ashath who are startled and taken back by the ferocity of Muslim bin Aqeel's fight. Muslim bin Aqeel single-handedly kills around 40 soldiers. The remaining soldiers disperse and Muhammad Ashath is forced to retreat.

Muhammad Ashath sends a message to Ubaydullah requesting reinforcements. Ubaydullah questions Muhammad Ashath as to why he would need reinforcements to arrest one man. Muhammad Ashath sarcastically tells Ubaydullah that he was not arresting some shopkeeper from Kufa, but he was fighting a man who was a descendant of the Prophet.

As the reinforcements arrive the soldiers make a plan to trap Muslim bin Aqeel. They dig a trench in one of the streets and conceal it with grass. Some soldiers climbed on the rooftops of the houses along the street and start throwing stones and shooting arrows at Muslim bin Aqeel. As he fights his way through the street he falls into the concealed trench. The soldiers start hitting Muslim bin Aqeel with their weapons as he is stuck in the trench. He is badly wounded and is bleeding profusely.

Muslim bin Aqeel is arrested and is brought before Ubaydullah, who charges him with treason and orders that he should be taken to the roof of the palace and beheaded. Muslim bin Aqeel is taken to the roof of the governor's palace where he requests that he should be allowed to do a short prayer to Allah (salah/namaz) before being killed. The request is granted, and as soon as Muslim bin Aqeel finishes his prayer he is made to position his head over the side of the roof, and he is beheaded. The head falls to the ground and his body is also thrown from the rooftop. The body is then dragged along the streets of Kufa to the market square of the city, where it is crucified to a wall as a warning to the people of Kufa not to revolt against the government or support Imam Hussain.

The barbarity of Yazid's forces is in full swing, and Muslim bin Aqeel becomes the first martyr linked to the tragedy of Karbala.

Next is the turn of Hani bin Urwa, who was earlier locked up in the dungeon under the palace. Hani bin Urwa is also taken to the market square and beheaded, as another lesson for the people of Kufa, in case they choose to support the grandson of the Prophet Imam Hussain.

Ubaydullah orders that the heads of these two martyrs should be sent to Yazid in Damascus. On receiving the heads of Muslim bin Aqeel and Hani bin Urwa, Yazid sends a letter to Ubaydullah stating the following:

> *'You have not gone beyond how I wanted you to be. You have acted with decision...you have satisfied me, been sufficient for the task.'*

- *p. 157, Al-Bidaya wa al-Nihaya. Hafiz ibn Kathir (d. 774 A.H.) Volume VIII.*
- *Maktaba al-Ma'arif, Beirut, Lebanon. 1999. p.64. The History of al-Tabari;*
- *The Caliphate of Yazid. b. Mu'awiyah. Volume XIX. Translated by I.K.A. Howard. State University of New York Press, USA, 1990. p. 157,*

Yazid declares his approval at the actions of Ubaydullah, that he is satisfied with how his newly appointed governor had put an end to the movement of Muslim bin Aqeel in support of Imam Hussain in Kufa.

14.5.10. Muslim bin Aqeel's Young Sons are Slaughtered too

The killing of Muslim bin Aqeel's sons is even more heart rendering. His two young sons Muhammad and Ibrahim were eight and ten respectively. They were scared and frightened and kept crying and searching for their father. The heartless men of Ubaydullah found and arrested the two young flowers. After being arrested both boys were imprisoned in terrible conditions with little food or water and were sentenced to be executed at a later date.

One of the prison guards who carries out the night duty is an old man and looked sympathetic. The two boys decide to speak to him one night and said to the guard:

> "We are from the progeny of your Prophet and are the sons of Muslim bin Aqeel. We have been in prison under you for a long time. You do not give us good food and you persecute us in the prison."
> - *Nafsul Mahmoon by Haj Shaikh Abbas Qummi*

The prison guard broke down and fell upon their feet and said:

> "May my life be your ransom O progeny of the chosen Prophet of Allah! The doors of this prison are open for you, you may go away to whichever place you desire."
> - *Nafsul Mahmoon by Haj Shaikh Abbas Qummi*

The little boys escape from the prison in the dead of the night, but there wasn't anywhere to go. They knock on the door of a house and an old lady comes out. They plead with her to let them stay for the night. She feels pity on the two young souls and she gives them food and water and shelters them in her house. Ubaydullah had put a bounty of one thousand dirhams on the head of each boy. The son-in-law of the old lady whose name was Harith comes home and sees the sons of Muslim bin Aqeel in the house. He cruelly ties the two young boys to a pillar and waits for dawn to break.

The two young boys suffer through the night and in the morning, he drags them to the river Euphrates to behead them and to collect his reward. The old lady pleads with her son-in-law to spare the little boys and fear the wrath of Allah. The little boys remind him that they are the progeny of the Prophet and are the sons of Muslim bin Aqeel, the ambassador of Imam Hussain. Harith shows no mercy and takes out his sword. The little boys start crying and with their eyes filled with tears they ask Harith to give them some time to pray before he kills them.

The elder brother Ibrahim says that he should be killed first as he would not be able to bear the sight of his younger brother being beheaded. Harith accepts his wish and beheads him first and puts his head in a bag. The younger brother is drenched in the blood of the older brother. On seeing the sight of his elder brother's gruesome murder, the younger brother is crying profusely and is traumatized beyond words. But Harith shows no mercy and beheads him too. He throws their bodies into the river Euphrates and takes the two little heads to Ubaydullah to collect his reward.

14.6. Hussain Starts his Journey

Imam Hussain is in Makkah mingling with the pilgrims. The season of Hajj is approaching fast. He is unaware of the atrocities that have been inflicted on Muslim bin Aqeel and his supporters in Kufa. As far as Imam Hussain is concerned the situation in Kufa is favourable, based on the letter that he had earlier received from Muslim bin Aqeel.

While Imam Hussain is in Makkah, Yazid sends assassins disguised as pilgrims to assassinate him. Imam Hussain finds out about the plot of Yazid. His first consideration is to preserve the sanctity of the Holy Kaaba, and to ensure that there is no bloodshed in the vicinity of Kaaba and in the holy city of Makkah. He immediately changes his intentions of performing the Hajj and performs an Umrah instead, since Yazid had planned to kill Imam Hussain during Hajj when Makkah is packed with pilgrims.

Imam Hussain tells his family that they would leave Makkah immediately after the Umrah, and they would be heading to the city of Kufa. The sudden departure in itself generates a lot of publicity, as people were asking as to why the grandson of the Holy Prophet is leaving Makkah just before the Hajj is about to begin.

As Imam Husain is about to leave, he gives a sermon to the people of Makkah. Below is an extract from the sermon of Imam Hussain:

> "……We (Ahlulbayt) shall be patient as we face His trial, and He shall give us in full the rewards due to those who persevere. The Prophet's offspring shall not deviate from His path. Rather, they shall be gathered before him in the presence of the most Holy One. ……. Anyone among you who is ready to sacrifice himself and is determined to meet Allah should join our departing party, for I shall depart in the morning if Allah Almighty so wills"

- Ibn Tawaas, Al-Luhauf, p. 33.
- Ibn Nama, p. 20.

Imam Hussain informs the people of Makkah that the family of the Prophet would stay patient in the face of trials and tribulations, but they would not deviate from the path of the Prophet. He then invites the people of Makkah to join his path of sacrifice and determination if they wish to do so.

The sermon of Imam Hussain had the desired effect. Around one hundred people join Imam Hussain on his way to Kufa. As Imam Hussain leaves Makkah, it is around the same time that Muslim bin Aqeel was being killed in Kufa. The distance between Makkah and Kufa is around eight hundred miles.

It is a long journey that Imam Hussain had embarked upon in search of friends and supporters. The journey of Imam Hussain is a journey of self-sacrifice to redeem the Sunnah of the Prophet.

14.6.1. Hussain Learns about the Killing of Muslim bin Aqeel

Imam Hussain eventually learns about the killing of Muslim ibn Aqeel when he was at a place called Thalabiyyah on his way to Kufa. Muslim ibn Aqeel was not just the ambassador of Imam Hussain, but he was Imam Hussain's cousin and a very dear friend too. Imam Hussain is shattered at the news of Muslim ibn Aqeel's brutal murder. Imam Hussain is also thinking about Muslim ibn Aqeel's two young sons as he had no idea if they were alive and safe.

Imam Hussain receives more bad news from Kufa. Another messenger of Imam Hussain Abdullah Yaqtar has been arrested and killed by Ubaydullah's men. He was found carrying a letter of Imam Hussain to the people of Kufa informing them that Imam Hussain was on his way to their city. As another lesson for the people of Kufa not to rise in support of Imam Hussain, Ubaydullah's men threw Abdullah Yaqtar from the roof of the governor's palace. His bones were crushed but he did not die immediately, so one of Ubaydullah's men stepped forward and slit his throat.

Imam Hussain gathers his supporters and informs them about the situation in Kufa in black and white. He tells them that what has befallen on Muslim bin Aqeel, Hani bin Urwa and Abdullah Yaqtar is awaiting them too. They should not entertain any hope of benefitting from the spoils of war or gaining a high office or a position of power in Kufa. Imam Hussain wants only the most dedicated and loyal supporters for his mission. He wants quality and not quantity, for this is a battle of conscience versus might.

Imam Hussain then offers his supporters to leave his movement if they wish to do so, and that they would still have his full support and blessings. It is said that out of one hundred people who joined Imam Hussain in Makkah, around thirty of them left Imam Hussain at this stage. Imam Hussain wants people who are dedicated and ready to sacrifice their lives for the sake of safeguarding the principles of Islam. He does not want people to join his movement for ulterior motives.

Imam Hussain wants the cream of the believers in his movement, to reflect the nature of his unique and distinguished stand.

Imam Hussain has taken a principled stand against the Caliphate of Yazid because the system of governance that the Umayyads had put in place had completely undermined and altered the Sunnah of the Prophet. Yazid was sitting on the pulpit of Prophet, but his character and his actions reflected everything that the Prophet of Allah stood against. Yazid wanted Imam Hussain to give him a personal oath of allegiance, so that he could justify his un-Islamic character and his forceful acquisition of the Caliphate.

Imam Hussain being the true representative of the Prophet was not prepared to fulfil the wish of Yazid.

14.6.2. Ubaydullah's Men Intercept the Caravan of Hussain

Ubaydullah knows that Imam Hussain and his caravan is on its way to Kufa. He dispatches an army to block any paths leading to the city of Kufa. The small caravan of Imam Hussain, which includes women and children is intercepted by Ubaydullah's army. They refuse to let the caravan of Imam Hussain enter the city of Kufa. Imam Hussain shows them the letters that he had received from the people of Kufa inviting him to their city.

Imam Hussain addresses the troops of Ubaydullah with these words.

> *"I have come because you (Kufans) wrote letters inviting me to come and unite you for the cause of truth and justice. But now if you have changed your mind and you dislike my presence here, I am ready to go back."*
> - *Ansab Al-Ashraf, vol.III, p.170*
> - *Al-Futuh, vol V, p.135*

Imam Hussain is not looking for a confrontation unnecessarily. He has made a principled stance that he would not give allegiance to the likes of Yazid, because if Imam Hussain accepts the Caliphate of Yazid it would mean that Imam Hussain has given his tacit approval to the corrupt and the cruel system of governance that the Umayyads had established, and Yazid was the head of that system at the time.

At the same time Imam Hussain is not looking to start a war either and offers an amicable solution. He says to Ubaydullah's men that he is prepared to go back to Makkah or to his home city of Madinah if his presence is not desirable in Kufa. The options offered by Imam Hussain to defuse the crisis are rejected by Ubaydullah. Ubaydullah is not prepared to let Imam Hussain go anywhere until Imam Hussain is captured or pledges allegiance to Yazid.

14.7. Hussain Arrives in Karbala

Imam Hussain continues his march in a direction that neither leads to Kufa or Madinah, and he ends up on the fateful plains of Karbala on the 2nd of Muharram. Imam Hussain does not know the name of this land. He asks the locals as to what this place is called. Some locals tell him that it is called Naynava, others told him that it is called Mariya. Imam Hussain asked if there was any other name for this place. An old man came forward and said that he had heard from his ancestors that this land is also called the land of Karbala.

When Imam Hussain heard the name Karbala he smiled, and thanked Allah and said:

> *"Surely this is the plain where my Holy Grandfather has prophesied that I, with my faithful companions shall lay slain….. We will not move from here - we have reached our destination."*
>
> - *Hussain The Saviour of Islam by S.V Mir Ahmad Ali (Al-Islam.org)*

Imam Hussain informs his companions that they have reached their promised destination. The word Karbala itself is composed of two separate words, "Karb" and "Bala". The word "Karb" means grief or sorrow and the word "Bala" means afflictions, so the word Karbala means a land of grief and afflictions.

Imam Hussain stops his caravan in Karbala and erects his tents next to the banks of the river Euphrates. Imam Hussain wants to buy this piece of land. He does not want to stay or be killed on someone else's land. Imam Hussain is an embodiment of the character of the Prophet. His wisdom and piety had come from his pure upbringing and lineage. He wants to show the world that the land he was going to be killed upon would be his own land, and Yazid's army would be trespassing on a land that does not belong to them.

This was the beauty of Imam Hussain's stand. It was unique in every sense.

14.7.1. Hussain Purchases the Land in Karbala

The people living in the area were from the tribe of Banu Assad. Imam Hussain purchases the land of Karbala from Banu Assad for 60,000 dirhams, and then to their surprise he immediately gifts it back to them with three requests:

- Firstly, he explains to the people of Banu Assad that soon he and his companions would be killed on this land and their bodies would be left unburied, so he requests the people of Banu Assad to bury them after the army of Yazid has gone.
- Secondly, he requests them that this land should remain a cemetery and not be cultivated.
- Thirdly, he requests the people of Banu Assad to be hospitable to the pilgrims who would come and pay their respects at the graves of the martyrs.

Following are the words of Imam Hussain as recorded in history:

> *"On the tenth of this month you will see our dead bodies lying on this plain with our heads severed and taken away. Please bury us and when our devotees come to visit our graves treat them with honour and point out to them the places of our burial."*
>
> - *The Arrival in Karbala (erfan.ir)*

Imam Hussain then turns to the women of the tribe and said:

> "O virtuous ladies! If your husbands, out of fear of Yazid do not bury us, then please encourage them to do so, or do it yourselves."

- *The Arrival in Karbala (erfan.ir)*

Finally, he turned to the children of Banu Assad and said:

> "O innocent ones! If your parents, out of fear of the ruler do not bury us, then by way of playing, bring some earth and throw it on our bodies to hide them."

- *The Arrival in Karbala (erfan.ir)*

This heartrending appeal of Imam Hussain reduced everyone to tears.

The people of Karbala to this day have honoured the request of Imam Hussain. I am myself a witness to the welcome and the hospitality offered by the people of Karbala when I visited the blessed shrine of Imam Hussain.

14.7.2. Hussain is Surrounded, Food and Water is Cut Off

Ubaydullah sends more troops to surround Imam Hussain at Karbala. By the seventh of Muharram some twenty thousand troops reach Karbala and encircle Imam Hussain and his small contingent.

Imam Hussain is left with two options:

- He either surrenders to Ubaydullah's forces and pledges allegiance to Yazid.
- Or he carries on with his principled stand against the Umayyads and prepares for death.

On the same day i.e., the seventh of Muharram the tyrannical army of Yazid under the command of Ubaydullah cuts off the water supplies to the tents of Imam Hussain. He sends five hundred troops to guard the banks of river Euphrates. Imam Hussain's caravan consists of women and children from the household of the Prophet. His youngest son Ali Asghar is only six months old. The children would not be able to survive without water in the scorching desert heat of Karbala, but the heartless men of Ubaydullah are determined to force Imam Hussain to pay allegiance to their Umayyad master Yazid.

One of Ubaydullah's men, al-Azdi taunts Imam Hussain with these words:

> "Don't you see the crystal water, as pure and transparent as the sky above? By God, you will not be allowed to taste a drop until your death."

- *Life of Imam Husayn [The Saviour], p. 149*
- *Imam Hussain & Tragic Saga of Karbala, p. 169-170*

We read in Sahih Bukhari.

> "Prophet once took Hussain and Hasan and proclaimed, 'O Allah! Verily I love these two, so you love them!'

- *Sahih al-Bukhari. Hadith no. 3464. Book of Superiorities. Chapter; the Superiority of Imam Hasan and Hussain.*

The Prophet is inviting Muslims to love and follow Imam Hussain, whereas the men of Yazid's army are threatening to kill Imam Hussain without giving him a drop of water. This is how far the Caliphate had come since the death of the Prophet, and the very family that the Prophet of Allah had ordered to be loved and revered is being threatened with the most brutal of the consequences.

We read the words of Allah in the verse of Affection (Mawaddah) in the Holy Quran:

> "...Say (O' Muhammad unto mankind): I do not ask of you any reward for it (preaching the message), but love for my relatives (Ahlulbayt)..."
>
> - Quran (42:23)

In this verse Allah has made the love of the Ahlulbayt mandatory and an Islamic duty for all the Muslims. But the army of Yazid is putting the members of the Ahlulbayt through all kinds of trials and tribulations, challenging and contradicting the clear commands of Allah.

They are denied food and water in the unbearable open desert of Karbala. The little children of Prophet's family are constantly screaming "Al-Atash", "Al-Atash", which means "The thirst", "The thirst". The children would come up to their parents with empty cups asking for water, and the parents are at loss to explain as to why they have no water to offer them. The sight of their children dying of thirst is intolerable. The family of the Prophet is struggling to stay alive with women and children barely able to walk and even stand.

The events are about to take an even more brutal turn for the Ahlulbayt. Imam Hussain and his small contingent was already going through the most unbearable form of torture, but the vicious Ubaydullah now instructs his army commander Umar ibn Saad to further increase the oppression against Imam Hussain.

Ubaydullah writes a letter to Umar ibn Saad with these instructions:

> '...I did not send you to Hussain to hold off from fighting him, to give him time, to promise him peace and preservation, or to be an intercessor on his behalf with me. Therefore, see that, if Hussain and his followers submit to my authority and surrender, you can send them to me in peace. If they refuse, then march against them to kill and disfigure them, for they deserve that. If Hussain is killed, make the horses trample on his chest and back, for he is a disobedient rebel, an evil man who splits the community. Not that I think he would feel any harm once he is dead, but I vowed to do this if I killed him. If you carry out our order concerning him, we will give you the reward due ....'
>
> - p.110. The History of al-Tabari; The Caliphate of Yazid. b. Mu'awiyah. Volume XIX. Translated by I.K.A. Howard. State University of New York Press, USA, 1990.

Ubaydullah makes it clear to Umar ibn Saad that unless Imam Hussain submits to the Umayyad authority, he should kill and disfigure Imam Hussain and trample his body with horses. He also calls Imam Hussain an evil man and a disobedient rebel.

Let's see what Prophet had said about Imam Hussain.

> Prophet said to Ali, Fatima, Hasan and Hussain 'I oppose those who oppose you, and I am peaceful to those who are peaceful to you.'
>
> - (Sunan al-Tirmidhi. Hadith no. 3705. Book of Superiorities. Chapter; What has been mentioned regarding the superiority of Fatima bint Muhammad.)

The words of Yazid's governor Ubaydullah negate the beautiful words of the Holy Prophet in the most disrespectful way. The Prophet had said that he is at peace with those who are at peace with Hussain. But Ubaydullah intends to disfigure Imam Hussain and trample his body with horses. On the Day of Judgment, Yazid and his governor will be brought to face the Prophet of Allah, and these words of disfiguring Imam Hussain would haunt them forever.

Despite the unimaginable hardship facing Imam Hussain and his family he remained resolute and firm in his belief and conviction. Imam Hussain was the grandson of the Prophet, and he was the son of Ali, who was the bravest of the warriors that Arabs had witnessed. Imam Hussain was a lion of man, and he was not going to capitulate to the threats of Ubaydullah bin Ziyad.

Imam Hussain famously said:

> "......... I look upon death as but the felicity of martyrdom and I regard life among oppressors and transgressors as nothing but agony and torture. By God I will never give you my hand like a man who has been defeated; nor will I flee like a slave."
>
> • Hadiyyat al-Ahbb, p. 111, where al-Bayhaqi's biography is detailed.

The words of Imam Hussain reflect the courage and the dignity of his upbringing in the household of the Prophet.

14.7.3. The Night Before the Battle

Umar ibn Saad informs Imam Hussain about the orders of Ubaydullah. The orders of Ubaydullah are unmistakable. He has given Imam Hussain two options i.e., either give allegiance to Yazid or face death. Imam Hussain requests that he should be given a night to ponder before he makes his decision. Umar ibn Saad consults with his officers and allows Imam Hussain an extra night to come to a decision.

Imam Hussain had absolutely no intention of giving allegiance to Yazid. If Imam Hussain had intended to give allegiance to Yazid then he would have done that in his home city of Madinah. Imam Hussain had not travelled hundreds of miles to Karbala to give allegiance to the Umayyads. However, Imam Hussain wants to postpone the battle for a night to invoke the conscience of the people on both sides.

Imam Hussain was the embodiment of Prophet's Sunnah. The whole stand of Imam Hussain against Yazid was based on reforming the Muslim Ummah as per the ideals of the Prophet's revolution. Imam Hussain wants both sides to reflect in the quiet of the night on what they are actually embarking upon the next morning.

The soldiers in the camp of Yazid are all psyched up for the battle. Imam Hussain wants them to reflect on what they are about to do to the family of the Prophet, and the consequences of their actions. He is giving them a chance to reconsider their position, so that they cannot give an excuse that they were overwhelmed by the momentum of the ensuing events.

The companions of Imam Hussain are also given a chance to decide if they truly want to sacrifice their lives for his principled stand against the Umayyads. Imam Hussain had embarked upon a path of self-sacrifice to redeem and rekindle the traditions of the Prophet. However, he does not want to force others to join his mission despite knowing the righteousness of his stand.

Imam Hussain wants his supporters to understand the magnanimity of his stand, without any influence or pressure from him. He gathers his supporters and draws their attention to the sounds coming from the camp of Yazid. It was the sound of war drums beating and armoury being sharpened. He tells his supporters that Yazid's men are after him and him alone, but they will not spare anyone who gets in their way, so if they wish to leave, they will be given a safe passage back to their homes.

He acknowledges and thanks them for their courage and support so far, and he says that he could not have wished for better companions and supporters, for they are the very best. He gives them his full blessings and permission to leave, and he promises them that he would not hold any grudges against them either in this world or in the hereafter.

He further says that should anyone be hesitant to leave because they might be ashamed, he was going to turn off the candles so that they could leave in the darkness of the night unnoticed. Imam Hussain then turns off all the candles to give his supporters a chance to leave. After some time, Imam Hussain lights up the candles again and he sees that not even a single person from his camp has left.

The people who accompanied Imam Hussain to Karbala were the cream of the believers!

And lastly, Imam Hussain wanted an extra night that he and his supporters could spend in worshipping Allah and in the recitation of the Holy Quran. History records that the sounds of the prayers like the humming of the bees was coming from the tents of Imam Hussain on the night before the tragedy of Karbala.

The approach of Imam Hussain is very different from the approach of a conventional leader who at this stage would be energizing his troops to stick together and fight the enemy. This is because the mission of Imam Hussain is very different from the mission of a conventional leader. Imam Hussain is not after the glory of this world. His aim is to invoke the conscience of the believers through the ultimate sacrifice of his family and his friends.

By the spilling of his blood, he wants the Ummah to recognize that the family of the Prophet was not going to tolerate the deviation and the injustices of the Umayyads. The Umayyads had gone too far against the traditions of the Prophet, and as the grandson of the Holy Prophet Imam Hussain prefers to die rather than give his hand of allegiance to Yazid, who was in charge of that corrupt and brutal system of governance at the time.

The night of reflection had the desired effect on both sides.

Eleven people from Yazid's army changed sides and joined the contingent of Imam Hussain in the morning. This includes Hurr ar-Riyahi who was a top lieutenant in Ubaydullah's army. He was the army commander who had intercepted the caravan of Imam Hussain outside the city of Kufa and forced Imam Hussain in the direction of Karbala.

The supporters of Imam Hussain had also renewed their pledges of allegiance to him. Abbas, the brother of Imam Hussain speaks on behalf of the family, and he gives a solemn promise that they would never part with Imam Hussain until the last drop of their blood.

Muslim bin Awsaja, an elder from Kufa and a signatory to the very first letter of invitation to Imam Hussain, speaks on behalf of the friends and the companions of Imam Hussain. He said that they were prepared to endure any sufferings on the battlefield of Karbala, and that they would fight until their last breath in order to protect Imam Hussain. Muslim bin Awsaja further adds that even if they had no weapons, they would support Imam Hussain by throwing stones at the enemy.

Zuhayr bin al-Qayn, another supporter of Imam Hussain from Kufa, says that even if they had to die a thousand times, they would still support the grandson of the Prophet against the Umayyads.

The family and the companions of Imam Hussain are committed to his cause until the last drop of their blood. They are willing to sacrifice their lives to preserve the just and the virtuous stand of Imam Hussain, and with this commitment from the contingent of Imam Hussain dawn breaks on the fateful Day of Ashura.

14.8. The Day of Ashura.

The Day of Ashura is the day when the battle of Karbala took place between the army of Yazid and the small contingent of Imam Hussain. It fell on the 10th of Muharram of the Islamic Calendar. In Arabic 10th is known as Ashara and hence this day is called the Day of Ashura.

In the camp of Imam Hussain, the Day of Ashura starts with the morning prayers (Fajar). Imam Hussain asked his son Ali Akbar to give the Adhan (call to the prayer). Imam Hussain chooses Ali Akbar for a particular reason. Ali Akbar was an image of the Prophet in every respect. He physically resembled the Prophet of Allah when Prophet was in his youth. He resembled the Prophet in the way he walked and in the way he spoke and even his voice resonated like the voice of the Prophet.

There were some companions of the Prophet who had joined the army of Yazid against Imam Hussain. The idea was to remind them that they are in fact fighting the army of the Prophet by siding with Yazid.

14.8.1. Hussain Identifies Himself

Imam Hussain identifies himself to the army of Yazid in case they had been fooled by the State authorities, who had been portraying Imam Hussain as a common rebel, and as someone who was out to create trouble for the Caliphate of Yazid. It was important that Imam Hussain makes his identity known, so that the soldiers of Yazid cannot later on claim that they were not aware about the identity of the person they were about to kill.

Imam Hussain addresses the army of Yazid with these words and also warns them about the crime that they were about to commit.

> '...Trace back my lineage and consider who I am. Then, look back at yourselves and remonstrate with yourselves. Consider whether it is right for you to kill me and desecrate my inviolability. Am I not the son of the daughter of your Prophet, the son of the executor of his will and his cousin, the first of the believers in God and the man who [first] believed in what His Messenger brought from his Lord? Was not Hamzah, the lord of the Martyrs, my uncle? Was not Ja'far, who flies with two wings in heaven, my uncle? Have you not heard the words that circulate among you that the Prophet of Allah said concerning myself and my brother: 'These are the two leaders of the youths of the inhabitants of heaven'?

- Al-Bidaya wa al-Nihaya p.179 Hafiz ibn Kathir (d. 774 A.H.) Vol. VIII.
- Maktaba al-Ma'arif, Beirut, Lebanon. 1999. pp. 123-124.
- The History of al-Tabari; The Caliphate of Yazid. b. Mu'awiyah. Volume XIX. Translated by I.K.A. Howard. State University of New York Press, USA, 1990.

Imam Hussain identifies himself to the enemy with these clear and simple questions.

- Am I not the grandson of your Prophet?
- Am I not the son of the daughter of your Prophet?
- Am I not the son of the executor of the will of the Prophet (meaning Ali)?
- Is Hamza the Lord of the Martyrs not my uncle?
- Is Jaffer who is flying with two wings in Paradise not my uncle?
- Did the Prophet not say that Hasan and Hussain are the leaders of the youths of Paradise?
- Am I not that Hussain?

The idea behind Imam Hussain's speech was to leave nobody in any doubt as to his identity and his stature. Imam Hussain is reminding the army of Yazid to recognize his stand in the light of his unique position in relation to the Prophet of Allah. Imam Hussain is reminding the enemy that his stand represents the stand of the Prophet, since Prophet had said that he was the leader of the youth of the Paradise. Imam Hussain with these words is inviting the army of Yazid to his side, and he is trying to persuade them not to spill his blood.

Imam Hussain then says to the enemy that he has never lied before and is not lying now. Imam Hussain also wants to identify their motive behind killing him. He asks them if he had killed any of their relations? Or if he had stolen their property? Or if he had hurt them in anyway other way? Imam Hussain wants to invoke their conscience to make them realize that they have embarked on a path of misguidance and tyranny.

Imam Hussain being a man of extreme courage and bravery tells the army of Yazid, while he is surrounded by them from all sides, that their leader Yazid was a criminal and a killer who had transgressed the laws of Allah.

Imam Hussain addresses the army of Yazid with these words:

> *"Yazid himself and his men who have gathered here are guilty of making innovations, discarding religious injunctions, indulging in worldly carnal pleasures, and mocking the messenger of Allah by saying that there is nothing but this life in this world, and that there is no accountability or reward or punishment and no life hereafter. Has not Yazid persecuted and killed several noble scholars who were pious Muslims? Do you then take sides with such men against me? Have you lost your sense of justice? Have you forgotten that Islam teaches austerity and piety? Is not this worldly life transitory and the gain you hope to get is not going to provide eternal comfort to you? Do you not realize the consequences of the evilness of your act in seeking to slay me?"*

- *The Hidden Truth about Karbala by A.K Ahmad (Al-Islam.org)*

The words of Imam Hussain reflected the truthfulness of his stand. He informs the army of Yazid of the crimes committed by their leader, and he challenges them not to side with him for worldly gains by killing the grandson of the Prophet.

He then offers the army of Yazid a way out. Imam Hussain says to the army of Yazid:

> *"Let me either return where I came from or let me live in this extensive land"*

- *Tarikh al-Kamil, vol. IV, p.54*
- *Tarikh al-Tabari, vol. II, p.182*

Even at this last stage Imam Hussain wants to avoid bloodshed, without compromising his stance of not giving the allegiance to Yazid. Imam Hussain says that he is ready to go back to Makkah or Madinah or to any other place in the extensive land of Allah.

Imam Hussain had taken a principled stance of not giving the allegiance to Yazid, as that would justify the innovations of the Umayyad rule on behalf of the Ahlulbayt. At the same time Imam Hussain is not seeking to initiate a war. He offers an amicable solution, where he maintains his principled stance of not giving the allegiance to Yazid but at the same time he avoids open conflict.

Imam Hussain's offer of a peaceful resolution to the crisis is rejected by Ubaydullah bin Ziyad. Imam Hussain is now left with only two options i.e., either to capitulate and pledge allegiance to Yazid, or face death on the battlefield against the Umayyads. Imam Hussain was not a man who was afraid of death, and there was no way that he was going to give allegiance to the likes of Yazid in exchange for a life under tyranny. Imam Hussain has now tried everything in his power to avoid bloodshed and to come to a peaceful resolution.

The battle is about to commence however it is not much of a battle. There are just over 100 people on the side of Imam Hussain including women and children, and the army of Yazid is around 30,000. The contingent of Imam Hussain has had no food or water for the last three days. They are hungry and thirsty, and the cries and the screams of women and children coming from the tents of Imam Hussain are resonating on the plains of Karbala. But their vigour and determination to support and die for the righteous cause of Imam Hussain is unshakeable.

14.8.2. The Discipline of Hussain's Contingent

The battle starts off in in the traditional Arab way of warfare. A soldier on either side identifies himself by his tribal lineage and challenges a single combatant from the opposite side. This is followed by a one-to-one combat until one of the fighters is killed, and his place is taken by another fighter. The fighting goes on until one side overpowers the other and becomes victorious.

Despite the extremely small number of fighters on the side of Imam Hussain their discipline is amazing and remarkable. Before any person steps forward for the duel he obtains permission from Imam Hussain, and only then he proceeds to the battlefield. Also, when a martyr falls Imam Hussain would personally go to honour him and hear his last words. Imam Hussain then collects the body of each martyr and brings it back to a makeshift tent, which he had setup before the battle commenced. This was to ensure that the bodies of the martyrs were not trampled upon by the horses as planned by the army of Yazid.

Umar bin Saad, who is the commander of Yazid's army observes that in one-to-one combat his side is losing more men than Imam Hussain's side. He immediately changes the rules of engagement and orders a general attack, which was contrary to the Arab tradition and was against all the accepted norms of warfare at the time. A unit of about five hundred archers shoot arrows simultaneously at the small army of Imam Hussain. It is reported that as many as fifty martyrs fell on the side of Imam Hussain as a result of this attack.

This attack against the traditions of warfare breaks the back of Imam Hussain's small army. Even on the battlefield Yazid's army does not keep to the ethics and the principles of warfare despite their huge numbers. The dreadful irony now facing the camp of Imam Hussain was that there were more bodies than people left to carry them. Imam Hussain and his handful of remaining supporters do their best to move the bodies of their fellow comrades to the makeshift tent.

As the time for afternoon (Zohar) prayer approaches Imam Hussain requests a suspension of the battle for the prayers, but his request is turned down despite pleas by three eminent people of Kufa namely Abu Thumama, Habib bin al-Muzahir and Hurr ar-Riyahi. Imam Hussain leads a shortened prayer which is performed in times of danger or war.

Two of Imam Hussain's companions Saeed Abdullah and Zuhayr Qayn stand as human shields in front of Imam Hussain while he leads the prayers. They die of their wounds from the arrows being thrown at Imam Hussain while he was praying. Both men fell in front of Imam Hussain as he ends his prayer. Imam Hussain speaks to the two martyrs and thanks them for their courage and sacrifice.

Even in these desperate moments Imam Hussain remembers Allah and does not neglect the obligatory prayers, unlike the other side which does not even give Imam Hussain a chance to pray in peace.

14.8.3. The Sacrifice of the Ahlulbayt and the Banu Hashim Begins

There is unanimity in the historical literature that the family members of Imam Hussain were martyred after all his companions had fallen. This proved that the companions of Imam Hussain were so resolute that as long as they were alive, they did not allow any harm to the family of the Prophet, and they defended the Ahlulbayt until the last drop of their blood.

After all the companions and the supporters of Imam Hussain were killed, the time finally arrived for the sacrifice of Banu Hashim and the Ahlulbayt.

The battle of Karbala was fought against the same enemy that the battles of Badr, Uhad and Moat were fought some fifty years ago. In those battles the Prophet of Allah would lead the Muslim army against the Quraysh of Makkah, who were dominated by the Umayyad clan. At that time, it was the Umayyad leader Abu Sufyan who used to lead the fight against the Prophet and the Muslims.

In Karbala it was Abu Sufyan's grandson Yazid who was fighting the grandson of the Prophet Imam Hussain. The Banu Hashim and the Ahlulbayt were still facing the same enemy, some fifty years after the death of the Prophet. The people that Ali had defeated to secure the revolution of Islam have again re-emerged after the counter-revolution of the Umayyads. And now it was the turn of Hussain, the son of Ali to stop the revolt of the Umayyads against the Sunnah of the Prophet.

The Banu Hashim and the family members now come to Imam Hussain one by one seeking his permission to go to the battlefield. As they fall on the battlefield Imam Hussain would personally go and honour them and collect their bodies just as he did for his companions.

I will briefly mention the story of some of the martyrs of Karbala.

14.8.4. Ali Akbar (Son of Imam Hussain)

Ali Akbar was the second son of Imam Hussain. He was around eighteen years of age. He was the first from among the members of Imam Hussain's family to go into the battle. When Ali Akbar went to his father seeking permission for the battle the Imam tearfully looked up at the sky and said:

> *"O Allah! Be a witness against these people, for now I send against them that son of mine who bears the most resemblance to your Messenger in features, character and speech. O Allah! He is the one at whom we look whenever we desire the sight of your Messenger."*
> - *(Maqtal al-Husayn al-Muqarram)*

Ali Akbar was well known for his distinct resemblance to the Prophet. In Madinah where Imam Hussain used to live, often the old companions of the Prophet would come and knock-on Imam Hussain's door, simply to look at Ali Akbar as he reminded them of the Prophet of Allah.

When Ali Akbar approached the battlefield, Yazid's army were so amazed at his resemblance to the Holy Prophet that some companions of the Prophet who were fighting on the side of Yazid thought that the Prophet had reappeared in this world to help his grandson. People were so anxious to see this enchantingly handsome young man that those who were at the back of the army would stand on their horses to catch a glimpse of Ali Akbar.

As Ali Akbar advanced towards the enemy, he broke their ranks and single-handedly fought against them without any fear. However, the forces of Ubaydullah began to surround him and started attacking him from all sides. As Ali Akbar was valiantly fighting surrounded by the enemy, Murrah ibn Munqidh Abdi, a soldier in the army of Umar ibn Saad vowed to a friend and said:

> *"I will strike such a blow to the chest of this youth as will cause his father's heart to bleed even if the sins of the Arabs fall upon me."*
>
> - *(Kibrit al-Ahmar)*

Amidst the raging swords and spears that were being driven into his blessed body, an arrow was shot that ripped apart his throat. As Ali Akbar fell to the ground drowning in the blood pouring from his throat, he cried out for his father Imam Hussain:

> *"O father! Accept the final salutations from your dying son. Here is my grandfather the Messenger of Allah, greeting you with peace and awaiting your arrival. He has quenched my thirst with his chalice. After that I will never feel thirst again."*
>
> - *(Maqtal al-Husayn al-Muqarram)*

Imam Hussain struggling with anguish and pain came to where Ali Akbar lay dying. Looking down at the state of his son who was the light of his eyes, and tears pouring down his cheeks and beard he cried:

> *"O son! The world has lost its appeal without you."*
>
> - *(Kitab al-Irshad)*

Imam Hussain then took the torn body of Ali Akbar in his arms and he said:

> *"O child! You have acquired rest from the grief and the miseries of this world and left your father alone and without any helpers."*
>
> - *(Maqtal al-Husayn by Abu Mikhnaf)*

Imam Hussain put his face against the blood covered face of Ali Akbar and cried and cried until his tears dried up. Struck with grief and pain Imam Hussain was unable to carry the body of Ali Akbar back to the makeshift tent. After all Ali Akbar was his eighteen years old young and handsome son. He called upon the remaining youth of Banu Hashim to help him carry the body of Ali Akbar.

As the body reached the tent of Lady Zaynab who was Imam Hussain's sister, she ran out lamenting:

> *"O brother! O 'Ali Akbar!" She ran to 'Ali Akbar's body and threw herself on to it. The Imam pulled Lady Zaynab away from the blood-soaked body that she was clinging to and took her back to the tent."*
>
> - *(Kitab al-Irshad)*

The army of Yazid had killed a young man who resembled the Prophet so much so that some old companions of the Prophet had thought that it was in fact the Prophet who had come back to help his grandson. The killing of Ali Akbar showed the enmity of Yazid's army towards the Prophet himself, that they were willing to kill anyone even if they were the direct descendants of the Prophet and even if they looked just like the Prophet.

14.8.5. Qasim (Son of Hasan)

Qasim was the eldest son of Imam Hasan, the elder brother of Imam Hussain. Qasim was in his early teens and had not reached the age puberty at time of his martyrdom in Karbala. As he sees Imam Hussain bring back martyr after martyr, he is eager to join their ranks too. Qasim approaches Imam Hussain and seeks permission to fight.

Imam Hussain says to Qasim:

> *"Qasim, you are young. You are the only child of your mother. Qasim, you are my brother's son. I have promised my brother to look after you. My darling Qasim, you are the image of my brother. You remind me of Hasan. No, Qasim, no. I cannot allow you to die."*
> - *Tears for Karbala by Liakat Dewji*

Qasim was heartbroken at the refusal of Imam Hussain. He approaches his mother Umm-e-Farwa and asks her to intervene. Umm-e-Farwa remembers that just before Imam Hasan died, he gave her a letter saying that if you ever find Qasim in a difficult situation then give him this letter.

She gives the letter to Qasim which read:

> *"My son Qasim, a day will come when my brother Hussain will be facing an enemy of tens of thousands. That will be the day when Islam will need to be saved by sacrifice. You must represent me on that day."*
> - *Tears for Karbala by Liakat Dewji*

Qasim smiles after reading the letter and rushes to Imam Hussain and gives him the letter. After reading the letter Imam Hussain embraces Qasim and starts weeping. Imam Hussain says to Qasim that how can I stop you now? You have given me the will of my brother.

Imam Hussain asks Qasim as to how he finds death? Qasim replies:

> *"O Uncle I find death sweeter than honey!"*
> - *Perspectives on Islamic Faith and History by Bashir A. Datoo*
> - *(Al-Waqa'i' wa-al-Hawadith)*

Imam Hussain asks his sister Lady Zainab to bring him the Turban (head gear) and the Abaa (cloak) of Imam Hasan. Imam Hussain dresses Qasim in the clothes of Imam Hasan as Qasim is representing his father on the plains of Karbala. After dressing up Qasim both Imam Hussain and Lady Zainab start crying as they remembered their brother Imam Hasan and the way he was poisoned by Muawiyah. They both looked at each other with their eyes full of tears and admired the youthful innocent looks of Qasim.

As Qasim walks out on to the battlefield his sword touches the ground and starts making a mark in the sand. His sword was longer than his legs. He was so young that he could not even mount the horse on his own. His uncle Abbas helped him mount the horse. As young Qasim rode to the battlefield of Karbala his feet would not reach the foot straps on the horse.

Like other children of Banu Hashim, Qasim was a handsome young boy. When the enemy saw Qasim they began to murmur as to how could they kill this young boy whose face was shining like the moon.

Humayd ibn Muslim who was in Yazid's army reported Qasim's death in the following way:

> "A young boy came out of the tents of al-Hussain and approached the battlefield. His face was like the first splinter of the new moon. He had a sword in his hand and was wearing a long shirt. As he entered the battlefield and engaged in fighting, 'Amr ibn Sa'd Azdi, who stood next to me, said, "By God! Let me attack this child!"
>
> I replied, "What cause do you have with him? He is only a child. Let those who surround him finish him off. By God! I would not lift a finger against him even if he was to strike me down with his sword."
>
> He repeated, "By God! Let me attack him and make life a misery for him." As Qasim ibn al-Hasan was fighting with the soldiers that surrounded him, 'Amr sneaked behind him and struck him on the head with a sword.
>
> Qasim's head split open as he fell from his mount onto his face and he cried out. " O uncle! Come to my aid."

- *The Earliest Historical Account of the Tragedy of Karbala by Abu Mikhnaf (Al-Islam.org)*
- *Al-Tabari (5:447)*
- *Al-Irshad (pg.239)*

As Qasim falls from the horse he is crying out for Imam Hussain: "O uncle, Accept My Last Salaam."

Imam Hussain had been standing and watching his nephew fight the soldiers of Umar ibn Saad. It is said that as soon as he heard the cries of Qasim he went towards Qasim like an eagle descends on its prey. In the ensuing confusion the horses galloped over Qasim's small body, and he was trampled to death by their hooves.

As the cloud of dust settled Imam Hussain was seen standing next to the broken body of Qasim, while Qasim was rubbing his heels on the ground as his soul was departing from his mutilated body. Tears flew from the eyes of Imam Hussain at this dreadful sight. Imam Hussain puts his cheek on the torn chest of Qasim crying and lamenting:

> "O child! It is unbearable that you called out to your old uncle and I could not come to your help. And when I did, it was to no avail."

- *Lamentations – The Tragedy of the Lord of the Martyrs by Shaykh Mohammad Ishtihardi*

Imam Hussain picks up the broken body of Qasim in his arms, but because the body had been trampled upon, as he walks back to the tenets the feet of Qasim were touching the ground and making a line in the sand. He takes the body of Qasim to the makeshift camp where the bodies of his other companions and family members were resting. He places Qasim's body next to his son Ali Akbar and says:

> "O my nephews! Persevere. O my children! Have patience. By Allah! You will not see any grief after this day."

- *A'yan al-Shi'ah*

Some reports suggest that Qasim's body was so badly mutilated by the hooves that Imam Hussain took off his abaa (clock), spread it on to the ground and gathered the pieces of Qasim as one gathers flowers from a garden, and then took it back to the tent.

Imam Hasan was poisoned by Muawiyah and Imam Hasan's son Qasim was killed by Yazid's army. The Umayyad dynasty had been systematically killing the progeny of the Prophet ever since they took over the reins of power.

14.8.6. Ali Asghar (Six Month Old Son of Hussain)

Ali Asghar was the youngest son of Imam Hussain. He was only six months old when he was martyred in Karbala.

On the Day of Ashura, the time for the late afternoon prayers (Asr) was approaching fast, and by this time Imam Hussain had lost all the men of fighting age from his companions and from his family. Imam Hussain was about to step into the battlefield himself, but before going into battle he came to see his sister Umm Kulthum and said to her:

> "O sister! Take great care of my suckling child Ali Asghar, He is only six months old."
> - *Lamentations – The Tragedy of the Lord of the Martyrs by Shaykh Mohammad Ishtihardi*

As Imam Hussain approaches the enemy all alone with no one left to support him, he deliberately makes a plea which has preserved the state of the Ummah forever in history. Imam Hussain looks at the battlefield and says:

> "Is there anyone to help me? Is there anyone left to help the grandson of the Holy Prophet?"
> - *Lamentations – The Tragedy of the Lord of the Martyrs by Shaykh Mohammad Ishtihardi*

The plea of Imam Hussain speaks a thousand words. Imam Hussain knows that there is no one out there to help him or support his cause. Also, Imam Hussain does not need anyone to help him either. He had already chosen his destiny when he left Makkah for Iraq.

But the words of Imam Hussain gives us a glimpse of the state of the Ummah at the time. In the vast empire of the Muslim Ummah which by that time had expanded to the shores of North Africa, there was no one left to support the grandson of the Prophet, and there is no one left who had the courage to take on the might of the Umayyad dynasty.

When Imam Hussain utters these words, he hears the sounds of crying and sobbing coming from his tents. Imam Hussain turns around and goes back into his tents and enquires about the reasons for the sudden crying.

Lady Zainab stood up and says to Imam Hussain:

> "My brother Hussain, when you called out, "Is there anyone to help me?", Ali Asghar fell from his cradle."
> - *Tears for Karbala by Liakat Dewji*

Imam Hussain knew exactly what Ali Asghar was trying to say.

Imam Hussain approaches Umm Rubab who was Imam Hussain's wife and Ali Asghar's mother. She was trying to comfort Ali Asghar in her lap. Imam Hussain picks up the baby and whispered something in his ear. Ali Asghar immediately stops crying. Imam Hussain tells Umm Rubab that he was going to take Ali Asghar to the battlefield to get him some water.

Umm Rubab dresses up her little warrior (mujahid) in the best possible clothes that she could find, with the hope that Yazid's army would show some mercy and Ali Asghar could quench his thirst. Ali Asghar is all dressed up and Imam Hussain carries him to the battlefield. It is extremely hot, so Imam Hussain covers Ali Asghar with his abaa (cloak) to protect him from the scorching sun.

Yazid's men see Imam Hussain approaching with something in his hand:

> "Look, Hussain is coming with the Quran. He has no one left to help him. With the help of the Quran he is hoping to win."
>
> - *Tears for Karbala by Liakat Dewji*

Imam Hussain is walking towards the enemy and as he comes closer to the soldiers of Yazid he moves his abaa (cloak) and exposes Ali Asghar. He then holds Ali Asghar high with both hands and says:

> "O soldiers of Yazid, you feel I have offended you, but what has this little child done to you? His mother's milk has dried up. He has not had a drop of water for three days. He is dying of thirst. I ask you to give water to this innocent little child"
>
> - *Tears for Karbala by Liakat Dewji*

Imam Hussain gets no response from the army of Yazid. No one steps forward with water for the little child that Imam Hussain has in his lap.

Imam Hussain makes another plea:

> "Maybe you think that when you bring the water for this child, I will drink it too. I will put this child on the plains of Karbala and you can give him the water yourself."
>
> - *Tears for Karbala by Liakat Dewji*

Imam Hussain places Ali Asghar on the burning sand of Karbala. Ali Asghar lay quietly on the hot sand with his head turned towards the enemy and his innocent eyes staring at Yazid's men. Still there is no response from the enemy, and Ali Asghar is struggling to stay alive. Imam Hussain picks up Ali Asghar and says:

> "My son Ali Asghar, my darling, you are too young to fight with a sword or a spear. My little Mujahid, my little soldier, you are the grandson of Ali. O' Ali Asghar, fight your Jihad with your tongue."
>
> "Asghar sticks his dry tongue out and moved it over his dry lips looking towards Yazid's men."
>
> - *Tears for Karbala by Liakat Dewji*

The actions of Ali Asghar caused a sudden uproar among the soldiers of Yazid. It touched their hearts as many of them had children of their own. They became restless and some even started crying. They spoke amongst themselves and said:

> "Hussain is saying the truth. What has this child done to us? Why is he punished like this? Let us give him some water."
>
> - *Tears for Karbala by Liakat Dewji*

Umar ibn Saad, who was commanding the army of Yazid in Karbala got worried that his soldiers might turn against him. He immediately orders his best archer by the name of Hurmalah to act.

> "Hurmalah! What are you waiting for? Silence the little child! Don't you know he is a grandson of 'Ali? Hurry, shoot your arrow, before it is too late."
>
> - *Tears for Karbala by Liakat Dewji*

On the instructions of Umar ibn Saad, Hurmalah aims a three-headed arrow at Ali Asghar. A three-headed arrow in those days was normally used to kill wild animals. Imam Hussain sees the arrow coming and tries to protect Ali Asghar with his arms. But the arrow rips open the neck of the little flower from one ear to the other, and also pierces the arm of Imam Hussain. Ali Asghar dies instantly in the arms of his father.

This was not the response that Hussain was expecting. Hussain had come to quench the thirst of his six-month old son but walks away with an arrow in his neck. Hussain is a father after all. He had already lost his elder son Ali Akbar earlier in the day. How is he now going to break the news of Ali Asghar's death to his mother?

Hussain gently pulls the arrow from Ali Asghar's tiny neck, a sight that no father would be able to bear.

As blood gushes out from Ali Asghar's neck, a voice comes from the plains of Karbala:

> *"No, Hussain no, do not let this blood fall to the ground, otherwise no crops will ever grow from this land"*
> - *Tears for Karbala by Liakat Dewji*

Imam Hussain looks up towards the sky, and a voice comes from the sky:

> *"No Hussain no, do not let this blood gush towards the sky, otherwise, no drop of rain will ever fall from the sky."*
> - *Tears for Karbala by Liakat Dewji*

Imam Hussain wipes the blood of Ali Asghar on his face, as neither the earth nor the sky is willing to accept this innocent blood.

Imam Hussain starts walking towards his tents. He sees Ali Asghar's mother Umm Rubab standing by the tent waiting anxiously for her little boy. Imam Hussain hasn't got the courage to face Umm Rubab. He struggles to walk as he does not know what to say to Umm Rubab? She had just dressed up Ali Asghar in his best outfit before giving him to Imam Hussain.

Imam Hussain walks forward and then turns back, he then again walks forward and turns back. He does this seven times while he is reciting the following:

> *"Inna Lillahi Wa Inna Ilaih Raja'oon! We are from Allah and to Him we shall return!"*
> - *Tears for Karbala by Liakat Dewji*

He finally reaches the tent where Umm Rubab was standing.

> *"Rubab, come and take your Ali Asghar. Rubab, your little soldier is back."*
> - *Tears for Karbala by Liakat Dewji*

Umm Rubab took her little boy and hugged him, and cried and cried and said:

> *"I had no idea that even children of this age are slaughtered!"*
> - *Tears for Karbala by Liakat Dewji*

Imam Hussain takes Ali Asghar back from his mother Umm Rubab. He then goes to the side of the tents where he digs a grave with his sword and buries Ali Asghar in a shallow grave. Imam Hussain then laments at the grave of Ali Asghar and sprinkles it with his tears.

One wonders as to what answer would Yazid and his army give to the Messenger of Allah on the Day of Judgment, as they had even slaughtered the youngest flower of Prophet's family.

14.8.7. Hussain, the Grandson of the Prophet

The time for the Asr prayer is approaching fast and by this time Imam Hussain is the only male adult left from his camp, except for his twenty two year old son Imam Zainul Abedeen (also known as Sajjad), who is extremely ill. His illness intermittently causes him to become unconscious, and for this reason he has not taken part in the jihad.

Imam Hussain looks around and he finds himself all alone. There is nobody left to support or help him anymore.

He sees the remains of his friends and companions such as Habib bin al-Muzahir, Muslim bin Awsaja and Zuhair ibn Qain. He sees the bodies of Awn and Muhammad, the two sons of Lady Zainab who were also martyred in Karbala. He looks at the trampled remains of Qasim, the son of his late brother Imam Hasan. He looks at the dreadful wounds in the chest of his handsome and beloved son Ali Akbar. He looks towards the banks of river Euphrates where he sees the commander of his army Abbas lay motionless. He looks towards the grave of Ali Asghar that he had just dug up.

The Imam is stricken with grief and tribulations, as a poet said:

> "O' Hussain you have been inflicted with so much suffering in just one day! With so many dead!".
> - *Tears for Karbala by Liakat Dewji*

The battle of Karbala began in the morning and since that time Imam Hussain had witnessed 72 of his companions and close family members being killed and slaughtered one after the other. Imam Hussain is tired, thirsty, and heartbroken, but his resolve is unshaken and firm, after all he is the son of Ali and the grandson of the Prophet of Allah.

14.8.8. Hussain Bids Farewell to his Son

Imam Hussain starts bidding farewell to his family who have also been suffering alongside him since the morning. Imam Hussain alongside Lady Zainab went to the tent of Imam Zainul Abedeen (Sajjad), who is lying unconscious on his bed. Bibi Zainab shook his shoulder and said:

> "Son, Sajjad! Your father has come to see you."
> - *Tears for Karbala by Liakat Dewji*

Imam Zainul Abedeen opened his eyes. He saw his father who is wearing white clothes marked with blood stains everywhere. Imam Hussain says to his son:

> "My son Sajjad! I have come to say farewell. I am going to the battlefield."
> - *Tears for Karbala by Liakat Dewji*

Imam Zainul Abedeen says:

> "Father, Father, why are you alone? Where is my uncle Abbas? Where is Ali Akbar? Where is Qasim? Where are all of your companions?"
>
> - *Tears for Karbala by Liakat Dewji*

Tears pouring down his cheeks, Imam Hussain says to his son:

> "My son, everyone is dead, except for you and me"
>
> - *Tears for Karbala by Liakat Dewji*

Imam Zainul Abedeen tries to get up from his bed and says:

> "O' Aunt Zainab! Give me my sword. I will go to the battlefield. I will save my father's life."
>
> - *Tears for Karbala by Liakat Dewji*

Imam Hussain responds:

> "No, son Sajjad, no! You are too sick for Jihad. Son Sajjad, your Jihad is still to come...."
>
> - *Tears for Karbala by Liakat Dewji*

Imam Hussain says good-bye to his son and asks him to look after the women and the children who were left behind. Imam Hussain had left behind one of his daughters in Madinah before he began his journey as she had been unwell. Imam Hussain was always mindful of Sughra and he asks his son Sajjad to take care of her too if he ever makes it back to Madinah.

Imam Hussain then advises Sajjad with these words:

> "You will have a lot of work to do after my death. You will face lots of hardship and suffering, my son Sajjad!.. Do not be afraid to fight for truth and justice!....Maintain your patience at all times, Allah is with people who remain patient. Patience, my son, patience."
>
> - *Tears for Karbala by Liakat Dewji*

14.8.9. Hussain Bids Farewell to the Women and Children

Imam Hussain now bids farewell to the women and children of his contingent. They had been incredibly patient and inspirational in their support to the Imam. Imam Hussain calls all the womenfolk of his family who gather around him. Imam Hussain then bids farewell to them all.

> "O' Zainab, O' Kulthoom, O' Sakina, O' Ruqayya, O' Rubaab, O' Fizza my greetings to you! and my Farewell to you all!"
>
> - *Tears for Karbala by Liakat Dewji*

The women come to the door of the tent and surround Imam Hussain. The women from his family began to kiss his Abaa (cloak) and his hands. Imam Hussain comforts them and asks them to return to their tents.

Imam Hussain then speaks to Lady Zainab as he is leaving the tent.

> "Sister Zainab My last will to you. Zainab, I am leaving you in charge of this caravan. Sister Zainab, take care of Imam Zainul Abedeen…..O' my sister Zainab! Look after my little Sakina. She will cry a lot after my death."
>
> - *Tears for Karbala by Liakat Dewji*

Sakina was the youngest daughter of Imam Hussain. She was four or five years of age when the tragedy of Karbala took place. On hearing the words of Imam Hussain, Lady Zainab breaks down in tears. Imam Hussain then comforts her by saying:

> "Bear patiently O Daughter of Ali for the time of crying will be lengthy."
>
> - *Tears for Karbala by Liakat Dewji*

Lady Zainab was struggling to part with Imam Hussain, and she wouldn't let him go to the battlefield. As Imam Hussain took a few steps towards his horse to head to the battle, Lady Zainab came out of the tent crying and said to Imam Hussain:

> "O' Brother! Wait for a moment that I may fulfil the last request of our mother Lady Fatima", "What request is that?" Asked the Imam as he paused."
>
> - *Lamentations – The Tragedy of the Lord of the Martyrs by Shaykh Mohammad Ishtihardi*

Lady Zainab said to the Imam:

> "Our Mother made her last will to me and said, when you sent off the light of my eyes for his final battle kiss his neck on my behalf."
>
> - *Lamentations – The Tragedy of the Lord of the Martyrs by Shaykh Mohammad Ishtihardi*

The neck of Imam Hussain was going to be severed by the army of Yazid.

Lady Zainab fulfils the will of her mother and kisses the neck of Imam Hussain and returns to her tent. The sounds of wailing and lamenting arouse from the tents as Imam Hussain heads to the battlefield.

Imam Hussain had helped all his companions and family members to mount their horses as they went into the battle. But now Imam Hussain is all alone and there is no one left to help Hussain mount his horse. As a sign of love and respect for her brother Lady Zainab again steps out of her tent and helps Imam Hussain mount the horse.

> "Brother Hussain, bring your horse nearer my tent. My brother, let me help you."
>
> - *Tears for Karbala by Liakat Dewji*

Lady Zainab held the reins as Imam Hussain mounts the horse. Imam Hussain gently strokes the horse's neck and says:

> "My faithful horse, I know you are thirsty. I know you are tired. You have been helping me carry the bodies from the battlefield since dawn. My faithful horse, for the last time take me to the battlefield….. "
>
> - *Tears for Karbala by Liakat Dewji*

But the horse of Imam Hussain does not move forward. As Imam Hussain looks down, he sees his four years old daughter Sakina clinging on to the hind legs of the horse. Sakina was Imam Hussain's youngest daughter, and she was heard murmuring something to the horse. She was saying:

> *"O horse! Do not take my father away. No, horse, no. You will not bring my father back. Since dawn, everyone who has gone to the battlefield has not come back. Please, horse, do not take my father away. I will not be able to live without my father. Please, horse, please."*

- *Tears for Karbala by Liakat Dewji*

On seeing his daughter Imam Hussain dismounts the horse and says:

> *'O' Sakina, you are the great granddaughter of the Holy Prophet! I love you so much that if you tell me not to go, I will not go. But how will I be able to face the Prophet of Allah on the Day of Judgment?' Fighting back her tears the four years old Sakina can only manage to say, 'Bismillah, father!' (go on father!), the four years old holds the reins as her father mounts the horse for the last time"*

- *Life History of Ahlulbayt and their families*

Imam Hussain mounts his horse and heads to the battlefield.

14.8.10. Hussain Heads to the Battlefield

As Imam Hussain heads to the battlefield, he is thirsty, he is tired, he is wounded and he is heartbroken, but he is invigorated with the desire to meet his Creator. As Imam Hussain rides towards the enemy, they shower him with arrows, but Imam Hussain carries on and attacks the enemy with such a vigour and intensity that they disperse in all directions.

Imam Hussain engages in fierce battles with the enemy and one by one he kills some of the finest fighters in the army of Yazid. The forces of Yazid are pushed back by the might of Hussain's attack. Imam Hussain carries the sword of Ali with him which was called al-Zulfikar. Ali had fought with this sword in the battles of Badr, Uhud, Hunayn, Moat and Khaibar, under the command of the Holy Prophet.

Despite all the tribulations and the grief that Imam Hussain had endured, and despite the fact that he hasn't had a sip of water for three days, he truly fights in a manner that reminded the enemy that he was indeed the true inheritor of Ali's bravery and velour. No one would dare approach Imam Hussain as he would attack the enemy at will. The soldiers of Yazid would flee in all directions as soon as they would see the Imam approaching.

Imam Hussain pushes the army back and reaches the banks of river Euphrates. Yazid's army had blocked the river to deny Imam Hussain and his supporters any water. But Imam Hussain does not drink the water as the women and children in his camp are still thirsty.

Humayd ibn Muslim gives an account of Imam Hussain's battle:

> *"By Allah I have not seen a person so harried by his adversaries, whose sons and companions have been slain and who is being attacked from all directions that fights with such strength. I saw him being attacked by the horse and foot yet he would fearlessly advance to them in a way that caused them to flee as a pack of foxes would flee and scatter from a raging lion."*

- *(Kitab al-Irshad)*

On seeing the bravery of Imam Hussain and the damage that he was inflicting on the troops, Umar ibn Saad who was the commander of Yazid's army in Karbala orders a full assault on Imam Hussain from all sides. Yazid's army is attacking Imam Hussain with arrows, with spears, with stones, but still nobody dares to come near the Imam.

A voice comes from the sky:

> "O' Hussain Allah is pleased with you…the time has come to put your sword down. Enough Hussain enough! Come to us! The Prophet awaits your arrival Hussain……"
> - *Tears for Karbala by Liakat Dewji*

Imam Hussain puts the sword into the sheath and lowers himself on the horse's back.

Seeing that Imam Hussain had sheathed his sword the enemy comes nearer and attacks him with whatever they could find. Some soldiers would throw stones at Imam Hussain while others would attack him with their swords and spears. Imam Hussain has hundreds of wounds and he is bleeding profusely. As Imam Hussain finally fell from the horse his body is pierced with so many arrows that he does not fully touch the ground.

While the body of Imam Hussain is resting on the arrows he supplicates to Allah:

> "O' You who preserves every soul with what it has earned, judge between me and them O' best of judges."
> - *Maqtal al-Husayn Al-Muqarram*

Hilal ibn Nafi, a commander in the army of Yazid narrates the moments when Imam Hussain descended to the ground.

> "By Allah I have not seen a slain man whose beard is covered with his blood, more admirable than him, nor a face more radiant than his. The beauty of his posture and the splendour of his face kept me from the thought of killing him."
> - *(A'yan al-Shi'ah)*

Shimr, who was considered to be the most brutal officer of Yazid's army walks towards Imam Hussain with a dagger in his hand.

Imam Hussain makes a request:

> "O' Shimr, I know your intention. I ask of you to give me a little time to do couple of Sajdas (prostrations)."
> - *Tears for Karbala by Liakat Dewji*

Imam Hussain does the first Sajdah (prostration) and says:

> "O' Allah! All Praise is to You and You Alone! I have abandoned the creation in Your loveI have orphaned my children so that I may see You. If the swords were to cut me into pieces in Your love even then my heart would not long for other than You"
> - *Lamentations – The Tragedy of the Lord of the Martyrs by Shaykh Mohammad Ishtihardi*

Imam Hussain lifts his head and went down to perform his second Sajdah. But Shimr does not allow Imam Hussain to lift his head again. He beheads the grandson of the Prophet while he is prostrating.

A voice rings out:

> "Quitalul Hussain o bay Karbala! (Hussain has been killed on the plains of Karbala!)"
> "Zabihal Hussain o bay Karbala! (Hussain has been slaughtered on the plains of Karbala!)"
> - *Tears for Karbala by Liakat Dewji*

Lady Zainab comes out of the tent and sees the head of Imam Hussain on a lance. She cries out:

> "O' Hussain! O' Hussain! O' Hussain! We are from Allah and to Him we will return!"
> - *Tears for Karbala by Liakat Dewji*

14.8.11. Hussain's Body is Trampled with Hooves

Readers would recall that Ubaydullah had written a letter to Umar ibn Saad asking him to disfigure Imam Hussain and to trample his chest and his back after he is killed.

> '...I did not send you to Hussain to hold off from fighting him, ...disfigure them, for they deserve that. If Hussain is killed, make the horses trample on his chest and back, for he is a disobedient rebel, an evil man .....'
> - *p.110. The History of al-Tabari; The Caliphate of Yazid. b. Mu'awiyah. Volume XIX. Translated by I.K.A. Howard. State University of New York Press, USA, 1990.*

As per the instructions of Ubaydullah, Umar ibn Saad called out on his men:

> "Whom from you will take charge to trample the chest and the back of al-Hussain under the hooves of their horses?"
> - *Al-Tabari (5:415)*
> - *al-Maqatil (pg.79) of Abu al-Faraj*
> - *Muruj al-Dhahab (3:72) of al-Mas'udi*

There were ten men from the army who offered to carry out this heinous crime against the grandson of the Prophet. They rode their horses upon the beheaded body of Imam Hussain and crushed every bone in his chest and back. After committing their crime, the men went to Ubaydullah to claim their reward.

Ubaydullah asked them as to what they have done to deserve this reward, they responded by saying:

> "We are the ones who rode on strong horses and crushed the bones in al-Hussain's chest and back. We are the ones who trampled his body until his chest became as soft as kneaded dough,"
> - *The Journey of Tears: From Karbala to Kufa, Maqtal by Qazi Dr. Shaikh Abbas Borhany al-Waleed*

The crimes against the family of the Prophet in Karbala saw no bounds!

The men of Umar ibn Saad did not just trample upon the body of Imam Hussain, but they also trampled upon the Sunnah of the Prophet. The Prophet had said:

> 'I am from Hussain and Hussain is from me. Allah loves the one who loves Hussain...'
> - *Sunan al-Tirmidhi. Hadith 3708. Book of Superiorities. Chapter; the Superiority of Imam Hasan and Hussain.*

Crushing the body of Imam Hussain was to crush the beautiful Sunnah of the Prophet.

Imam Hussain's body was robbed of his turban, his sword, his shoes, and even all his clothes were stripped off his body. They left his body naked and unburied on the plains of Karbala. Such despicable treatment of a dead person was unheard off in Arabia, even during the pre-Islamic days such atrocities were not committed.

The soldiers of Yazid behave in the most inhuman, outrageous and deplorable way towards the family of the Prophet. Umar ibn Saad orders that the head of Imam Hussain which was mounted on a lance is immediately sent to Ubaydullah in Kufa. An army officer by the name of Kholi takes the severed head of Imam Hussain to Kufa. Before taking the head of Imam Hussain to Kufa it is displayed to the joyous army of Yazid who were already celebrating the defeat of Hussain.

Contrary to the celebrations in the camp of Yazid on the killing of Imam Hussain, the actions of the Prophet on the Day of Ashura tell us a different story. Ibn Abbas who was the uncle of the Prophet saw a dream about the tragedy of Karbala, in which he saw the Prophet on the Day of Ashura, where the Prophet was collecting the blood of Hussain and his companions. Ibn Abbas narrates his dream in the following words:

> *'One afternoon I dreamt of Holy Prophet (saw) standing with his hair disturbed and with dust tangled in them and he was holding a phial filled with blood. I said to the Prophet (saw): 'O Allah's Prophet, what are you holding?' The Prophet (saw) replied: 'This is the blood of Hussain and his companions that I have been collecting all the day long." They did calculation and found out that he (Hussain) was killed a day before it (the day of dream).*

- Al-Hakim in Al-Mustadrak Ala Sahihayn. Vol. 4, Pg. # 439-440.
- Ahmad ibn Hanbal in Musnad Ahmad ibn Hanbal. Vol. 4, H. # 2165, Pg. # 59 - 60.
- Al-Albani in Mishkatul Masabih of Al-Albani. Vol. 3, Pg. # 1741-1742.

The Prophet had been collecting the blood of Hussain and his companions all day long on the fateful Day of Ashura. Prophet was seen with his hair disturbed and with dust tangled in them while he was collecting the blood of Hussain. Prophet had immense love for Imam Hussain. Prophet used to play with Imam Hussain when he was a child. He used to make Imam Hussain sit on his shoulders and back and carry him around. Prophet could not possibly leave his grandson alone on the Day of Ashura. He was present on the plains of Karbala collecting every single drop of Hussain's blood.

A similar tradition is also narrated by the wife of the Prophet Umm Salma.

> *I went to Umm Al-Salama and she was crying. So I asked what makes you cry? She said: I saw the Messenger of Allah (saw) in a dream, and there was dust on his head and beard." I said: 'What is wrong O Messenger of Allah (saw)?' He said: "I just witnessed the martyrdom of Hussain (a.s).*

- Siyar A'lam An-Nubala. Vol. 3, Pg. # 316

The wife of the Prophet Umm Salma also saw the messenger of Allah in a dream where he was present on the plains of Karbala witnessing the martyrdom of his grandson Hussain, with dust in his head and beard, implying that the Prophet was extremely disturbed and distressed at seeing the atrocities committed against his children.

No doubt, on the Day of Judgment the Prophet of Allah will present the innocent blood of Hussain in the highest of the courts, and the perpetrators of this crime would face the everlasting justice of Allah.

14.9. The Tyranny Against Hussain's Women and Children

Imam Hussain was killed in the most inhumane of the ways, but despite such brutality the tyranny against the family of the Prophet and its supporters did not end. Umar ibn Saad wants all the bodies of the companions and the family members of Imam Hussain to be beheaded, so that the heads of the martyrs can be taken to Ubaydullah in Kufa and later to Yazid in Damascus. Every single martyr is beheaded on the orders of Umar ibn Saad and their heads are dispatched to Ubaydullah.

The soldiers were unable to find the body of Ali Asghar as Imam Hussain had buried him by one of his tents. The orders were given to pierce the ground with spears until the body of Ali Asghar is uncovered. A successful hit finds the little boy, his body plucked out from the ground with a spear. He is then beheaded like the rest. All the heads are then mounted on spears and distributed amongst the army officers to be taken back to Kufa. These heads will be paraded through the streets of Kufa as a lesson and a reminder to anyone who plans to challenge the authority of Yazid.

The survivors among the contingent of Imam Hussain are his son Imam Zainul Abedeen (who is ill), the womenfolk of his family and the accompanying children. Sources indicate that this is a group of around forty people.

The next target for the tyrannical army of Yazid were the tents and the residence of Imam Hussain. After beheading all the martyrs, the enemy sets its sights on the camp of Imam Hussain. With no one left to defend, the soldiers of Yazid marched into the tents where the women and children of Prophet's family were sheltering. They were already shattered and traumatized but these grief-stricken ladies were subjected to even more torment and indignity.

Yazid's soldiers ransacked the tents of Imam Hussain. They would lay their hands on anything that they would find of value or interest. The family of the Prophet was even stripped off the little items they had in their possession. They even snatched the jewellery that some ladies and young girls were wearing. The soldiers even took away simple items and clothes, some of which had been stitched by Lady Fatima (mother of Imam Hussain) with her own hands. The heartless soldiers even stole those few possessions of sentimental value from the family of the Prophet.

14.9.1. Sakina, the Beloved Daughter of Hussain

Imam Hussain was very close and attached to his youngest daughter Sakina. We saw how she clung on to the horse of Imam Hussain as he has heading to the battlefield. She would often sleep on the chest of Imam Hussain and wouldn't let go off him all night. Imam Hussain had bought her some earrings which she always used to wear.

As the beleaguered family of Imam Hussain was being robbed of all their belongings a man from the army of Yazid approaches the little girl. Sakina is scared and frightened and wants to run away, but the man gets hold of her and slaps her across the face. He is after her earrings. The little girl pleads with the man not to harm her and not to touch her earrings. But the cruel solider forcefully pulls off her earrings, leaving her earlobes torn and bleeding. The little girl is in excruciating pain, and she runs off to her aunt Lady Zainab who tries to comfort her.

Such was the callous behaviour of Yazid's army that even the defenceless children of Imam Hussain were not spared.

The Prophet had not only asked the Muslims to love and follow his Ahlulbayt, but he had also warned them about mistreating his family.

The Prophet had said:

> "............ I am leaving in you the Two Valuables: The Book of God and the members of my House. The Almighty informed me that they will never part with each other until they join me at the Basin (on the Day of Judgment). Beware how you shall treat them after me........"

- *Imam Ahmad Al-Musnad part 3 p. 17, narrated by Abu Sa-eed Al-Khidri.*

It seems as if the army of Yazid was determined to undermine and make a mockery of every single word that Prophet had said about his family.

14.9.2. Headscarves are Snatched from the Women of the Prophet's Family

On the orders of Umar ibn Saad, the army of Yazid commits another huge crime, probably the biggest crime in the entire tragedy of Karbala. Angry at the lack of war booty, they start snatching the veils and headscarves from the pious women of Prophet's family. Out of shame the women of Imam Hussain's family were hiding behind each other as the soldiers would step forward to remove their veils. This humiliation and indignity were too much to bear, and it was a step too far for the family of the Prophet.

The faces and the hair of the daughters of the Holy Prophet were exposed for all to see.

Even today if somebody forcefully pulls off the hijab (head scarf) of a Muslim lady, it is a huge crime in the eyes of Islam. Muslims would never accept such indecency, and the culprit of such a crime would be severely punished. But this crime was committed against the family of the Prophet in Karbala. It was committed against the daughters of Ali and Fatima. It was committed against the very family that had in fact introduced the practice of hijab (head scarf) to this world.

The crimes of the Umayyad's will not go unanswered on the Day of Judgment, and Allah will see to each and every crime that they had committed against the defenceless family of the Prophet.

Not satisfied with the atrocities that they had already committed against the family of the Prophet, Umar ibn Saad orders his army to burn the tents of Imam Hussain. As the soldiers starts burning the tents the terrified ladies of Prophet's family would gather their children and run from one tent to the other, trying to escape the burning flames. When the last tent was also set on fire the family of the Prophet had no choice but to come out in the open, without their veils and without their headscarves.

These were moments of untenable humiliation for the daughters of the Prophet. These pious ladies had never been out in public without their full Islamic dress code. But now these shy and virtuous ladies were in full view of the soldiers of Yazid. It was something that was unthinkable for the family of the Prophet. This was an act of an outrageous indignity on part of the Umayyads, on top of all the other sufferings and tribulations that they had put the family of the Prophet through.

Even the tents of Imam Hussain which were the only shelter left for the family of the Prophet was burned down. The Prophet's Household was dispossessed of everything that they had. The survivors spent the night under the open sky, with nothing to protect them from the dust and the desert wind blowing on the plains of Karbala. Lady Zainab gathered all the women and children in one place. They huddled together as a group surrounded by the army of Yazid, who were awaiting the orders from Ubaydullah for their next atrocity.

14.9.3. The Parading of Women and Children from the Prophet's Family

The family of the Prophet is now under the captivity of Ubaydullah's forces, the governor of Yazid in Kufa. As a show of victory for his men and as a show of ultimate humiliation for the family of the Prophet, Ubaydullah orders the public parading of the family of the Prophet through the streets of Kufa. The aim was twofold, firstly to rub salt into the wounds of the Ahlulbayt, and secondly it was a lesson for anyone else who might be thinking of opposing the Umayyads or challenging the might of Yazid.

The family of the Prophet now only comprises of women and children expect for Imam Zainul Abedeen, who is the only surviving adult male member of Hussain's family.

The orders of Umar ibn Saad who is the commander of Ubaydullah's forces in Karbala were harsh and brutal. The women and children were to be tied with ropes to be backs of the camels without any saddles, so as to cause them maximum pain and discomfort. The punishment for Imam Zainul Abedeen was even more severe. His hands and feet were chained, and an iron collar with inward spikes put around his neck. He was then made to walk all the way to Kufa, while the men of Umar ibn Saad would lash him if he slowed down.

These are not just fairy tales from the Islamic history, but these are the actual atrocities that were committed against the family of the Prophet in Karbala.

The journey for the family of the Prophet as captives of the Umayyads begins in Karbala on the 11th of Muharram, a day after the martyrdom of Imam Hussain. The captives reach the outskirts of Kufa on the same night, but they are not allowed to enter the city. Ubaydullah, the governor of Kufa sends a message that the captives must spend the night outside the city of Kufa, as he wants to stage-manage their entry as a victory parade which must be witnessed and celebrated by the locals in broad daylight.

Ubaydullah also orders that the heads of all the martyrs should be paraded alongside the captives. The head of Imam Hussain and the 72 other martyrs are sent on lances to the outskirts of Kufa, to join the captives who had been waiting there all night. The people of Kufa were told that a group of people who had rebelled against the government of Yazid had been killed, and their women and children would be paraded through the streets in the morning.

Being the cunning and the devious man that Ubaydullah was, he did not inform the people of Kufa that Imam Hussain and his companions had been killed in Karbala, so as to avoid any untoward reaction from the locals. At this stage very few people in Kufa had any idea as to what had actually taken place in Karbala.

Readers would recall that Imam Hussain was stopped on the outskirts of Kufa and was not allowed to enter the city. Also, Imam Hussain's messenger Abdullah Yaqtar who was carrying Imam Hussain's letter for the people of Kufa was killed before he could reach the city. Most of the people of Kufa had no idea about the whereabouts of Imam Hussain or if he had been killed in Karbala.

On the morning of the 12th of Muharram the parade of the captives starts from the outskirts of Kufa and wiggles its way through the streets and proceeds to the governor's palace where Ubaydullah bin Ziyad is residing. At the front are the heads of the martyrs mounted on spears, followed by the women and children from the family of the Prophet, who are bound by ropes on the backs of the camels. Imam Zainul Abedeen, the only remaining son of Hussain is still on foot and his hands and feet are bound in chains.

The ladies from the family of the Prophet are barefaced and bare head with no scarf or veil to cover their dignity.

The soldiers of Ubaydullah are beating the drums and waving the flags in a show of victory. The crowd that has gathered is cheering the soldiers and jeering the captives. As the parade makes its way through the streets of Kufa some women ask the captives about their identity. When they find out that these women are from the family of the Prophet and were in the contingent of Imam Hussain, they are shocked and are in disbelief. The people of Kufa had been misinformed about the identity of the captives and they had no idea as to who these prisoners were.

Once the captives reached Ubaydullah's palace he insults, taunts and ridicules them to further humiliate and disgrace the family of the Prophet. The captives i.e., the women and the children from the family of the Prophet are then imprisoned in Kufa, until the orders are received from Yazid to send them to Syria (Damascus).

The tyranny against the family of the Prophet sees no end.

The Prophet of Allah had said:

> *"Acknowledgment of Aale-Muhammad (the family of Muhammad) means salvation from the fire, and love for them is a passport for crossing the bridge of the Siraat, and obedience to them is a protection from divine wrath."*
> - Kitab al-Shafa, by Qadhi 'Ayadh, published in 1328 AH, v2, p40
> - Yanabi al-Mawaddah, al-Qundoozi al-Hanafi, section 65, p370

The Prophet had informed the Muslims that the love and the obedience of Ahlulbayt would keep them on the path of Salvation and would allow them to cross the bridge of Siraat on the Day of Judgment. But the actions of Yazid's army completely negated the words and the Sunnah of the Prophet in all its manifestations.

14.9.4. The Women and Children are Paraded Again in Damascus

The whole exercise of humiliating and shaming of the captives is again repeated, but this time on a much larger scale. Yazid orders Ubaydullah to send the captives to Syria (Damascus) so that they could be paraded at the seat of his power. The aim again is twofold, firstly to humiliate the family of the Prophet as much as possible, and secondly to warn any potential opponents not to step out of line.

The streets of Damascus are decorated with ornaments, silk, and colourful flags. Drums are being played on the streets. The people are all dressed up and look their best. The whole city of Damascus is in a festive and a carnival mood. People are told that the festivities are to celebrate the victory of Yazid over the rebels.

As the family of the Prophet arrives in Damascus, they are made to wait for three days outside the gates of the city, while the streets are being decorated and while the preparations for the victory parade are underway.

Finally, after three days of waiting the parade of victory gets underway. It snakes through the crowded streets of Damascus and heads to the palace of Yazid. Just like in Kufa at the front of the parade is the head of Imam Hussain followed by the heads of the other martyrs. Behind the heads of the martyrs is the family of the Prophet who are being jeered all the way. The same atrocities that were committed in Kufa are being repeated in Damascus. The women and the children are tied to the backs of the camels with ropes and without any saddles. Imam Zainul Abedeen is made to walk with his hands and feet chained and an iron collar around his neck which has inward spikes.

Yazid has gathered his government ministers, dignitaries, ambassadors, and key members of the public at his palace to share the festivities of victory. The head of Imam Hussain and the heads of the other martyrs are brought to the palace and are laid out in trays. The women and children are also chained, as they are paraded in front of Yazid and his guests in his magnificent palace. The women are absolutely mortified at this public dishonouring. They try and hide behind each other to avoid the limelight. They are bare head and barefaced in front of Yazid and his entourage with no head scarfs or veils to cover their dignity.

As Yazid sits on his chair he takes out a stick and starts disrespecting the head of Imam Hussain. He strikes the lips of Imam Hussain with the stick, while he taunts, insults, and ridicules the family of the Prophet, who are bound in chains and are being paraded in his palace. On seeing Yazid's behaviour a companion of the Prophet, Abu Barzah al-Aslami who was among the audience says to Yazid:

> *'Take your cane away! By God! How often have I seen the Messenger of Allah kiss that mouth!'*

- *p.76. The History of al-Tabari;*
- *The Caliphate of Yazid. b. Mu'awiyah. Volume XIX. Translated by I.K.A. Howard. State University of New York Press, USA, 1990. Reports say that Ibn Ziyad too showed the same gross and heinous behaviour of poking his teeth with a cane. See, p.165. The History of al-Tabari;*

Despite Abu Barzah al-Aslami reminding Yazid that it was the Sunnah of the Prophet to kiss the lips of Imam Hussain, Yazid carries on with his insults against the grandson of the Prophet.

14.9.5. The Imprisonment of the Prophet's Family

As if the atrocities had not gone far enough Yazid now orders the imprisonment of the family of the Prophet. Imam Zainul Abedeen, and all the women and children of Prophet's family are imprisoned in an old building which has no roof. The torture that Yazid had planned for the family of the Prophet was to expose them to the blazing sun throughout the day, and after sunset they would have to endure the chill of the night. He also gives orders that the heads of the martyrs are to be put on a public display. The heads of all the martyrs including that of Imam Hussain is hung from the palace gate for three days, as a show of victory and as a lesson to any opponents who might be thinking of challenging Yazid.

Apart from imprisoning the family of the Prophet out in the open they are also subjected to food rationing. This brutal punishment had a devastating effect on all the family members especially the children. After months of imprisonment many of the family members are barely able to stand and walk, as they had lost so much weight and had become so weak.

Sakina, the youngest daughter of Imam Hussain who was slapped across the face and whose earrings were snatched, leaving her earlobes bleeding, was unable to stand this new form of torture. She was only five years of age, and she could not bear the heat of the day and the cold of the night. She used to miss Imam Hussain terribly and was at loss at his death. She became seriously ill and suffered for many weeks before she eventually died in that prison. As there was nowhere else to bury her, Imam Zainul Abedeen made a small grave inside the prison and buried the little girl there.

14.9.6. A Place to Remember and Mourn the Tragedy

As news began to spread about the tragedy of Karbala and how Imam Hussain and his companions were killed, and subsequently how the family of the Prophet had been imprisoned, people begin to react against this atrocity. In many provinces of the Islamic State people started turning against Yazid who was now coming under increasing pressure to release the captives.

As a result of public pressure and to save his own Caliphate Yazid decided to set the captives free after one year of imprisonment.

The captives requested for a place where they could mourn and remember the martyrs of Karbala, for until now they get beaten by the prison guards whenever they mourn or recall the events of Karbala. A house was allocated where the family of the Prophet could mourn and lament over the tragedy of Karbala and remember their loved ones.

This in fact marked the birth of the institution of "Azadari" or "Majalis", as we know it today, where people would gather to mourn the tragedy of Karbala. It was a practice that was started by the family of the Prophet after they were set free. It was the very first thing they did after gaining their freedom from the tyranny of Yazid.

To this day the followers of Ahlulbayt have kept this practice alive by mourning the tragedy of Karbala during the first ten days of the month of Muharram, since Imam Hussain arrived in Karbala on the second of Muharram and he was killed on the tenth of Muharram. The mourning ceremonies are done to honour the Sunnah (tradition) of the family of the Prophet, which they had established upon their release from the captivity of Yazid.

14.10. How could this Happen?

The question now arises as to how could this possibly happen? How was it possible that the leadership of the Islamic State could slaughter the entire family of the Prophet? After all this was the very Islamic State that Prophet of Allah had founded and nurtured. How could it be possible that Hussain who was the grandson of the Holy Prophet and who was among the Ahlulbayt was beheaded on the orders of a Muslim Caliph? Even the women and children of Prophet's family were not spared. Ali Asghar, who was only six months old was struck down with an arrow and then beheaded.

The women of Prophet's family who were the most honourable ladies were dishonoured in the most appalling way. Their headscarves were snatched forcefully, and they were taken as captives and paraded on the streets bare faced and bare headed. The same women and children from Prophet's family were then imprisoned in a building without a roof, where they were exposed to the heat of the day and to the chill of the night.

Surely the family of the Prophet did not deserve such a treatment.

The Prophet of Allah had not only instructed the Muslims to love and respect his family, but he had also instructed the Muslims to follow in their footsteps. The Prophet had classed his Ahlulbayt alongside the Holy Quran as a source of knowledge and guidance for the Muslim Ummah. The Prophet had compared his Ahlulbayt to the Ark of the Noah, implying that anybody who follows the Ahlulbayt would be saved and would stay on the path of salvation.

The Prophet had clearly said on many occasions that he was at war with those who were at war with his Ahlulbayt. The Prophet had specifically said about Imam Hussain that Hussain was from him, and he was from Hussain.

Leaving aside the issue of following, loving, or respecting the Ahlulbayt, the leadership of the Islamic State ends up slaughtering and killing the entire family of the Prophet including their children.

Something must have gone wrong somewhere!

The key question now arises as to how was it possible that the Islamic State which was founded and headed by the Prophet of Allah could end up in the hands of a person like Yazid? Yazid had no assemblance of Islam in him and was an absolute tyrant. How could he possibly become the head of the Muslim Ummah? How was it possible that a person who was an open sinner and a person who would openly ridicule the tenets of Islam would become the head of the very Islamic State that was established to be ruled by the book of Allah and the Sunnah of the Prophet?

How was it possible that a person who was sitting on the pulpit of the Prophet i.e., the place where the Prophet of Allah used to sit would in fact kill the entire family of the Prophet? How could it be possible that the Umayyad's who had fought the Prophet for almost two decades, would end up becoming the leaders of the very Islamic State that Prophet had established as a base to secure the future of the Muslims?

The answers to all these thought-provoking questions unfortunately lie in the fateful meeting of Saqifah!

The regression of the Caliphate did not happen overnight. But without a shadow of a doubt, it began with the meeting of Saqifah where the nominee of the Prophet was side-lined to choose a candidate who would be more acceptable to the majority of the Qurayshite tribes. The Quraysh of Makkah had been the sworn enemy of the Prophet. The Quraysh were not willing to see a candidate who was from the same clan as the Prophet to rule over them. The Qurayshite clans did not want to see the leadership of the Muslims confined to the clan of the Prophet i.e., the Banu Hashim. Hence, they opposed the leadership of Ali who happened to be from the same clan as the Prophet.

This decline at the very top of the Islamic State began when the person who was trained by the Prophet for twenty-five years to lead the Muslims i.e., Ali, was ignored in favour of an older and a more politically acceptable figure i.e., Caliph Abu Bakr. The downfall began when instead of merit the principle of Shura (Consultation) was used to side-line the clear Sunnah of the Prophet. The downturn started when the trend of al-ijtihad (independent judgment) was given precedence over the traditions of the Prophet.

As Abu Bakr became the first Caliph the leadership of the Muslim Ummah slipped away from the Ahlulbayt, in complete contradiction to the wishes and the plan of the Prophet, and it eventually ended up in the hands of the Umayyads, a tribe who had been the biggest enemy of Islam and Muslim during the time of the Prophet.

Caliph Abu Bakr had justified his Caliphate to Ali by insisting that the meeting of Saqifah had taken place so suddenly that he did not have the time to consult or call upon Ali. However, when Caliph Abu Bakr had the time and the opportunity to choose his successor, he nominated Caliph Umar who was his right-hand man, and he decided to ignore Ali all together.

Despite knowing the past of the Umayyads and the history of their enmity towards the Prophet, Caliph Umar appointed Muawiyah as the governor of Syria. Muawiyah was the son of Abu Sufyan and Abu Sufyan had been the biggest enemy of the Prophet. Abu Sufyan had fought the Prophet of Allah for almost twenty years until he was defeated at the Conquest of Makkah. Muawiyah's mother had mutilated the body of Prophet's uncle and had made anklets out of it.

Caliph Umar was generally very strict with his governors, but he gave Muawiyah the kind of freedom that he had not given to any of his other governors. This enabled Muawiyah to consolidate his power base even further in Syria.

As the reign of Caliph Umar came to an end, he formed a committee of six people which was heavily biased towards the Umayyad's to choose the next caliph. The committee made an unprecedented demand of following the Sunnah of the first two Caliphs as a condition for becoming the third Caliph. The reason for this innovation was to again deny Ali and the Ahlulbayt their right. The unwarranted innovation was simply used to side-line Ali and to give the leadership of the Muslims to Caliph Uthman, who was another key Umayyad leader.

On acquiring power Caliph Uthman began the systematic process of empowering the Umayyads. The key provinces in the Islamic State which were full of resources such as Basra, Kufa and Egypt were all given to the fellow Umayyads. Caliph Umar had appointed Muawiyah as the governor of Syria, but Caliph Uthman added Palestine, Homs and Quneitra to Muawiyah's authority too. The fortunes of Muawiyah had doubled under Caliph Uthman's rule and Muawiyah became the governor of what can be termed today as greater Syria.

The influence of Muawiyah had started to grow during the Caliphate of Umar. However, under the leadership of Caliph Uthman, Muawiyah's influence and authority in Syria became almost absolute and free of any supervision from the central government. Within a space of few years Syria almost became an autonomous region within the Islamic State, and Muawiyah became a political powerhouse of the Muslim world. Muawiyah's authority and influence had grown so much that he was able to muster an army of around one hundred thousand (100,000) men into the battlefield.

As the Caliphate of Uthman came to a violent end and Ali became the next Caliph, Muawiyah refused to accept Ali's authority as the new leader and embarked on a plan to bring down Ali's Caliphate. Ali needed some support at that stage to take on the Umayyad strongman Muawiyah. However instead of supporting Ali, Lady Aisha and other prominent companions launched a war against Ali, on the pretext that Ali had not brought the killers of Caliph Uthman to justice. This severely weakened Ali's hand both politically and militarily, and as a result Ali was unable to defeat the insurgency led by Muawiyah.

After Ali was killed his elder son Hasan briefly took over the reins of power, however Muawiyah had other ideas. Muawiyah could not accept the leadership of Muslims to be in the hands of Banu Hashim especially in the hands of the Ahlulbayt. Muawiyah bribed and coerced Imam Hasan's army into submission forcing Imam Hasan to sign a peace treaty.

After acquiring power Muawiyah broke all the conditions that he had signed in the treaty, which had in fact categorically barred Muawiyah from appointing a successor. Contrary to the conditions of the treaty with Imam Hasan, Muawiyah forcefully appointed his son Yazid as the new Caliph over the Muslims.

Yazid was an open sinner and a transgressor of the Islamic laws who would openly flout the Sunnah of the Prophet. Yazid had absolutely no assemblance of Islam in his character. The words of corruption and nepotism are way too insignificant to define the Caliphate of Yazid. He not only used the Islamic treasury as his personal wealth, but he also ruled with an iron fist and killed his opponents with impunity.

The early Muslims who had worked tirelessly for the establishment of the Islamic State could not have imagined that a person like Yazid would one day be at the helm of the Islamic State. But this is exactly what took place in the Islamic history, and it happened because the participants of Saqifah had ignored the plan devised by the Prophet for the leadership of the Muslim Ummah.

The participants of Saqifah used their own ijtihad (independent judgment) to choose someone who they believed would be acceptable to the Quraysh, rather than to choose someone who was appointed by the Prophet.

If the participants of Saqifah had followed the directive of the Prophet, then the likes of Muawiyah and Yazid would have never become the Caliphs. Muawiyah had absolutely no power or influence until Caliph Umar appointed him as the governor of Syria. And Caliph Umar himself was appointed by Caliph Abu Bakr and Caliph Abu Bakr was chosen in the fateful meeting of Saqifah.

After becoming the Caliph Yazid demanded form Hussain that he gives him allegiance as the new Caliph and the leader of the Muslim Ummah, since Yazid knew that the real authority of the Islamic leadership rested with the Ahlulbayt. Hussain being the son of Ali and the grandson of the Holy Prophet refused to give allegiance to a character like Yazid.

On Hussain's refusal Yazid ordered the killing of the entire family of the Prophet and imprisoned the women and children of Prophet's household, to show that he is the one who has the authority over the Muslims and not the Ahlulbayt.

We as Muslims living in 21st century cannot undo the tragedy of Karbala, nor can we reverse and unfold the suffering and the tribulations that the family of the Prophet went through. However, we can distance ourselves from the events that caused and led to the tragedy of Karbala.

Leaving all the other arguments aside, a simple observation of the historical chain of events that led to the tragedy of Karbala, prove beyond any doubt that the path adopted by history against Ali was flawed and disastrous. This path eventually brought the enemies of the Prophet i.e., the Umayyad's to become the undisputed rulers of the Muslim Ummah.

It is only logical and reasonable to expect that as followers of Prophet's Sunnah, we recognize Ali as the true successor of the Prophet, and we distance ourselves from the injustice that took place in Saqifah against the nominee of the Prophet, since it was that injustice which eventually resulted in the killing and the imprisonment of the entire family of the Prophet. A family that Prophet had in fact asked to be followed, loved, and revered after his death.

This would be the most appropriate way to pay homage and tribute to the martyrs of Karbala, whose innocent blood still awaits the recognition and the acknowledgement that it deserves from the wider Muslim Ummah. The innocent blood of Hussain and his companions demands from the Muslims that we recognize that what happened in Karbala was in fact set in motion in Saqifah.

14.11. Defaming the Stand of Hussain

It is most unfortunate and sad to see that there is a segment of the Muslim population who claim to be the Ahl-e-Sunnah, the followers of the Sunnah, but they try their up most to defame and weaken the significance of the stand of Imam Hussain. They try and confuse the minds of the ordinary Muslims with a variety of theories which would take the shine away from the virtuous and the principled stand of Imam Hussain.

They try and move the focus away from the actual reasons that prompted Imam Hussain to take such a stand and move it in a direction that essentially protects the Umayyad's from any wrongdoing. They cleverly try to shift the focus of the tragedy of Karbala to the invitation that Imam Hussain had received from the people of Kufa. They advocate that it was the people of Kufa who had invited Imam Hussain, and they are ones who betrayed him, and they are the ones who had killed him.

This narrative is cleverly used to undermine the stand of Imam Hussain with two key objectives. Firstly, it exonerates the Umayyads and the likes of Muawiyah and Yazid from any responsibility in the killing of Imam Hussain. Secondly, it dilutes the actual stand of Imam Hussain as it gives the impression that Imam Hussain was killed because of a betrayal by the people of Kufa, rather than the actual stand that he had taken against the Umayyads.

Along similar lines the supporters of the Umayyads would use yet another theme to undermine the principled stand of Imam Hussain. They would say that Imam Hussain was advised by the elders of the

Muslim Ummah such as Ibn Abbas, Abdullah ibn Umar, and Abdullah ibn Zubair not to pursue the path that he had embarked upon. And since Imam Hussain did not listen to the advice of these key Islamic personalities he eventually got killed in Karbala. The aim is to portray Imam Hussain as a stubborn and an emotional individual who would not heed the advice of his elders.

Some supporters of Muawiyah and Yazid would even claim that Imam Hussain was actually after the Caliphate, and Imam Hussain was indeed a rebel, since he had challenged the legitimate Caliphate of Yazid which the rest of the Muslim Ummah had already accepted.

The aim of all these narratives is to damage and malign the magnificent stand of Imam Hussain, by diverting the attention from the actual reasons that prompted Imam Hussain to take such a stand into an area of history that has no relevance to the principled stand taken by Imam Hussain.

The simple reason why such narratives are put forward is to protect the system of governance which had enabled a personality like Yazid to come to the helm of power. The advocates of these narratives know full well that Yazid did not miraculously became the Caliph. It wasn't as if Allah had thrown Yazid from the sky and he had landed on the seat of the Caliphate. There was a history of fifty years in the making which brought a character like Yazid to the pulpit of the Prophet.

The virtuous stand of Hussain had shown beyond any doubt that the system which had brought Yazid to power had digressed from the path of the Prophet, and this decline in the institution of Caliphate did not happen at the hands of the non-Muslims. It happened due to the actions and the policies of the companions of the Prophet who choose to ignore the clear commands of the Prophet with respect to the leadership of the Muslim Ummah.

The aim of these narratives is to protect the actions of those companions who had transgressed the Sunnah of the Prophet, and to put the focus of the killing of Hussain on other factors which were insignificant in the principled stand of Imam Hussain.

Unfortunately, the advocates of these narratives do not realize that as a Muslim we have not been instructed by Allah or his Prophet to defend the actions or the policies of every single companion. Our duty in this life is to simply submit to the commands of Allah and to the Sunnah of the Prophet. If a companion had made a mistake and had gone against the commands of Allah, or had transgressed the Sunnah of the Prophet, then Allah would hold those companions accountable on the Day of Judgment, and not us. There is no need and no reason for us to defend the wrong actions of a companion or any other individual for that matter as we would not be held accountable for someone else's actions.

14.11.1. Was the Stand of Hussain Initiated by the People of Kufa?

Those who put the focus of the tragedy of Karbala on the people of Kufa have done a great disservice to the history itself. They try and imply that the people of Kufa prompted and initiated Imam Hussain to take a stand, by inviting him to their city and by asking him to lead them against Yazid.

Those of us who have read the history without trying to defame the magnificent stand of Imam Hussain would confirm that Imam Hussain took his stand against Yazid in the city of Madinah, well before any invitation was received from the people of Kufa. In fact, the people of Kufa were not even aware at the time that Imam Hussain had taken a stand against the Caliphate of Yazid in Madinah.

The letters of invitation from Kufa came to Imam Hussain in Makkah, long after he had left the city of Madinah. As Imam Hussain travelled to Makkah the news spread throughout the Muslim Ummah that Imam Hussain had not given allegiance to Yazid and has moved to the city of Makkah. It was at that point that Imam Hussain started receiving the letters from the people of Kufa, because the people of Kufa realized that Imam Hussain had already refused to accept the Caliphate of Yazid and has even left his home city. The people of Kufa saw an opportunity that Imam Hussain could potentially come to their city and lead them.

The stand of Imam Hussain against Yazid was initiated in Madinah, and not in response to the letters of invitation from the people of Kufa. The stand of Imam Hussain was initiated in response to the demand of allegiance from Yazid through his governor Walid bin Utba, in the city of Madinah. Yazid had demanded that Imam Hussain accepts him as a Caliph of the Muslim Ummah, something that Imam Hussain could not accept.

If Yazid had not demanded the allegiance from Imam Hussain then there would have been no invitation from the people of Kufa either, since Imam Hussain would have never left his home city of Madinah. The invitations from the people of Kufa came while Imam Hussain was in Makkah, way after Imam Hussain had already taken his principled stand against the Caliphate of Yazid in Madinah.

14.11.2. Hussain could have been Killed in Madinah

The supporters of the Umayyads argue that Imam Hussain was killed in Karbala because the people of Kufa had invited him to Iraq, and when Imam Hussain reached Iraq they betrayed him, and he ended up in a place called Karbala where he was killed.

Let's see what the Umayyads had planned for Imam Hussain.

The Umayyads had in fact planned to kill Imam Hussain in Madinah. Yazid writes to his governor Walid bin Utba in Madinah with these instructions.

> "Seize Hussain, Abdullah bin Umar, Abdullah bin Zubair to give the oath of allegiance. Act so fiercely that they have no chance to do anything before giving the oath of allegiance........."

- (p. 146-7, Al-Bidaya wa al-Nihaya. Hafiz ibn Kathir (d. 774 A.H.) Vol. VIII.
- Maktaba al-Ma'arif, Beirut, Lebanon. 1999. See also pp.1-2.
- The History of al-Tabari; The Caliphate of Yazid. b. Mu'awiyah. Volume XIX. Translated by I.K.A. Howard. State University of New York Press, USA, 1990.)

Walid bin Utba consults with his advisor Marwan bin Hakam who advises Walid with these words.

> "I consider that you should send immediately to this group (Hussain, Abdullah bin Umar, Abdullah bin Zubair), and summon them to give the oath of allegiance and enter into obedience .... If they refuse, you should take hold of them and execute them before they learn of the death of Muawiyah"

- The History of al-Tabari; The Caliphate of Yazid. b. Mu'awiyah. Volume XIX. p. 2-3 -Translated by I.K.A. Howard

As per the words of the chief Umayyad advisor Marwan bin al-Hakam, Imam Hussain was to be killed in Madinah if he refuses to give allegiance to Yazid, and Imam Hussain was to be killed even before he could find out that Muawiyah had died.

And when Imam Hussain had refused to give allegiance to Yazid in front of Walid bin Utba, Marwan bin Hakam again advised Walid to seize the opportunity and kill Imam Hussain there and then.

> *"Should he (Hussain) part with you now without swearing it, you will never be able to secure it from him again till many of your people are killed, but confine the man till he either swears the oath of allegiance, or you kill him."*

- al-Tabari, Tarikh, Vol. 6, p. 189.

Yazid and his Umayyad advisors had planned to kill Imam Hussain in Madinah. The only reason they could not kill Imam Hussain in Madinah was because Imam Hussain had left Madinah overnight, and he had avoided a direct confrontation with the Umayyads in the city of the Prophet to preserve its sanctity.

The invitation from the people of Kufa came much later and it would have been completely irrelevant, since Imam Hussain would have been killed in his home city of Madinah, and the people of Kufa wouldn't have even known that Imam Hussain had taken a stand against the Caliphate of Yazid.

The Umayyad intention to kill Imam Hussain had been there since the inauguration of Yazid as the new Caliph. However, history took such a course that Imam Hussain eventually ended up in Karbala. But the Umayyads had planned to kill Imam Hussain anywhere they would find him.

The invitation from the people of Kufa had made no difference to the eventual outcome i.e., the actual killing of Imam Hussain. Because the killing of Imam Hussain would have happened anyway once he had refused to accept the caliphate of Yazid.

14.11.3. Hussain could have been Killed in Makkah

Yazid had planned to kill Imam Hussain in Makkah during the Haj pilgrimage.

Imam Hussain was all set to perform the Haj rituals, however he receives the news that Yazid had appointed Amr ibn Said ibn al-Aus as the head of the army to take charge of the Haj caravans. The aim of Yazid with the new appointment was to kill Imam Hussain while he was performing Haj.

Amr ibn Said had sent men disguised as pilgrims to kill Imam Hussain when the Holy Mosque of Makkah would have been packed with worshippers. These henchmen of Amr ibn Said were hiding swords and daggers under their clothes to attack Imam Hussain whenever they would get the opportunity.

Imam Hussain's upmost concern was to prevent the bloodshed in the Holy Kaaba. The Umayyads obviously had no qualms about the sanctity of Kaaba, but Imam Hussain did, so he changed his Haj into an Umrah and hastily left Makkah to preserve its sanctity.

Imam Hussain said the following words while leaving Makkah.

> *"My father told me once that there is a ram in Mecca through which its sanctity would be violated, and I do not like to be it. Should I be killed outside Mecca even the distance of a span, it is better for me than being killed inside it"*

- Al-Azraqi's Tarikh Mecca, Vol. 2, p. 150.

Imam Hussain leaves Makkah without performing Haj to avoid being killed by the Umayyads in the Holy Kaaba.

As evident from the above events of history Imam Hussain could have easily been killed in Makkah if he had not changed his plans, and the invitation from the people of Kufa would have had no bearing on his killing. The issue was the intention of the Umayyads to kill Imam Hussain rather than the invitation from the people of Kufa. The Umayyads eventually managed to corner Imam Hussain in Karbala and killed him there, but he could have been killed in any of the cities in the Muslim Ummah.

The real issue was the Umayyad demand of allegiance that Imam Hussain had refused which eventually resulted in his killing, and not the invitation from the people of Kufa.

14.11.4. Hussain could have Returned Home from the Outskirts of Kufa

When the caravan of Imam Hussain approached the outskirts of Kufa, the army of Ubaydullah bin Ziyad intercepted his caravan and would not allow it to enter the city.

At that juncture Imam Hussain asked the army of Ubaydullah to allow him to go back to his home city.

> *"I have come because you (Kufans) wrote letters inviting me to come and unite you for the cause of truth and justice. But now if you have changed your mind and you dislike my presence here, I am ready to go back."*
> - Ansab Al-Ashraf, vol.III, p.170
> - Al-Futuh, vol V, p.135

But the request of Imam Hussain to go back to his hometown was declined by the army of Ubaydullah, and Imam Hussain was forced to go in the direction of Karbala where he was eventually killed.

The life of Imam Hussain could have easily been spared if Ubaydullah had agreed to the proposal of Imam Hussain. The invitation from the people of Kufa would have once again become irrelevant as Imam Hussain would have survived, and no harm would have been done to him.

The reason why Imam Hussain was not allowed to return home was because he had refused to accept the Caliphate of Yazid, and not because the people of Kufa were treacherous. The killing of Hussain was a result of his refusal to pay allegiance to Yazid and not the invitation from the people of Kufa.

14.11.5. Hussain's Life could have been Spared in Karbala

At the very last minute just before the tragedy of Karbala was about to unfold, Imam Hussain once again offered a way out to the enemy, and once again the proposal of Imam Hussain was declined.

Imam Hussain offers an amicable solution without pledging allegiance to Yazid. Imam Hussain says:

> *"Let me either return where I came from or let me live in this extensive land"*
> - Tarikh al-Kamil, vol.IV, p.54
> - Tarikh al-Tabari, vol.II, p.182

The offer of Imam Hussain was pretty reasonable. Imam Hussain was proposing to either return home or live a quiet life in some far away land without pledging allegiance to Yazid. The offer of Imam Hussain could have easily prevented his killing, but the offer was turned down.

Apart from avoiding the bloodshed in Karbala the offer of Imam Hussain was also intended to preserve his principled stance against Yazid. Because the Muslim Ummah would realize that the grandson of the Prophet had left for a faraway land, but he had not recognized Yazid as a legitimate Caliph, proving that the Caliphate of Yazid and the Umayyad rule were unjust and un-Islamic.

The Umayyads however refused to budge and declined every offer of Imam Hussain. The reason for their refusal was simple, the Umayyads were looking for complete capitulation from Imam Hussain, since their intention was to legitimize their rule with the allegiance from Hussain who was the grandson of the Prophet.

The tragedy of Karbala could have easily been averted even in the final stages. The letters of invitation from the people of Kufa would have had little relevance as Imam Hussain would have survived. But the Umayyads choose to pursue the path of violence because Imam Hussain had refused to pledge allegiance to their leader.

The only difference that the invitation from the people of Kufa had made was that the killing of Imam Hussain had moved from the city of Makkah or Madinah to the plains of Karbala. But the killing itself would have happened regardless of the town or the city where Imam Hussain would have been residing.

In the next few sections I will further delve into some of the other narratives that are used to dilute and divert the attention from the actual stand of Imam Hussain.

14.11.6. The Shias of Kufa Invited, Betrayed and Killed Hussain

As mentioned previously the aim of all such narratives is to belittle and devalue the principled stand of Imam Hussain. The supporters of the Umayyads would lay the blame for the Killing of Imam Hussain on the people of Kufa, especially the Shias of Kufa. They would argue that since the Shias of Kufa had written letters to Imam Hussain inviting him to their city, and since they were the very people who deserted him in the hour of his need, the blame for the killing of Imam Hussain falls on their shoulders.

The ordinary Muslims who have either no knowledge of the tragedy of Karbala or have not read the Islamic history objectively could perhaps be swayed by such clever narratives. But people who have spent time in researching and analysing the history of Islam could easily see through the facade.

Imam Hussain was the grandson of the Prophet, and he was part of the Ahlulbayt. He was fifty-seven years of age when he received the letters from the Shias of Kufa inviting him to their city. Prophet had declared the Ahlulbayt to be one of the two weighty things alongside the Book of Allah. Imam Hussain was not an ordinary personality. He was the pinnacle of Islamic knowledge and wisdom and that is why the Umayyads were desperate that he accepts their man Yazid as the true leader of the Muslim Ummah.

When Imam Hussain accepts the invitation from the Shias of Kufa and heads to their city, then this action in itself clarifies a few key points.

- Imam Hussain must have considered the Shias to be his own people, to be his friends, to be his well-wishers and to be his followers and hence he accepted their invitation. If Imam Hussain had not considered Shias to be his own group and to be his supporters, he would have never accepted their invitation.
- The Shias as a sect or as a group who consider Ali to be the rightful successor of the Prophet are not misguided or deviant, since if that was the case then Imam Hussain who was the grandson of the Prophet would have never accepted their invitation or sent his ambassador Muslim bin Aqeel to Kufa.
- The Shias were the only people or the only group who at that time were willing to support the stand of Imam Hussain. This support may only have been on paper i.e., in the form of letters which they had written to Imam Hussain, but at least in principle they were willing to support the grandson of the Prophet.

Now whether the Shias of Kufa ditched Imam Hussain in the end and eventually deserted him is a separate story. But the fact that Imam Hussain being the grandson of the Prophet accepted the invitation from the Shias of Kufa, clearly proves that he considered Shias to be his creed and to be his own people and to be his friends.

Before I go any further, I will clarify the actual meaning of the term "Shia". Because the term "Shia" in the timeframe of the tragedy of Karbala and the term "Shia" in 21st century has a very different meaning. This clarification itself will show the unjust nature of the narrative that the Shias had invited, betrayed, and killed Imam Hussain.

14.11.7. The Shias of Kufa and its History

The word Shia in Arabic simply means a party, a group, or a follower. For example, if someone says that Ahmed is a Shia of Saleh, it means that Ahmed is from the party or the group of Saleh, or Ahmed is a follower of Saleh.

The term Shia was first coined to refer to the group of companions and Muslims who considered Ali to be the rightful successor of the Prophet. During the Caliphate of the first three Caliphs i.e., Caliph Abu Bakr, Caliph Umar and Caliph Uthman, any companions or Muslims who accepted the narrative that Prophet had appointed Ali to lead the Muslim Ummah were referred to as the party or the followers of Ali i.e., the Shias of Ali.

The rest of the Muslims in the time period of the first three Caliphs i.e., all the non-Shia Muslims had no specific name for their creed. The term "Sunni" or the term "Ahl al-Sunnah wal-Jama'ah" did not exist at that time. This does not mean that the Sunni view did not exist, but what it means is that the non-Shia Muslims were not referred to as Sunni Muslims in that era. So, you were either a Shia Muslim or a non-Shia Muslim at that time.

The city of Kufa was founded during the reign of Caliph Umar. He planned and constructed the city of Kufa during his Caliphate (Al-Faruq Vol.2 p.96-97). Caliph Umar appointed Saad Ibn Abi Waqqas, the famous companion of the Prophet as the governor of Kufa and made him responsible for establishing and organizing the city. As Kufa was founded by Caliph Umar many non-Shia Muslims began to settle in the city of Kufa from other parts of the Muslim world, and Kufa became a well-known city in the Muslim Ummah.

When Ali became the fourth Caliph, he moved his administration from Madinah to the city of Kufa, so many Shias of Ali also moved to the city of Kufa from other parts of the Muslim Ummah. However, the Shias of Ali were a minority in Kufa as the original inhabitants were non-Shia Muslims, who were far more numerous.

When Lady Aisha launched the first civil war (the battle of Jamal) against Ali, the Muslim Ummah got divided even further. The Muslims who sided with Lady Aisha were referred to as the Shias of Uthman i.e., the party of Uthman, since they were demanding that the killers of Caliph Uthman be apprehended and brought to justice. The Uthmani Shias were extremely anti Ali and would openly attack him from the pulpits.

> *"The Uthmani Shias were openly hostile towards Ali from pulpit"*
>
> - *Minhaj al Sunnah, Volume 1 page 178*

All the Muslims who fought on the side of Ali against Lady Aisha were also termed as the Shia of Ali. However, the Shia of Ali now became a much broader group. The Shias of Ali now consist of two distinct groups. The first group consisted of the original Shias who considered Ali to be the rightful successor of the Prophet. Then there was a second group of the Shias of Ali who were previously non-Shia Muslims, but since they fought alongside Ali in the battle of Jamal they were now also referred to as the Shia of Ali.

However, this new group of the Shias of Ali does not consider Ali to be the rightful successor of the Prophet. They had only sided with Ali against Lady Aisha because Ali had now become the fourth Caliph. They had previously given allegiance to Caliph Abu Bakr, Caliph Umar and Caliph Uthman, and have now given allegiance to Ali on the basis of him holding the office of the fourth Caliph.

Ali himself confirms this notion.

> *"Verily those who took the oath of allegiance to Abu Bakr, Umar, Uthman have sworn allegiance to me"*
> - Imamah wal Siyasa Vol 1 Page 93
> - Abdul Fareed Vol 4 Page 322
> - Nahjul Balagha letter 6

This is also confirmed in Al Mizan.

> *The justifying conclusion is that the Shias of Kufa accepted the Caliphate of the Sheikain (i.e. Umar and Abu Bakr)*
> - Al Mizan Vol 1, Page 118-119

This new group of the Shias of Ali which came about after Ali became the fourth Caliph can be termed as the political Shias of Ali, since they only began to side with Ali after he acquired the political office of the Caliphate. In the same context the original Shias of Ali who believed that Ali was the rightful successor of the Prophet could be classed as the theological Shias of Ali, since they had accepted Ali as the rightful successor of the Prophet even when he did not hold the political office of the Caliphate.

The basis on which the theological Shias of Ali gave allegiance to Ali was very different from the basis on which the political Shias of Ali had given allegiance to Ali. The theological Shias of Ali had given allegiance to Ali not because he was chosen by the Ummah as the fourth Caliph, but because they believed that he was chosen by the Prophet to lead the Ummah.

One of the theological Shias of Ali by the name of Khuzaymah ibn Thabit said the following after Ali became the fourth Caliph.

> *"We have elected someone who was chosen for us by the Messenger of Allah."*
> - Al-Mi'yar wa al-Muwazanah by Abu Jaffar al-Iskafi (d. 240 H), page 51

So, the Muslim Ummah is now divided into three groups, the theological Shias of Ali, the political Shias of Ali and the Shias of Uthman, who sided with Lady Aisha against Ali in the battle of Jamal.

After the Caliphate of Ali and the brief Caliphate of Imam Hasan, Muawiyah becomes the Caliph and rules for around twenty years. Over a span of two decades Muawiyah creates a loyal group of supporters who were referred to as the Shia of Muawiyah i.e., the party of Muawiyah. The Shia of Muawiyah also fought against Ali in the battle of Siffin. The people who fought on the side of Ali were still called the Shias of Ali, and they comprised of both the theological and the political Shias of Ali.

When Yazid became the Caliph, he referred to his supporters in Kufa as the Shias of Yazid.

> *".... My Shia (followers) among the people of Kufa have written to me to inform me that Muslim ibn Aqeel is in Kufa gathering units in order to spread rebellion among the Muslims...."*
>
> - (p.31. The History of al-Tabari; The Caliphate of Yazid. b. Mu'awiyah. Volume XIX. Translated by I.K.A. Howard. State University of New York Press, USA, 1990.)

The Shias of Yazid were essentially the Shias of Muawiyah since Shias of Muawiyah were now supporting the Caliphate of Yazid. As part of this discussion, I would refer to Shias of Yazid as the Shias of Muawiyah, since that is what they were originally called.

Therefore, at the time of the tragedy of Karbala there were four different kinds of Shias, the theological Shias of Ali, the political Shias of Ali, the Shias of Uthman, and the Shias of Muawiyah.

The key point that comes out from the above discussion is the fact that every Muslim in that era was called a Shia! At the time of the tragedy of Karbala a Muslim would either be a theological Shia of Ali, a political Shia of Ali, a Shia of Uthman, or a Shia of Muawiyah. The term "Sunni" or "Ahl al-Sunnah wal-Jama'ah" was not used to refer to any group of Muslims at that time.

However, the Muslim world today is broadly divided into two groups i.e., the Sunnis and the Shias. The theological Shias of Ali from that era are the ancestors of the Shia Muslims of 21st century, whereas the political Shias of Ali, the Shias of Muawiyah and the Shias of Uthman are the ancestors of the Sunni Muslims of 21st century.

The theological Shias of Ali have kept their original name and are still known as the Shia of Ali, or in short, they are known as the Shia. The political Shias of Ali, the Shias of Uthman and the Shias of Muawiyah adopted the name Sunni or Ahl al-Sunnah wal-Jama'ah for their group, but this was adopted much later in the history, long after the tragedy of Karbala.

The study of sects and their development is beyond the scope of this book. However, I have tried to give a very brief and a rough overview of the groups that existed at the time of the tragedy of Karbala. The aim was to inform the reader about the composition of the Muslim Ummah that existed at the time of the killing of Imam Hussain.

The city of Kufa just like the Muslim world today comprised of both the Shia and the Sunni Muslims. The Shia Muslims being the theological Shias of Ali and the Sunni Muslims being the political Shias of Ali, the Shias of Muawiyah, and the Shias of Uthman. Since the Sunni Muslims came from three different groups, they were the majority in the city of Kufa just as they are the majority in the Muslim world today. The Shia Muslims of today whose predecessors were the theological Shias of Ali were a minority in the city of Kufa, just as they are a minority in the Muslim world today.

When the supporters of Muawiyah and Yazid in 21st century use the narrative that Imam Hussain was invited, betrayed, and killed by the Shias of Kufa, they do not specify which Shia group invited Imam Hussain, which Shia group betrayed Imam Hussain, and which Shia group killed Imam Hussain.

They just say it was the Shia who killed Imam Hussain!

And this is done deliberately, to not only dilute the actual Stand of Imam Hussain, but to also implicate the present-day Shia Muslims in the killing of Imam Hussain, despite knowing full well that the term Shia in that era was a generic term, which incorporated all the Muslims groups including the Sunni Muslims of today.

The Sunni Muslims at the time of the tragedy of Karbala were also known as Shia.

14.11.8. The Invitation of Hussain to Kufa

Let us see which Shia group had invited Imam Hussain to Kufa, and which Shia group had betrayed him, and which Shia group had killed him.

I will start my discussion with the reign of Muawiyah and his policies towards the Shias of Ali in Kufa, as this would clarify and put into context the reasons as to why the Shias of Ali chose to invite Imam Hussain to their city.

Muawiyah had killed many Shias of Ali in Kufa during his twenty-year rule. Most of the Shias that were killed were the theological Shias of Ali like Hujr bin Adi and Amr bin Hamiq, but some political Shias of Ali were also killed if they didn't toe the government line. Many theological Shias of Ali were thrown out of their homes and were forced to migrate to other lands. And their properties and businesses were taken over by the supporters of Muawiyah i.e., the Shias of Muawiyah.

> *"When the people of Iraq agreed to recognise Muawiyah as Caliph after Ali, Muawiyah took to expelling from Kufa those who had been passionate in the cause of Ali, and to settle in their homes those people of Syria and Basra who were passionate in his (Muawiyah's) cause"*
> - Tabari Vol 10 Page 97

When Muawiyah forcefully appointed Yazid as the new Caliph in breach of the peace agreement with Imam Hasan, there was a lot of resentment among the Shias of Ali in Kufa. This included both the theological and the political Shias of Ali. They were dismayed that Muawiyah had not only broken the peace agreement, but he had also changed the Caliphate into an Umayyad dynasty.

Soon after Yazid became the Caliph news started reaching Kufa that Imam Hussain had refused to pay allegiance to Yazid, and had taken a stand against his Caliphate, and had even left Madinah and had moved to Makkah. The theological Shias of Ali in Kufa saw this as an opportunity where they could invite Imam Hussain to their city, rally behind him as their leader and support his principled stand against the Caliphate of Yazid.

A meeting was held in the house of Suleman bin Surad al-Khuzai to discuss the feasibility of inviting Imam Hussain to Kufa. Suleman bin Surad al-Khuzai was a companion of the Prophet and had fought alongside Ali in the early battles of Islam. He was one of the key leaders of the theological Shias of Ali in Kufa. The meeting was also attended by Al-Musayyab bin Najaba, Rifa bin Shaddad, Habib bin al-Muzahir, and Muslim bin Awsaja, who were the other key Shia players in the city. It was agreed by all the leaders that Imam Hussain would be invited to Kufa and that they would support his stand against Yazid.

The very first letter of invitation to Imam Hussain was written and signed by this group of theological Shias of Ali from Kufa, who were led by Suleman bin Surad al-Khuzai. However, as the news spread that the grandson of the Prophet was being invited to Kufa, the political Shias of Ali also joined the movement, since they had been a victim of Umayyad tyranny too, and they had no reason to support the Caliphate of Yazid either.

The letters of invitation to Imam Hussain suddenly shot up and the movement in support of Imam Hussain quickly became a populace movement in the city of Kufa. It no longer remained a pure movement of the theological Shias of Ali, since the political Shias of Ali i.e., the Sunnis of our times also joined in, and were just as enthusiastic about inviting Imam Hussain to their city as the theological Shias of Ali were. The political Shias of Ali i.e., the Sunnis in Kufa also wrote thousands of letters to Imam Hussain pledging their support and inviting him to their city.

The political Shias of Ali (Sunnis) had previously fought alongside Ali and against both Lady Aisha and Muawiyah in the battles of Jamal and Siffin, and they were willing to side with Imam Hussain against Yazid too.

Contrary to the myth which is propagated that the Shias had invited Imam Hussain to Kufa, it was in fact both the Shias and the Sunnis who had invited Imam Hussain to Kufa. The Shias being the theological Shias of Ali and Sunnis being the political Shias of Ali. The likes of Suleman bin Surad al-Khuzai, who was a theological Shia of Ali was no doubt the founder of the movement in favour of Imam Hussain in Kufa, but the Sunnis also joined his movement just as enthusiastically as the Shias did, once it had been initiated.

However, the Sunnis were divided into three groups i.e., the political Shias of Ali, the Shias of Uthman. and the Shias of Muawiyah. The Sunnis who belonged to the Shia of Uthman and the Shia of Muawiyah groups were supporting the Umayyads and the Caliphate of Yazid. They obviously did not join the movement of the theological Shias of Ali or wrote letters of invitation to Imam Hussain. It was only the political Shias of Ali from the Sunni side who wrote the letters of invitation to Imam Hussain.

In fact, the Sunnis who were the Shia of Uthman and the Shia of Muawiyah wrote a letter to Yazid, stating that unless something is done to stop the movement of Shias of Ali in Kufa, Yazid stands to lose the city to Imam Hussain.

> *"Abdallah b. Muslim. B. Said al Hadrami an ally of the Banu Umayyah…went out and wrote the following letter to Yazid b. Muawiyah: 'Muslim bin Aqeel has come to al-Kufa and the Shia have given the allegiance to him on behalf of al-Husayn b. Ali b. Abi Talib. If you have any need of Kufa send a strong man there, who would carry out your orders in the same way you would at against your enemy. Al-Nauman b. Bashir is a weak man or he is acting like a weak man". He was the first to write to him (Yazid). Then Umarah b. Uqbah wrote to him in a similar vein. As did Umar b. Sad b. Abi Waqqas"*
>
> - *History of Tabari, Volume 19 page 30*

Many Shias of Muawiyah wrote letters to Yazid informing him of the dangerous situation in Kufa, They informed Yazid that the Shias of Ali in Kufa were giving allegiance to Muslim bin Aqeel, the ambassador of Imam Hussain, and that Nauman Bashir who was the governor of Kufa was a weak man, and that he wasn't doing enough to stop the movement of Imam Hussain in Kufa.

Readers would recall that after receiving these letters Yazid replaced Nauman Bashir with Ubaydullah bin Ziyad as the governor of Kufa, who changed the balance of power in Kufa in favour of Yazid.

So, some Sunnis i.e., the political Shias of Ali wrote letters to Imam Hussain inviting him to their city, whereas other Sunni groups such as the Shias of Muawiyah wrote letters to Yazid urging him to crush the movement of Imam Hussain in Kufa. The Sunnis of Kufa were divided in their stance towards the grandson of the Prophet.

Then there was a group of people from Kufa who neither could be placed into the Sunni or the Shia camps. They were the opportunists, who were simply looking to benefit from the politics of the day. As the level of support began to increase for Imam Hussain in Kufa they also began writing to him and invited him to their city believing that he would become the winning party in Kufa.

14.11.9. The Betrayal of Hussain

Broadly speaking, the society of Kufa was divided into three distinct opinions in terms of their support for the movement of Imam Hussain. The theological and the political Shias of Ali were supporting the movement of Imam Hussain. The Shias of Muawiyah and the Shias of Uthman were opposing the movement of Imam Hussain. The opportunists or the mercenaries were on the side of Imam Hussain to begin with, but their aim was to support the winning side.

The word betrayal is too strong to be used for the entire population of Kufa, considering it had many loyal supporters of Imam Hussain, but the circumstances changed to such a degree that many of them were unable to support the movement of Imam Hussain in the way that they had promised.

14.11.9.1. What Actually Happened?

Both the theological Shias of Ali and the political Shias of Ali had invited Imam Hussain to their city, and they were ready to support his principled stance against Yazid and they became part of his movement. However, the situation in Kufa took an unprecedented turn against the supporters of Imam Hussain, and their movement was completely crushed by the Shias of Muawiyah and the Shias of Uthman.

The life was taken out from the movement in favour of Imam Hussain in Kufa with the following tactics.

- As the Shias of Ali welcomed the ambassador of Imam Hussain to Kufa with open arms and around 8,000 of them pledged allegiance on the hand of Muslim bin Aqeel, this changed the calculus of the Umayyads towards the Shias of Ali in Kufa.
- The Shias of Muawiyah and the Shias of Uthman wrote to Yazid informing him that he stands to lose Kufa unless something was done swiftly to crush the movement of Shias of Ali in Kufa.
- Yazid's non-Muslim advisor Sir John advised him to use Ubaydullah bin Ziyad, who was one of the most vicious and brutal men in Yazid's arsenal to crush the supporters of Hussain.
- The movement of Imam Hussain was flourishing under the governorship of Noman Bashir, but he was replaced by Ubaydullah bin Ziyad who was a ruthless dictator.
- Ubaydullah was a Shia of Muawiyah. He enters the city under the cover of darkness with a cloth on his face and dressed up as Imam Hussain.
- Both the theological and the political Shias of Ali stream out in their thousands to welcome Imam Hussain, but it turns out to be the devious Ubaydullah.
- This was a huge physiological setback for the supporters of Imam Hussain. They were completely deceived and demoralized by the cunning tactics of Ubaydullah.
- All the key supporters of Imam Hussain had been exposed to Ubaydullah, who was known to cut the hands and legs of his opponents and crucify them on the doors of their homes.

- The movement in favour of Imam Hussain was forced to go underground and as a result lost its populace appeal.
- The ambassador of Imam Hussain in Kufa, Muslim bin Aqeel who was openly rallying support for Imam Hussain was now moving from one safe house to another, simply trying to keep the movement alive until Imam Hussain arrives in the city.
- Ubaydullah hires an experienced spy who manages to infiltrate the underground network of Imam Hussain's supporters, giving a death blow to the movement of Shias of Ali in Kufa.
- The ambassador of Imam Hussain, Muslim bin Aqeel was captured and taken to the roof of the palace and was beheaded. His body was dragged through the streets and crucified in the market square as a lesson for the rest of the Shias of Ali.
- The other key leaders of the movement had either been killed, imprisoned, or were hiding to avoid death or capture.
- Without their leaders and without the network of support that they had enjoyed both the theological and the political Shias of Ali in Kufa had lost their sense of direction.
- The head of the movement and the ambassador of Imam Hussain in Kufa i.e., Muslim bin Aqeel had been killed. Hani bin Urwa had been beheaded. Sulemain al Surd al Kuzai who had invited Imam Hussain was imprisoned, and so was Mukthar al Taqavi, whose house had been used as a base in Kufa for all the activities.
- Once the key leaders had been taken out, the movement in favour of Imam Hussain lost its vigour and viability in the eyes of the public, and the ordinary supporters of Imam Hussain were subdued and forced into hiding.
- The messengers of Imam Hussain to the city of Kufa were also beheaded and thrown from the rooftops of the palace.
- When Imam Hussain actually arrived in Kufa he was not even allowed to enter the city. The caravan of Imam Hussain was forced from the outskirts of Kufa in the direction of Karbala, in order to avoid any direct contact between Imam Hussain and the people of Kufa, as the presence of Imam Hussain in the city could rekindle his movement.

The Shias of Muawiyah and the Shias of Uthman had managed to brutally and cleverly crush the movement of the theological and the political Shias of Ali in Kufa. In the context of 21st century, a segment of Sunni population had overpowered another segment of the Sunni and the Shia population of Kufa, and had crushed their movement in favour of Imam Hussain in the city.

The supporters of Imam Hussain were unable to take on the organised brutality of the Umayyad State. They were threatened with death, they were threatened with the killing of their family members, and they were threatened with the loss of their livelihoods. It was in these circumstances that the movement of Shias of Ali in favour of Imam Hussain was crushed and defeated in Kufa.

It wasn't a case of betrayal as suggested by the defenders of Muawiyah and Yazid. It wasn't as if the people of Kufa had simply ditched Imam Hussain on his arrival in their city. In fact, Imam Hussain was never even allowed to enter the city of Kufa. His caravan was stopped on the outskirts of Kufa by the army of Ubaydullah. The people of Kufa never met or saw Imam Hussain.

On the other hand, when the news broke that Imam Hussain had arrived in Kufa, hundreds of Shias from Kufa went out to greet and welcome Imam Hussain to their city, but it turned out to be the cunning Ubaydullah, proving that the Shias of Ali were sincere in their invitation to Imam Hussain.

Coercion, deceit, intimidation, killings, barbarity and threatening of livelihoods were just a few of the tactics used by Ubaydullah to end the support that people of Kufa had pledged for Imam Hussain. Ubaydullah had used every trick in the book to crush the movement of Imam Hussain in Kufa.

The Shias of Ali in Kufa were average human beings like me and you. They were not Prophets or super humans, and neither were the people of Kufa chosen by Allah as role models for mankind. Like most people in this world when the tide turned against them, they faltered, and their movement in favour of Imam Hussain was crushed. This would have happened to any other people anywhere in the world if they were put through such extreme conditions.

14.11.9.2. Brief Analysis

The people who try and put the blame for the tragedy of Karbala on the people of Kufa have completely ignored and neglected the fact that at least the people of Kufa had invited the grandson of the Prophet to their city. The other cities in the Muslim Ummah had completely fallen under the thumb of the Umayyads. The people in those cities would not even dare to speak up against the Umayyads.

At least in Kufa there was a resistance movement against the Umayyad rule, and this was due to the presence of a significant number of the theological Shias of Ali in the city. At least the people of Kufa had the guts and the courage to write to Imam Hussain and invite him to their city, something that was visibly missing from any other city in the Muslim Ummah.

The Umayyads had already pacified the rest of the cities in the Islamic State. This was done by the way of coercion, bribery and through the use of force and threats against the local population. Muawiyah had been laying the groundwork for an Umayyad dynasty ever since he took over the seat of the Caliphate.

The city of Kufa was the last bastion where people took a stand against the Umayyad rule. At least the Shias of Ali had the courage to stand-up to the oppressive and the corrupt Umayyads in that era, even though their stand was unsuccessful in the end.

The critics of the Shias of Ali in Kufa tend to forget that Kufa was just one city in the entire Muslim Ummah. Yazid was in complete control of the whole Islamic State which had expanded from Persia to the shores of North Africa. The Islamic State at the time comprised of twenty-three or twenty-four provinces, and Kufa was only one city in the province of Iraq. All the other big and small provinces and cities in the Islamic State were under the complete authority of the Umayyads. For instance, Makkah, Madinah, Syria, Egypt, Yemen, Iran, Iraq (Basra) were all under the thumb of the Umayyads.

Even if the entire population of Kufa had somehow managed to support the stand of Imam Hussain, the final outcome i.e., the tragedy of Karbala and the killing of Imam Hussain could not have been averted. Yazid had a massive army at his disposal. He could have easily used the army from the other regions to crush the revolt coming from the city of Kufa.

The only way the killing of Imam Hussain could have been averted was for him to give allegiance to Yazid, the Ummayad caliph of the time.

As it happened Yazid used Ubaydullah to crush the movement of Shias of Ali in Kufa. Ubaydullah did exactly what he was tasked to do by his Umayyad master. However, on the Day of Judgment Ubaydullah's file will reopen, and the atrocities that he had committed against the supporters of Imam Hussain would be read out to him one by one. He would not be able to bribe, threaten, intimidate, or coerce anybody on that day. He would be all alone with a long charge sheet against his name, and no doubt the justice of Allah will be swift and everlasting.

14.11.10. The Killing of Hussain

Let us see who actually killed Imam Hussain in Karbala. The Shias of Ali certainly invited Imam Hussain to their city and it is also true that they were not able to support Imam Hussain in the way that they had promised him in their letters, and this was due to the organized brutality that the Umayyads had employed against the Shias of Ali in Kufa. However, they were not the ones who killed Imam Hussain as portrayed by the supporters of Muawiyah and Yazid.

14.11.10.1. Who Killed Hussain?

The answer to this key question is well documented in the books of history. Imam Hussain was killed by the Shias of Muawiyah and the Shias of Uthman because he had refused to accept the legitimacy of Yazid's Caliphate. Imam Hussain was killed on the orders of Yazid through Ubaydullah bin Ziyad who was Yazid's governor in Kufa.

Ubaydullah wrote to Yazid after killing Imam Hussain and stated:

> "Praise be to God …….. He has given victory to the Commander of the Faithful Yazeed ibn Muawiyah, and his party. He has killed the liar (Hussain) who is the son of a liar (Ali), al-Hussain bin Ali and his Shi'ah"

- Al-Tabari, Volume 19 page 167-169, English translation by I.K.A. Howard.

Ubaydullah happily writes to his Umayyad master Yazid that he had killed Imam Hussain and his Shias. The Shia here refers to the Shias of Ali.

Ubaydullah was a Shia of Muawiyah. Muawiyah had made Ubaydullah's father Ziyad bin Abih his real brother by deliberately going against the Islamic law. After making Ziyad bin Abih his real brother Muawiyah then used him to crush the Shias of Ali in Basra and Kufa during his rule of twenty years. Yazid did exactly the same during his reign as the Caliph. He used Ziyad bin Abih's son Ubaydullah bin Ziyad to crush Imam Hussain and the movement of Shias of Ali in Kufa.

Ubaydullah bin Ziyad admitted to his crime of killing Imam Hussain on more than one occasion. Ubaydullah said that he had killed Imam Hussain on the orders of Yazid, because if he didn't kill Imam Hussain then Yazid would have killed him.

> "I killed Al Hussain on the orders of Yazid ……. otherwise he (Yazid) would kill me therefore I chose to kill Hussain"

- Tareekh Kamil, Volume 4 page 55 (Egypt)

On another occasion Ubaydullah again confesses that he had killed Imam Hussain. And he says that he killed Imam Hussain because Imam Hussain had refused to give allegiance to Yazid.

> "I killed Al Hussain due to the reason that he revolted against our Imam [Yazid] and the very Imam [Yazid] sent me the message to kill Al Hussain. Now if the murder of Hussain is a sin then Yazid is responsible for it"

- Akhbaar Tawaal, page 279 (Egypt) by Ahmed Bin Daud Abu Hanifa Dinwari

Although Ubaydullah admits to the killing of Imam Hussain, but he puts the blame for the killing on the shoulders of Yazid. He says that it was Yazid who had ordered him to kill Imam Hussain.

The famous historian Suyuti also confirms that Yazid had ordered the killing of Imam Hussain through his governor Ubaydullah bin Ziyad.

> "Yazid wrote his ruler in Iraq Ibn Ziyad for the murder of Hussain"
> - Tareekh Khulfa, page 182, Allamah Jalaluddin Suyuti

Contrary to the propaganda of the people who try and put the blame for the killing of Imam Hussain on the Shias of Ali in Kufa, the killers of Imam Hussain have themselves confessed to his killing. Yazid and Ubaydullah bin Ziyad were not Shias of Ali. They were both Shias of Muawiyah.

Similarly, Umar ibn Saad who was the commander in chief of Ubaydullah's army in Karbala had proudly confessed to be the first one who attacked Imam Hussain and fired arrows at his tents. Umar ibn Saad said to his army:

> "My warriors! Bear witness before God and people that it is me, Umar son of Saad, who is the first to attack al-Husayn."
> - History of al Tabari, Volume 19 page 129

Umar ibn Saad then shot the first arrow towards the camps of Imam Hussain signifying the commencement of the battle of Karbala.

Umar ibn Saad was the son of the famous companion of the Prophet Saad ibn Abi Waqqas. Caliph Umar, who was the founder of the city of Kufa had appointed Saad ibn Abi Waqqas as its governor and made him responsible for constructing the city. Caliph Umar was extremely close to Saad ibn Abi Waqqas. Caliph Umar had also made Saad ibn Abi Waqqas a candidate for the third Caliphate, by adding his name to the six-member Shura which was responsible for choosing the third Caliph.

Saad ibn Abi Waqqas's son Umar ibn Saad had not only joined the camp of Yazid, but he was also one of those individuals from Kufa who wrote to Yazid warning him about the rising tide of the Shias of Ali in Kufa. Umar ibn Saad wrote to Yazid that unless Yazid does something to stop the movement of Shias of Ali in Kufa he stands to lose the city to Muslim bin Aqeel.

Subsequently, Yazid wrote to Ubaydullah bin Ziyad urging him to crush the rebellion of Shias of Ali in Kufa, and declared that his own Shia from Kufa i.e., the likes of Umar ibn Saad have written to him about the activities of Muslim bin Aqeel in the city (History of Tabari, Vol 19 Page 31).

Yazid declared Umar ibn Saad to be his Shia in Kufa, and Umar ibn Saad eventually led the army which crushed the small contingent of Imam Hussain and his supporters in Karbala.

> He (Ubaydullah bin Ziyad) ordered Umar ibn Saad to stay put in Karbala and extract the allegiance for Yazid from Hussain. Umar replied that Husain would never give his allegiance. Ibn Ziyad replied that he would not have it any other way except that he puts Husain and his small army to sword.
> - (Tarikh-e-Tabari, vol. 6, p. 234)

Imam Bukhari writes in his book Tarikh al-Saghir.

> "When Hussain arrived in Karbala, Umar bin Saad was the first individual who cut the ropes of the tents (i.e. the tents of Hussain)"

- Tarikh al-Saghir Volume 1 page 75

Umar ibn Saad was initially in two minds if he should fight Imam Hussain or not, but Ubaydullah bin Ziyad offered him the governorship of Raiy, which is present-day Tehran the capital of Iran. Even in those days it was a priceless jewel in the Muslim Ummah. Umar ibn Saad eventually agreed and decided to kill Imam Hussain because he wanted to become the governor of Raiy. He chose the life of this world over the life of the grandson of the Prophet.

Ubaydullah bin Ziyad used another tactics to incite people against Imam Hussain. It was the same tactics that Muawiyah had previously used to incite people against Ali. Ubaydullah bin Ziyad incited the Shias of Uthman to kill Imam Hussain with these words:

> "Become an obstacle between Hussain and water and treat them in the same way that the pious, righteous and oppressed Amee'rul Momineen Uthman was treated"

- Al Bidayah wal Nihayah, Volume 8 page 1058
- Tabari Volume 19 page 107

Ubaydullah bin Ziyad incites the Shias of Uthman to treat Imam Hussain in the same way that Caliph Uthman was treated. Readers would recall that when protestors gathered outside the house of Caliph Uthman in Madinah to protest against his policies, they had cut off his water supply. However, the deception of Ubaydullah bin Ziyad could not be more ironic, as it was in fact Imam Hussain and Imam Hasan who took the water to Caliph Uthman on the instructions of their father Ali, after the water supply had been cut off from the house of Caliph Uthman by the protestors.

But this was the legacy of Muawiyah against Ali that many Muslims at that time believed that it was Ali who had indeed killed Caliph Uthman. And it was for this very reason that many Shias of Uthman used to openly curse and abuse Ali from the pulpits.

> "The followers (Shias) of Uthman used to abuse Ali openly from the Mosque pulpits"

- Minhaj al Sunnah, Volume 6 page 201

Ubaydullah bin Ziyad was inciting the supporters of Caliph Uthman in the army of Umar ibn Saad to avenge the killing of Caliph Uthman from the son of Ali. Because in that deeply tribal society the Shias of Uthman were led to believe (through the propaganda of Muawiyah) that it was Ali who had killed their Umayyad leader Uthman.

In fact, when the battle of Karbala began, as per the Arab tradition the fighters on either side would identify their creed and lineage as they would step forward to fight. This indeed clarified who were the actual killers of Imam Hussain and who were his actual supporters.

When Nafi bin Hilal al Jamali, who was in the army of Imam Hussain entered the battle in Karbala he identified himself with the following words.

> "I am al-Jamali. I believe in the religion of Ali"

- Tabari Volume 19 pages 136-137

The religion of Ali here signifies that the individual was a Shia of Ali, since there was no separate religion that Ali had created.

A man called Muzahim al Hurayth stepped forward from the army of Umar ibn Saad against Nafi bin Hilal al Jamali, and declared:

> "I follow the religion of Uthman"
>
> • Tabari Volume 19 pages 136-137

Again, the religion of Uthman signifies that the individual was a Shia of Uthman.

Muzahim al Hurayth who was a Shia of Uthman killed Nafi bin Hilal al Jamali who was a Shia of Ali. The people who were fighting Imam Hussain in Karbala were the Shias of Uthman and the Shias of Muawiyah. The killers of Imam Hussain had identified their own creed by clearly stating that they belonged to the camp of Uthman or the camp of Muawiyah and not to the camp of Ali.

Many such statement were made in the battle of Karbala where the companions of Imam Hussain would identify themselves to be the Shia of Ali and the Shia of Hussain, to show that they belonged to the camp of the Ahlulbayt. On the other hand, the fighters in the army of Yazid would identify themselves as the Shia of Uthman or the Shia of Muawiyah, to show that they belonged to the Umayyad camp.

When Ubaydullah bin Ziyad broke the news of the killing of Imam Hussain the women from the clan of Banu Hashim raised their voices and started lamenting. On hearing the lamentation of the women of Banu Hashim, Umro bin Saeed who was an associate of Ubaydullah bin Ziyad stated:

> "This is the revenge for the lamentation of the wives of Uthman bin Affan"
>
> • Al Bidayah wal Nihayah (Urdu), Volume 8 page 1097

Again, the Shias of Uthman believed that they did the right thing by killing Imam Hussain the son of Ali.

This was the legacy of Muawiyah that the killing of Caliph Uthman had been attributed to Ali, and Ubaydullah bin Ziyad had incited the Shias of Uthman in killing the son of Ali, to avenge the killing of their Umayyad Caliph Uthman.

It becomes crystal clear from the historical analysis that Imam Hussain was killed by the Shias of Muawiyah and the Shias of Uthman, and not by Shias of Ali as propagated by the defenders of Yazid and Muawiyah.

14.11.10.2. The Opportunist Killers of Hussain

On the Day of Ashura just before the battle commenced Imam Hussain gave a sermon in which he identified some of the people who were standing in the army of Umar ibn Saad. These individuals had written letters to Imam Hussain inviting him to Kufa with promises of their support but now they were standing in the opposite camp.

Imam Hussain directly addresses these individuals and calls out their names.

> "O` Shabath ibn Rab`i, Hijar ibn Abjar, Qais ibn Ashaf, Zaid ibn al-Harith, did you not write to me saying come for the fruits are ripe and the dates have gone green and you will come to the troops ready for your command"
>
> • Tarikh al-Tabari Vol 6 Page 243

These individuals had written to Imam Hussain claiming that the fruits were ripe and that there was an army ready to support Imam Hussain. However, when the time came to support Imam Hussain they were standing with the forces of Umar ibn Saad, ready to kill Imam Hussain.

I will use Shabath ibn Rabi who was the first individual that Imam Hussain had addressed, as an example to see if he was a theological Shia of Ali, a political Shia of Ali, a Shia of Muawiyah or a Shia of Uthman.

Shabath ibn Rabi had a history of switching sides when the balance of power would change. Shabath ibn Rabi was not a young man. Readers will be surprised to know that Shabath ibn Rabi was one of those individuals who had a hand in the killing of Caliph Uthman (Al-Fiqat vol 1 page 448). He was in the camp of Lady Aisha, Talha and al-Zubair against Caliph Uthman, when they launched their ferocious movement against the third Caliph.

However, after the death of Caliph Uthman he paid allegiance to Ali when Ali became the fourth Caliph. He even fought alongside Ali in the battle of Siffin and thus became a political Shia of Ali. When Ali was returning form the battle of Siffin he rebelled against Ali and joined the Khawarij, and became a leader of the Khawarij (Talbis Iblis page 40 by Ibn Jauzi).

Later he repented and again joined Ali and fought alongside Ali against the Khawarij in Naharwan.

When Muawiyah acquired power and became the Caliph he joined the camp of Muawiyah and became his supporter. However, when the tide turned against Yazid in Kufa he rejected the Caliphate of Yazid and invited Imam Hussain to Kufa.

When Muslim bin Aqeel arrived in Kufa he paid allegiance to Muslim bin Aqeel as the movement in favour of Imam Hussain was on the rise at the time. However, when the tide turned against Muslim bin Aqeel in Kufa he again joined the camp of Yazid against Imam Hussain.

Shabath ibn Rabi was not a Shia of Uthman since he was involved in the killing of Caliph Uthman. He became a political Shia of Ali until the battle of Siffin. Then he joined the ranks of Khawarij and became one of their leaders and became an enemy of Ali. As Ali's party remained the strongest group he repented and re-joined the camp of Ali, and again became a political Shia of Ali.

When Muawiyah came to power, he joined the camp of Muawiyah and became a Shia of Muawiyah. When the movement of Shias of Ali was in its ascendency in the city of Kufa, he ditched the camp of Muawiyah and re-joined the camp of Ali. As the tide turned against the Shias of Ali in Kufa he again became a Shia of Muawiyah and joined the camp of Yazid. It is said that after the killing of Imam Hussain he ditched the camp of Yazid too.

Shabath ibn Rabi was not a Shia of Uthman, he was not a Shia of Ali, and he was not a Shia of Muawiyah either. He was simply a Shia of this world who was willing to side with any party that was most likely to win on the day.

The people who try and divert attention from the virtuous stand of Imam Hussain portray that individuals such as Shabath ibn Rabi were the Shias of Ali, which indeed is most absurd and regrettable. Since people like Shabath ibn Rabi were the men of this world who were not ideologically committed to any camp, let alone the camp of Ali.

People who put individuals such as Shabath ibn Rabi among the Shias of Ali have not done their due diligence in the history of these individuals. The people like Shabath ibn Rabi were the opportunist and the mercenary killers of Imam Hussain, who had no qualms about ditching or siding with anyone as long as it benefited their personal and political interests.

Even the letter that Shabath ibn Rabi wrote to Imam Hussain kind of gives the game away. It had a reflection of his insincerity towards the cause of Imam Hussain. He painted such a rosy picture of Kufa to Imam Hussain by stating in his letter that the fruits were ripe, and the dates were green, and an army was waiting to be led by the grandson of the Prophet.

In reality there was no army waiting to be led by Imam Hussain in Kufa. There was certainly support in favour of Imam Hussain among the people of Kufa, but there was no army that was waiting for the arrival of Imam Hussain.

This is why Imam Hussain challenged Shabath ibn Rabi on the Day of Ashura and showed him his letter where he had exaggerated the claims about the people of Kufa, and even worse he had now switched sides and was standing in the camp of Yazid. Imam Hussain was taking Shabath ibn Rabi to task for his lies and deception in order to show his real face to the world.

Imam Hussain certainly reminded individuals like Shabath ibn Rabi about their betrayal on the Day of Ashura. But the stand of Imam Hussain against Yazid was not based on the letters of invitation from the people of Kufa. Imam Hussain had taken a stand against the Caliphate of Yazid in Madinah, way before any letters were ever written to him. The letters of invitation from the people of Kufa were only written after they found out that Imam Hussain had already taken a stand against the Caliphate of Yazid.

The letters from the people of Kufa had no bearing on the actual stand of Imam Hussain. The stand of Imam Hussain was simply based on the fact that Yazid represented a system that was opposed to the system of governance established by the Prophet of Allah.

14.11.10.3. The Individuals Switching Sides

At the time of the tragedy of Karbala there were individuals who had switched sides from one camp to the other, either for the love of this world or for the love of the hereafter. However, the switching of the sides by these individuals had no impact on the eventual outcome of the tragedy of Karbala.

For instance, the commander of Ubaydullah's army in Kufa was Al-Hur bin Yazid al Riyahi. Ubaydullah sent Al-Hur with one thousand soldiers to intercept the caravan of Imam Hussain as it approached the city of Kufa. Al-Hur prevented Imam Hussain from reaching Kufa on the orders of Ubaydullah and forced him in the direction of Karbala.

Al-Hur was a Shia of Muawiyah and was in the camp of Yazid. However, on the eve of Ashura, the night before the tragedy of Karbala he switched sides and came to the tents of Imam Hussain repenting for his crime. Imam Hussain welcomed him with open arms, and he became one of the first martyrs from the side of Imam Hussain on the Day of Ashura.

Similarly, we have the example of Zuhayr bin al-Qayn who was a diehard Shia of Uthman. He was coming back with his wife from Haj to the city of Kufa when he encountered the caravan of Imam Hussain. After meeting Imam Hussain, he switched sides and became a Shia of Ali.

When Zuhayr went out to fight on the side of Imam Hussain on the Day of Ashura he was taunted by the army of Ubaydullah, who reminded him that he was previously a Shia of Uthman.

> *"Zuhayr according to us you were not the Shi'ah from this family (bayt). You used to be a supporter of the party of Uthman………"*

- *History of al-Tabari Volume 19 page 113*

Although for individuals like Al-Hur and Zuhayr it was a great honour to be martyred on the side of Imam Hussain, but their martyrdom did not avert the tragedy of Karbala or stop the killing of Imam Hussain. This is because the acts of individual courage and bravery or switching of sides to the camp of Imam Hussain were no match for the organised brutality that Ubaydullah bin Ziyad had put in place for the supporters of Imam Hussain.

Just as some individuals had switched sides to the camp of Imam Hussain there were also individuals who had moved to the camp of Yazid. These individuals choose the life of this world over the life of hereafter.

We have examples of individuals like Azrah bin Qays and Shimr bin Thu al Jawshan who had fought alongside Ali in the battle of Siffin, but now they were standing in the camp of Yazid. However, it has to be said that these individuals were the political Shias of Ali. They took the side of Ali in the battle of Siffin because Ali was the Caliph of the time and Ali held the political office of the Caliphate. As the political office of Caliphate moved to Yazid these individuals' switched sides and moved to the camp of Yazid.

In case of Shimr he did switch sides, but he moved to the camp of Yazid very early on. He did not switch sides right at the end. Shimr had always been part and parcel of Ubaydullah's entourage. Shimr was also that criminal who dealt the final blow to Imam Hussain and he was the one who beheaded the grandson of the Holy Prophet.

Since Shimr was once a political Shia of Ali and was on the side of Ali in the battle of Siffin, the supporters of the Umayyads argue that Imam Hussain was killed by a Shia of Ali, and in this guise, they also try and implicate the present-day Shia Muslims in the killing of Imam Hussain, despite knowing full well that the political Shias of Ali are in fact the Sunni Muslims of today.

The supporters of the Umayyads use every opportunity to malign the lovers of the Ahlulbayt.

They also do not realize that once you have switched sides you no longer remain part of the old camp, but instead you become part of the new camp that you have joined. For instance, Al-Hur who was the commander of Ubaydullah's army in Kufa was a Shia Muawiyah, but once he switched sides and moved to the camp of Imam Hussain, he no longer remained a Shia of Muawiyah, but instead he became a Shia of Ali.

Similarly, when Shimr fought alongside Ali in the battle of Siffin he was a Shia of Ali, but once he moved to the camp of Yazid he no longer remained a Shia of Ali, and instead he became a Shia of Muawiyah. So, when Shimr dealt the final blow to Imam Hussain and beheaded him, at that point in his life Shimr was not a Shia of Ali, he was a Shia of Muawiyah.

If a Muslim today leaves the path of Islam and becomes a Christian and starts drinking alcohol, one can no longer associate his actions of drinking alcohol with his Muslim heritage, because he no longer subscribes to the religion of Islam. He now subscribes to the religion of Christianity where drinking alcohol is allowed, and his actions now would be associated with his new religion.

Similarly, once Shimr left the camp of Ali and joined the camp of Yazid he no longer remained a Shia of Ali, and his actions of killing Imam Hussain can no longer be associated with his past. His actions of killing Imam Hussain are now associated with his new camp which was the camp of Yazid.

In any case, the actions of these individuals had no bearing on the actual outcome of the tragedy of Karbala. If Shimr had not joined the camp of Yazid then Ubaydullah would have used someone else from his army to kill Imam Hussain. There were many individuals like Shimr in the army of Ubaydullah bin Ziyad. He could have easily used any one of those criminals to kill the grandson of the Holy Prophet.

The actions of Ubaydullah bin Ziyad however were decisive as far as the tragedy of Karbala is concerned. He changed the course of history after he arrived in the city of Kufa. He changed the politics of the day and stifled the movement in favour of Imam Hussain in the city of Kufa. The movement of Muslim bin Aqeel was at its peak when Ubaydullah bin Ziyad arrived in Kufa.

People like Ubaydullah bin Ziyad had indeed changed the course of events, and he gave Kufa back to the Umayyads.

14.11.10.4. Ubaydullah Prevents the Supporters of Hussain

When Ubaydullah bin Ziyad devised a plan to kill Imam Hussain he gathers the Shias of Uthman, the Shias of Muawiyah and the opportunists in Kufa to join his army, while on the other hand he prevents the Shias of Ali in Kufa from reaching Karbala where Imam Hussain had been cornered.

Once Imam Hussain was forced towards Karbala, Ubaydullah effectively sealed off the city of Kufa, so that nobody could enter or leave the city without being arrested or killed by the security forces. The aim was simple, no one should be allowed to reach Imam Hussain or support his stand in Karbala.

The city of Kufa was placed under strict curfew and people were not allowed to move from one district to another. There was a complete blackout on any news and information coming in and out of Kufa, which meant that people had no idea as to what was actually happening. Many people were not even aware that Imam Hussain had been forced towards Karbala, and those who were aware were prevented from reaching him.

Imam Hussain enquired about the situation in Kufa from one of the people who lived in the desert outside Kufa. He said to Imam Hussain.

> "By Allah we don't know anything except the fact that neither we can exit nor can we enter (Kufa)"
> - History of Tabari Volume 19 page 84

Kufa was completely blocked off from Karbala. Ubaydullah bin Ziyad placed around five hundred soldiers under the command of Zabar bin Qais al Jaufi, who was tasked with patrolling all the routes from Kufa leading to Karbala. Anyone who was caught on route to Karbala would either be killed or imprisoned.

The Shias of Ali faced a similar situation on the borders of Kufa and Basra too. The Shias of Ali who were coming from Basra to support Imam Hussain were prevented from entering Kufa altogether, since Ubaydullah had placed his men on this border as well (History of Tabari Volume 19 page 83).

Ubaydullah used another cunning strategy to prevent the supporters of Imam Hussain from reaching Karbala. He introduced forced conscription into the army for all able-bodied men in the city of Kufa. All men of fighting age were given two choices i.e. either to join the army and fight Imam Hussain or be killed alongside their family.

As a result of this decree many Shias of Ali in Kufa went into hiding, to avoid being recruited into the army of Ubaydullah bin Ziyad. Also, many Shias of Ali who were forcefully recruited into the army of

Ubaydullah would disappear into the desert, as the army made its way to Karbala to avoid fighting against Imam Hussain.

To show to the people of Kufa that Ubaydullah meant what he had stated he killed a man from Syria who had come to Kufa on a personal matter. The man pleaded that he had nothing to do with this fight and refused to join the army of Ubaydullah, but Ubaydullah killed him and made an example out of him for the people of Kufa (Akhbar Tawal, page 252).

Ubaydullah used another effective tactic to blunt the support for the grandson of the Prophet. He used local leaders as spies to arrest and incarcerate anyone who was willing to support and join Imam Hussain in Karbala. He appointed local heads in each district of Kufa with the task of reporting anyone who had any links with the movement of Imam Hussain. These local heads were threatened with crucifixion on the doors of their homes if they did not comply with the orders of Ubaydullah (History of Tabari Volume 19 page 34).

As a result, anyone who was even suspected of having any links with the movement of Imam Hussain was arrested and imprisoned. Ubaydullah himself testified that he had imprisoned almost everyone who was a suspected of being a supporter of Imam Hussain.

> *"There was no individual who about whom were suspicions that he might oppose the government that was not imprisoned"*
> - *Tarikh Tabari Volume 7 page 18*

The supporters of Imam Hussain had either been killed, imprisoned or were under the curfew of Ubaydullah's security forces in Kufa. While some supporters of Imam Hussain had gone into hiding to avoid being forcefully recruited into the army of Ubaydullah.

It was under these circumstances that the Shias of Ali were prevented from joining Imam Hussain in Karbala.

Unlike the false narrative of the defenders of Muawiyah and Yazid who advocate that the Shias of Ali in Kufa had betrayed and killed Imam Hussain, the reality could not be more different. The Shias of Ali were in fact prevented from joining and supporting Imam Hussain in Karbala. They were in fact prevented from saving the life the grandson of the Prophet rather than killing him.

The killing of Imam Hussain was orchestrated by Ubaydullah bin Ziyad on the orders of Yazid, in a calculated and an extremely well thought out plan. Ubaydullah forced Imam Hussain away from Kufa in the direction of Karbala which was an open desert. He then gathered all the enemies of Imam Hussain in Karbala and prevented his supporters from reaching him, ensuring that Imam Hussain was killed with the minimum of the efforts.

It is the height of injustice on part of the supporters of Muawiyah and Yazid that they accuse the Shias of Ali for the killing of Imam Hussain, when in fact it was the Shias of Muawiyah and the Shias of Uthman who had killed Imam Hussain.

The real aim of the defenders of Muawiyah and Yazid is to actually kill three birds with one stone.

Firstly, they try and undermine the actual stand of Imam Hussain by moving the focus of the tragedy of Karbala away from the crimes of the Umayyads to the issue of the invitation of Imam Hussain by the people of Kufa.

Secondly, by putting the blame of the killing of Imam Hussain on the Shias of Kufa they try and relieve Yazid from having any hand in the killing of Imam Hussain.

Thirdly, by blaming the Shias of Kufa for the killing of Imam Hussain they also try and implicate the present-day Shia Muslims in the killing of Imam Hussain to try and malign their reputation too.

14.11.11. In Present Day Terms

The supporters of Muawiyah and Yazid very cleverly play with the term "Shia", knowing full well that the word "Shia" at the time of the tragedy of Karbala was used in a completely different context. At the time of the tragedy of Karbala every Muslim group was known as a Shia of someone, including the Sunni Muslims of today. The word "Sunni" or "Ahl al-Sunnah wal-Jama'ah" was not used to refer to any group of Muslims in that era.

The Sunnis at the time of the tragedy of Karbala were also known by the term "Shia". They were either called the Shia of Muawiyah, the Shia of Uthman, or the Shia of Ali (which included both the theological and the political Shias of Ali). The word "Sunni" or "Ahl al-Sunnah wal-Jama'ah" was coined much later in history, long after the tragedy of Karbala.

The ancestors of present-day Sunni Muslims at the time of the tragedy of Karbala were the Shias of Muawiyah, the Shias of Uthman, and the political Shias of Ali. It was in fact two groups within the Sunni Islam i.e., the Shias of Muawiyah and the Shias of Uthman who had killed Imam Hussain in Karbala.

The ancestors of the present-day Shia Muslims were the theological Shias of Ali in Kufa. They had certainly invited Imam Hussain to their city, but they were not the ones who had killed him. Imam Hussain was killed by the ancestors of the present-day Sunni Muslims, and this is a reality which is clear to any student of Islamic history.

The aim here certainly is not to implicate the present-day Sunni Muslims in the killing of Imam Hussain. The aim here is to simply state the historical facts. The groups which were involved in the killing Imam Hussain i.e., the Shias of Muawiyah and the Shias of Uthman, later on in history came under the broader umbrella of "Ahl al-Sunnah wal-Jama'ah" or Sunni Muslims.

In fact, it is for this historical reason that there has always been a difference of opinion within Sunni Islam with regards to the stand of Imam Hussain in Karbala. There are Sunni Muslims who would support and admire the stand of Imam Hussain against Yazid, whereas there are Sunni Muslims who would only partially support the stand of Imam Hussain and would not fully condemn or blame Yazid for his killing. Then there are those extreme groups within Sunni Muslims who consider Imam Hussain to be a rebel and Yazid to be the righteous Caliph.

The present-day Shia Muslims or their ancestors i.e., the theological Shias of Ali never had any such ambiguity about the principled stand of Imam Hussain. They have always been clear in their position towards the grandson of the Prophet. Throughout history and to the present day they have considered the stand of Hussain to be righteous and exemplary, and worthy of praise in every sense.

Some Sunni scholars have even taken hadith from the killers of Imam Hussain and have considered those narrators to be truthful and trustworthy.

For instance, we find that a famous Sunni scholar Ibn Hajar Asqalani who wrote the sharah (explanation) of Sahih Bukhari, says that Umar ibn Saad was truthful. Umar ibn Saad was the commander-in-chief of Ubaydullah's army in Karbala that killed Imam Hussain.

> *Umar ibn Sa'ad bin Abi Waqqas Al-Madani 'Truthful.'*
>
> - Source: Taqreeb Al-Tahdeeb. Pg. # 351, Person # 4903.

Ibn Hajar further says that Umar ibn Saad narrated traditions of the Prophet from his father and from Abu Saeed Al-Khudri, and Umar ibn Saad's children and grandchildren then narrated those traditions from him.

> *Umar ibn Sa'ad bin Abi Waqqas …. lived in Kufa. He narrated traditions from his father and Aboo Sa'eed Al-Khudri. His son Ibraheem and grandson Aboo Bakr bin Hafs ibn Umar….. and others have narrated traditions from him.*
>
> - Source: Tahdeeb Al-Tahdeeb. Vol. 3, Pg. # 227.

Another famous Sunni scholar Al-Mizzi reports that Umar ibn Saad was a trustworthy Tabiee.

> *Ahmad bin Abdullah Al-Ijlli said: "He (Umar ibn Saad) used to narrate traditions from his father, and the people narrated from him, and he is the one who killed Al-Hussain, and he is Trustworthy Tabi'ee."*
>
> - Tahdeeb Al-Kamal. Vol. 21, Pg. # 357.

The Arabic word "Tabiee" means a disciple of the companions of the Prophet or the generation of Muslims that came after the companions. Umar Ibn Saad was the commander in-chief of Yazid's army in Karbala, and he is considered to be a trustworthy disciple of the companions, which indeed is most unfortunate and tragic.

It becomes abundantly clear that because of the historical indifference within Sunni Islam towards the stand of Imam Hussain, some Sunni scholars have even accepted the killers of Imam Hussain as trustworthy narrators in their books of hadith.

The people who try and implicate the Shias of Ali in the killing of Imam Hussain with the aim of maligning even the present-day Shia Muslims, should realize that some of their own scholars have even taken and accepted the traditions of the Prophet from the killers of Imam Hussain, whereas the Shias have no such discrepancy about their narrators of hadith.

14.11.12. The Shias of Ali in Kufa and the Companions of the Prophet

The people who criticise the Shias of Ali in Kufa should read the history of nations to broaden their vision and see how human beings behave when the political or military tide would turn against them. These critics should at least read the history of the companions of the Prophet i.e., the first generation of Muslims, who had the honour of seeing and meeting the Prophet of Allah and spending time in his company.

The following incident from the time of the Prophet highlights the human behaviour and phycology in terms of one's temptations and perceived self-interest, despite the fact that these individuals were in the midst of a Friday sermon given by the Prophet of Allah.

This famous incident happened in the Holy Mosque of the Prophet in Madinah. The Prophet of Allah was giving the Friday sermon (Khutbah), a trade caravan approached with drums and fanfare selling merchandise, food and other items. The companions of the Prophet who were listening to his sermon left him standing alone in the mosque and rushed towards the trade caravan and started doing business with the traders.

Allah reprimanded the companions with these words.

> *When they saw the fanfare along with the caravan, they (almost all) flocked to it, leaving you (O Prophet) standing on the pulpit. Say, "What is with Allah is far better than amusement and merchandise. And Allah is the Best Provider."*
> - *(Quran 62:11)*

This incident is also narrated by Jabir ibn Abdullah with these words.

> *We were praying with the Prophet, peace and blessings be upon him, as a caravan arrived carrying food. They turned their attention to it until none remained with the Prophet but twelve men. Thus, the verse was revealed, "When they saw trade or diversion, they rushed to it and left you standing." (62:11)*
> - Ṣaḥīḥ al-Bukhari 936
> - Ṣaḥīḥ Muslim 863

The companions ditched the Prophet of Allah while he was in the middle of a Friday sermon and left him standing alone on the pulpit, to do business and for amusement as they could hear the fanfare and the beating of the drums.

If the Shias of Kufa had left the movement of Imam Hussain in face of extra ordinary brutality of the Umayyads where they were threatening people with crucifixion at their doorsteps, then surely the Shias of Ali in Kufa were no worse than the companions of the Prophet, who in peace times and without any threat to their lives or livelihoods had ditched the Prophet of Allah, while he was standing right in front of them giving the Friday sermon!

The companions of the Prophet and the Shias of Ali in Kufa were ordinary Muslims and human beings like me and you. When the companions of the Prophet saw that they could make some money and have some fun they left the Prophet to follow their desires. Similarly, when the Shias of Ali in Kufa were threatened with death alongside the death of their family members they also left the movement of Imam Hussain to save their lives.

However, neither the companions of the Prophet and nor the Shias of Ali in Kufa were chosen by Allah to lead the Muslim Ummah. They are not our role models, except those companions who had supported the mission of the Prophet throughout his lifetime, and except those Shias of Ali who had perished in the path of Imam Hussain, only they are our role models.

The Prophet had chosen the Ahlulbayt to lead the Muslim Ummah, so the honour of leading the Muslims belonged to Imam Hussain, and our aim should be to follow the path of Imam Hussain and not the path of others.

14.11.13. The First Attempt to Avenge the Killing of Hussain Fails

After the killing of Imam Hussain there was a lot of anger and unease among the people of Kufa, especially among the theological Shias of Ali, the ones who had written the very first letters of invitation to Imam Hussain. They were extremely angry at the Umayyads and at the same time they had an immense sense of guilt and remorse that they had invited Imam Hussain to their city, and he was killed in their neighbourhood, but they were not able to support him or join him in Karbala.

As the political and the military situation began to ease in an around Kufa, and the hold of the Umayyads began to loosen, the Shias of Ali began to regroup to avenge the killing of Imam Hussain.

Readers would recall that the first meeting to invite Imam Hussain to the city of Kufa was held in the house of Suleman bin Surad al-Khuzai, who had been imprisoned during the tragedy of Karbala. The very first letter of invitation to Imam Hussain was signed by Suleman bin Surad al-Khuzai and his group, which included Al-Musayyab bin Najaba, Rifa bin Shaddad, Habib bin al-Muzahir and Muslim bin Awsaja.

Two of the signatories on this letter i.e., Habib bin al-Muzahir and Muslim bin Awsaja had already been martyred alongside Imam Hussain in Karbala, as they did manage to leave Kufa and join Imam Hussain in Karbala, whereas the other three were unable to reach Imam Hussain.

The remaining three members of this movement i.e., Suleman bin Surad al-Khuzai, Al-Musayyab bin Najaba and Rifa bin Shaddad, alongside a few other notable Shia leaders of Kufa began to plan their next moves to bring the killers of Imam Hussain to justice. A meeting was again held in the house of Suleman bin Surad al-Khuzai, this time to try and formulate a plan to avenge the killing of Imam Hussain.

Here is an extract from one of the speeches made at the house of Suleman bin Surad al-Khuzai.

> *They were pulling him (Hussain) violently on the ground, not thinking of God in regard of him nor his relationship to the Prophet. Eyes have never before seen the like of this. By God, Husayn b. 'Ali, what a betrayal of truth, forbearance, trust, nobility, and resolution: the son of the first Muslim (Ali) in Islam and the son of the daughter of the Messenger of the Lord of the Worlds. Around him his defenders were few, and his attackers were in multitudes. His enemies killed him while his friends deserted him. Woe to the killers and reproaches to the deserters! God will accept no excuse from those who killed him, nor any argument from those who deserted him except that the latter should sincerely repent before God and fight against the killers and repudiate and eliminate the unjust and the corrupt. Only then, perhaps, God may accept our repentance and remove our guilt. We invite you to the Book of God and the Sunna of his Prophet, to vengeance for the blood of his [Prophet's] family and to war on the heretics and deviators from the true religion. If we are killed, there is nothing better for the pious than to be with their God; if we are successful, we will restore power to the Ahl al-Bayt of our Prophet.*
>
> - *Tabari, volume II, pp. 507-8*

The above extract sums up the feelings of Shias of Ali in Kufa after the killing of Imam Hussain. There was an overwhelming feeling of bewilderment and disbelief that Imam Hussain had been killed in their midst, and that they were not able to support him in the way that they had promised him. They felt that they had broken their promise to Imam Hussain as they were still alive while he had been brutally murdered in their midst.

Although all of this happened under duress and in the face of extra ordinary steps taken by Ubaydullah bin Ziyad against the Shias of Ali in Kufa, the Shias still felt an immense sense of guilt and a sense of responsibility, since they had invited Imam Hussain to their city but were not able to aid him in Karbala.

They felt that the only way they could redeem themselves was to first repent, and then avenge the killing of Imam Hussain from the deviators and the heretics i.e., from the Umayyads and their supporters, who were the actual killers of Imam Hussain. As they first repented i.e., they did Tawbah, this movement was known as the movement of Tawwabun (the penitents).

The Shias of Ali began to regroup under Suleman bin Surad al-Khuzai who was appointed as their leader. They began to collect money to form an army that could take on the might of the Umayyads. Suleman bin Surad al-Khuzai wrote to the Shia leaders in other parts of Iraq for assistance, so that they could also join his movement and avenge the killing of Imam Hussain. The response from the Shias of Ali was overwhelmingly positive. They promised support and money to avenge the killing of Imam Hussain at the hands of Umayyads.

Suleman bin Surad al-Khuzai gathered an army of around three thousand die hard Shias of Ali in Kufa. The aim was to find and annihilate the killers of Imam Hussain. The army under the command of Suleman bin Surad al-Khuzai first went to the grave of Imam Hussain in Karbala. They spent the night by his grave, lamenting and grieving over his tragic and barbaric killing. They made solemn promises at the grave of Imam Hussain that they would either bring his killers to justice or die in this path.

Next day the army left for the Syrian border and finally arrived at a place called Ayn al-Warda. The Umayyads had already sent an army of thirty thousand men under the command of Ubaydullah bin Ziyad to take on the Shias of Ali led by Suleman bin Surad al-Khuzai. Despite being hugely outnumbered the Shias of Ali fought one of the fiercest and the most violent battles in the history of Islam.

The battle lasted for around three days and a huge damage was inflicted on the Umayyad army. However, the Umayyads with their superior numbers finally managed to overpower the supporters of Imam Hussain, and unfortunately the Shias of Ali once again lost to the Umayyads. Almost the entire army of three thousand men was wiped out. Suleman bin Surad al-Khuzai and Al-Musayyab bin Najaba, who were both leading the army and were the founders of the initial movement in favour of Imam Hussain in Kufa, were brutally killed in this battle.

Only Rifa bin Shaddad survived from the original group which had invited Imam Hussain to Kufa. He and a handful of Shias who survived the battle returned back to Kufa and joined the movement of Mukthar al Taqavi, who would later mount another attempt to avenge the killing of Imam Hussain.

Contrary to the narrative advocated by the defenders of Muawiyah and Yazid, the actions of Shias of Ali in Kufa, after the killing of Imam Hussain clearly prove that they had absolutely no hand in his killing. They certainly invited Imam Hussain to their city and could not give him the kind of support that they had promised, but they were not his killers.

On the contrary, they in fact gave their lives trying to avenge his killing. Almost every single one of them was killed in this path, proving beyond any doubt that they were sincere in their invitation to Imam Hussain. The Umayyads did manage to subdue them temporarily in Kufa for a period of time, but their sincerity to the path and the mission of Imam Hussain was never in doubt, and this fact was vindicated by their actions in the battle of Ayn al-Warda, which took place some four years after the killing of Imam Hussain.

14.11.14. The Second attempt to Avenge the Killing of Hussain Succeeds

The first attempt by the Shias of Ali to avenge the killing of Imam Hussain had failed with a huge loss of life. Almost three thousand Shias had lost their lives in the battle of Ayn al-Warda. The remaining Shias of Ali under the leadership of Rifa bin Shaddad went back to Kufa and later joined the movement of Mukhtar al Taqavi. Mukhtar would lead the second uprising against the Umayyads in Kufa with the aim of avenging the killing of Imam Hussain.

Mukthar was the first Shia leader in Kufa who had hosted the ambassador of Imam Hussain i.e., Muslim bin Aqeel in his house when he arrived in Kufa. Mukthar was imprisoned by Ubaydullah bin Ziyad at the time of the tragedy of Karbala.

Readers would recall that after the killing of Imam Hussain the women and children from his family alongside the heads of the martyrs were paraded on the streets of Kufa, as a show of victory by the Umayyads.

It is said that Mukhtar either witnessed this event from his prison cell or heard the captives from the caravan of Imam Hussain as they passed by his prison. This event truly shock Mukthar and he cried and wept uncontrollably on witnessing the heads of the martyrs, and on the treatment being meted out to the widows and the orphans from the family of the Prophet. Mukhtar at that point made a promise that he would not rest until he would find and punish all the main culprits who were involved in the killing of Imam Hussain.

Mukhtar was a political and a military strategist unlike Suleman bin Surad al-Khuzai. Mukthar had advised Suleman bin Surad al-Khuzai not to take action against the Umayyads so soon after the tragedy of Karbala. Mukhtar was in prison when the Tawwabun launched their movement against the Umayyads. Mukhtar had suggested to the Tawwabun from his prison cell that they should wait until he was out before taking on the Umayyads.

But Suleman bin Surad al-Khuzai declined the offer of Mukhtar. The Tawwabun became emotional and had no proper plan or strategy to take on the Umayyads, they were kind of on a mission of self-sacrifice. They had decided to avenge the death of Imam Hussain at any cost, without necessarily taking into account the correct political or military strategy. However, the approach of Mukhtar was very different, he waited for the right opportunity to strike the Umayyads, and as a result he was extremely successful.

Once Mukhtar was released from prison he initially went to Makkah and then he returned back to Kufa, where he began his uprising with the motto "Ya la-Tharat al-Hussain", which means "O the avengers of Hussain". Under the leadership of Mukhtar, the Shias of Ali quickly took over the city of Kufa. The State's police force and the soldiers were forced to surrender, while the governor of Kufa escaped to Hijaz.

Mukhtar went to the pulpit of the grand mosque in Kufa and asked people to give him allegiance on three principles. Mukhtar stated that he would rule by the Book of Allah, the Sunnah of the Prophet, and he would seek to avenge the blood of the grandson of the Prophet. After acquiring the governorship of Kufa Mukhtar began to systematically search and kill the perpetrators of the tragedy of Karbala.

One of Mukhtar's key lieutenants was Ibrahim al Ashtar who was the son of Malik al Ashtar. Readers would recall that Malik al Ashtar was a key supporter of Ali. Malik al Ashtar had argued for the right of Ali to become the third Caliph against Caliph Uthman. Muawiyah later poisoned Malik al Ashtar and killed him in Egypt. Malik al Ashtar's son Ibrahim al Ashtar became an instrumental figure in the army of Mukhtar which would seek vengeance for the blood of Hussain.

One of the first people that Mukhtar captured were the ten horsemen who had trampled upon the blessed body of Imam Hussain after he had been beheaded. These horsemen had secured lavish rewards form Ubaydullah bin Ziyad for trampling the body of Imam Hussain. They were all captured and killed by Mukhtar.

The man by the name of Khooli who took the blessed head of Imam Hussain to his house, and then boasted his actions to Ubaydullah bin Ziyad in order to get a bigger reward was captured, after his wife gave away his whereabouts to Mukhtar. He was also executed by Mukhtar's men.

The commander in chief of Ubaydullah's army in Karbala was Umar ibn Saad. He had proudly announced that he was the first person who had fired arrows at the tents of Imam Hussain, and he was the one who indeed began the battle of Karbala. Umar ibn Saad was married to Mukhtar's sister. But Mukhtar paid no attention to his family links. He was looking to kill Umar ibn Saad wherever he could find him. Umar ibn

Saad was scared and frightened, he was hiding in Kufa and was moving from house to house to save his life. But Mukhtar located his whereabouts and sent Khayan to kill him. Umar ibn Saad was sleeping when Khayan approached him. As he woke up and tried to run Khayan strikes Umar ibn Saad and killed him.

Shimr bin Thu al Jawshan who beheaded Imam Hussain was hiding in Basra and was also moving from place to place to avoid being caught by Mukhtar's men. Shimr wrote a letter seeking help to save his life from Mukhtar, but his letter was intercepted revealing his whereabouts. Mukhtar sent his men to Basra who caught Shimr and executed him.

Seeing the rise of Mukhtar, the Umayyads sent an army from Syria towards Kufa, under the command of Ubaydullah bin Ziyad to kill Mukhtar and to take the city of Kufa back from him. Mukhtar sent an army under the command of Ibrahim al Ashtar to take on the advancing army from Syria, with specific instructions to kill Ubaydullah bin Ziyad.

Ibrahim al Ashtar the son of Malik al Ashtar was a brave warrior from Kufa. As the two armies met Ibrahim al Ashtar recognised Ubaydullah bin Ziyad on the battlefield from a specific perfume (mask) that he used to wear. Ibrahim al Ashtar made most of this rare encounter and killed Ubaydullah bin Ziyad. Ibrahim ibn al Ashtar then beheaded Ubaydullah bin Ziyad and brought his head to Mukhtar, just as Imam Hussain's head was brought to Ubaydullah bin Ziyad.

The killing of Ubaydullah bin Ziyad was a huge moment for the Shias of Ali in Kufa. He had been Yazid's top henchman in Iraq. He had killed and arrested thousands of Shias of Ali in Kufa and Basra. He was responsible for killing the grandson of the Prophet and enslaving the women and children of Prophet's family. He was also responsible for capturing and killing Muslim bin Aqeel the ambassador of Imam Hussain in Kufa, who was thrown from the rooftop of Ubaydullah's palace. The killing of Ubaydullah had brought a huge sense of relief and happiness to the Shias of Ali in Kufa.

But Mukhtar was seeking one man in particular, and his name was Hurmalah bin Khail. Hurmalah was a master of archery, and his crime was absolutely unforgivable. He had deliberately shot an arrow at the neck of Imam Hussain's six months old baby Ali Asghar, while Imam Hussain was seeking water for him. The arrow had pierced the neck of Ali Asghar who was instantly killed in the arms of Imam Hussain.

Mukhtar was seeking Hurmalah with a vengeance. Hurmalah had been running away from Mukhtar as he knew what his fate would be if he was caught. Hurmalah was finally arrested and was brought to Mukhtar. Hurmalah revealed that on the Day of Ashura he had directed many arrows towards the camps of Imam Hussain, but there were four arrows which were of great significance.

The first arrow of significance was directed towards the eyes of Al-Abbas who was the commander in chief of Imam Hussain's army in Karbala. He was also Imam Hussain's stepbrother. He was blinded in one eye by Hurmalah's attack. The second arrow was directed at Qasim who was the thirteen-year old son of Imam Hasan, while he was fighting on the battlefield of Karbala. The third arrow was directed towards Ali Asghar, the six months old baby of Imam Hussain, who died in the arms of his father. The fourth arrow was aimed at the forehead of Imam Hussain during the final moments of his life in Karbala.

Mukhtar killed Hurmalah like the rest of the killers of Imam Hussain.

They Shias of Ali were the avengers of Imam Hussain's blood. They were not his killers. Mukhtar successfully led the Shias of Ali in Kufa in avenging the killing of the grandson of the Prophet, proving beyond any doubt that the Shias of Ali were sincere in their love and support for Imam Hussain. They were temporarily subdued by the brutality of Ubaydullah bin Ziyad and his henchmen, but as soon as the Umayyads hold on the city of Kufa eased they began to regroup and asserted their authority.

Also, the Shias of Ali in Kufa were the only group in the Muslim Ummah who had avenged the killing of Imam Hussain in Karbala. No other group in the entire Muslim Ummah had the courage or the will to avenge the killing of the grandson of the Prophet from the Umayyads.

14.11.15. Hussain did not Listen to the Advice of the Key Companions

The defenders of Yazid and Muawiyah look for any excuse to try and defame the courageous and the principled stance of Imam Hussain against the Umayyads. They would try all kinds of tactics to try and poison the minds of the ordinary Muslims about the tragedy of Karbala. Apart from blaming the Shias for the killing of Imam Hussain they would also argue that Imam Hussain did not listen to the advice of the key companions who had advised him against travelling to Iraq.

They would point out that personalities like Abdullah Ibn Abbas, Muhammad ibn al-Hanafyyia, Abdullah Ibn Zubair and others had advised Imam Hussain against travelling to Iraq, but he ignored their advice and still went ahead with his plans and travelled to Kufa.

The aim of propagating such a notion is pretty clear. Firstly, the aim is to undermine the magnificent stand of Imam Hussain against the Umayyads, since the advocates of such notions support the key Umayyad leaders like Muawiyah and Yazid. Secondly, they try to portray Imam Hussain as an emotional and a stubborn individual who paid no attention to the advice that was given to him by his elders.

The people who propagate such notions about Imam Hussain either do not know or do not realize the position and the status of Imam Hussain in the eyes of the Prophet. Imam Hussain was no ordinary personality. The Prophet of Allah had declared that Imam Hussain was a leader of the paradise.

> 'Hasan and Hussain are the leaders of the youth in Paradise...'
> - (Sunan al-Tirmidhi. Hadith no. 3701. Book of Superiorities. Chapter; the Superiority of Imam Hasan and Hussain)

When Prophet of Allah declares someone to be a leader of the paradise, then this distinguished status must be based on some unique merit or some distinct achievement of that individual. The Prophet of Allah could not simply declare Imam Hussain to be a leader of the paradise just because he was his grandson. Such a pronouncement would inevitably be seen as clannish and tribal in nature, and as something that would be contradictory to the principles of Islam.

When Prophet declared Imam Hussain to be a leader of the paradise, Imam Hussain was around six or seven years of age and was still a child. This means that Imam Hussain was going to do something unique and distinct in his future life which would justify his unique status as a leader of the paradise.

When the key Islamic personalities advised Imam Hussain against travelling to Kufa and Iraq, Imam Hussain gave them an answer which history has preserved.

Imam Hussain said:

> *"Verily I had a dream, in which I saw the Prophet. He ordered me to do something, which I will implement. And I will not tell anyone of it until I complete this ordered task."*
> - p. 5 Tarikh al-Islam. Hafiz Shams al-Din Muhammad ibn Ahmad ibn Uthman al-Dhahabi (d. 748 A.H.) Vol.:Years 61-80 A.H. Dar al-Kutub al-Arabi, Beirut, Lebanon, 1998.
> - p.73. The History of al-Tabari; The Caliphate of Yazid. b. Mu'awiyah. Volume XIX. Translated by I.K.A. Howard. State University of New York Press, USA, 1990.
> - p. 163, Al-Bidaya wa al-Nihaya. Hafiz ibn Kathir (d. 774 A.H.) Volume VIII. Maktaba al-Ma'arif, Beirut, Lebanon. 1999.

Imam Hussain had seen a dream in which the Prophet of Allah ordered him to do something. Imam Hussain informed the people who were advising him against travelling to Iraq that he would implement the plan of the Prophet, but he would not tell anyone as to what that plan or task was until he had completed the task.

The decision of Imam Hussain to travel to Iraq, despite the advice of the notable Islamic personalities, clearly tell us the actual task that Prophet of Allah had set out for his grandson. The mission set out by the Prophet for Imam Hussain was a mission of self-sacrifice. It was a mission to redeem the Sunnah of the Prophet which had been changed and undermined by the corrupt rule of the Umayyads.

The task of Imam Hussain was to write with his own blood that the path which had been adopted by the Islamic leadership was against the traditions of its founder. The task of Imam Hussain was to take a stand against the despotic Umayyad rule and to rejuvenate the fire of Islam in the hearts and minds of the believers. The task of Imam Hussain was to sacrifice his entire family including his six months old son to awaken the conscious of the Muslim Ummah against the tyranny of the Umayyad rule.

The task of Hussain was to draw a clear line between right and wrong which had been blurred by the gradual decline of the Islamic Caliphate. The task given to Imam Hussain by the Prophet of Allah was to challenge the status quo which nobody else at the time had the courage to do so. The task ordained by the Prophet was to show to the entire Muslim Ummah that the people who were chosen as the custodian of his Sunnah i.e., the Ahlulbayt, would indeed one day justify their unique status by sacrificing everything that they had in its path, including their children.

Prophet had declared Ahlulbayt to the guardians of his faith. The Prophet stated:

"Behold! My Ahlul-Bayt are like the Ark of Noah. Whoever embarked in it was SAVED, and whoever turned away from it was PERISHED."

- *al-Mustadrak, by al-Hakim, v2, p343, v3, pp 150-151 on the authority of Abu Dhar. al-Hakim said this tradition is authentic (Sahih).*
- *Fadha'il al-Companions, by Ahmad Ibn Hanbal, v2, p786*
- *Tafsir al-Kabir, by Fakhr al-Razi, under the commentary of verse 42:23, Part 27, p167*
- *al-Bazzar, on the authority of Ibn Abbas and Ibn Zubair with the wording "drowned" instead of "perished".*
- *al-Sawa'iq al-Muhriqah, by Ibn Hajar Haythami, Ch. 11, section 1, p234 under Verse 8:33. Also in section 2, p282. He said this Hadith has been transmitted via numerous authorities.*
- *Tarikh al-Khulafaa and Jami' al-Saghir, by al-Suyuti al-Kabir, by al-Tabarani, v3, pp 37,38 al-Saghir, by al-Tabarani, v2, p22*
- *Hilyatul Awliyaa, by Abu Nu'aym, v4, p306*
- *al-Kuna wal Asmaa, by al-Dulabi, v1, p76*
- *Yanabi al-Mawaddah, by al-Qundoozi al-Hanafi, pp 30,370*

This was a huge honour that Prophet had bestowed upon the Ahlulbayt. But with every honour comes responsibility too. The higher the honour the bigger is the responsibility.

When things began to fall apart at the helm of the Islamic State and when the Sunnah of the Prophet became a toy in the hands of the Umayyads, it became the responsibility of the Ahlulbayt to step up to the plate and justify their status of being the guardians of the faith, through a unique and an unrivalled sacrifice which was not expected of the others in the Muslim Ummah.

The people who were advising Imam Hussain against travelling to Iraq were sincere in their advice, but they were not members of the Ahlulbayt. Prophet had not made them responsible for steering the ship of Islam in his absence. They were not aware of the responsibility that Prophet had placed on the shoulders of his grandson in his dream.

The Prophet of Allah had predicted the killing of Imam Hussain on many occasions, in order to prepare his grandson for the ultimate sacrifice. The Prophet used to cry whenever he would make the prophecy about the tragedy of Karbala. This is why on the Day of Ashura when Imam Hussain was actually killed, the Prophet with the will of Allah was present in Karbala, collecting the blood of his grandson.

Ibn Abbas narrates his dream in the following words:

> 'One afternoon I dreamt of Holy Prophet (saw) standing with his hair disturbed and with dust tangled in them and he was holding a phial filled with blood. I said to the Prophet (saw): 'O Allah's Prophet, what are you holding?' The Prophet (saw) replied: 'This is the blood of Hussain and his companions that I have been collecting all the day long." They did calculation and found out that he (Hussain) was killed a day before it (the day of dream).

- Al-Hakim in Al-Mustadrak Ala Sahihayn. Vol. 4, Pg. # 439-440.
- Ahmad ibn Hanbal in Musnad Ahmad ibn Hanbal. Vol. 4, H. # 2165, Pg. # 59 - 60.
- Al-Albani in Mishkatul Masabih of Al-Albani. Vol. 3, Pg. # 1741-1742.

Imam Hussain was neither stubborn nor emotional, and neither was he naive and nor was he a fool, as suggested by the supporters of Muawiyah and Yazid. Imam Hussain went to Iraq to fulfil the prophesy of the Prophet and to carry out the task that Prophet of Allah had ordained for him.

Imam Hussain was not under any illusions. At numerous points in his journey to Iraq he had asked his supporters to leave his cause, as it was a mission of self-sacrifice for him and him alone. On his way to Iraq when the news came that his brother and his ambassador Muslim bin Aqeel had been killed in Kufa, he gathered his supporters and informed them of the fate that was awaiting them.

He knew what the situation was like in Iraq. But he was duty bound to respond to the invitations of the people of Kufa. Imam Hussain had clarified his position with regards to the people of Kufa.

> "I shall not be blamed by Allah for shrinking from the religious duty of training and guiding people to be pious and simple. If the people of Kufa prove disloyal and if I am killed in the discharge of my duty, my position will be much nearer to God …."

- Life of Husayn the Saviour, P. 124.

Imam Hussain informed the people who were advising him against travelling to Iraq that if the people of Kufa prove to be disloyal, and if he is killed in this path then his position would have been much nearer to Allah, as he would have discharged his duty of guiding and leading the people to the right path.

The real agenda of the supporters of Yazid and Muawiyah is to simply undermine the magnificent and the principled stand of Imam Hussain against the Umayyads, in order to protect and defend the actions of some of the key companions especially Muawiyah.

If Imam Hussain had declined the invitation of the people of Kufa and had remained in Madinah or Makkah as per the advice of the key Islamic personalities, then it was almost certain that he would have been killed in either one of those cities. The supporters of Yazid and Muawiyah would then argue that Imam Hussain was killed in Makkah or Madinah because he was naive and stubborn, since he declined the invitation of thousands of his supporters and well-wishers from Kufa, and he had refused to go to a city where he had so much support and following.

The supporters of Yazid and Muawiyah would always be able to find an argument to belittle and undermine the stand of Imam Hussain.

However, the stand of Imam Hussain was not based on the invitations from the people of Kufa. Imam Hussain was fully aware of the political situation in Iraq, especially after Muslim bin Aqeel had been killed in Kufa. Imam Hussain had witnessed at first hand that when his own father Ali became the fourth Caliph, he could not subdue Muawiyah despite being the Caliph of the time. Imam Hussain had also witnessed how Muawiyah had turned the tables against his brother Imam Hasan, who was forced to sign a peace treaty.

Imam Hussain knew that he was not going to end the Umayyad rule or become the Caliph of the Muslims. Imam Hussain's mission was to simply write a note of protest with his blood, to awaken the conscious of the Muslim Ummah, and to show that the path adopted in Saqifah against the Sunnah of the Prophet eventually undid the revolution of Islam, and it allowed the enemies of the Prophet such as the Umayyads to acquire the leadership of the Muslim Ummah.

The task set out by Prophet for Imam Hussain in his dream was a replica of the task set out by Allah for Prophet Ibrahim in his dream. Prophet Ibrahim had a dream that Allah had ordered him to sacrifice his son Ismail. Prophet Ibrahim went ahead and fulfilled his dream and slaughtered his son Ismail, but Allah saved Ismail and a sheep was slaughtered instead.

Although Ismail was saved but since Prophet Ibrahim fulfilled the commands of Allah, it became a celebration (Eid ul Adha) for the entire Muslim Ummah. In case of Hussain, he also fulfilled his dream and followed the commands of the Prophet, but he was not so lucky. He paid the ultimate price with his blood and with the blood of his children and wrote a history of sacrifice that is yet be matched.

Prophet Ibrahim blindfolded himself as he could not bear to see the blood of his son Ismail. But Hussain witnessed the blood of his eighteen-year-old son Ali Akbar in his lap, and Hussain witnessed the blood of his six months old son Ali Asghar in his arms. The sacrifice of Hussain was unique and distinct.

Let's not defame the magnificent stand of Imam Hussain in order to defend the decisions made in Saqifah, or defend personalities like Yazid and Muawiyah whose hands were stained with the blood of the Ahlulbayt. It is not going to get us any mileage on the Day of Judgment.

Hussain was even a star among the Ahlulbayt. His sacrifice is unmatched even within the family of the Prophet. The Prophet of Allah for this very reason had said.

'I am from Hussain and Hussain is from me…..'

- (Sunan al-Tirmidhi. Hadith 3708. Book of Superiorities. Chapter; the Superiority of Imam Hasan and Hussain)

14.11.16. When Hasan Signed a Deal then Why did Hussain Take a Stand

As I have said on a number of occasions the aim is to somehow find any excuse to discredit Imam Hussain and pick holes in the path adopted by the grandson of the Prophet. The goal is to malign and vilify the stand of Imam Hussain by injecting a variety of thoughts and notions in the minds of the ordinary Muslims.

The supporters of Yazid and Muawiyah would argue that when Imam Hasan had signed a deal with Muawiyah and eventually accepted his Caliphate, then why did Imam Hussain not take the same approach? Why did Hussain not come to some kind of an agreement with Yazid? And why was there a discrepancy in the approach of the two brothers, when both of them were members of the Ahlulbayt?

The individuals who try and dismiss the stand of Hussain with such naive and childish slur have not paid any attention to the sequence of events which led to the signing of the peace treaty between Muawiyah and

Imam Hasan, and the sequence of events which led Imam Hussain to take a stand against the tyrannical Caliphate of Yazid. The politics of the day were not so simple or straightforward that both Imam Hasan and Imam Hussain should have taken the same approach.

The situation facing Imam Hasan was completely different to the scenario facing Imam Hussain. Imam Hasan was the Caliph of the time, and Muawiyah offered him a peaceful resolution to an ongoing war, by offering him a peace treaty. However, in case of Imam Hussain, Yazid was the Caliph of the time, and was demanding unconditional allegiance form Imam Hussain. The two scenarios were totally different and poles apart . Hence the approach of Imam Hasan and Imam Hussain was also different.

Muawiyah gave Imam Hasan a blank piece of paper to sign, where Imam Hasan was given complete authority to write down any conditions that he wanted to in the peace treaty. Obviously, we now know that later on Muawiyah did not comply with any of the conditions that he had agreed, but at time when he offered the peace deal to Imam Hasan, he gave Imam Hasan a blank cheque, and Imam Hasan was allowed to write down anything that he wanted to in the peace treaty.

But in case of Imam Hussain, Yazid demanded total capitulation from Imam Hussain from the word go. He never gave Imam Hussain any diplomatic option. He only gave Imam Hussain two choices i.e., either to pay allegiance or face death. The scenarios facing Imam Hasan and Imam Hussain had no similarities, except the fact that Imam Hasan was facing Muawiyah who was the father and Imam Hussain was facing his son Yazid.

Also, in case of Imam Hasan he had political authority being the Caliph of the time. He was responsible for the lives of millions of Muslim subjects under his authority, including the army personnel under his command. He had witnessed the battle of Siffin at first hand which was fought between his father Ali and Muawiyah. The battle of Siffin had cost the lives of some seventy thousand Muslims.

So, when Muawiyah offered the peace deal to Imam Hasan to stop the war, Imam Hasan being the leader of the Muslim Ummah was obliged to respond to Muawiyah's proposal positively, to potentially save the lives of thousands of his subjects, despite what the intentions of Muawiyah may have been at the time. Imam Hussain on the other hand had no such responsibility. He held no political office when Yazid demanded allegiance from him. Imam Hussain was only responsible for his own life, his family's life, and the lives of his few die-hard supporters.

The decision of Imam Hasan had to reflect the interests of all his subjects who were under his authority, whereas Imam Hussain did not face such a scenario.

Furthermore, the peace treaty between Imam Hasan and Muawiyah was done on specific points. It wasn't an approval of Muawiyah's character or his policies, as some supporters of Muawiyah try to portray. On the contrary the aim of the deal was to reverse the policies of Muawiyah and tie him down to a specific set of conditions, to ensure that Muawiyah rules by the Quran and the Sunnah of the Prophet, which he wasn't doing in Syria where he was the governor.

There was no compromise on the principles of Islam by Imam Hasan in the peace treaty signed with Muawiyah. The treaty in fact was meant to push Muawiyah to follow the Islamic path. The only compromise that Imam Hasan made was to lose his political authority after tying Muawiyah down to a very specific code of conduct.

In case of Imam Hussain there was no political authority that he could have potentially lost, hence his approach was different. The ultimate thing that Imam Hussain could have lost was his life, so he compromised his life and defended the principles of Islam.

Also, legally speaking the stand of Imam Hussain was completely legitimate and within the rules of the peace treaty signed by Imam Hasan. Imam Hussain abided by the peace treaty with Muawiyah throughout the duration of Muawiyah's Caliphate. Only when Muawiyah broke the very last condition of the treaty and appointed his son Yazid as the new Caliph, Imam Hussain took a stand and refused to accept the illegal Caliphate of Yazid.

So, the stand of Imam Hussain against Yazid was completely legitimate and justified even from a legal point of view. Imam Hussain only took a stand against the Umayyads once Muawiyah had broken every single condition in the treaty that he had signed.

Although the approach of Imam Hasan and Imam Hussain was very different at a practical level i.e. Imam Hasan signed the peace deal with Muawiyah and Imam Hussain took a stand against the Caliphate of Yazid, but the outcome of both approaches was the same. Both Imam Hasan and Imam Hussain exposed Muawiyah and Yazid as un-Islamic characters with no interest in ruling by the Book of Allah or the Sunnah of the Prophet. Muawiyah was exposed as an unprincipled man who would break his promise, and Yazid as a cruel dictator who was willing to go to any length to prolong his illegal rule.

Also, the approach adopted by both Imam Hasan and Imam Hussain clearly showed that they considered Muawiyah and Yazid to be their enemies. In case of Imam Hasan, he signed the peace treaty with Muawiyah, proving that Muawiyah was an enemy. Because peace deals are only signed between enemies, especially an enemy that you have been at war with. And in case of Imam Hussain, he refused to give allegiance to Yazid, again proving that he not only considered Yazid to be his enemy but an enemy of Allah too.

And last but not least, the approaches adopted by Imam Hasan and Imam Hussain were indeed prophesized by the Messenger of Allah. The Messenger of Allah had said about Imam Hasan that this son of mine would make peace between two Muslim groups.

> *"This son of mine is a chief, and Allah may make peace between two groups of Muslims through him."*
>
> - Sahih al-Bukhari 7109
> - Sahih Al-Bukhari, Book of "Afflictions," #6629, vol.6

And for Imam Hussain the Prophet had prophesized that this son of mine would be killed on the plains of Karbala.

> *"……. Prophet said: Jibril came to me and said that very soon, some people from my Ummah will kill this son (Hussain) of mine. I asked: O Prophet, will they kill this prince? The Holy Prophet said: Yes and Jibril gave me the red sand of that place (Karbala)"*
>
> - Sunan Bayhaqi- Dalaail Un Nubuwwah, Hadith No: 2805
> - Mishkaat Ul Masabeeh, Vol. 2, Pg No. 572
> - Zujajatul Masabeeh, Vol. 5, Pg No. 327/328

It is impossible that Prophet of Allah would make such prophecies without actually agreeing with the actions of his grandsons. The Prophet of Allah was fully aware of the approach that Imam Hasan and Imam Hussain were going to take, and he still made them the leaders of the paradise, proving beyond any doubt that the approach adopted by both Imam Hasan and Imam Hussain had the seal of approval of the Prophet.

The Prophet of Allah had said:

> 'Hasan and Hussain are the leaders of the youth in Paradise...'

- *(Sunan al-Tirmidhi. Hadith no. 3701. Book of Superiorities. Chapter; the Superiority of Imam Hasan and Hussain)*

Those who question the approach of Imam Hasan and Imam Hussain with respect to Muawiyah and Yazid, should perhaps pose the question to the Prophet of Allah on the Day of Judgment.

14.11.17. Hussain was Going for Power and was After the Caliphate

When all else fails to stick against the unique and the wonderful stand of Imam Hussain, the extreme supporters of the Umayyads would even claim that Imam Hussain was going for power, and Yazid was right to crush the rebellion spearheaded by Hussain.

The people who make such accusation towards the grandson of the Prophet have completely lost their sense of justice and fair play.

If Imam Hussain was truly going for power, then Imam Hussain would have initiated the challenge to the authority of Yazid, since Imam Hussain would have been looking to replace Yazid as the new Caliph. But Imam Hussain did not initiate any challenge to the rule of Yazid. It was Yazid who demanded allegiance from Imam Hussain once he became the Caliph.

It was Yazid who was looking to consolidate his power after acquiring the seat of the Caliphate, rather than the myth propagated by the supporters of the Umayyads that Imam Hussain was seeking power. It wasn't Imam Hussain who initiated the crisis that led to the tragedy of Karbala. It was Yazid who initiated this crisis by demanding allegiance from the grandson of the Prophet to solidify his rule. It was Yazid who made the first move not Hussain.

Yazid knew the position and the status of Imam Hussain within the Muslim Ummah. Imam Hussain being the last surviving member of the Ahlulbayt commanded a huge amount of love and respect among the Muslim masses. Yazid was also fully aware of the position of Imam Hussain in relation to the Prophet. Yazid knew that Prophet had made the Ahlulbayt the guardians of his faith. It was Yazid who needed allegiance from an individual like Imam Hussain to approve his caliphate, rather than the baseless accusation that Imam Hussain was going for power.

Also, Yazid knew full well that his Caliphate was illegal and was forced onto the Muslim Ummah by his father Muawiyah. Muawiyah had broken the peace treaty with Imam Hasan where Muawiyah had promised that he would not appoint a successor, but Muawiyah appointed his son Yazid as his successor and made him the Caliph of the Muslim Ummah. Yazid wanted to legitimize and justify his Caliphate in the eyes of the Muslim Ummah by seeking allegiance from Imam Hussain. Because if Imam Hussain pays allegiance to Yazid it means that the Ahlulbayt had given their seal of approval for the Caliphate of Yazid.

Even the travel of Imam Hussain to Iraq was not his own idea. It was initiated by the people of Kufa. It was the people of Kufa who had invited Imam Hussain to their city. Imam Hussain did not write to the people of Kufa suggesting that he wanted to lead or guide them. It was the people of Kufa who had asked Imam Hussain to come to their city and become their leader.

Also, the invitation from the people of Kufa was a reaction to the demand of allegiance from Yazid. The invitation by the people of Kufa was only made after they heard that Yazid was demanding allegiance from Imam Hussain, and Imam Hussain had refused to give allegiance to Yazid and had taken a stand against his Caliphate.

It was Yazid who triggered this whole sequence of events by demanding allegiance from Imam Hussain, since it was him who was looking to consolidate his rule rather than Imam Hussain vying for power.

Furthermore, the actions of Imam Hussain throughout the crisis of Karbala clearly show that he wasn't interested in acquiring power, and nor was he seeking the Caliphate of the Muslim Ummah. Because if Imam Hussain was truly after the Caliphate and if he was genuinely looking to dislodge Yazid, then Imam Hussain would have been rallying his troops to fight the army of Yazid to win the battle of Karbala.

But Imam Hussain kept offering his supporters to leave his path and save their lives. Even on the eve of the battle of Karbala, the night before the battle was about to commence Imam Hussain puts out all the candles and offers his troops to leave him in the guise of darkness, to relieve them from any sense of guilt. This was not a path to acquire power by any stretch of the imagination. This was a path of self-sacrifice on part of Imam Hussain, a path that was ordained by the Prophet, in order to redeem his Sunnah.

The readers would also recall that while Imam Hussain was on his way to Kufa he received the news that his ambassador Muslim bin Aqeel had been killed there. If Imam Hussain was truly seeking the Caliphate with the support and the backing of the people of Kufa, then surely Imam Hussain would have known at that point that he could not count on the people of Kufa to support his movement, since if the people of Kufa were unable to defend and protect his ambassador, then it was unlikely that they would support his movement to dislodge the Caliphate of Yazid.

Surely at that point Imam Hussain would have stopped and turned back and would have dropped the idea of expecting any support from the people of Kufa in removing Yazid from power. However, after receiving the news that Muslim bin Aqeel had been killed in Kufa, Imam Hussain did not stop but instead he continued his journey, because the mission of Imam Hussain was not to acquire the Caliphate. The mission of Imam Hussain was to write a note of protest with his blood, to show to the Muslim Ummah that what was happening at the helm of the Islamic State was against the Book of Allah and the Sunnah of the Prophet.

The goal of Imam Hussain was to awaken the conscious of the Muslims with a unique and distinct sacrifice. The actions of Imam Hussain completely negate the notion that he was going after the political office of the Caliphate.

Also, the people who accuse Imam Hussain of going after the Caliphate should perhaps cast an eye on the size and the makeup of Imam Hussain's contingent. The entire contingent of Imam Hussain was no more than one hundred and twenty people. This included around forty women and children who were also part of his caravan. The army at the disposal of Yazid was in tens of thousands of men.

Surely, if Imam Hussain was after the political office of the Caliphate, then he would have realized that the troops at his disposal had no chance of delivering that goal. And surely, Imam Hussain was wise enough to know that he was not going to defeat the army of Yazid with the handful of supporters that he had. But since Imam Hussain was not after the political office of the Caliphate, the size and the makeup of his contingent made no difference, and he still took a stand against the Caliphate of Yazid, to show to the Muslim Ummah that the path adopted by the Islamic leadership was contrary to the path laid out by the Prophet of Allah.

The aim of Imam Hussain was to rekindle the ideological fire of Islam in the hearts of the believers which had been dampened by decades of Umayyad rule.

14.11.18. The Fabricated Story of Imam Baqir

Another strategy used by the supporters of Yazid and Muawiyah to discredit the magnificent stand of Imam Hussain is to propagate a fabricated story in the name of Imam Baqir, who was the grandson of Imam Hussain. This fabricated story is heavily relied upon by the Salafis to poison the minds of the ordinary Muslims about the tragedy of Karbala.

I have seen this story being propagated heavily in the South Asian countries. Following are some of the main contours of this fabricated story.

When Imam Hussain received the news of the killing of Muslim bin Aqeel he wanted to go back and end his stand against Yazid, but his cousins who were part of his caravan insisted that they should avenge the killing of Muslim bin Aqeel, and hence Imam Hussain continued his journey to Kufa.

As always, the aim with such notions is to simply discredit the principled and the courageous stand of Imam Hussain, and to give the impression that Imam Hussain's mission in Karbala was not based on his disapproval of the Caliphate of Yazid, but it was based on avenging the killing of his brother Muslim bin Aqeel.

As part of this fabricated story, it is further said that Imam Hussain was willing to pay allegiance to Yazid, however Imam Hussain wanted to pay allegiance to Yazid in person, but Ubaydullah rejected this demand of Imam Hussain because Ubaydullah wanted Imam Hussain to give him allegiance first, since he was the governor of Kufa. As Imam Hussain rejected this demand of Ubaydullah, he ordered the killing of Imam Hussain in Karbala.

Again, the aim is to simply tarnish and defame the magnificent stand of Imam Hussain by claiming that Imam Hussain was actually willing to pay allegiance to Yazid, and it was Ubaydullah who created this whole mess by insisting that Imam Hussain should pay allegiance to him first.

The goal of this fabricated story is to firstly smear and belittle the stand of Hussain and secondly to protect Yazid from any wrongdoing.

The reason why they try and blame Ubaydullah is to protect Yazid, because if Yazid is implicated in the killing of Imam Hussain then it means that his father Muawiyah would also be implicated in the killing of Imam Hussain. Since Yazid did not just land on the seat of the Caliphate out of thin air. It was Muawiyah who forced his brutal son Yazid on the Muslim Ummah. The blame for the killing of Imam Hussain would inevitably fall on the shoulders of Muawiyah too, so the aim really is to protect Muawiyah, and this is done by cleverly shifting the blame from Yazid to Ubaydullah.

And the reason why they want to protect Muawiyah is because Muawiyah was a companion of the Prophet, and they feel religiously obliged to protect and defend the actions of every single companion, regardless of whether those actions were in line with the Sunnah of the Prophet or not. They have in fact made this as part of their religion, that they should defend the actions and decisions of each and every companion, regardless of what those companions ever did in their lifetimes.

They don't care that Muawiyah was one of those companions who not only destroyed the Sunnah of the Prophet, but he almost undid the entire revolution of the Prophet by changing the Islamic Caliphate into an Umayyad dynasty. It is clear that for these supporters of the Umayyads defending the actions of one of the most corrupt and ruthless companions such as Muawiyah takes precedence over the life of the grandson of the Prophet.

It is true that as a general rule of thumb we should respect the companions of the Prophet. But that does not mean that we should place the status of a companion above the Book of Allah or the Sunnah of the Prophet. If a companion breaks the laws laid out by Allah and his Prophet, then we must distance ourselves from the actions of that companion, and instead we should support the Book of Allah and the Sunnah of the Prophet.

This whole story which is attributed to Imam Baqir who was the grandson of Imam Hussain was fabricated by Khalid bin Abdullah al Kasri. Al Kasri was a governor of the Umayyads in Makkah. He was one of those extreme haters of Ali who would curse and abuse Ali from the pulpits of Makkah. Imam Dhahabi also declared him to be a nasibi, which means a person who was an enemy of Ali and the Ahlulbayt.

There is a book called Giyat al Marah which mentions the history of the governors of Makkah. This book sheds light on the character and the hatred of Al-Kasri towards Ali and the family of the Prophet. This fabricated story was first narrated in Al-Tabari by Zakaria bin Yahya Zalil. All the other historians and hadith recorders have copied this story from Al-Tabari.

The narrator of this story i.e. Zakaria bin Yahya Zalil has been classed as Majhool in the science of Hadith. Majhool in terms of the science of Hadith means an unknown narrator i.e. a person who is not known to the Hadith recorders or the historians, and they have no idea about the identity of this individual.

So not only has this story been fabricated by an enemy of the Ahlulbayt but the main narrator of this story is also an unknown individual. Nobody even knows if this narrator ever existed in history.

It is a real shame that some Muslims could scope so low that they would use a story which has been fabricated by an Umayyad governor, who was a known enemy of the Ahlulbayt and where even the narrator of the story is unknown, and then attribute this story to Imam Baqir who was the grandson of Imam Hussain, with the sole aim of making the story sound believable.

The propagators of this story don't even realize that if this story was in fact true and if Imam Hussain had indeed agreed to give allegiance to Yazid, then there would have been no reason for the tragedy of Karbala, and Yazid would have won without throwing a single arrow towards Imam Hussain.

Ubaydullah was the governor of Yazid in Kufa. Yazid had not promised Ubaydullah huge rewards for Imam Hussain to pay allegiance on his governor's hand. Yazid had promised reward for Ubaydullah to convince Imam Hussain to pay allegiance to him as the new Caliph.

If Imam Hussain had indeed changed his mind and had agreed to give allegiance to Yazid then Ubaydullah would have been the first person to take Imam Hussain to the palace of Yazid, since Yazid would have showered Ubaydullah with a huge reward for convincing Imam Hussain to give him allegiance. The entire dispute between Imam Hussain and Yazid would have been over.

Furthermore, many propagators of this fabricated story also consider Imam Hussain to be a rebel, since according to them Imam Hussain had refused to accept the legitimate Caliphate of Yazid. If this story is in fact true, then the issue of Imam Hussain being a rebel is also resolved. Because according to this story Imam Hussain had agreed to give allegiance to Yazid, which clearly means that Imam Hussain was no longer a rebel, and his killing was completely unjustified.

The truth is that Hussain was not only oppressed in Karbala, but he is still being oppressed by the arrows of injustice. Let's not oppress Hussain anymore with such fabricated and childish stories and give Hussain the credit that he truly deserves.

14.11.19. Yazid was Forgiven by the Prophet

To add insult to injury and to further discredit and tarnish the stand of Imam Hussain it is said that Prophet had said that Yazid would be forgiven. A tradition of the Prophet is quoted from Bukhari to justify this narrative. The tradition of the Prophet goes like this:

> *"Paradise will be granted to the first batch of my followers who will undertake a naval operation in the war of Constantinople (Qustuntuniya)"*
> - Sahih Bukhari, Kitab ul jihad, hadith no 2924

The above tradition of the Prophet is basically a prophecy, which states that the first Muslim army that attacks Constantinople (present day Istanbul) would be forgiven. Constantinople at that time was part of the Roman Empire.

The supporters of the Umayyads say that it was Yazid who led the first army battalion to Constantinople, and hence as per the above tradition of the Prophet he is forgiven. They give the following tradition as evidence for Yazid's participation in the first army that attacked Constantinople.

> *"...... one of whom was Abu Ayyub, the companion of Allah's Messenger in the battle in which he (Abu Ayyub) died and Yazid bin Mu'awiya was their leader in Roman Territory"*
> - Sahih Bukhari, Kitab ul Tahujjud, Hadith no. 1185

Let us see if the assertion of the supporters of Yazid that he had been forgiven because he took part in the first army expedition to Constantinople is correct.

The above tradition of the Prophet which is given as evidence for Yazid's participation in the army that first attacked Constantinople also states that a companion of the Prophet by the name of Abu Ayyub Ansari died in that expedition. So, this expedition would have been the last expedition for Abu Ayyub Ansari, since he died in this expedition.

However, there is another tradition in Sunan Abu Dawood which would prove that the expedition led by Yazid to Constantinople was not the first expedition to Constantinople.

> *"..... We went out on an expedition from Medina with the intention of (attacking) Constantinople. Abdur Rahman ibn Khalid ibn al-Walid was the leader of the company..... Abu Ayyub (who was part of the expedition) said: This verse was revealed about us, the group of the Ansar (the Helpers) ..... Abu Ayyub continued to strive in the cause of Allah until he (died and) was buried in Constantinople"*
> - Sunan Abu Dawood, Kitab ul Jihad, Hadith no. 2512

The above tradition states that Abul Rehman led an expedition to Constantinople while Abu Ayyub Ansari was still alive. Since during this expedition Abu Ayyub Ansari was explaining the verses of the Quran to others. This means that the expedition in which Abu Ayyub Ansari died and was led by Yazid must have been after this expedition.

In other words, the army expedition led by Abdul Rehman to Constantinople must have been before the expedition led by Yazid.

So, the expedition to Constantinople led by Yazid could not have been the first one. At best it could have been the second one. The prophecy of the Prophet for forgiveness is only for the members of the very first expedition to Constantinople, and Yazid was not part of that expedition.

The tradition in Sunan Abu Dawood actually clarifies this issue even further. It states that Abu Ayyub Ansari continued to strive in the path of Allah, meaning that he took part in many expeditions to Constantinople until he finally died in one of those expeditions. So, the expedition in which Abu Ayyub Ansari died was led by Yazid, but his previous expeditions to Constantinople were led by others, such as Abul Rehman.

Yazid was part of one of the army expeditions to Constantinople, but he was not part of the first army that attacked Constantinople, contrary to what the supporters of the Umayyads advocate. This defence card for Yazid was first used by an individual called Ibn Taymiyyah, and the supporters of Yazid have been blindly following him for centuries without even checking the historical facts.

It is most unfortunate and sad to see that there are Muslims living in 21st century who would try and defend a character like Yazid, rather than support the grandson of the Prophet who had sacrificed everything that he had in the path of Allah including his children.

In the course of our discussion so far, I have assumed that the prophecy of the Prophet about the first army that attacked Constantinople is in fact genuine and authentic. Since I wanted to show that even if Prophet had made such a prophecy, it could not be used in favour of Yazid. However, if one looks at the chain of narrators of this tradition it is extremely likely that this tradition of the Prophet was fabricated during the era of the Umayyads.

This tradition of the Prophet has only been narrated by a single person, whose name is Umm Haram bint Milhan. Nobody else other than Um Haram has narrated this tradition of the Prophet. Also, in the chain of narrators all the individuals are from Syria (Sham). No Muslim in any other part of the Muslim Ummah such as Makkah, Madinah, Iraq etc had ever heard of this tradition.

Syria was the province of the Islamic State where Muawiyah had built his empire, and Umayyads had fabricated many traditions of the Prophet in favour of their leaders, in order to justify their acquired positions of authority in the Muslim Ummah. A tradition which is only narrated by the people of a certain persuasion i.e., a tradition which is only narrated by the Syrians, who were the supporters and followers of the Umayyads in those days, is likely to be fabricated and cannot be used as an alibi for Yazid, since he was an Umayyad too.

In that era of tribalism, the people of Syria were bound to side with Muawiyah and Yazid as they were the leaders of their clan. The testimony of Syrians alone in favour of Muawiyah or Yazid cannot be relied upon, unless it was reported by Muslims of other regions too.

Also, among the chain of narrators of this tradition are individuals like Saud Bin Yazid al Kalahi, who were open haters of Ali. Saud Bin Yazid al Kalahi used to curse Ali, and he would justify his actions by stating that how could he possibly like Ali when Ali had killed his grandfather in the battle of Siffin. The sword of Ali had created many enemies, both during the lifetime of the Prophet and also in the intra-Muslim wars that took place after the death of the Prophet.

The enemies of Ali had fabricated many such traditions in that era, in order to protect the Umayyad leaders from the heinous crimes that they had committed against the family of the Prophet. Such traditions were a way of saving the stature and the reputation of the Umayyad leaders in the eyes of the ordinary Muslims.

14.11.19.1. The Attack on Madinah

Those who argue for the forgiveness of Yazid should realize that the crimes of Yazid were not limited to the tragedy of Karbala alone. The killing of Imam Hussain and taking the family of the Prophet captive was undoubtedly his biggest crime. However, Yazid had committed many other unforgivable crimes against the Muslim Ummah during his Caliphate.

Readers would recall that Ansar (natives of Madinah) had been side-lined ever since the Caliphate of Abu Bakr. Caliph Abu Bakr had offered to make the Ansar his advisors in Saqifah, but he never fulfilled his promise when he actually became the Caliph. Subsequently, Caliph Umar also barred the Ansar from the leadership of the Muslim Ummah when he formed the six-member Shura to choose the next Caliph after him.

As a consequence of this approach the Ansar rallied behind Ali after the killing of Caliph Uthman, since they saw him as the only viable person who could protect their rights. The Ansar for this reason had a soft corner for Ali and his children. Also, both Imam Hasan and Imam Hussain had grown up in Madinah, so there was a lot of support and respect for the family of the Prophet in the city of Madinah.

When the news reached Madinah that Imam Hussain had been killed by the Umayyads and his family had been taken captive, there was a lot of anger and unease in the city. A sort of a rebellion began to take shape in Madinah and many inhabitants of Madinah revoked their pledge of allegiance from Yazid. These pledges of allegiance for Yazid were taken forcefully in the first place when Muawiyah had appointed Yazid as the new Caliph.

Yazid could not possibly afford to lose Madinah, so he launched an attack on city to pacify its citizens. Thousands of Umayyad troops entered Madinah, and nothing was spared including the mosque of the Prophet.

The commander of Yazid's army Muslim ibn Aqabah gave sweeping powers to his soldiers.

> *"Your hands are open and you are free to do whatever you want. You must plunder and loot Medina for three days."*
> - Al-Imamah wa al-Siyasah, vol. 1, pp. 220-221.

Many companions of the Prophet were put to the sword alongside many ordinary residents of Madinah. The Ansar were also butchered in droves and even some notable Qurayshites were killed in the brutal attack. Hundreds of Muslim women were raped and taken as slaves and their honour violated. As a result of the violation of the women of Madinah hundreds of illegitimate children were born in the city of the Prophet (Ibn Athir, Vol 3, pp. 310-13).

Here is a brief account of what the army of Yazid did to the city of the Prophet.

> *"The army that Yazeed had sent to Medina comprised of 60,000 horsemen and 15,000 foot soldiers. For three days they shed blood freely, 1000 women were raped and 700 named Quraysh and Ansar were killed. Ten thousand women and children were made slaves. Muslim bin Uqba forced people to give bayya to Yazeed in such a manner that people were enslaved and Yazeed could sell them as he pleased, none of the Sahaba that were present (with the Prophet) at Hudaibiya were spared".*
> - Aujaz al masalik by Shaykh al hadith Muhammad Zakaria

The mosque of the Prophet where he used to give sermons and lead the prayers was attacked as well, and its sanctity violated. The army of Yazid tied their horses inside the mosque of the Prophet as they took over the city. The attack on Madinah lasted for three days and during this time even the calls to the prayers were barred from the mosque of the Prophet.

The city of Madinah was plundered and ransacked beyond recognition by the army of Yazid, in a clear sign of Yazid's contempt for the Prophet and his city. It seems as if Yazid wasn't satisfied with the killing of the Ansar alone, and he wanted to destroy the city of Madinah itself to show his contempt for the Prophet too (Sahih Muslim, Hadith 1851).

Yazid had indeed killed the entire family of the Prophet in Karbala, so destroying the sanctity of the city of the Prophet wasn't a big deal for him. This terrible event is known as the event of Harrah.

The Prophet had in fact invoked the curse of Allah on an individual like Yazid, rather than prophesied for his forgiveness. The Prophet had said:

> "Whoever terrorizes the people of Medina with oppression, then Allah will terrorize him. The curse of Allah, the angels, and the people altogether will be upon him. Allah will not accept his obligatory or voluntary good deeds on the Day of Resurrection."
> - Musnad Ahmed 6498

The Prophet had stated that a person who terrorizes and frightens the people of Madinah would invoke the curse of Allah and the angels. And Yazid was indeed that individual who not only terrorized the people of Madinah, but he had killed and raped the people of Madinah too.

14.11.19.2. The Attack on Makkah

As if the attack on Madinah wasn't enough Yazid now turns his attention to Makkah, the city of the Holy Kaaba.

Readers would recall that Al-Zubair was in Makkah when Imam Hussain was leaving Makkah for the city of Kufa. By now Al-Zubair had established his government in Makkah and its surroundings. Yazid was not going to allow Al-Zubair to establish a base in the heart of Arabia. Muawiyah had already warned Yazid about the political ambitions of Al-Zubair and had asked Yazid to kill Al-Zubair whenever he gets the opportunity to do so.

> ".... the man who will attack you with full force, like a lion attacks his prey, and who will pounce upon you, like a fox when it finds an opportunity to pounce, is Abd Allah b. az-Zubair. Whenever you get a chance, cut him into pieces."
> - (Iqd al Fareed, Volume 4 page 226)

As per the advice of Muawiyah the army of Yazid not only attacked the city of Makkah to kill Al-Zubair, but his troops also attacked the Holy Kaaba with fireballs. The cloth of Kaaba was burned and the Holy Kaaba itself was damaged by the army of Yazid. The horns of the sheep that came as a sacrifice for Prophet Ismail were preserved on the walls of Kaaba at that time. Those horns were also burned down in this attack.

> "......They (Yazid's army) stoned the Ka'aba with their cannons, burnt it & started singing thus: "We (Yazid's army) have tremendous power & courage, we stone this Masjid with cannons."
> - Tarikh Kamil, Volume. 3, Page. No. 464

It was the most despicable attack on the Holy Kaaba after the coming of Islam. Even an ordinary Muslim with limited knowledge of Islam could confirm that person who attacks the Holy Kaaba and destroys its sanctity does not have much hope of forgiveness.

Yazid had initially asked Ubaydullah bin Ziyad to attack Makkah, but even he refused to follow the orders of Yazid.

> "When Yazid wrote to Ibn Ziyad that he should go to Makkah and besiege Abdullah Ibn Zubayr he refused to do so and said: By Allah I will not combine two things for a Fasiq (i.e. Yazid). I have already killed the son of Prophet's daughter (on his order) and now (he asks me to) wage war on Bayt ul Harram? ....."

- Al-Bidayah Wal Nihayah, Volume 8, Page No 279

The above incident also confirms the fact that it was Ubaydullah who had killed Imam Hussain on the orders of Yazid, rather than the Shia of Kufa as claimed by the supporters of the Umayyads.

The attack on the Holy Kaaba, the destruction of the city of Madinah, the killing of the entire family of the Prophet in Karbala, clearly prove that after the debacle of Saqifah where the leadership of the Muslim Ummah was diverted away from the Ahlulbayt, eventually enabled the enemies of the Prophet in the form of the Umayyads to take over the leadership of the Muslim Ummah.

This was indeed a catastrophe and a calamity to say the least.

14.12. Hussain the Magnificent

The Islamic history is full of warriors and conquerors who have fought and conquered huge swathes of land and expanded the borders of the Muslim Empire. One such conqueror was Tariq ibn Ziyad who led the conquest of Spain.

The army of Tariq ibn Ziyad arrived on boats on the shores of Spain at a place called Gibraltar, later to be called Jabl Tariq (mountain of Tariq). Once the troops had landed in Gibraltar, Tariq ibn Ziyad ordered his troops to burn their boats, so that they had no means of escape left. The troops were left with two choices i.e., either to fight the enemy and win the battle, or be pushed out into the ocean and drown.

On the other hand, we have the example of Imam Hussain the grandson of the Prophet. The night before the battle of Karbala Imam Hussain is surrounded by the enemy, but he offers his troops to leave his camp in the guise of the darkness and save their lives, unlike Tariq ibn Ziyad who forces his troops to fight. This is because Hussain was no ordinary conqueror.

Hussain was out to conquer the hearts of the believers!

Hussain had gone out to preserve the ideals of Prophet's revolution, whereas conquerors like Tariq ibn Ziyad were out to conquer swathes of land. Their aim was to expand the borders of the Muslim empire (there was no harm in that), but the battle of Hussain was different. The battle of Hussain was to preserve the ideological message of Islam. A message which had been diluted by the counter-revolution of the Umayyads.

Hussain does not need to force anyone to fight on his side. The conquest of Hussain was a conquest of self-sacrifice. Hussain knew that his destiny was in Karbala, just as Prophet Ismail knew that he was going to be sacrificed by his father Prophet Ibrahim.

When Imam Hussain was born Allah sent Angel Gabriel to inform the Prophet about the killing of his grandson on the plains of Karbala.

Umme Fadhl Ibnt Haris, who was Prophet's aunt narrates:

> "…. Fatima was blessed with Imam Hussain and he was placed in my (Umme Fadhl) lap, as the Holy Prophet had said. Then one day, I went to the Holy Prophet and placed Imam Hussain before Him. What I saw! That the Holy Prophet's eyes were full of tears. Upon seeing this, I asked: O Prophet of Allah…..what is the reason of your crying? The Holy Prophet said: Jibril came to me and said that very soon, some people from my Ummah will kill this son of mine. I asked: O Prophet, will they kill this prince? The Holy Prophet said: Yes and Jibril gave me the red sand of that place"

- Sunan Bayhaqi- Dalaail Un Nubuwwah, Hadith No: 2805;
- Mishkaat Ul Masabeeh, Vol. 2, Pg No. 572;
- Zujajatul Masabeeh, Vol. 5, Pg No. 327/328

Allah had informed the Prophet about the killing of Imam Hussain when he was born. The Prophet of Allah could not control his emotions and was reduced to tears when he heard that his grandson would be killed by his Ummah. The destiny of Imam Hussain was settled at his birth.

The Prophet of Allah had informed Imam Hussain about the sacrifice that was expected of him. Imam Hussain confirms his destiny before heading to Iraq.

> "Verily I had a dream, in which I saw the Prophet. He ordered me to do something, which I will implement. And I will not tell anyone of it until I complete this ordered task."

- p. 5 Tarikh al-Islam. Hafiz Shams al-Din Muhammad ibn Ahmad ibn Uthman al-Dhahabi (d. 748 A.H.) Vol.:Years 61-80 A.H. Dar al-Kutub al-Arabi, Beirut, Lebanon, 1998.
- p.73. The History of al-Tabari; The Caliphate of Yazid. b. Mu'awiyah. Volume XIX. Translated by I.K.A. Howard. State University of New York Press, USA, 1990.
- p. 163, Al-Bidaya wa al-Nihaya. Hafiz ibn Kathir (d. 774 A.H.) Volume VIII. Maktaba al-Ma'arif, Beirut, Lebanon. 1999.

The task of Imam Hussain was to sacrifice his life in Karbala as ordained by the Prophet. Those who undermine the magnificent stand of Imam Hussain by blaming the Shias of Ali in Kufa, or by using all sorts of unscrupulous arguments, should pay heed to the above tradition of the Prophet and review their stance.

The Prophet of Allah had no sons of his own. He used to call Imam Hasan and Imam Hussain his sons and he used to love them dearly. Even when the Prophet was in a state of prayer and if Imam Hasan or Imam Hussain would approach him, he would oblige, and he would give them the attention that they were seeking.

There is a famous story from the childhood of Imam Hussain when Prophet was leading the congregational prayers, and Imam Hussain climbed over his back and shoulders while he was prostrating. Instead of asking Imam Hussain to leave he extended his prostration until Imam Hussain left on his own accord. Such was the love and closeness that Prophet had with his grandsons.

Allah tests his Prophets in the most amazing ways. He asked Prophet Ibrahim to slaughter his own son, to see if he was willing to sacrifice his most precious gift in the path of Allah. In case of Prophet Mohammad, Allah informed him that his grandson would be killed by his Ummah, to see if he was willing to sacrifice his own family members in the way of Allah.

The Prophet was informed about the killing of Imam Hussain on more than one occasion. As a test, the angel who came to inform the Prophet about the killing of Imam Hussain on one of the occasions even asked the Prophet as to how much he loved his grandson, before breaking the news that he would be killed in Karbala.

> " …. the Angel of Rain took permission from his lord to visit the Prophet so He gave him permission. The Prophet told Umm Salamah (his wife) to watch the door so no one could come in. Al-Hussain came wanting to enter and I (Umm Salamah) stopped him. But he jumped, entered, and started sitting on the back of the Prophet, and on his shoulders. Then the angel asked the Prophet, "Do you love him?". He (Prophet) said, "yes". The angel said, "Indeed your Ummah will kill him, and if you wish, I can show you the place where he will be killed". Then, he (angel) struck with his hand and came with red clay. So Umm Salamah took it and tied on it in her veil …... "it has reached us that it's (the sand is from) Karbala".
>
> - Musnad al-Imam Ahmad, vol. 3, p. 242

So, Allah had not only informed the Prophet that his grandson Hussain would be killed, but he also informed the Prophet as to who would in fact kill his grandson and exactly where he would be killed. Allah told the Prophet that his own Ummah would kill his grandson i.e., Hussain would be killed by fellow Muslims, and not by Christians or Jews, and Hussain would be killed in Karbala which is a city in present day Iraq.

Despite knowing these facts Prophet did not stop Imam Hussain from travelling to Karbala. On the contrary Prophet encouraged Imam Hussain to fulfil the prophecy and travel to Iraq, to show that he (the Prophet) was willing to sacrifice his own children in the path of Allah.

However, Prophet could not leave his beloved grandson Hussain to die alone. He was present in Karbala with the will of Allah and was collecting the blood of Hussain and his companions.

Prophet's Uncle Ibn Abbas narrates:

> 'One afternoon I dreamt of Holy Prophet (saw) standing with his hair disturbed and with dust tangled in them and he was holding a phial filled with blood. I said to the Prophet (saw): 'O Allah's Prophet, what are you holding?' The Prophet (saw) replied: 'This is the blood of Hussain and his companions that I have been collecting all day long." They did calculation and found out that he (Hussain) was killed a day before it (the day of dream).
>
> - Al-Hakim in Al-Mustadrak Ala Sahihayn. Vol. 4, Pg. # 439-440.
> - Ahmad ibn Hanbal in Musnad Ahmad ibn Hanbal. Vol. 4, H. # 2165, Pg. # 59 - 60.
> - Al-Albani in Mishkatul Masabih of Al-Albani. Vol. 3, Pg. # 1741-1742.

When Allah chooses someone to be sacrificed in his path then that individual has to be the most pious and the most worthy in the eyes of Allah.

Even when ordinary Muslims like us choose an animal to be sacrificed in the path of Allah, we try and find an animal that is free of faults and is as perfect as possible within our limited budgets. For instance, when we choose an animal for the auspicious occasion of Eid-ul-Adha, we look for an animal that is healthy, an animal that is disease free and an animal that looks well all around.

However, our choice can have flaws, but when Allah chooses someone to be sacrificed in his path, then his choice is flawless, and he chooses the very best among his creation to be sacrificed in his path. The Prophet and his family were the best of the creation, and that is why Allah had chosen them to be sacrificed in his path.

The people who are the very best in the eyes of Allah and the people who have been given the highest of the honours, are also chosen for the steepest of the tests. The Prophet made his family to be at par with the Book of Allah, the Prophet chose his family to be the custodian of his Sunnah, and the Prophet made his family to be the ark of the salvation.

When Prophet of Allah had bestowed all those honours on to his family, then they also had to justify their elevated status with one of the most distinguished sacrifices in the history of Islam. The higher the honour the greater is the responsibility of the individual.

This is why when the ideological message of Islam was being challenged and threatened by the Umayyad dynasty, it was the family of the Prophet who rose to the occasion and justified their unique status as the custodian of Prophet's Sunnah, with a unique and a distinguished sacrifice which is unrivalled in history. And it was the grandson of the Prophet who stood up and took on the might of the Umayyad Caliph.

The rest of the Ummah had either been bought or had been pacified by the fear of the Umayyad sword. The children and the grandchildren of all the other companions were alive, but nobody had the courage to stand in the path of the Umayyad innovations. Only the family of the Prophet took that step, despite knowing full well that the path they had chosen was the path of certain death.

It was for this reason that Prophet had left his Sunnah in the hands of his family, as they were the very best among his Ummah, who would one day sacrifice everything that they had in the way of Allah.

The magnificent stand of Hussain opposed the dictatorial and the corrupt system of governance established by the Umayyads in the guise of the Islamic Caliphate. The unwavering stand of Hussain supported the revolution of the Prophet at a time when everyone else in the Ummah had been silenced.

Just as we had witnessed at the start of the revolution of Islam that it was the sword of Ali which was the differentiating factor in all the key battles of Islam, we would once again witness that when the revolution of Islam was being threatened by the Umayyads, it was the son of Ali who stood up and rekindled that revolution with his blood.

14.13. Visiting the Shrine of Hussain

When Imam Hussain arrived in Karbala the very first thing that he did was to purchase the land of Karbala. Imam Hussain was not going to be killed on someone else's land. Imam Hussain was going to be killed on his own land and Yazid's army would be trespassing on Hussain's land, and this is where the shrine of Imam Hussain has been built. The land of Karbala is the land of Hussain.

When Imam Hussain purchased the land of Karbala from the tribe of Banu Assad, he made the following plea to the people of Banu Assad.

> "On the tenth of this month you will see our dead bodies lying on this plain with our heads severed and taken away. Please bury us and when our devotees come to visit our graves treat them with honour and point out to them the places of our burial."

- *The Arrival in Karbala (erfan.ir)*

The plea of Imam Hussain was indeed his will, where he requested the people of Banu Assad to honour his devotees who would come and visit his grave. The people of Karbala to this day have honoured the will of Imam Hussain to the letter. They serve and honour the visitors of Imam Hussain in the most incredible of the ways. It is something that can only be experienced when one actually visits the blessed shrine of Imam Hussain.

After Hussain's innocent blood was spilt on this land, the land of Karbala has become a land of eternal inspiration for the lovers of the Ahlulbayt. The will of Hussain is an open invitation for all the Muslims to come and visit this sacred land.

This is the land where the revolution of the Prophet was rekindled by the ultimate sacrifice of his family. This is the land where the grandson of the Prophet stood alone and faced an army of some 30,000 men. This is the land where the blood of the family of the Prophet was spilt in the most callus of the ways. This is the land where the battle for the defence of the Sunnah of the Prophet was won against the innovations of the Umayyads.

This is the land where the prophecy of the Prophet about Hussain had come true. This is the land where despite three days of hunger and thirst Hussain fought in a manner that revived the honour of Ali's sword. This is the land where the son of Ali stood alone and challenged the might of the Umayyad dynasty. This is the land where the bravery of Ali could be witnessed at every step that Hussain took.

This is the land where Hussain had dug the grave of Ali Asghar, his six months old son. This is the land where every single male member of Prophet's family was beheaded except one. This is the land where thirteen years old son of Imam Hasan was beheaded. This is the land where the veils and the scarfs of the daughters of the Prophet were snatched by fellow Muslims. This is the land where the family of the Prophet including the women and children were taken captive.

This is the land where the family of the Prophet proved with their blood that they were the true custodians of Prophet's Sunnah. This is the land where the sacrifice of the family of the Prophet negated the verdict of Saqifah. This is the land where the blood of Hussain had vindicated the plan that was devised by the Prophet for the leadership of the Muslim Ummah.

This is the land where the Umayyads had won the battle but lost the war. This is the land of Hussain, and this is the land where the greatest sacrifice in the history of Islam took place. The land of Karbala is the land of martyrs.

The land of Karbala has not only become a magnet for the believers after the tragedy of Karbala, but it was visited by the members of the Ahlulbayt even before the event of Karbala. When Ali was travelling to the battle of Siffin to take on the forces of Muawiyah, he passed through the land of Karbala. As Ali realized that he was in Karbala he stopped his army on this sacred land and wept for his son Hussain before continuing his journey to the battlefield.

> *"When Ali passed by Karbala in his march to Siffeen and lined up with Nainawa - a village on the Euphrates - he stopped and called one of them men: Tell aba 'Abdullah (al Hussain) what this land is called? He said: Karbala. Then he cried until the earth was wet from his tears. He (Ali) then said: I entered on the messenger of Allah and he was crying. So I said: What makes you cry?*
> *He said: Gabriel was with me, just now, and informed me: that my son al-Hussain will be killed at the banks of Euphrates in a location called Karbala. Then Gabriel grabbed a handful of dirt and let me smell it. So I could not help it, my eyes overflowed."*
>
> - *Musnad al-Imam Ahmad, vol. 1, p. 85*
> - *al-Tabaqat al-Kubra, Ibn Saad*
> - *al-Musannaf, Ibn Abi Shaibeh, v.12*
> - *al-Moejam al-Kabeer, al-Tabarani, v.1*

Ali wept on the land of Karbala even before the killing of Imam Hussain until the soil of Karbala was wet with his tears. As can be seen in the above tradition that the Prophet of Allah was also crying when he informed Ali about the killing of Imam Hussain in Karbala.

Crying for Hussain is indeed the Sunnah of the Prophet!

Just as Ali had passed through Karbala the Prophet of Allah also visited the land of Karbala. He was present in Karbala on the day of Ashura when Imam Hussain was being killed by the army of Yazid. The Prophet with the will of Allah was not only present in Karbala but he was in fact collecting the blood of Hussain and his companions.

> One afternoon I dreamt of Holy Prophet (saw) standing with his hair disturbed and with dust tangled in them and he was holding a phial filled with blood. I said to the Prophet (saw): 'O Allah's Prophet, what are you holding?' The Prophet (saw) replied: 'This is the blood of Hussain and his companions that I have been collecting all the day long." They did calculation and found out that he (Hussain) was killed a day before it (the day of dream).
>
> - Al-Hakim in Al-Mustadrak Ala Sahihayn. Vol. 4, Pg. # 439-440.
> - Ahmad ibn Hanbal in Musnad Ahmad ibn Hanbal. Vol. 4, H. # 2165, Pg. # 59 - 60.
> - Al-Albani in Mishkatul Masabih of Al-Albani. Vol. 3, Pg. # 1741-1742.

This is why visiting the land of Karbala is a huge honour and a blessing for any Muslim. Millions of Muslims across the Muslim Ummah pay their respects to the grandson of the Prophet every year, and visit his shrine especially on the Day of Ashura when the tragedy of Karbala took place, mimicking the footsteps of the Prophet on that day.

A visit to the shrine of Imam Hussain reminds a Muslim of the cost that the family of the Prophet had to pay to defend his blessed Sunnah. The Prophet of Allah had lost both his grandsons to the Umayyad dynasty. Imam Hasan was poisoned by Muawiyah and Imam Hussain was killed by Yazid in Karbala.

A visit to the shrine of Hussain inevitably reignites the fire of Islam in the hearts of the believers and brings them closer to the path established by the Prophet of Allah. A visit to the shrine of Hussain takes a Muslim back in time, a time when Hussain stood alone on the plains of Karbala and rekindled the revolution of the Prophet with his blood.

A visit to the shrine of Hussain forces a Muslim to ponder over the events of history that led to the killing of the entire family of the Prophet. A visit to the land of Karbala undoubtedly enables a Muslim to choose between the traditions of Saqifah and the blessed traditions of the Prophet. A visit to the shrine of Hussain opens the hearts of the believers to the love of the Prophet and his family.

A visit to the shrine of Hussain would be an honour and a privilege for any Muslim who can afford to make the trip to the city of Karbala which is located in present day Iraq.

15. A Logical Approach

15.1. The Best Man

As we come to the end of this book, we can clearly see how the Caliphate was diverted away from the members of the Ahlulbayt and it eventually ended up in the hands of the Umayyads, who had been the biggest enemy of the Prophet and Muslims until they were defeated at the conquest of Makkah.

We know that Islam as an Ideology values merits and achievements and rewards an individual for their contribution in the path and in the service of Allah.

If we go back to the time of the Prophet, we know that Prophet began preaching the message of Islam in Makkah and his mission finally ended with his death in the city of Madinah.

Even if we leave aside the fact that Prophet had appointed Ali as his successor, by simply looking at the life of Ali until the death of the Prophet, and by comparing it to the life of any other companion in the same timeframe, we can clearly see that the merits, the achievements and the contribution of Ali in the service of Islam was far superior than any other companion. The companions of the Prophet are no doubt worthy of our respect, but the successor of the Prophet can only be someone who was distinguished and distinct among all the companions.

A companion of average achievements and contribution cannot be given precedence over someone whose career in the path and in the service of Islam was unique and unrivalled. This would be tantamount to breaking the very basic ethos of the Islamic ideology.

Ali began the defence of Prophet and his mission as a child, an honour which no other companion shares with Ali. Ali had slept in Prophet's bed on many occasions to save Prophet's life from would be assassins of Quraysh. In the night of Hijrah Ali again defied the warriors of Quraysh and put his life in harm's way to save the life of his mentor.

The biggest and the most critical project that Prophet had undertaken during his lifetime was to establish the Islamic State of Madinah. It was a strategy that the Prophet of Allah had devised to secure the future of the Muslims and to frustrate the enemies of Islam.

Ali was the star performer in the establishment and in the defence of the Islamic State of Madinah. Ali took part in some 18 battles and expeditions alongside the Prophet and Prophet never placed Ali under anybody else's command. In every battle that Ali took part, his performance was the differentiating factor which brought the outcome in favour of Islam and the Muslims. The battles of Badr, Uhud, Moat and Khaibar were a testament of his unrivalled bravery and skill on the battlefield, which no other companion can claim to match.

These battles were truly decisive battles for the destiny of Islam. If Muslims had been decisively beaten or taken out in any of these battles, the message of Islam would have been wiped out from the Arabian Peninsula. It was the unique and distinct contribution of Ali in these battles which ensured that the Muslim camp came on top against all the odds.

Ali's success was not limited to the battlefield alone. When the Christian of Najran challenged the ideological message of Islam and when the truthfulness and the piety of the Prophet was being questioned, Prophet picked Ali among all the companions to take on the Christian delegation, proving that the ideological closeness of Ali with Prophet was just as unique and distinguished as the performance of Ali on the battlefield.

The supremacy of Ali's knowledge was even acknowledged by his political rivals. In their reigns as Caliphs, both Caliph Abu Bakr and Caliph Umar would come to the door of Ali seeking answers on issues that they were unable to resolve on their own. Ali in fact demonstrated the words of the Prophet in practice, where Prophet had said that he was city of knowledge and Ali was its gate.

When Prophet arrived in Madinah, he established brotherhood among all the Muslims. He made Caliph Abu Bakr the brother of Caliph Umar, since both Caliph Abu Bakr and Caliph Umar were companions of similar status and stature. But he chooses Ali to be his own brother, because Ali was closest to him in every sense, especially in terms of his wisdom and intellect, since Ali had acquired those traits from the Prophet himself.

Just like everything else, the companionship of the Prophet with Ali was unlike his companionship with any other companion. It began with the birth of Ali when Ali had opened his eyes in the lap of the Prophet, and it ended with Ali lowering the body of the Prophet into the grave. Even when the debacle of Saqifah was underway Ali was next to the Prophet washing and preparing his body for burial, while others were arguing in Saqifah as to who should succeed the Prophet.

One may ask as to why was it that Ali was unique and distinguished among all the companions, when Prophet had thousands of companions. Ali was only one of the many companions of the Prophet. What was the reason that Ali had these merits while others didn't?

Ali had himself given an answer to this question in one of his famous speeches. Ali said:

> *"The Holy Prophet brought me up in his own arms and fed me with his own morsel. I followed him wherever he went like a baby-camel following its mother. Each day a new aspect of his character would beam out of his noble person and I would accept it and follow it as a command"*
>
> - *Nahjul Balagha*

The reason why Ali was unique and distinguished was because Prophet had chosen to train and teach Ali in a manner that he did not train or taught any of the other companions. The other prominent companions used to meet the Prophet in the Mosque or when Prophet was in public. They would listen to his sermons, they would hear his words, they would witness his actions and they would try and follow his path as best as they could.

There is no doubt that the other companions had also learned and benefited from the company of the Prophet and had the honour of being his companions. But the situation of Ali was different, Prophet had specifically prepared and trained Ali in all aspects of human excellence by bringing him up in his own house, which wasn't the case for any of the other companion.

As Ali said:

> *"every day he showed me part of his moral acts and ordered me to do likewise"*
>
> - *Nahjul Balagha*

Every day Prophet would show Ali some of his excellence and then he would order Ali to follow it. Everyday Prophet would raise the bar for Ali and everyday Ali would have to touch it. This is how Ali became unique and distinguished from the rest of the companions. Prophet had not imparted such training and guidance to any of the other companions.

The reason why Prophet was training and teaching Ali specifically and not the other companions, was because he wanted Ali to succeed him and take over the mantle of the Islamic leadership. He wanted his successor to resemble him in manners, in truthfulness, in bravery, in piety, in knowledge, in wisdom and in all the other disciplines of life. He wanted to raise Ali to a level where he could successfully lead the ideological and the intellectual revolution of Islam.

It was the Prophet who created this difference between Ali and the rest of the companions. This was in fact the Sunnah of the Prophet. This was part of his plan and strategy for the safety and the future of the message of Islam. He was teaching and guiding all the Muslims and companions around him, but their training was at a general level, however, the training and teaching of Ali was specific, so that he could lead and guide the Muslim Ummah in Prophet's absence.

Ali was being trained and taught to be the leader, the guide, and the custodian of the message of the Prophet, hence, his training had to be different, whereas the rest of the companions were being trained to be good Muslims, hence one could see the obvious difference.

One of the key honours of Caliph Abu Bakr was that he was the companion of the cave i.e., he stayed with the Prophet in a cave on the night of the Hijrah.

In the below speech Ali says:

> "Every year he used to take me to Hira....So I saw the light of revelation and the message and smelt the fragrance of prophecy"
> - Nahjul Balagha

Hira was a cave where Prophet used to receive the revelations from Allah through angle Gabriel. This was where much of the Quran had been revealed to the Prophet. Ali had not only been the companion of the Cave on many occasions, but Ali had also witnessed the revelations of Allah coming to the Prophet, another honour that no other companion shares with Ali.

Also, the true character and the calibre of a leader is not only judged when they have acquired power, but in fact the true character of a leader comes out when they have actually lost power. The actions and the deeds of Ali after losing the Caliphate to Abu Bakr prove beyond any doubt that Ali was in fact the choice of the Prophet.

Ali declined the lucrative offer of Abu Sufyan to fill the streets of Madinah with cavalrymen, in order to bring down the Caliphate of Abu Bakr, an offer which only the very best of the characters would be able to refuse.

History is a witness that only a few years later when the opportunity arose to bring down the Caliphate of Uthman, the politically ambitious companions like Talha, Zubair and Lady Aisha left no stone unturned in making the most of the opportunity to further their own political goals. But the character of Ali again stood out in sharp contrast to the character of an average companion, where Ali did everything he possibly could to resolve the crisis and preserve the unity of the Muslims, even though it was Ali who had lost out to Caliph Uthman and not Talha or Zubair.

Caliph Abu Bakr had acquired the Political leadership of Muslims after Saqifah, but the title of being the Successor of the Prophet could only go to the very best of the characters, a character that was nurtured and cultivated by the Prophet of Allah himself.

Allah had chosen the best of the angels (Angel Gabriel) to reveal the holy Quran to the Prophet. The Prophet of Allah was the best of the creation ever to grace the earth. It was only logical that Prophet would also choose the very best of the companions to lead the movement of Islam in his absence.

15.2. The Majority and the Minority

After the meeting of Saqifah ended Caliph Abu Bakr was chosen as the leader of the Muslims. The news of Caliph Abu Bakr's selection as the new Caliph and the leader of the Muslims spread far and wide. Muslims were informed that a Shura (Consultation) had taken place by the leaders of the Ansar and the Muhajireen and it has been agreed that Caliph Abu Bakr would now be the new leader (Ameer) of the Muslims.

The trend of al-ijtihad (independent judgment) which was a minority among the companions but had taken root in some key companions prevailed in Saqifah, and as a result managed to acquire the leadership of the Muslims and the Islamic State.

As a consequence, the Muslim Ummah was immediately divided into two groups, one which had acquired power and was destined to rule and extend its influence to include the majority of the Muslims, while the other group which was forced away from power and was destined to exist as an opposing minority within the wider Muslim Ummah.

This minority was in fact the Shia of Ali i.e., the supporters of Ali.

The supporters of Ali were those companions who supported the nominee of the Prophet and believed that it was Ali's right to lead the Muslims after Prophet's death. These companions believed in strictly adhering to the Sunnah of the Prophet, as opposed to the companions who believed in the trend of al-ijtihad.

The word Shia literally means supporters, friends, a group, or a party. The companions of the Prophet who supported the right of Ali to succeed the Prophet were simply referred to as the Shia of Ali i.e., the party of Ali. This was the historical name given to the group of companions who opposed the order of Saqifah after the death of the Prophet, and who supported Ali's right to succeed the Prophet. The term "Shia of Ali" in short became simply as "Shia".

The Shia thought was not formed because of some alleged Jewish conspiracy against Islam, and nor was it formed as a result of some sectarian prejudice to divide the Muslims.

The Shia thought was a natural response to the trend and the thought which had prevailed in Saqifah, a trend that the Shia thought believed had breached the clear Sunnah of the Prophet.

The Shia trend believed that the Prophet would not leave the ideological revolution of Islam to the events of Saqifah. They believed that Prophet had trained and prepared Ali to lead that revolution after his death. They believed that Ali had also earned this position as result of his service and contribution in the path of Islam. They believed that Ali was unique and distinguished among all the companions to be the rightful successor of the Prophet. They believed that Ali was the custodian of Prophet's knowledge and mandate as per many traditions of the Prophet.

The Shia thought believed that the participants of Saqifah had done injustice to the nominee of the Prophet. They believed that the trend of al-Ijtihad was a contradiction of the Sunnah of the Prophet.

The prominent companions of the Prophet who believed in the Shia thought were Ammar bin Yasir, al-Miqdad bin al-Aswad, Salma al-Farsi, Abu Dharr al Ghifari and others. However, as a result of Saqifah they not only found themselves in a minority, but also having no say or influence in the decision-making process of the Islamic State.

The Shia companions of the Prophet did not have the political clout or the tribal standing of their counterparts such as Caliph Abu Bakr and Caliph Umar. Their tribal lineages were unimpressive in an era of tribal dominance and supremacy, and hence they had no sway or influence on the politics of the day.

As a consequence, the trend of al-ijtihad which had succeeded in Saqifah began its domination of the Muslim Ummah, whereas the trend which supported the nominee of the Prophet found itself on the wrong side of history.

Since the Shia companions and the Shia thought became a minority after the meeting of Saqifah, it gave the impression that the real and the actual Islamic thought was with the trend that had prevailed in Saqifah, and Shia were the exception, who must have developed as a result of separating from the main body of the Muslims to oppose the order of the day.

Because of the numerical strength of the non-Shia Islam, it was seen as the true manifestation of the Sunnah of the Prophet, whereas the Shia were seen as a group that was formed as a result of some internal friction or as a result of some outside conspiracy to harm the religion of Islam from within.

However, the reality could not be more different. The Shia trend believed in following the directive of the Prophet in all circumstances and scenarios, whereas the non-Shia trend accepted the permissibility of al-ijtihad (independent judgment) against the clear Sunnah of the Prophet.

Hence, the non-Shia trend sided with the view of Quraysh in Saqifah and choose Caliph Abu Bakr against the clear directive of the Prophet in favour of Ali.

Because the Shia thought became a minority after Saqifah and the non-Shia trend acquired the leadership of the Muslim Ummah, all kinds of illogical and unjustifiable accusations were labelled against the Shias of Ali, in order to poison the minds of the ordinary Muslims who had no knowledge of what had actually taken place in Saqifah. This view of the Shia is unfortunately still prevalent among many Muslims who are ignorant about the historical events and have no idea as to what actually happened after the death of the Prophet.

Just like the thousands of companions who had gathered at the mosque of the Prophet to find out who would succeed the Prophet, millions of Muslims today are given the same news that Caliph Umar gave to those companions, that an agreement and a consensus was reached on the Caliphate of Abu Bakr. And just like the thousands of good companions, millions of good Muslims today have no reason not to accept the verdict of Saqifah.

However, in this age of knowledge and information when the facts have become so clear, we can certainly make a more informed choice. Should we believe in the news that came out of Saqifah or should we follow the news that Prophet had given to the Muslims, regarding the position and the status of Ali on so many occasions.

15.3. Our Approach

It is imperative to appreciate that this book is written in a historical context, primarily discussing the events which took place in the very early Islamic History. It should not be confused in any way with the apparent Sunni-Shia conflict that we see in some parts of the Muslim Ummah today. I believe that the present-day strife has more to do with the global politics, controlling of wealth, power, and influence in the Middle East, rather than the religion itself.

The religion is simply being used as a tool to further the interests and agendas of the key power brokers in the region, at the expense of the Muslim masses. We must distance ourselves from such conflicts and pray for peace and tranquillity to return to our lands.

The call of this book is set in the age of the Prophet, when the revolution of Islam began to take root in the Arabian desert, and when the Prophet of Allah was establishing a State to secure the future and the destiny of the Muslims.

The call of this book is set in the era when Prophet was reaching the end of his life, and when he wanted the ideological revolution of Islam to be led by the most deserving and capable individual, an individual whose contribution has been the differentiating factor in making the new ideology a success.

The call of this book is set at a time when Ali was preparing the body of the Prophet for burial, while others were advancing the views of the Quraysh in Saqifah. The call of this book is set at a time when the trend of al-ijtihad (independent judgment) had taken over the leadership of the Muslim Ummah, against the clear Sunnah of the Prophet.

The call of this book is against the notion of a political adjustment which took place between the Ansar and the Muhajireen in the hastily organized gathering of Saqifah. The call of this book is against the idea that on one hand the Prophet of Allah would establish a State to secure the future of the Muslims, but on the other hand he would remain passive about the future leadership of that very State.

The call of this book is against the notion that Prophet would allow a criterion other than merit, or service in the path of Islam to be used as a means of choosing his successor.

The call of this book is to distance ourselves from the course of history which gave the leadership of the Muslims to the unscrupulous Umayyads, a clan who had been the biggest enemy of the Prophet during his lifetime. The call of this book is to challenge the path which brought individuals like Muawiyah and Yazid to the helm of the Islamic State. The call of this book is against the course of history which led to the killing of Imam Hussain, the grandson of the Prophet on the plains of Karbala.

The call of this book is in favour of the idea that since Islam was an ideological revolution sweeping the Arabian Peninsula, and the only way that Prophet could guarantee that the best and the most able person was chosen, was to hand pick someone from his own team to lead the reformatory movement of Islam. Since any other system or method to choose a successor could not guarantee that the best and the most deserving individual would come on top.

The call of this book is in line with the fact that Prophet chose someone from an early age, trained him for twenty-five years in the ideals of Islam, kept him away from the Jahilliyah (backward) traditions of the time, specifically prepared him for this role so that one day he could take over the religious, intellectual, and political leadership of the Muslim Ummah.

The call of this book supports the trend which believed that Ali was the rightful successor of the Prophet, a trend which became a minority after the spontaneous meeting of Saqifah. The call of this book is against the trend established by the companions who supported the Qurayshite view of the Caliphate, contrary to the plan and the strategy of the Prophet.

The call of this book supports those companions who found themselves in a minority as a consequence of the meeting of Saqifah, and due to the numerical strength of the majority were seen as opposing the order of the day. The call of this book supports the idea that the successor of the Prophet could come from the same clan as the Prophet i.e., the Banu Hashim, unlike the view of Quraysh which dominated the proceedings of Saqifah.

The call of this book supports the notion that our approach and responsibility is to follow the course of history which the Prophet had wished and hoped for, rather than the course of history which was established in Saqifah. Prophet had nominated and appointed Ali to lead the revolutionary movement of Islam in his absence, whereas Caliph Umar had nominated Caliph Abu Bakr in Saqifah to lead the Muslim Ummah. The call of this book supports the traditions of the Prophet as opposed to the traditions of Saqifah.

The call of this book confirms the real reason as to why Ali was not selected in Saqifah. Caliph Umar who was the main architect of Caliph Abu Bakr's Caliphate and a key player in the meeting of Saqifah, confirmed the actual reason as to why Ali was denied the Caliphate. Following is the conversation that Caliph Umar had with Ibn Abbas a few years after the meeting of Saqifah.

> *Caliph Umar: "Do you know why the people did not elect you (the family of the Prophet) to the Caliphate?"*
> *Ibn Abbas: "No, I do not know."*
> *Caliph Umar: "I know what the reason was."*
> *Ibn Abbas: "What was it?"*
> *Caliph Umar: "The Quraysh was unwilling to let you (the Hashimites) have the honour of both Prophethood and Caliphate. If that would have happened you would have wronged the people! Quraysh chose for itself, it succeeded and made the right decision."*

- Tarikh al-Tabari, 5:30
- Qasas al-Arab, 2:263
- Ibn al-Atheer al-Kamal fil-Tarikh, 3:63
- Tarikh e Islam: 481-482, by Akbar Shah Najibabadi

Caliph Umar confirmed that the real reason as to why Ali was not chosen was because the Quraysh were not willing to accept the leadership of Islam to be confined to the clan of Banu Hashim i.e., the clan of the Prophet. They were not willing to accept that the Prophet and his successor could come from the same clan.

The call of this book is to enforce the notion that we cannot possibly support the view of Quraysh today, since we will not be able to justify our stance to the Prophet of Allah on the Day of Judgment. The call of this book supports the idea that on the Day of Judgment we will not be questioned about the meeting of Saqifah or its outcome, but we will be asked if we had followed the Sunnah of the Prophet.

The event of Saqifah took place some fourteen centuries ago. If some prominent companions supported the views of Quraysh in Saqifah to justify their Caliphate, then we leave their judgment, their decisions. and their intentions with Allah. We will not be questioned about the decisions or the choices that Caliph Abu Bakr or Caliph Umar made in the meeting of Saqifah.

However, we will be asked about the choice and the decisions that we make in our lifetimes.

We cannot change the course of history or turn back the clock. But in this age of freedom and choice we can choose to follow the nominee of the Prophet rather than the nominee of Saqifah.

Caliph Abu Bakr, who immediately succeeded the Prophet was at best a good Muslim and a companion of the Prophet, but he was not the ideological successor of the Prophet. Caliph Abu Bakr had accepted Islam at the age of forty, whereas Ali had been brought up in house of the Prophet since the age of four. The ideological upbringing and the grooming of Ali was unique and distinct, and it was unlike the upbringing of any other companion.

The Ahle Sunnah by their very definition must do justice to the Sunnah of the Prophet, especially when they can clearly see that the Prophet could not have left the choice of his successor to a spontaneously organized meeting like Saqifah.

Muslims who are proud to be called the Ahle Sunnah, the followers of the Sunnah are dually invited to pay allegiance to the Sunnah of the Prophet. The Ahle Sunnah, more than any other group have an obligation to follow the nominee of the Prophet rather than the nominee of Saqifah. Allegiance to Ali is allegiance to the Sunnah of the Prophet and allegiance to Saqifah is a negation of the Sunnah of the Prophet.

The true lovers of the Prophet who are willing to lay down their lives in the defence and the honour of the Prophet, should honour the Sunnah of the Prophet and accept Ali as the rightful Successor of the Prophet.

The Ahle Sunnah are commonly known as Sunni Muslims or Sunnis in this day and age. A true Sunni, a person who follows the Sunnah of the Prophet is in fact a Shia, a person who accepts Ali as the rightful successor of the Prophet. And a true Shia, a person who accepts Ali as the rightful successor of the Prophet is in fact a Sunni, a person who follows the Sunnah of the Prophet.

16. A Couple of Additional Topics for Completeness

After concluding the book, I felt it was necessary that I clarify and discuss some important points and topics which for years have been used to poison the minds of the ordinary Muslims against the leadership of Ali and the Ahlulbayt.

In the first section I will discuss the absurd logic and reasoning used by the advocators of Saqifah to justify the Caliphate of Abu Bakr with various themes and notions which have no relevance to the events of history, but it is simply used as a smoke screen to blur the overwhelming evidence in favour of Ali's leadership.

In the second section I will discuss the notion of a Jewish conspiracy which is used by certain groups to deny Ali his right of leadership of the Muslim Ummah, and to also confuse the minds of ordinary Muslims regarding Ali's status and stature in the eyes of the Prophet.

16.1. The Justification of Saqifah

Despite the overwhelming traditions of the Prophet and the evidence of history in favour of Ali's right to lead the Muslim Ummah, there are many Muslim scholars who are still adamant to defend and justify the outcome of Saqifah, a meeting that was held some fourteen centuries ago without the consent or the consensus of its contemporaries.

If there was a single individual who had the most influence in the final outcome of Saqifah then that individual was none other than Caliph Umar. Caliph Umar was not only one of the key participants in the meeting of Saqifah, but he was in fact the main architect of the Caliphate of Abu Bakr in Saqifah.

Caliph Umar was the one who informed Caliph Abu Bakr about the meeting of Saqifah. He was the one who nominated Caliph Abu Bakr in the meeting of Saqifah and he was the first one to pay allegiance to him in that meeting, and he was also the one who had urged the companions who had gathered in the mosque of the Prophet to accept Abu Bakr as the first Caliph.

Caliph Umar, more than anyone else knew exactly what took place in the meeting of Saqifah. In later life when Caliph Umar had time to think about the meeting of Saqifah, he gave his own verdict on the event of Saqifah which is preserved in history.

I will give a few different versions of his sentiments and feelings about the gathering of Saqifah.

Caliph Umar says:

> "The pledge of allegiance given to Abu Bakr was an un-premeditated spontaneous affair which was (then only later) ratified."

- (Sahih Bukhari, Volume 8, Book 82, Number 817)

> Caliph Omar said: "Abu-Bakr's bay`ah was a 'falta' or something done without thinking about it. Even then, Allah spared us from His anger. Again if someone follows this method, he must be killed."

- Treekh-Al-khulafa p51,
- Bidaya wa Nehay by ibn katheer: 5/215
- Musnad Ahmad Bin Hanbal 1/323

In a slightly longer version Caliph Umar says:

> "By Allah, apart from the great tragedy that had happened to us (i.e. the death of the Prophet), there was no greater problem than the allegiance pledged to Abu Bakr because we were afraid that if we left the people, they might give the Pledge of allegiance after us to one of their men (the Ansar), in which case, we would have given them our consent for something against our real wish, or would have opposed them and caused great trouble. So, if any person gives the Pledge of allegiance to somebody (to become a Caliph) without consulting the other Muslims, then the one he has selected should not be granted allegiance, lest both of them should be killed."

- (Sahih al-Bukhari: Volume 8, Book 82, Number 817, also in al-Musnad: vol.1, Narration 391)

It becomes clear that according Caliph Umar

- Saqifah was a spontaneous event, something that just happened at the spur of the moment.
- It wasn't a thought through process, and it happened without due diligence.
- The event of Saqifah took place without consulting other Muslims.
- In future if anyone conducts a meeting (Shura) like Saqifah then it would not only be unacceptable, but anyone who receives or gives allegiance in this manner should be killed.

It is impossible to think that Caliph Umar could be any more explicit about his disapproval of the event of Saqifah.

After such a clear verdict from Caliph Umar who was an eyewitness to the entire episode of Saqifah, it is futile for anyone else especially people who came in later generations to try and justify the proceedings and the choice of Saqifah. It makes no sense and serves no purpose.

The proceedings and the outcome of a meeting which was spontaneous in its very nature are unjustifiable by this fact alone. The meeting of Saqifah happened out of the blue, it wasn't a thought through process, hence the outcome of such a meeting is not necessarily based on logic or reason, let alone Quran and Sunnah.

Despite these clear facts people still try and justify the outcome of a spontaneous gathering which took place some fourteen centuries ago, to deny Ali his right. I will mention some key themes that are still put forward to justify the meeting of Saqifah with the sole aim of denying the actual position of Ali in relation to the Prophet.

16.2. The Consensus of the Ummah (Ijma)

The consensus of the Ummah (Ijma) is one of the classical theories put forward by the supporters of Saqifah, when they have no other rational means left to justify the proceedings or the outcome of that meeting.

They would simply say that there has been a consensus of the Ummah or the consensus of the scholars on the Caliphate of Abu Bakr, essentially saying that the Ummah has given its consent to the trend of al-ijtihad (independent judgment) to this day, against the clear Sunnah of the Prophet.

Our discussion is not about the consensus of the Ummah that took place on Abu Bakr's Caliphate after the meeting of Saqifah. As I have explained earlier that the consensus at that time primarily came about due to the tribal vote, and the speech of Caliph Umar at the mosque of the Prophet, where he urged all the companions to accept the verdict of Saqifah.

Our discussion is about the consensus of Muslims on the Caliphate of Abu Bakr who are not his contemporary i.e., Muslims who came in later generations like us.

It will be worthwhile to briefly recap how the Caliphate of Abu Bakr was selected in Saqifah.

- The Ansar organized a spontaneous gathering in Saqifah immediately after the death of the Prophet.
- The Ansar did not inform any of the other stakeholders about the meeting.
- The Muhajireen i.e., Caliph Abu Bakr and Caliph Umar managed to find out about the meeting in Saqifah, but they also did not inform anyone else about this meeting.
- No one in the Muslim Ummah knew about the timing or the location of the meeting except its participants.
- Only four candidates who were physically present in the meeting were nominated for the position of the Caliphate.
- Ali, the family of the Prophet (Ahlulbayt) were not represented or present in the meeting of Saqifah.
- In the end a political adjustment (deal) between the Ansar and the Muhajireen enabled Caliph Abu Bakr to become the first Caliph of the Muslims.
- Caliph Abu Bakr had offered the Ansar the position of Vazirs (advisors) to the Caliph to pacify their political ambitions, but this position was never actually created for the Ansar.

Today, the Muslim Ummah and its scholars cannot possibly justify consensus on a meeting which was organized without any consensus in the first place. The Ansar had decided to organize the meeting of Saqifah without the consensus of the Muhajireen, the family of the Prophet and the Banu Hashim. How can we possibly reach consensus on behalf of the people who were missing from that meeting? It is simply impossible to give consensus to a meeting which was held without any consensus in the first place!

Saqifah was a spontaneous meeting organised by the Ansar on hearing the news of the death of the Prophet. The meeting of Saqifah took place even without the consensus of the people who were contemporary to the meeting. How can the later generations of Muslims possibly reach consensus on a meeting which took place without the consensus of its contemporaries?

There can be no justification for a consensus on Saqifah in this day and age when the meeting itself was conducted some fourteen centuries ago without the consensus of the key stakeholders at the time.

Consensus can only be achieved on issues which were done with consensus in the first place.

Leaving aside the debate that Prophet had chosen Ali as his successor, if the meeting of Saqifah would have taken place with the consent and with the approval of all the key stakeholders where everybody was given a fair chance to present their case, then the consensus or the Ijma that would have taken place could be classed as valid and fair.

Even then, the later generations would not be obliged to follow that consensus (Ijma), because they were not party to that consensus, even though the consensus that took place was fair and just.

The stick of consensus (Ijma) is simply used to justify the actions of the prominent companions in the meeting of Saqifah, which denied Ali the right that was given to him by the Prophet.

As I have said before that we leave the actions of the companions who took part in Saqifah with Allah. At the same time, we are responsible for our own actions in our lifetime, and we cannot possibly become party to the injustice of Saqifah.

If we accept the consensus and the Ijma of Saqifah, it means that we accept and give our consent to the following:

- An unannounced meeting of the Ansar on hearing the news of the death of the Prophet rather than participating in his funeral.
- The decision of the Muhajireen i.e., Caliph Abu Bakr and Caliph Umar not to inform anyone else in the Muslim Ummah about the meeting (shura) of Saqifah.
- That Ali and the Ahlulbayt were neither informed and nor was Ali even nominated as a candidate in the meeting while he was preparing the body of the Prophet for burial.
- The tactical voting of the al-Khazraj tribe of the Ansar against al-Aws to win favour in the eyes of the new Caliph.
- Caliph Abu Bakr not making the Ansar his advisors despite his promise in Saqifah as part of the political deal.

People who try and justify such a consensus have chosen to ignore even the very basic Islamic spirit of justice and fair play. Muslims living today cannot possibly give their consent to the above points. We will not be able to justify our consensus to the Prophet of Allah on the Day of Judgment.

We cannot do another injustice today to simply justify the outcome of Saqifah.

16.3. Bottom of the Pile

Apart from the consensus (Ijma) on Saqifah, Muslims are also informed that the best of the companion was Caliph Abu Bakr, then it was Caliph Umar, and then it was between Caliph Uthman and Ali, but the stronger opinion suggests that Caliph Uthman was superior to Ali. Ali is placed at the bottom of the pile to justify the political order of the Caliphate.

There are two aims with such statements.

Firstly, it reinforces the consensus on the Caliphate of Abu Bakr among the Muslims, implying that since he was the best companion of the Prophet, so he also deserved to be the first Caliph.

Secondly, even the merits of Ali are denied based on the order set out in Saqifah. As Ali became the fourth Caliph, then he must have been the least virtuous out of the four companions to be given that slot.

The injustice of Saqifah is topped up with yet another even bigger injustice, where the merits of the person who was trained for twenty-five years by the Prophet are denied, to justify the choice of Saqifah.

I will discuss this topic in two parts.

16.3.1. The Order of Saqifah

I have already gone through these points in previous chapters but for the completeness of this section I will reiterate some of the relevant points from the meeting of Saqifah.

- The Ansar had almost finalized Saad ibn Ubaadah as the new Caliph.
- Caliph Abu Bakr was not even invited to the meeting.
- Once in the meeting, Caliph Abu Bakr nominates Caliph Umar and Abu Ubaydah al-Jarrah for the position of the Caliphate.
- Caliph Umar in turn proposes Caliph Abu Bakr and eventually gives him the allegiance.

If the Ansar (companions from Madinah) had their way, then Caliph Abu Bakr would have never become the first Caliph. They neither invited him to the meeting, nor did they have any intention of selecting him for the position of the Caliphate.

In the meeting itself there were four potential candidates and any one of them could have been selected as the new Caliph. The Ansar had proposed Saad ibn Ubaadah as their candidate. Caliph Umar had proposed Caliph Abu Bakr to be his nominee, and Caliph Abu Bakr had proposed Caliph Umar and Ubaydah al-Jarrah as his choice in Saqifah.

There was no guarantee that Caliph Abu Bakr would have come on top. It just happened that Caliph Umar made a smart move and used the principle of allegiance in favour of Caliph Abu Bakr, which gave him the Caliphate.

The order of Saqifah could have been very different, since the gathering of Saqifah was a spontaneous event, where any one of the candidates could have won on the day.

Also, the outcome of Saqifah was not based on the merits of the candidates or their contribution in the path of Islam. It was simply based on the fact that the candidates happen to be at the right place at the right time. And to win on the day Caliph Abu Bakr offered the Ansar a position of being his advisors, and the Ansar as a compromise reluctantly accepted him as the first Caliph.

Those who insist that Caliph Abu Bakr was the best of the companions because of the order of Saqifah, have either not read the history of Saqifah or have chosen to ignore it completely.

Also, towards the end of his Caliphate Caliph Umar had set up a committee to choose his successor. Caliph Umar had proposed six candidates for the position of the third Caliphate. The candidates proposed by Caliph Umar were Ali, Uthman, Abdul Rahman, Saad, Al-Zubeir and Talhah. Again, any one of these candidates could have easily become the third Caliph, and there was no guarantee that Caliph Uthman would have come on top and would have definitely become the third Caliph.

The order of the Caliphs that we see in history could have been very different. Hence, it cannot possibly be used as a basis to put Ali at the bottom of the pile.

Also, the order created by Saqifah has no value in the eyes of the Prophet or in the eyes of Allah, because that order was never established with their permission or command.

This is just another injustice in a series of injustices that history has panned out against Ali and the Ahlulbayt.

16.3.2. The Merits

If Ali has been put at the bottom of the pile because of his merits and not because of the order of Saqifah, then I think it is only fair to have quick comparison between the merits of the first four Caliphs.

I will take a brief look at a few key merits.

16.3.2.1. Companionship with the Prophet

- Ali had opened his eyes in the lap of the Prophet, the first thing that Ali saw was the immaculate face of the Prophethood.
- Ali was brought by the Prophet himself and lived in Prophet's house all his life, an honour that no other companion shares with Ali.
- The other companions would meet the Prophet in the Mosque or outside in the streets of Madinah, but Ali was always with the Prophet.
- Ali was the only companion who knew how Prophet lived his life at home, and what his Sunnah was when he was in the confinement of his house.
- Ali was the companion of the cave of Hira on many occasions, where Quran was revealed to the Prophet, Ali became a witness to the revelations of the Holy Quran, again an honour that no other companion can claim to have.
- Ali remained the companion of the Prophet in the battle of Uhud, when the tables turned against the Muslims, and on seeing the danger the majority of the Companions fled including Caliph Umar, but Ali stayed back and saved the Prophet from certain death.
- On hearing the news of the gathering of Saqifah, both Caliph Abu Bakr and Caliph Umar left the body of the Prophet, but when Ali heard that Caliph Abu Bakr had been selected as the new Caliph in Saqifah, he still remained with the Prophet until the Prophet was laid to rest in his grave.
- The companionship of Ali and the Prophet began with the birth of Ali and ended with the burial of the Prophet.
- The companionship of Ali with the Prophet was different in every sense. No other companion including the participants of Saqifah shared this unique companionship that Ali had with the Prophet.
- This is why the Prophet had famously said that nobody knows me except Allah and Ali, and nobody knows Ali except Allah and me.

16.3.2.2. Piousness and Piety

- Proving someone's piousness or piety is very difficult as they are inner traits of a person, and only Allah knows if a person's heart is indeed pure.
- When the Christians of Nijran came to the Prophet for a dialogue, Allah revealed the verse 3:61, challenging the Christians for a Mubahila, where each side prays against the other, and the side which is most pious and truthful prevails.
- On the commands of Allah out of all the companions Prophet choses Ali along with the rest of the Ahlulbayt to take on the Christian of Najran.
- On seeing the piousness and piety on the faces of the Prophet, Ali and the rest of the Ahlulbayt, the Christian delegation declined the challenge of Mubahila and accepted the supremacy of Prophet's side.

- This was a unique distinction of Ali that even when the test of piousness and piety came, a trait which is only known to Allah, Prophet chooses Ali, proving his superiority even on this hidden merit.

16.3.2.3. Knowledge and Wisdom

- Ali was renowned for his amazing knowledge and wisdom, even the first two Caliphs would come to his door looking for answers on issues which they could not resolve on their own.
- During his reign, Caliph Umar had sentenced a woman to be stoned to death on finding out that she was giving birth after six months of marriage, the woman kept pleading her innocence, but Caliph Umar refused to pardon her. Finally, the matter was brought to the attention of Ali, who gave a judgment from Quran.
- Ali said, Allah says: "And the mothers should suckle their children for two years" (2:233) and in another place Allah says: "And the bearing of him and the weaning of him is thirty months" (46:15). If the period of weaning which is two years (24 months) is subtracted from thirty months (which is overall period of bearing & weaning), there remains only six months. This proves that pregnancy period can be for six months.
- The innocent woman who was facing death by stoning as a result of Caliph Umar's verdict was saved by the Quranic knowledge of Ali.
- Two women were fighting over a baby boy each claiming to be his mother, the case was brought to Caliph Umar, he was unable to resolve the dispute and decide which woman was the real mother. He asked Ali to resolve the issue for him.
- When Ali came, he looked at both the woman and suggested that he was going to cut the baby into half, so each woman can have her share. The real mother immediately screamed and offered the baby to the other woman. On seeing her response Ali gave the baby to the real mother.
- By simply using a little wisdom Ali resolved another tricky dispute which Caliph Umar was struggling to deal with.
- A Jewish man came to Caliph Abu Bakr seeking answers on Tauheed. Caliph Abu Bakr's responded that Allah is in Heaven on his throne, the Jewish man was puzzled and confused and asked if the God of earth and the heaven were different?
- As he was leaving the town he met Ali, who not only explained the proper concept of Tauheed in Islam, but also verified it from a conversation that Musa had with an angle which was found in Torah. The man was so impressed that he inquired as to why was Ali not the Caliph!
- The Prophet had not only taught Quran to Ali, but the Prophet also gave him the knowledge of the previous scriptures too.
- There is no evidence from history to suggest that Ali ever turned to another companion for an answer on an Islamic issue, whereas there are tens of instances where the ruling Islamic leadership felt it necessary to consult Ali, in spite of their reservations in this matter.
- This is why Prophet had famously said that I am the city of knowledge and Ali is the gate.

16.3.2.4. Bravery and Contribution in the Service of Islam

- Even the supporters of Saqifah would not dispute that the bravery and contribution of Ali in the decisive battles where the fate of Islam hung in balance was head and shoulders above the rest of the companions.
- When Amr Ibn Abd Wudd crossed the Moat and challenged the companions for a duel, no one had the courage to take him on. His challenge was for all the companions, but only Ali stepped up to the mark and not only accepted the challenge but quickly disposed him off.
- If Amr Ibn Abd Wudd wasn't stopped at that moment, then the rest of the Qurayshite army would have also crossed the Moat, and with their invasion the Islamic State of Madinah would have ended.
- This is why the Prophet had said that the duel of Ali against Amr Ibn Abd Wudd at the Battle of the Moat outweighs the good deeds of the entire nation until the Day of Judgment.

- In the battle of Uhud as the tables turned against the Muslims, the vast majority of the companions fled the battlefield to save their lives, but Ali stayed with the Prophet and saved him from certain death. The death of the Prophet in the battle of Uhud would have ended the revolution of Islam itself.
- In the battle of Badr Ali alone had killed close to 40% of the enemy fighters whereas the rest of the companions had killed the remaining 60%.
- The individual contribution of other companions did not make a difference to the outcome of the battle of Badr, but the performance of Ali was decisive in tipping the scales in favour of Islam and the Muslims.
- Similarly, in the battle of Khaibar the Muslim army had laid the siege for weeks without any results. Both Caliph Abu Bakr and Caliph Umar came back empty handed when they were given the flags of the Muslim army.
- Ali was not even well at the time and was exempt from jihad, but Prophet had no choice except to call upon him and hand over the flag of the Muslim army to his most trusted commander.
- Ali not only killed Marhab, the most celebrated Jewish warrior, but Ali also conquered their fortresses and defeated the enemy on its home soil, completely eliminating the Jewish threat to the newly established Islamic State.
- All together Ali took part in 18 battles and expeditions and Prophet never placed Ali under anybody's command or authority.
- In every battle that Ali took part his performance was the differentiating factor, and he tipped the scales of every battle in favour of Islam and the Muslims.

The unique thing about the merits of Ali is that they are in fact proven by the actual events of history, unlike the academic merits of some of the companions which are mentioned in the books but have no relevance to the key events that shaped early Islamic history.

It would be interesting to find out as to what merit was it? Or what discipline was it? that Ali was at the fourth position behind Caliph Abu Bakr, Caliph Umar or Caliph Uthman?

Obviously in the four merits or disciplines that I have mentioned above Ali was certainly not at the bottom of the pile. On the contrary, he was way ahead of the rest in every sense.

Regardless of the answer that the supporters of Saqifah may choose to give, the Prophet of Allah had already given his verdict on the position of Ali in comparison to the companions.

We read in Al-Seerat Al-Halabeyah that:

> Prophet created brotherhood between Caliph Abu Bakr and Caliph Omar, and between Caliph Abu Bakr and Kharijah Ibn Zeid, and between Caliph Omar and Atban Ibn Malik.
> Then he held the hand of Ali Ibn Abu Talib and said: "This is my brother"
> - (Ali Ibn Burhanudeen Al-Halabi, Biography of the Prophet Part 2, p. 97)

Similarly, we read in Biography of the Prophet (Seerah) by Ibn Husham

> "The Prophet, after the Hijrahh said to the Muslims: Be brothers in God. Every two should be brothers. Al-Hamzah, and Zeid Ibn Haritha became brothers and Abu Bakr and Kharijah Ibn Zuhair became brothers. Omar Ibn Al-Khattab and Atban Ibn Malik became brothers....
> Then he held Ali Ibn Abu Talib's hand and said: "This is my brother"
> - Ibn Husham, Part 1, p.505.

Also, we read in Al-Tirmidhi, Vol 2, Page 143

"O `Ali! You are my brother in this world and in the Hereafter."

As we can clearly see that Prophet made Caliph Abu Bakr the brother of Caliph Umar. He also makes Caliph Abu Bakr the brother of Kharijah Ibn Zuhair and makes Caliph Umar the brother of Atban Ibn Malik.

This is because in the eyes of the Prophet these companions were of similar calibre and stature. Their merits and virtues were comparable. For instance, the merits and virtues of Caliph Abu Bakr were similar and comparable to Caliph Umar, and hence the Prophet created brotherhood between the two. The actions of the Prophet of Allah were not without a reason or without wisdom.

But Prophet chooses Ali to be his brother. He does not compare Ali with any of the other companions, nor does he make Ali the brother of another companion. He only makes Ali his own brother. Because the virtues and merits of Ali were a result of Prophet's training and upbringing, and hence were unique and distinct. He could not possibly compare Ali to another companion because it would have been unfair for both Ali and that companion, since they never had the kind of upbringing that Ali had.

And this is why Prophet had said that Ali was his brother in this world and in hereafter.

Prophet had never compared Ali to any of the companions. On the contrary the Prophet had famously said:

> *"He who wants to see Noah in his determination, Adam in his knowledge, Abraham in his clemency, Musa in his intelligence and Isaa in his religious devotion should look at Ali Ibn Abi Talib."*

- *Tafsir al-Kabir, by Fakhruddin al-Razi, commentary of the Verse of Imprecation (Mubahilah), v2 p700*
- *Ibn Muttahar al-Hilli recorded the hadith in his "Minhaj al-karamah"*
- *Ibn Asakir narrated it in his history (12/ 140/ 2)*
- *Ibn Asakir narrated from Anas (12/ 133/ 2)*

Ali's determination could be seen on the battlefield. Ali's knowledge could be judged when the Caliphs of the time would come to his door looking for answers. Ali's religious devotion could be seen during the event of Mubahila when the Christians refused to take on the truthfulness of his stance.

Prophet is comparing Ali to the likes of Mosa, to the likes of Isaa, to the likes of Noah and to the likes of Adam. He does not compare Ali to the companions because Ali was trained to lead the companions, Ali was trained to guide the companions and to keep them on the path of the Sunnah of the Prophet.

Let's not do another injustice and even deny the merits of Ali, simply because he became the fourth Caliph.

This would be the mother of all injustices.

16.4. Burden, Binding, an Indication, and an Indirect Appointment

This is another classic theme that is used to justify the meeting and the appointment of Saqifah.

Muslims are informed that the Prophet did not explicitly appoint a successor because the words of the Prophet were binding, and if Prophet had explicitly appointed a successor then Muslims would have been obliged to follow his successor too, and this would put an extra and an unnecessary burden on the Muslim Ummah!

As bizarre and as absurd as it may sound, this is one of the arguments put forward by the followers of Saqifah.

Interestingly, the justification of Saqifah does not end at the above argument. It is further added that although the Prophet did not explicitly appoint a successor, but he gave an indication in favour of Caliph Abu Bakr, and some even say that he indirectly appointed Caliph Abu Bakr by letting him lead the prayers in his absence.

The main reason for putting such arguments is to simply defend the trend of al-ijtihad, which existed among the prominent companions at the time of the death of the Prophet. Since the participants of Saqifah did not consider the words of the Prophet binding and used their own judgment to choose the successor of the Prophet, Muslims are informed that the Prophet did not explicitly appoint a successor because it would extra burden on the Muslims.

It is unfortunate that such weak and feeble arguments are still used to defend the choice of Saqifah.

16.4.1. Burden and Binding

The reality of the argument of burden and binding could not be more flawed. If the Prophet did not appoint a successor than he would have put the entire burden of choosing his successor on the newly established Muslim Ummah! The Muslims would have been totally responsible for not only choosing the successor of the Prophet on their own, but they would also be responsible for ensuring that the successor of the Prophet adheres to the Holy Quran and the Sunnah of the Prophet.

However, if Prophet chooses his own successor than he removes that burden from the Ummah all together. Muslims would no longer be responsible for choosing Prophet's successor, nor would they be responsible for the subsequent actions and decisions of the Caliph. They would only be obliged to follow the nominee of the Prophet.

If Muslims Choose a Caliph, then the Muslims would have to ensure that the Caliph works within the limits set out by the Holy Quran and the Sunnah of the Prophet. But when Prophet chooses an individual to lead the Muslims then the entire burden is on the shoulders of the Prophet.

In fact, the group which considered the nominee of the Prophet to be a burden was the Quraysh of Makkah. They could not bear the thought of the leadership of the Muslims staying in the clan of Banu Hashim, and especially for Ali to head the Islamic State as they considered him to be their biggest enemy. Since Ali had killed some of their finest fighters in the battles of Badr, Uhad and Moat.

Unfortunately, the participants of Saqifah were influenced by the sentiments of Quraysh and did not nominate Ali for this very reason, as they considered the nomination of Ali to be a burden for the Qurayshites.

In later part of his Caliphate, Caliph Umar also confirmed this notion in a conversation that he had with Ibn Abbas.

> *Caliph Umar: "The Quraysh was unwilling to let you (the Hashimites) have the honour of both Prophethood and Caliphate. If that would have happened you would have wronged the people! Quraysh chose for itself, it succeeded and made the right decision."*

- *Tarikh al-Tabari, 5:30*
- *Qasas al-Arab, 2:263*
- *Ibn al-Atheer al-Kamal fil-Tarikh, 3:63*

- *Tarikh e Islam: 481-482, by Akbar Shah Najibabadi*

Unfortunately, the burden that the Qurayshite clans would have felt as a result of Ali's Caliphate is still being used as a reason to deny Ali his right, by claiming that if the Prophet had chosen a successor to lead the Muslim Ummah, then he would have put an unnecessary burden on the Muslims, because the choice of the Prophet would have been binding on the Muslims.

Ironically, the people who use the argument of "Burden and Binding" seem to completely ignore the burden that was put on the family of the Prophet as a result of Abu Bakr's Caliphate. According to the supporters of Saqifah, Prophet had not chosen anybody to be his successor but had only given an indication in support of Caliph Abu Bakr by allowing him to lead the prayers.

However, as Ali had not gone to the mosque of the Prophet to pay allegiance to Abu Bakr after he became the Caliph, Caliph Abu Bakr sends Caliph Umar to forcefully demand allegiance from Ali and the family of the Prophet, putting the burden of allegiance on the very person who also had a claim to the Caliphate.

As for Caliph Umar, he not only demands allegiance but also threatens the family of the Prophet with the burden of burning down their house if they refuse to pay allegiance.

> *When Umar came to the door of the house of Fatimah, he said: "By Allah, I shall burn down (the house) over you unless you come out and give the oath of allegiance (to Abu Bakr)."*

- *History of Ibn Athir, v2, p325*
- *al-Isti'ab, by Ibn Abd al-Barr, v3, p975*
- *Tarikh al-Kulafa, by Ibn Qutaybah, v1, p20*
- *Tarikh Abul Fida, 1:156*

Considering that the Prophet had only given an indication in favour of Abu Bakr, the actions of Caliph Umar seem a little extreme to say the least.

The burden of Abu Bakr's Caliphate on the family of the Prophet did not end there either. The land of Fadak which was a major source of income for the Prophet and his family was also confiscated by Caliph Abu Bakr on becoming the head of the Islamic State, adding financial burden on the family of the Prophet on top of interfering in their right of the Caliphate.

In fact, after the death of the Prophet if there was any case of putting the "Burden", then surely it was put on the family of the Prophet, on a mere indication in favour of Caliph Abu Bakr.

Interestingly, the supporters of the argument of "Burden and Binding" have no issue with the appointment of Caliph Umar by Caliph Abu Bakr as the next Caliph and the head of the Islamic State.

When it comes to Caliph Abu Bakr appointing a successor, the argument of "Burden and Binding" is reversed. The supporters of Saqifah would now argue that since the words of Caliph Abu Bakr were not binding on Muslims, he could appoint a successor, but Prophet couldn't.

Let see if Caliph Abu Bakr had agreed with such logic.

When Caliph Abu Bakr was in his final ailment and was about to die, he nominated Caliph Umar as his successor and the future leader of the Muslims.

We read the words of Caliph Abu Bakr in Tareek Al-Tabaree:

> *Abu Bakr Stood up before the people and said to them, 'Are you pleased with the person that I have appointed over you? Verily, I have thought long and hard before making this decision, and I did not appoint a relative; instead, I appointed over you Umar Ibn Al-Khattab, so listen to him and obey him.' They said, 'We hear and we obey.'*
>
> - *Tareekh At-Tabaree (4/248)*

Caliph Abu Bakr not only appoints a successor but also instructs the Muslims to follow and obey his choice. Caliph Abu Bakr tells the audience that they must listen to and obey Caliph Umar. Caliph Abu Bakr had certainly considered his words binding on all the Muslims and hence he was asking them to obey and listen to his nominee.

This is contrary to the argument given by the supporters of Saqifah that the words of Caliph Abu Bakr were not binding on the Muslims.

Also, Caliph Abu Bakr had not given Muslims a choice between a few candidates for his successorship. The only candidate put on the table for being the next Caliph was Caliph Umar. Muslims were not allowed or given the freedom to appoint anyone else other than Caliph Umar as the successor of Caliph Abu Bakr.

Even when companions complained about Caliph Umar that he had an extremely harsh personality, and hence he was unsuitable for being the Caliph, Caliph Abu Bakr did not change his mind and dismissed the criticism and insisted on appointing Caliph Umar as his successor.

Talha and other companions complained to Caliph Abu Bakr's about the choice of Caliph Umar as the next Caliph.

Tallha said to Caliph Abu Bakr:

> "What will you say to your Lord tomorrow? You have chosen a severe, harsh man to govern us. People run away from him and their hearts beat because of him".
>
> - History of the Prophets and Kings pp. 2138-9 al-Tabari

Caliph Abu Bakr replied:

> "...... "Do you try to scare me with Allah? If I am asked about it tomorrow I will say: 'I selected the best of your people to rule them".
>
> - History of the Prophets and Kings pp. 2138-9 al-Tabari

Caliph Abu Bakr dismissed his critics by saying that he has chosen the best of the companions to rule over them. Caliph Abu Bakr did not offer the Muslims any freedom when it came to choosing his successor, because he had considered his choice to be binding on all the Muslims.

The argument that Caliph Abu Bakr's words were not considered binding, and hence he could appoint a successor, falls flat on its face as the actions of Caliph Abu Bakr tell a different story.

In any case, based on the logic of "Burden and Binding", if Prophet had not appointed a successor and had only given an indication, since it would become binding on the Muslims to follow his nominee, a burden which the Muslims could not possibly handle, then surely nobody else had a right to appoint a successor either, because they would be unnecessarily burdening the Ummah with their appointment, especially when they are also binding the Muslims to obey their appointee.

Just like the Prophet, Caliph Abu Bakr should have also left the choice of his successor to the Ummah, since according to the followers of Saqifah, it was the Sunnah of the Prophet to leave the choice of his successor to the Ummah or at best give an indication in someone's favour. If Prophet had chosen not to burden the Ummah with his successor, then by explicitly choosing a successor and instructing the Muslims to follow him not only tantamount to putting extra burden on the Ummah, but it is also a clear breach of the Sunnah of the Prophet.

It's a real shame that even in this era of logic and reason such indefensible theories are still propagated to justify the outcome of Saqifah.

Similarly, when Caliph Umar was about to leave this world, he setup a committee to choose his successor with some very specific and harsh instructions.

> "O group of Muhajireen! Verily, the Apostle of God died, and he was pleased with all six of you. I have, therefore, decided to make it (the selection of khalifa) a matter of consultation among you, so that you may select one of yourselves as khalifa. If five of you agree upon one man, and there is one who is opposed to the five, kill him. If four are one side and two on the other, kill the two. And if three are on one side and three on the other, then Abdur Rahman ibn Auf will have the casting vote, and the khalifa will be selected from his party. In that case, kill the three men on the opposing side. You may, if you wish, invite some of the chief men of the Ansar as observers but the khalifa must be one of you Muhajireen, and not any of them. They have no share in the khilafat. And your selection of the new khalifa must be made within three days."

- (Al-Tabari, Vol 3, pp. 294-295)

Caliph Umar not only forms a committee to choose his successor, but he also orders the killing of the minority group within the committee. He certainly did not believe in simply giving an indication in favour of another companion, as the followers of Saqifah suggest was the Sunnah of the Prophet.

He not only puts the burden of death on the committee members, but he also expects the choice of the committee to be binding on the entire Muslim Ummah.

Needless to say that based on the assertion that if Prophet had left the choice of his successor to the Ummah, then the Sunnah of the Prophet was once again in tatters, because Caliph Umar had setup a committee to choose his successor and he did not leave the decision to the Ummah.

Also, when the committee setup by Caliph Umar meets, it puts the burden of following the Sunnah of both Caliph Abu Bakr and Caliph Umar as a condition for Ali to become the third Caliph. A burden, which Ali refuses to accept, and as a result was denied the third Caliphate.

It would be advisable for people who use the argument of burden and binding to objectively read Islamic history before proposing such naive theories.

16.4.2. An Indication or an Indirect Appointment

The Prophet of Allah had asked Caliph Abu Bakr to lead the prayers while he was unwell.

Carrying on from the theme of "Burden and Binding", some supporters of Saqifah even go a step further, and say that by asking Caliph Abu Bakr to lead the prayers the Prophet of Allah had in fact indirectly appointed Caliph Abu Bakr as his successor. They further add that because of this indirect appointment of Caliph Abu Bakr by the Prophet of Allah, he was chosen by the Muslims as the first Caliph.

The notion that Prophet had given an indication in favour of Caliph Abu Bakr or had indirectly appointed him as the future leader of the Muslims, by the virtue that Prophet had chosen him to lead the prayers, was completely rejected by Caliph Abu Bakr himself in the gathering of Saqifah.

On reaching Saqifah, Caliph Abu Bakr never suggested that he should be chosen as the Caliph because Prophet had chosen him to lead the prayers. In fact, Caliph Abu Bakr's argument against the Ansar was solely based on the theme that the Caliphate was the right of Muhajireen as the Qurayshites would not recognize the leadership of any other tribe.

Here is what Caliph Abu Bakr said in Saqifah to convince the Ansar:

> *"(O Ansar) you are our brethren in Islam and our partners in religion…but the Arabs will not submit themselves except to this clan of Quraysh…we (the Quraysh) are in the centre among the Muslims with respect to our position…"*
>
> - *(The History of al-Tabari, Volume 9, p.193)*
>
> *"The people of Arabia are not aware of anyone's political leadership except that of the Quraysh."*
>
> - *(Musnad Ahmad, vol 1., p.56)*

Caliph Abu Bakr clarifies exactly the issue that was at stake in Saqifah. Leading or not leading the prayers was irrelevant.

Caliph Abu Bakr said to the Ansar that although you are our brothers in Islam, but the Arabs will not recognize the political leadership of anyone except that of a Qurayshite clan. To justify the right of Quraysh to lead the Muslims, Caliph Abu Bakr further adds that we (the Quraysh) are the centre among the Muslims with respect to our position.

Caliph Abu Bakr's argument was not based on the fact that he had led the prayers in Prophet's absence. Caliph Abu Bakr's augment was entirely based on the fact that Arabs would only recognize the leadership of a Qurayshite leader and not someone who was an inhabitant of Madinah.

Caliph Abu Bakr had never considered leading the prayers as an indication for his own Caliphate, otherwise he would have used this indication in his favour in Saqifah, as he had used the fact that he was from the Qurayshite tribe just like the Prophet, and hence deserved more to lead the Muslims than the Ansar.

On the contrary, in Saqifah Caliph Abu Bakr had indeed proposed Caliph Umar and Abu Ubaydah al-Jarrah as the potential candidates for the position of the Caliphate. However, neither Caliph Umar and nor Abu Ubaydah al-Jarrah had ever led the prayers in Prophet's absence, but both of them were Qurayshite Muslims who would potentially be accepted to the wider Arabs as the new Caliphs.

Caliph Abu Bakr said to the Ansar:

> *He (Abu Bakr) said: "All the good that you have said about yourselves (O Ansar) is deserved. But the Arabs will recognize authority only in this clan of Quraysh, they being (considered) the best of the Arabs in blood and country.*
> *I offer you one of these two men (Umar and Abu Ubaydah al-Jarrah): accept whom you please.'"*
>
> - *Ibn Ishaq, Seerah Rasool-Allah*

The actions of Caliph Abu Bakr in the meeting Saqifah confirmed beyond any doubt that he had never considered leading of the prayers as an indication for his Caliphate or an indirect appointment by the Prophet, because if that was the case then he would have never proposed Caliph Umar or Abu Ubaydah al-Jarrah for the Position of the Caliphate.

The real issue in Saqifah was not about who had or hadn't led the prayers in Prophet's absence, it was all about who would be acceptable to the Quraysh as the new Caliph based on his tribal lineage.

Caliph Abu Bakr had not intervened in the meeting of Saqifah because Prophet had given an indication in his favour or because Prophet had indirectly appointed him as a successor. Caliph Abu Bakr had thwarted the plans of Ansar in Saqifah because in his view the Quraysh would not accept a leader from the Ansar to head the Islamic State. Caliph Abu Bakr was simply advocating the views of Quraysh in Saqifah.

The Ansar also had no qualms about who had or hadn't led the prayers. They did not even invite Caliph Abu Bakr to the meeting of Saqifah, despite the fact that he had led the prayers in Prophet's absence. On the contrary, the Ansar had in fact finalized their own candidate Abu Ubaydah as the new Caliph when Caliph Abu Bakr reached Saqifah. Abu Ubaydah obviously had not led the prayers in Prophet's absence, but he was acceptable to the Ansar as the new Caliph since he was an inhabitant of Madinah.

Caliph Abu Bakr won the day in Saqifah because he came from a clan of Quraysh, and the Quraysh were not willing to allow the leadership of the Islamic State to be in the hands of the Ansar, or anybody else for that matter. It was the view of Quraysh on Caliphate that dominated the proceedings and the outcome of Saqifah.

The Ansar had in fact suggested that there should be two Caliphs one from them and one from the Muhajireen, despite the fact that their candidate had not led the prayers.

The Ansar said:

> *"O Quraysh. There should be one ruler from us and one from you."*
> - *(Sahih Bukhari, Volume 8, Book 82, Number 817)*

The Muhajireen rejected the proposal of Ansar and said:

> *"How preposterous! Two swords cannot be accommodated in one sheath. By Allah, the Arabs will never accept your rule…"*
> - *(History of al-Tabari, p.194)*

On seeing that the Ansar were not being swayed and were still sticking to their guns, Caliph Abu Bakr made a counteroffer to the Ansar. He offered them to become the advisors to the Caliph and said that the Muhajireen would not make any decisions without consulting the Ansar.

> *We (the Muhajirs) are the leaders, and you (Ansars) are the advisors/ministers; matters shall not be settled without consultation, nor shall we decide on them without you."*
> - *(The History of al-Tabari, Vol.10, pp.4-5)*

Based on the political adjustment offered by Abu Bakr, the Ansar eventually accepted the leadership of the Muhajireen.

> *"What you say is correct: we are your advisors and you are our rulers."*

- *Musnad Ahmad, Vol.1, p.5*

Even at this stage the Ansar had not accepted the leadership of Abu Bakr, they had only accepted the leadership of the Muhajireen as a group. They had only given consent for the Muhajireen as a whole to rule over the Muslim Ummah.

On seeing this shift in the position of the Ansar Caliph Umar seized the opportunity, and immediately gave allegiance to Caliph Abu Bakr by saying that since Caliph Abu Bakr had led the prayers he deserved to be the Caliph.

Leading the prayers was simply a statement that Caliph Umar had uttered in favour of Caliph Abu Bakr while he paid allegiance to him. It wasn't something that was even discussed or debated in the meeting of Saqifah. It was only a comment made by Caliph Umar right at the end as he paid allegiance to Abu Bakr.

The assertion that Prophet had given an indication in favour of Abu Bakr, or had indirectly appointed him as a successor, and hence Muslims choose him as their leader has no historical basis. The proceedings of Saqifah do not support such a notion or a theory.

The evidence of history points to a compromise that Caliph Abu Bakr had offered to the Ansar, by making them his advisors, which eventually convinced the Ansar to accept the leadership of the Muhajireen. It was this compromise which had formed the basis of Abu Bakr's Caliphate, and not the fact that he had led the prayers. Once the Ansar had accepted the offer of being the advisors the fight was over at that point and the Ansar were willing to accept any one from the Muhajireen to become the new Caliph.

Despite such clear facts, the supporters of Saqifah to this day not only insist on burdening the Ummah with the Caliphate of Abu Bakr, but also consider it binding on all the Muslims.

The very people who consider the nomination of Ali to be a burden on the Ummah, regard any Muslim who goes against the Caliphate of Abu Bakr as a deviant or even a Kafir (a non-Muslim), simply because he or she has negated the choice of Saqifah.

Even the burden of Kufar and deviation is put on fellow Muslims in order to justify the outcome of Saqifah.

Muslims who believe in the Tawheed (Oneness) of Allah, and not only consider Prophet Mohammad as the final Messenger of Allah, but the best of the creation are placed outside the fold of Islam, on the grounds that they have refused to accept the Caliphate of Abu Bakr.

The institution of Caliphate is put above the institution of Tawheed and Prophethood, which indeed is most unfortunate and tragic.

16.5. Our Approach

Our approach on the issue of Saqifah should be based on true historical facts and the notion of fair play. If for tribal, political, or social reasons the nominee of the Prophet was considered a burden by the first generation of Muslims (companions), then surely in the 21st century where we have the freedom of thought and expression in most parts of the world, there should be no burden on us today if we decide to follow the nominee of the Prophet.

We are not bound by the same tribal or social order that the early generation of Muslims were, and certainly there is no Qurayshite influence on any of us today, which could be given as a justification for not accepting Ali as the rightful successor of the Prophet.

In this day and age there would be no extra burden on us if we decide to accept Ali as the successor of the Prophet. There is no reason as to why we cannot today accept the path laid down by the Prophet of Allah rather than the path laid out by Saqifah.

16.6. The Jewish Conspiracy

There are certain sections of the Muslim Ummah which promote and propagate the theme of a Jewish conspiracy against Islam, by claiming that the entire notion that Prophet had appointed Ali to be his successor had been coined by a man of Jewish heritage.

The aim of such themes is obvious. It is a cheap attempt to belittle the status and the stature of Ali in the eyes of the Muslim masses, so it appears that Ali was no different to any other companion and it was in fact a Jewish man who had elevated the status of Ali as the successor of the Prophet. Apart from lowering the status of Ali in the eyes of the Muslims the other aim is to malign the present-day Shia Muslims as well, by implying that they are in fact following in the footsteps of a Jewish man, since they believe that Ali was the rightful successor of the Prophet.

The Jewish conspiracy theme is very cleverly used to deny Ali his right and to justify the spontaneous gathering of Saqifah, by stating that the whole notion and the concept of Ali being the successor of the Prophet was indeed first introduced by a Yemeni Jew whose name was Ibn Saba. Many absurd theories are attributed to this fictitious Jewish character. However, the biggest allegation made against him is the fact that he was the first person in history to have introduced the idea that Ali was the successor of the Prophet.

And since it was Ibn Saba the Yemeni Jew who had invented this whole idea of Ali's successorship, any person who accepts this theory is in fact following a misguided Jew.

The supporters of Saqifah try not to leave any stone unturned in their quest to justify their historical stance on the issue of Caliphate.

However, it has to be said here that most of the scholars from the Sunni school of thought do not believe in the fairy tale of Ibn Saba, nevertheless a strong and an influential minority primarily in the form of the Salafis, insists that it was a Yemeni Jew who founded the theory of Ali being the successor of the Prophet.

The Muslim world in general is pretty susceptible to conspiracy theories. The easiest way to dismiss an ideology or a notion is to simply link it to the Jews, and class it as a Jewish conspiracy against Islam. In this specific case playing the Jewish card is really the last form of defence in the face of overwhelming evidence and clear Sunnah of the Prophet in favour of Ali's successorship.

When all else fails and when all the evidence and the key historical events negate the choice of Saqifah, the idea that a Jewish man had cooked up the entire theory of Ali's leadership is put forward to deny the clear Sunnah of the Prophet, and to justify the trend of al-ijtihad (independent judgment) that existed among the prominent companions.

The reason why the Jewish conspiracy card tends to be effective is because historically there has been mistrust between the Jews and the Muslims. Also, during the time of the Prophet Muslims had quite a few skirmishes and battles with the Jews of the Arabian Peninsula, most notably of them being the battle of Khaibar. As a result, historically there is a suspicion and misgivings between the people of the Jewish faith and the Muslims. In the present era unfortunately because of the policies of the Israeli government towards the Palestinians, the whole Jewish nation is still seen in a negative light in the Muslim Ummah.

So, the most effective way to create doubt in the minds of the ordinary Muslims about an issue is to create a Jewish link. This is commonly done by using words like the "Jewish agents", or a "Jewish conspiracy" against Islam and Muslims. The aim is to kill two birds with one stone. Firstly, it is a very convenient way of blaming all the ills on a foreign entity, and secondly it relives Muslims of any responsibility and blame.

The allegation that Ibn Saba (a Jew) had invented the idea of Ali being the successor of the Prophet should be seen in this light.

I will divide this topic into three sections, and it will be a slightly lengthy discussion due to the nature of the allegation.

In the first section I will discuss the theories that have been attributed to Ibn Saba, and we will see if he was really the first person who had come up with those notions. In the second section I will shed light on the historical character of Ibn Saba and see if such a character in fact existed in history. In the third section I will discuss the Saba'iya group, a name which is often given to the alleged followers of Ibn Saba.

16.7. The Theories Attributed to Ibn Saba

Although there are many ludicrous and illogical theories and notions that have been attributed to Ibn Saba, however for our discussion we will pick three such theories which are most relevant to our topic.

Also, in this section we will assume that the Yemeni Jew Ibn Saba had in fact existed in history, and then we will see that despite his existence was he really the first person to have come up with the theories that have been attributed to him.

Here is what the Salafis say about Ibn Saba in general.

Abdullah ibn Saba was a Jew who came from Yemen. He embraced Islam during the reign of the third Caliph Uthman. He roamed through the Muslim world causing dissent, and corrupting Muslims with fabricated ideologies and notions. He launched his campaign from Hijaz then travelled to Basra, Kufa and Syria and finally settled in Egypt. He led Muslims astray and caused division and fitna by exalting Ali and the Ahlulbayt. He manipulated the companions and the generations after them and caused wars, instability and fitna which engulfed the best of the nation …….He was instrumental in campaigning against Caliph Uthman, and he gained many followers known as Sabaies who eventually killed and brought down the Caliphate of Uthman.

Following are the three key theories which are alleged to have been founded by Ibn Saba.

- Ibn Saba predicted the idea that Prophet Mohammed would return to earth. He based this theory on the return of Jesus. He said: "if Jesus could return then why can't Mohammed?"
- Ibn Saba was the first person in history to have come up with the idea that Ali was the rightful successor of the Prophet. Hence, the whole notion that Prophet had appointed a successor had indeed come from a Yemeni Jew.
- Ibn Saba had heavily criticized the government of Caliph Uthman and was instrumental in causing the rebellion against him which eventually led to the killing of the third Caliph.

16.7.1. The Return of the Prophet.

It is alleged that Ibn Saba had predicted the idea of the return of the Prophet i.e., Prophet Mohammed would return to this world after his death.

People who have read Islamic history objectively would immediately recognize that the first person who had in fact predicted the return of the Prophet was none other than Caliph Umar. All historians agree that after the death of the Prophet, Caliph Umar stood at the mosque of the Prophet and said:

> *"There are hypocrite men who allege that the Messenger of God has died. Certainly, the Messenger of God did not die, but he went to his Lord as Musa, son of Imran, went to his Lord (for receiving the Heavenly commandments). By God, Muhammad will return as Musa returned, and he shall sever the hands and legs of the men who alleged that the Messenger of Allah has died."*

- *(Ibn Hisham, Al-Sirah al-Nabawiyyah, part 2, page 655)*

According to the Salafis Ibn Saba became a Muslim during the time of Caliph Uthman. However, Caliph Umar predicted the return of the Prophet soon after the death of the Messenger of Allah. Hence, the first person who suggested the return of Prophet Mohammed was indeed Caliph Umar and not Ibn Saba.

If the character of Ibn Saba had indeed existed, then it was possible that he had borrowed this idea from the speech of Caliph Umar which he had made after the death of the Prophet!

It is difficult to ascertain as to why Caliph Umar would come up with such a notion, as we have not seen any evidence or narrations where the Prophet had predicted his own return. Nevertheless, the claim that Ibn Saba had invented the concept of Prophet's return is incorrect, since this theory was first put forward by Caliph Umar way before the alleged appearance of Ibn Saba on the scene, which is said to have happened during the reign of the third Caliph Uthman.

16.7.2. Ali is the Successor of the Prophet

The claim that Ibn Saba was the first person to have come up with the idea that Prophet had appointed Ali to be his successor is not just preposterous but is also insane.

According to the advocators of Ibn Saba he appeared during the reign of Caliph Uthman.

However, the idea that Ali was the successor of the Prophet could have come from any of the following events, which took place way before the reign of the third Caliph.

For instance:

- The first event which could have given the idea that Ali was the successor of the Prophet was in fact the very first call to Islam that Prophet had made to his clan. During this call Prophet had prepared a feast for his clan and then invited them to the path of Islam. Prophet had asked the audience if there was anybody who would support him in his mission. The only person who offered his unconditional support to the Prophet was Ali. Prophet then held Ali's hand and declared him to be his brother and his successor. So, in fact the very first call to Islam could have given the idea that Prophet had appointed Ali to be his successor. Even if Ibn Saba existed in history, his existence starts from the Caliphate of Uthman, he was not present when the first call

to Islam was made, but the theory of Ali being the successor of the Prophet was bubbling around even at that time. (See chapter 6 for the details of this event).
- The narration of the Prophet where he had stated to Ali that you are to me like Harun was to Musa except that there would be no Prophet after me, could also have been seen as an intention of the Prophet to appoint Ali as his successor. Again, this theory was proposed way before the coming of Ibn Saba in the books of history.
- The tradition of the Prophet at Ghadeer Khum where the Prophet had raised the hand of Ali and said to the audience of thousands of Muslims, that whoever accepts me as their Mawla (Guardian) should also accept Ali as their Mawla (Guardian). This position that Prophet had given to Ali could certainly be perceived as a plan by the Prophet to appoint Ali as his successor. And of course, this plan was also hatched long before the inception of Ibn Saba in the works of history.
- The advice of the Prophet where he had explicitly asked the Muslims to follow the two valuable assets after his demise, i.e., the Book of Allah and his Ahlulbayt, could be viewed as a proposal to deem Ali as the successor of the Prophet, since in the absence of the Prophet Ali was the head of the Ahlulbayt. Again, this advice was made well before the existence of Ibn Saba, proving that Ibn Saba was not the inventor of the notion of Ali's leadership.
- Another tradition of the Prophet where he had compared his Ahlulbayt to the Ark of the Noah and said that whoever embarked on it was saved, could be interpreted as a theory for the leadership of Ali, since Ali was the head of the Ahlulbayt after the Prophet and whoever followed Ali would be saved. Like the other traditions this tradition was also relayed well before the advent of Ibn Saba, clearly proving that the concept of Ali's leadership was present long before the presences of Ibn Saba.
- The narration of the Prophet that do not be ahead of the Ahlulbayt for you will perish, and do not turn away from them for you will perish, and do not try to teach them since they know more than you, could also be seen as a pointer to the leadership of Ali among the Ahlulbayt. Again, the appearance of Ibn Saba in history happened way after the above tradition of the Prophet, proving once more that the first person who suggested that Ali was the successor of the Prophet was not Ibn Saba.
- The coming of the Prophet to the door of Ali every day for six months and praying for his righteousness and purification, could also be seen as an intention of the Prophet to ensure that the leadership of the Muslim Ummah stays in the hands of Ali. Again, this expression of Prophet's intent to choose Ali as his successor was made way before the coming of Ibn Saba in history.
- In the distinguished event of Mubahila where Christians had challenged the ideological message of Islam, Prophet took Ali as a representation of his own truthfulness. This event could easily be symbolized as a plan of the Prophet to endorse the truthfulness of Ali's leadership. The event of Mubahila took place long before the alleged notion of Ibn Saba that he was the one who had introduced the concept of Ali's leadership.
- The fact that Prophet had adopted Ali as a child and brought him up in his own house, kept him away from the Jahilliyah traditions of the time, ideologically trained and groomed him in the spirit of Islam for twenty-five years, could be envisaged as an intention of the Prophet to appoint Ali as his ideological successor. Clearly, even if Ibn Saba had come of age at the time of Caliph Uthman, the perception and the notion of Ali being the ideological successor of the Prophet was ingrained way before in the pages of history.
- Ali was the differentiating factor among all the companions in the establishment and in the defence of the Islamic State of Madinah. Without the establishment of the Islamic State Muslims would have never been able to expand and grow. The killing of Amr Ibn Abd Wudd in the battle of Moat, saving the life of the Prophet in the battle of Uhud, wiping out 40% of the enemy in the battle of Badr, defeating the Jews in the battle of Khaibar, could all be seen as a way of Ali earning the title of being the successor of the Prophet. Again, all these key events took place long before the alleged notion that Ibn Saba had introduced the theory of Ali's leadership.

- The explanation given by Caliph Abu Bakr to Ali where he tries to justify his own Caliphate by stating that there wasn't enough time to call Ali to the meeting of Saqifah, clearly gives an indication that Ali also had a claim to the Caliphate. Once again, the justification given by Caliph Abu Bakr took place long before the alleged arrival of Ibn Saba in history.
- The instructions of the Prophet to Caliph Abu Bakr and Caliph Umar to leave Madinah for a military expedition, while keeping Ali in Madinah in the final days of his life, could easily be seen as a gesture of the Prophet in favour of Ali to take over the leadership of the Muslims after his demise. By keeping Ali in Madinah, the Prophet clearly amplifies his intentions in favour of Ali's leadership, way before Ibn Saba is supposed to have come up with this idea.
- The fact that Ali did not accept the leadership of the Islamic State for six months after the inauguration of Caliph Abu Bakr, could have easily given the impression that Ali had also considered himself to be the successor of the Prophet, way before Ibn Saba was supposed to have invented this theory.
- The conversation between Caliph Umar and Ibn Abbas where Caliph Umar explains that the reason why Ali was not selected in Saqifah was because he belonged to the same clan as the Prophet, clearly shows that the idea of Ali's right to the Caliphate existed even during the meeting of Saqifah, and was confirmed by Caliph Umar who was the architect of Abu Bakr's Caliphate. And of course, the event of Saqifah took place well before the time of Ibn Saba, who was alleged to have appeared during the caliphate of Uthman.

Assuming, that Ibn Saba did exist in history, it is certainly possible that he may have borrowed this idea from any of the above events. But in no way was he the first person to have founded this notion, or to have come up with the idea that Ali was the successor of the Prophet.

The thought and the concept that Prophet had appointed a successor had been around since the birth of Islam itself. It is a separate debate whether one accepts this theory and considers Ali to be the rightful successor of the Prophet, but the concept or the notion that Prophet had appointed Ali to be his successor had been floating around since the very first invitation to Islam.

Not following the notion that Ali was the successor of the Prophet is one thing but claiming that it was a Jewish conspiracy is a step too far. People who have crossed these limits and have equated the Sunnah of the Prophet to a Jewish conspiracy would no doubt be held accountable for their actions on the Day of Judgment.

And surely the people who claim to love the Prophet and are proud to be called the Ahle Sunnah would distance themselves from such baseless theories.

16.7.3. Ibn Saba and the Caliphate of Uthman

It is alleged that Ibn Saba was a main critique of Caliph Uthman's government and was instrumental in causing the rebellion against him, which eventually led to the killing of the third Caliph. It is also said that during the reign of Caliph Uthman, Ibn Saba roamed through the Muslim world causing dissent, and corrupting the Muslims with fabricated ideologies and notions. He launched his campaign from Hijaz then travelled to Basra, Kufa and Syria and finally settled in Egypt. He manipulated the companions of the Prophet and caused wars and instability which engulfed the best of the nation. He played a lead role in campaigning against Caliph Uthman, and he gained many followers known as Sabaies who eventually killed and brought down the Caliphate of Uthman.

It is possible that a person who has not read Islamic history might buy into the clandestine character of Ibn Saba, where somehow, he secretively plotted against Caliph Uthman, unfairly criticized his government, and launched a rebellion against him which eventually resulted in his killing.

However, a person who has read Islamic history with facts would beg to differ. The downfall of Caliph Uthman's administration was a result of his blatant nepotism and corruption, as already detailed in Chapter 12 (The legacy of Saqifah).

Caliph Uthman had showered his Umayyad relatives with huge sums of money and gifts from the Islamic treasury, even though they were least adherent to the path of Islam. He gave many of his relatives, friends, and supporters vast pieces of public land in and around Hijaz.

During the reign of Caliph Uthman, the Umayyad's put their hands on the two key sources of power within the Islamic State i.e., the authority of its key provinces and their treasuries. The main power and the wealth of the Islamic state was concentrated in three provinces i.e., Syria, Iraq, and Egypt. During Caliph Uthman's rule these vast provinces became Umayyad Kingdoms. All the governors of these key provinces were fellow Umayyad's who were personally appointed by Caliph Uthman.

As a result of Caliph Uthman's attitude towards the Islamic treasury, most of the officials appointed by him also misused and embezzled public funds, in proportion to the level of authority that they had enjoyed, and the Islamic Caliphate resembled an Umayyad kingdom under his rule.

The Umayyad clan exploited and abused the third Caliphate as far as they possibly could, and Caliph Uthman allowed it to happen under his leadership without taking any measures or steps to stop them. In fact, he played right into their hands and simply became a tool of the Umayyads. He turned the Islamic State established by the Prophet into an Umayyad State.

The policies of misusing public funds and appointing unqualified relatives to the top positions finally came to haunt Caliph Uthman. The opposition to Caliph Uthman's rule came from many quarters within the Muslim Ummah. The most decisive opposition against the rule of Caliph Uthman began in Madinah itself, and it was led by some of the most influential and renowned personalities of the Muslim world.

The most prominent and outspoken critics of Caliph Uthman were Talhah, Zubair, Lady Aisha, Amr Ibn Al-Auss and Ammar Ibn Yasir. These were the public faces of the opposition that had flared up against Caliph Uthman.

Are the proponents of Ibn Saba suggesting that all the above opposition figures, which included both the prominent companions and the wife of the Prophet were in fact working under the influence of Ibn Saba, a Yemeni Jew? Since publicly there was no individual by the name of Ibn Saba who was criticizing or opposing the Caliphate of Uthman.

All the prominent opposition personalities like Talhah, Zubair and Lady Aisha who were leading the public opposition against Caliph Uthman had obviously accepted Islam during the lifetime of the Prophet.

Assuming that Ibn Saba was behind the campaign which had brought down the administration of Caliph Uthman. Are the advocators of Ibn Saba implying that instead of teaching and guiding a newly converted Jew to the path of Islam, these early Muslims who were the public face of the opposition were influence by a Yemeni Jew and became his followers, and ended up killing a fellow companion of the Prophet, who also happen to be the Caliph at the time?

The people who try to blame Ibn Saba for organizing the revolt against Caliph Uthman and accuse him of adversely criticizing the third caliph have completely ignored the facts on the ground. This imaginary Jew had no role in the killing of Caliph Uthman. The revolt against Caliph Uthman began in Madinah by the most notable Islamic personalities mentioned above.

16.7.3.1. The Reasons for the Jewish Card

The Jewish card is primarily played for two reasons:

- Firstly, it gives Caliph Uthman an alibi that his administration was indeed clean and upright, and it was a Yemeni Jew who caused all the trouble, clearing Caliph Uthman of any wrongdoings during his reign.
- Secondly, it clears the opposition from any wrongdoing too, including the murder of Caliph Uthman. Since they allege that it was a Yemeni Jew who had plotted the rebellion against Caliph Uthman, it removes the blame for the killing of the third Caliph from the shoulders of the prominent personalities like Lady Aisha, Talhah and Zubair, who in fact were leading the opposition against Caliph Uthman's rule and were calling for his head.

Any genuine student of history would agree that the opposition against Caliph Uthman was not led by Ibn Saba. Even if one assumes that there was a character like Ibn Saba who existed during the time of Caliph Uthman, his role in opposing the third Caliph would have been insignificant compared to the role played by the key opposition figures like Lady Aisha, Talhah, Zubair, Abdur Rahman ibn Auf, Amr Ibn Al-Auss and Ammar Ibn Yasir.

As mentioned in detail in chapter 12 (The legacy of Saqifah), there were three different forms of opposition against Caliph Uthman.

16.7.3.2. The Genuine opposition

This form of opposition was led by companions like Ammar ibn Yasir, Abdullah Ibn Masud, Abu Dhar and Malik al Ashtar. These people were genuinely opposed to the administration of Caliph Uthman for its breach of the Sunnah of the Prophet and for its violation of the Book of Allah.

16.7.4. The Politically Motivated Opposition

This form of opposition was led by prominent companions like Talhah, al-Zubair and the wife of the Prophet Lady Aisha. Although, they were also using the policies of Caliph Uthman as a pretext for opposing him, but their motives were merely political and were based on their own ambition of acquiring the Caliphate.

16.7.4.1. The Opportunistic Opposition

This form of opposition was led by companions like Amr ibn-Aluss who held a grudge against Caliph Uthman after he was dismissed as the governor of Egypt. Such individuals were looking for any opportunity to bring down the Caliph, and the policies of Caliph Uthman gave them ample opportunity to avenge their earlier treatment.

16.7.4.2. Lady Aisha, Talhah and Zubair

Talhah was one of the biggest and the most dangerous agitators against Caliph Uthman, he was at the forefront of opposing the rule of the third Caliph. His opposition against Caliph Uthman was far more violent and pronounced than any Jewish character possibly lurking in the background. Talhah was using his own house as a base for the opposition activities where large number of people would gather to challenge the Caliphate of Uthman.

Along similar lines the wife of the Prophet Lady Aisha became one of the most influential and high-profile agitators against Caliph Uthman. She would openly criticize Caliph Uthman and would accuse him of transgressing the Sunnah of the Prophet. She would occasionally display the garment of the Prophet, saying that the garment of the Prophet had not yet deteriorated, but Caliph Uthman had brought the precepts of the Prophet into disrepute.

She used to call Caliph Uthman a Naathal which means a heavily bearded Jew who was opposed to the religion of Allah. Lady Aisha also used to say that she wished she could put Caliph Uthman in a sack and throw him into the sea. Lady Aisha openly supported her cousin Talhah in his opposition of Caliph Uthman. She would also ask other influential personalities like ibn Abbas not to deter people from joining the opposition movement against Caliph Uthman. She was hoping that her cousin Talhah would succeed Caliph Uthman and he would follow the path of her father Caliph Abu Bakr.

The reach and influence of Lady Aisha or Talha in instigating ordinary Muslims against Caliph Uthman was far more effective than the influence of any Jewish character that may have been around at the time. The theory of Jewish conspiracy against the Caliphate of Uthman has no legs, unless of course we accept that the key opposition figures like Lady Aisha, Talhah, Zubair, Abdur Rahman ibn Auf, Amr Ibn Al-Auss and Ammar Ibn Yasir were all acting on the orders of a Yemeni Jew called Ibn Saba, who was manipulating them covertly behind the scenes.

Since publicly there was no character by the name of Ibn Saba to be seen anywhere.

16.7.4.3. The Events Dispel the Existence of Ibn Saba

The events which took place in the last few days of Caliph Uthman's life would itself dispel the whole notion of Ibn Saba or the presence of any kind of a Jewish conspiracy. Readers would recall from chapter 12 (The legacy of Saqifah) that Ali had successfully managed to bring about a reconciliation agreement between the opposition and the administration of Caliph Uthman.

This agreement itself proves that the opposition was not acting on the orders of Ibn Saba or was under some kind of Jewish influence. Because if it was the case then the opposition would have never agreed to reconcile with Caliph Uthman, since their whole intention would have been to simply bring down his Caliphate or kill him.

It was Caliph Uthman who went back on his promises that he made to the opposition, under the influence of his chief advisor Marwan bin al-Hakam. It was Marwan who had thwarted the reconciliation process, and not the opposition, proving that most of the opposition was genuine in their demands, and was not under the influence of some fictitious Jew.

The politically motivated opposition also fell in line once the genuine opposition agreed to reconcile, since the genuine opposition had the majority of the Muslims with them.

Also, if Ibn Saba was the instigator of the rebellion against Caliph Uthman, then the protestors who came from various provinces would have come with a pre-planned mind-set of Killing the Caliph. They would not have besieged his house for forty days before killing him, they would have immediately attacked and killed him.

The reason why the protestors besieged the house of Caliph Uthman was to pressurize him to meet their demands. The main demand of the protestors was to get Caliph Uthman to change his monetary policy and to remove his Umayyad relatives from his administration.

The siege of Caliph Uthman's house continued for forty days. Caliph Uthman had ample time to meet the demands of the protestors, or at least start some form of reforms in his administration. If Caliph Uthman would have met the demands of the protestors, reformed his administration, and changed his monetary policy, the protests against his administration would have subsided, and he would have survived.

If Ibn Saba was the organizer of the revolt against Caliph Uthman, then he would not have given so much time to the Caliph, he would have quickly taken the Caliph out once the protestors had entered Madinah, nor would he have allowed the opposition to reconcile with Caliph Uthman.

The invention of Ibn Saba and the invention of a Jewish conspiracy against Caliph Uthman is simply done to remove any blame of corruption or nepotism from his administration. The aim of such theories is to clear Caliph Uthman of any wrongdoing, in the guise that it was all a Jewish conspiracy that had brought down the government of Caliph Uthman which led to his killing.

However, such illogical and absurd theories cannot blind a genuine student of history from the facts on the ground.

It is evident from the above discussion that even if Ibn Saba did exist, the theories that have been attributed to him are baseless. For instance, he was not the first person to have predicted the return of the Prophet, nor was he the first person to have come up with the idea of Ali being the successor of the Prophet, and neither was he the cunning figure who had manipulated the companions and led a rebellion against Caliph Uthman.

16.8. Ibn Saba in the Eyes of History

In his section we will shed light on the existence of Ibn Saba in history. We will analyse the historical evidence which is given to justify the presence of such a character.

16.8.1. Ibn Saba according to Sunni History

The name of Ibn Saba appears in Sunni history from two sources, Sayf Ibn Umar and Ibn Asakir.

16.8.1.1. Sayf Ibn Umar

The portrayal and the sketch of Ibn Saba which is mostly advocated and which we have discussed so far comes from Sayf Ibn Umar.

Sayf Ibn Umar is the source which depicts Ibn Saba as a Yemeni Jew who appeared during the reign of Caliph Uthman, predicted the return of the Prophet, claimed that Ali was the successor of the Prophet, travelled throughout the Muslim Ummah manipulating the beliefs of the Muslims causing dissent, and launched a rebellion against Caliph Uthman which resulted in his killing.

The above picture of Ibn Saba appears in several Sunni books, however the source of all these stories is Sayf Ibn Umar.

Let us see what the famous Sunni scholars and historians say about Sayf Ibn Umar:

- Al-Albaani declared him a liar (Silsila Sahiha, v3 p184)
- Ibn Hajar declared him weak (Taqrib al-Tahdib, v1 p408)
- Imam Al-Nesai declared him weak (Al-Du'afa, p187)

- Al-Salehi al-Shami declared him very weak (Subul al-Huda wa al-Rashad, v11 p143)
- Imam Ibn Haban said: 'He narrates fabricated traditions' (Al-Majrohin, v1 p345).
- Imam Abu Daud said that he was nothing (Sualat al-ajeri, v1 p214)
- Imam Ibn al-Jawzi said: 'He is accused of fabricating hadith' (Al-Mudu'at, by ibn al-Jawzi, v1 p222).
- Allamah Sibt Ibn al-Ejmi said: 'He used to fabricate hadith' (Al-Kashf al-Hathith, p131)
- Al-Hakim said: 'Sayf is accused of being a heretic. His narrations are abandoned.' (Tarikh al-islam, v11 p161).
- Al-Dhahabi says: "Sayf Ibn Umar wrote two books, which have been unanimously rejected by scholars". (Al-Mughani fil Dhufa, page 292).

As mentioned above, Sayf is considered to be a liar and a fabricator by many prominent Sunni scholars and historians. He has been deemed as unreliable, weak, a liar, and even a heretic. His narrations have either been abandoned, disregarded, or are considered to be a forgery.

Sayf Ibn Umar al-Tamimi lived in the second century after the Hijrah and died during the rule of Haroon al-Rashid. He was considered a chronicler, or a storyteller as opposed to a hadith recorder. He wrote two books which have now perished. His books used to be around at the time of the Umayyad's and the scholars who read those books had unanimously rejected them.

It is also said that Sayf had invented several imaginary companions of the Prophet from his own tribe, to exalt the status of his tribe over others. He also distorted the biographies of many companions to please the Umayyad's who were the rulers of his time.

This is the reason why most Sunni scholars consider the story of Ibn Saba to be a fairy tale. However, a minority primarily in the form of Salafis still insist on Ibn Saba's existence, and to this day they advocate the baseless theories attributed to him.

The story of ibn Saba was fabricated by Sayf Ibn Umar to please the Umayyad rulers of his time. The Umayyad's were the biggest enemy of Ali and the Ahlulbayt since the time of the Prophet. The Umayyads could never accept Ali to be the rightful successor of the Prophet. The moment Ali became the Caliph, the most influential Umayyad leader of the time Muawiyah began plotting against his Caliphate. Muawiyah fought against Ali in the battle of Siffin to weaken Ali's rule and destroy his government.

Later, Muawiyah challenged Ali's elder son Imam Hasan when he briefly took over the reins of the Caliphate. He bribed Imam Hasan's army into submission and contrary to his agreement with Imam Hasan he forced his cruel son Yazid to be the next Caliph. Yazid starved and brutally murdered the entire family of the Prophet including his grandson, Imam Hussain. The hatred of the Umayyads towards Ali and the household of the Prophet was not hidden from anybody.

The Umayyad's did everything they could to undermine the leadership of Ali and the school of Ahlulbayt. It was very convenient for people like Sayf Ibn Umar to come with such fictitious stories and get into the good books of the rulers. Introducing Jewish element to distort the clear Sunnah of the Prophet (i.e., Ali was the successor of the Prophet), was just another ploy to poison the minds of the masses from the leadership of Ali.

Unfortunately, we see the same technique being used today by some so-called scholars.

For historians, the simple fact that there is no record of Ibn Saba in the battle Siffin disproves the entire theory of the existence of Ibn Saba. Since, if ibn Saba did really exist and was not a fictitious character, then there would have been some evidence of his presence in Siffin. It is not possible that he would have simply disappeared from the face of history during this battle.

It becomes abundantly clear to people who have read history objectively that the character of ibn Saba as a Yemeni Jew, who accepted Islam during the reign of third Caliph Uthman is nothing more than the imagination of one man called Sayf Ibn Umar al-Tamimi, who is considered to be a liar, a fabricator, and a foregoer.

16.8.1.2. Ibn Asakir

Among all the Sunni historians there was only one historian by the name of Ibn Asakir who had collected some reports about Ibn Saba, where the source of the traditions is not from Sayf Ibn Umar or Sayf ibn Umar is not in the chain of the narrators. These few traditions which number no more than fifteen are found in the book of Ibn Asakir called Tarikh Madinatul Damishq.

However, the sketch and the picture portrayed of Ibn Saba by Ibn Asakir is very different from the portrayal of Ibn Saba by Sayf Ibn Umar.

According to the reports collected by Ibn Asakir, a man by the name of Ibn Saba appeared during the Caliphate of Ali and claimed that Ali was God and divine. Ali asked Ibn Saba to repent but he insisted on his claim of Ali's divinity and as a result Ali killed him.

Unlike the Ibn Saba of Sayf Ibn Umar the Ibn Saba documented by Ibn Asakir:

- Appeared during the Caliphate of Ali rather than the reign of Caliph Uthman.
- Played no part in the rebellion against Caliph Uthman since he was not even present at that time.
- Did not claim that Ali was the successor of the Prophet but claimed that Ali was God.
- And was Killed by Ali due to his apostasy.

It is clear that these were two separate characters in history with the same name. The Character of Ibn Saba depicted by Sayf Ibn Umar was simply his own imagination, whereas the Ibn Saba described by Ibn Asakir may have been a reality.

However, it has to be said that Ibn Asakir was a historian from the 6th century, and the Ibn Saba that he had portrayed who claimed Ali was God appeared in the 1st century. There was a gap of 500 years between the appearance of Ibn Saba and the time when he was documented by Ibn Asakir. During these five centuries many renowned Sunni scholars and historians had appeared such as Bukhari, Muslim, Abu Hanifa, Imam Shafiyee, Imam Malik and many others, but none of them had collected any reports about Ibn Saba.

Nevertheless, there is no reason to completely deny the existence of the Ibn Saba who appeared during the reign of Ali and claimed that he was God. However, this Ibn Saba has no bearing on the theories which were attributed to the fictitious Ibn Saba of Sayf Ibn Umar.

So, it is possible that an individual who claimed that Ali was God did appear during Ali's caliphate and was killed by Ali himself.

16.8.2. Ibn Saba according to Shia History

The three Shia scholars who had originally mentioned Ibn Saba in their works are:

- Sa'ad Ibn Abdullah al-Ash'ari al-Qummi in his book "al-Maqalat wal-Firaq"
- Hasan Ibn Musa al-Nawbakhti in his book "al-Firaq"
- Al-Kashi in his book "Rijal al-Kashi"

All the other reports in Shia books have come from the above three sources.

The first two historians i.e., Qummi and Nawbakhti have mentioned Abdullah Ibn Saba, but they have not provided any sources or references for their claim. For instance, they have not mentioned any chain of narrators for their story, or the chain of narrators is broken in their books. As a result, these reports about Ibn Saba are not considered authentic, since they have no reference whatsoever.

However, the reports mentioned in al-Kashi seem more authentic as they are mentioned with a chain of narrators. Although, it must be said that among all the Shia scholars and historians between the 1st and the 4th century, Al-Kashi was the only scholar who reported some traditions mentioning Ibn Saba, which did not have Sayf Ibn Umar as the source. There are only five such traditions found in his book called Rijal al-Kashi.

Here is one such tradition from Al-Kashi about Ibn Saba:

> *Hisham bin Salim, who said that he heard it from Imam Abu `Abd Allah (as) when he told that `Abd Allah bin Saba called (to people) the lordship/divinity of Imaam `Ali (as). Upon that 'Ali ordered him to repent, but he refused. Then Ali let him burn in fire."*
>
> - Al-Kashee, Rijaal, pg. 107, hadeeth # 171

The reports from Al-Kashi paint the following picture of Ibn Saba.

Ibn Saba was a person who came to Ali in the mosque of Kufa and claimed that Ali was divine or God. Ali asked him to repent, but he persisted in his extremism and Ali eventually killed him for his apostasy. Some reports also suggest that he claimed Prophethood for himself while claiming divinity of Ali.

Based on the above description:

- Ibn Saba did not emerge in the time of Caliph Uthman but appeared during the Caliphate of Ali.
- He did not say that Ali was the successor of the Prophet but stated that Ali was God.
- He played no part in the revolt against Caliph Uthman or manipulated any of the companions of the Prophet.
- He may have claimed Prophethood for himself while claiming divinity of Ali.
- He was condemned and killed by Ali.

As we can see, the portrayal of Ibn Saba from Shia sources is similar to the depiction of Ibn Saba by Ibn Asakir from the Sunni side.

In both the cases i.e., in case of Al-Kashi and Ibn Asakir, Ibn Saba appeared during the Caliphate of Ali as an extremist (Ghulat), who claimed that Ali was God rather than claiming that Ali was the successor of the Prophet. He also played no role in the rebellion against Caliph Uthman, since he did not even exist at that time.

An individual with the name of Ibn Saba, who is described as an extremist (Ghulat) and who appeared during the Caliphate of Ali, seems more genuine and may have existed. But this Ibn Saba has nothing to do with the fictitious Ibn Saba who was invented by Sayf Ibn Umar as a Jewish conspiracy against Islam.

Needless to say, that the Ibn Saba mentioned by Al-Kashi and by Ibn Asakir had no influence on the Shia thought, as Shias do not believe in the divinity of Ali and nor do they believe that Ali is God.

16.8.3. An Interesting Theory

Ammar bin Yasir verses Ibn Saba.

The character of Ibn Saba was the imagination of Sayf Ibn Umar. However, there is a real character in history who had many similarities with Ibn Saba except the Jewish link. This character was none other than Ammar bin Yasir, the famous companion of the Prophet.

The following similarities exist between the imaginary Ibn Saba and the companion of the Prophet i.e., Ammar bin Yasir:

- Ibn Saba is alleged to have come from Yemen and so did Ammar bin Yasir. They were both from the Saba'iya tribe of Yemen.
- Ibn Saba depicted by Sayf Ibn Umar is also referred to as Ibn Sauda which means son of the black woman. Ammar bin Yasir's mother was also black. In the battle of Siffin Amr ibn-Aluss refers to Ammar bin Yasir as Ibn Sauda, the son of the black woman.
- It is alleged that Ibn Saba was one of the main organizers of the revolt against Caliph Uthman. History informs us that Ammar bin Yasir was one of the key agitators against Caliph Uthman and was one of his strongest opponents. He also called for Caliph Uthman's downfall, alongside Lady Aisha, Talha and other prominent companions.
- It is alleged that it was Ibn Saba who claimed that Ali was the successor of the Prophet. Ammar bin Yasir was one of the staunchest supporters of Ali's right to the Caliphate, he considered Ali to be the rightful successor of the Prophet. For instance, Ammar bin Yasir publicly argued against Abu Sarh to choose Ali rather than Uthman for the third Caliphate.

Considering all the above similarities, it is certainly possible that Sayf Ibn Umar had based the imaginary character of Ibn Saba on Ammar bin Yasir, a prominent companion of the Prophet. To add spice to the fictitious character he injected the Jewish element to his fairy tale!

16.9. The Mythical Saba'iya Group

Just as the myth of Ibn Saba is advocated to deny Ali his right and to cover up the mismanagement of Caliph Uthman's administration, another mythical group or a sect is invented by the name of Saba'iya, or Saba'i or Sabaites.

It is alleged that the followers of Ibn Saba who was the imagination of Sayf Ibn Umar were called Saba'iya, or Saba'i or Sabaites. The Sabaites being Ibn Saba's followers were the ones who had besieged the house of Caliph Uthman and they were the group who eventually killed him.

Some advocators of Ibn Saba even claim that those who consider Ali to be the successor of the Prophet were originally Saba'iya, i.e., followers of Ibn Saba, and are now known as the Shia.

Like all the other myths around Ibn Saba, the myth of a group or a sect called Saba'iya or Sabaites is just as baseless as the fabrication of Ibn Saba itself.

When one reads the history of Arabs, we find that Arabs were broadly categorized into three different groups.

16.9.1. The Perishing Arabs

These Arabs no longer exist as they have perished over the course of history and hence are known as perishing Arabs. There are some references to these Arabs in Quran too. They perished due to genocide or natural calamities, but little is known about this group or tribe.

16.9.2. The Adnaniya Arabs

The Arabs who came from the progeny of Prophet Ismael, the first son of Prophet Ibraheem are known as Adnaniya Arabs. The Prophet Mohammed was an Adnaniya Arab. The Adnaniya Arabs are also know by the following two names.

- Nazariya
- Mudhariya

16.9.3. The Qathanian Arabs

These Arabs came from the Yemeni side of the Arabian Peninsula and were from the progeny of Ya'rub. The grandson of Ya'rub was called Saba. All the Yemeni tribes trace their ancestry from the grandson of Ya'rub called Saba. The Qathanian Arabs are known by three different names.

- Qahtaniya
- Yamaniya
- Saba'iya

16.9.4. Saba'iya is an Ethnic Group

This is where the name Saba'iya in fact originates from and not from Ibn Saba (who was the imagination of Sayf ibn Omar). The Yemeni Arabs were known as Saba'iya or Saba'i. This is there tribal and ethnic name. The Saba'iya does not signify a sect or set of beliefs. It refers to an ethnic group or a tribe which came from Southwestern Arabia.

For instance, the first leader of al-Khawarij was called Abdullah bin Wahab al-Saba'i. Abdullah bin Wahab al-Saba'i led an army against Ali in the battle of Naharwan. He was called Saba'i because he was from the Sabai'ya tribe, this was his ethnic background. He wasn't called a Saba'i because he was a follower of Ibn Saba, on the contrary he was an enemy of Ali. He was the leader of al-Khawarij, the group that killed Ali.

In fact, the word Saba is still being used to refer to the Yemeni Arabs. Many organizations that work in present day Yemen use the name Saba to signify their ethnicity. For example, today a news group in Yemen is called sabanew (https://www.sabanew.net/home/en). It is not called sabanew because the Muslims of Yemen are followers of Ibn Saba. It is called sabanew because Saba is their ethnicity.

Similarly, a well-known shipping company in Yemen goes by the name of sabashipping (http://www.sabashipping.com

). Again, the owners of the shipping company have not added Saba to their company name because they are the followers of some fictitious character called Ibn Saba. The name of their company clearly represents their ethnic origins.

But Sayf Ibn Umar twisted the facts and claimed that Saba'iya was a sect whose leader was Ibn Saba. However, in reality Saba'iya was a tribe and an ethnic group who traced their ancestry from Saba the grandson of Ya'rub, who came from the Yemeni part of Arabia.

The simple reason for propagating such myths and falsehood is to poison the minds of ordinary Muslims from accepting Ali as the rightful successor of the Prophet.

There were no followers of Ibn Saba, or a group called Saba'iya or Sabaites who had besieged the house of Caliph Uthman. The house of Caliph Uthman was besieged for forty days by the companions of the Prophet and by ordinary Muslims, who had come from all parts of the Muslim world to protest against his policies. Unfortunately, he refused to budge as he was completely under the thumb of Marwan bin Hakam, his chief advisor. His refusal to heed the demands of the protestors resulted in violence which ended his life.

Surely, at some point the proponents of Ibn Saba must come to the realization that the conspiracy theory of Ibn Saba is unlikely to achieve its objectives in the factual world of 21st century.

16.10. Why would a Jew Exalt Ali?

As I wrap up this discussion it would be interesting to find out from the advocators of Ibn Saba as to why would a man of Jewish origin only glorify Ali. The Prophet of Allah had thousands of companions, and when there were so many companions of the Prophet to choose from, then why would a man of Jewish faith only pick out Ali and exalt his status among all the companions?

As far as the history informs us Ali had no soft corner for the Jews of his time due to their animosity towards Islam. On the contrary he was their sworn enemy. Ali had been at the forefront of all the wars and battles against the Jews of Arabia, alongside the Prophet of Allah. The most famous of them being the battle of Khaibar. The Jews had settled in Khaibar and its numerous fortresses which was about eighty miles from Madinah. They represented a great danger to the safety and the security of the Islamic State of Madinah.

The Prophet decided to remove the Jewish threat and led an army of around sixteen hundred men which besieged the fortresses of Khaibar for days without any success. Both Caliph Abu Bakr and Caliph Umar had failed to break the siege when Prophet had given them the flag of Islam. The Prophet of Allah then specifically called upon Ali for this key battle against the Jews.

We read in Sahih al-Bukhari and Sahih al-Muslim:

> "The Messenger of God said at Khaibar: I shall give this banner to a man through whom God will bring the victory. He loves God and His Messenger and God and His Messenger love him. ……. The Prophet gave Ali the banner and Ali asked: "Messenger of God shall I fight them until they become Muslims like us?" The Messenger said: "Go on until you reach their dwelling. Invite them to Islam and inform them of their duty towards God and Islam. …………"
>
> - *Sahih Al-Bukhari Part 5 p. 171 and Muslim in his Sahih Part 15 pp. 178-179*

Ali went towards the Jewish fortress of Khaibar carrying Prophet's banner and leading the army from the front. One of the most feared Jewish warriors of the time known as Marhab challenged Ali for a dwell. Ali struck a single blow with his sword splitting Marhab's head into two. The killing of Marhab capitulated the Jewish hearts, they retreated into the fortress and tried to defend it by locking its doors.

Ali broke the gate and entered the fortress bringing an end to the siege of Khaibar.

The Jews of Arabia could never get over their defeat of Khaibar at the hands of Ali. They held a grudge and an animosity towards Ali as long as he lived. For people of logic and reason this point alone should be enough to disprove the entire myth of Ibn Saba.

A man of Jewish faith could have never claimed the supremacy of Ali over others, a person of Jewish origin could have never glorified Ali. There was no reason as to why any person of Jewish faith would have taken Ali's side in that era. The notion that a Jewish man exalted the status of Ali completely contradicts the events of history and flies in the face of logic and reason.

With such bloodletting between Ali and the Jews, there was no possibility that a man of Jewish background would have exalted or glorified Ali. In fact, this whole notion of Jewish conspiracy has been advocated to lower the status of Ali, by claiming that the idea of Ali being the successor of the Prophet was a Jewish innovation.

It is a real shame that some supporters of Saqifah can stoop so low that they end up equating the traditions of the Prophet to a fictitious Jew, simply to justify their stance. It seems as if everything is justifiable and a fair game in the defence of Saqifah. However, these supporters of Saqifah seem to forget that on the Day of Judgment they will not be asked about the event of Saqifah or the fictitious character of Ibn Saba, but they will be asked about the traditions of the Prophet in support of Ali's leadership.

16.11. Caliph Umar and Jewish Influence

Although Ibn Saba was a mythical figure both in terms of the theories attributed to him and also in terms of his character in history, however there was a man by the name of Kaab ibn Mati al-Humyari who actually existed in the history and was a prominent Jewish rabbi. He came to Madinah from Yemen during the rule of Caliph Umar and became a Muslim.

He was also known by the names of Abu Ishaq or Kaab al-Aḥbar and is counted among the tabaeen. Tabaeen were the generation of Muslims who came after the death of the Prophet. This newly converted Muslim who was a former Jewish rabbi quickly gained the confidence and trust of the second Caliph Umar.

As time passed his influence grew among the early Muslims and prominent companions. He narrated many tales and stories claiming that they were from the Old Testament.

Many famous companions reported stories from him including the following.

- Abu Huraira
- Abdullah Ibn Umar
- Abdullah Ibn Amr Ibn al-Aas

One of the companions of the Prophet by the name Qais Ibn Kharshah (known as al-Qaisi) reported that Kaab al-Ahbar said:

> *Every event that has taken place or will take place on the earth, is written in the Tourat (Old Testament), which Allah revealed to his Prophet Moses (as).*
> - *Ibn Abdul Barr - al-Istiab, v3, p1287, Printed in Cairo 1380 A.H*

This is obviously not true, no book in the world contains all the events that have already taken place or will take place. The Old Testament certainly does not have this information.

16.11.1. Caliph Umar and Kaab Al-Ahbar

It is said that when Caliph Umar entered Jerusalem, he was accompanied by Kaab al-Ahbar who travelled with him from Madinah. Caliph Umar became very close to Kaab al-Ahbar especially towards the end of his Caliphate. This is evident from the fact that Kaab al-Ahbar even predicted the death of Caliph Umar, for instance al-Tabari reports the following conversation that took place between Kaab al-Ahbar and Caliph Umar.

> *Kaab: Amir al-Mumineen (Umar), you ought to write your will because you will die in three days.*
> *Umar: How do you know that?*
> *Kaab: I found it in the Book of God, the Taurat (Old Testament).*
> *Umar: By God do you find Umar Ibn al-Khattab in the Old Testament?*
> *Kaab: By God, no. But I found your description in the Old Testament and your time is coming to an end.*
> *Umar: But I do not feel any pain or sickness.*

On the following day Kaab al-Ahbar came to Caliph Umar and said:

> *Amir al-Mumineen (Umar), one day has passed and you have only two more days.*

The following day Kaab al-Ahbar came to him and said:

> *Amir al-Mumineen (Umar), two days have gone and you have only one day and one night remaining.*

The following morning Abu Lulu appeared carrying a dagger and stabbed Caliph Umar six times which eventually resulted in his death.

- History of al-Tabari, v4, p191, Printed by Dar al-Maarif - Cairo

It is obvious that none of this is actually found in the Old Testament and Kaab al-Ahbar was probably part of the conspiracy and the plot to kill Caliph Umar. By announcing the event beforehand and claiming that it was found in the Old Testament, he positions himself as a reliable source of information for predicting future events.

The unfortunate thing here is not what Kaab al-Ahbar is stating but the response of Caliph Umar. He literally believes everything that Kaab al-Ahbar mentions. If Caliph Umar had bothered to check the Old Testament, he would have realized that Kaab al-Ahbar was simply lying.

16.11.2. The Advice of the Prophet to Caliph Umar

Caliph Umar was one of the earliest companions of the Prophet who had adopted Islam in Makkah and had spent a great deal of time in the company of the Prophet. It was expected that Caliph Umar during his Caliphate would in fact try and guide a newly converted Jew to adopt the teachings of Islam, rather than getting influenced by the fairy tales that he was making up based on his previous faith.

In fact, the Prophet had specifically told Caliph Umar not to believe in or follow the teachings of the Old Testament. The following tradition of the Prophet is directly addressing Caliph Umar to refrain from the doctrine of the Old Testament.

> *Umar ibn al-Khattab brought to Allah's Messenger a copy of the Torah and said: Allah's Messenger, this is a copy of the Torah. He (Allah's Messenger) kept quiet and he (Umar) began to read it. The (colour) of the face of Allah's Messenger underwent a change, whereupon Abu Bakr said: Would that your mother mourn you, don't you see the face of Allah's Messenger? Umar saw the face of Allah's Messenger and said: I seek refuge with Allah from the wrath of Allah and the wrath of His Messenger. We are well pleased with Allah as Lord, with Islam as religion, and with Muhammad as Prophet. Whereupon Allah's Messenger said: By Him in Whose hand is the life of Muhammad, even if Moses were to appear before you and you were to follow him, leaving me aside, you would certainly stray into error; for if (Moses) were alive (now), and he found my prophetical ministry, he would have definitely followed me.*
>
> - Al-Tirmidhi Hadith 194 Narrated by Jabir ibn Abdullah

Despite such clear words of the Prophet and despite the Prophet directly confronting Caliph Umar, he still choses to listen to the words of Torah, while he was at the end of his Caliphate, clearly proving that even at that late stage in his life he didn't consider the words of the Prophet binding!

Even though Prophet was absolutely furious with Caliph Umar about following the previous scriptures, Caliph Umar chose to ignore the commands of the prophet and still believed in the stories of Torah (Old Testament) which weren't even true.

I have only given a snapshot of one the conversations that Caliph Umar had with Kaab al-Ahbar. Caliph Umar had many such conversations with the former Jew on various topics and issues concerning the Muslim Ummah, and inevitably his decisions were influenced by the likes of Kaab al-Ahbar and other such individuals.

The people who fabricate the story of Ibn Saba to deny Ali the right of leadership, and who also accuse Shia Muslims of borrowing Jewish teachings should read Islamic history objectively, and they would realize that it was indeed Caliph Umar and other prominent companions who were actually influenced by the Jewish thought, rather than the Shia view which was strictly based on the traditions of the Prophet.

In any case the attitude and the behaviour of Caliph Umar towards Kaab al-Ahbar was neither surprising and nor usual, we had seen the same pattern of behaviour from Caliph Umar on previous occasions too, where he adopts a path contradictory to the Sunnah of the Prophet, the most notable of them being the meeting of Saqifah, where he proposes Caliph Abu Bakr rather than to accept the leadership of Ali as commanded by the Prophet.

Also, prior to this Caliph Umar had challenged the Prophet on the Treaty of Hudaybiyya, he had refused to bring pen and paper to the Prophet when he wanted to write a will, and he had refused to join Usama's army despite Prophet's clear instructions to do so.

The trend of al-ijtihad (independent judgement) which had plagued the prominent companions was clearly evident from their actions even towards the end of their lives.

Fortunately, we are not bound by the actions of Caliph Umar or any other companion for that matter. We are only bound by the traditions of the Prophet which are our guiding stars, and they inevitably point to the leadership of Ali with an absolute and an unwavering clarity.

www.ingramcontent.com/pod-product-compliance
Lightning Source LLC
Chambersburg PA
CBHW080048190426
43201CB00036B/2273